Hong Kong
and Macau

THE ROUGH GUIDE

Other guides available in this series

Amsterdam
Andalucia
Australia
Barcelona & Catalunya
Berlin
Brazil
Brittany & Normandy
Bulgaria
California
Canada
Corsica
Crete
Cyprus
Czech & Slovak Republics
Egypt
England
Europe
Florida
France
Germany
Greece
Guatemala & Belize

Holland, Belgium &
  Luxembourg
Hungary
Ireland
Italy
Kenya
Mediterranean
  Wildlife
Mexico
Morocco
Nepal
New York
Nothing Ventured
Paris
Peru
Poland
Portugal
Prague
Provence
Pyrenees
San Francisco

Scandinavia
Scotland
Sicily
Spain
St Petersburg
Thailand
Tunisia
Turkey
Tuscany & Umbria
USA
Venice
Wales
West Africa
Women Travel
Zimbabwe & Botswana

Forthcoming titles
India
Malaysia & Singapore
Classical Music
World Music

Rough Guide Credits

Text Editor:	Jules Brown
Series Editor:	Mark Ellingham
Editorial:	Martin Dunford, John Fisher, Jonathan Buckley, Greg Ward, Kate Berens, Graham Parker
Production:	Susanne Hillen, Gail Jammy, Andy Hilliard, Vivien Antwi, Melissa Flack, Alan Spicer
Publicity:	Richard Trillo
Finance:	Celia Crowley

Acknowledgements

This edition owes a great deal to the sleuth-like efforts of Michael Mackey, who climbed every mountain and forded every stream in the pursuit of esoteric information and big dinners. His help, and that of Mark Harris (who deserves a medal for concise note-taking, never mind a degree), is greatly appreciated.

For other **assistance**, special thanks must go to the MTIB (Paul Hoskins in London and Brian Cuthbertson in Hong Kong) for their generous help in Macau; and, in Hong Kong, to Amanda Loui and Allen Chan of the *Hotel Victoria*, Stephen Yam of the *Ambassador Hotel*, and Gabrielle C. Keep and the Hong Kong Youth Hostels Association. It was a pleasure to catch up with Lucy and Mike Simmonds (and Freddie); and thanks are also due to Clare Dargan at *Campus Travel*, to staff at *STA Travel*, to Jeanne Muchnick and David Reed, to Huw Molseed at *BookTrust*, all of whom plugged information gaps with their customary efficiency, and to Sam Kirby for new maps. The **Rough Guides** crew did its usual excellent job: thanks in particular to Pat Yale for painstaking proofreading and additional comments, and to Susanne, Gail and Jonathan whose input is always welcomed and appreciated.

At home, continued thanks are owed to Ken, Jean and Joanna Brown for their unflagging support; to Colette Doyle, who at this rate will soon need a separate shelf for her book credits; to Capt. I. Little, who knows as much about Hong Kong as he does about the law; to Ally Scott, who kept the burglars at bay; and to my friends Greg Ward and Sam Cook.

Finally, from the **first edition**, I'd like to thank Helen Lee, without whom this book would never have been written in the first place; the Lee family for their hospitality; Michael Lee for his Chinese calligraphy; Martin Dunford for help and encouragement; and the friends I made in China and kept in the real world: Anna Hanley, Alan Brooks, Cheryl Taylor, Alex van Paasen and Nicola Jones. This book is still dedicated to the memory of Liu Yuk Hing (1944–1988).

This second edition published 1993 by Rough Guides Ltd, 1 Mercer Street, London WC2H 9QJ.
Reprinted twice 1994.

Distributed by the Penguin Group:

Penguin Books Ltd, 27 Wrights Lane, London W8 5TZ
Penguin Books USA Inc., 375 Hudson Street, New York 10014, USA
Penguin Books Australia Ltd, 487 Maroondah Highway, PO Box 257, Ringwood, Victoria 3134, Australia
Penguin Books Canada Ltd, 10 Alcorn Avenue, Toronto, Ontario, Canada M4V 1E4
Penguin Books (NZ) Ltd, 182–190 Wairau Road, Auckland 10, New Zealand

Originally published in the UK by Harrap Columbus Ltd, 1991.
Previous edition published in the United States and Canada as *The Real Guide Hong Kong and Macau*.

Printed in the United Kingdom by Cox & Wyman Ltd (Reading).
Typography and **original design** by Jonathan Dear and The Crowd Roars.
Illustrations throughout by Edward Briant.

British Library Cataloguing in Publication Data
A catalogue record for this book is available from the British Library.
ISBN 1-85828-066-4

Hong Kong
and Macau

THE ROUGH GUIDE

Written and researched by
Jules Brown and Helen Lee

WIth additional contributions by
Michael Mackey and Mark Harris

THE ROUGH GUIDES

Contents

Introduction

Hong Kong is a beguiling place to visit: a land whose aggressive capitalistic instinct is tempered by an oriental concern with order and beauty. Indeed, whatever you've heard about it, the most important thing to remember is that Hong Kong is, and always has been, Chinese. Although all the legal trappings of British colonial rule will remain in place until 1997, in fact Hong Kong has a cosmopolitan veneer through which shines the inescapable fact that the vast majority of its people and customs are thoroughly Chinese. The ultra-modern skyline imitates others throughout the world; the largest department stores are Japanese-owned; you can take English high tea to the accompaniment of a string quartet; there's cricket and horse-racing, pubs and cocktail lounges. But for most of the Chinese locals – 98 percent of the six-million-strong population – life still follows a pattern that many of the mainland Chinese would recognise as their own: food from teeming markets and street stalls; hard work and cramped housing; a polytheistic religion celebrated in the home and in smoky temples; annual, intense, stylistic festivals. Above all, for visitors new to the scene, there's the bizarre juxtaposition of the all-consuming noise and smell of the East in one of the world's most clinically up-to-date cities.

As 1997 approaches, which is the date the colony – or "territory" as it's now known – is due to be handed back officially to the Chinese government, Hong Kong is undergoing its last painful manoeuvres under colonial rule. The British have been here since 1841 and are finding it difficult to fulfil their obligations to the citizens of this vibrant, thriving colony; the Chinese government, for its part, hasn't yet found the key to reassuring Hong Kong that there's a place for its naked free enterprise economy in a largely unreconstructed socialist society. Caught between these two stools, the people of Hong Kong are variously worried, or angry, or unconcerned as long as the dollars keep flowing in.

Because all that's Chinese is found in Hong Kong, you need have no fear that a visit to the territory is somehow second-best to seeing China itself. Most people, in fact, do make at least a day trip to neighbouring Guangzhou (Canton), but it's not an essential requirement. More important is that you throw away any preconceived notion that all there is to do in Hong Kong is go shopping while on the way to more exciting parts of Asia. The city is dense with interest: the **architecture** is an engaging mix of styles, from stunning, modern banks to ramshackle town housing and centuries-old Chinese temples; the markets and **streetlife** are always compelling; the **shopping** – if no longer the bargain it once was – is eclectic, from open-air stalls to glittering, hi-tech malls. Hong Kong is also *the* place in the world to eat **Chinese food** (and a good many other food styles besides), while the Western influence on the territory throws up a mean selection of **bars and nightspots**. If there's a downside, it's that straightforward consumption tends to dominate life: **cultural** matters have been less well catered for, though a superb Cultural Centre, several new museums, and an increasing interest in and awareness of the **arts** – both Chinese and Western – is changing even that.

Outside Hong Kong, the obvious move is the sixty-kilometre trip west across the Pearl River estuary to **Macau**, which makes Hong Kong look like the gaudy *arriviste* colony it is, the Portuguese having arrived in southern China in the early sixteenth century, setting up base here in 1557. This gave the Portuguese almost three hundred years start on the British, and although Hong Kong and its harbour soon surpassed the older territory in terms of trading importance, Macau absorbed its Portuguese links and culture in a way that Hong Kong never did with Britain.

On a much smaller scale than its better-known neighbour, Macau is more immediately attractive, and though it, too, is due to be handed back to China, in 1999, for the time being it remains a fascinating contrast to the madness across the way in Hong Kong.

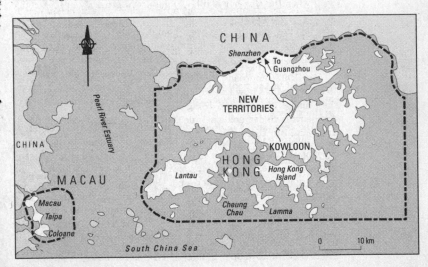

It's one of Asia's most enjoyable spots for a short visit, its Chinese life tempered by a Catholic, almost Mediterranean, influence, manifest in the ageing churches, hilltop fortresses and a grand seafront promenade. Of course, like Hong Kong, Macau is Chinese, and 95 percent of its population speak Cantonese. All the temples and festivals of southern China are reproduced here, but few come to Macau to pursue them, believing – perhaps rightly – that such things are done bigger and better in Hong Kong. Instead, two main draws bring tourists to Macau: the food and the gambling. Eating in Macau is one of the highlights of any trip to the region, so much so that, even with only a couple of days in Hong Kong, it's worth taking the jetfoil over for a meal: Macanese food is an exciting combination of Portuguese colonial cooking, with dishes and ingredients taken from Portugal itself, Goa, Brazil, Africa and China, washed down with very cheap, imported Portuguese wine, port and brandy. And with gambling illegal in Hong Kong, except for horse-race betting, the Hong Kong Chinese look to Macau's several casinos to cater to their almost obsessive interest in the matter.

The closest major city in China to both Hong Kong and Macau is Guangzhou (Canton), reachable from either territory by land or sea, and the best place for a short glimpse of the mainland. There are several other Chinese destinations which can also be reached directly from Hong Kong and Macau; for full details see "Onwards Travel", p.365.

When to go

Hong Kong and Macau's climates are broadly similar – subtropical in character, which means that apart from a couple of months a year when the weather is reliably good, it's generally unpredictable and often downright stormy. The heat is always made more oppressive by the humidity: in very humid weather you'll get hot and sticky very quickly, and will find your strength sapped if you try to do too much walking around. You'll need air-conditioning in your hotel room, or – at the very least – a fan. Macau, though, does have the bonus of the cool breeze off the sea in summer, which makes nursing a beer on the waterfront the pleasant experience it rarely is in Hong Kong.

The best time is undoubtedly the autumn, when the humidity is at its lowest, and the days bright, clear and hot without being stifling. In winter, things get noticeably cooler (you'll need a jacket) and though the skies do often stay clear, there'll be periods of wind and mist – don't expect constant decent views from The Peak at this time. Spring sees a rise in temperature and humidity, but there's little improvement as far as the skies go; they stay grey and there are frequent showers and heavier rain. The summer is dramatically different: it's terribly hot and humid (about the worst possible time for extended walking in either territory, in the city or countryside);

you'd be wise not to come at this time. If you do visit in the spring or summer, you'll need an umbrella; raincoats are hot and aren't much use in heavy downpours.

The summer also sees the **typhoon season**, which lasts roughly from July to September. Getting stuck in a typhoon can be quite an experience. The word is from the Chinese *dai foo*, or "big wind", an Asian hurricane, and over the years typhoons whistling through Hong Kong have had a devastating effect – scores of people dead and millions of dollars' worth of damage. Listen to the radio or TV weather broadcasts to find out what's happening and check the box below for Storm Signal details.

Average Temperatures and Humidity

Note that the figures below are *averages*. In summer, the temperature is regularly in the 90s (and higher), as is the humidity. The winter is comparatively chilly, but the temperature rarely drops below 60°F.

	Average Temperature (°F)	Average Humidity	Monthly Rainfall (mm)
Spring (March to May)	70	84%	137
Summer (June to mid-Sept)	82	83%	394
Autumn (mid-Sept to mid-Dec)	73	73%	43
Winter (mid-Dec to Feb)	60	75%	33

Storm Signals

Once a typhoon is in full swing (after the no. 8 signal has been announced), planes will start to be diverted, local transport (like the buses and cross-harbour ferries) will eventually stop running, and you would be wise to stay indoors and away from exposed windows.

Storm Signal 1 means a tropical cyclone (and thus the wind, or typhoon, associated with it) is within 800km of Hong Kong.

Storm Signal 3 indicates winds are expected across Hong Kong of 60km/hr, with gusts up to 110km/hr. This generally means a typhoon is on its way: you're supposed to tie things down on balconies and rooftops, and check transport availability.

Storm Signal 8 means be prepared for storm force winds of between 63 and 117km/hr and gusts up to 180km/hr.

Storm Signal 9 indicates storm force winds are set to increase significantly.

Storm Signal 10 means there will be a hurricane of 118km/hr and upwards, with gusts up to and above 220km/hr.

Part 1

The Basics

Getting to Hong Kong and Macau from Britain and Ireland

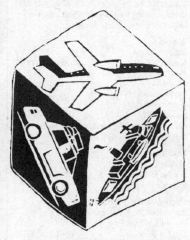

The simplest way to reach both territories from Britain and Ireland is to fly. Until Macau's airport becomes operational (in 1995 at the earliest), all routings are to Hong Kong in the first instance; for details of travel on to Macau from Hong Kong, see p.291. Always ring around to find the best deals on flights and try to plan as far ahead as you can, certainly if you're travelling at a popular time.

There's also the possibility of following one of the world's classic overland trips, by train from London, through Russia and Mongolia to China, and from there to the end of the line in Hong Kong. Travelling this way takes at least 12–14 days and requires making the necessary travel and visa arrangements well in advance, but as a route it has few equals.

Flights from Britain

The least demanding way to reach Hong Kong is to **fly non-stop** with one of the three major airlines – just under a thirteen-hour flight **from London** Heathrow. *British Airways* flies non-stop twice daily; *Cathay Pacific* and *Virgin* both have a once-daily non-stop service. Prices, though, are high. With the cheapest PEX fares, you must stay a minimum of seven days and a maximum of three months. Low-season fares cost from around £640 return, shoulder season around £100 more, while in high season (mid-June to Sept, Christmas, New Year and Easter), you'll pay around £850–900. *Cathay Pacific* also flies non-stop **from Manchester** five times weekly, PEX fares starting at around £750 return, rising to just under £1000 in high season.

Non-direct flights are a little cheaper, but can take sixteen to twenty hours. Several airlines fly to Hong Kong and, depending on the time of year, flights cost from around £550–600 return, though seats at Christmas, Chinese New Year and Easter are hard to come by: try and book well in advance. You'll touch down two or three times on the way, sometimes giving the opportunity of a stopover: the Middle East and Southeast Asia are standard stops, while *Air China* (China's national airline) flies via Beijing. You can try the airlines (see the list below) for their current prices: some don't sell tickets directly to the public and will point you in the direction of their appointed agent. Or ring an **agent** which specialises in discounted air fares, some of which – like *Campus Travel, Council Travel* and *STA Travel* – offer special deals for students and those under 26; prices can sometimes go as low as £500 return. You'll find the agents listed, with their latest prices, in the Sunday newspapers, in the weekly London listings magazine *Time Out* or London's *Evening Standard*; and in Manchester's weekly listings magazine *City Life*. We've listed some of the more reliable agencies below.

Most of the specialist agents will also be able to sell you a **Round-the-World** ticket, routed out of London, which often includes Hong Kong in the itinerary. These are, of course, much more expensive – the current cheapest including a stop in Hong Kong costs around £1000 – but, as they're usually valid for 6 to 12 months, they're just the thing if your Hong Kong visit is part of a longer world trip.

Airlines

Air China
c/o CTS, 24 Cambridge Circus
London WC2   ☎ 071/836 9911
*Good deals on flights to Beijing, where you can
change for Hong Kong.*

Air India
17 New Bond St
London W1   ☎ 071/491 7979
Stopovers in Delhi/Bombay.

Bangladesh Biman
17 Conduit St
London W1   ☎ 071/629 0252
Flies via Dacca; no direct sales to the public.

British Airways:
156 Regent St
London W1   ☎ 071/434 4700
Offices, too, at Victoria Station, London SW1;
101 Cheapside, London EC2;
19–21 St Mary's Gate, Market St
Manchester M1   ☎ 061/832 6896

Cathay Pacific
Reservations   ☎ 071/747 8888
Office at 52 Berkeley St
London W1 (personal callers only);
4th Floor, Arkwright House, Parsonage Gardens,
Manchester M3   ☎ 061/833 9266

China Airlines
41 Piccadilly
London W1   ☎ 071/434 0707
*Flies via Amsterdam, Bangkok and Taipei. No
direct sales to the public; try* Crystal Travel *(see
opposite) for fares.*

Gulf Air
Jet Air House, 188 Hammersmith Rd
London W6   ☎ 081/970 1510
*Usually among the cheapest flights; stopovers
in Bahrain, Muscat and Bangkok.*

Qantas
182 The Strand
London W1   ☎ 0345/747767
Flies via Bangkok.

Royal Brunei
49 Cromwell Rd
London SW7   ☎ 071/584 6660
*Flies via Brunei. No direct sales to the public;
try* Globepost *(see opposite) for fares.*

Thai International
41 Albemarle St
London W1   ☎ 071/491 7953
Flies via Bangkok.

Virgin Atlantic
Sales office, *Virgin Megastore*
Tottenham Court Rd
London W1   ☎ 0293/747747

Finally, a couple of **courier** firms offer cheap flights to Hong Kong – around £350–450 return – though often you're only allowed to take hand baggage, and there'll be some restrictions on when you can travel and how long you can stay. Tickets are usually valid for just 10 to 15 days and you should book at least two months in advance.

Bear in mind that whatever ticket you buy, you'll be subject to a HK$150 (£12.50/US$22) airport **departure tax** when leaving Hong Kong on an international flight; it's payable when you check in.

Package Tours

The other option from Britain is to travel to Hong Kong on an inclusive **package tour**, something that can be very good value out of season. For a week (ie, two nights on a plane and five nights in Hong Kong), including flights and accommodation, you can expect to pay from around £650 per person. Obviously, the price goes up in the high season (mid-June to Sept and Christmas),

and according to which class of hotel you choose to stay in – at peak times, the same holiday will be more like £1000. However, all the hotels used are more than adequate and you can sometimes get extremely good deals for a stay in the very best hotels; in low season *Kuoni* can book you a return flight and five nights in the *Mandarin Oriental* for around £850.

Several **specialist operators**, like *Voyages Jules Verne*, offer all-inclusive Far Eastern tours which often include China and Hong Kong in the itinerary. These are usually very expensive – £2000 and upwards – and only worth considering if you don't have the time to make your own way in China. You can see what they'll show you of Hong Kong much more cheaply on a regular package or by simply buying a return flight.

Overland: By Train

The **overland train route from London** passes through eastern Europe, Russia and Mongolia to China and Beijing, from where trains run south to the end of the line in Hong Kong. It's a

Discounted Flight Agencies

Campus Travel
52 Grosvenor Gardens
London SW1 ☎ 071/730 8111

14 Southampton St
London W1 ☎ 071/836 3343

90–98 Corporation St
Bull St Subway
Birmingham B4 ☎ 021/233 4611

5 Emmanuel St,
Cambridge ☎ 0223/324 283

5 Nicholson Square,
Edinburgh ☎ 031/668 3303

166 Deansgate
Manchester M3 ☎ 061/833 2046

13 High St
Oxford ☎ 0865/242 067

and in YHA shops and university
campuses all over Britain.

Council Travel
28a Poland St
London W1 ☎ 071/437 7767

Crystal Travel
9 Rathbone Place
London W1 ☎ 071/830 0600

Far East Travel Centre
33 Maddox St
London W1 ☎ 071/414 8844

2 Gerrard Place
London W1 ☎ 071/437 8164

Globepost Ltd
324 Kennington Park Rd
London SE11 ☎ 071/587 0303

STA Travel,
74 & 86 Old Brompton Rd
London SW7 ☎ 071/937 9962

117 Euston Rd
London NW1 ☎ 071/937 9962

36 George St
Oxford ☎ 0223/66966

25 Queen's Rd, Bristol;

38 Sidney St, Cambridge;

75 Deansgate, Manchester;

and offices at the universities of Birmingham,
Kent, Loughborough and London (all colleges).
All offices for personal callers only; phone the
London or Oxford number for telephone sales.

Trailfinders
42–48 Earls Court Rd
London W8 ☎ 071/938 3366

58 Deansgate
Manchester M3 ☎ 061/839 6969

Travel Bug
597 Cheetham Hill Rd
Manchester M8 ☎ 061/721 4000

Travel Cuts
295a Regent St
London W1 ☎ 071/255 2082

Courier Firms

Courier Travel Service ☎ 071/351 0300
Polo Express ☎ 081/759 5383

Tour Operators

British Airways Holidays
Atlantic House,
Hazelwick Ave,
Three Bridges,
Crawley.
West Sussex RH10 ☎ 0293/613777

China Travel Service (*CTS*)
24 Cambridge Circus
London WC2 ☎ 071/836 9911

Far East Travel Centre
33 Maddox St
London W1 ☎ 071/414 8844

2 Gerrard Place
London W1 ☎ 071/437 8164

Globepost Ltd
324 Kennington Park Rd
London SE11 ☎ 071/587 0303

Jade Travel
1st Floor, 5 Newport Place
London WC2 ☎ 071/494 2461

Kuoni Travel
Kuoni House
Dorking, Surrey ☎ 0306/740 500

Thomas Cook Holidays
PO Box 36, Thorpe Wood
Peterborough PE3 ☎ 0733/332255

Voyages Jules Verne
Travel Promotions Ltd,
10 Glentworth St
London NW1 ☎ 071/486 8751

supremely satisfying – though exacting – journey, but it doesn't save you any money; count on around £300–450 one-way, just for the Moscow to Beijing route; fares are highest from June to September. You'll have to do some serious advance planning as far as getting the necessary visas goes. It's also a very long haul: from London to Moscow is two days, Moscow to

Beijing takes around a week, and it's at least another two solid days from there to Hong Kong. There's no direct train service between Beijing and Hong Kong – you have to change in Guangzhou – though a direct service is expected to be in operation by 1996.

If this doesn't put you off, you'll have to decide upon the route and train you want to take – services are operated by both the Russians and Chinese, either passing through, or bypassing, Mongolia (for which you need a separate visa). To sort it all out, an invaluable read is the *Trans-Siberian Handbook* by Bryn Thomas (Lascelles), which specifies all the routes, prices and procedures. *Campus Travel* (see Tour Operators box for address) has student/youth rail tickets from Moscow to Beijing from around £220; a flight from Beijing back to London with them adds around another £390. The *China Travel Service* also sell rail tickets to independent travellers;

organised trips, from London, start at about £1200 per person.

Travelling via Southeast Asia and China

With **Southeast Asia** opening up as a long-haul package destination, particularly from Britain, cheap flights to cities other than Hong Kong are now a distinct possibility. At most times of the year you should be able to find a flight from London to Bangkok for around £400–450 return, and flights to Singapore and Indonesia are usually only slightly more expensive. To use these destinations as a springboard for Hong Kong you'll need to have plenty of time, but lingering is no hardship if you're on a longer tour. Once there, **discounted air tickets** to Hong Kong are no problem: try the very useful *STA Travel* offices in Bangkok (at the *Thai Hotel*, 78 Prajathipatai Rd,

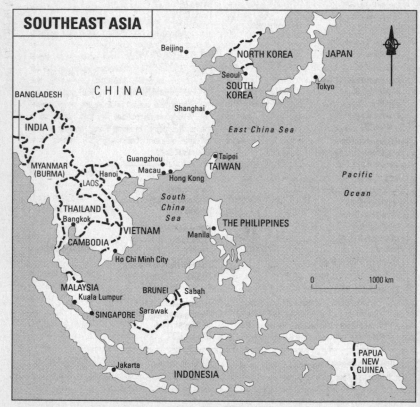

SOUTHEAST ASIA

Beijing • NORTH KOREA JAPAN

CHINA Seoul• SOUTH KOREA Tokyo•

BANGLADESH

Shanghai•

INDIA *East China Sea*

MYANMAR (BURMA) Guangzhou• Taipei• Hanoi• Macau• TAIWAN

LAOS Hong Kong • *Pacific*

THAILAND *South China Sea* *Ocean*

Bangkok• VIETNAM THE PHILIPPINES

CAMBODIA Manila•

Ho Chi Minh City•

0   1000 km

MALAYSIA BRUNEI Sabah Kuala Lumpur• Sarawak

SINGAPORE•

PAPUA NEW GUINEA

Jakarta• INDONESIA

Banglamphu; ☎6622815314/5); Kuala Lumpur (*MSKL Travel*, 1st Floor, *Asia Hotel*, 69 Jin Rd H| Hussin 50300; ☎6032989722); Singapore (02-17 *Orchard Parade Hotel*, Tanglin Rd; ☎7657345681); or Bali (*Carefree Bali Holidays*, Kuta Beach Club, Kuta Beach; ☎51261 x80). For one-way onward flights you can expect to pay in the region of £80/US$120 from Bangkok, and £120/US$180 from Singapore.

An alternative is to fly first to **China**, specifically to Beijing, and travel on to Hong Kong from there, either overland (two to three days by train) or by air. Current air fares to Beijing from London cost from around £470 return, rising to over £600 in the summer; *China Travel Service* generally has the cheapest flights, with *Air China*, or try the discounted flight agents listed on p.5.

Flights from Ireland

British Airways flies to Hong Kong from Dublin (via London Gatwick) and Belfast (via Heathrow), the flight time around 15 hours – though this stretches depending on how long you have to wait in London for the connection. The smoothest connections are **via Belfast/Heathrow**, for which you'll pay a high season PEX fare of around £1000 return. A specialist agent like *USIT* (see box below for address) can often find students, under 26s and independent travellers better deals than this – though you're still looking at return fares of between IR£680 (from Dublin) and IR£710 (Shannon/Cork).

In practice, this means that you're better off taking advantage of the cheap air fares between Ireland and Britain and picking up an onward flight from London with another airline. *Cathay Pacific* in London can arrange an add-on fare from Ireland in conjunction with their regular London–Hong Kong flights, but these are usually much higher than fares you can book yourself with a variety of airlines. There are numerous daily flights **from Dublin**, operated by *Ryanair*, *Aer Lingus*, and *British Midland* – the cheapest, on *Ryanair*, cost from around IR£60 for a return to Luton or Stansted, though the cost of the bus and underground journeys across London may make the total cost greater than *Aer Lingus* or *British Midland* fares to Heathrow. **From Belfast**, there are *British Airways* and *British Midland* flights to Heathrow, but the cheapest service is the *Britannia Airways* run to Luton, at around £70 return.

From Dublin, you can slightly undercut the plane's price by getting a **Eurotrain** ticket (around IR£50 return), but from Belfast you'll save nothing by taking the train or ferry.

Alternatively, check with your local travel agent (*Thomas Cook* addresses given below) for details of **inclusive holidays**, on which the Ireland to Britain section of your trip will be included in the overall price. At the time of writing, a one week holiday (ie, two nights on a plane, five nights in Hong Kong), staying in one of the pleasant Causeway Bay hotels, cost around IR£879.

Airlines and Agencies in Ireland

Aer Lingus
42 Grafton St
Dublin 2   ☎01/794 764

46 Castle St
Belfast   ☎0232/245 151

British Airways
Call Linkline   ☎0345/222111

British Midland
54 Grafton St
Dublin 2   ☎01/798 733

Suite 2, Fountain Centre
College St
Belfast   ☎0232/225 151

Britannia Airways
no reservations office in Ireland –
bookings from Luton Airport,
Luton, Beds   ☎0582/424 155

Ryan Air
College Park House
20 Nassau St   ☎01/797 444
Dublin 2   or ☎01/770 444

Thomas Cook
118 Grafton St
Dublin   ☎01/6771721

11 Donegall Place
Belfast   ☎0232/240 833

USIT
Aston Quay
O'Connell Bridge
Dublin 2   ☎01/679 8833

Fountain Centre
College St
Belfast   ☎0232/324073

Getting to Hong Kong and Macau from North America

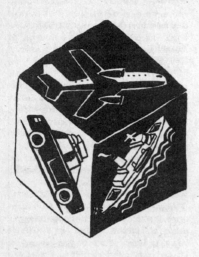

There are any number of possible routes to Hong Kong from the US, all of which involve flying at some point. Whichever method you choose will probably not be particularly cheap, but if you shop around and allow yourself time to plan then it's possible to find some real bargains, and also some very inventive routes.

Direct from the USA

Cathay Pacific, United, and *Northwest* all fly non-stop **from the West Coast** to Hong Kong: *United* and *Northwest* return fares run from around $890 (low season) to $1150 (high season); *Cathay Pacific* fares are usually around $150 higher.

From the East Coast, you're looking at from $1200–1450 return with *United* and *Northwest,* $150 or so more with *Cathay Pacific.* Due to the presence of the Pacific the only viable **stopover** destinations when flying to Hong Kong are Alaska and Hawaii. Flying with *Northwest* or *United* you can often call in at the latter for no more than the regular round-trip fare.

Airlines

Canadian Airlines
Canada ☎ 800/665-1177;
USA ☎ 800/426-7000.

Cathay Pacific
☎ 800/233-2742.
Flies direct to Hong Kong daily from Los Angeles

China Airways
☎ 800/227-5118.
Flies into Hong Kong via Taipei, Taiwan from Los Angeles, San Francisco, and New York. The New York flight makes an additional stop in Anchorage, Alaska.

Korean Air
☎ 800/438-5000.
Flies to Hong Kong via Seoul.

Northwest Airlines
☎ 800/447-4747.
Flies to Hong Kong via Tokyo or Seoul. Departures from New York, Detroit, Los Angeles, and Seattle.

United Airlines
☎ 800/538-2929.
Flies direct to Hong Kong from San Francisco and LA seven days a week.

For the most up-to-date prices and current special offers, you should phone the airlines (most have toll-free numbers), or see a travel agent.

Student and Discount Flights

For student and discount fares, try the organizations listed overleaf, many of which from time to time offer genuine bargains. There are plenty of agents to choose from, and you should be able to turn up fares from the West Coast as low as $800–900 round-trip. Also worth checking are the travel pages of the Sunday papers, the *New York Times,* and the *Washington Post.* The airlines offer occasional excellent promotional and vacation deals.

Council Travel in the US

Head Office
205 E 42nd St
New York, NY 10017   ☎ 212/661-1450

Emery Village, 1561 N Decatur Rd
Atlanta, GA 30307   ☎ 404/377-9997

2000 Guadalupe St, Suite 6
Austin, TX 78705   ☎ 512/472-4931

2486 Channing Way
Berkeley, CA 94704   ☎ 510/848-8604

729 Boylston St, Suite 201
Boston, MA 02116   ☎ 617/266-1926

1138 13th St
Boulder, CO 80302   ☎ 303/447-8101/
905-5777

1384 Massachusetts Ave,
Suite 206,
Cambridge, MA 02138   ☎ 617/497-1497

1153 N. Dearborn St
Chicago, IL 60610   ☎ 312/951-0585

1093 Broxton Ave., Suite 220
Los Angeles, CA 90024   ☎ 310/208-3551

6363 Charles St
New Orleans, LA 70118   ☎ 504/866-1767

198 W 4th St
New York, NY 10011   ☎ 212/254-2525

895 Amsterdam Ave
New York, NY 10025   ☎ 212/666-4177

715 SW Morrison, Suite 600
Portland, OR 97205   ☎ 503/228-1900

171 Angell St, Suite 212
Providence, RI 02906   ☎ 401/331-5810

530 Bush St, Suite 700
San Francisco, CA 94108   ☎ 415/421-3473

1314 Northeast 43rd St, Suite 210
Seattle, WA 98105   ☎ 206/632-2448

1210 Potomac St, NW
Washington, DC 20007   ☎ 202/337-6464

STA Travel in the US

273 Newbury St
Boston, MA 02116   ☎ 617/266-6014

914 Westwood Blvd
Los Angeles, CA 90024   ☎ 310/824-1574

48 E 11th St
New York, NY 10003   ☎ 212/477-7166

166 Geary St, Suite 702
San Francisco, CA 94108   ☎ 415/391-8407

Travel Cuts in Canada

Head Office
87 College St
Toronto, Ontario M5T 1P7   ☎ 416/979-2406

12304 Jasper Ave
Edmonton T5N 3K5   ☎ 403/488-8487

6139 South St
Halifax B3H 4J2   ☎ 902/424-7027

Université McGill
3480 rue McTavish
Montréal H3A 1X9   ☎ 514/398-0647

1613 rue St Denis
Montréal H2X 3K3   ☎ 514/843-8511

1 Stewart St, Suite 203
Ottawa K1N 6H7   ☎ 613/238-8222

96 Gerrard St E
Toronto M5B 1G7   ☎ 416/977-0441

1516 Duranleau St,
Granville Island
Vancouver V6H 3S4;   ☎ 604/689-2887

Student Union Building
University of British Columbia
Vancouver V6T 1W5   ☎ 604/822-6890

University Centre
University of Manitoba
Winnipeg R3T 2N2   ☎ 204/269-9530

Nouvelles Frontières

12 E 33rd St
New York, NY 10016   ☎ 212/779-0600

1001 Sherbrook East, Suite 720
Montréal, H2L 1L3   ☎ 514/526-8444

Packages, Round-the-World Tickets and Courier Flights

If you're planning a short stay and want a pre-planned **package vacation**, there are a number of companies that offer airfare and five-day hotel stay for the same price as a regular air ticket. *Interpacific Tours* (111 East 15th Street, New York, NY 10003; ☎ 800/221-3594) and others offer bare bones packages of flight and five-night hotel stays (West Coast departures) for $995–1255 depending on the season; information is available at travel agents.

A popular way to see the Far East is on a **Round-the-World (RTW) ticket**, on which only flight and destinations are reserved in advance, leaving you to your own devices to plan your itinerary. Most tickets use a combination of major air carriers, stopping in Hong Kong as well as cities like Delhi, London, and New York. *Airbrokers International* (☎800/883-3273) can supply an RTW ticket, including Hong Kong, for around $1350–1450.

Possibly the cheapest, but also the most restrictive way of getting to Hong Kong is by taking a **courier flight**. New York-based *Now Voyager* (☎212/431-1616) and Los Angeles agency *Way To Go Travel* (☎213/466-1126) sometimes offer flights for less than half the standard fare to Hong Kong. Bear in mind that availability of flights and dates of departure may be restricted, along with the amount of baggage

you're allowed to carry, and that this method shouldn't be relied on for last-minute flights.

From Canada

Canadian Airlines (see box on p.8 for telephone number) flies daily from Toronto to Hong Kong, making a stop in Vancouver. **From Vancouver**, fares range from Can$1320–1545, **from Toronto**, Can$1570–1795, depending on the season. Other than this, most of the major US airlines have connecting flights from Toronto and Vancouver linked to their direct Hong Kong flights originating in Los Angeles, San Francisco, and Seattle.

Getting to Hong Kong and Macau from Australasia

A fairly wide selection of airlines offers all sorts of flights between Australasia and Hong Kong, as well as Round-the-World tickets which include the territory. To sort them all out you'd do best to use one of the specialist independent travel agents, the best in both countries being the long-established *STA Travel*. Look, too, in the travel sections of the weekend newspapers, which carry adverts for other agents and operators. It's as well to know from the outset that scheduled flights aren't particularly cheap from either Australia or New Zealand, and you'll pay much more if you want to travel in December or January.

From Australia, *Qantas* flies to Hong Kong from Sydney, Brisbane, Melbourne or Adelaide for around A$1230 return; it's a couple of hundred dollars cheaper from Perth. Youth/student fares offer a slight saving on these prices. However, you should be able to undercut these fares with

other airlines, particularly if you're just looking for a one-way flight to Hong Kong as part of a longer world trip: one-way fares range from A$490 with *Royal Brunei* from Darwin or Perth to A$700 from Sydney with *Garuda*. Possible **stopovers** to bear in mind are Bali and Jakarta with *Garuda*; Brunei with *Royal Brunei*; Bangkok with *Thai Airways*; and Singapore with *Singapore Airlines*. Or, if Hong Kong is your only destination, consider an **inclusive package**. *Qantas* currently offers a return airfare from Sydney and six nights' accommodation in Hong Kong for around A$1300.

From New Zealand, a low-season (June and July) *Qantas* fare from Auckland to Hong Kong is around NZ$1200 return. This obviously increases during peak season, but shop around and you should be able to find all-year-round fares of around NZ$1500 return (with *Singapore Airlines*) from Auckland or Christchurch.

Red Tape and Visas

Most people need only a valid passport to enter Hong Kong or Macau. Depending on your nationality, you'll be allowed to stay for various periods, from three days to a year without a visa.

Hong Kong

British citizens will be given a stamp in their passports on entry allowing them to stay for up to one year. Citizens of **Eire, Canada, Australia, New Zealand**, all other **Commonwealth** passport holders and citizens of most **European** countries can stay for up to three months. **American** citizens can stay for up to thirty days, as can South African, Japanese, German and Greek passport holders.

Everyone else should consult the relevant British Embassy, Consulate or High Commission in their country of origin for visa requirements; some are listed below. If in any doubt, write to the **Immigration Department**, 7 Gloucester Rd, Wan Chai, Hong Kong ☎ 829 3000.

There shouldn't be any trouble with the **immigration officers**, all of whom speak English. You may be asked how long you intend to stay, and if it's for a fairly lengthy period, for referees in Hong Kong and to prove that you can support yourself without working. Remember that the questions are designed to see if you're intending to work in Hong Kong: if you are, and you don't have an employment visa (see p.276), on no account say so.

Given the length of time most people are allowed to stay in Hong Kong, you shouldn't need to **extend your stay** if you're just a tourist: in any case, go to Macau or China for the weekend and come back, and nine times out of ten you'll just

British Embassies and Consulates Abroad		Germany	
Australia		Friedrich-Elbert-Allée 51	
Commonwealth Avenue		Bonn 1	☎ 0228/23 40 61
Yarralumla, Canberra, ACT 2600	☎ 2706666	Unter den Linden 32–34	
		Berlin 1080	☎ 220 2431
Canada		**Ireland**	
Room 901, 1155 University St		31–33 Merrion Rd	
Montréal H3B 3A7	☎ 514/866-5863	Dublin 4	☎ 01/695 211
80 Elgin St		**Netherlands**	
Ottawa K1P 5K7	☎ 613/237 1303	General Koningslaan 44	
		Amsterdam	☎ 020/676 4343
China		**New Zealand,**	
11 Guang Hua Lu	☎ 532 1961	Reserve Bank Building	
Jian Guo Men Wai	or ☎ 532 1930	9th Floor, 2 The Terrace	
Beijing 100600	or ☎ 5321938	Wellington 1	☎ 726 049
244 Yong Fu Lu		**USA**	
Shanghai 20031	☎ 330 508	3100 Massachusetts Ave NW	
		Washington DC	☎ 202/986-0205
Denmark		845 Third Ave	
Kastelsvej 36–40		New York	☎ 212/745 0202
DK-2100, Copenhagen	☎ 35/26 4600		

get another period stamped in your passport. If you want to ensure a longer stay, though, you'll need to apply for a visa from the Immigration Department (see above); as you will if you're intending to stay on and work in the territory, for details of which see "Staying On", p.276.

If you're in trouble or lose your passport, or you want details of the visas necessary for travel on to neighbouring countries, consult the relevant **foreign consulate in Hong Kong** – there's a list on p.280–281. And for specific visa requirements for **travel to China**, see "Onwards Travel", p.365.

Customs

You're allowed to bring the following **duty free goods** into Hong Kong: 200 cigarettes (or 50 cigars or 250g of tobacco), 1 litre of wine, 60ml of perfume and 250ml of toilet water. Apart from spirits, which are all taxed, you can take most other things into Hong Kong with little difficulty – though transporting electrical goods into the territory is rather like taking coals to Newcastle. **Prohibited items** include all firearms and fireworks, while if you're caught carrying any kind of **drugs** you can expect very tough treatment. Indeed, if you're arriving from anywhere in Southeast Asia that has a high drugs profile, and are young and scruffy, or have long hair, your baggage might come in for some extra attention.

Macau

Citizens of Britain, Australia, New Zealand, Canada, USA and most European countries need only a **valid passport** to enter Macau, and can stay up to ninety days. Hong Kong residents can stay for twenty days; other nationals, including citizens of Eire, don't need a visa either, but can only stay three days. Irish citizens wanting to stay more than three days can buy an **individual visa** on arrival, valid for twenty days. If you're a national of a country which doesn't have diplomatic relations with Portugal, you need a visa in advance from an **overseas Portuguese Consulate** – for the address of the Portuguese Consulate in Hong Kong, see p.281.

If you need to extend your stay (and this is unlikely, given the size of the place), the simplest thing is to return to Hong Kong and re-enter Macau at a later date.

You'll barely notice the **customs** officials as you arrive in Macau, though there might be the odd spot check, with the same severe penalties as Hong Kong for any drugs or firearms offences. Otherwise, the only thing to watch for is when **returning to Hong Kong**: there's no export duty on goods taken out of Macau, though the Hong Kong authorities will only allow you to bring in one litre of the cheap wine (or spirits) sold in Macau, and 50 cigarettes.

Information and Maps

Both Hong and Macau maintain tourist offices in several cities abroad, where you can pick up information, maps, brochures and leaflets before you go. Don't go mad, though: once you're there, you'll get better, more detailed information from **local tourist offices**. For addresses and opening hours, see Hong Kong, p.36, Macau, p.294.

Maps

The **street plans** given away by the tourist offices are fairly good, but if you want more detailed

Tourist Offices Abroad

Hong Kong Tourist Association (HKTA)

Australia
Level 5, 55 Harrington St
The Rocks
Sydney, NSW 2000 ☎ 02/251 2855

Canada
Suite 909, 347 Bay St
Toronto
Ontario M5H 2R7 ☎ 416/366 2389

France
38 Avenue George V (entrance at
53 rue François 1er, 7th Floor)
75008 Paris ☎ 47/20 39 54

Germany
Wiesenau 1
D-6000 Frankfurt am Main ☎ 069/722 841

New Zealand
PO Box 2120
Auckland ☎ 09/521 3167

Singapore
10 Collyer Quay, No. 13-08
13th Floor, Ocean Building
Singapore 0104 ☎ 65/532 3668

UK
5th Floor, 125 Pall Mall
London SW1 ☎ 071/930 4775

USA
Suite 2400, 333 North Michigan Ave
Chicago IL 60601 ☎ 312/782 3872

590 Fifth Ave, 5th Floor
New York, NY 10036 ☎ 212/869 5008

10940 Wishire Blvd, Suite 1220
Los Angeles, CA 90024 ☎ 310/208 4582

Macau Tourist Information Bureau (MTIB)

Australia
449 Darling St
Balmain
Sydney, NSW 2041 ☎ 02/555 7548

Canada
Suite 305, 1530 West 8th Avenue
Vancouver, BC ☎ 604/736 1095

5059 Yonge St
Ontario M2 ☎ 416/733 8768

Europe
Contact the relevant Portuguese National
Tourist Offices for information.

New Zealand
PO Box 42-165, Orakei
Auckland 5 ☎ 64/520 3317

Singapore
11-01 A PIL Building
140 Cecil St
Singapore 0106 ☎ 65/225 0022

UK
6 Sherlock Mews
Paddington St
London W1 ☎ 071/224 3390

USA
Suite 316, 70a Greenwich Ave
New York, NY 10011 ☎ 212/206 6828

3133 Lake Hollywood Drive
PO Box 1860
Los Angeles, CA 90078 ☎ 213/851 3402
for toll-free information: ☎ 800/331 7150

UK & North American Map Outlets

London
Daunt Books, 83 Marylebone High St, W1 ☎071/224 2295.

National Map Centre, 22–24 Caxton St, SW1 ☎071/222 4945.

Stanfords, 12–14 Long Acre, WC2 ☎071/836 1321.

The Travellers' Bookshop, 25 Cecil Court, WC2 ☎071/836 9132.

Chicago
Rand McNally, 444 North Michigan Ave, IL 60611 ☎312/321 1751.

New York
The Complete Traveler Bookstore, 199 Madison Ave, NY 10016 ☎212/685 9007.

Rand McNally, 150 East 52nd St, NY 10022 ☎212/758 7488.

Traveler's Bookstore, 22 West 52nd St, NY 10019 ☎212/664 0995.

San Francisco
The Complete Traveler Bookstore, 3207 Filmore St, CA 92123.

Rand McNally, 595 Market St, CA 94105 ☎415/777 3131.

Seattle
Elliot Bay Book Company, 101 S Main St, WA 98104 ☎206/624 6600.

Toronto
Open Air Books and Maps,
25 Toronto St, M5R 2C1 ☎416/363 0719.

Vancouver
World Wide Books and Maps, 1247 Granville St.

regional **maps** of Hong Kong and Macau or Southeast Asia, visit one of the map outlets listed in the box above. On the whole, though, you'd do better to wait until you get to Hong Kong as there's a wider available selection in the bookshops there; see p.262 for more details.

Costs and Money

It's difficult to pinpoint an average daily cost for staying in Hong Kong and Macau, though it's broadly true to say that both places come more expensive than most other Southeast Asian destinations in terms of food and accommodation. If you've just come from China or Thailand, for instance, you're in for a substantial increase in your daily budget. The details below should help you plan exactly how much to allow for.

The easiest and safest way to carry your money is as **travellers' cheques**, available for a small commission (usually one percent of the amount ordered) from any bank and some building societies, whether or not you have an account, and from branches of *American Express* and *Thomas Cook*. **Paying for things** with travellers' cheques and credit cards is widely accepted, though the major scam you'll encounter when paying for things with plastic is the 3–5 percent **commission** that lots of travel agencies and shops add to the price. It's illegal, but there's not much you can do about it except shop around: always ask first if there's an extra commission charge with a credit card. And inform your credit card company when you get home.

You can get cash advances from banks on all the major **credit cards** – *Visa, Access (Mastercard), American Express* and *Diners Club* – as well as using them in return for goods and services. In addition, *American Express, Mastercard* and *Visa* cardholders can use the **automatic teller machines** (ATMs) at various points in both territories to withdraw local currency; details from the companies direct.

If you need to **transfer money from overseas**, go to one of the major international banks (preferably one which is linked with your bank back home) and get them to have your bank telex the money to a specific branch in Hong Kong. This will probably take a day or so, and you'll be charged a small handling fee.

For **banking information and opening hours** in both territories, see Hong Kong, p.280, Macau, p.333.

Hong Kong

The vast consumer choice in Hong Kong leads to a few contradictions in terms of how much things cost. There is no limit to the amount of money you could spend; certain hotels, restaurants and shops are among the priciest in the world. But the overwhelming majority of the population doesn't command the same income as the super-rich, and consequently it's possible to survive as they do: eating well and cheaply, travelling for very little and staying in low-cost accommodation.

At the bottom end of the scale, staying in hostels and dormitories costs from around £5/$7.50 a night, and cheap Chinese meals at street stalls and in cafés go for another £2–3/$3–4.50 a time. **Living frugally** this way, for a fairly short time, you could survive on around £7–10/$11–15 a day.

Eat out more in fancier restaurants, take a taxi or two, have a drink in a bar, and an average day easily costs £20/$30 or more. Upgrade your accommodation to a room in a guest house with a small bathroom, eat three meals a day and don't stint on the extras and this figure at least doubles: a reasonable estimate for a good time in the territory, without going over the top, is anything from **£35–50/$50–75 a day**. Obviously, if you're planning to stay in one of the very expensive hotels, this figure won't even cover your room – but then you probably won't be bothered about sticking to any kind of budget.

The bonus of Hong Kong is that once you've accounted for your room and a decent meal every day, most of the extras are very cheap: snacking as you go from the street, or lunching on *dim* sum, is excellent value; public transport costs are among the lowest in the world; the museums and galleries are mostly free; and the active, colourful street life doesn't cost a penny either.

Currency

The unit of **currency** is the Hong Kong dollar, often written as HK$, or just $, and divided into 100 cents (written as c). Bank notes are issued by two banks, the *Hongkong and Shanghai Banking Corporation* and the *Standard Chartered Bank*, and are of slightly different design and size, but they're all interchangeable. **Notes** come in denominations of $10, $20, $50, $100, $500 and $1000; **silver coins** as $1, $2 and $5; and **bronze coins** as 10c, 20c and 50c. It's a good idea to buy at least a few Hong Kong dollars from a bank before you go; that way you don't have to use the airport exchange desk (which has poor rates) when you arrive.

The current **rate of exchange** fluctuates around $11–12 to the pound sterling/$7.50–8 to the US$. There's no black market and money can be freely taken in and out of the territory.

Macau

You'll find **living costs** in Macau similar to those in Hong Kong, though there are significant differences. You'll pay slightly more for the very cheap-est beds, but will get much better value in the larger hotels – which drop their prices even further in midweek; it's always worth shopping around. Meals, too, are particularly good value: wine and port is imported from Portugal and untaxed, and an excellent three-course Portuguese meal with wine and coffee can be had for as little as £10/$15. Transport costs are minimal, since you can walk to most places, though buses and taxis are in any case extremely cheap. All in all, you can live much better than in Hong Kong on the same money, or expect to be around 10–20 percent better off if you watch your budget.

The unit of **currency** is the *pataca*, made up of 100 *avos*. You'll see prices written in several ways, usually as M$100, MOP$100 or 100ptcs (as in this book), which mean the same thing. **Coins** come as 10, 20 and 50 *avos*, and 1 and 5ptcs, **notes** in denominations of 10, 50, 100, 500 and 1000ptcs.

The *pataca* is pegged to the Hong Kong dollar (see above), though officially worth roughly three percent less. In practice, **you can use Hong Kong dollars (notes and coins) throughout Macau** to pay for anything, on a one-for-one basis, though you can't use *patacas* in Hong Kong – in fact, you'll find them almost impossible to get rid of there, so spend all your *patacas* before you leave Macau.

Health and Insurance

You don't need to have any inoculations to enter Hong Kong or Macau. The only stipulation is that if you've been in an area infected with cholera and typhoid during the fourteen days before your arrival, you'll need certificates of vaccination against the two diseases. These requirements might change, so ask your doctor if you're unsure about what constitutes an infected area. If you're travelling elsewhere in Asia or China, before or after Hong Kong and Macau, it's a good idea to make sure that all your inoculations (against typhoid, cholera, tetanus, polio and hepatitis) are up-to-date; for the addresses of **vaccination centres** in Hong Kong, see p.285; in Macau, see p.335.

Insurance

Medical services, particularly in Hong Kong, are good, but you'll have to pay for all your treatment (and it can be enormously expensive), so taking out an **insurance policy** is vital. Make sure that the medical cover is high enough – ie sufficient to get you home under supervision if you fall really ill. A good policy should also include insurance against loss or theft of money and personal belongings. **UK citizens** can ask about policies at any bank or travel agency, or use a specialist, low-priced firm like *Endsleigh* (97 Southampton Row, London, WC1; ☎071/436 4451) or *Campus Travel* (address on p.5). A couple of weeks' cover starts at around £31, a month around £40, with either.

Before purchasing any insurance, **US and Canadian citizens** should check what they have already, whether as part of a family or student policy – you may find yourself covered for medical expenses and loss or damage to valuables while abroad. Bank or charge accounts often have certain levels of medical or other insurance included, as do home owners' or renters' insurance. Only after exhausting these possibilities might you want to contact a specialist travel insurance company; your travel agent should be able to recommend one – *Travelguard* is a good policy.

For medical treatment and drugs, keep all the **receipts** so that you can claim the money back later. If you have anything stolen, register the loss immediately with the **police**, since without their report, you won't be able to claim. For the address of the main **police stations** in Hong Kong, see p.283, in Macau, p.334.

Health Problems

You shouldn't encounter too many problems during your stay. The **water** is fit for drinking everywhere (except from old wells on some of Hong Kong's outlying islands), though bottled water always tastes nicer. Other than washing or peeling fruit and vegetables from the market, you needn't worry about the **food** either: Cantonese food is usually so fresh it's alive, and the only real problem is with shellfish that's often dredged out of the sometimes less-than-clean bays and waters around the islands.

The **heat** is more likely to lay you low. Hong Kong and Macau can be terribly humid and hot, and skin rashes are not uncommon, something you can combat by showering often and using talcum powder, renting a room with air-conditioning and wearing light cotton clothing. If you come down with **stomach trouble**, the best advice is not to eat anything for 24 hours, to drink lots of water or weak tea, and to take it easy until you feel better. Once on the mend, start on foods like soup or noodles, though if you don't improve quickly, get medical advice.

More sinister is the fact that **AIDS** figures are set to rocket throughout Southeast Asia in general. Thus far, the territories have escaped fairly lightly as places like Bangkok have superseded them as a holiday sex centre. Nevertheless, there's a growing awareness of the threat caused by the virus and TV advertising campaigns and educational programmes have been set in motion. As the latest posters in Hong Kong have it: "Condoms: Less Risky, More Happy!"

Pharmacies, Doctors and Hospitals

For anything more serious than an upset stomach and the like you'll need specialist help. **Pharmacies** can advise on minor ailments and will prescribe basic medicines: they're all registered, will often employ English speakers (especially in the centre of Hong Kong, less so in Macau), and are generally open daily 9am–6pm.

At some stage, even if it's just to look, go into one of the **Chinese herbal medicine shops**, found throughout Hong Kong and Macau, which are stacked from floor to ceiling with lotions, potions and dried herbs. The people in these shops are less likely to speak English, but if you can describe your ailment they'll prescribe and mix for you a herbal remedy that might or might not cure it. Opinions – Western opinions certainly – divide on whether or not the herbal cures really work. On balance, though, there's a strong case to be made for the holistic approach of Chinese medicine. Nevertheless, remember that Chinese herbalists need no formal training to set up shop and are not registered.

For a **doctor**, look in the local phone directories' Yellow Pages (under "Physicians and Surgeons" in Hong Kong; "Medicos" in Macau), or contact the reception desk in the larger hotels. Most doctors have been trained overseas and often speak English. You'll have to pay for a consultation and any medicines they prescribe; ask for a receipt for your insurance.

Hospital treatment is infinitely more expensive, which makes it essential to have some form of medical insurance. Casualty visits are free, however, and hospitals in both territories have 24-hour casualty departments. Finally, both doctors and **dentists** are known as "doctor" in Hong Kong, so be sure you're not wasting your time at the wrong place. Having dental work done costs a lot, so if you possibly can, wait until you get home for treatment.

Opening Hours, Holidays and Festivals

Hong Kong has a fairly complicated set of different opening hours for different shops and services. Generally, though, **offices** are open Monday–Friday 9am–5pm, Saturday 9am–1pm; **banks**, Monday–Friday 9am–4.30pm, Saturday 9am–noon; **shops**, daily 10am–7/8pm, though later in tourist areas (see p.261 for more details); and **post offices**, Monday–Friday 8am–6pm, Saturday 8am–2pm. **Museums** are open various hours, but are usually closed one day a week; check the text for exact details. **Temples** often have no set hours, though are usually open from early morning to early evening; again, the text has full details.

In **Macau**, opening hours are more limited than in Hong Kong, with government and official offices open Monday–Friday 8.30/9am–1pm and 3–5/5.30pm, Saturday 8.30/9am–1pm. Shops and businesses are usually open throughout the day and have slightly longer hours.

On **public holidays** and some religious festivals (see below) most shops and all government offices in both territories will be closed. Annual public holidays in Hong Kong and Macau are listed over the page; Macau has several more than Hong Kong, due to its Portuguese (and consequently Catholic) colonial heritage.

Festivals

You're in luck if you can time a visit to coincide with one of the many **festivals** that bring whole streets or areas in both Hong Kong and Macau to a complete standstill. At the most exuberant festival of all – Chinese New Year – the entire population takes time out to celebrate. With roots going back hundreds (even thousands) of years, many of the festivals are highly symbolic and are often a mixture of secular and religious displays and devotions. Each has its own peculiarities and attractions: not all are as vibrant and lively as New Year, but each offers a unique slice of Hong Kong and Macau and, by extension, China.

Confusingly, not all the festivals are also public holidays, when most things will be closed. But all mean a substantial increase in the number of people travelling on public transport, higher prices for certain services and large crowds in the festival centres. Also, as the Chinese use the **lunar calendar** and not the Gregorian calendar, many of the festivals fall on different days, even different months, from year to year. The likely months are listed below, but for exact details contact the HKTA or MTIB. And for a description of what happens at each major festival in each territory, turn to p.255 (Hong Kong) and p.332 (Macau).

Chinese Festivals

January/February: Chinese New Year; Yuen Siu (Lantern Festival).

April: Ching Ming Festival.

April/May: Tin Hau Festival.

May: Birthday of the Lord Buddha; Tai Chiu Festival.

June: Tuen Ng (Dragon Boat Festival).

July: Birthday of Lu Pan.

August: Maiden's Festival; Yue Lan Festival.

September: Mid-Autumn (Moon Cake) Festival; Birthday of Confucius.

October: Cheung Yeung Festival.

Public Holidays

Hong Kong

January 1: New Year.

January/February: three days' holiday for Chinese New Year.

March/April: Easter (holidays on Good Friday and Easter Monday).

April: Ching Ming Festival.

June: Dragon Boat Festival.

June: Queen's Birthday (public holidays on a Sat and following Mon).

August: Liberation Day (public holidays on Sat preceding last Mon in Aug, and on last Mon in Aug itself).

September: Mid-Autumn Festival.

October: Cheung Yeung Festival.

December 25 and 26: Christmas.

Macau

January 1: New Year.

January/February: three days' holiday for Chinese New Year.

March/April: Easter (holidays on Good Friday and Easter Monday).

April: Ching Ming Festival.

April 25: anniversary of the 1974 Portuguese revolution.

May 1: Labour Day.

June 10: Camões Day and Portuguese Communities Day. Commemorating Portugal's national poet.

June: Dragon Boat Festival; also Feast of St John the Baptist.

September: Mid-Autumn Festival.

October 5: Portuguese Republic Day; to mark the establishment of the Portuguese Republic in 1910.

October: Cheung Yeung Festival.

November 2: All Souls Day.

December 1: Portuguese Independence Day.
8: Feast of Immaculate Conception
22: Winter Solstice.
25 and 26: Christmas.

Post and Phones

As befits one of the world's greatest business centres, Hong Kong's communications are fast and efficient. The phones all work and the postal system is good, sending mail home is quick and relatively cheap, and even receiving poste restante letters is fairly painless. Macau is slightly more laid back, but you should have few problems getting in touch.

Hong Kong

Post offices throughout the territory are open Monday–Friday 8am–6pm, Saturday 8am–2pm. Letters sent **poste restante** will go to the GPO building in Central (see p.283 for address) – take your passport along when you go to collect them. Letters and cards sent **airmail** take five days to a week to reach Britain or North America. **Surface mail** is slower, in weeks and not days; the rates are listed in a leaflet available from most post offices.

If you're sending **parcels** home, they'll have to conform with the post office's packaging regulations, so take your unwrapped parcel along to a main post office – together with your own brown paper and tape – and follow their instructions. It's a good idea to **insure** your parcels, too: the post office will have the relevant forms, as well as the **customs declaration** form that you'll have to fill in for all goods sent abroad by post. Your parcel will go by surface mail unless you specify otherwise – and the price obviously increases the bigger the parcel and the further it has to go.

The Hong Kong **telephone** system – operated by *Hongkong Telecom* – works well, perhaps inspired by the fact that everybody, roadmenders to millionaires, seems to have their own portable phone. Making a **local call** from a private phone, which means throughout the territory of Hong Kong, is free. Public **Coinphones** cost HK\$1 for an unlimited call, while there are also **Creditcard phones** and **Cardphones**. You'll find phones at MTR stations, ferry terminals, in shopping centres and hotel lobbies, while most shops and restaurants will let you use the phone for free. You can buy **phone cards** from *HK Telecom Service Centres* (see below) and from tourist offices and *7-Eleven* stores; they come in units of \$50, \$100 and \$250.

Making a call is easy: on every pay and card phone there are instructions in English – the ringing, engaged and number unobtainable tones are similar to those used in Britain. All telephone numbers contain seven digits and there are no area codes. For **long distance** (ie, international) calls, use the International Direct Dialling (IDD) phones found around the territory, or go to one of the several **Hong Kong Telecom Service Centres** throughout the territory; there's a list of the central ones on p.284. Here you can make overseas calls, including **reverse charge** ("collect") calls, and

---

Telephone Numbers

The Hong Kong Chinese consider certain phone **numbers** to be unlucky, principally because the words for some of the numbers sound like more ominous words, for example, 4 (*sei*), which sounds like the Cantonese word for "death". Lots of people won't accept the private numbers they're allocated by the telephone company for this reason, and there's a continuous struggle to change numbers. Conversely, other numbers are considered lucky because they sound fortuitous – particularly 3 (longevity), 8 (prosperity) and 9 (eternity) – and people will wheedle, pay or bribe to have these included in their telephone number. The same applies, incidentally, to car number plates: each year there's a government auction of the best ones, some of which fetch thousands of dollars.

To phone Hong Kong from abroad
From UK ☎ 010 852 (country code) + number
From USA ☎ 011 852 + number

To phone abroad from Hong Kong
Dial ☎ 001 + IDD country code (see below) +
area code minus first 0 + subscriber number

IDD country codes
Australia ☎ 61   Macau ☎ 853
Canada ☎ 1   New Zealand ☎ 64
China ☎ 86   UK ☎ 44
Ireland ☎ 353   USA ☎ 1

Home Direct codes
Australia 800 0061
Canada 800 1100
Ireland 800 0353
Macau 800 0853
New Zealand 800 0064
UK (BT numbers only) 800 0044
USA   (AT&T) 800 1111
         (MCI) 800 1121
         (Sprint) 800 1877
         (TRT/FTC) 800 1115

send telexes and faxes. Another method of making cashless international calls is to use Hong Kong's **Home Direct** service (see box above), which gives you access to an operator in the country you're calling, who can either charge calls collect or to an **overseas telephone card**. These include the **BT Chargecard** or the card issued by **AT&T Direct Service**. Both cards are free and they work in the same way – just ring the company's international operator (*BT* ☎ 172 0044; *AT&T* ☎ 172 1011), who will connect you free of charge and add the cost of the connected call to your domestic bill.

For a list of **useful telephone numbers** in Hong Kong, see p.284.

Macau

The main **post office** in Macau (see p.334 for address) is open Mon–Fri 9am–1pm and 3–5.30pm, Sat 9am–12.30pm. Otherwise little booths all over Macau sell **stamps**, as do the larger hotels, and there's a post office on each of the two outlying islands, Taipa and Coloane. Letters and cards sent from Macau to Europe and North America take around the same time as from Hong Kong, ie between five days and a week.

The Macanese **telephone system** is operated by *Companhia de Telecomunicações de Macau* (*CTM*). **Local phone calls** from a pay phone cost 1ptca, though like in Hong Kong, local calls are free from a private phone or from the courtesy phones in shops and restaurants. There are no

area codes; just dial the five or six figure number given. You can make **international calls** from the telephone office at the back of the main post office; some of the staff speak English. As in Hong Kong, there's a **Home Direct** service (*Pais Directo*), which gives you access to an operator in the country you're calling, who can either charge calls collect or to your overseas phone card (see "Hong Kong" above). For a round-up of **useful and emergency telephone numbers** in Macau, see p.335.

To phone Macau from abroad
From UK ☎ 010 + 853 (country code) +
number
From USA ☎ 011 853 + number

To phone abroad from Macau
Dial the IDD country code (given below), the
area code (minus its first 0) and finally the
subscriber number
Australia ☎ 0061
Canada ☎ 001
Ireland ☎ 00353
New Zealand ☎ 0064
UK ☎ 0044
USA ☎ 001

to Hong Kong – classed as an international
call – dial ☎ 01 + number.

Home Direct Codes
Australia 0800-610
Canada 0800-100
Hong Kong 0800-852
USA 0800-111

Police and Trouble

Hong Kong and Macau are both relatively safe places for tourists, certainly compared to other Asian cities. The only thing to be really concerned about is the prevalence of pickpockets: the crowded streets, trains and buses are the ideal cover for them. To guard against being robbed in this way, keep money and wallets in inside pockets, sling bags around your neck (and not just over your shoulder) and pay attention when getting on and off packed public transport.

Apart from this, **avoiding trouble** is a matter of common sense. Most of the streets are perfectly safe, as is Hong Kong's MTR underground system, which is clean, well-lit and well-used at night. Taxis, too, are considered to be reliable, though there have been cases of late-night attacks on women by the odd driver: either try not to travel on your own at night, or only get in if you feel comfortable; and only use registered taxis from proper taxi ranks.

In both territories, it's rare that you'll be wandering around areas of the city at night that are a bit dodgy and if you are, there's nothing you can do to avoid standing out. The best advice if you're lost, or somewhere vaguely threatening, is to look purposeful, don't dawdle, and stick to the main roads. If you are **held up and robbed** – an extremely unlikely event – hand over your money and *never* fight back: local villains have large knives which they have few compunctions about using.

More common problems are those associated with **drunkenness** in Hong Kong. If it's your scene, be careful in bars where the emphasis is on buying hugely expensive drinks for the "girls": if you get drunk and can't/won't pay, the bar gorilla will help you find your wallet. And unless you like shouting and fighting, try and avoid the bars when the sailors of various fleets hit the city.

Police and Offences

Probably the only contact you'll have with the green- or blue-uniformed **Royal Hong Kong Police** (who are armed) is if you have something stolen, when you'll need to get a report for your insurance company. On the street, police officers who speak English wear a red flash under their shoulder number. Otherwise, contact one of the police stations, whose addresses are given on p.283. In **Macau**, police wear a dark blue uniform in winter, and sky-blue shirts and navy blue trousers in summer. The main police station, where you should go in the event of any trouble, is listed on p.334.

There are a few **offences** you might commit unwittingly. In Hong Kong, you're required to carry some form of **identification** at all times: if you don't want to carry your passport around, anything with your photograph will do, or your driving licence. Residents (and those thinking of staying and working in Hong Kong) need a special ID card – see p.278 for details of how to get one. It's not likely that you'll be stopped in the street and asked for ID, though you might be involved in the occasional police raid on discos and clubs, when they're usually looking for known Triad members, illegal immigrants and drugs. They'll prevent anyone from leaving until they've taken down everyone's details from their ID.

Buying, selling or otherwise being involved with **drugs** is of course extremely unwise. If you're caught in possession, no one is going to be sympathetic, least of all your consulate. And you can expect to be held in fairly unpleasant conditions for a considerable length of time.

Other than these things, you'll be left pretty much alone, though don't think of **bathing topless** on any of Hong Kong or Macau's beaches: you'll draw a lot of attention to yourself, offend some people and in any case it's illegal.

Sexual Harassment

As a **woman travelling in Hong Kong and Macau**, you're more likely to be harassed by sexist foreign expats than by Chinese men, which at least has the advantage of being more familiar and so easier to deal with. You're not likely to mistake unwelcome advances from a Westerner as cultural inquisitiveness, and the same tactics as at home are the ones to use to get rid of creeps. To minimise what physical risks there are, try and avoid travelling alone late at night in taxis and on Hong Kong's MTR; don't be tempted by any work offers as "hostesses" (see "Staying On", p.276); and generally use your

common sense. For local womens' organisations in Hong Kong, see p.285.

Organised Crime: the Triads

Much of the lurid crime you read about every day in Hong Kong's English-language newspapers is related to the **Triads**, organised crime societies (similar to the Mafia) who appear to be stepping up their illegal activities in the run-up to the handing over of the territory to China. The historical reasons for the Triads' existence is discussed in "History" (p346), but at street level they're directly and indirectly responsible for all the drug dealing, prostitution, corruption and major crime in the territory. Needless to say, you won't come into contact with any of it while you're in Hong Kong, though the drug addicts support their habit by pickpocketing and mugging, and the shop you bought your camera from almost certainly pays protection money to one Triad society or another.

Religion

Most major **religions** are represented in Hong Kong and Macau, though it's the three Chinese and Eastern ones – Taoism, Confucianism and Buddhism – that are of most interest to visitors. Everywhere, you'll come across temples and shrines, while many of the public holidays are connected with a particular religious occasion. The whole picture is further confused by the contemporary importance attached to superstition and ancestor worship. The information below should help sort out some of the main themes, and add some interest as you look around the temples and shrines covered in the book.

The Religions

The main local religion, **Taoism**, dates from the sixth century BC. A philosophical movement, it advocates that people follow a central path or truth, known as *Tao* or 'The Way', and cultivate an understanding of the nature of things. This search for truth has often expressed itself in Taoism by way of superstition on the part of its devotees, who engage in fortune telling and the like. The Taoist gods are mainly legendary figures, with specific powers – protective or otherwise – which you can generally determine from their form: warriors, statesmen, scholars, etc. Taoist temples are generally very colourful, hosting the rowdiest of the annual festivals.

Confucianism also began as a philosophy, based on piety, loyalty, education, humanitarianism and familial devotion. In the 2500 years since Confucius died, these ideas have permeated every aspect of Chinese social life, and the philosophy has acquired the characteristics of a religion. However, it's the least common of the Eastern religions in Hong Kong, with few temples and fewer regular observances. Rather it's a set of principles, adhered to in spirit if not in practice.

Also represented in Hong Kong and, to a lesser extent, Macau, is **Buddhism**, which isn't Chinese at all, but originally came from India to China in the first century AD. It recognises that there is suffering in the world, which can be relieved only by attaining a state of personal enlightenment, *nirvana*, or extinction, at which point you will find true bliss. The method of finding this enlightenment is by meditation. There are lots of different Buddhist sects following slightly different practices, and in Hong Kong the situation is made more complicated by the way in which deities from various religions are worshipped in each other's temples – it's common for Buddhist deities to be worshipped in Taoist temples, for example. Buddhist temples are relaxed places, less common and less bright than Taoist, but often built in beautiful, out-of-the-way places and with resident monks and nuns.

Inside a Temple: the Deities

You'll find descriptions of many Chinese temples in Hong Kong and Macau throughout the text, and as the majority are Taoist what goes on inside is fairly similar everywhere. Most temples are **open** from early morning to early evening and people go in when they like, to make offerings or to pray; there are no set prayer and service times.

The **roofs** of Taoist temples are usually decorated with colourful porcelain figures from Chinese legend, while inside you'll find stalls selling joss sticks, and slow-burning **incense** spirals which hang from the ceiling. In most temples there's a stall or special room for **fortune telling**, most commonly achieved by shaking sticks in a cylinder until one falls out: there's a fortune paper attached to the stick, which has to be paid for and interpreted by the fortune teller at the stall. Go with someone who can speak Chinese if you want to try this, or visit Hong Kong's massive Wong Tai Sin temple in Kowloon (see p.122), where fortune telling takes place on a much more elaborate scale: here you'll find lots of long-established fortune tellers, as well as palmists and phrenologists, who are used to foreign tourists, and lots of explanatory notes.

Obviously, coinciding with one of the main religious **festivals** (see "Opening Hours, Holidays and Festivals", above) is an invigorating experience, and this is when you'll see the various temples at their best: lavishly decorated and full of people. There'll be dances, Chinese opera displays, plenty of noise and a series of **offerings** left in the temples – food, and paper goods which are burned as offerings to the dead.

Gods and Goddesses

You'll find further information about the following **deities** throughout the text, usually under the entry for the main temple in which they're worshipped. For the most part, the Chinese gods and goddesses honoured in Macau are the same as in Hong Kong, with occasional variations in spelling and importance. One to watch for is A-Ma, celebrating the goddess of the sea, who corresponds exactly to Hong Kong's Tin Hau.

Tin Hau: goddess of the sea, and one of the most popular deities, unsurprising in a land where fishing has always been important; known as A-Ma in Macau.

Kuan Ti (or Kuan Yue): god of war; a warrior.

Kuan Yin (or Kwun Yum): Buddhist goddess of mercy.

Pak Tai: god of order and protection; also known as Emperor of the North.

Pao Kung: god of justice.

Wong Tai Sin: a god who cures illness and brings good fortune.

Sui Tsing Paak: a god who cures illness; also known as the "Pacifying General".

Tai Sui: a series of sixty different gods, each related to a year in the Chinese calendar.

Shing Wong: a city god, who's responsible for people living in a certain area.

Disabled Travellers

Physically disabled travellers, especially those reliant upon wheelchairs, will find **Hong Kong** easier to manage than they might have imagined. There are special access and toilet facilities at the airport, as well as on the main Kowloon–Canton Railway (KCR), though other forms of public transport – buses, trams and the MTR underground system – are virtually out of bounds. However, wheelchairs are able to gain access to the lower deck of cross-harbour and outlying island ferries, taxis are usually obliging, and there's a special bus service, *Rehabus*, which operates on a dial-a-ride system – see p.281 for details.

All other facilities for the disabled in public buildings, hotels, restaurants and recreational buildings are listed in a very useful and comprehensive free booklet, **A Guide for Physically Handicapped Visitors to Hong Kong**, distributed by the Hong Kong Tourist Association. This also includes information about the fewer facilities for visually disabled visitors.

On the whole you'll find people willing to help as you go. If you can, use the telephone numbers given in the text to phone ahead if you think there's likely to be a problem with access at any hotel, restaurant or public building. There's a list of **useful numbers** given on p.281 if you require more information when in Hong Kong.

Macau is far less easy to negotiate for most physically disabled travellers The streets are older, narrower, rougher and steeper, and there isn't the same hi-tech edge – overhead rampways, wide, modern elevators, etc – that makes Hong Kong relatively approachable. Visitors in wheelchairs will first have to contact the *STDM* office in Hong Kong (in the Shun Tak Centre; see p.291), which can assist with travel arrangements on the Jetfoils. Some of the larger hotels are also geared towards disabled visitors; contact the MTIB for more information.

In **Britain**, the best sources of information are *Radar*, 25 Mortimer St, London W1 (☎071/637 5400) and *Mobility International*, 228 Borough High St, London SE11 (☎071/403 5688). In the **US**, you can get information and advice from *Mobility International USA*, PO Box 3551, Eugene, OR 97403 (☎503/343 1284) or the *Society for Advancement of Travel for the Handicapped*, 347 Fifth Ave, Suite 610, New York, NY 10016 (☎212/447 7284).

Hong Kong

Chapter 1

Introducing Hong Kong

Amainland peninsula and 235 islands of assorted shape and size on the southeastern tip of China make up the **territory of Hong Kong**, which has a total land area of just under 1100 square kilometres. Over six million people live here, but despite the congestion on the roads and in the urban areas, it's fairly easy to get around: you could travel the 40km from the Chinese border in the north to the south coast of Hong Kong Island in a couple of hours or so. Indeed, it's compact enough to make seeing the whole territory in just a few days eminently possible – though the geographical and cultural diversity packed in between could take weeks of careful exploration if you had the time or the inclination.

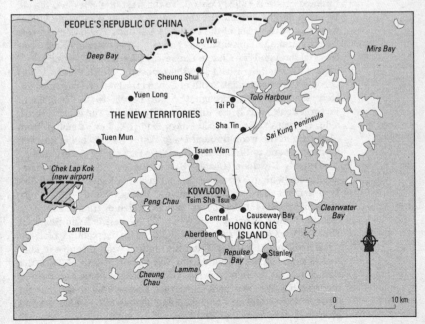

Hong Kong Island, which later gave its name to the entire territory, was the original British settlement – at its widest points, around 15km from east to west and 11km north to south. If you're on the island, you're "Hong Kong-side". The southern part of the Kowloon peninsula (just 12 square kilometres) was added in 1860, but this gave the British control of the deep-water harbour between the two: here, you're "Kowloon-side". At a certain point beyond Kowloon (actually, north of Boundary Street) lie the New Territories, acquired in 1898: they stretch right to the Chinese border and, together with the outlying islands, also added to the colony in 1898, make up the rest of Hong Kong. These distinctions will last only until 1997 when Hong Kong becomes a Special Administrative Region (SAR) of the People's Republic of China.

If your time is at all limited in Hong Kong, you'll do nearly all your sleeping, eating and sightseeing on the island or in Kowloon, crossing between the two on the cross-harbour ferries or on the MTR underground system. However, if you stay on the island and in Kowloon, you're only seeing a fraction of Hong Kong, and – arguably – little of the real Chinese part of the territory.

Orientation

Most visitors start with **Hong Kong Island** (Chapter 2), whose main business centre is called **Central**. To the west, it shades into the old **Western** district, around the area called Sheung Wan, while further west still, at the edge of the island, is **Kennedy Town**. Moving east from Central, the built-up areas change little in outer appearance as they run through **Wan Chai** to **Causeway Bay**, though beyond here – certainly beyond the island's northernmost tip, **North Point** – things become more residential. South of Central the land becomes immediately steeper, rising through the **Mid-Levels** to the heights of **Victoria Peak**, usually just known as "The Peak". The island's **south side** is characterised by its bays and beaches, running from **Aberdeen** in the west, through **Deep Water Bay**, **Repulse Bay** and **Stanley**, around to **Shek O** and **Big Wave Bay** on the eastern side.

Cross to **Kowloon** (Chapter 3) and you leave the island geography firmly behind. The tip of the peninsula is known as **Tsim Sha Tsui** and it's here – along its spine, **Nathan Road** – that every consumer durable under the sun is sold, stolen or traded; here, too, that you'll most likely sleep and eat. To the east is **Tsim Sha Tsui East**, a new area of flash hotels and shopping centres built on reclaimed land, and **Hung Hom** train station; while a couple of kilometres north of Hung Hom is **Kai Tak** airport. North of Tsim Sha Tsui, you head through crowded, gridded streets which become less recognisably Western and more recognisably Asian as you go: through noisy residential and shopping centres like **Yau Ma Tei** and **Mongkok**, 3km from Tsim Sha Tsui.

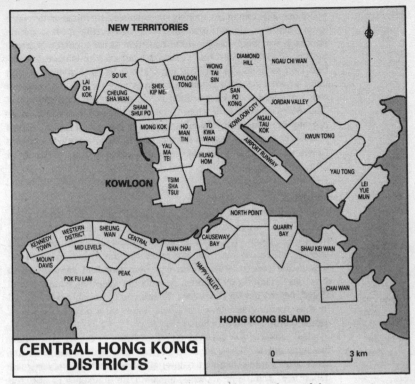

CENTRAL HONG KONG DISTRICTS

0   3 km

You should try and make at least one trip to the **outlying islands** (Chapter 5), the southwestern group especially – **Lamma, Lantau, Cheung Chau** and **Peng Chau** – only around an hour away from Central by ferry. But it's the **New Territories** (Chapter 4) that give an insight into the real Hong Kong: they feed the colony, and provide it with water, labour and enterprise. New towns, like **Sha Tin, Tsuen Wan, Tuen Mun** and **Yuen Long**, are all easily reached by public transport; or you can take the New Territories train line (the KCR) from Hung Hom to **Sheung Shui** – the end of the line on the Hong Kong side of the border – for a fifty-minute tour through the region. To the east, the **Sai Kung peninsula** is a glorious region of country parks, islands, bays and beaches. In the west, traditional Chinese fishing villages, like **Lau Fau Shan**, are also easily reached on a good day out from central Hong Kong.

Arriving in Hong Kong

As most old hands will tell you, arriving in Hong Kong by air is one of travel's most thrilling experiences, the plane swooping down onto the city from over the South China Sea, skimming the high-rise buildings and pulling up quickly on a runway surrounded by water in the heart of Hong Kong. This will remain the most common approach for most visitors until the new airport, currently being built on Chek Lap Kok, one of the outlying islands, is operational – that isn't expected to be until after 1997. Sadly, arriving by ship from anywhere outside Southeast Asia is only for the spectacularly rich, cruise ships docking at the ritzy Ocean Terminal, on the tip of Tsim Sha Tsui. However, there's a distinct chance that you'll arrive in Hong Kong by water if you're staying in the region for any length of time, as there are regular ferry connections with both Macau and China, while overland travellers can also arrive by train or bus from China.

By Air

Planes touch down at **Hong Kong International (Kai Tak) Airport**, on the Kowloon peninsula about 5km from Tsim Sha Tsui. There's a foreign exchange office in the Buffer Hall (with poor rates), a left luggage office, as well as an office of the Hong Kong Hotel Association (see p.193), which can help you find somewhere to stay. The Hong Kong Tourist Association (see "Information and Maps", below) has an office too, though you'll probably be accosted by their roaming assistants, who will hand you a plastic bag full of tourist literature and brochures.

Helicopter arrivals from Macau with East Asia Airlines touch down on the helipad above the Macau Ferry Terminal (see "By Sea" below), where you'll clear customs.

The cheapest way into the city is by bus. For the **Airbus**, follow the signs out of the terminal to the bus and taxi ranks: there are three main routes, detailed below, all of which have very regular departures, and there's plenty of room for luggage. To use the cheaper city buses, take the footpath to the right after leaving the airport and follow the signs to Ma Tau Cheung Road – any of the double-deckers, including the #101 and #111, will take you to Central for around a third of the Airbus price (though using the city buses in the rush hour, with luggage, is madness).

Airbus Routes

• **#A1** to Tsim Sha Tsui via Nathan Road, stopping at the Kowloon-side Star Ferry terminal (daily 7am–midnight, every 15min; $9). Travels via *Miramar Hotel, Mirador Mansions, Chungking Mansions/Holiday Inn Golden Mile/Sheraton, YMCA/The Peninsula, New World/Regent.*

• **#A2** to Hong Kong Island via Wan Chai and Central, stopping at the Macau Ferry Terminal (daily 6.50am–midnight, 11.30pm on Sun, every 12–15min; $14). Travels via *China Harbour View Hotel, Grand Hyatt, Harbour View International House, Island Shangri-La/Conrad/Marriott, Furama/Hilton, Mandarin Oriental, Victoria Hotel.*

• **#A3** to Hong Kong Island, stopping in Causeway Bay (daily 6.55am–midnight, every 15min; $14). Travels via *Excelsior, Park Lane Radisson, Lee Gardens.*

Taking a taxi into the city isn't expensive either. The approximate fares are posted on boards at the taxi rank: the taxis themselves are metered and reliable (see "Getting Around", below, for more details). You might want to get the tourist office in the Buffer Hall to write down the name of your hotel or guest house in Chinese characters for the driver, though drivers will usually know the names of the big hotels in English. It costs roughly $45 to get to Tsim Sha Tsui or the hotels in Tsim Sha Tsui East, around twice that to reach Hong Kong Island, since you have to pay the cross-harbour tunnel toll on top. If you're **staying in New Kowloon or the New Territories**, take a taxi from the airport to Kowloon Tong, a $35 ride and ten minutes west, where you can change onto the underground (MTR) and overground (KCR) train systems.

Note that **rush-hour traffic** can slow down journey times considerably, particularly if you're using the cross-harbour tunnel to Hong Kong Island. Depending on where you're aiming for, and the amount of luggage you're carrying, it's sometimes quicker to take the bus/taxi to the Star Ferry terminal on Kowloon-side and cross that way – or cross the water by MTR from Tsim Sha Tsui.

By Sea

Almost all the various jetfoil and ferry services from Macau arrive at the **Macau Ferry Terminal**, in the Shun Tak Centre, 200 Connaught Road, Hong Kong Island. The MTR (from Sheung Wan station, accessed directly from the Shun Tak Centre) links with most places from there; or you can pick up Airbus #A2 from outside the centre if you're heading for hotels in Central and Wan Chai. Some services from Macau (hoverferries and Jetcats) dock instead at the **China Hong Kong Ferry Terminal** at 33 Canton Road, in Tsim Sha Tsui, behind Kowloon Park, from where it's walking distance to most of the city's accommodation.

From China you'll arrive at the China Hong Kong Ferry Terminal (see above) – on the ferry and Jetcat services from **Guangzhou**, the hoverferry from **Shekou** (close to Shenzhen), the catamaran service from **Zhuhai** (west of Macau) and ferry from **Shanghai**.

By Train and Bus

Express trains from Guangzhou arrive at **Hung Hom Railway Station**, east of Tsim Sha Tsui, also known as the **Kowloon–Canton Railway Station** (or KCR). Signposted walkways lead from here to a bus terminal, taxi rank and the Hung Hom Ferry Pier: for Tsim Sha Tsui East, you can walk from the station, following the signs; for Tsim Sha Tsui itself, take bus #1K, #5C, #8 or #8A to the Star Ferry; for Hong Kong Island, take the cross-harbour ferry to Wan Chai or Central. **Local trains** from Guangzhou drop you at the Chinese border city of Shenzhen, from where you walk across the border to Lo Wu on the Hong Kong side and pick up the regular

KCR trains to Kowloon: it's a fifty-minute ride, the trains following the same length of track to Hung Hom station.

You might conceivably arrive by bus from a couple of Chinese cities, though the services are more used by the local Chinese. The *CTS* bus from Guangzhou drops you at Jordan Road Ferry Terminal, Kowloon, from where it's a cross-harbour ferry to Central or a short walk to Jordan MTR station. From Shenzhen, the *Citybus* stops at the corner of Middle Road and Kowloon Park Drive, Tsim Sha Tsui (behind the YMCA).

Information, Maps and Addresses

At the airport HKTA assistants will sidle up to you and hand over a plastic bag full of brochures. If you miss out, visit the the HKTA information office in the Buffer Hall (daily 8am–10.30pm).

In central Hong Kong there are two more information centres: at Shop 8, Basement, Jardine House, 1 Connaught Place, Central (Mon–Fri 9am–6pm, Sat 9am–1pm); and at the Star Ferry Concourse, Tsim Sha Tsui (Mon–Fri 8am–6pm, Sat & Sun 9am–5pm). They are both staffed by English-speakers and have a wealth of printed information to dish out: transport timetables, accommodation brochures and sightseeing manuals. The most useful things to pick up are the magazine *Hongkong This Week*, which has "what's on" listings; the separate guides to Sightseeing and Culture, Shopping, and Dining and Entertainment; the factsheets on individual temples, sights and areas; and the monthly *Official Hong Kong Guide*, which changes its restaurant recommendations each month and covers current festivals and events.

There's a general, English-language HKTA Telephone Information Service on ☎801 7177 (Mon–Fri 8am–6pm, Sat & Sun 9am–5pm).

Maps

Our maps of Hong Kong should be good enough for most purposes; taken together with the free HKTA map of Tsim Sha Tsui and Central to Causeway Bay, you shouldn't go far wrong. For anything more detailed you'll need one of the commercial maps and gazetteers, vital if you're intending to do any serious travelling around the territory. Best is the paperback format *Hong Kong Guidebook*, a couple of hundred pages of indispensable maps, street and building indexes, transport timetables and other listings. There are various editions, but you should pick one up for around $50–60 from large bookstores which sell English-language books (see p.262).

You might also want to visit the Government Publications Centre, on the ground floor of the General Post Office Building, Connaught Place, Central (Mon–Fri 9am–6pm, Sat 9am–1pm). As well as government publications, this sells the *Countryside Series* of maps ($20–25 each), which come in very useful if you plan to go hiking on the outlying islands or in the New Territories. They have various scales, with good inset maps of the smaller islands and areas.

Finding an address

Finding your way around Hong isn't particularly difficult, though there are certain local peculiarities to be aware of. **Addresses** make great use of building names – often designated "Mansions" – as well as street names and numbers, and usually specify whether the address is in Hong Kong (ie, on Hong Kong Island) or Kowloon. Abbreviations to note are HK (Hong Kong Island), Kow (Kowloon) and NT (New Territories).

If you're looking for a shop or office in a large building, the **numbering system** generally follows this format: no. 803 means no. 3 on the 8th floor; 815 is no. 15 on the 8th floor; 2212 is no. 12 on the 22nd floor, and so on. And floors are numbered in the British fashion: ie, the bottom floor is the ground floor.

To maximise the convenience of the guide, we've listed hotels and many of the restaurants and bars under subheadings which correspond to various districts covered in the guide: eg, Tsim Sha Tsui, Central, Wan Chai, Causeway Bay. These are all served by **MTR underground stations** (see below), called by the same name, which is the easiest way to reach the various districts. Occasionally, a district has more than one MTR station – Tsim Sha Tsui is also served by Jordan MTR; Causeway Bay by Tin Hau MTR – so it's always worth checking which is the nearest. We've marked MTR exits and entrances on our maps.

Getting Around

Hong Kong has one of the world's most efficient integrated public transport systems – from trams and buses to underground and overground trains and ferries – connecting up almost every part of the territory. Moreover, services are extremely cheap and simple to use, which encourages you to roam far and wide. Two problems are universal, whatever type of transport you use. Travelling in the rush hour anywhere in the urban area is a slow and crowded business, worth avoiding; while travelling outside the urban areas, don't expect too many people to speak English – sorting out your route back in advance is a good idea.

The Mass Transit Railway (MTR)

Hong Kong's transport pride and joy, the **Mass Transit Railway** – always shortened to MTR – opened in 1979 and is in a state of constant, and speculative, expansion. It's the city's underground system, running on three lines for over 43km: the **Island Line**, which runs along the north side of Hong Kong Island; the **Tsuen Wan Line**, crossing under the harbour from Admiralty on the island and reaching out to Tsuen Wan in the western New Territories; and the **Kwun Tong Line**, linking Yau Ma Tei in Kowloon with Kwun Tong to the east, and then running back under the harbour to connect with Quarry Bay on Hong Kong Island. The latest plans are for a link with the new airport at Chek Lap Kok, not due to be operational until the airport comes on stream after 1997.

The MTR is the fastest means of public transport in the territory, and the most expensive – the harbour crossing, from Central or Admiralty to Tsim Sha Tsui costs around $6, considerably more than the Star Ferry. However, it is also air-conditioned, fully automated, sparkling clean and very easy to use: the **interchange stations** between lines are clearly marked on maps and boards at the stations and there's a handy interchange at Kowloon Tong (Kwun Tong Line) with the Kowloon–Canton Railway.

The MTR's **hours of operation** are daily from 6am to 1am, with trains running every few minutes; the first and last train times are posted on boards at the stations. The times to avoid using the MTR are the morning and evening **rush hours** (8–9.30am and 5.30–7pm); in the morning especially, the crowds piling onto the escalators and trains are horrendous, and the MTR authorities have taken to hiring people to "help" passengers onto trains and get the doors closed. If you're shoved inside by someone wearing a red sash, don't get cross; there will, in any case, be plenty of shoving going on elsewhere to get worked up about. Incidentally, don't even think about taking heavy luggage onto the train during the morning rush hour.

There's a **no smoking** policy on all trains; you're not supposed to eat anything either. There are also **no toilets** on any of the MTR platforms. However, everything is marked and signposted in English, as well as in Chinese characters, so you shouldn't get lost. See the MTR map (opposite) for all line and station details; for the **MTR Passenger Information Hotline**, call ☎ 750 0170.

Tickets

Tickets cost from $3.50 to $9 for a one-way journey. There are no returns and tickets are only valid for ninety minutes, so don't buy one for your return journey at the same time. The ticketing system is electronic: feed the right amount into the machines on the station concourse and you'll get your ticket, which looks like a plastic credit card. The machines don't give change (the next person gets any credit left), but there are small change machines in the stations, and you can change notes at the information desks. **Children** under twelve need a special Child Ticket from similar machines, which are half-price.

To **use the system**, you feed your ticket into the turnstile, walk through and pick it up on the other side. When you've completed your journey, the turnstile at the other end will retain the ticket.

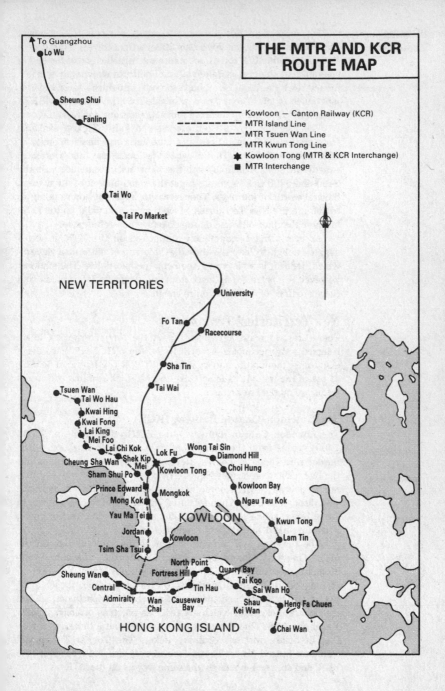

THE MTR AND KCR
ROUTE MAP

Kowloon — Canton Railway (KCR)
MTR Island Line
MTR Tsuen Wan Line
MTR Kwun Tong Line
★ Kowloon Tong (MTR & KCR Interchange)
■ MTR Interchange

To Guangzhou
Lo Wu

Sheung Shui
Fanling

Tai Wo
Tai Po Market

NEW TERRITORIES
University

Fo Tan
Racecourse

Sha Tin
Tai Wai

Tsuen Wan
Tai Wo Hau
Kwai Hing
Kwai Fong
Lai King
Mei Foo
Lai Chi Kok
Cheung Sha Wan
Shek Kip
Mei
Sham Shui Po
Prince Edward
Mong Kok
Yau Ma Tei
Jordan
Tsim Sha Tsui

Lok Fu
Kowloon Tong
Mongkok

Wong Tai Sin
Diamond Hill
Choi Hung
Kowloon Bay
Ngau Tau Kok
Kwun Tong
Lam Tin

KOWLOON
Kowloon

Sheung Wan
Central
Admiralty
Wan
Chai
Causeway
Bay

North Point
Fortress Hill
Tin Hau

Quarry Bay
Tai Koo
Sai Wan Ho
Shau
Kei Wan
Heng Fa Chuen
Chai Wan

HONG KONG ISLAND

For more than one journey, there's a souvenir MTR **Tourist Ticket**. It costs $25, but gives only $20 worth of travel on the system (it's valid on the KCR too). Feed it into the turnstile and at the end of each journey the cost is deducted, the indicator showing how much money is left on the ticket, though for your last ride it doesn't matter how much is left. The ticket is available from MTR stations, HKTA offices, the *Hang Seng* banks in the major stations and KCR stations.

You can also buy a **Common Stored Value Ticket**, available from station booking offices and automatic machines in units of $50, $100 and $200. This is what the locals use, and works on exactly the same principle, with the same last ride bonus; with the $100 and $200 tickets you also get the small benefit of a few extra dollars' worth of journeys. They're worth buying if you're going to travel into the New Territories, since they're also valid on the KCR, but note that unused value on the tickets is non-refundable.

As everything is completely automated on the MTR, it seems simple enough to leap the turnstiles and **travel without a ticket** – which, indeed, is what you'll see some people doing. The stations, however, are patrolled by inspectors and swept by TV cameras, and there are fines of $3000 if you're caught.

New Territories' Trains

There are two **train networks** out in the New Territories, again referred to by acronyms – the KCR and the LRT. You'll have occasion to use them both, particularly the KCR, if you intend to do a bit of out-of-the-way sightseeing. Like the MTR, all stations, signs and trains are marked in English.

The Kowloon–Canton Railway (KCR)

The Kowloon–Canton Railway – the KCR (information on ☎602 7799) – runs from the Hung Hom train station in Kowloon to the border with China at Lo Wu. Regular, electric stopping trains use the line, calling at various New Territory towns on the way – a fifty-minute journey – while some non-stop express trains run right the way through to Guangzhou (Canton). Even if you're only staying in Hong Kong, a ride on the KCR is thoroughly recommended, giving you a first-hand view of New Territories life.

More details on using the KCR to leave Hong Kong are given in "Onwards Travel", p.365.

The ticketing and turnstile system is the same as that on the MTR. One-way **tickets** cost from $3.50 (the Kowloon Tong–Mongkok section) to $7.50 (for the journey from Kowloon to Sheung Shui). **Children** under three travel for free, those under twelve pay half-fare, and there's a **first-class** compartment, staffed by a guard, tickets for which are twice as much as ordinary tickets. You'll pay a $80 **fine** if caught travelling without a ticket, or travelling first-class with an ordinary ticket. The Tourist Ticket and Common Stored Value Ticket (see above) are both valid on the KCR, and are used in exactly the same way as on the MTR.

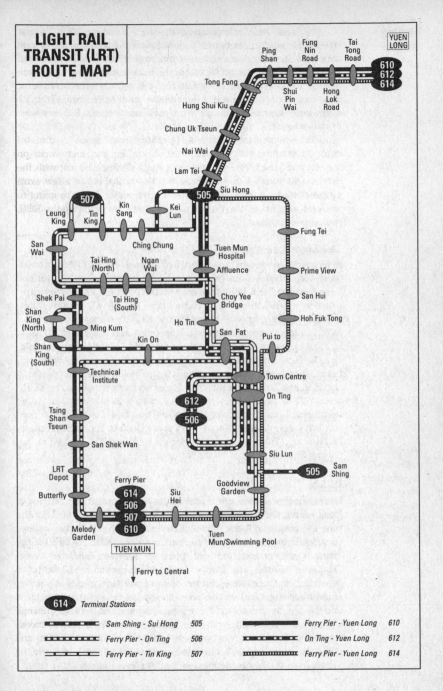

LIGHT RAIL TRANSIT (LRT) ROUTE MAP

YUEN LONG

610
612
614

Ping Shan
Fung Nin Road
Tai Tong Road

Tong Fong
Shui Pin Wai
Hong Lok Road

Hung Shui Kiu

Chung Uk Tseun

Nai Wai

Lam Tei

505   Siu Hong

507   Kin Sang   Kei Lun

Leung King   Tin King

San Wai

Ching Chung

Tai Hing (North)   Ngan Wai

Tuen Mun Hospital

Affluence

Fung Tei

Prime View

San Hui

Shek Pai

Tai Hing (South)

Choy Yee Bridge

Hoh Fuk Tong

Shan King (North)

Ming Kum

Ho Tin

San Fat

Shan King (South)

Kin On

Pui to

Technical Institute

Town Centre

612   On Ting

506

Tsing Shan Tseun

San Shek Wan

Siu Lun

LRT Depot

505   Sam Shing

Ferry Pier

Goodview Garden

Butterfly

614   Siu Hei

506

507

610

Melody Garden

Tuen Mun/Swimming Pool

TUEN MUN

↓ Ferry to Central

---

614   *Terminal Stations*

▬▬▬▬▬	*Sam Shing - Sui Hong* 505	▬▬▬▬▬ *Ferry Pier - Yuen Long* 610
▪▪▪▪▪	*Ferry Pier - On Ting* 506	▬▪▬▪▬ *On Ting - Yuen Long* 612
▬┼┼┼▬	*Ferry Pier - Tin King* 507	▥▥▥▥▥ *Ferry Pier - Yuen Long* 614

As far as the **stations** are concerned, **Kowloon Tong** is the interchange station for the MTR; just follow the signs to switch rail networks. More importantly, **Sheung Shui is the last Hong Kong stop** that you can get off at on the KCR. Although most trains run through to **Lo Wu**, which is still in Hong Kong, it's a restricted area and you'll need to have travel documents valid for entering China to alight here (and a special Lo Wu ticket, which costs $25 one-way from Kowloon).

The air-conditioned trains **operate** from around 6am to midnight, running every ten minutes or so. They're generally much less crowded than the MTR trains (except during rush hour at the Kowloon stations – Kowloon Tong and Mongkok), but be aware that **pickpockets** tend to ply their trade on this route. Again, there's **no smoking** and no eating on board, but there are **toilets** on all the station concourses.

The Light Rail Transit (LRT)

A second train system, the **Light Rail Transit** – LRT (information on ☎468 7788) – links two towns in the western New Territories, Tuen Mun and Yuen Long (see map on the previous page). There are plans to extend the system further into the New Territories and possibly to link it up with the MTR and KCR networks in the future. At the moment, though, it's the rail system you're least likely to use.

The trains are electric, running alongside – and down the middle of – the New Territories' roads, and the system is zoned. Automatic ticket machines on the platforms tell you which zone your destination is in and how much it'll cost. Fares are comparable to the KCR, around $3–5 per journey; feed your money in and wait for your ticket. One branch of the line starts at **Tuen Mun Ferry Pier**, which you can reach direct by hoverferry from Central; the northernmost LRT station, **Yuen Long**, is connected by bus #76K and #77K to Sheung Shui (the end of the KCR line).

Buses

Double-decker buses are operated by three companies: on Hong Kong Island, the *China Motor Bus Company* (*CMB*; ☎565 8556) runs the cream and blue buses, *Citybus* (☎736 3888) the orange ones; while the *Kowloon Motor Bus Company* (*KMB*; ☎745 4466) operates the cream and red ones in Kowloon and the New Territories. **Fares** are low – from $2 to around $10 a trip, depending on the route – and the amount you have to pay is posted at most bus stops and on the buses as you get on. Put the exact fare into the box by the driver; there's no change given, so always keep a supply of coins with you. The buses run on fixed **routes** from various terminals throughout the city, from around 6am to midnight: some of the main **bus terminals**, and the buses which depart from them, are detailed below; for more information check

USEFUL BUS ROUTES: NUMBERS AND TERMINALS

Each double-decker bus is marked with the destination in English and a number. A "K" after the number means that the bus links with a stop on the KCR line; an "M"-suffixed bus stops at an MTR station; ones with an "R" only run on Sunday and public holidays; and "X" buses are express buses with limited stops.

Hong Kong Island

Central Bus Terminal (Exchange Square): to Aberdeen #7 and #70; Causeway Bay #11; Mid-Levels #15; Ocean Park #90; The Peak #15; Repulse Bay #6, #61, #260; Stanley #6, #260; Tiger Balm Gardens #11; Wan Chai #11 .

Central Government Pier: to Cotton Tree Drive (Hong Kong Park) #3; Happy Valley #1 .

City Hall (Edinburgh Place): *maxicabs* to Admiralty MTR #7 (not Sun); Happy Valley, #7 (not Sun); Ocean Park #6 (not Sun); The Peak #1. Also *express bus* to Ocean Park (Sun) #71M; and free *shuttle bus* to Lower Peak Tram terminus.

Macau Ferry Terminal: to Airport #A2; Shau Kei Wan #2.

Kowloon

Jordan Road Ferry: to Lai Chi Kok #12; Sheung Shui #70; Star Ferry #8, #8A; Tuen Mun #60X; Wong Tai Sin temple #11; Yuen Long #68X.

KCR (Hung Hom) Station: to Jordan Road #8A; Kowloon Park #26; Mong Kok #1K; Star Ferry #1K, #5C, #8, #8A; Tsim Sha Tsui East #1K; Whampoa Gardens #8A.

Star Ferry: to Airport #A1, #1A, #5C, #9; China Ferry Terminal #8A; Jade Market #6, #6A, #7, #9; Jordan Rd Ferry #8; KCR station (Hung Hom) #2K, #5C, #8; Kowloon Park #1, #6, #6A, #7; Lai Chi Kok #6A; Mongkok (up Nathan Rd) #1K; Science Museum #5, #5C, #8; Sung Dynasty Village #6A; Temple St Night Market #1,

#6, #6A, #7, #9; Waterloo Road (for YMCA) #7; Whampoa Gardens #8A. Also *maxicabs* to Tsim Sha Tsui East #1, #1M.

Cross-Harbour Services

There are around a dozen cross-harbour bus services: ones you might use include the #170 (Ocean Park/Hennessy Rd/Causeway Bay/Waterloo Rd/Sha Tin KCR), #111 (Chatham Rd North/Wan Chai/Admiralty/Central/Macau Ferry Terminal) and #103 (Waterloo Rd/Wan Chai/Admiralty/Cotton Tree Drive). Otherwise, the two that use the cross-harbour tunnel all night are #121 (Macau Ferry Terminal–Choi Hung) and #122 (North Point Ferry Pier–So Uk).

New Territories

Choi Hung to Clearwater Bay #91; Pak Tam Chung #96R; Sai Kung #92.

Fanling to Hok Tau Wai #52K; Luen Wo Market and Sha Tau Kok #78K; Luk Keng #56K.

Pak Tam Chung to Wong Shek #95R.

Sai Kung to Nai Chung #99; Pak Tam Chung #94; Wong Shek #94.

Sha Tin to Sai Kung, via Nai Chung #89R.

Tai Po Market to Tai Mei Tuk (for Plover Cove) #75K.

Sheung Shui: to Jordan Road Ferry #70; Lok Ma Chau 76K or minibus #17; Yuen Long #76K and #77K.

Tsuen Wan: to Kam Tin #51; Sham Tseng #34B or minibus #96M; Yuen Long, via Tuen Mun (for Ching Chung Koon Temple and Mui Fat Monastery) #68M.

Yuen Long: to Jordan Road Ferry #68 and #68X; Kam Tin #54; Lau Fau Shan #655; Sheung Shui (via Lok Ma Chau) #76K; Sheung Shui (via Kam Tin) #77K; Tai Po Market KCR #64K; Tuen Mun #68M.

the text. Most buses are not air-conditioned (those that are cost more), not particularly well sprung, and can get very crowded during rush hour. However, on longer journeys, to the south of Hong Kong Island and out in the New Territories, they're an excellent way to see the countryside.

Minibuses are red and yellow and seat 14–16 people. They run very regularly on fixed routes throughout the territory, but will stop (within reason) wherever you flag them down or ask to get off. The main problem is that as they're almost exclusively used by the locals, the destination card on the front of each one is in Chinese characters, with a tiny English version above it that is not always visible. Either make sure you know the number that you want to catch (given in the text where necessary) or flag them all down until you strike the one that you want. They're quicker than the double-deckers, the fares are roughly similar and posted inside the bus ($2–8; pay the driver when you get off), and they can be really useful for jumping short distances (up Nathan Rd, say) when you're in a hurry. When they want to get off, the Chinese shout *yau lok*; in practice, you can say almost anything as long as you make it clear you want to get off. On Sundays, public holidays, race days and when it's raining, the fares shoot up to around twice the normal rate. Hours of operation are from around 6am until well after midnight on some routes.

The green and yellow minibuses are called **Maxicabs**, seating the same number of people but running on fixed routes and stopping at marked maxicab stops. Some useful routes are given in the box, and detailed in the text, and the fares are fixed: again, from around $2 to $8 depending on distance, but paid to the driver as you get on. Operative hours are around 6am to midnight.

The HKTA puts out some very useful free **timetables** listing bus routes, frequencies, fares and the Chinese characters for all the major destinations on Hong Kong Island, in Kowloon and the New Territories. Timetables are also posted at most bus stops.

Trams

The north shore of Hong Kong Island has retained its ninety-year-old tram line, with rickety **trams** running from Kennedy Town in the west to Shau Kei Wan in the east, via Western, Central, Wan Chai and Causeway Bay; some detour around Happy Valley too. Not all of them run the full distance, so check the destination (marked in English) on the front and sides before you get on. From Central, east to Shau Kei Wan takes around fifty minutes, west to Kennedy Town around half an hour.

Climb aboard at the back. If you're staying on for a long journey, head upstairs for the views. Otherwise, start working your way through to the front and when you get off, drop the **flat fare** ($1 for adults, 50c for kids) in the box by the driver: there's no change

given. Trams operate from 6am to 1am, though some routes finish
earlier; avoiding the rush hours is essential if you actually want to
see anything as you go – seats are in short supply. For travel **information**, call *Hong Kong Tramways* ☎559 8918.

The most famous tram of all is the **Peak Tram**, not really a tram
at all but a funicular railway, which climbs swiftly from Garden
Road (behind the *Hilton* in Central) to the Peak Tower on Victoria
Peak. Tickets cost $10 one-way, $16 return (children under 12, $4
and $6 respectively), and the service operates from 7am to
midnight, every ten to fifteen minutes; see p.77 for more details.
Information from *Peak Tramways* ☎522 0922.

Ferries and Hoverferries

The one enduring image of Hong Kong is that of the countless
ferries and boats zipping across the harbour. The views are rightly
lauded, and on a clear day the ferries provide an unforgettable first
sight of Hong Kong Island. All the services are very cheap and reliable: the only days to watch out for are in **typhoon** season when the
crossings sometimes become very choppy, though at really blustery
times, they will be suspended altogether.

Of all the **cross-harbour ferry services**, the quickest and most
famous is the **Star Ferry** (information on ☎366 2576), a seven-
minute crossing **between Tsim Sha Tsui and Central** on one of the
ten double-decker, green and white passenger ferries. The service
runs every three minutes at peak hours and operates from 6.30am
to 11.30pm; it currently costs just $1.50 to travel on the upper

---

MAIN CROSS-HARBOUR AND NEW TOWN SERVICES

Hong Kong Island

From Blake Pier: hoverferry to
Tuen Mun (7am–6.30pm, every
10–20min).

**From Central Harbour Services
Ferry Pier**: to Sham Shui Po
(6.30am–7.50pm, every 20min);
Tai Kok Tsui (6am–10pm, every
20min).

From Central Star Ferry Pier:
to Tsim Sha Tsui (6.30am–
11.30pm, every 3–5min); Hung
Hom (7am–7.20pm, every 10min).

From Government Pier: hoverferry to Tsuen Wan (7.20am–
6.20pm, every 10–20min).

From Queen's Pier: hoverferry to
Tsim Sha Tsui East (7am–7pm,
every 20min); *walla-wallas* across
harbour to Kowloon Public Pier.

From Vehicular Ferry Pier: to
Jordan Road (6.15am–midnight,
every 12–15min).

Kowloon

From Hung Hom Ferry Pier: to
Central (7am–7.20pm, every
10min); Wan Chai (6.20am–10pm,
every 20min); North Point
(6.15am–10.45pm, every 20min).

From Jordan Road Ferry Pier:
to Central (6.15am–midnight,
every 12–15min); Wan Chai
(6.30am–10.30pm, every 20min).

**From Tsim Sha Tsui Star Ferry
Pier**: to Central (6.30am–
11.30pm, every 3–5min); Wan
Chai (7.30am–11pm, every
10min).

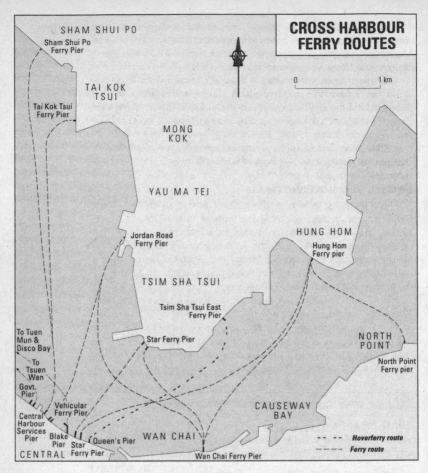

CROSS HARBOUR
FERRY ROUTES

SHAM SHUI PO

Sham Shui Po
Ferry Pier

TAI KOK
TSUI

Tai Kok Tsui
Ferry Pier

MONG
KOK

YAU MA TEI

Jordan Road
Ferry Pier

HUNG HOM

Hung Hom
Ferry pier

TSIM SHA TSUI

Tsim Sha Tsui East
Ferry Pier

Star Ferry Pier

To Tuen
Mun &
Disco Bay

To
Tsuen
Wan

Govt.
Pier

Central
Harbour
Services
Pier

Vehicular
Ferry Pier

Blake
Pier Star
Ferry Pier

CENTRAL

Queen's Pier

WAN CHAI

NORTH
POINT

North Point
Ferry pier

CAUSEWAY
BAY

Wan Chai Ferry Pier

- - - Hoverferry route
- - - Ferry route

0   1 km

deck, $1.20 on the lower deck. Check you're in the right channel at
the ferry pier, feed your coins into the relevant turnstile and join the
waiting hordes at the gate, which swings open when the ferry docks.
It all looks chaotic, but the numbers allowed on board are
controlled, and if there are too many people you'll have to wait for
the next ferry – though this will never be more than a few minutes
behind. There's one other very useful Star Ferry cross-harbour
service, the fifteen-minute Central–Hung Hom crossing (for the
KCR station). The *Hong Kong Ferry Company* (☎542 3081) also
operates a series of cross-harbour services, the most useful the
Tsim Sha Tsui–Wan Chai run; some of the others are detailed
below and in the text where relevant. While you may have no real
cause to use these, they're worth thinking about simply as trips in
their own right: splendid, cheap sightseeing.

Quicker harbour crossings are provided by a fleet of
hoverferries, most usefully the one that links Central (next to the
Star Ferry pier) with Tsim Sha Tsui East, stopping at the pier in
front of the *Shangri-La Hotel*: this runs every twenty minutes or so,
from 7am to 7pm, and costs $4. Hoverferries also run to the new
towns of Tsuen Wan and Tuen Mun, in the New Territories, and
details are given in the text. There's another series of ferries and
hoverferries that serve the outlying islands from Central and elsewhere: all the details for those are given on p.164–165.

After midnight, when the ferries stop running, you can cross the
harbour on one of the motorised sampans that you'll have seen
scuttling back and forth. Usually known as kaidos (or *walla-
wallas*), they can be hired from Queen's Pier, Central, and Kowloon
Public Pier – the prices comparing well with the taxi fare late at
night.

Taxis

Hong Kong's taxis are relatively cheap: you can flag them down in
the street, or pick one up at the ranks you'll find at major MTR and
KCR stations, both Star Ferry terminals, the KCR train station and
Jordan Road Ferry Terminal. If a cab is for hire there's a red "For
Hire" flag in the windscreen; at night the "Taxi" sign on the roof is
lit. Make sure the driver turns the meter on when you get in (though
rip-offs are rare). On Hong Kong Island and Kowloon, taxis are
red: minimum charge is $9 (for the first 2km) and then it's 90c for
every 200m. In the New Territories, taxis are green and slightly
cheaper. The island of Lantau has its own taxi service, though
there's no taxi service on any other island.

There are a few drawbacks to taxis. They can be extremely
hard to come by when it rains, on race days, after midnight, and at
driver changeover time (around 9.30am and again at 4pm). Many
drivers don't speak English, although they'll know the names of
major hotels – and they should have a card somewhere in the cab
with major destinations listed in Cantonese and English. Otherwise
you'll need to have someone write down where you're going on a
piece of paper and show it to the driver.

The other gripe is that although the red taxis are supposed to
work on Hong Kong Island and in Kowloon, drivers will often only
pick up fares on one side or the other. In practice, this means that if
you want to use the cross-harbour tunnel, the driver is allowed to
charge you double the $10 toll (ie another $20 on top of the fare),
since they assume they won't get a fare back. More annoying is the
practice of drivers heading back to base and putting a sign in their
window saying either "Hong Kong" or "Kowloon", depending on
where they are; they'll only take you if you're headed their way, but
more often than not will still charge you double the actual toll. Ask
before you set off, and if they want $20 kick up a fuss and get out:

it's a rip-off. On the subject of tolls, you'll also have to pay them on top of your fare at the other tunnels in the territory: the Aberdeen tunnel ($5) and the Lion Rock tunnel to Sha Tin ($6). You'll also have to pay an extra $4 for each piece of luggage.

There's a **Taxi Complaints Hotline** (☎527 7177): take a note of the taxi number if you want to pursue a complaint.

Renting Cars and Bikes

There are comparatively few private cars in Hong Kong: only nineteen percent of the territory's vehicles are privately owned and run; the rest are public transport, goods' and works' vehicles. And you soon get an idea of who does drive when you look at the other figures: there are more Rolls Royces in Hong Kong per head of the population than anywhere else in the world, and more *in number* than everywhere except Britain and the US.

Accordingly, there isn't a circumstance when **renting your own car** in Hong Kong is a sensible idea. The public transport system is so good that it's rarely quicker to drive, and in any case, one dose of rush-hour traffic would put you off for ever. If you really need a car, out in the New Territories, say, or on Lantau, it's always cheaper just to take a taxi. There's also the problem of parking: finding a space in the centre is nigh impossible, and the multi-storey car parks are generally expensive and located where you least want them. If you're determined, turn to p.280 for the addresses of **car rental agencies and central car parks**.

Bike rental is a more likely possibility, though again, not in central Hong Kong or Kowloon. There are several places in the New Territories where it's fun: there are cycle lanes around Sha Tin and stretching all the way along Tolo Harbour to Tai Po. To use these, go to Tai Wai KCR station and rent a bike from the open space next to the amusement park there; the cheapest are only a few dollars an hour (for more, see p.130). You can also rent bikes at the Plover Cove country park, near Tai Po; see p.138. The best place, though, for bikes are the less congested outlying islands: there are some for hire at Mui Wo on Lantau.

Walking and Hiking

All the above means of transport will combine during your stay with the best way of getting around much of the territory: **walking**. It's unavoidable on nearly all the outlying islands, good fun in the country parks of the New Territories and essential on the view-laden round-Peak tour. In the city, parts of Central and Western on the island, and Kowloon, are fascinating places to stroll around, and in Central there's a hi-tech edge to walking: step off the Star Ferry and head up the nearest set of steps and you don't need to touch the ground again for hundreds of metres as you walk above the traffic on **footbridges and escalators** – in fact, you can keep above ground right the way from the Star Ferry to the Macau Ferry Terminal in the west and Admiralty in the east.

More energetically, all the possible long-distance hikes are covered in the text. The three main routes are the **Lantau Trail** (p.176); the 100km-long **MacLehose Trail** in the New Territories (p.127), from Pak Tam Chung to Tuen Mun; and the **Hong Kong Island Trail** (p.53), which runs from east to west across Hong Kong Island.

Rickshaws and Helicopters

Every time you step off the Star Ferry on Hong Kong Island, you'll pass the idle red rickshaws in the concourse, survivors of a trade that was once the only way around Hong Kong, certainly for the monied classes. The old blokes squatting next to their vehicles are touting for custom, though what this generally means is a photo-opportunity: bargain before you snap away and expect to pay around $50 for a picture. You *can* ask them to take you around the block, something that with bargaining will cost around twice that. But try to get them to take you any further and, whatever you pay them, you could end up on manslaughter charges, as most of them don't look fit enough to blow their own noses.

If you're really intent on wasting your cash on frivolous transport, you could always charter a helicopter (for five people or less) for a jaunt over Hong Kong Island, Lantau or the New Territories. Prices start at $2100 for a fifteen-minute jaunt with *Heliservices* ☎ 802 0200.

Organised Tours

There are more **organised tours** of Hong Kong than you can shake a stick at and even if you have a general antipathy to this kind of operation, with only a couple of days in Hong Kong, some are worth considering – certainly the more exotic tram- and boat-related extravaganzas. Some of the better ideas are detailed below. Also, if you really can't bear to make your own arrangements, a whole range of companies will organise your trip to Macau or China, though this is so easy to do yourself these days it makes falling off a log look tricky. For more help, turn to the list of **travel agencies** on p.284.

China Travel Service, 2nd Floor, China Travel Building, 77 Queen's Rd, Central ☎ 525 2284; 1st Floor, Alpha House, 27–33 Nathan Rd, Tsim Sha Tsui ☎ 721 1331. Local tours and China trips with the Chinese state organisation.

Detours Ltd, 1st Floor, Carnarvon Mansion, 3A, 10 Carnarvon Rd, Tsim Sha Tsui ☎ 311 6111. Ninety-minute harbour tours on the Duk Ling junk, four times daily Mon–Sat. Around $200 per person including drinks.

Organised Tours and Museums

The Gray Line, 5th Floor, Cheong Hing Building, 72 Nathan Rd, Tsim Sha Tsui ☎723 5262 or ☎368 7111. An international organisation whose Hong Kong arm runs predictable coach tours ($200 upwards) plus longer trips to Macau and China.

Hong Kong Archeological Society, Block 58, Kowloon Park, Tsim Sha Tsui ☎723 5765. Field trips, lectures and excavations. Contact the Honorary Secretary.

HKTA Any of the HKTA offices can book you onto one of their tours, which include everything from escorted visits to various attractions to harbour cruises and full-day New Territories tours. Some of the more offbeat itineraries include a *dim sum* lunch served on an antique tram; an evening cruise with unlimited free drinks; a Family Insight Tour, including a visit to a public housing estate; a day at the races; and a day's sport at the Clearwater Bay Golf and Country Club. From around $120 a head upwards; more expensive China day-trips, too.

Wan Fu, *Hong Kong Hilton*, 2 Queen's Road, Central ☎523 3111 x2009. The *Hilton*'s rigged sailing ship, the *Wan Fu*, is available for hire for lunch, dinner and general cruises. From $300–600 a head, including barbecue meals and drinks.

Watertours, Salisbury Rd, between Kowloon-side Star Ferry and Ocean Terminal, outside Star House; and Blake Pier, Central ☎525 4808 or ☎730 3031. From around $140 for a two-hour harbour cruise. Most of their tours include at least a few drinks; the expensive ones come with dinner and unlimited booze.

Museums

The alphabetical list of Hong Kong's museums below includes full details of current opening hours, admission and concessionary prices, telephone contact numbers and public transport links. The page references refer to specific accounts of the particular museums. Note that on **public holidays** (there's a list on p.20), museum adopt Sunday opening hours, while most are closed for a few days over Christmas and Chinese New Year.

Chinese University Art Gallery, Chinese University, Sha Tin, New Territories ☎609 7416. Open Mon–Sat 10am–4.30pm, Sun 12.30–4.30pm; free. University KCR. See p.135.

Fung Ping Shan Museum, University of Hong Kong, 94 Bonham Rd ☎859 2114. Open Mon–Sat 9.30am–6pm; closed Founder's Day 16 March; free. Bus #3. See p.74.

Lei Cheng Uk Museum, 41 Tonkin St, Sham Shui Po ☎386 2863. Open Mon–Wed & Fri–Sat 10am–1pm & 2–6pm, Sun 1–6pm; free. Cheung Sha Wan MTR. See p.123.

Museum of Art, Cultural Centre Complex, 10 Salisbury Rd, Tsim Sha Tsui ☎734 2167. Open Mon–Wed & Fri–Sat 10am–6pm, Sun 1–6pm; $10, children and senior citizens $5. Tsim Sha Tsui MTR. See p.109.

Museum of Chinese Historical Relics, 1st Floor, Causeway Centre, 28 Harbour Rd, Wan Chai ☎827 4692. Open Mon–Sat 10am–6pm, Sun 1–6pm; free. Bus #10A or ferry to Wan Chai. See p.84.

Museum of History, Kowloon Park, Haiphong Rd, Tsim Sha Tsui ☎367 1124. Open Mon–Thurs & Sat 10am–6pm, Sun 1–6pm; $10, children and senior citizens $5. Tsim Sha Tsui MTR. See p.115.

Museum of Teaware, Flagstaff House, Hong Kong Park, Cotton Tree Drive, Central ☎869 0690. Open daily except Wed 10am–5pm; free. Admiralty MTR, bus #3. See p.66.

Police Museum, 27 Coombe Rd, Wan Chai Gap ☎849 6018. Open Tues 2–5pm, Wed–Sun 9am–5pm; free. Bus #15. See p.82.

Railway Museum, On Fu Rd, Tai Po Market, New Territories ☎653 3339. Open daily except Tues 9am–4pm; free. Tai Po Market KCR. See p.136.

Sam Tung Uk Museum, Kwu Uk Lane, Tsuen Wan, New Territories ☎411 2001. Open daily except Tues 9am–4pm; free. Tsuen Wan MTR. See p.145.

Science Museum, Science Museum Rd, Tsim Sha East ☎732 3232. Open Tues–Fri 1–9pm, Sat & Sun 10am–9pm; $25, children and senior citizens $15. Minibus #1. See p.116.

Sheung Yiu Folk Museum, Pak Tam Chung, Sai Kung Country Park, New Territories ☎792 6365. Open daily except Tues 9am–4pm; free. Choi Hung MTR, bus #92 to Sai Kung and then bus #94. See p.159.

Space Museum, Cultural Centre Complex, 10 Salisbury Rd, Tsim Sha Tsui ☎734 2722. Open Mon & Wed–Fri 1–9pm, Sat & Sun 10am–9pm; $10, children & senior citizens $5. Tsim Sha Tsui MTR. See p.112.

Chapter 2

Hong Kong Island

To many people – visitors and residents alike – **Hong Kong Island** *is* Hong Kong. Seized by the British in 1841, the colony took its name from the island (*Heung Gong* in Cantonese, or "Fragrant Harbour") and created its initial wealth here, despite Lord Palmerston's famous disappointment that all Britain had grabbed was a "barren rock" in the South China Sea. The rich, industrious and influential carried on their business around the enormous harbour, building warehouses, offices and housing, in support of which communications, roads and transport developed as best they could. The island still doesn't look planned, though it has taken a kind of mad, organisational genius to fit buildings into the space allowed by the terrain. First impressions are of an organic mass of concrete and glass, stretching back from the water to the encroaching green hills behind. This is **Central**, the economic hub of the island and territory. Like Manhattan, which it superficially resembles, film and TV familiarity does nothing to prepare you for the reality of a walk through Central's streets, which hold as tightly constructed a grouping of buildings as can be imagined: there's little available space to drive, walk or even breathe at ground level, and the only way left to build is up.

The wealth generated in this urban concentration is part of the reason that Hong Kong exists as a British territory, and brash, commercial Central is interesting for just that – though the island also encompasses the more traditional districts of **Western** and **Wan Chai**, and the tourist and shopping zone of **Causeway Bay**. There are rural pockets and walks, too, that make Hong Kong Island an attractive target for a few days' gentle sightseeing. When it's tough going in the city, half an hour's bus ride leaves you on the island's **south side** or **east coast** for a diverse series of attractions: beaches, small villages and seafood restaurants, an amusement park, markets and walks. Closer to Central, you can escape the city by getting on top of it, either by a walk through residential **Mid-Levels** or **Wan Chai Gap**, or by going one better and scaling **Victoria Peak** itself, the highest point on the island, reached by the famous Peak Tram, a perilously steep funicular railway.

Central

The financial, business and administrative heart of the territory, **CENTRAL**, is crammed into a tight web of streets on the northern side of Hong Kong Island. It forms the southern edge of Victoria harbour and is just a few minutes from the mainland by ferry. Still technically the "capital" of Hong Kong, the district was originally named Victoria, following the planting of the Union Jack just to the west of here in 1841, claiming the island for Britain. The name still survives with the harbour, but the district's no-nonsense, latter-day tag reflects what this part of Hong Kong has become in the last fifty years: the most expensive bit of real estate in the world, supporting a few of the planet's priciest (and most exciting) buildings and a skyline for the twenty-first century.

Packed into a short stretch of land (much of it reclaimed over the years) that only reaches a few blocks back from the harbour, Central is emphatically a place to walk around. You can see much of the area from elevated walkways and escalators that pass above the snarling streets and construction jackhammers. This way, without touching the ground, you can head along the harbour front or through the shopping malls and lower floors of the skyscrapers that stack back from the water. Nearly all the sights are contemporary, relating to the buildings and views, shops and consumption. But it's an appealing concoction: markets and street traders rub shoulders with the monolithic financial slabs and towers; the **harbour** is a mass of activity; while a few rare **colonial buildings** survive, one – Flagstaff House – hosting Central's only **museum**. This lies within the boundaries of the territory's newest park, **Hong Park Park**, and it's here – and in the nearby **Zoological and Botanical Gardens** – that the district gets as close as Hong Kong ever does to winding down.

Around the Star Ferry Pier

The cheapest, greatest ferry ride in the world, the *Star Ferry* across the harbour from Tsim Sha Tsui, lands you right in Central at the **Star Ferry Pier**. If you're staying in Tsim Sha Tsui, make this seven-minute ride as soon as you can after arrival: the sight of Central's

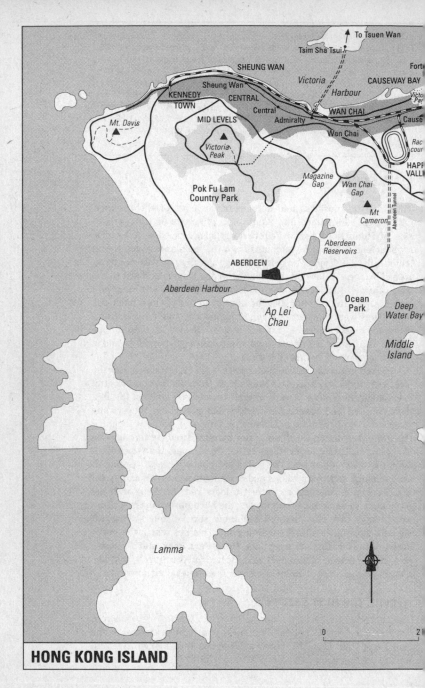

To Tsuen Wan

Tsim Sha Tsui

Fort

SHEUNG WAN

Victoria

CAUSEWAY BAY

Sheung Wan

Victo
Par

KENNEDY
TOWN

CENTRAL

Harbour

WAN CHAI

Central

Admiralty

Cause

Mt. Davis

MID LEVELS

Wan Chai

Rac
cour

Victoria
Peak

HAPP
VALL

Magazine
Gap

Wan Chai
Gap

Pok Fu Lam
Country Park

Mt
Cameron

Aberdeen Tunnel

Aberdeen
Reservoirs

ABERDEEN

Aberdeen Harbour

Ap Lei
Chau

Ocean
Park

Deep
Water Bay

Middle
Island

Lamma

N

0   2

HONG KONG ISLAND

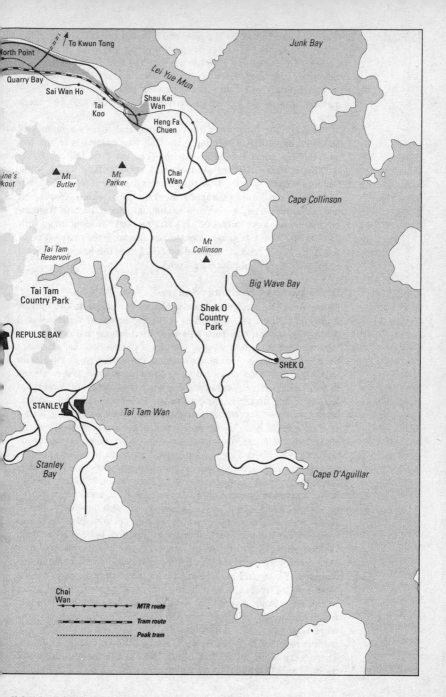

tower blocks, framed by the hills and looming up as the ferry skips across the channel, is one of the most thrilling images of Hong Kong – one you're unlikely to forget in a hurry. The ferries themselves (so-called because each ferry is named after a star: "Morning Star", "Evening Star", etc) have been running since 1898, the diesel-operated, double-decker ferries carrying around 100,000 passengers a day.

Step off the ferry onto the concourse and there's a huddle of buildings immediately to hand. City Hall (see below) is to the left past the car park; the long and low **General Post Office** (GPO) building is to the right of the pier; and, rising behind it, the white building with the hundreds of portholes is **Jardine House**, the head-quarters of the Jardine company. Built in 1972, within ten years it had been completely covered in aluminium, since the tiles from its original facing kept falling off. It's still marked on some maps with its old name, the Connaught Centre, and contains the main office of the **Hong Kong Tourist Association** (HKTA) in the basement (Shop 8; Mon–Fri 9am–6pm, Sat 9am–1pm).

Blake Pier and Exchange Square

Either from the Star Ferry concourse or the steps at the end of Connaught Place, you can climb up to the **elevated walkway and footbridge** system that runs alongside the harbour and deeper into Central. Best for a first view of the city is the section that stretches for a half-kilometre or so above Connaught Road, west to the Macau Ferry Terminal, escalators dropping down at intervals to give access to the various ferry piers along the way. The section of footbridge leading to the first pier adjacent to the Star Ferry, **Blake Pier**, is a home for those for whom Hong Kong's economic miracle hasn't worked, people lying under cardboard on the concrete walkway. At Blake Pier itself, the lower level is the departure point for the hover-ferries to Discovery Bay (Lantau) and Tuen Mun (New Territories). On the upper level, a roof garden with benches gives fine views over the harbour, most enjoyable if you ensconce yourself in the café/bar at the end of the pier and sink a beer as the sun goes down.

In an almost obscene juxtaposition with the down-and-outs of Blake Pier, the adjacent pastel-pink, marble and glass buildings house Hong Kong's **Stock Exchange**, ranking behind New York, London and Tokyo in world importance. The territory's four exchanges were merged in April 1986 and found a new home in this complex, Swiss architect Remo Riva's **Exchange Square**, whose three towers, open spaces and fountains add a rare touch of grace to the waterfront. Everything here is computer-operated: you can watch the latest gold prices on video screens, the buildings' environment is electronically controlled, and the brokers and others who work here whisk between floors in state-of-the-art talking elevators. There's exhibition space, too, inside **The Forum**, the restaurant and meeting area that splits the complex.

Victoria Harbour

Central is the best place to ponder the magnificent **Victoria Harbour**, one of the major reasons that the British took possession of Hong Kong Island in the first place. This was once the best and busiest deep-water harbour in the world, though the waterfront warehouses – or "godowns" – are long gone, and the money-making has shifted into the office blocks of Central, many of which are built upon land reclaimed from the sea. In 1840, the harbour was 2km wide: the latest reclamation project under discussion will add another 300m to the island's north shore, halve the original width of the harbour and drastically reduce its natural capacity for flushing itself. This could prove catastrophic since the harbour is already dangerously polluted, as a peer over the side of any *Star Ferry* will prove – 1.5 million cubic litres of untreated sewage are discharged here daily. It's still difficult to beat the thrill of crossing the harbour by ferry, but even that is at risk from a mooted plan to build a pedestrian footbridge from Central to Tsim Sha Tsui.

Apart from the *Star Ferry*, there are several other **ferry** routes and **harbour cruises** to take, and you get a fine sight of the capacity of the port every time you arrive by ferry from one of the outlying islands or Macau. Or simply park yourself on a bench on Blake Pier and watch the comings and goings of the junks, ferries, motorboats, container ships, cruise liners, hoverferries and sailing boats. Twenty thousand ocean-going ships pass through the harbour every year, with scores of thousands of smaller boats heading from here on their way to the Pearl River Estuary and China.

Underneath Exchange Square (reached by escalators) is Hong Kong's **Central Bus Terminal**, also referred to as Exchange Square Bus Terminal – a handy place to know about if you want to head further afield. Buses leave from here for Aberdeen, Stanley, Repulse Bay and The Peak among other places; see p.43 for details.

City Hall to HMS Tamar

To the left of the Star Ferry Pier, the two blocks of the **City Hall** are a mean exercise in 1960s' civic architecture, given the grand mid-nineteenth-century French classical structure that was its forerunner – and which was knocked down with little care for aesthetics, like so much in Hong Kong. The Low Block, to the front, has a theatre and a concert hall (and a *dim sum* restaurant with harbour views), as well as an enclosed garden through which parade regular wedding parties. The High Block to the rear holds a succession of libraries, a recital hall and various committee rooms.

It's useful to know that the City Hall Low Block houses clean, free public toilets.

In front of City Hall, **Queen's Pier** has a hoverferry service across to Tsim Sha Tsui East. This is also where the corporate junks belonging to the local businesses tie up. If you're here at around 6pm on Friday and Saturday evening, the quayside is jammed with motorised yachts jockeying for position.

The area just to the east of here was until recently the site of the British Naval Headquarters – known as **HMS Tamar** after the naval supply ship that docked here in 1878 and became the Royal Navy's administrative HQ in 1897. The ship was scuttled during World War

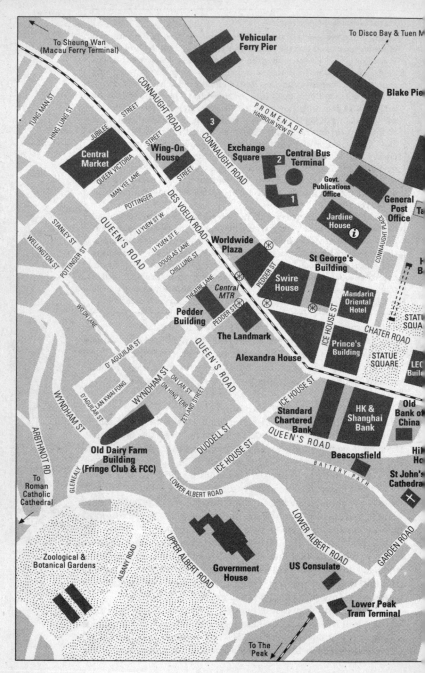

To Sheung Wan
(Macau Ferry Terminal)

Vehicular
Ferry Pier

To Disco Bay & Tuen M

Blake Pie

CONNAUGHT ROAD

STREET

TUNG MAN ST

HING LUNG ST

JUBILEE STREET

STREET

PROMENADE
HARBOUR VIEW ST

3

Wing-On
House

CONNAUGHT ROAD

Central
Market

QUEEN VICTORIA

MAN YEE LANE

Exchange
Square

2

Central Bus
Terminal

Govt.
Publications
Office

General
Post
Office

Ta

POTTINGER

DES VOEUX ROAD

LI YUEN ST W

LI YUEN ST E.

Jardine
House

i

STANLEY ST

WELLINGTON ST

POTTINGER ST

QUEEN'S ROAD

DOUGLAS LANE

CHIU LUNG ST

Worldwide
Plaza

St George's
Building

H
B

THEATRE LANE

PEDDER ST

Swire
House

Mandarin
Oriental
Hotel

STATI
SQUA

Central
MTR

WO ON LANE

Pedder
Building

PEDDER ST

CHATER ROAD

The Landmark

Prince's
Building

STATUE
SQUARE

ICE HOUSE ST

D'AGUILAR ST

QUEEN'S ROAD

Alexandra House

LEC
Buile

WYNDHAM ST

LAN KWAI FONG

ON LAN ST

ON HING TERR

ZETLAND STREET

ICE HOUSE ST

Standard
Chartered
Bank

HK &
Shanghai
Bank

Old
Bank of
China

D'AGUILAR ST

DUDDELL ST

QUEEN'S ROAD

Hi
Ho

Old Dairy Farm
Building
(Fringe Club & FCC)

GLENEALY

ICE HOUSE ST

Beaconsfield

BATTERY PATH

St John's
Cathedra

ARBUTHNOT RD

To
Roman
Catholic
Cathedral

LOWER ALBERT ROAD

LOWER ALBERT ROAD

GARDEN ROAD

Zoological &
Botanical
Gardens

ALBANY ROAD

UPPER ALBERT ROAD

Government
House

US Consulate

Lower Peak
Tram Terminal

To The
Peak

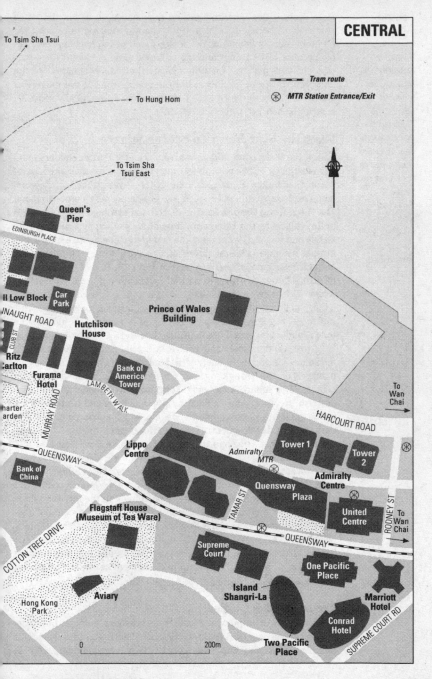

CENTRAL

To Tsim Sha Tsui

To Hung Hom

⚞⚟ Tram route

⊛ MTR Station Entrance/Exit

⊕N

To Tsim Sha Tsui East

Queen's Pier

EDINBURGH PLACE

II Low Block

Car Park

Prince of Wales Building

NNAUGHT ROAD

Hutchison House

CLUB ST

Ritz Carlton

Furama Hotel

Bank of America Tower

LAM BETH WALK

MURRAY ROAD

harter arden

To Wan Chai

HARCOURT ROAD

Lippo Centre

Tower 1

Tower 2

QUEENSWAY

Admiralty MTR

Admiralty Centre

⊛

Bank of China

Quensway Plaza

United Centre

RODNEY ST

To Wan Chai

TAMAR ST

⊛

Flagstaff House (Museum of Tea Ware)

QUEENSWAY

COTTON TREE DRIVE

⊛

Supreme Court

One Pacific Place

Marriott Hotel

Island Shangri-La

Aviary

Hong Kong Park

Conrad Hotel

SUPREME COURT RD

Two Pacific Place

0 ——————— 200m

Central

Transport: between City Hall and the adjacent Edinburgh Place car park, there's a free double-decker shuttle-bus to the Lower Peak Tram Terminal; while the #1 minibus from the same place goes to The Peak.

II, to prevent the Japanese getting their hands on it, but the name continued to be used. In May 1993, the Navy moved to a new base on Stonecutter's Island, at the western end of the harbour, ostensibly because HMS Tamar and the adjacent naval dockyard form part of a planned land reclamation scheme. Indeed, reclamation of the dockyard will soon go ahead, but the real reason for the move was almost certainly to deprive the Chinese navy of a politically sensitive base in the heart of Central after 1997.

From the Star Ferry to Statue Square

Follow the pedestrian underpass from the Star Ferry concourse and you emerge by the **Cenotaph** war memorial, which – after the massacre at Tiananmen Square in June 1989 – was decked in flowers, banners, letters and poems left by pro-democracy demonstrators. The **Hong Kong Club**, a bastion of colonial privilege since Victorian times, still faces the Cenotaph, though it's no longer housed in the stately building that went up at the end of the nineteenth century, but instead occupies several floors of a newish tower. Opposite, the **Mandarin Oriental Hotel** was built in 1963, the first of the new wave of luxury hotels in Hong Kong and candidate for "best hotel in the world" almost every year since – though it hides its riches well inside a fairly dull box-like structure. Taking tea inside is one way for riff-raff to get a glimpse (see p.213), or you can march in and use the toilets, almost the last word in urinary comfort.

Cross Chater Road and you're in **Statue Square**, the statue in question – typically – that of a banker, Sir Thomas Jackson, a manager of the Hongkong and Shanghai Bank in the nineteenth century. The square once gave Hong Kong its colonial focus, open down to the water, surrounded by fine buildings and topped with a statue of Queen Victoria, but it's lost almost all its character to twentieth-century development. (Even a cricket pitch once adorned the square, but this, too, had to move.) The square does come to life, though, on Sunday, when it and the surrounding streets and spaces are packed with the territory's Filipina maids, who gather here on their day off. People from the Philippines form the largest immigrant grouping in Hong Kong and have been coming to the territory since the ending of Spanish colonial rule in their country a century ago. Most are women who come to work here as maids, sending money back home to support their families. They descend upon Statue Square at the weekend, setting out picnics on matting, and reading and singing – a scene Jan Morris likened, memorably, to an "assembly of starlings".

The Legislative Council

One of the most important of Central's surviving colonial buildings sits on the eastern side of Statue Square. Built in the first decade of this century as the **Supreme Court**, the granite building, with its

Hong Kong's Government

Until 1997, when Hong Kong becomes a Special Administrative Region of the People's Republic of China, the territory will retain its British colonial structure. The head of government, the **Governor**, is appointed by the Queen and serves in office without limit. Traditionally, the Governor has been appointed from the ranks of senior British civil servants or diplomats. The current incumbent, Chris Patten, appointed in 1992, after the Conservative Party's general election victory – but following his own personal defeat in his British parliamentary seat – is unique in that he's the first career politician to hold the post.

As Governor, he is head of both the **Executive Council** (known as Exco), which advises the Governor on his day-to-day decisions, and of the **Legislative Council** (Legco), which formulates the territory's laws and controls its expenditure. The only matters the Governor has no responsibilty for are defence and foreign relations, which remain in the hands of the British government. The other governmental body is the **Urban Council**, which raises local taxes to finance municipal services like markets, sports and cultural faciltities.

In the past, both Exco and Legco were staffed solely by appointed and ex-officio members, approved by the Governor. However, following direct elections in September 1991 – the territory's first – roughly a third of Legislative Council members were elected, most of them belonging to Hong Kong's main pro-democracy political party, the United Democrats. They're opposed in Legco, and outside, by the Liberal Democratic Federation, a conservative pro-China political grouping. It's the future of Legco's democratically elected members that is now the point at issue between and the Governor (and, by extension, Britain) and China. The Governor has made it clear that he regards an extension in the franchise in Hong Kong as of paramount importance: elections are proposed in 1995 which would increase the number of directly and indirectly elected Legco members and widen the franchise from around 2000,000 voters to around 2.7 million. China, for its part, is equally keen that the democratic content of Hong Kong's "parliament" be as muted as possible when it takes control of the territory in 1997. For the moment, the issue is unresolved – though for more on the manouvreings of both sides, see p.351.

dome and colonnade, is the only extant structure from earlier times left in the square. It's as safe from future development as anything can be in Hong Kong, renovated since the Court moved to new, modern, premises nearby and now used as the meeting place of Hong Kong's **Legislative Council**. You can't go into what is effectively Hong Kong's parliament, currently the scene of much of the wrangling taking place between Governor Chris Patten, Britain and China over exactly what democratic machinery will be in place by the time the territory is handed back to China in 1997.

The Hongkong and Shanghai Bank and around

Over Statue Square and crossing busy Des Voeux Road puts you right underneath one of Hong Kong's most extraordinary buildings, Norman Foster's headquarters for the **Hongkong and Shanghai**

Banking Corporation, first opened in 1986. Depending on who you believe, it's the most expensive building in the world, costing around a billion US dollars to complete, although the structure itself is far more impressive than any statistics. Wearing its innards on the outside, the ladder-like construction hangs from towers like a suspension bridge, the whole building supported on eight groups of four pillars. Walk under the glass canopy and you look up through the glass underbelly into a sixty-metre-high atrium, the floors linked by long escalators that ride through each storey, open offices ranged around the central atrium. No one minds you riding the first couple of escalators from the gallery underneath the bank to have a look.

On a less hi-tech note, all buildings in Hong Kong have to conform with the dictates of the geomancer, called in with the planning of every building to ensure that spirits aren't disturbed and that the building is favourably sited – and the Hongkong and Shanghai Bank is no exception. The stone lions guarding the entrance are from the bank's previous HQ, torn down to make way for this one, while even the angle of the escalators was fixed according to the instructions of the geomancer.

The Standard Chartered Bank and the Bank of China

There's been a recent spate of bank building around here, each architect keen to outdo the other. Next door to the Hongkong and Shanghai Bank, the **Standard Chartered Bank** put up its own new headquarters, a fairly anonymous thin tower squeezed between opposing blocks that – by design – just topped out above the Hongkong and Shanghai's building.

But the only serious conceptual rival to Foster's creation is the Chinese-American architect I.M. Pei's **Bank of China Tower** further along the road, which succeeded a solid stone predecessor which passes almost unnoticed, opposite the Supreme Court. At seventy storeys high (or around a thousand feet), Pei's blue-trimmed, spear-like building was the territory's highest until Central Plaza went up in Wan Chai (see p.84). However, it doesn't have the compelling interest of the Hongkong and Shanghai Bank, except in its complete domination of the Central skyline – a soaring advertisement for the strength of Communist China, which owns the bank.

Along Queen's Road and Des Voeux Road

Queen's Road is Central's main street, as it has been since the 1840s when it was just above the water and described by contemporaries as a "grand boulevard" (or *dai ma lo* in Cantonese, a name by which it's still known by the Chinese). Running west from **Chater Garden**, the first road to cross it is **Ice House Street**, named for a building that once stored blocks of ice for use in the colony's early hospitals, imported from the United States since there were no commercial ice-making facilities in Hong Kong. A wander up Ice

House Street to the junction with Lower Albert Road gives you a view of a later storage building, the early twentieth-century **Old Dairy Farm Building**, in brown and cream brick, which today houses the Fringe Club (see "The Arts and Media", p.250) and the Foreign Correspondents' Club, a members-only retreat for journalists. On the way, opposite a hospital, you'll also pass two gas street lamps, almost miraculous survivors from earlier times.

To the west, beyond Ice House Street, Queen's Road and parallel **Des Voeux Road** take in some of the most exclusive of the territory's shops and malls, including **The Landmark**, on the corner of Pedder Street and Des Voeux Road. Open since 1980, this is an enormous and very pricey shopping complex, with an impressive fountain in the huge atrium. The complex is one you'll doubtless pass through since it's part of the **pedestrian walkway** system that cuts above this area of Central, linking all the major buildings with the Star Ferry and the harbour.

It's worth leaving the indoor galleries to reach **Pedder Street** itself at some stage – where the turn-of-the-century **Pedder Building**, filled with shops and businesses, is a solid old structure that's somehow escaped demolition over the years. Back across the street, between no. 3a and The Landmark, you should be able to make out a plaque which marks the line of the 1841 waterfront – a remarkable testament to the amount of land reclamation that has taken place since then.

West to Central Market

It doesn't matter which of the two main streets you follow west from Pedder Street, though it's useful to know that **trams** run straight down Des Voeux Road, either into Western or east into Wan Chai. Stay on foot, though, until you've walked the few hundred metres up to Central Market (see below), and you'll pass the parallel cross alleys of **Li Yuen Street East** and **Li Yuen Street West**, which run between the two main roads. Both are packed close with stalls touting clothes and accessories: the East alley sells mostly women's clothes, including silk wear, and accessories; the West alley has more of the same, as well as fabrics and kids' clothes. Emerge from Li Yuen Street East on Queen's Road and you're opposite the more upmarket shopping experience of **Lane Crawford**, one of the city's top – and most staid – department stores, with a smart café up top and aisles full of heavily made-up charge-card queens.

A little further on, the district's western end is marked by **Central Market**, which – like all markets in Hong Kong – is about the best fun you can have outside a hospital operating room. Fish and poultry get butchered on the ground floor, meat on the first, with the relative calm of the fruit and veg selling taking place one floor higher. It's virtually all over by midday, so aim to get here early and (if you've the stomach for it) take a break at one of the food stalls inside.

South of Queen's Road: Lan Kwai Fong

There's a network of streets south of Queen's Road – Stanley Street, Wellington Street, D'Aguilar Street and Wyndham Street – that supports a fancy array of shops, galleries, restaurants and bars, in which the emphasis is firmly European and American. Sedan chairs and rickshaws used to park at the bottom of **Wyndham Street** as late as the 1950s; on foot, you can follow this street right the way up to the zoological gardens if you wish (see below).

Alternatively, try and grab a table in the **Luk Yu Teahouse** at 24–26 Stanley Street, a traditional Chinese tea house relocated here in 1975, using the lovely wooden furniture and decorations from the original building, which had stood on Wing Kut Street since the 1930s.

Apart from the Luk Yu Teahouse (details on p.216), the other famous Cantonese restaurant in the area is the Yung Kee, 32–40 Wellington Street (p.219), a great spot for lunch.

If you've got the money, you may well find yourself eating and drinking in this area at other times, particularly off D'Aguilar Street on a sloping L-shaped lane known as **Lan Kwai Fong**, where there's a burgeoning set of Hong Kong's happening pubs, bars, restaurants and clubs: full details in chapters 7 and 8. They're mostly frequented by expats and well-to-do Chinese yuppies (called, predictably enough, "chuppies") and a night out here doesn't come cheap, though the after-work Happy Hour generally redresses the balance a little, at which time all the bars are packed. Every year at the end of August, the area resounds with the sounds of the **Lan Kwai Fong Street Festival**: several days' worth of outdoor events, food promotions in the restaurants and general good times. During street celebrations in Lan Kwai Fong for New Year's Eve in 1992, panic set in among the 20,000 or so people crowded into the area. In the ensuing crush, twenty people died, a sobering thought as you trawl around the various bars.

There is one small, traditional enclave amidst this contemporary barrage of bars and restaurants. **Wo On Lane**, off the western side of D'Aguilar Street, retains an Earth God shrine, a couple of basic cafés and a working street-barber – a rare sight these days.

From the Zoological Gardens to St John's Cathedral

Perching on the slopes overlooking Central are the two halves of the **Zoological and Botanical Gardens**, open since 1864 (daily 6am–10pm; free); the main entrance is on Upper Albert Road. The views of the harbour disappeared years ago, replaced by spectacular close-ups of the upper storeys of the Bank of China Tower and the Hongkong and Shanghai Bank. Early in the morning it's a favourite venue for people practising *tai chi*, a balletic discipline in which the protagonists are reminiscent of someone walking through treacle. The Botanical Gardens, together with the aviary, are the nicest retreat, replete with pink flamingos, cranes, toucans and all kinds of ducks. Cross the road using the underpass and the Zoological

Buses #3 or #12 run directly to the gardens from stops along Connaught Rd; get off at the Caritas Centre.

section is much less worthy, its unhappy captives – including stir-crazy simians – sitting bored in cramped cages.

An exit through turnstiled gates from here and a right turn down the steep hill, followed by a left up a driveway, leads to the city's **Roman Catholic Cathedral**, finished in 1888 and financed largely by Portuguese Catholics from Macau. It's currently undergoing restoration, but if it's finished you should be able to get in for a look around, particularly to see the stained-glass west windows, made in Toulouse.

Government House and the Cathedral

Beneath the gardens, on Upper Albert Road, **Government House** has been the official residence of Hong Kong's Governors since 1855. It's a strange conglomeration of styles, with several additions made over the years, the most unusual those of a young Japanese architect who was commissioned to redesign the building during the Japanese occupation of Hong Kong in World War II.

The main building was retouched and the central Asian-influenced tower added, making it the one colonial building that's seen spirited adaptation rather than destruction. You can't normally get into the house (though Governor Patten has recently opened up some of the rooms for public concerts; watch the local press for details). One Sunday every spring, however, you're allowed to extend your tour through the Botanical Gardens to take in Government House's flowering gardens, famous for their rhododendrons and azaleas.

Down Garden Road, past the **Lower Peak Tram Terminal** (see p.77), is the other dominant symbol of British colonial rule, the Anglican **St John's Cathedral**, founded in 1847 but damaged during World War II when the Japanese army took it over. It's been restored since and despite being dwarfed by almost everything around, its pleasant aspect gives you an idea of the more graceful proportions of colonial Hong Kong. The main doors, incidentally, were made from the wood of the supply ship *HMS Tamar*, which was docked down at the harbour for nearly fifty years until 1941 (see above), and which lends its name to the British Naval HQ.

You can regain Central's lower grid by walking on down Garden Road, past the L-shaped wedge of the **Hilton** hotel, but it's more direct to stroll across the small, leafy cathedral grounds to the early nineteenth-century redbrick building at the top of the hill, known as **Beaconsfield** after Disraeli, the Earl of Beaconsfield. This has had several uses: once the French Mission Building, for years it housed Victoria District Court, and now it's the Government Information Services Department. During business hours, if you want to see its original early twentieth-century interior, including a mosaic floor, you might ask someone inside to let you have a quick look. From Beaconsfield, a path drops down to Queen's Road and the Hongkong and Shanghai Bank building.

Hong Kong Park

The other route from the Zoological Gardens is to branch to the right down **Cotton Tree Drive**, which sounds charmingly rural, but is in fact choked with traffic. However, beyond the Lower Peak Tram Terminal, on the eastern side of the drive, is the territory's newest urban park project, the remarkably attractive **Hong Kong Park** (daily 7am–11pm; free), which incorporates the colonial Flagstaff House and its museum of tea ware (see below).

Heading straight for the park, bus #3 from along Connaught Rd stops near the entrance; get off at the first stop on Cotton Tree Drive.

Opened in 1991, and beautifully landscaped in tiers up the hillside, the park contains an interesting **conservatory** with dry and humid habitats for its plants and trees, as well as a superb **aviary** (daily 9am–5pm; free) – an enormous mesh tent which incorporates a tropical rainforest and its attendant bird species. Wooden walkways lead you through and above the trees, bringing you face-to-face with exotically coloured hooting birds; signs point out which ones are currently rearing chicks. The rest of the park features ornamental lakes, a visual arts display centre, a children's playground and a bar-restaurant. It's also a popular wedding spot (there's a registry office inside the park), so bridal parties framed by Central's surrounding skyscrapers are a common sight.

Flagstaff House: The Museum of Teaware

Also within the park, in the northern corner, is **Flagstaff House**, in the lee of the massive Bank of China building. Built in 1844, this was the residence of the Commander of the British Forces in the territory for well over a century, and it survives as an impressive piece of colonial architecture – a cool, white, shuttered building, its simple pillars and surrounding garden an elegant contrast to the skyscrapers all around. That it still stands is down to the donation by one Dr. K.S. Lo of his fine teaware collection to the Urban Council, which promptly restored the house and opened the **Museum of Teaware** inside (daily except Wed 10am–5pm; free). The house alone – with high-ceilinged rooms and polished wooden floors – is worth seeing, but the displays of teaware and related items from China throughout the ages are engaging, too, and there are explanatory English notes.

If you want to pick up the MTR, Admiralty MTR has several entrances in the neighbourhood, one at the Lippo Centre itself, another at Queensway Plaza.

Admiralty

Latterly, Central has expanded eastwards, with a batch of striking new buildings down **Queensway**, beyond Hong Kong Park, in an area known as **ADMIRALTY**; all the buildings are connected by overhead walkways which you can join from the bottom of Cotton Tree Drive. The **Lippo Centre** is the most obvious structure, formerly owned by the troubled Australian entrepreneur Alan Bond (after whom it used to be named). Supported on huge grey pillars, interlocking steel and glass spurs trace their way up the centre's twin towers, while in the central lobby a ten-metre-high stone relief of a dragon and junk

dominates. A time capsule placed behind the sculpture in 1988 is due
to be opened in the year 2000, the next year of the dragon.

Walkways connect the Lippo Centre to more office and retail
buildings, like Queensway Plaza, the gold block of the **NEC** building
(the one that looks like a giant cigarette lighter) and **Hutchison
House**, from where you can get back to the other footbridges that
lead around Central's office blocks. There are also walkways across
Queensway to the modern **Supreme Court** building – a disappoint-
ingly squat, grey block – and, along from it, to the vast development
of **Pacific Place**, with yet more shops, offices, restaurants and three
luxury hotels; the *Island Shangri-La*, the *Conrad* and the *Marriott*.

Western District: Sheung Wan To Kennedy Town

The oldest settled parts of Hong Kong Island are all in **Western
District**, which starts only a few hundred metres from the heart of
Central's skyscrapers and office blocks. Not long after the seizure of
the island, the British moved out of Western, leaving what was a
malarial area to the Chinese, who have been living and trading here
ever since. Full of traditional businesses, small temples and crowded
residential streets and fronted by a working harbour, it has a claim to
be the most characterful part of the island, but it's by no means an
homogeneous mass, and encompasses several quite distinct areas.

Sheung Wan, closest to Central, is what's generally thought of
as "Western", a web of street markets and traditional shops that
unfolds back from the **Macau Ferry Terminal**. You can reach the
terminal by the footbridge from Star Ferry in Central; Sheung Wan
also marks the western end of the MTR Island Line. South of Sheung
Wan, climbing up the island's hillside, **Hollywood Road** is one of
the more important of the district's thoroughfares, where you'll find
the famous **Man Mo Temple**; nearby, the **Tai Ping Shan** district
conceals a set of lesser-known temples. Further west, you can skip
the less appealing bits of Western by taking the bus to the
University of Hong Kong, where there's the fine **Fung Ping Shan
Museum** of Chinese art. Or take the tram direct to **Kennedy Town** –
the island's westernmost point of interest – which retains much of
its mid-nineteenth-century character in a series of streets and warehouses alive with the trade based around its harbour.

Sheung Wan

SHEUNG WAN begins immediately west of Central Market, its
streets a more Chinese mixture of traditional shops and merchants,
tucked into the narrow lanes that run between the main roads. You
can follow the routes outlined below, or simply wander into the
district: it's difficult to get lost since the main roads are always

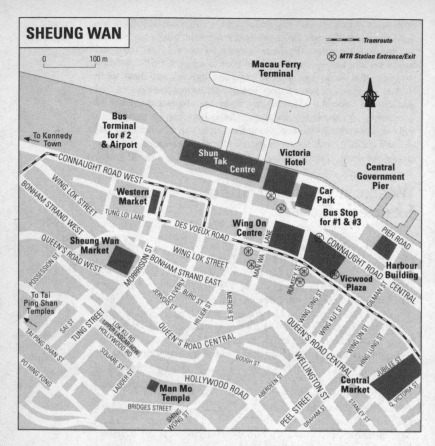

SHEUNG WAN

Tramroute

⊗ MTR Station Entrance/Exit

0   100 m

Macau Ferry Terminal

To Kennedy Town →

Bus Terminal for # 2 & Airport

CONNAUGHT ROAD WEST

Shun Tak Centre

Victoria Hotel

Central Government Pier

Car Park

Bus Stop for #1 & #3

PIER ROAD

WING LOK STREET

Western Market

TUNG LOI LANE

DES VOEUX ROAD

Wing On Centre

MAN WA LANE

CONNAUGHT ROAD CENTRAL

BONHAM STRAND WEST

Sheung Wan Market

QUEEN'S ROAD WEST

POSSESSION ST

MORRISON ST

WING LOK STREET

BONHAM STRAND EAST

RUMSEY ST

WING SING ST

Harbour Building

Vicwood Plaza

GILMAN ST

To Tai Ping Shan Temples

SAI ST

TUNG STREET

JERVOIS ST

CLEVERLY ST

BURD ST

HILLIER ST

MERCER ST

WING SING ST

WING KUT ST

WING ON ST

QUEEN'S ROAD CENTRAL

HING LUNG ST

TAI PING SHAN ST

LOK KU RD

UPPER LASCAR ROW

HOLLYWOOD RD

SQUARE ST

QUEEN'S ROAD CENTRAL

GOUGH ST

WELLINGTON ST

JUBILEE ST

PO HING FONG

LADDER ST

Man Mo Temple

HOLLYWOOD ROAD

ABERDEEN ST

PEEL STREET

GRAHAM ST

Central Market

STANLEY ST

Q. VICTORIA ST

BRIDGES STREET

SHING WONG ST

close by, and once you start climbing you know you're heading away from the harbour.

From Wing On Street to Man Wa Lane

Heading down Des Voeux Road, a couple of blocks up on the left is **Wing On Street**, formerly known as "Cloth Alley" because of the fabric stalls that used to cluster here. They've all been relocated to Western Market, for which, see below. Further up Des Voeux Road is **Wing Sing Street**, a dark and unpromising alley that's the haunt of Hong Kong's egg sellers. It's lined with gloomy, fetid warehouses stuffed and stacked with racks of eggs, which are distributed daily to the territory's restaurants and shops. Apart from the fresh eggs – from ducks, quails, pigeons and geese, as well as chickens – which are inspected under a light by the traders for their freshness, the street also contains a massive range of preserved eggs. The so-called "hundred-year-old eggs" in particular have a fascinating production process. Duck eggs are covered with a thick mixture of lime, ash and tea leaves, soaked for a month and then wrapped in ash and rice husks for around six months, when they are peeled and eaten with pickled ginger. They're an acquired taste: green and black inside, with a strong odour, they have a jelly-like consistency and a rich yolk. Salted eggs, too, are produced here, covered with a black paste made from salt and burnt rice – you'll see men plunging the eggs into murky vats of the paste and stirring slowly. These eggs are Cantonese delicacies, which you can try in plenty of restaurants as an appetiser. Failing that, buy a moon cake during the Mid-Autumn Festival (see "Festivals", p.255), which uses the preserved yolk as a filling.

At the Des Voeux Road end of Wing Sing Street, Wing Lok Street leads down to the stalls of **Man Wa Lane**, where another old Chinese trade is practised – carving seals, or "chops", as the carved name stamps they make here are called. They're used to tourists coming down here to get their personal chop made, and lots of the stalls have their methods and prices marked in English, so if you're tempted it's easy enough to arrange. The craftsmen will translate your name or message into Chinese characters, which are then carved onto the seal you've picked, usually made of wood, soapstone or porcelain. The process takes around an hour, making it possible to wander round the rest of Sheung Wan while you're waiting.

If you're looking for a dim sum lunch, Sheung Wan has some fine, authentic restaurants: try the Diamond Restaurant, *267–275 Des Voeux Rd (p.215).*

Around the Macau Ferry Terminal

Down at the waterfront, catamarans and jetfoils to Macau leave from the **Macau Ferry Terminal**, part of the massive red-trimmed **Shun Tak Centre**, a shopping mall, hotel and apartment complex. If you want to circle back to Central from here, head inside up the main shopping level and from the eastern section (by the *Victoria Hotel* entrance) an **elevated walkway** runs right the way along the harbour, past the outlying island ferry piers, to the Star Ferry terminal, a fifteen-minute walk.

Across Connaught Road from the Shun Tak Centre, **Western Market** (daily 10am–7pm), built in 1906, retains its Edwardian shell but has undergone a marked interior transformation. A Chinese food market for over eighty years, much like Central Market to the east, it was renovated and in 1991 re-opened as an arts and crafts centre – which means it has retained its fine original brick- and ironwork but replaced the noisy market with a two-floor shopping mall. Ground-floor stalls sell arts and crafts, while the first floor is devoted to the cloth shops that moved here from Wing On Street; the second floor is a galleried restauant (which stays open until 11pm).

For a traditional Chinese market, you don't have to venture very far from Western Market. Head up Morrison Street and the large white complex on the right is the **Sheung Wan Market**, packed full of meat, fish, fruit and vegetable stalls. The second floor is a cooked food centre (open 6am–2am), with *dai pai dongs* in operation almost around the clock – a very cheap place for a bowl of noodles.

Wing Lok Street and Bonham Strand

There's more sustained interest in the long streets to the south and west, which provide glimpses of the trades and industries that have survived in this area since the island was settled. **Wing Lok Street**, in its lower reaches at least, retains some of its older, balconied buildings and a succession of varied shops and businesses that merit a browse. Two to look for are *Lam Kie Yuen* tea shop, at no. 78, which features a variety of teas in boxes and tins, as well as ceramic tea pots and cups; and at no. 133 there's an ornamental lantern shop.

Bonham Strand runs parallel and is the centre of the flourishing **snake shop business**, most in evidence from October through to February, when you're considered to need the extra strength that the snake products provide to live through the winter months. The snakes themselves lie coiled up in cages outside the shops, inside which you can buy a wine made out of snakes' gall bladders, and out of snake bile, too: the more poisonous the snake, the better it is for you. There's a typical snake shop at 127 Bonham Strand East; and a slither along Jervois Street and Hillier Street reveals more snake-related businesses, including restaurants serving snake soup.

Even outside the winter season, this area of Sheung Wan repays a visit. It's also known as **Nam Pak Hong** – "North–South Trading Houses" – and many of the businesses are herbal and medicinal wholesalers, with snake recipes just one of their many products. Glass cases fronting Bonham Strand contain a whole host of Chinese medicinal ingredients, of which **ginseng** is the most famous – and one of the most expensive. The root of a plant found in Southeast Asia and North America, there are over thirty different varieties of ginseng, including the pricey red from North Korea, white from the United States and wild from mountainous northeast China. It's prescribed for a whole host of problems, from saving those faced with imminent death by illness (which wild ginseng is purported to delay for three days) to curing hangovers (take white ginseng in boiled water). Some of the larger ginseng trading companies have their offices along **Bonham Strand West**, the most venerable ones boasting impressive interiors of teak and glass. Here you'll see people sorting through newly arrived boxes of ginseng root, chopping it up and preparing it for sale.

Bonham Strand West is quite a modern street, but at its western end **Ko Shing Street** is very different, the bustling artery of the wholesale medicinal trade. Great sacks and wicker baskets are taken off a line of trucks by men carrying a wicked hook in one hand: they spear the sacks and hoist them onto their shoulders, dumping them onto the pavements where others unload and sort their contents. The shops here, open to the street, display ginseng alongside antlers, crushed pearls, dried sea-horses, birds' nests and all the assorted paraphernalia of Chinese **herbalists**. In keeping with the traditional nature of the trade, some of the names are straight from the nineteenth century – one company here has a sign proclaiming it to be the *Prosperity Steamship Company*.

Ko Shing Street bends back round to Des Voeux Road, becoming **Sutherland Street**, along which you'll find a row of street-barbers. Once much more common on the territory's streets, these are among the last, dispensing pudding-bowl haircuts and shampoos and shaves. Back on the main **Des Voeux Road** (along which the tram runs), the stretch between Sutherland Street and Ko Shing Street is devoted to stores selling salted and preserved fish and seafood, dried squid, oysters, scallops and seaweed. They make for colourful displays, and even if the pricey preserved scallops are out of your range, you could always pick up a bottle of homemade oyster sauce.

Along and around Hollywood Road

Hollywood Road, running west from the end of Wyndham Street in Central, and the steep streets off it, forms one of Western's most interesting areas, a run of secondhand and antique shops, curio and furniture stores. There's some wonderful Asian applied art here – blackwood furniture, ceramics, painted screens, prints, figurines and statues – and although most of the shops are firmly geared towards tourists there are any number of smaller places that sell (basically) junk. Hollywood Road is also known for its coffin sellers, and there are a few surviving shops as well that sell funeral clothes for the dead, made from silk.

Man Mo Temple

Follow Hollywood Road west and just before the junction with Ladder Street is the **Man Mo Temple** (daily 7am–5pm), one of Hong Kong's oldest, built in the 1840s and equipped with impressive interior decorations from mainland China. It's dark and smoky, the hanging, pyramidal incense coils belching out scented fumes, but it's not intimidating and no one will mind you poking about the interior. It's generally busy, too, as plenty of people pop in to pay their respects to the two gods honoured here, while others are having their fortunes told by shaking inscribed sticks out of bamboo cylinders. The name of the temple means "civil" (Man) and "martial" (Mo) and it's dedicated to these two characteristics which are represented by separate gods. The "civil" aspect belongs to the God of Literature, Man Cheong, who protects civil servants (he's the red-robed statue wielding a writing brush); the "martial" is that of the God of War, Kuan Ti (represented by another statue, in green, holding a sword). Kuan Ti, particularly, is an interesting deity, worshipped by both Buddhists and Taoists, and a protector of – among other things – pawn shops, policemen, secret societies and the military. Close to the main altar, the carved nineteenth-century sedan-chairs in the glass cases were once used to carry the statues through the streets at festivals. The other altars in the temple are to Pao Kung, the God of Justice, and to Shing Wong, a God of the City, who protects the local neighbourhood.

Ladder Street to Possession Street

Outside the temple, Hollywood Road is crossed by **Ladder Street**, not so much a street as a steep flight of steps linking Caine Road with Queen's Road. Built to ease the passage of sedan-chair bearers as they carried their human loads up to the residential areas along Caine Road in the nineteenth century, it's the only surviving street of this kind, one of several that used to link Central and Western with Mid-Levels. It retains some of its older, shuttered houses, their balconies jutting over the steps.

Turn right, down the steps, and immediately on the left, **Upper Lascar Row** is what's left of the area known to the late nineteenth-century citizens of Hong Kong as "Cat Street". The names have various interpretations: "lascar" is an Urdu word, meaning an East Indian seaman, and the area is probably where these seamen lived, the "Cat Street" tag probably deriving from its consequent role as a red-light area. The other theory is that Cat Street was a "thieves' market", all the goods at which were provided by cat burglars. Whatever the derivation, these days Upper Lascar Row is mostly a small-scale flea market, with old banknotes, coins, jade, watches and jewellery spread out on the ground alongside broken TVs, chests and other junk. All the pricey antique stuff has shifted into the plush **Cat Street Galleries** (Mon–Sat 9am–6pm, Sun 11am–5pm), halfway along the Row, with antique and craft showrooms on several floors.

Hollywood Road continues west past **Possession Street**, where in 1841 the British landed, claiming the island by planting the Union Jack – though the street's name is the only reminder of this symbolic act. The only interesting thing about Possession Street, in fact, is how far inland it is today, land reclamation having pushed the shoreline hundreds of metres north over the years.

A little further on, Hollywood Road meets **Queen's Road West**, which carries another mix of age-old shops and trades. You can follow Queen's Road right back into Central, a long walk past wedding shops full of embroidered clothes and goods; shops selling paper offerings, burnt at various religious festivals; art supply shops, with calligraphy sets, paper and ink; tea shops and all manner of other traditional trades, conducted from a variety of gleaming windows and dusty shop fronts.

Tai Ping Shan

Up Ladder Street from the Man Mo Temple and off to the right lies the district of TAI PING SHAN or "Peaceful Mountain". One of the earliest areas of Chinese settlement after the colony was founded, it was anything but peaceful, notorious for its overcrowded housing and outbreaks of plague, and known as a haunt of the early Hong Kong Triad societies. Tai Ping Shan is a less dramatic place these days, but it's worth a stroll down **Tai Ping Shan Street** itself, beyond Bridges Street, to see the neighbourhood's surviving temples, which cluster together at the junction with Pound Lane.

Raised above the left-hand side of the street, the temples are easily missed, more like part of someone's house than a place of worship, an impression that persists until you see the incense sticks and get hassled for money by the old women sitting outside. First is the **Kuan Yin Temple**, the smallest, dedicated to the Buddhist Goddess of Mercy and reached by climbing the steps. The green-tiled **Sui Tsing Paak Temple**, next door, has a main hall whose altar holds a statue of the god Sui Tsing Paak, known as the "Pacifying General" and revered for his ability to cure illnesses: the statue was brought here in 1894 during a particularly virulent outbreak of plague. One of the rooms off the main hall is used by fortune tellers, and you should also look for the rows of *Tai Sui* in the temple – a series of statues of sixty different gods, each one related to a specific year in the sixty-year cycle of the Chinese calendar. In times of strife, or to avert trouble, people come to pray and make offerings to the god associated with their year of birth.

The most interesting temple is further down the street, past the little red Earth God shrine at the junction with Pound Lane, which protects the local community. The **Paak Sing** ("hundred names") ancestral hall was originally established in the mid-nineteenth century (and rebuilt in 1895 after the buildings in the area were razed because of plague), to store the bodies of those awaiting burial back in China, and to hold the ancestral tablets of those who had died in Hong Kong, far from their own villages. Usually such halls are for the sole use of one family or clan, but this one is used by anyone who wishes to have an ancestral tablet made for their relatives – there are around 3000 people commemorated here. Several small rooms hold the ancestral tablets – little wooden boards with the name and date of birth of the dead person written on them, and sometimes a photograph, too. Behind the altar there's a courtyard, whose incinerator is for burning the usual paper offerings to the dead, on the far side of which is a room lined with more tablets, some of them completely blackened by years of incense and smoke.

West to Kennedy Town

If you've followed the route through Western district this far, you won't want to walk on to Kennedy Town as it's a long haul from Central. Either head straight there on the tram, down Des Voeux Road, or follow the route outlined below, which takes you most of the way there by bus, and allows you to stop off at a couple of points of interest along the way.

The Fung Ping Shan Museum

Bus #3 from the stop in front of the Connaught Centre, on Connaught Road Central, takes around ten minutes to run along Caine Road and Bonham Road. Get off opposite St Paul's College, at the university, and the **Fung Ping Shan Museum** is at 94 Bonham Road (Mon–Sat 9.30am–6pm; free), opposite an old, yellow-plastered house of the type that once lined this residential road.

An impressive museum of Chinese art, the Fung Ping Shan is a rare find in Hong Kong, a quiet collection that's rich in interest. Certainly, it will not be crowded, and its ceramics and bronzes especially are worth the detour on the way to Kennedy Town – not to mention some interesting scroll paintings and character scrolls, and a set of inlaid, carved chairs and tables, all beautifully and precisely executed.

The bronzes are on the **first floor**, including bronze mirrors from the Early Warring States period (475–221 BC) through to the Tong Dynasty (seventh to tenth century AD), and a large, impressive Six Dynasties' bronze drum. There are also swords, vessels, bird figures and decorative items, but the most remarkable exhibit here is a unique group of Nestorian bronze crosses, relics of the Yuan Dynasty (1271–1368 AD) from the Ordos region of northern China. There are 966 crosses in all, each just a few centimetres across and every one different, though only a fraction of the collection is displayed here. The bronzes were decorations for a heretic Christian group, which had survived in central and east Asia since the fifth century AD, and most are cruciform in shape, though a few are bird-shaped (also a Christian symbol), star-shaped or circular, or use a swastika pattern. Each has a flat back and a fixed loop, designed to be attached to a leather thong and probably worn as a pendant.

Upstairs on the **second floor** is the ceramics collection, from Neolithic pottery right through the Dynasties. Fine pieces here include the three-coloured, glazed Tang pottery – dishes, jars, even an arm rest and head rest. There's white ceramic ware from the Sui to the Song Dynasties, too (like the delicate spittoons); a coloured Tang camel, with arched neck; and Song Dynasty ceramic pillows, one round and one rectangular and decorated with black and white line drawings. More colourful are the polychromatic Ming Dynasty bowls and dishes, displaying rich blues, greens and reds. Outside China, the museum takes in ceramics from Vietnam, Thailand and Korea as well, while contemporary work is represented by early twentieth-century Buddhist monk figurines.

From the University to Lu Pan Temple

From the museum, you can walk up into the car park and through the grounds of the **University of Hong Kong**, whose buildings have stood here since its foundation in 1912, when it had less than a hundred students (today it has 8000, in nine faculties).

Architecturally, it's less than gripping, though you might as well walk around to Loke Yew Hall on your left, inside which some quiet cloisters planted with high palm trees make for a bit of a break from the traffic outside.

Follow the road through the grounds, cross Pokfulam Road by the footbridge and then walk up the right-hand side of Pokfulam Road (you'll have to dodge under a subway initially). A few hundred metres up, after no. 93, a flight of steps leads down on the right to a terrace overlooking the elaborate, multicoloured roof carvings of figures and dragons on top of the **Lu Pan Temple**. It's the only temple in Hong Kong dedicated to Lu Pan, the "Master Builder", blessed with miraculous powers with which (according to legend) he repaired the Pillars of Heaven and made carved birds which could float in the air. He's commemorated every year on the thirteenth day of the sixth moon (see "Festivals" p.255), when building and construction workers take some time off to have a feast and make offerings to him in the temple here. At most other times of the year it's dark and empty inside, but take a look at the interesting carvings on either side of the door and above the two internal doors.

From the temple's terrace, steps continue downwards and turn into a wide, stepped path, Li Po Lung Path, which descends to Belcher's Street, at which point you're in Kennedy Town.

Kennedy Town

Most people come out to **KENNEDY TOWN** for a ride on the tram, and then catch the first one back again to Central, which certainly gives you good enough views of the moored junks and warehouses. But it doesn't begin to give you the real flavour of the place, which is a sort of down-at-heel Sheung Wan, supporting a fascinating series of sea- and market-related businesses. Much of the district (named after Sir Arthur Kennedy, Governor from 1872–77) is built on reclaimed land, piled high with decrepit tenements, the streets busy with traders and jammed traffic. Since the mid-nineteenth century, it's seen its goods arrive and leave by sea, at a curved harbour that still retains its working edge.

If you've walked down from the University, make for the **tram terminus**, which is away to your left at the end of Catchick Street. Here, where the trams turn round before heading back to Central, is the **Kennedy Town Wholesale Market**, the warehouses in the vicinity constantly busy – one filled with coconuts, another occupied by men sorting and boxing fresh clams. The waterfront strip a couple of blocks down is known as the **Praya**, a Portuguese word (used more commonly in Macau) that's evidence of the once-strong Portuguese influence in the whole of the South China Sea. The Praya is lined with ships unloading by crane into the waterfront **godowns**, or warehouses, and there are scores of junks moored offshore, painted in traditional reds and greens. The tram runs back along part of the Praya, but before you go take a walk through the small streets back from the shore. One of them, **North Street**, has a lively food market, and everywhere there are loads of basic restaurants and cafés where you can get a cheap bowl of noodles or a plate of roast meat with rice.

HONG KONG ISLAND

Victoria Peak and Around

As one of Hong Kong's main attractions, you have to visit **Victoria Peak** (or simply "The Peak") sooner or later, and since you're going up primarily for the views, make sure you do so on a clear day. It's a fine ride up, by bus or tram, and the little network of paths and gardens at the top provides one of the world's most spectacular cityscapes – little wonder that this is *the* place to live in the territory, and has been since the mid-nineteenth century.

Yet even on the murkiest days The Peak is worth a journey. It's cooler up here, there's badly needed foliage and birdlife to immerse yourself in, and a series of paths gives you a choice of quiet, shady walks – both around The Peak and away from it. Bring a picnic and it easily beats struggling through the crowds below.

The area halfway up The Peak, back from the flat strip around the harbour, is known – reasonably enough – as **Mid-Levels**. It, too, has been a popular residential area almost as long as the colony has existed and while it's generally a less grand address than The Peak, Mid-Levels is still fairly exclusive – a leafy set of roads with good enough views over Central and a few places of interest along the way. Over to the east of The Peak, more shaded paths and roads wend across the hillside to **Wan Chai Gap**, another decent target for a walk and with one of the territory's more offbeat museums close by.

Victoria Peak

The 550m heights of **VICTORIA PEAK** give you the only perspective that matters in Hong Kong – down to the outlying islands, the blocks of Mid-Levels and Central and the magnificent harbour that frames the island. It didn't take long for the new British arrivals to flee the malarial lower regions of Hong Kong Island and set up cool summer homes here. The first path up to The Peak, as everyone soon learned to call it, was made in 1859 and within twenty years it was a popular retreat from the summer diseases and heat below. Access was difficult at first, by sedan-chair only, something that ensured it would remain the preserve of the colony's wealthy elite; and it originally had just the cool air to recommend it, since the bare rock was only gradually transformed by the planting of trees and shrubs. Things changed in 1888 with the opening of the Peak Tram, and the first road connection was made in 1924, since which time the territory's power brokers and administrators have settled it properly with permanent houses – and latterly, apartment blocks – that rival each other in terms of position, views and phenomenal rentable value. Along the racist lines of other British colonial haunts elsewhere in the world, the Chinese weren't allowed on The Peak, unless it was to carry up overweight Europeans and supplies on their backs, and it didn't see its first Chinese-owned house until well into modern times. Now, of course, money is the only qualification necessary for residence here. Among the super-rich currently maintaining houses up here are Martin Lee, barrister and leader of the United Democrats; the chairman and deputy chairman of the Hongkong bank; members of the Hotung family, the first Chinese people to live on The Peak; and various Consul-Generals, businessmen and assorted celebrities; while there are also official residences for Hong Kong's Chief Secretary, Attorney General and Chief Justice, and the Commander of the British forces.

Getting there: the Peak Tram and other routes

Since 1888, the **Peak Tram** – actually a funicular railway – has been transporting passengers from a terminal close to St John's Cathedral to the end of the line at Victoria Gap, close on a 1400m-long ride up to around 400m above sea level. It's an extraordinary sensation, the 27-degree gradient providing an odd perspective of the tall buildings of Central and Mid-Levels, which appear to lean in on the tram as it makes its speedy journey. The terminals at either end have been renovated over the years, and in 1989 there was a complete overhaul of the tram system itself, replacing the old cars with computer-controlled ones and increasing their capacity. Fundamentally, though, there's been little change in its operation: it's still the same route that was followed in the late nineteenth century and it's still reputed to be the safest form of transport in the world. There's never been an accident yet, and the track-brakes fitted to the wheels can stop the tram on the steepest part of the system within six metres.

Most tourists take the tram right to the top, which disguises the fact that for the whole of its life it's been primarily a commuter system. There are four intermediate stops at which you can flag the tram down – at Kennedy, Macdonnell, May and Barker roads – but unless you've been up before and have time to explore on the way, stick with the journey, since the views are remarkable.

Catch the tram from the **Lower Peak Tram Terminal**, in Garden Road, just up from the *Hilton* hotel in Central. It runs daily from 7am to midnight, every ten to fifteen minutes, and **tickets** cost $16 return (under 12s, $6) and $10 one-way (under 12s, $4). If you've just come from the Star Ferry, rather than walk you can head over to the City Hall car park and catch the **free shuttle bus** from there to the Lower Terminal; it runs daily, every twenty minutes from around 9am to 7pm. Be warned that on Sundays and public holidays the queues at the terminal can be maddening: get there early.

Victoria Peak and Around

You can also reach Victoria Gap by **bus**, a route worth considering in its own right, whatever the queues are like for the tram. Bus #15 runs from the Central Bus Terminal, underneath Exchange Square (every 15–30min; 6.15am–11pm), a splendid ride up the switchback road to The Peak and offering arguably even more spectacular views than those from the tram; it costs around half as much too, though count on the journey taking at least half an hour. The other service is the #1 minibus from the City Hall car park (Edinburgh Place), a slightly quicker bus ride, though a bit pricier. You can do the trip by **taxi** as well, though this costs around $50 from the Star Ferry.

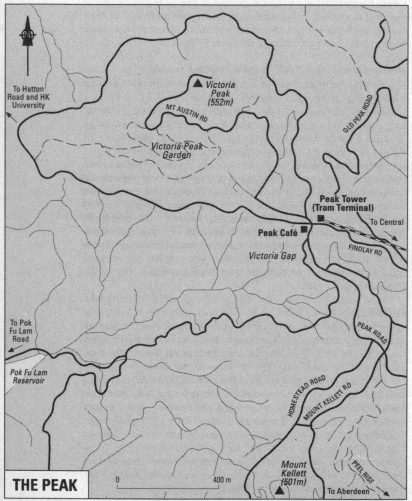

THE PEAK

Walks around The Peak

The trams pull up at the **Upper Peak Tram Terminal**, while buses and taxis stop at the ranks in the adjacent car park. The Peak Tower complex here is currently being redeveloped; when it re-opens, expect excellent views, a café-restaurant and other facilities.

The first thing to know is that you're not yet at the top of The Peak itself. Three roads pan out from the tower, one of which, **Mount Austin Road**, leads up to the landscaped **Victoria Peak Garden** – all that remains of the old Governor's residence here which was destroyed by the Japanese during their occupation of the territory in World War II. It's a stiff climb, but is rewarded by more of those views that leave your stomach somewhere in Central.

Nearly everyone will then want to make the circuit of The Peak, a circular walk that takes around an hour depending on how many times you stop for photo calls. Opposite Peak Tower, a noticeboard details the various possible walks: basically, you follow the green arrows up to Victoria Peak Garden, the blue arrows if you want to follow Old Peak Road down to May Road tram station, and the yellow arrows for the Harlech and Lugard Roads walk.

Start at **Harlech Road** and you'll get the very best views at the end. It's a shaded path for most of the route, barely a road at all, and you'll be accompanied by birdsong and cricket noises as you go: other wildlife is less conspicuous, certainly the mythical monkeys that are said to frequent the trees, but you might catch sight of the odd alarmed snake. First views are of Aberdeen and Lamma, and as you turn later into **Lugard Road**, eventually Stonecutter's Island, Kowloon and Central come into sight – with magnificent views of the latter especially, just before you regain the Peak Tower. It's a panorama that is difficult to tire of, and if you can manage it, come up again at night when the lights of Hong Kong transform the city into a glittering box of tricks, the lit roads snaking through the buildings and Kowloon glinting as gold in the distance.

Walks from The Peak

More adventurous types can make one of several **walks from The Peak** which will take you down to both sides of the island in steep scrambles. Each one won't take more than a couple of hours, but you'll need to carry some water if you're going to tackle them during the heat of the day, as there are no facilities en route.

Head down Harlech Road from the Peak Tower and after about five minutes a signposted path runs down to **Pok Fu Lam Reservoir**, a couple of kilometres away to the south and a decent target for picnics and barbecues. You can reach the same place by way of Pok Fu Lam Reservoir Road, which starts close to the car park. Either way, once you're there, the path runs past the reservoir and joins the main Pok Fu Lam Road – from where you can catch any of several buses back to Central.

The Peak Café, *opposite the tram terminal, is a good place for lunch or a weekend barbecue; see p.232.*

You could also do this walk and then catch a bus in the other direction, on to **Aberdeen**, but it's more fun to walk there direct from The Peak. To do this, follow Peel Rise (down, and then off, Peak Road) for around an hour, a lovely shaded – and signposted – walk down the valley, passing an immense cemetery on the way into Aberdeen. Huge swathes of graves are strung across the terraces, which are cut into the hillside above the town, and from here there are great views of the town's harbour.

Finally, if you follow Harlech Road to just past the junction with Lugard Road, **Hatton Road** makes a steep descent down to the streets above the **University of Hong Kong**, one possible approach to Kennedy Town (see "West to Kennedy Town" in the previous section) or Mid-Levels (see below).

Mid-Levels

Although a notch or two down the social scale from The Peak, **MID-LEVELS** retains a definite cachet. A forest of swanky apartment blocks and the odd grand house line the narrow roads which run across the hillside, midway between the waterfront and The Peak itself, and though Mid-Levels is only a short, steep climb from the crowded streets of Western, there's a world of difference in atmosphere in this mostly dull, if affluent, neighbourhood.

Mid-Levels begins just above **Caine Road**, which leads past the Roman Catholic Cathedral (p.65) to Shelley Street, a left turn up which – at no. 30 – is the **Jamia Mosque**, or Shelley Street Mosque, an important place of worship for the territory's 50,000 Muslims. A mosque has stood on this site since the 1850s, though this building dates from 1915, a pale green structure, set in its own quiet, raised courtyard above the surrounding terraces. The cool interior isn't always open, but the courtyard behind should be accessible, flanked by three-storeyed houses with wooden, railed balconies strung across with drying washing. The Mosque and Islamic Society accounts are pinned to the doors, enabling the faithful to see how much has been spent on maintaining the hearse and sending the Imam on overseas trips.

This part of Mid-Levels is very peaceful, with plenty of incidental interest in the peeling residential terraces around. One of the terraces off the other side of Shelley Street is **Rednaxela Terrace**, an unlikely name even for Hong Kong until you reverse the letters – actually a misspelling of Alexandra and named after the wife of King Edward VII, Queen Victoria's son.

Go up Shelley Street to the top and follow the other streets around and you'll come out on busy **Robinson Road** with its prestigious apartment blocks. Head west along here and at no. 70 a driveway leads down to the **Ohel Leah Synagogue**, finished in 1902, the territory's only synagogue. The name means "Tent of Leah" and it was built by the wealthy Sassoon family in memory of their mother.

It lurks in its own leafy hollow below the main road and there should be a door open into the quiet, oak-carved interior if you want to take a look.

The final Mid-Levels attraction is Hong Kong at its most modern, a convoluted series of elevated walkways, escalators and travelators designed to provide direct access to Mid-Levels from Central. The 800-metre-long **Hillside Escalator Link** runs from Central Market (at the footbridge across Queen's Road, at the corner of Jubilee Street), climbing through Cochrane Street, Hollywood Road and Robinson Road to Conduit Road. It cost over HK$200 million, and is capable of carrying 30,000 people a day on a one-way system, which changes direction throughout the day depending on the flow of passengers.

Wan Chai Gap

The other hillside section of town is a better bet for an extended stroll: the tree-planted paths leading to **WAN CHAI GAP** offer some fine views and a couple of rather peculiar points of interest. As the approach to the walk is by the #15 bus, again it's a tour you can make on your way back from The Peak if you wish.

Along Bowen Road

Get off the #15 bus on Stubbs Road at the stop closest to the *Highcliff Apartments* and *Monte Rosa*, two apartment blocks you can't miss if you're watching out for them. Steps opposite the apartments lead down to **Bowen Road**, which runs westwards above the city, right the way back to the Peak Tram line.

Just down from Stubbs Road, a red-railed path runs up to the right to an **Earth God shrine**, a painted red image on the rock below the road, fronted by a neat altar where there are usually incense sticks burning and small food offerings lying about. Protectors of the local community, Earth Gods have been worshipped for centuries on the mainland; in Hong Kong you still find them tucked into street corners and against buildings, but this is easily the most spectacularly sited, with views falling away over the Happy Valley racecourse below and the gleaming, teeming tower blocks beyond.

Keep on shaded Bowen Road – a marvellous walk at rooftop level – and after about fifteen minutes the so-called **Lover's Stone Garden** is home to more shrines, a steep landscaped area through which steps lead up past a motley succession of red-painted images, tinfoil windmills (representing a change in luck), burning incense sticks and porcelain religious figures. At the top is the **Yan Yuen Sek**, "Lover's Rock", a nine-metre-high rock pointing into the sky from the top of the bluff. It's one of several focuses of the Maiden's Festival, held in mid-August, and since the nineteenth century unmarried women, wives and widows, have been climbing up here to pray for husbands and sons.

The Maiden's Festival: the Legend

While you're considering the wonderful views from Lover's Stone Garden, over Wan Chai and the harbour beyond, you can muse on the legend commemorated by the festival. A cowhand stole the clothes of a weaving girl, a daughter of the Kitchen God, while she was bathing, and having seen her naked, had to marry her, after which they lived together happily. But the gods ordered her to return to heaven to continue her weaving, and said that the couple could meet only once a year. The cowhand died and became an Immortal, but to prevent the couple meeting in heaven, the Queen of Heaven created the Milky Way, leaving the weaving girl on one side and the cowherd on the other. Although they can see each other, they only meet on the seventh day of the seventh moon, when magpies form a bridge so that they might cross to each other.

Beyond the garden, passing various other small shrines along the way, it's about another ten minutes to the junction with **Wan Chai Gap Road**, where a sharp right leads down into Wan Chai itself, past the Pak Tai Temple (p.85). The left turn heads back up to Stubbs Road to Wan Chai Gap proper, and the Police Museum.

The Police Museum

The #15 bus from Central Bus Terminal stops close to the Police Museum, at the junction of Stubbs Road and Peak Road.

Back up to Stubbs Road, a signpost points you to the **Police Museum** (Tues 2–5pm, Wed–Sun 9am–5pm; free), 100m up Coombe Road at no. 27, on the hill to the right behind the children's playground. One room charts the history of the Royal Hong Kong Police Force, with lots of old photos, uniforms and guns, as well as police statements, seized counterfeit cash and a tiger's head (a beast shot in Sheung Shui in 1915). Beyond here things improve as another room displays every kind of drug you've ever heard of and (unwittingly) shows you exactly how to smuggle them – hollowed-out bibles and bras and girdles stuffed with heroin are just some of the more obvious methods. There's also a mock-up of a heroin factory, and there's a Triad room, complete with ceremonial uniforms and some very offensive weapons retrieved by the police.

Back on Peak Road, you can hang around for the #15 bus up to The Peak, or follow Wan Chai Gap Road all the way down into Wan Chai. Coombe Road itself climbs on to **Magazine Gap**, another of the hillside passes, from where – if you've got a decent map and lots of stamina – you can eventually strike The Peak from another direction.

HONG KONG ISLAND

Wan Chai

East of Central, long, parallel roads run all the way to Causeway Bay, cutting straight through **WAN CHAI**, a district noted for its bars, restaurants and nightlife. Wan Chai first came to prominence as a red-light district in the 1940s, though its real heyday was twenty years later when American soldiers and sailors ran amok in its bars and clubs while on R&R ("rest and recreation") from the wars in Korea and Vietnam. Richard Mason immortalised the area in his novel, *The World of Suzie Wong*, later made into a fairly bad film, whose eponymous heroine was a Wan Chai prostitute. (Oddly, when the film was made in 1960, Wan Chai itself wasn't deemed to be properly photogenically sleazy, filming taking place around Hollywood Road instead.)

Set against those times, present-day Wan Chai is fairly tame, though its eastern stretch is still a decent venue for a night out – packed with places to eat and drink, from *dai pai dongs* on the street corners to restaurants and bars; full of local colour during the day and vibrant at night. However, the westernmost part of Wan Chai, beyond Queensway, belies its traditional, rather seedy good-time image. As the rents have increased in Central, the office blocks and businesses have moved into the area, giving the local yuppies the chance to tag it "East Central". It's a development that has acquired its own momentum since the opening of the enormous **Convention and Exhibition Centre** in 1988; the latest, spectacular addition is **Central Plaza**, Asia's tallest building.

Walking through Wan Chai you can follow one of three parallel main roads – Lockhart Road, Jaffe Road or Hennessy Road – all of which reach down to Causeway Bay. If you're going by tram, note that it detours down Johnston Road instead, which is fine for the Pak Tai Temple and Queen's Road East, but not so handy if you're aiming for the Arts Centre, Convention and Exhibition Centre or the water-front – for these, take the #18 **bus** (not Sun) from Connaught Road Central or the **Star Ferry** from Tsim Sha Tsui to Wan Chai Ferry Pier.

The tram from Central to Causeway Bay, via Wan Chai, follows this route: Des Voeux Rd, Queensway, Johnston Rd, Hennessy Rd, Yee Wo St.

The Arts Centre and Academy for Performing Arts

Since 1976 much of Hong Kong's arts and drama has been centred on the fifteen-storey **Hong Kong Arts Centre** at 2 Harbour Road, in Wan Chai. Despite the competition posed by the Cultural Centre in Tsim Sha Tsui (see p.108), it's still a leading venue for drama, film and various cultural events, and also contains the fifth-floor *Pao Sui Loong Galleries* (daily 10am–8pm; free), which maintain temporary exhibition space for contemporary art: local and international painting, photography and sculpture. It's always worth dropping in to see what's on, especially as you can take advantage of the Arts Centre's coffee shop or restaurant, which both feature views of the harbour.

For events and box office details for the Arts Centre and Academy for Performing Arts, see p.249–250.

Backtracking a little, to Gloucester Road, the building with the triangular windows houses the **Academy for Performing Arts** (APA). Here the majority of the productions are performed by the students themselves – local works to Shakespeare – though you'll also come across visiting shows, as well as modern and classical music and dance. Other than performances, the facilities are only open to the students, though once a year (usually May or June) an open day allows visitors to tour the wardrobe rooms, library and backstage areas.

The Convention and Exhibition Centre and around

Massive development over recent years has changed the Wan Chai harbourfront. Enormous new buildings loom over the water, grandest of all the gigantic **Convention and Exhibition Centre**, the largest of its kind in Asia, flanked by landscaped gardens. Other record-breaking claims include the building's use of the world's largest glass curtain wall – the centre's first five floors are open to view and cross-hatched by escalators which grant superb harbour views. The centre is topped by two luxury hotels, the ultra-flash *Grand Hyatt* and *New World Harbour View*, aimed firmly at the expense-account businesspeople here to wheel and deal at the centre's various trade exhibitions.

The Wan Chai Ferry Pier is across from the Convention and Exhibition Centre, for services to Tsim Sha Tsui (7.30am–11pm) or Hung Hom (6.20am–10pm).

Further east, there's the **China Resources Building**, over Harbour Road, worth walking through for its department store in the Low Block, which displays a grand mixture of Chinese arts and crafts. A little enclosed Chinese garden sits in the middle of the block, while the adjacent building, the Causeway Centre, has some interest in its **Museum of Chinese Historical Relics** (1st Floor, 28 Harbour Rd; Mon–Sat 10am–6pm, Sun 1–6pm; free), with more Chinese painting and handicrafts, and plenty of rare historical pieces on display.

Central Plaza

With the completion of **Central Plaza** in October 1992, Hong Kong acquired the latest high-tech, high profile addition to its already cluttered skyline. Sited across from the Convention and Exhibition Centre, at 18 Harbour Road, it pipped Central's Bank of China Tower by topping out at 78 storeys, to become Asia's tallest building and the fourth tallest building in the world. It's built of reinforced concrete (which, almost interestingly, makes it the world's tallest reinforced concrete building), though more impressive is its height – 374 metres to the top of its mast – and its extraordinary design and exterior cladding. Triangular in shape, it's topped by a glass pyramid from which a 64-metre mast protrudes: the locals, always quick to debunk a new building, promptly dubbed it "The Big Syringe". As if this wasn't distinctive enough, the American design team swathed the reflective glass curtain walls with luminous neon panels, while the glass pyramid shoots out computer-controlled light. At night, there's no question that Central Plaza is the dominant feature of the skyline, lit up like a beacon from almost anywhere you care to look.

You can go inside the split-level, thirty-metre-high lobby, whose marble and sandstone interior is enlivened by soaring palm trees; and from here, you're connected to the elevated walkways that run deep into Wan Chai and back to Central. To get back to Central by bus, take the #10A, #20, #21 or #104, which run from Gloucester Road, or alternatively walk back around to the water to the Wan Chai Ferry Pier, for ferry services to Tsim Sha Tsui and to Hung Hom.

Along Lockhart Road

If Wan Chai has a main street it's **Lockhart Road**, which runs west–east through the district and finishes up in Causeway Bay. For many, Lockhart Road epitomises Wan Chai. The street's heady days as a thriving red-light district, throbbing with US marines on leave, are now behind it, but although the bite has gone out of Lockhart Road, that's not to say that the area has become gentrified, or anything approaching it. Lots of the bars and clubs still make a living from fleecing tourists, and a walk down the street at night is a fairly lively experience even now. Most of the pubs between Luard Road and Fleming Road are rowdy until the small hours, and it's easier to get a late meal in the hundreds of restaurants along and around Lockhart Road than anywhere else in Hong Kong. If there's a merchant or naval fleet in town, Wan Chai occasionally echoes with the sounds of yesteryear, though the most pleasant experience is to stroll down here on Sunday. This is a day off for the Filipina housemaids all over the territory, and after meeting in Central, many head for Wan Chai, where the bars and clubs around Lockhart Road open their doors early for some wild singing and dancing.

Queen's Road East and around

There's a more sustained pocket of interest in Wan Chai's southern streets, particularly around **Queen's Road East**, which you can reach from Central on buses #6, #260 or #15: get off at **Wan Chai Market**, another of the island's indoor municipal meat, fish, fruit and veg markets.

The Pak Tai Temple

From the market, Stone Nullah Lane ("nullah" is a ravine) leads uphill; off to the left, down Lung On Street, is the **Pak Tai Temple**, decorated with handmade, colourful roof pottery. The temple is dedicated to Pak Tai, the Military Protector and Emperor of the North, whose task it is to maintain harmony on earth, and he's represented inside the main hall by a tall, seventeenth-century copper statue, seated on a throne facing the door. Behind, four figures of warriors and scholars guard the ebony-faced and bearded god, who is resplendent in an embroidered jacket with a tiger-face motif. A room off to the left, as you leave the main hall, is one to linger in. Here you'll find craftsmen practising an age-old Chinese art, making **burial offerings** from paper and bamboo, delicate works of art that are burned in order to prepare and equip the deceased for the afterlife. Around the walls hang half-finished and finished items: a car, a block of flats, houses, money, furniture and aeroplanes, all painted and coloured. From the temple, you can continue up to the main Kennedy Road, and take a left turn up Wan Chai Gap Road, to join the walk described under "Wan Chai Gap", above.

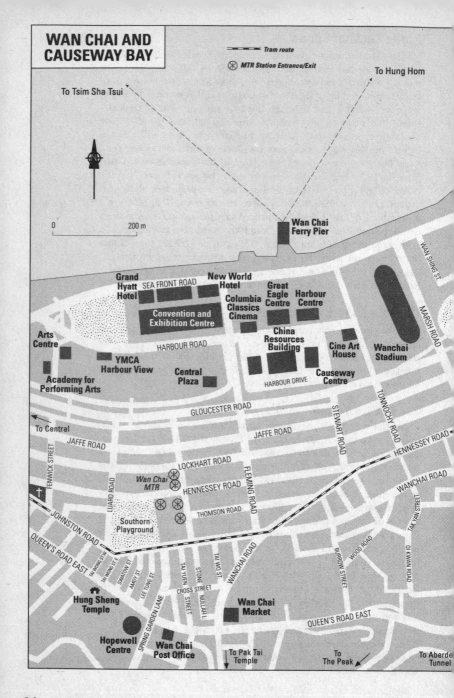

WAN CHAI AND CAUSEWAY BAY

Tram route

⊗ MTR Station Entrance/Exit

To Tsim Sha Tsui

To Hung Hom

N

0   200 m

Wan Chai
Ferry Pier

WAN SHING ST

MARSH ROAD

Grand
Hyatt
Hotel

SEA FRONT ROAD

New World
Hotel

Great
Eagle
Centre

Harbour
Centre

Columbia
Classics
Cinema

Convention and
Exhibition Centre

China
Resources
Building

Arts
Centre

HARBOUR ROAD

Cine Art
House

Wanchai
Stadium

YMCA
Harbour View

Central
Plaza

Academy for
Performing Arts

HARBOUR DRIVE

Causeway
Centre

TONNOCHY ROAD

GLOUCESTER ROAD

STEWART ROAD

To Central

JAFFE ROAD

JAFFE ROAD

HENNESSEY ROAD

FENWICK STREET

LOCKHART ROAD

WANCHAI ROAD

LUARD ROAD

Wan Chai
MTR

HENNESSEY ROAD

FLEMING ROAD

TAK YAN STREET

⊗

⊗ ⊗

THOMSON ROAD

⊗

Southorn
Playground

JOHNSTON ROAD

WOOD ROAD

BURROW STREET

OI KWAN ROAD

QUEEN'S ROAD EAST

DA WONG ST/W

PA WONG ST/W

SWATON ST

AMOY ST

LEE TUNG ST

TAI YUEN
STREET

STONE
NULLAH L.

CROSS STREET

TAI WO ST

WANCHAI ROAD

Hung Sheng
Temple

SPRING GARDEN LANE

Wan Chai
Market

QUEEN'S ROAD EAST

Hopewell
Centre

Wan Chai
Post Office

To Pak Tai
Temple

To
The Peak

To Aberde
Tunnel

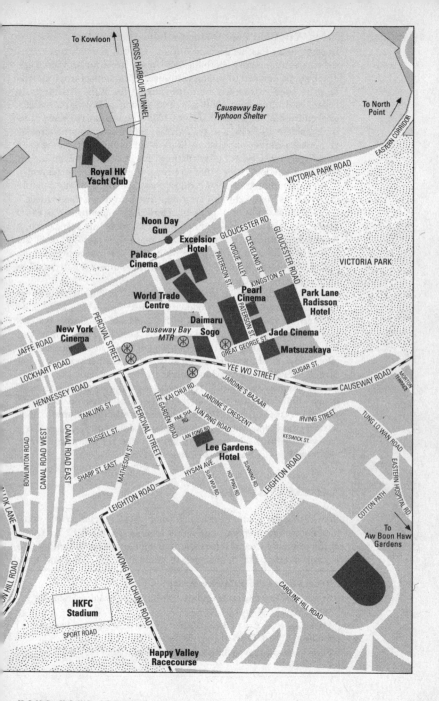

To Kowloon

CROSS HARBOUR TUNNEL

Causeway Bay
Typhoon Shelter

To North
Point

EASTERN CORRIDOR

**Royal HK
Yacht Club**

VICTORIA PARK ROAD

VICTORIA PARK

**Noon Day
Gun**

GLOUCESTER RD.

GLOUCESTER ROAD

**Excelsior
Hotel**

**Palace
Cinema**

PATERSON ST.

VOGUE ALLEY

CLEVELAND ST.

KINGSTON ST.

**World Trade
Centre**

**Pearl
Cinema**

**Park Lane
Radisson
Hotel**

PATERSON ST.

Daimaru

**New York
Cinema**

PERCIVAL STREET

*Causeway Bay
MTR*

Sogo

Jade Cinema

JAFFE ROAD

GREAT GEORGE ST.

Matsuzakaya

LOCKHART ROAD

YEE WO STREET

SUGAR ST.

CAUSEWAY ROAD

MORTON TERRACE

HENNESSEY ROAD

JARDINE'S BAZAAR

KAI CHUI RD.

JARDINE'S CRESCENT

IRVING STREET

TUNG LO WAN ROAD

TANLUNG ST.

LEE GARDEN ROAD

PAK SHA RD.

YUN PING ROAD

KESWICK ST.

CANAL ROAD WEST

RUSSELL ST.

LAN FONG RD.

**Lee Gardens
Hotel**

EASTERN HOSPITAL RD.

CANAL ROAD EAST

PERCIVAL STREET

SHARP ST. EAST

MATHESON ST.

HYSAN AVE.

SUN WUI RD.

SUNNING RD.

HOI PING RD.

LEIGHTON ROAD

BOWLINTON ROAD

LEIGHTON ROAD

COTTON PATH

To
Aw Boon Haw
Gardens

WONG NAI CHUNG ROAD

CAROLINE HILL ROAD

OK LANE

ON HILL ROAD

**HKFC
Stadium**

SPORT ROAD

**Happy Valley
Racecourse**

Wan Chai

From Wan Chai Post Office to Johnston Road

Queen's Road East leads back towards Central, a route that traces the nineteenth-century shoreline. It's a good street for browsing, lots of the shops devoted to selling **rattanware** products, a tropical cane or palm used extensively here for making furniture. It's all fairly cheap, and often very elaborate. You'll soon pass the old, white-washed front of the **Wan Chai Post Office**, opened in 1915 and positively ancient by Hong Kong standards, before reaching the circular **Hopewell Centre**, once Hong Kong's tallest building; though it's dwarfed by more recent constructions, it's still worth taking the lift to the sixtieth floor, where there's a revolving *dim sum* restaurant.

A hundred metres or so further along, the **Hung Sheng Temple** at no. 131 is built right into the rocks that bear down upon Queen's Road East at this point, with boulders dotted amongst the altars inside. A long, narrow temple, with the room on the far right reserved for fortune tellers and palm readers, it started life in the mid-nineteenth century as a shrine by the sea: the scholar Hung Sheng is a patron saint of fishermen because of his reputed skill in forecasting the weather.

Opposite the temple, over the main road, **Tai Wong Street West** runs through to Johnston Road, the bottom half of the alley filled with bird cages and the air thick with the calls of songbirds, budgies and their dinner – crickets tied up in little bags. It's not as big as Yau Ma Tei's bird market (p.119), but if you haven't seen one before, take a slow stroll through. A couple of streets further up is **Gresson Street**, which has a produce market where you can buy freshly peeled bamboo shoots and preserved eggs among the more usual items, while over the road at the junction of Johnston Road and Fenwick Street, the red-brick **Chinese Methodist Church** nods towards the Orient with a rooftop pagoda. Johnston Road itself is a handy place to finish, because you can catch the tram from here, either back to Central or on to Causeway Bay.

HONG KONG ISLAND

Causeway Bay

Completing the short list of Hong Kong Island's major tourist destinations, everyone spends half a day or so in **CAUSEWAY BAY**, one of the original areas of settlement in the mid-nineteenth century. It's a small district, but it manages to pack in more shops and busi-

---

Tram Routes From Causeway Bay

From Causeway Bay to Central: Yee Wo St, Hennessy Rd, Johnston Rd Queensway, Des Voeux Rd.

From Causeway Bay to Happy Valley: Percival St, Wong Nai Chung Rd, Morrison Hill Rd, Ting Lok Lane, Hennessy Rd.

From Causeway Bay to Shau Kei Wan: Causeway Rd, King's Rd, Shau Kei Wan Rd.

---

nesses than just about anywhere else in the territory. Indeed, shopping – or at least window-shopping – is the only real reason to come, although once here there are a few low-key attractions which help pad out your day, and the rattling tram ride from Central is pleasant enough to warrant the journey in the first place.

The Bay and the Noon Day Gun

Before land reclamation, Causeway Bay was just that – a large, natural bay, known as *Tung Lo Wan* in Chinese, that stretched back into what's now Victoria Park and the surrounding streets. The British settled here in the 1840s, erecting warehouses along the waterfront and trading from an area they called East Point. Filled in since the 1950s, all that's left of the bay is the **typhoon shelter**, with its massed ranks of junks and yachts, and **Kellet Island**, now a thumb of land connected to the mainland and harbouring the *Royal Hong Kong Yacht Club*. Development around here really got under way with the opening of the two-kilometre-long **Cross-Harbour Tunnel** in the early 1970s, which runs under Kellet Island to Kowloon. With the greater access that this brought (though massive congestion at peak hours threatens its benefit these days), hotels, shops and department stores moved in, effectively making Causeway Bay a self-perpetuating tourist ghetto. White high-rises now girdle the typhoon shelter, but if it's not the prettiest of the territory's harbour scenes, there's something stirring in the hundreds of masts and bobbing boats that carpet the water.

In front of one of the modern hotels, the **Excelsior** on Gloucester Road, stands one of Hong Kong's most well-known monuments, the **Noon Day Gun**, made famous by one of Noel Coward's better lyrics:

> *In Hong Kong*
> *They strike a gong*
> *And fire off a noonday gun*
> *To reprimand each inmate*
> *Who's in late*
> (from *Mad Dogs and Englishmen*)

Apart from a few local street names, this is the only relic of the influence that the nineteenth-century trading establishments wielded in Causeway Bay, in particular *Jardine, Matheson & Co*, which had its headquarters here. The story is suitably vague, as all legends should be, but it's said that the small ship's gun was fired by a Jardine employee to salute one of the company's ships, an action which so outraged the Governor – whose traditional prerogative it was to fire off salutes – that he ordered it to be fired every day at noon for evermore. Some of the short harbour cruises (see "Organised Tours", p.49) take in the daily noon firing of the gun, and there's a more elaborate ceremony every New Year's Eve, when

impeccably dressed Jardine's managers fire the thing off at midnight.
The whole story is recorded on a plaque by the gun, which you reach
by crossing Gloucester Road: the easiest way is to go through the
grey steel door next to 297 Gloucester Road and follow the tunnel,
which comes up right next to the gun. After all the fuss in print,
though, it's simply a rather tiresome gun in a railed-off garden.

From the gun, walk further up the tatty promenade towards
Victoria Park, where you can negotiate the hire of a **sampan** with the
women from the typhoon shelter who'll be hanging about. Settle on a
price and you'll be paddled into the shelter, whereupon other
sampans will appear to sell you fresh seafood and produce, which is
cooked in front of you and washed down with beer bought from other
boats – not a bad way to spend an evening, though hardly the bohe-
mian night out it once was. You'll need to bargain every step of the
way.

Victoria Park

The eastern edge of Causeway Bay is marked by the large, green
expanse of **Victoria Park**, one of the few decent open-air spaces in
this congested city. Built on reclaimed land, it's busy all day, from
the crack-of-dawn *tai chi* practitioners to the old men spending an
hour or so strolling with their songbirds in little cages along the
paths. There's a swimming pool and sports facilities here, too, and if
you wander through you might catch a soccer match or something
similar, while a couple of times a year the park hosts some lively
festivals – a flower market at Chinese New Year, and a lantern
display for the Mid-Autumn Festival.

At the park's eastern corner, up Tin Hau Temple Road (by the
Tin Hau MTR station), lies Causeway Bay's **Tin Hau Temple**, a
couple of centuries old, sited on top of a little hill which once
fronted the water. These days it's surrounded by tall apartment
blocks, but the temple is one more indication of the area's strong,
traditional links with the sea.

Shopping in Causeway Bay

*For lunch, try
the* Sogo *or*
Daimaru
*supermarkets,
which have
cheap takeaway
sushi and
sit-down
Japanese snack
bars; each store
has a coffee
shop, too.*

Doing your shopping in Causeway Bay means splitting your time
between two main sections. The grid of streets to the north, closest
to Victoria Park, contains the modern shops and businesses, many
of them owned by the Japanese who moved in here in the 1960s.
There are large **Japanese department stores** on and around the
main Yee Wo Street – *Sogo* on Hennessy Road, *Daimaru* on Great
George Street and *Matsuzakaya* on Paterson Street – stuffed with
hi-tech, high-fashion articles, open late and normally full of big-
spending customers. The other main store here is *China Products*,
on Yee Wo Street, one of the biggest of the stores specialising in
products from the PRC, another Aladdin's Cave of bargains and rip-
offs. For designer clothes and shoes, visit **Vogue Alley**, a covered,

Art-Nouveau-style mall with fountains running between Kingston Street and Gloucester Road. It used to be known as Food Street, when it featured restaurants instead; it remains to be seen whether the clothes theme will last any longer.

The area **south** of Yee Wo Street is immediately different. It's the original Causeway Bay settlement and home to an interesting series of inter-connected markets and shopping streets. **Jardine's Bazaar** and **Jardine's Crescent**, two narrow, parallel lanes off Yee Wo Street, have contained a street market since the earliest days of the colony (their names echoing the trading connection) and they remain great places to poke around: cheap clothes abound, while deeper in you'll find *dai pai dongs*, a noisy little market and all manner of traditional shops and stalls selling herbs and provisions. There are similar sights the further back into these streets you go: **Pennington Street**, **Irving Street**, **Fuk Hing Lane** and others all reward making a slow circle through them, perhaps stopping for some tea or to buy some herbal medicine.

Aw Boon Haw Gardens

The last stop in Causeway Bay is at the gross **Aw Boon Haw Gardens** (daily 9.30am–4pm; free), a landscaped nightmare also known as the "Tiger Balm Gardens" and which is another of Hong Kong's accredited "sights". It's not strictly in Causeway Bay, though you could easily walk here, up Tai Hang Road. Direct from Central Bus Terminal, the #11 bus takes about twenty minutes, stopping right outside the gardens by a row of souvenir stalls.

The person responsible for the gardens was Mr Aw Boon Haw, a millionaire who made his money by manufacturing *Tiger Balm* ointment (hence the gardens' other name), which you'll see on sale everywhere in Hong Kong: it's a bit like *Vick* vapour rub, used for soothing aches and pains. Aw Boon Haw blew his cash in 1935 on this landscaped concoction of coloured statues from religious tales, pagodas, garish staircases, animals and grottos; there are bilingual signs on most explaining their significance. There's a good view from the top of the Tiger Pagoda (which alone cost a cool million dollars in the 1930s), but otherwise what charm the place had is entirely lost under the daily deluge of visitors. The only vaguely interesting part, the Haw Par Mansion at the gates, which the founder's family still owns, is closed to the public.

Happy Valley

HONG KONG ISLAND

Travel south on the branch tram line from Causeway Bay and you're soon in **HAPPY VALLEY**, or Wong Nai Chung. After Western district, which was soon discovered to be rife with malaria, Happy Valley was one of the earliest parts of the island to be settled, in the hope that it would be healthier and more sheltered. Plenty of posh

Happy Valley houses were built before the "yellow mud stream" that gave Happy Valley its Chinese name appeared with a vengeance – the settlers had unknowingly built on a fever-ridden swamp. Everyone moved out, the land was drained and the flattest part turned into a racecourse in 1846, which survives and thrives famously today.

The only legal gambling allowed in Hong Kong is on horseracing, and the **Happy Valley Racecourse** is the traditional centre of this multimillion-dollar business (though there's a second racecourse now, in Sha Tin in the New Territories). It's controlled by the *Royal Hong Kong Jockey Club*, one of the colony's power bastions since its foundation in 1884, with a board of stewards made up of the leading lights of Hong Kong big business. A percentage of the profits go to social and charitable causes – you'll see Jockey Club schools and clinics all over the territory – and such is the passion for betting on horses in Hong Kong (or indeed betting on anything) that the money involved defies comprehension: the racing season pulls in over HK$45 *billion*. The season runs from September to May and there are meetings on the synthetic surface at Happy Valley twice a week, on Wednesday night and at the weekend. Entrance to the public enclosure is $10, and bilingual staff at the various information desks can help make some sense of the fairly intricate accumulator bets that Hong Kong specialises in. Or give the HKTA's pricey **racing tour** a whirl. They'll take you there, feed you before the races, get you into the members' enclosure and hand out some racing tips: you need to be over eighteen, have been in Hong Kong for less than three weeks, and take your passport to any of the HKTA offices at least a day before the race.

You can book the racing tour at any of the HKTA offices; see p.36 for addresses. It costs over $400 per person.

The cemeteries

It's tempting to think that the series of **cemeteries** staggered up the valley on the west side of the racecourse is full of failed punters. In fact, they provide an interesting snapshot of the territory's ethnic and religious mix: starting from Queen's Road East and climbing up, the five mid-nineteenth-century cemeteries are officially Muslim, Catholic, Colonial (the largest, with a berth for Lord Napier, the first Chief Superintendent of Trade with China), Parsee and Jewish. For a closer look, the #15 bus (to The Peak from the Central Bus Terminal) runs past them, up Stubbs Road, though the best views are the virtually airborne ones from Bowen Road, the path that runs to Wan Chai Gap (see "Wan Chai Gap", above).

The South Side

HONG KONG ISLAND

Apart from The Peak, the other great escape from the built-up north side of Hong Kong Island is to the **south side**, a long, fragmented coastline from Aberdeen to Stanley punctured by bays and inlets. Unfortunately, everyone in Hong Kong escapes there, too, particlarly at the weekend, but it's worth braving the crowded buses and roads for some of the territory's best **beaches** and a series of little villages which pre-date the arrival of the British in the mid-nineteenth century – though none of them are exactly traditional or isolated these days. Most have somewhere to eat and you needn't worry about getting stuck as the **buses** are all very regular, and run until late in the evening.

The quickest and most obvious trips are to **Aberdeen** and **Repulse Bay** in the west, and most will find time to move on to **Stanley**, too, which is probably the most interesting place to aim for if you've only got the time for one excursion. If you have children in tow, then **Ocean Park** – Hong Kong's biggest theme and adventure park – is a must.

Aberdeen

ABERDEEN was one of the few places on the island already settled when the British arrived in the 1840s, the bay here was used as a shelter for the indigenous local people – the Hoklos and Tankas who fished in the surrounding archipelago. It's still really the only other

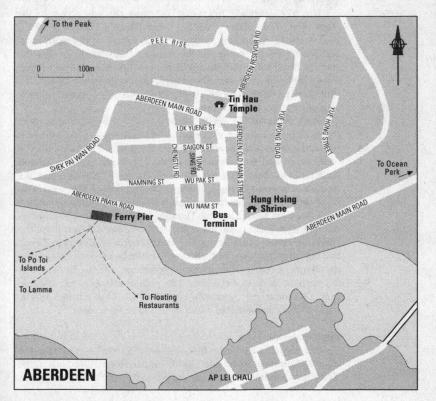

large town on the island, with around 60,000 people, several thousand of them living as they've done for centuries, on sampans and junks tied up in the harbour (though they're gradually being moved into new housing estates). The British named the town that grew up here after their Colonial Secretary, the Earl of Aberdeen, but the Chinese name – *Heung Gong Tsai* – gives the better hint as to its water-based character: "Little Hong Kong", reflecting the attractions of its fine harbour.

Arriving by bus, you'll either be dropped at the Bus Terminal or on Aberdeen Main Road, but it makes no difference since the central grid of streets is fairly small. It's best to make your way down to the **harbour** first, if you want to understand the importance of the water to the town. Cross the main road by the pedestrian footbridge to the long waterfront and you'll soon be accosted by women touting **sampan rides** through the typhoon shelter, a good way to take a closer look at the floating homes that still clog the water. A bit of bargaining should get you a twenty- or thirty-minute ride for around $50 a head. More sampans and ferries at the harbour take you to other nearby destinations: to Lamma Island (p.166) and the Po Toi group (see below).

If you're especially interested, sampans also run across to the large island just offshore, **Ap Lei Chau** (Duck's Tongue Island) – there's also a connecting bridge – which is one of the main boat- and junk-building centres in the territory. Wandering around the yards is fascinating, particularly if you can find someone to tell you what's going on. The workshops here are mostly family-owned, the skills handed down through generations, with only minimal reliance on proper plans and drawings.

Back in town, the small centre is worth a look around, over-touristed these days but with some interesting shops and businesses that can enliven a spare hour or so. At the junction of Aberdeen Old Main Street and Aberdeen Main Road, the **Hung Hsing Shrine** is dedicated to a local god who protects fishermen and oversees the weather. Towards the top of town, at the junction of Aberdeen Main Road and Aberdeen Reservoir Road, a hollow in the ground contains the more important **Tin Hau Temple**, built in 1851, with circular-cut doorways inside leading to the furnace rooms. From here, the energetic could continue up the main Aberdeen Reservoir Road, looking for a left turn, **Peel Rise**, which climbs up over the town to the stepped terraces of an immense **cemetery**, offering fine views of the harbour and Ap Lei Chau. The path continues ever upwards from the cemetery, eventually reaching The Peak, though this is really only a climb for those with their own oxygen tents.

Practicalities

It's around half an hour by **bus** to Aberdeen from Central: take the #7 (via Kennedy Town, getting off on Aberdeen Main Rd) or the #70 (via Aberdeen Tunnel, getting off at the end of the line) from

the Central Bus Terminal; or bus #72 from Yee Wo Street in
Causeway Bay. Aberdeen's **Bus Terminal** is off Wu Nam Street at its
eastern end, close to the water.

There's plenty of choice if you want **something to eat** in
Aberdeen. The traditional thing to do here is to take the free shuttle
ferry from the harbourfront across to the two **floating restaurants**,
the *Jumbo* and the *Tai Pak*, which are moored in the yacht bays over
to the east of the harbour; see p.221 for details. Or you can take the
kaido across to **Lamma** and its seafood restaurants (p.168): the
regular service stops in the early evening, but it's always easy to find
a sampan to take you across and pick you up again after a couple of
hours, something that shouldn't cost more than $120 for the boat.
There are, of course, restaurants in Aberdeen town, too, though
they're nothing special. For something more traditional, look out for
the *Tse Kee*, a basic fishball noodle shop, where you can get a tasty
and inexpensive bowl of food: it's at 82 Old Main Street (just up from
the bus terminal) and open from 10.30am to 6pm.

The Po Toi Islands

Aberdeen harbour is jumping-off point for a visit to the southerly **Po
Toi Islands**, an hour's ferry ride away. Like all the minor outlying
islands, their population is dwindling, but the main island, with its
rock carvings, is good for an isolated stroll. Fans of John Le Carré
will know that this island is where the denouement to his *The
Honourable Schoolboy*, a thriller largely set in Hong Kong, takes
place. **Ferries** leave Aberdeen on Tuesday, Thursday and Saturday at
9am, and there are five ferries on Sunday; phone ☎554 4059 for
more details.

Deep Water Bay and Ocean Park

East of Aberdeen, the road cuts across a small peninsula to **DEEP
WATER BAY**, one of Hong Kong Island's better beaches; you can get
there on bus #73 from Aberdeen. Hong Kong suffered one of its periodic shark scares at Deep Water Bay in 1989, when two people were
pulled out of the water with flesh wounds. Investigations revealed
that they had actually been attacked by moray eels, which usually live
among rocks and don't encroach upon sand beaches. The area was
subsequently cleared of eels, some of them more than a metre long.
It was, no doubt, all fairly unpleasant for the people attacked, but the
signs erected on the beach at the time, "Danger: Eel Attack!", didn't
quite have the fearful ring about them that was intended.*

---

* The last real shark attack in Hong Kong was in August 1979, when an illegal
immigrant from China made the dangerous mistake of trying to swim across
Mirs Bay, in the northeast of the territory, to freedom: he never made it. More
recently, in 1986 there was a barracuda attack on a surfboarder off Shek O
beach, and in 1985 and 1986 several people were stung by Portuguese Men
O'War at Clearwater Bay.

Ocean Park

The adjacent peninsula is wholly taken up by **OCEAN PARK** (Mon–
Sat 10am–6pm, Sun 9.30am–6pm; $140, under 11s half-price), a
thoroughly enjoyable open-air theme park, fun fair and oceanarium.
It opened in 1977 and the massive complex is divided into three
sections joined by a cable-car and outdoor escalator – big enough in
fact to take up most of a day.

The ticket price seems steep but includes all the rides, shows
and displays on offer. A couple of **warnings**, though: there's food on
sale inside, but it's plastic and pricey (hot dogs, burgers and the
like), so you might want to take your own picnic; and try and go early
if you're determined to get your money's worth. It'll take a good four
hours to see all parts of the park, queue for a couple of rides and see
the marine shows – with kids, and in the busy summer season, expect
it to take longer, and expect to have to wait for all the popular rides.

The first section, the **Lowland** area, is a landscaped garden with
greenhouses, a butterfly house, various parks, a theatre and a
kiddies' adventure playground. It's also the departure point for
about the scariest ride in the complex, the **cable-car**, which hoists
you a kilometre-and-a-half up the mountainside, high above Deep
Water Bay in a flimsy capsule, to the **Headland** section. Here,
there's a mix of rides (including a truly frightening roller-coaster
that travels at 80km per hour) and marine displays – a massive
aquarium, a seal, sealion and penguin sanctuary, and Ocean
Theatre, where the performing sharks and whales are put through
their paces a couple of times a day. Looming over the lot is the
Ocean Park Tower, 200m above sea level, giving superb views
from its viewing platform. After this, you can head down the other
side to the **Tai Shue Wan** area, by way of the world's longest

---

Bus Routes to Ocean Park

Unless otherwise shown, buses run every ten to fifteen minutes right up
until around midnight, though check the Ocean Park opening times above.

From Aberdeen
#48 and #73 from Aberdeen Main
Rd run past the park.

From Admiralty MTR
Citybus to Ocean Park every
30min. You can also buy an all-in-
one bus and entrance ticket for
around $160 (children half-price)
on this route.

From Causeway Bay
#72 from Yee Wo St; get off just
after emerging from Aberdeen
Tunnel and follow the signs
along Ocean Park Rd; on Sun the

bus stops right outside Ocean
Park.

From Central Bus Terminal
#4 to Wah Fu Estate, from where
you catch the #48 right to the
park.
#70: get off just after emerging
from Aberdeen Tunnel and follow
the signs along Ocean Park Rd.
#90: same as the #70, except on
Sat and Sun the bus goes right to
Ocean Park.

From Hong Kong-side Star Ferry
#6 minibus (daily except Sun).

outdoor escalator. There are more fine views on the way down, more rides at the bottom, and access to **Middle Kingdom**, a Chinese theme park with pagodas, traditional crafts and all the associated entertainment, including Chinese opera performances.

Back at the main entrance to the Lowland site, you'll find a separate entrance for the adjacent **Water World** (April, May, Sept & Oct daily 10am–5pm; June 10am–10pm; July & Aug 9am–10pm; $70, children $45). This is a water-based fun park – slides and chutes – which gets incredibly packed in the summer, but is just the place to cool down after tramping around Ocean Park.

Repulse Bay

The next bay along, **REPULSE BAY**, has lost whatever colonial attraction it once had, when the grand *Repulse Bay Hotel* stood at its centre, hosting graceful tea-dances and cocktail parties. The hotel was torn down without ceremony in the 1980s (the only surviving portion the ludicrously expensive *Verandah* restaurant, at 109 Repulse Bay Rd) and the hill behind the bay is now lined with flash high-rise apartments. The **beach** itself is clean and wide, though the water quality isn't all it could be, and it's backed by a concrete promenade containing some unmemorable cafés and a garish two-in-one *McDonalds* and *Kentucky Fried Chicken*. It's all fairly nasty and you needn't worry about missing out on anything if you skip it, though kitsch connoisseurs will want to amble down to the little Chinese garden at the end of the prom, where a brightly painted group of goddesses, Buddha statues, stone lions and dragons offer some tempting photo-opportunities. All in all, it doesn't take great imagination to work out the derogatory, locally inspired tag the bay has acquired over the years – Repulsive Bay, for the really slow ones.

For Repulse Bay, take bus #6, #61 or #260 from the Central Bus Terminal; or the #73 from Aberdeen/ Stanley. Buses #6 or #260 continue through Repulse Bay to Stanley, a fine ride.

Those people packing the beach are mostly oblivious to Repulse Bay's fairly grim history during World War II. The old hotel was used as a base by British troops, but the Japanese stormed straight through in 1941, capturing and executing many of the defenders and sticking the rest in Stanley prison camp to the east. The bay here had always been an attractive target for new arrivals: the name itself comes from the ship *HMS Repulse*, from which the nineteenth-century British mopped up the local pirates operating out of the area. If the beach is too crowded for comfort you can try the nearby beaches at **MIDDLE BAY** and **SOUTH BAY**, fifteen minutes' and thirty minutes' walk around the bay respectively.

Stanley

The major attraction on the south coast is the village of **STANLEY**, sited on its own little peninsula and with much more appeal than all the other villages along the coast of the island. If you have the time, spending a day here wouldn't be too long, certainly if you're planning to do any shopping in the good market.

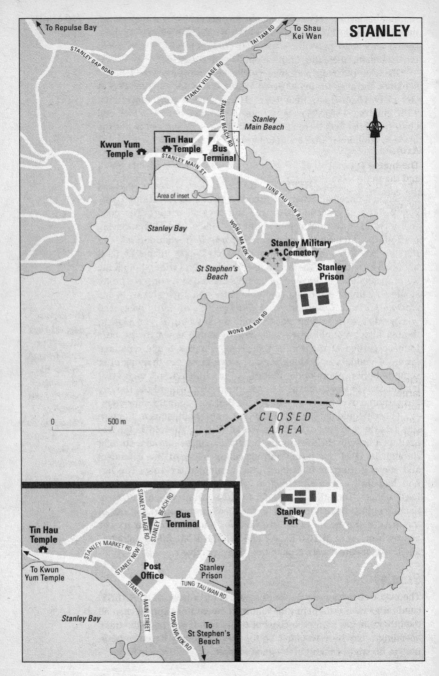

STANLEY

To Repulse Bay

STANLEY GAP ROAD

TAI TAM RD

To Shau Kei Wan

STANLEY VILLAGE RD

STANLEY BEACH RD

Stanley Main Beach

Kwun Yum Temple

Tin Hau Temple

Bus Terminal

STANLEY MAIN ST

Area of inset

Stanley Bay

TUNG TAU WAN RD

Stanley Military Cemetery

Stanley Prison

St Stephen's Beach

WONG MA KOK RD

WONG MA KOK RD

0   500 m

CLOSED AREA

Stanley Fort

Tin Hau Temple

STANLEY VILLAGE RD

STANLEY BEACH RD

Bus Terminal

STANLEY MARKET RD

STANLEY NEW ST

To Kwun Yum Temple

Post Office

To Stanley Prison

TUNG TAU WAN RD

Stanley Bay

STANLEY MAIN STREET

WONG WA KOK RD

To St Stephen's Beach

Stanley has been one of the main areas of settlement throughout the island's history, and in 1841 there were 2000 people living here, earning a decent living from fishing. Today, it's very much a small residential place, popular with Westerners as it's only 15km from Central, and fairly lively at most times of the year. The name, incidentally, is down to another nineteenth-century Colonial Secretary, Lord Stanley, but as with Aberdeen the original Chinese name is much more evocative – *Chek Chue* or "robber's lair", after the pirates who once used the village as a base.

Around the village

The bus will drop you at the **bus terminal** on Stanley Village Road, and the **main beach** is just a couple of minutes' walk away, down on the eastern side of the peninsula. This is narrow and stony, ringed by new development, and for swimming there's actually a much better one, St Stephen's Beach, about ten minutes out of the centre in the opposite direction (see below).

Much of Stanley's attraction lies in its **market** (daily 10am–7pm), which not surprisingly straddles the streets and alleys around Stanley Market Road, just a step over from the bus terminal. It's famous for its cheap clothes (though they're not actually that cheap), and rooting around turns up all sorts of fake designer gear, silk, T-shirts, good sportswear and jeans, as well as the more usual market items – food, household goods, crockery and the rest. When you've done, you can follow Stanley Main Street around the bay to the small **Tin Hau Temple**, which overlooks the western side of the peninsula. It's old by Hong Kong standards, built in 1767, and survived the Japanese bombing of Stanley in the last war, though a large tiger, the skin of which hangs on the wall inside, was less fortunate: he got his at the hands of an Indian policeman in 1942. Lanterns and model ships decorate the rest of the inside, reminding you of Tin Hau's role as protector of the fishermen, though there's precious little fishing done from Stanley any more.

Past the temple, a path leads up to **MA HANG VILLAGE**, the original Chinese settlement here, with a clutch of old houses spreading up the hillside that are gradually becoming dwarfed by the surrounding new apartment blocks. Look for a red-bricked gate on the left, five minutes up from the Tin Hau temple, where a lane leads up to the **Kwun Yum Temple** gardens, whose main feature is the six-metre-high statue of the Goddess of Mercy, Kwun Yum (or Kuan Yin), set in a pavilion from where you can look out over the bay.

To St Stephen's Beach and Stanley Fort

The other route through Stanley is to follow Wong Ma Kok Road south through the village, down the peninsula. After about ten minutes (just after the playing field), steps lead down to **St Stephen's Beach**, a nice stretch of clean sand with a water sports centre, barbecue pits and decent swimming. If you miss the steps to

the beach, you can take the side road on the right a little further on,
by St Stephen's School.

A few minutes on down the main road, the **Stanley Military
Cemetery** has some graves dating back to the mid-1840s, but is
mostly full of those killed defending Hong Kong from the Japanese
in 1941 and later in the war. It's a poignant spot to stop and remember the brave stand that many of the soldiers took, especially since
the other significant landmark, **Stanley Prison** – where hundreds of
civilians were interned in dire conditions by the Japanese during the
war – is just over the way. Nowadays, it's a maximum-security
prison, housing among others forty convicted murderers who were
on Hong Kong's death row until 1993, when capital punishment was
finally removed from the statute books. The death sentence hadn't
been carried out since 1966 – it was always commuted to terms of
imprisonment – but the worry was that China might have carried
out the penalty after 1997 if it had remained in law. The prison
gallows are destined for one of the territory's museums.

The road continues past the cemetery, climbing up to **Stanley
Fort**, base of a British regiment and closed to the public (signs here
say "Caution – Troops Marching"), though there's nothing to stop
you going as far as you're allowed for the views over Stanley Bay.

Practicalities

Stanley isn't far beyond Repulse Bay, reached on **bus #6** or **#260**
(an express) from the Central Bus Terminal, the **#73** from Aberdeen/
Repulse Bay, or – coming around the other side of the island – the
#14 from Shau Kei Wan (which is on the MTR and tram route; see
below). The bus takes about forty minutes from Central and is a
terrific ride, the road sometimes swooping high above the bays.

You can get something cheap to **eat** at the *dai pai dongs* on
both sides of Stanley Market Road – noodles and the like, though
there's fresh fruit on sale, too. More formally (and expensively),
there are three good **restaurants** – *Stanley's French Restaurant*
(p.229), *Stanley's Oriental Restaurant* (p.232) and *Il Mercato*
(p.232) – reviewed on the respective page numbers. Stanley being
the *gweilo* hangout it is, there's also a couple of **pubs** on Stanley
Main Street; the *Smuggler's Inn* and, more attractively, with seats by
the pavement, *Lord Stanley's Bar* – both serve reasonable British
pub food too. If you need them, you'll also find a **post office** in
Stanley (2 Wong Ma Kok Rd), a couple of **banks** and a **supermarket**.

The East Coast

HONG KONG ISLAND

There's little incentive to travel much further **east** than Causeway
Bay, although the tram ride is fairly entertaining – along King's
Road, through **North Point**, the northernmost point of Hong Kong
Island, and the residential areas of **Quarry Bay** and **Taikoo Shing**

before reaching **Shau Kei Wan** at the end of the line. Once, this whole stretch was lined with beaches, but the views these days are of high-rise apartments and housing estates. The various developments here have increased in popularity with improvements in the transport system: the **Eastern Island Corridor** is a highway built above and along the shoreline, providing some impressive views if you're speeding along it in a car; the newly tunnelled **MTR** link across the harbour gives much quicker access to Kowloon. Probably the best combination is to go out on the tram, which will take around half an hour from Causeway Bay to the end of the line, and return by MTR; each place along the tram route also has its own MTR station.

Beyond Shau Kei Wan, heading south, you soon escape into more rural surroundings. Some of the island's best beaches are those on its east coast, the ones around **Shek O** particularly recommended, while you've a better chance of avoiding the crowds if you take one of the high hill walks from **Tai Tam Reservoir** which run over the centre of the island.

North Point

If you're going to jump off the tram anywhere before Shau Kei Wan, **NORTH POINT** is as good a place as any. It doesn't get many tourists, which isn't surprising since the apartment blocks and busy main road don't hide any real attractions, but there is a good **market** on Marble Street, a couple of blocks up from North Point Ferry Pier. It sells very cheap T-shirts and light summer clothes, and has a good produce section. Down at the ferry pier, there's a fresh fish market, too, while the **ferries** run across to Hung Hom or Kwun Tong in Kowloon. The ferry pier is also good for picking up a couple of buses: the #10 to Kennedy Town and the #65 to Stanley.

Quarry Bay, Taikoo Shing and Sai Wan Ho

Further east, the tram runs through **QUARRY BAY**, where the second cross-harbour tunnel comes up on the island. The MTR link under the water means that you can switch lines here if you wish, crossing to Kowloon and the Kwun Tong Line.

If you're on the tram, the only other stop you might want to make is at **TAIKOO SHING**, a massive new development just beyond Quarry Bay. If you don't have time to see one of the New Territories' sparkling, instant cities that have sprung up over the last few years, then Taikoo Shing will do just as well – a large-scale residential city with its own monster shopping and entertainment complex, **Cityplaza**, featuring shops, skating rinks (ice- and roller-), restaurants, free children's shows and lots more indoor entertainment. It's not a bad place for a wet day, and decked out in the glossy, hi-tech fashion loved by the Hong Kong Chinese. Taikoo Shing has its own MTR station, from which you can walk straight into *Cityplaza*.

A few minutes' further on, at **SAI WAN HO**, you can catch a ferry across the Lei Yue Mun channel to Sam Ka Tsuen ferry pier, near which is one of the best places in Hong Kong to eat fresh seafood, Lei Yue Mun. For more details see p.125.

Shau Kei Wan

The tram finishes its run in **SHAU KEI WAN**, which is an important transport terminus as well as somewhere you could profitably spend an hour before heading back. Close to the tram terminus you'll find a Taoist **Shing Wong Temple**, dedicated to the local City God, while further up by the water – close to the fish market – there's the **Tam Kung Temple**, dedicated to a lesser-known fishermen's god, Tam Kung. The temple was built at the turn of this century and is the venue of a lively festival, usually at the beginning of May, when it's decorated and there are processions around the whole area. You could take a look around Shau Kei Wan's market stalls, too, before either catching the tram or the MTR back into Central. The **bus terminal** is outside the MTR station; from here the #2 runs into Central.

Shek O and around

The easternmost limb of land on the island holds the enjoyable beach and village of **SHEK O**, reached by taking bus #9 from Shau Kei Wan bus terminal (see above), a glorious half-hour ride down a winding road, taking in splendid views of Tai Tam reservoir, as well as Stanley and the south coast.

The bus drops you at the small bus station in Shek O village. Walk down the road to the roundabout and the **beach** is ahead of you, behind the car park. It's one of Hong Kong's best: wide, with white sand and fringed by shady trees, though it can get very full at the weekend. There's a mini-golf course next to the beach to help while away the afternoon; bikes for rent from the back of the car park; and a few **restaurants** in the village, including a decent one right on the roundabout and a recommended Thai place (see p.235). There's a pub here, too, and on Sunday extra shops and stalls open up, serving food and snacks to the crowds who come down to swim.

The bucket-and-spade shops and basic restaurants in the village don't give the game away, but Shek O is actually one of the swankiest addresses in Hong Kong, and there are some rich houses in the area. You can get a flavour of things by walking through the village and following the path up to **Shek O Headland**, where you'll be faced with yet more sweeping panoramas. To the right is **Cape D'Aguilar**, and to the left, **Rocky Bay**, a nice beach, though with heavily polluted water – which means the sand is generally empty.

Heading back to Shau Kei Wan from Shek O, you don't have to return to the bus station but can instead take a **minibus** from the car park: they're more frequent and a little quicker.

Big Wave Bay

A smarter move if you want more space and less people is to head
further north to **Big Wave Bay**, where there's another good beach
(that, unlike Rocky Bay, you can swim from), barbecue pits and a
refreshment kiosk. You'll have to walk from Shek O, which will take
you about half an hour: if you're heading straight here, get off the
bus on the way into Shek O at the fork in the road just before the
village.

Turtle Cove and Tai Tam Reservoir

The second of the bus routes which operate down the **east side of
the island**, the #14 (also from Shau Kei Wan), runs down the other
side of Tai Tam Harbour to Stanley, calling at TURTLE COVE, a
popular beach with all the usual facilities.

On the way back you could call at **Tai Tam Reservoir**, the first in
Hong Kong and starting point for several excellent hill **walks**. The
easiest is northwest to Wong Nai Chung Gap, a two-hour walk along
Tai Tam Reservoir Road to the Gap, just beyond which is Happy
Valley (walk on to Stubbs Road and you can pick up the #15 bus into
Central). Longer is the walk due north along Mount Parker Road,
between Mount Butler and Mount Parker, to Quarry Bay, from where
you can pick up the MTR or tram back into Central.

Chapter 3

Kowloon

The peninsula on the Chinese mainland, which became part of Hong Kong in 1860 – almost twenty years after the British nabbed the island over the water – is called **Kowloon**, an English transliteration of the Cantonese words, *gau lung*, "nine dragons". The dutiful historical explanation of the name is that the fleeing boy-emperor of the Song Dynasty, who ran to the Hong Kong area to escape the Mongols in the thirteenth century, counted eight hills here, purported to hide eight dragons – a figure which was rounded up to nine by sycophantic servants who pointed out that an emperor is also a dragon. Since that flurry of imperial attention, Kowloon's twelve square kilometres have changed from a rolling green peninsula to one of the most built-up areas in the world.

There was an unruly Chinese village here, at the tip of the peninsula, since the very earliest days of the fledgling island colony across the harbour, alongside fortified walls and battlements protecting a Chinese garrison. But after the peninsula was ceded to the British, development gathered pace, and colonial buildings and roads were laid out as the growing population spread across from Hong Kong Island. Today, that gradual development – from village to colonial town – has been subsumed into the packed, frenetic region of Kowloon that is **Tsim Sha Tsui**, which takes up the tip of the peninsula. This is where many visitors stay, eat and – almost Tsim Sha Tsui's *raison d'être* – shop, finding endless diversion in a commercial pack of streets that has few equals anywhere in the world.

But there's also a more traditional side to Kowloon, seen in the areas to the north – **Yau Ma Tei** and **Mongkok** – where there are older, explorable streets and buildings. There are similar sights and smells over to the east, around **Kowloon City**: if you fly into Hong Kong, this is the first area you'll see, the plane banking and turning between the buildings in order to straighten up for its descent into nearby **Kai Tak airport**.

Kowloon proper ends at **Boundary Street**, about 4km north of the harbour. In 1860, before the New Territories were added to the colony (in 1898), this formed the frontier between Hong Kong and China. Nowadays, although officially part of the New Territories, the areas immediately above Boundary Street are more usually known as **New Kowloon**, and have a few attractions for the visitor. Mostly, they're densely populated shopping and residential areas, but people ride out here for the amusement park and Chinese cultural village at **Lai Chi Kok**, to the west; for a scattering of **temples** and minor **museums**; and to the seafood-eating village of **Lei Yue Mun**, to the east.

Tsim Sha Tsui

If lots of tourists think Hong Kong Island is the only place in the territory worth seeing, then an equal number swear that **TSIM SHA TSUI** is the only place to shop – both mistakes, but both understandable given the HKTA's virtual encouragement of such beliefs in all its literature. Even beyond the brochures, though, Tsim Sha Tsui works hard to maintain the myth that all tourists like nothing better than to spend money: most of its notable monuments are swish commercial developments, and in the kilometre or so from the waterfront to the top of Kowloon Park a devoted window-shopper could find every bauble, gadget and designer label known to humanity – as well as a few pirated by the locals for good measure.

If it all sounds gruesomely commercial, well, it is. But it would be churlish to knock it, since the enterprise and endeavour shown in Tsim Sha Tsui are the main reason Hong Kong exists at all. There's an infectious vibrancy in the "get rich, get ahead" mentality that pervades the streets, and it rubs off in the countless restaurants, bars and pubs that make Tsim Sha Tsui one of the best places in Hong Kong for a night out. Look close enough, and amid the morass of consumerism are pockets of culture – an excellent Cultural Centre and a museum or two – that can provide a bit of serious relief. It's all a long way, though, from the "sharp, sandy point" that gave Tsim Sha Tsui its Chinese name. Hard to believe now, but in 1860, when the peninsula was ceded to Britain, Chatham Road was a beach and the point of Tsim Sha Tsui an abandoned sandy spit.

Around the Star Ferry

Walk down the gangway off the **Star Ferry** into its Kowloon-side terminal, and you're in the best possible starting place for a tour of Tsim Sha Tsui. The Concourse is full of newspaper sellers and hawkers; there's an HKTA office (Mon–Fri 8am–6pm, Sat & Sun 9am–5pm), and outside there's a major bus terminal and taxi rank.

For bus routes from the Star Ferry, see p.43.

On the waterfront, next to the Star Ferry terminal, tour boats are tied up, and beyond here steps and escalators lead up into an immense, gleaming, air-conditioned shopping centre, reputedly the

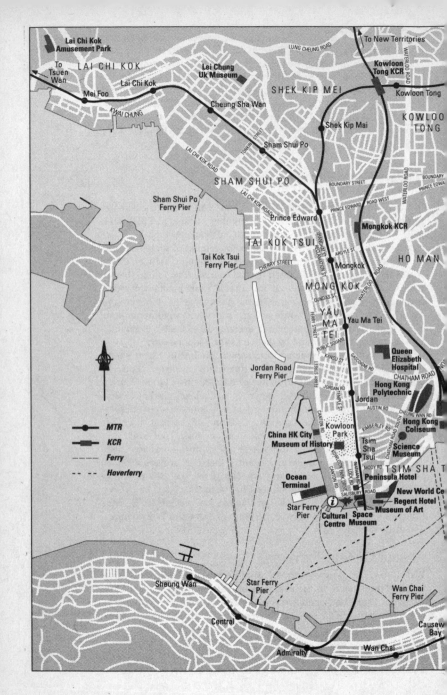

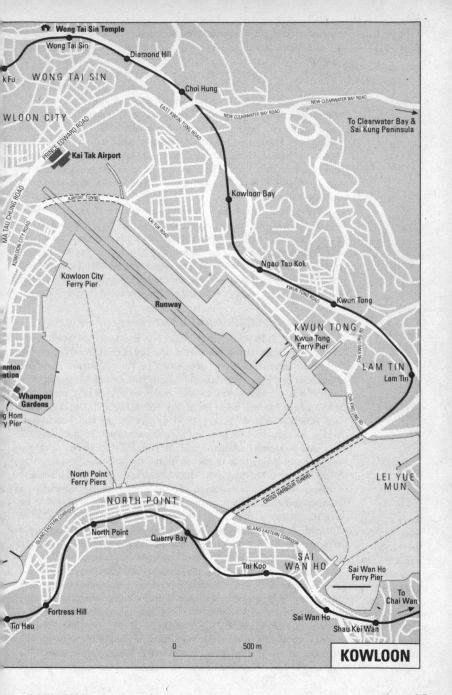

biggest in Asia (although that's not a unique claim in Hong Kong) – all marble, fountains, swish shops and bright lights. It's actually several inter-connected centres which run along the western side of Tsim Sha Tsui's waterfront, with luxury apartments studding the upper levels and commanding priceless views over the harbour. The first section, **Ocean Terminal**, which juts out into the water, is where the cruise ships dock; there's a passport control here for the passengers, who usually spend a night or two in Hong Kong before sailing on. Exclusive boutiques line the endless and confusing galleries that link Ocean Terminal with the adjacent **Ocean Centre**, and, the next block up, **Harbour City** – more shops, a couple of swanky hotels, and clothes and shoes the price of a small country's defence budget.

If you want to get back down to street level, signs everywhere will direct you out on to **Canton Road**, which runs parallel to the water. Continue up it, northwards, past Harbour City, and you'll pass the **Hong Kong China Ferry Terminal**, a block of shops and restaurants around the ticket offices and departure lounges for ferry and hoverferry trips to China and Macau; further up is the adjacent **China Hong Kong City** – more of the same though without the ferries.

The Hong Kong Cultural Centre

Back at the Star Ferry, over Salisbury Road, the slender **clock tower**, 45m high, dates from 1921, the only remnant of the grand, columned train station that once stood on the waterfront here, the beginning of the line that stretched from Hong Kong to Beijing. The station was demolished in 1978 to make way for a new waterfront development, whose latest stage, the **Hong Kong Cultural Centre**, was officially opened in late 1989 by the Prince and Princess of Wales. Its construction put the cat firmly amongst the architectural pigeons. Given six hundred million Hong Kong dollars and *the* prime harbourside site in the territory, the architect managed to come up with a building that, originally at least, had few friends and – astonishingly – no windows. The plain exterior is shaped like a vast winged chute which, among other interpretations, is said to be a bird's wings enshrouding the egg that is the adjacent Space Museum. A brick skirt runs around the entire complex, forming a sort of wedge-shaped cloister, while out in the landscaped plaza, a line of palm trees sit either side of a man-made water channel.

There are free foyer programmes and exhibitions at the Cultural Centre most days; also see Chapter 10 for other events and box office details.

Whatever you think of it, it's certainly bold, and the contentious design aside, the Cultural Centre represents a welcome commitment to making Hong Kong one of Asia's major cultural centres. Inside, the smart, state-of-the-art interior contains three separate venues – a concert hall, grand theatre and studio theatre – while adjacent blocks harbour a superb new art museum, a library, cinema and restaurants. If you're unable to catch a performance inside the Cultural Centre, consider instead taking one of the **guided tours** of the complex – in English on Wednesday and Saturday at 12.30pm (adults $10, children and senior citizens $5). Tickets are available in advance from the Enquiries Counter in the main foyer (☎734 2009). The box office is here, too, if you want to call in and pick up an events brochure.

Museum of Art

With the opening of the Cultural Centre came the eagerly awaited establishment of Hong Kong's **Museum of Art** (Mon–Wed & Fri–Sat 10am–6pm, Sun 1–6pm; $10, children and senior citizens $5), six beautifully appointed galleries on three floors, behind the main building. For years, most of the exhibits were crammed into unsuitable, temporary galleries in Central's City Hall, but now they have surroundings equal to their undoubted artistic value. As well as the galleries described below, there's space for touring exhibitions and a fine **museum shop**, by the entrance, with an adjacent gallery for sales of contemporary Hong Kong art and sculpture.

The museum galleries begin on the second floor with the **Xubaizhai Gallery of Chinese Painting and Calligraphy**, primarily featuring a series of hanging scrolls of ink on silk, some up to four metres high. Many depict rural Chinese scenes, though there are simpler representations, too – Jin Nong's podgy and overweight "Lone Horse" (1761) an appealing example. Next door, the **Contemporary Art Gallery** features changing exhibitions of silk-screen painting, modern calligraphy, ceramics, and Western and Chinese painting by Hong Kong artists.

These galleries are captivating enough, but up on the third floor are the museum's real highlights. The gallery devoted to **Chinese Antiquities** alone contains over 3000 exhibits, from daily artefacts and decorative items to burial goods. The Han Dynasty (206 BC–220 AD) ceramics are particularly interesting– look out for a green-glazed watch tower, just over a metre high. Pot-bellied tomb figures from the Tang Dynasty (618–907 AD), and an entire side gallery of carved bamboo brush pots and ornamental figures, complete the collection. The Antiquities section shades into the **Chinese Decorative Arts** gallery, laden with carved jade, ivory and glass-ware, as well as a series of Ming Dynasty ceramics unearthed from a pit on Lantau in 1990.

Also on the third floor, you'll find the **Historical Pictures Collection**, a fascinating array of over a thousand oils, watercolours, drawings and prints that trace the eighteenth- and nineteenth-century development of Hong Kong, Macau and Guangzhou as trading centres. The first painting in the gallery is in fact the earliest known painting of Hong Kong, dated 1816 and executed by William Havell – it depicts a waterfall near Aberdeen. Other works are by army draughtsmen, traders and local professional painters (called "China trade painters") and have acute historical interest: an 1854 oil painting of Victoria, as Central was then called, shows just a few

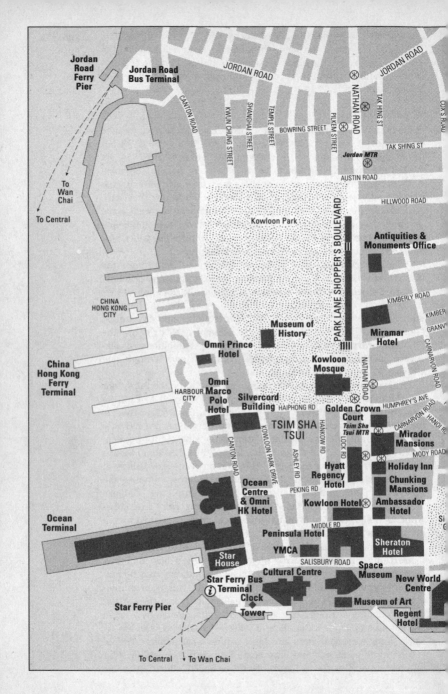

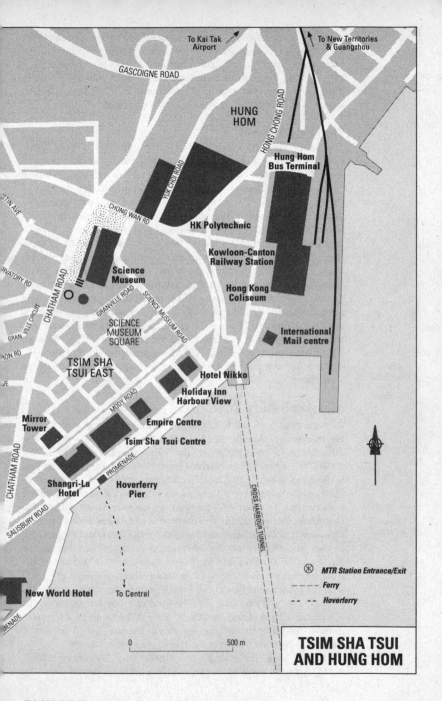

To Kai Tak Airport

To New Territories & Guangzhou

GASCOIGNE ROAD

HUNG HOM

HONG CHONG ROAD

Hung Hom Bus Terminal

YUK CHOI ROAD

CHONG WAN RD

HK Polytechnic

Kowloon-Canton Railway Station

CHATHAM ROAD

'STIN AVE

'RVATORY RD

Science Museum

GRAN'VILLE ROAD

GRAN'VILLE ROAD

SCIENCE MUSEUM ROAD

Hong Kong Coliseum

International Mail centre

SCIENCE MUSEUM SQUARE

GRAN'VILLE CIRCUIT

'ION RD

'VE

TSIM SHA TSUI EAST

Hotel Nikko

MODY ROAD

Holiday Inn Harbour View

Mirror Tower

Empire Centre

Tsim Sha Tsui Centre

CHATHAM ROAD

PROMENADE

Shangri-La Hotel

Hoverferry Pier

SALISBURY ROAD

CROSS HARBOUR TUNNEL

New World Hotel

To Central

'PROMENADE

⊛   MTR Station Entrance/Exit

— — —   Ferry

— — —   Hoverferry

0   500 m

TSIM SHA TSUI AND HUNG HOM

score buildings ranged along the empty waterfront; while contemporary paintings of Guangzhou show it as a thriving centre of warehouses and junks, its buildings sporting the flags of various trading nations. The museum ends on the fourth floor with the **Chinese Fine Art** gallery, rounding up a selection from 3000 works, including modern Chinese art, animal- and bird-paintings.

The Space Museum

The **Space Museum** (Mon & Wed–Fri 1–9pm, Sat & Sun 10am–9pm; $10, children and senior citizens $5) marked the first stage of the Cultural Centre, built in 1980 and devoted to a hands-on display of space- and astronomy-related objects and themes; the entrance is on Salisbury Road. The *Exhibition Hall* is well laid out, with push-button exhibits, video presentations, telescopes and picture boards which take you through astronomical and space history, with a perhaps understandable Chinese bias – you learn that the Chinese were the first to spot Halley's Comet, the first to plot star movements, the first to use gunpowder, etc. Upstairs, the *Hall of Solar Sciences* is duller, a brief introduction to all things solar, with explanations of eclipses, sun spots and the like. Most people (certainly most children) want to catch one of the regular daily showings at the *Space Theatre* ($20, 6–15-year-olds, students and senior citizens $13), which has a choice of films shown on the massive Omnimax screen, providing a thrilling sensurround experience – worth going to if you've never seen one before. Call ☎ 734 2722 for show times.

Along Salisbury Road

Over the road from the Space Museum stands an equally recognisable monument, though this time it's one of Tsim Sha Tsui's few throwbacks to colonial times: the **Peninsula Hotel**. Built in the 1920s, its elegant wings reaching around a fountain, it used to lord it over the water before land reclamation robbed the hotel of its harbourside position – a high, new central block, currently under construction, is designed to regain its harbour views. It was the *Peninsula* that put up the travellers who had disembarked from the Kowloon–Canton railway, and for decades the glitterati frequented it as they also frequented the other grand Asian colonial hotels, the *Taj Mahal* in Bombay and *Raffles* in Singapore. It's still one of the most expensive places to stay in Hong Kong, certainly the hotel with the most social clout, and even if your budget won't stretch to a room here, you can drop into the opulent lobby for afternoon tea – serenaded by a string quartet. It's worth knowing that if you're dressed "inappropriately" (no shorts or sandals) you'll be gently steered to the door whatever the size of your bank balance.

If you book far enough in advance (see "Accommodation", p.204), you can get a room at the **YMCA** building, next door to the

Peninsula, which apes the grand hotel in its solid design but is a fraction of the price. Stay anywhere else along Salisbury Road and you're still going to spend an enormous amount, from the *Sheraton* at the bottom of Nathan Road to the *New World* and the *Regent* over the road, the latter two part of the waterfront **New World Centre** – a hotel and shopping complex built on reclaimed land. Actually, the New World Centre isn't a bad place to linger: the lobby of the *Regent* has forty-foot-high windows looking out over the harbour, which make a humble drink there a spectacular affair; and if you work your way outside to the waterfront **promenade**, you can walk all the way up to Hung Hom.

Nathan Road

Between the *Peninsula* and the *Sheraton* hotels, **Nathan Road** is Tsim Sha Tsui's – and Kowloon's – main thoroughfare, running north from the waterfront right the way to Boundary Street. This is the commercial artery for the whole area, tall buildings crowding to a point in the distance, festooned with neon signs so bright and numerous that they're not allowed to flash at night in case incoming planes mistake Nathan Road for the airport runway. It's always packed and noisy, split by fast-moving traffic which stops occasionally at the periodic lights to allow an ocean of people to cross from side to side.

Turn-of-the-century photographs show Nathan Road as a tree-lined avenue, with grass verges and no traffic. Built originally in 1865 (and called Robinson Road), there was little prospect of its development until Sir Matthew Nathan, a professional engineer, took up the Governorship of Hong Kong in 1904. Under his orders the road was widened and extended as far north as Yau Ma Tei, but even with the gradual enlargement of Tsim Sha Tsui, the road remained so underused it gained the soubriquet "Nathan's Folly". Not until the 1960s was there real development, when large hotels began to appear in Tsim Sha Tsui and the shopping arcades sprouted.

Today, other than eating and drinking in the surrounding streets, most pedestrians on Nathan Road are intent on trawling the shops that have provided the road with its modern tag, the "Golden Mile". It's not just the neon along here that glitters, but the windows too – full of gold and silver, precious stones, hi-fi and cameras, watches and calculators, clothes, shoes and fine art. Window-shopping can be more of a struggle than usual since, apart from the crowds, you also have to contend with the pavement hawkers, who are selling goods at knock-down (and knock-off) prices – you'll soon tire of the insistent offers of a "copy watch".

As well as the mainstream jewellery and hi-fi shops, Nathan Road has its own **shopping centres**, some of which – in the hotel galleries – are as impressive as those anywhere else. It also has a

Buses that head up and down Nathan Road include the #1, #1A, #1K, #2, #6, #6A, #7 and #9. The MTR is less useful for short hops; the five stops on Nathan Rd are Tsim Sha Tsui (for Chungking Mansions and Kowloon Park), Jordan (at Jordan Rd), Yau Ma Tei (Waterloo Rd), Mongkok (Argyle St) and Prince Edward (Prince Edward Rd) – with around 3km between the first and last.

selection of often fairly grim mansion blocks, whose crumbling corridors contain numerous shops and stalls – fun to browse through even if you don't find a real bargain. The best known is **Chungking Mansions**, at nos. 36–44, on the right before the *Holiday Inn*, which is notorious for its plethora of cheap guest houses, and Indian and Pakistani cafés and restaurants, as well as some great places to buy cheap silk, T-shirts and other clothes; all the shops are on the ground and first floors. If you're into slum shopping, **Mirador Mansion**, further up on the same side of the road (nos. 56–58), is more of the same; while the side streets off both sides of Nathan Road are alive with similar possibilities – just saunter around and take your pick.

The Antiquities and Monuments Office

Opposite Kowloon Park, at 136 Nathan Road, the former Kowloon British School – built in 1902 – is now an exhibition hall for the **Antiquities and Monuments Office** (Mon–Fri 9.30am–12.30pm & 2–4.30pm, Sat 9.30am–noon). The two-storey Victorian villa, with wrap-around verandahs and high ceilings, puts on temporary displays relating to Hong Kong's history – and you can call in and pick up a full set of brochures detailing various archeological and historical sites around the territory. You might also ask here about visiting the Royal Observatory, behind the school, another colonial building, though one which doesn't always take kindly to speculative visits by tourists.

Kowloon Park

There's breathing space close by in **Kowloon Park** (daily 6.30am–11.30pm), which stretches along Nathan Road between Haiphong Road and Austin Road. Typically, for such a built-up territory, it's not actually at ground level, but suspended above a "Shoppers' Boulevard"; steps lead up into the park from Nathan Road. Although it's lost a few hundred metres around the edges recently to new buildings, it remains a handy place to rest your legs, parts of it landscaped and styled as a Chinese garden with fountains, rest areas and a chess garden, and an aviary (daily 6.30am–8pm; free). A Sculpture Walk features work by local artists.

The most obvious focus, though, is the large **Kowloon Mosque** in the southeastern corner, built in the mid-1980s for nearly $30 million to serve the territory's 50,000 Muslims (of whom about half are Chinese). It replaced a mosque orginally built in 1894 for the British army's Muslim troops from India, and retains its classic design, with a central white marble dome and minarets – surprisingly, it doesn't look out of place, standing above the street. However, sadly, unless you obtain permission in advance (☎724 0095), you're not allowed in for a further investigation of the mosque and Islamic Centre it encompasses.

You'll have to make do with visiting the park's other building, a converted colonial barracks which does duty now as the informative **Museum of History** (Mon–Thurs & Sat 10am–6pm, Sun 1–6pm; $10, children and senior citizens $5). Exhibitions here attempt to show a cross-section of the museum's enormous archeological and ethnographical collection, and displays cover the story of Hong Kong, from Neolithic times to the present day. Highlights include a model sampan (which you can board), a Hakka house and costumes, even a street reconstruction from the mid-nineteenth century with its medicine shops and opium dens. Old photographs, prehistoric finds and other cultural relics, and video displays on various periods in the colony's history all add up to an hour or so well spent here. There's a full range of public activities held at the museum, which you might find interesting – lectures and film shows particularly – though most are conducted in Cantonese: check at the reception desk for details.

Leave the park at the southern end and you can drop down to Haiphong Road and its covered **market** at the Canton Road end (daily 6am–8pm) – a good place to pick up food, and where Chungking Mansions does its shopping.

Tsim Sha Tsui East and Hung Hom

After the rambling streets and businesses of Tsim Sha Tsui, **TSIM SHA TSUI EAST** couldn't be more different. Starting at the New World Centre, all the land east of Chatham Road is reclaimed, and the whole of the district has sprung up from nothing over the last decade. It is almost exclusively a wedge of large hotels, connected shopping centres and expensive restaurants and clubs, which you can bypass by sticking to the **waterfront promenade** that follows the harbour around from the Cultural Centre. You can get good views of the dragon boat racing from here in June (see "Hong Kong's Festivals", p.256), year-round photo-opportunities across the harbour to the island, and the chance to be horribly fascinated by whether or not the people fishing off the promenade are actually going to eat what they haul out of the vile water. Halfway up, outside the *Shangri-La* hotel, there is a small pier from where you can catch a **hoverferry** over to Queen's Pier on Hong Kong Island.

Hung Hom

Keep to the promenade, past the line of hotels, and eventually (beyond the International Mail Centre) steps take you up into the labyrinthine corridors and overhead walkways which feed into one of several destinations in **HUNG HOM**, the next neighbourhood to the north. All told, it's a fifteen- to twenty-minute walk from the beginning of the promenade.

The most noticeable building is the **Hong Kong Coliseum**, an inverted pyramid which contains a 12,000-seater stadium, used for sports events and concerts. Signs also point you to the **Kowloon–Canton Railway (KCR) Station**, built in 1975 once it had been decided to demolish the old station down by the Star Ferry. This is where you have to come if you want to take the train to China, a route which has been in existence since 1912 and which provides a link with London, through the trans-Siberian railway. The present building is of no architectural merit, but from here there are KCR trains to the New Territories, as well as to China.

Heading directly for the KCR Station, take buses #2K, #5C, #8 and #8A from the Star Ferry; minibus #1M runs from Star Ferry to Tsim Sha Tsui East.

A signposted walkway leads you down to the water and around the harbour to the **Hung Hom Ferry Pier**, another ten minutes' walk from the station, for services across to Central, Wan Chai or North Point. Hung Hom itself is a recognised shopping area, with factory outlets selling clothes and jewellery in the block of streets northeast of the KCR station (between Man Yue St and Hok Yuen St).

If you're coming down this way, it's worth taking the time to head as far as **Whampoa Gardens**, behind the ferry pier, a new housing and commercial development built around an old dry dock. The Kowloon Dockyard operated on this site from 1870–1984, but with the land filled in around it, the dock now supports an impressive hundred-metre-long concrete "ship", open to the public and stacked with more shops, restaurants and recreational facilities. Climb up to the top deck for a surreal view of the surrounding buildings – across to tenth-floor apartments from a ship that looks like it could sail at any minute.

The UCC Coffee Shop, in the Whampoa Gardens ship, serves 23 different types of coffee, as well as iced tea and snacks.

The Hong Kong Science Museum

Back in Tsim Sha Tsui East, Hong Kong's newest museum is worth setting aside a few hours for – certainly if you have children to amuse. The **Hong Kong Science Museum** (Tues–Fri 1–9pm; Sat & Sun 10am–9pm; $25, children, students and senior citizens $15), at 2 Science Museum Road, is an enterprising venture comprising three floors of hands-on exhibits designed to take the mystery out of all things scientific. Since this includes things like explaining how kitchen and bathroom appliances work, as well as going into the finer points of robotics, computers, cellular phones and hi-fi equipment, even the most Luddite of visitors should be tempted to push buttons and operate robot arms with abandon. Avoid Sundays if you can, and try to go early or late in the day, since the attraction palls if you have to queue for a turn at the best of the machines and exhibits.

Yau Ma Tei and Mongkok

North up Nathan Road, beyond Jordan MTR, you enter an older part of Kowloon, **YAU MA TEI**, one of the first areas to be developed after 1860 and with plenty of interest packed into its tight grid of streets. The name of the district recalls the sesame seed farming that the first inhabitants made their living from (*ma* is sesame). The most interesting streets are the long straight ones north of Jordan Road, on the west side of Nathan Road.

Yau Ma Tei and Mongkok

Yau Ma Tei is a 20-min walk up Nathan Rd; or take the bus (see p.43), the MTR to Jordan, or the cross-harbour ferry from Central to Jordan Rd Ferry Pier.

Jordan Road to Waterloo Road

Like Western district on Hong Kong Island, the streets of Yau Ma Tei conceal a wealth of traditional shops, businesses and *dai pai dongs* that repay investigation. **Canton Road**, close to Jordan Road Ferry Pier, runs north, an interesting mix of businesses, from jade and ivory shops (*mahjong* sets a speciality) at the bottom end, to a section (Dundas St to Soy St, near Yau Ma Tei MTR) lined with mechanical and electrical shops – ships' chandlers' goods, hardware, engines and engineering works piled high at the side of the road.

Shanghai Street is similarly eclectic, with shops selling bright red Chinese wedding gowns, embroidered pillow cases and wedding decorations. At the junction of **Waterloo Road** and **Reclamation Street**, there's a large fruit market, with tiered boxes of oranges stacked under shelters; while Reclamation Street itself, north of the market, specialises in Buddhist utensil and decoration shops – shrines, joss sticks, urns and pictures by the windowful.

Before you leave, call into the **Tin Hau Temple** (daily 8am–6pm) that serves this harbour district, though following land reclamation it's now a little way inland, just back from Nathan Road, between Public Square Street and Market Street. A small park fronts the complex, usually teeming with men gambling at backgammon and *mahjong*, and the line of low buildings is heralded by people seeking alms as you enter. The main temple, around a century old, is dedicated to Tin Hau, but there are three other temples here, too: the one to the left is dedicated to Shea Tan, protector of the local community; to the right are ones to Shing Wong, the City God, and Fook Tak, an Earth God.

The Markets

Yau Ma Tei is famous for its **markets**, of which there are three main ones – two busy during the day, one at night. The one most people have heard of is the **Jade Market** (daily 10am–4pm), which you'll find underneath the Gascoigne Road flyover on Kansu Street (Jordan or Yau Ma Tei MTR). Several hundred stalls display an enormous selection of coloured jade, from earrings and jewellery to statues, and though there's some serious buying and bargaining going on here between dealers, it's a lot of fun just to poke around the stalls to see what you can turn up. All the best stuff goes before lunch, and if you're serious about buying real jade, you should get hold of the HKTA's factsheet about the market, which tells you what colour and quality to look out for. Otherwise, you can pick up small trinkets for just a few dollars if all you want is a souvenir.

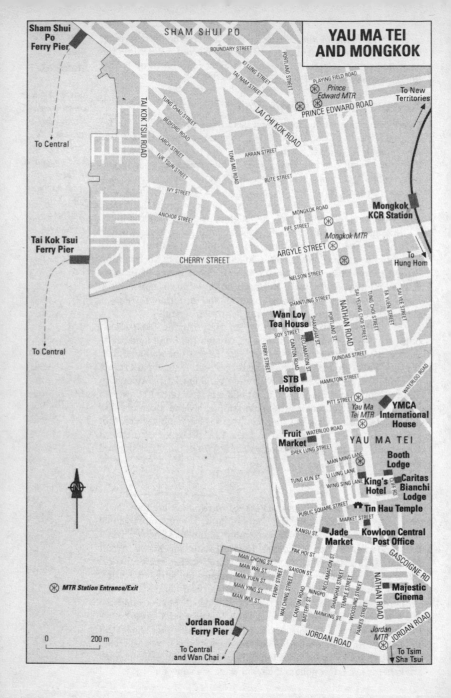

YAU MA TEI
AND MONGKOK

SHAM SHUI PO

Sham Shui Po Ferry Pier

BOUNDARY STREET

KI LUNG STREET

TAI NAM STREET

PORTLAND STREET

PLAYING FIELD ROAD

Prince Edward MTR

PRINCE EDWARD ROAD

LAI CHI KOK ROAD

To New Territories

To Central

TAI KOK TSUI ROAD

TUNG CHAU STREET

BEDFORD ROAD

LARCH STREET

FUK TSUN STREET

TONG MEI ROAD

ARRAN STREET

BUTE STREET

IVY STREET

ANCHOR STREET

MONGKOK ROAD

FIFE STREET

Mongkok MTR

Mongkok KCR Station

Tai Kok Tsui Ferry Pier

CHERRY STREET

ARGYLE STREET

To Hung Hom

NELSON STREET

SHANTUNG STREET

SAY YEUNG CHOI STREET

TUNG CHOI STREET

FA YUEN STREET

SAI YEE STREET

NATHAN ROAD

To Central

FERRY STREET

Wan Loy Tea House

SOY STREET

SHANGHAI ST

PORTLAND ST

RECLAMATION RD

CANTON ROAD

DUNDAS STREET

HAMILTON STREET

STB Hostel

WATERLOO ROAD

PITT STREET

Yau Ma Tei MTR

YMCA International House

Fruit Market

SHEK LUNG STREET

YAU MA TEI

MAN MING LANE

Booth Lodge

TUNG KUN ST

U LUNG LANE

WING SING LANE

King's Hotel

CLIFF RD

Caritas Bianchi Lodge

PUBLIC SQUARE STREET

Tin Hau Temple

MARKET STREET

KANSU ST

Jade Market

Kowloon Central Post Office

PAK HOI ST

GASCOIGNE RD

MAN CHONG ST

MAN WAI ST

MAN YUEN ST

MAN YING ST

MAN WUI ST

FERRY STREET

SAIGON ST

WOOSUNG STREET

RECLAMATION RD

SHANGHAI STREET

TEMPLE STREET

PARKES STREET

NATHAN ROAD

Majestic Cinema

WAI CHING STREET

CANTON ROAD

BATTERY ST

NINGPO

SHANGHAI ST

Jordan MTR

JORDAN ROAD

⊗ MTR Station Entrance/Exit

N

0   200 m

Jordan Road Ferry Pier

NANKING ST

JORDAN ROAD

To Central and Wan Chai

To Tsim Sha Tsui

Head further up into Yau Ma Tei and follow Shanghai Street north. At the junction with Soy Street (on the right), you'll find the *Wan Loy* tea house – three floors of wooden benches and men taking tea. It looks a bit basic and intimidating, with great brass spittoons at every bench, but climb the stairs and find a space. Poles along the windows are lined with bird cages, left there by their owners while they have a drink and a chat, and amid the birdsong you can flag down the geriatric waiters who totter around with *dim sum* on trays. Just around the corner is the reason for the tea house's popularity with bird fanciers, a noisy **bird market** (daily 10am–6pm), down a narrow alley called Hong Lok Street, between Shanghai Street and Portland Street (the nearest MTR is Mongkok). It's filled to the brim with caged songbirds, a fascinating strip which also features crickets tied up in little plastic bags, birdseed barrels, and men varnishing newly made and elaborate bamboo cages. Sadly, redevelopment plans threaten this whole area; the market may not be here much longer.

Temple Street Night Market

A more general market unfolds in the area at night up Temple Street (from the junction with Jordan Rd northwards). From around 6pm to 11pm, **Temple Street Night Market** is alive with activity, its stalls selling cheap clothes, household goods, watches, cassette tapes and jewellery. If you're lucky, there'll be impromptu performances of Cantonese opera, while fortune tellers and herbalists set up stalls in some of the surrounding streets. About halfway up you'll see stalls laden with an amazing array of shellfish. A couple of plates of sea snails, prawns, mussels or clams, with a beer or two, won't be expensive and it's a great place to stop awhile and take in the atmosphere. More formal meals, though hardly more expensive, can be found a little further up, where there's a covered *dai pai dong*. Again, fish and seafood are the speciality and some of the stalls here even have English menus if you want to know exactly what you're getting.

Mongkok

North of Yau Ma Tei is **MONGKOK**, one of the oldest and most dilapidated sections of Kowloon, and – in a territory of extremes – probably the most densely populated area in the world. Almost within touching distance across the roads, the decrepit apartment blocks here are stuffed to the gills with people living in some fairly grim conditions, though, as elsewhere in Hong Kong, attempts to move them out of their traditional homes have foundered. There's nothing to see here, and outsiders are unlikely to pick up on the reputed community spirit that keeps the inhabitants determined to remain in their peeling apartments, but you might walk through, certainly if you're staying at one of the religious guest houses nearby.

The one draw is along **Tung Choi Street**, where a women's clothes market (sometimes known as "Ladies' Market"; daily noon–10pm) stretches for four blocks between Argyle Street and Dundas Street. It's a good place to pick up bargain skirts, dresses, T-shirts and children's clothes; and there are *dai pai dongs* here, too.

The nearest MTR for Ladies' Market is Mongkok (eastern Nelson St exit).

Further north, at the western end of Argyle Street, you could use the regular cross-harbour ferry to Central from the **Tai Kok Tsui Ferry Pier**. From here, although there's nothing to see, you're within striking distance of **Boundary Street**, which until 1898 and the acquisition of the New Territories marked the boundary with China, and would have done again in 1997 if Britain and China hadn't agreed on returning the whole territory to Chinese rule when the lease on the New Territories expires.

Kowloon City and around

The northeastern edges of Kowloon, beyond the airport, have much less going for them than the shopping streets of Tsim Sha Tsui and Yau Ma Tei, but if you've got the time there are one or two destinations that show a different side of Hong Kong.

Boundary Street, Prince Edward Street and Argyle Street all run west from Mongkok, converging on **KOWLOON CITY**, the area immediately surrounding **Kai Tak airport**. There's been an airport here since the 1930s, though it wasn't until 1956 that the impressive runway was built right into the middle of Kowloon Bay: almost 4km long, it stretches down as far as Kwun Tong. It's an odd sensation to hear and feel the planes just a few score feet overhead, though you might bear in mind a report which estimated that a "worst case scenario" plane crash over Kowloon City would kill up to 5000 people – one of the reasons that the new airport on Chek Lap Kok is so eagerly awaited. That's unlikely to be operational until 1997, so in the meantime Kai Tak remains one of the world's most demanding runway approaches. It requires pilots to make a manual descent from 200m up above the city, with a final 47-degree turn to line up with the runway – what British journalist Mark Lawson has called "the 747 pilot's equivalent to running with the bulls at Pamplona".

For details of Kowloon City's Thai restaurants, see p.235.

With time on your hands at the airport, the best place to head for is the main Prince Edward Road: you can get there by walking through the lobby of the *Regal Meridien* airport hotel and dropping down a couple of floors to the hotel's *China Coast Pub*; the main road is out the main door, on your left. In the streets nearby (particularly Kai Tak Rd) there are several excellent **Thai restaurants**, which sometimes put tables outside so that you can wave at the people in the planes as they lurch past. There's a small **bird market** on Prince Edward Road itself (between the hotel and Kai Tak Rd), and a *dai pai dong*, too, so you should be able to occupy yourself for an hour or two if you're waiting for a flight.

Kowloon Walled City

For years, one of the more notorious districts of Hong Kong lay close to the airport, down Carpenter Road. Beyond Boundary Street and strictly in the New Territories, **Kowloon Walled City** was a slum of gigantic proportions, which had occupied an anomalous position in Hong Kong since 1898, when the Chinese retained judicial control over it by a legal sleight of hand. Originally the site of a Chinese garrison, and walled in (hence the name), it developed into a planned village, rife with disease but thriving from the trade that a nearby wharf brought. There was constant friction between the British authorities and the residents, who felt able to call on the Chinese government whenever they were threatened with resettlement, and the Walled City became a bizarre enclave, virtually free from colonial rule. During the Japanese occupation of Hong Kong, the walls were dismantled and used to extend the airport, and many of the buildings were destroyed. But any hope that the British had of taking over the district were dashed after the end of the war, when thousands of refugees from the Chinese mainland moved into the Walled City and made it their own. Compromise plans came to nothing and for years the Walled City remained a no-go area for the police, becoming a haunt of Triad gangs and fugitive criminals, leading some to call it the "cancer of Kowloon".

Sweat-shops and unlicensed factories employed the refugees, who never left the Walled City in case they were arrested; wells were sunk to provide water and electricity was tapped from the mains; every inch of its tattered surface was covered with wire cages tacked on by the inhabitants to create extra space; there was even a temple and basic restaurants. But life in the city took place amidst the most primitive surroundings imaginable: in gloomy, wet corridors, lined with festering rubbish, and with little semblance of order, let alone law. Things improved slightly in the 1970s and 1980s, when residents' associations got together and began to clean up the brothels, abortion clinics, unlicensed medical and dental shops, drinking, drugs and gambling dens that infested the six-hectare site. Finally, in 1987 a planned evacuation programme was agreed with the 30,000 residents, and by 1991 all of them had been rehoused elsewhere and compensated. The site was levelled and turned into a park, ending one of the more unsavoury of the territory's historical quirks.

Lok Fu

Just to the northwest of the airport, the district of **LOK FU** sees few tourists, but a couple of offbeat attractions might tempt you away from Kowloon's more usual draws. It's a large-scale residential area with huge apartment blocks towering close to the Lok Fu MTR station. Leave the station by exit A and aim for **Wang Lok House** (above the bus terminal), where – on level 1 – the Government Housing Department has constructed a series of model, single-room apartments open to the public. It's a rare opportunity to delve behind the tourist facade of Hong Kong and examine the cramped conditions in which much of the population lives; the sixteenth floor provides the best view over the **Chinese Christian Cemetery**, spread across a pyramid-shaped hill, that you'll see just before you land in Hong Kong at Kai Tak airport.

Kowloon City and around

A map at the MTR station also directs you to Junction Road, behind the Lok Fu Shopping Centre, and up to **Lok Fu Park**, the green, wooded hill behind the station. This is a terrific place to come and watch the planes landing at Kai Tak, so close to the aiport that one side of the hill has been shaved off to accommodate a red-and-white chequered sign to guide the pilots in. To reach the view-point, walk up Junction Road, take the first left and head up the tree-lined road past the barrier; turn left by the water service reservoir, walk to the end of the road and make your way down the dirt path by the side of the fence.

Kowloon Tong

West of the airport, **KOWLOON TONG** is a wealthy, residential area, packed with English and American kindergartens and expensive schools like *St George's*, while nearby **Broadcast Drive** is home to most of the radio and TV stations in the territory. You are hardly likely to find yourself strolling around here, though Kowloon Tong is the site of the **interchange** between the MTR and KCR train systems. More oddly, Kowloon Tong is also noted for its nest of euphemistically tagged "short-time hotels", though given the area, they're anything but seedy. Drive along Waterloo Road and down the adjacent side streets and you can't miss them: all sumptuously decorated and equipped, sitting behind security cameras and grilles.

Wong Tai Sin Temple

There are more strange goings-on a couple of MTR stops east of Kowloon Tong, about a kilometre north of the airport, where the entrance to the massive and colourful **Wong Tai Sin Temple** (daily 7am–5pm; small donation expected) is next to the station exit. Built in 1973, it's one of the territory's major Taoist temples, dedicated to Wong Tai Sin, whose image was brought to Hong Kong in 1915 from the mainland and moved here from a temple in Wan Chai six years later. Over three million people come to pay their respects here every year. The god, a mythical shepherd boy with the power of healing, has an almost fanatical following, primarily because he's famous for bringing good luck to gamblers, and there are always crowds at the temple, which shows no restraint in its decoration and lavish grounds. As you enter, you'll be besieged by women selling lucky cards, paper money and joss sticks; it's considered polite to buy something – they're so insistent, you'll be lucky to get away empty-handed anyway.

You're not always allowed into the main temple building, but you'll be able to see the altar, which supports the portrait of Wong Tai Sin brought from China, through the open doors. After that, the other shrines and halls, and the landscaped Nine Dragon Wall Garden (a copy of the famous mural in Beijing; $1 to enter) are good for an hour or so; just watching people here, making offerings and praying for good luck, is diverting enough.

On the way to the main entrance you'll have noticed a covered street of booths, whose occupants are there to tell fortunes, and read palms, bumps and faces. It's a thriving industry in Hong Kong and many of these **fortune tellers** have their testimonials of authenticity and success pinned to the booths, with prices and explanations displayed for the sceptical. Some of the people here speak English, so if you want to find out whether or not you're going to win at the races, this is the place to ask. Busiest days at the temple are around Chinese New Year, when luck is particularly sought, and at Wong Tai Sin's festival, on the twenty-third day of the eighth lunar month (usually in September).

New Kowloon: Cheung Sha Wan to Mei Foo

North of Boundary Street, in so-called **NEW KOWLOON**, there are two or three places close enough to tack onto the beginning or end of a day's sightseeing. All are still firmly in built-up parts of the city, in the districts of Cheung Sha Wan (which means "long, sandy bay", giving you an idea of the land reclamation in this area) and Mei Foo – access is easiest by MTR.

There's a map of the MTR system on p.39.

The Lei Cheng Uk Branch Museum

In 1955, between the districts of Sham Shui Po and Cheung Sha Wan, a couple of kilometres north of Mongkok, workmen flattening a hillside in order to build a new housing estate unearthed Hong Kong's oldest historic monument – a Han Dynasty tomb almost 2000 years old. It's been preserved *in situ* and now forms the major part of the **Lei Cheng Uk Branch Museum**, 41 Tonkin Street (Mon–Wed & Fri–Sat 10am–1pm & 2–6pm, Sun 1–6pm; free), an offshoot of the Museum of History in Tsim Sha Tsui.

In all truth, the small museum is a bit disappointing, though you can drop in on the way to Lai Chi Kok (see below) rather than make a specific journey. There's a brief explanation of how the tomb was found, with photographs and a few funerary exhibits, and out in the garden is the glass-fronted tomb itself, encased in concrete under the hill to preserve it. It's simple enough to make out the central chamber, which is crossed by four barrel-vaulted brick niches, but the best idea of what it looked like can be gleaned from the diagrams back inside.

To reach the museum, either take **bus #2** from the Star Ferry to Tonkin Street, or the **MTR** to Cheung Sha Wan and walk the five minutes up the street, past grim factories and some fairly dense housing. Heading back to the centre, you could always wheel down

through Cheung Sha Wan's waterfront wholesale market district to
Sha Shui Po ferry pier: it's around a kilometre or so, and there's a
ferry from there across to Hong Kong Island.

Lai Chi Kok: Tsui Museum of Art, Sung Dynasty Village and Amusement Park

One stop further on the MTR is the district of LAI CHI KOK, where
the Tsui Museum of Art (Mon–Sat 10am–4.30pm; free) houses
around 2000 Chinese antiquities, the best of which is a 500-piece
ceramic display. The museum is on the 10th Floor of Rediffusion
House, at 822 Lai Chi Kok Road, five minutes' walk from the MTR
station (take the Cheung Sha Wan Plaza exit). Few people bother to
stop off here (perhaps understandably, given the excellence of the
Cultural Centre's rival collection), preferring instead to keep on to
Mei Foo MTR, where a cultural "theme park" and amusement park
are sited next to each other.

The Sung Dynasty Village (daily 10am–8.30pm; $110, children
$60; weekends and public holidays 12.30–5pm $75, children $30)
is an attempt to recreate a Chinese village of Sung Dynasty times –
960–1279 AD. It's a small place, with immaculately reproduced
shops, houses, craft workshops and a tea house, based around a
village square and a pond, "villagers" milling about in traditional
costume and providing entertainment of sorts throughout the day –
a wedding parade, martial arts displays and traditional Chinese
music and dance. It's aimed squarely at tour groups, who arrive in
buses throughout the week and pay handsomely for an introduction
to traditional Chinese life that, frankly, you can do without if you're
going on into China or even staying any length of time in Hong
Kong. Unless you coincide with the free shows you'll be hard
pushed to get an hour's worth of entertainment for your steep entry
fee. Still, your ticket gets you a discount in the expensive restaurant,
and entrance to the dismal Waxworks Museum (otherwise daily
10am–9pm; $10, children $5; entry from the amusement park), a
cosmetic tour of Chinese history from the dynasties to Mao – who,
neutrally, on his name card, was simply "founder of the PRC and a
very important figure in Chinese history".

It would be nice to be able to say that the Lai Chi Kok amusement park (Mon–Fri noon–9.30pm, Sat 11am–10.30pm, Sun 10am–
9.30pm; $10, children $5, free entry from the Sung Dynasty Village)
next door, raises the spirits a little, but it's a tatty collection of side-
shows, tame rides and a small and unpleasant zoo. Even sensible
children disdain it, since all the big, scary rides are over at Ocean
Park, but there's a certain amount of amusement to be derived from
the Chinese roller disco.

From Mei Foo MTR, both "attractions" are a ten-minute signposted walk away. Or catch bus #6A from the Star Ferry, which
stops right outside the village and park.

East: to Lei Yue Mun

The other New Kowloon destination is entirely gastronomic in character – a trip to the village of Lei Yue Mun to eat seafood. You can approach from two directions: either direct by **ferry** from Sai Wan Ho on Hong Kong Island (see p.102), or, more interestingly, by taking the MTR and bus southeast through some largely unseen parts of Kowloon.

Coming this way, take the MTR as far as **KWUN TONG**, a massive residential and industrial area opposite the end of the airport runway. Follow the signs outside to Kwun Tong Road and pick up **bus #14C** which runs through the new cross-harbour tunnel site at **LAM TIN**; an MTR station here (with Hong Kong's longest escalator) links Kowloon with the island via the cross-harbour track to Quarry Bay. The bus eventually runs down to **SAM KA TSUEN** typhoon shelter, which is where the ferry from Sai Wan Ho docks. From behind the ferry terminal, you can take a sampan across to the village of **LEI YUE MUN**, passing through moored and inhabited fishing boats.

The village sits at the narrowest entrance to the harbour; its name means "carp fish gate". Like Lau Fau Shan in the New Territories, it's more or less a line of restaurants and seafood shops, though Lei Yue Mun is probably the biggest and most commercialised of the places to come and eat seafood in Hong Kong. There are around 25 restaurants in a row, and as many fresh fish shops, the slabs and tanks twitching with creatures shortly to be cooked. The recognised procedure is to choose your fish and shellfish from a shop, where it will be weighed and priced, and then take it (or you'll be taken) to a restaurant, where it's cooked to your instructions: you generally pay the bill at the end; one to the fishmonger and one to the restaurant for cooking the fish and for any rice and other dishes you may have had. The strongest warnings possible about **rip-offs** are applicable here. You *must* ask the price of the fish you choose before it's bashed on the head and carted off to a restaurant, or you're just inviting someone to choose the most expensive creature for you. Even prawns and the like are not terribly cheap, so make sure you know what you're ordering: a good way is to name a price to the fishmonger that you want to spend; or if there's a group of you, get the tourist office or a Chinese friend to ring one of the restaurants before you go, sorting out a set, fixed-price menu, which can work out fairly inexpensively. Evenings are the best time to come, when you can sit at the restaurant windows and look out over the typhoon shelter.

Chapter 4

The New Territories

Too many visitors miss out on the best that Hong Kong has to offer – namely the 740 square kilometres of mainland, beyond Kowloon, leased to Britain in 1898 and known as the **New Territories**. Around half of the colony's population lives here, in both large new cities and small, traditional villages, and the area is the source of much of Hong Kong's food and water. It's in the New Territories, too, that you'll find the most resonant echoes of the People's Republic over the border. Massive housing estates built around gleaming New Towns don't completely obscure the rural nature of much of the land, and although it's not as easy as it once was to spot water buffalo in the New Territories, some country roads still feature teeming duck farms and isolated houses, while in several corners, decrepit walled villages survive, surrounded by their ancestral lands and with their traditional temples and meeting halls intact. What's more, large parts of the New Territories, east and west, have been designated as Country Parks, and peninsular tracts sustain excellent hiking opportunities. The **Sai Kung peninsula**, to the east, is the best example, though the adventurous could see the whole of the New Territories from a hiker's viewpoint by following the cross-territory **MacLehose Trail** (see below) from Sai Kung to the far west.

Don't expect it to be all peace and quiet. Parts are as busy and boisterous as anywhere in Kowloon, though there is at least always the *impression* of more space. Some of the **New Towns** are sights in their own right, built from bright, white stone on view-laden sites and containing all the energy and industry of the city centre. In between the new structures and roads you'll come across nineteenth-century temples, some fascinating museums and traditional markets – as well as the coastal fishing villages and interior walled villages that have managed to retain an identity amid the rapid development. You can get a glimpse of the modern New Territories by riding the MTR to the end of the line, to **Tsuen Wan**, from where buses connect up with the other major western towns, **Tuen Mun** and **Yuen Long**. Equally rewarding is the KCR train route north, through interesting towns like **Sha Tin** and **Tai Po**, to the Chinese border. The last stop on the Hong Kong side, the town of **Sheung Shui**, is currently teetering between a traditional Chinese life and full-blown Hong Kong-style development.

Public transport is excellent everywhere in the New Territories, by both train and bus. You use minibuses more than usual to get around, but there isn't any one place that you can't get to and back from in a day if you're based in Kowloon or on the island; pick up the HKTA's bus route leaflet for the New Territories, which prints many of the destinations in Chinese characters. There are also some ferry connections between the New Territories and a few of the outlying islands, and hoverferry services between Central and Tsuen Wan and Tuen Mun. Note that you can rent **bikes** at a couple of places, too, particularly at Tai Wai, which is easily reached on the KCR.

For full transport details, check the text and see "Getting Around", p.37.

In one day, you could tour the greater part of the central and western New Territories on a **circular route** using the KCR and the buses; it would take at least another day to see some of the smaller eastern section, where the going is slower. However, you really need to give yourself more time than this to appreciate the land and its importance to Hong Kong. **Accommodation** is limited to a small number of youth hostels and campsites, which are detailed where appropriate and listed fully in Chapter 6. If you're out for the day, you shouldn't have too much trouble finding somewhere to eat. Some of the New Territories' towns have excellent restaurants (especially Sha Tin), though bear in mind that if you're camping or using the youth hostels, you should take plenty of food and a bottle of water with you as the more remote villages and countryside are poorly served as far as eating out is concerned.

The MacLehose Trail and the Country Parks

The **MacLehose Trail** (named after a former Governor) is a 100km-long hiking route which stretches from Pak Tam Chung on the Sai Kung peninsula to the new town of Tuen Mun. It's divided into ten different signposted stages, each of which connects with public transport and some of which are provided with campsites, so that you can make a day's hike or complete the whole trail, as you wish. There's one official *IYHF* youth hostel right on the trail at Tai Mo Shan, as well as a couple close to the trail at Wong Shek. You could do the whole trail in three or four days, but most people take it slower, particularly if they're attempting it in the summer, when the going is hot. There's a sketch map of the trail on p.158–159.

Pick up information on the trail, and on the Country Parks throughout the New Territories, from the **Country Parks Authority** (Agriculture and Fisheries Dept, 12th Floor, 393 Canton Rd, Kowloon; ☎733 2132); trail maps – with a scale of 1:10,000 – are available.

Other useful **maps** for the New Territories are those of the *Countryside Series*, available from the Government Publications Centre in Central (see "Information, Maps and Addresses", p.36). Sheets 4, 6 and 7 cover the area of the MacLehose Trail, and sheet 5 covers the northeast New Territories. Many bookshops, too, stock maps of the Sai Kung peninsula, worth buying if you're going to spend more than a day in the area.

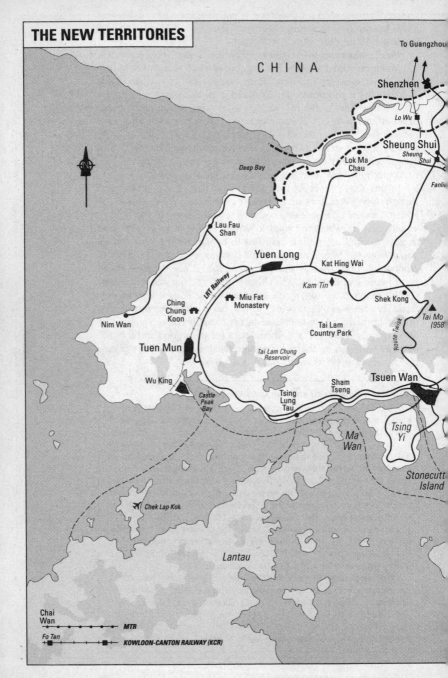

THE NEW TERRITORIES

CHINA

To Guangzhou

Shenzhen

Lo Wu

Sheung Shui

Sheung Shui

Lok Ma Chau

Deep Bay

Fanlie

Lau Fau Shan

Yuen Long

Kat Hing Wai

Kam Tin

LRT Railway

Miu Fat Monastery

Shek Kong

Ching Chung Koon

Tai Mo (958

Nim Wan

Tai Lam Country Park

Route Twisk

Tuen Mun

Tai Lam Chung Reservoir

Wu King

Sham Tseng

Tsuen Wan

Castle Peak Bay

Tsing Lung Tau

Tsing Yi

Ma Wan

Stonecutt Island

✈ *Chek Lap Kok*

Lantau

Chai Wan
●━●━●━●━●━● **MTR**

Fo Tan
■━┼┼┼┼━■ **KOWLOON-CANTON RAILWAY (KCR)**

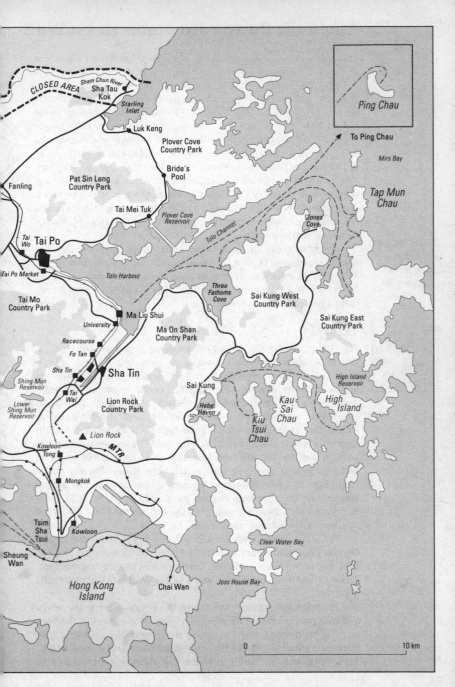

THE NEW TERRITORIES

The KCR Route: Kowloon to Lo Wu

The best way to see a large chunk of the New Territories quickly is to take the **Kowloon–Canton Railway** (the KCR) from its terminus in Hung Hom north to the Chinese border. The whole trip to Sheung Shui, the last stop you can make on the Hong Kong side as a day-tripper, takes around fifty minutes. The route passes through some typical New Towns, like **Sha Tin** and **Tai Po**, which have mush-roomed from villages (and sometimes from nothing) in a matter of a few years. In between, there are several temples and markets, while the stop at the Chinese University gives the choice of a scenic ferry ride or a visit to one of the territory's better art galleries. **Sheung Shui** itself is probably the most interesting place at which to break your journey, while from Tai Po and **Fanling** it's only a short bus ride into some quite beautiful countryside to the east, at **Plover Cove** and **Starling Inlet**.

For full details and ticket prices on the KCR, see p.40.

If you're going on into China later, you'll pass through the border crossing at Lo Wu, at the end of the Hong Kong part of the KCR line, an otherwise restricted area. Visitors can also peer over the border at a couple of points, particularly **Lok Ma Chau**, where there's been a lookout post for years.

THE NEW TERRITORIES

Tai Wai

The first stop after the MTR/KCR interchange at Kowloon Tong is TAI WAI, nowadays less a town in its own right (though there's been a village here since the fourteenth century) than an extension of Sha Tin. Its most obvious attraction is easy to spot from the train: **Amah Rock** (*Mong Fu Shek* in Cantonese), to the right across the valley after emerging from the tunnel – though it's debatable to what extent it looks like the human figure it's supposed to be. In legendary times, a woman climbed up the hill with her baby on her back to wait for her husband to return from fishing, but when he failed to appear the gods turned her into stone. There's still a pilgrimage up here by young women at the time of the annual Maiden's Festival (in early August; see p.257); if you want to clam-ber up yourself, there's a path from the end of Hung Mui Kuk Road which runs east of the train station.

The other immediately noticeable thing in Tai Wai is the **Happy Dragon Recreation Park** right by the station, which should be open daily but doesn't always bother midweek and during bad weather. There are the usual rides here, and a Water World with chutes that's good fun.

The huge open space over the way is always busy at the week-end with people renting **bicycles**. Cycle paths start next to the park and run up through Sha Tin, along the river, before skirting Tolo Harbour all the way to Tai Po – a popular route and a good way to get to grips with the New Territories. The bikes cost around $10 an hour, $40 a day, though there's room to bargain at the several stalls which line the park.

Che Kung Temple

A five-minute walk from Tai Wai station, the **Che Kung Temple** is a small Taoist temple dedicated to the Chinese general Che Kung, who is supposed to have beaten off the plague which once stalked this valley. From the KCR station, follow the signs for *Che Kung Miu* to the main road, turn left and then use the subway to cross it; the temple is in a small hollow further up the road, approached over a bridge. The entrance is guarded by extremely persistent old women, who are after your dollars in return for the lucky red paper symbols they'll press into your hand. It can be quite a fight to get through. Che Kung's festival is held on the third day of Chinese New Year, when this temple is packed with people coming here to pray for good luck, which they help along by turning the bronze prayer wheel in front of the altar clockwise.

Come out of the temple and keep on up the main road – Che Kung Miu Road – towards Sha Tin and, after another hundred metres or so on the right, you'll find a little garden containing a **Four-Faced Buddha Shrine**. This is a symbol more commonly found in Thailand: you're supposed to pray to each face, moving around the shrine in an anti-clockwise direction.

Tsang Tai Uk

From the shrine it's only a few more minutes up the main road to one of the New Territories' lesser-known walled villages, **TSANG TAI UK**, curiously dwarfed by the modern apartment blocks on nearby Sha Tin's riverfront. To get there, follow the main road (which becomes Tai Chung Kiu Rd as it approaches Sha Tin) and look for Sha Kok Street on the right: walk down here and the village is behind the recreation ground to the right, under a green bank of hills.

The name, Tsang Tai Uk, means "Tsang's Big House", though in effect it's a rectangular, greystone walled village, built in the mid-nineteenth century to shelter members of the Tsang family clan. It's survived well and bears comparison with the more frequently visited villages in the Kam Tin area near Yuen Long (see p.151). The thick walls incorporate separate rooms with grilled windows, and at each corner there's a tall, square watchtower, adorned with faded stone decoration. High doorways lead into the "village", based around a central courtyard, with wide alleys running its length split by a network of high-ceilinged rooms and storerooms. Most of the Tsang family have moved out, attracted abroad or by jobs in central Hong Kong, but even so there's a powerful atmosphere here – kids scuttling along the corridors, and washing and cooking going on in corners, much as it has always done.

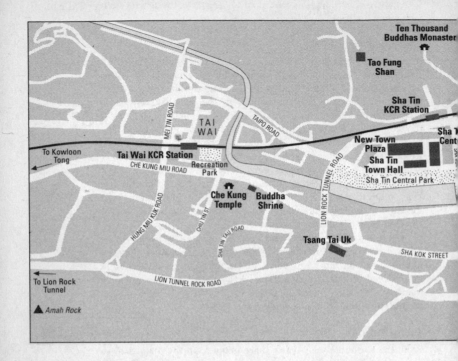

Sha Tin

THE NEW TERRITORIES

Built on both sides of the Shing Mun river in the southern New Territories, **SHA TIN** is one of the most interesting stops on the KCR line. Just 11km out of Tsim Sha Tsui, there's a similar echo in the name, which means "sandy field", a relic of the days when this area consisted of arable land made fertile by the sediment washed down by the river. This productive land supported farming villages, like Tai Wai, for centuries, though it's only since the 1970s that Sha Tin has taken on its ultra-modern appearance. Much of the New Town building here has occurred on land reclaimed from the mud and sand, which you can still see and smell in the murky channelled river.

The town – due to house 700,000 people by the end of the 1990s – splits into several distinct areas served by separate KCR stations: Tai Wai is covered above; to the north is Fo Tan, a residential area overlooking the racecourse; while Sha Tin town itself is reached from the central station, also called Sha Tin. From here, signs point you into the **New Town Plaza**, a huge shopping and recreation centre on several floors. It's as good an introduction as

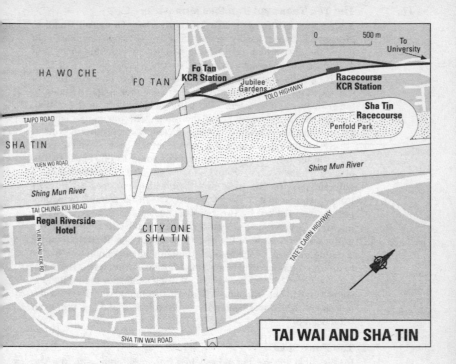

TAI WAI AND SHA TIN

any to town life in the New Territories: solidly Chinese, the restaurants here are good value and the shops crowded at all times with local families. There's a big cinema (*UA6*), bowling alleys and swimming pools, and if you're here around noon or in the evening, you can join the crowds of kids who gather to watch the central musical fountain do its stuff with its coloured lights and thirty-foot sprays.

Walk through the plaza, past the immense *Yaohan* department store (Japanese-owned and the biggest in Hong Kong), and there are walkway connections to other nearby shopping centres, as well as Sha Tin Town Hall and the riverside park. However, the town is known mainly for **Sha Tin Racecourse**, probably the most modern in the world, and, together with the one at Happy Valley, providing the only legal betting opportunity in Hong Kong. It's packed on race days (the season is from September to May) and the details for entry are the same as at Happy Valley; see p.92. It's even got its own KCR station, Racecourse, to which trains only run on race days. At other times, you can get into **Penfold Park** (closed Mon), in the middle of the track, by taking the KCR to Fo Tan – the track and park are behind the Jubilee Garden estate.

Sha Tin is one of the few places outside central Hong Kong that you might want to stay; the Regal Riverside *hotel is reviewed on p.206.*

The Ten Thousand Buddhas Monastery

A little way northwest of Sha Tin is the **Ten Thousand Buddhas Monastery**, known locally as *Man Fat Sze*, a temple complex high above the town which can only be reached by climbing more than 400 steps. It's a reasonably steep, twenty-minute climb: exit from Sha Tin KCR following the sign for "Buses", and go down the ramp to the left of the bus terminal, where there are more signs pointing to the path for the monastery. The path leads away from the station, through the fields to the left, and then steps take you up past bamboo groves and a few refreshment stalls, crickets sounding around you.

Eventually you emerge on a terrace, at the back of which stands the main temple, which actually contains some 13,000 small statues of the Buddha. Each is around a foot high, black or gold, and has a different posture; the walls are lined with them, stacked in rows from floor to ceiling. The courtyard outside is fronted by a pink pagoda, and flanked by two rows of much taller statues: Buddha's followers, a huge, malevolent-looking elephant and a blue dragon-griffin creature. Some of the best views yet of Sha Tin's skyscrapers are from the edge of the terrace, though you can climb even higher to an upper terrace which contains four smaller temples. The right-hand one here is home to both Hong Kong's tallest standing Buddha statue, and to the embalmed body of the monk who founded the monastery, which has been covered in gold leaf and lies preserved behind glass.

Tao Fung Shan

Up the same hillside, but approached from a different path, the **Tao Fung Shan** Christian Centre offers a different perspective over the town. At the bottom of the ramp by the bus terminal, instead of walking straight on for the Ten Thousand Buddhas Monastery, turn sharp left through Pai Tau village: look for the blue arrow on a post. The path leads up above the village, and, after about ten minutes' climb, the main Tao Fung Shan Road. Keep on up the road for another fifteen minutes or so and you can't miss the centre.

It's a complex of buildings built in the 1930s in Chinese style, though this time the pagoda at the top holds a small Christian chapel. A marked path leads through pretty grounds to a large, white stone cross which faces directly out over the river. Away to the left are the blocks of Sha Tin and Fo Tan, while just visible through the apartment buildings at the foot of the hills opposite is Tsang Tai Uk village, a low, grey splash among the towers.

The views aren't the only reason to make the climb. In the grounds you'll find a **porcelain workshop** (Mon–Fri 8.30am–12.30pm & 2–5pm, Sat 8.30am–12.30pm), where you can see good quality porcelain being hand-painted – a fair proportion of the items on display showing secular themes. The decorated plates run to hundreds of dollars, but you can pick up a souvenir here – a cup and saucer, jug or decorated tile – for $30–60.

Eating in Sha Tin

You could do worse than plan a day in the New Territories to include lunch or dinner in Sha Tin, since there's a fine selection of local restaurants. Turn to Chapter 7 for reviews of all the following places:

City Restaurant, 659–668, 6th Floor, New Town Plaza ☎606 4141; p.226. Cantonese hot-pots.

Laisan Korean BBQ, New Town Plaza, 6th Floor, 657–658; p.234. Korean.

Lung Wah Hotel and Restaurant, 22 Ha Wo Che ☎691 1594; p.222. Cantonese pigeon specialist.

Regal Riverside, Tai Chung Kiu Rd ☎649 7878; p.228. Asian buffet lunch and dinner.

Sha Tin Treasure Restaurant, New Town Plaza, 6th Floor, 602–637; p.217. *Dim sum.*

Steps from the centre lead down to the **cemetery**, below the stone factory, just outside the main entrance, where there's the grave of Tao Fung Shan's founder, a Norwegian evangelist, Karl Ludwig Reichelt (1877–1952), whose idea it was to convert Buddhist monks to Christianity. In part, this explains the centre's orthodox Buddhist look: Reichelt hoped that the buildings would dupe wandering Buddhist monks seeking sanctuary, and it certainly worked – until World War II, Tao Fung Shan was a prosperous Christian centre.

University, Ma Liu Shui and Tolo Harbour

THE NEW TERRITORIES

Beyond Sha Tin, the train runs upriver before turning to hug the edge of Tolo Harbour. Just before the turn, there's a stop called **UNIVERSITY** (the Chinese characters translate as "Big School"), which serves Hong Kong's **Chinese University**, the campus spread back from the harbour up the hillside. There's still a lot of construction going on around here, in an otherwise fairly windswept place, but there are a couple of reasons to alight.

For lunch, or just a drink, drop in at the Yucca de Lac restaurant, above the Tolo Highway; see p.222 for details.

A shuttle bus from outside the station runs every half-hour up the steep hill to the main campus: if you get off at the second stop, at the top by the Sir Run Run Shaw Hall, the university's **Art Gallery** (Mon–Sat 10am–4.30pm, Sun 12.30–4.30pm; free) is over to the left, in the middle of a block of buildings surrounding a square. The well-lit, spacious split-level galleries usually display items from its own wide collection of Chinese paintings, calligraphy and sculpture, dating from the Ming Dynasty onwards. Mainland Chinese museums often send touring exhibitions here, too, of art and archeological pieces.

Ma Liu Shui

The other reason to get off is for the short walk from the station to the ferry pier at **MA LIU SHUI**: follow the "Ferry Pier" sign out of the KCR, cross the highway by the flyover and descend to the waterfront, a fifteen-minute walk. From here, you can catch the ferry through **Tolo Harbour** and the Tolo Channel, either staying on board for the scenic round-trip or jumping off at Tap Mun Chau island or other very minor stops along the way; see the account on p.161 for details.

Ping Chau

Ferries also run from Ma Liu Shui to the island of **Ping Chau**, which is about as far away from central Hong Kong as you can get – which explains why hardly anyone goes there. Way to the northeast, beyond Tap Mun Chau and close to the Chinese coast, it's long been abandoned by its inhabitants, all of whom must have been glad to be off the isolated speck. It's a flat place, its highest point precisely 37m high, but there are some good beaches and the odd overgrown trail along its banana-shaped 4km length. Certainly, you could swim here in the clean water of Mirs Bay; in recent times, people have been known to swim *to* the island, escapees from the Chinese mainland.

There's only one **ferry** a week, which leaves Ma Liu Shui on Saturday at 11.15am: buy tickets up to a week in advance from the Central Harbour Services Pier on Hong Kong Island. The ferry doesn't return until Sunday, departing Ping Chau at 1.10pm, so you'll need to come equipped with **camping gear** and everything else necessary for a pleasant night's stay. Like an enormous bottle of something alcoholic. The campsite is at Kang Lau Shek, at the eastern end of the island, and there's no fresh water source.

Tai Po and Plover Cove

THE NEW TERRITORIES

At **TAI PO**, on the western point of Tolo Harbour, you're roughly halfway up the KCR line. A market town since the seventeenth century, the manageable town centre is gradually being overwhelmed by the new industrial and housing developments going up all around. Nonetheless, there's enough to warrant a short stroll through Tai Po, and regular buses from the station – called Tai Po Market – give you the first opportunity to escape into the peaceful country surroundings, to the unspoiled hiking and picnic areas around Plover Cove.

The Town

The town's **market** is the principal thing to see, at the end of the main road, Heung Sze Wui Street, a large covered run of stalls that's at its lively best in the morning. On the far side a gate leads up into the **Hong Kong Railway Museum** (daily except Tues 9am–4pm; free), which occupies the site and buildings of the old Tai Po Market Railway Station, built in 1913. A small exhibition in the main building includes photographs of the opening ceremony of the Kowloon–Canton Railway, and outside on the preserved tracks you can clamber through a series of railway coaches dating back to 1911.

TAI PO MARKET

For the rest of Tai Po's points of interest, you have to cross the river which splits the old town from the new industrial developments. Over the bridge, Ting Kok Road leads up to the town's **Tin Hau Temple**, a few hundred metres up on the left – a particularly old relic, built around 280 years ago, and reflecting Tai Po's traditional importance as a fishing centre. It's also one of the main centres for celebration and devotion around the time of the annual Tin Hau festival (late April/May), when the whole place is decorated with streamers, banners and little windmills: come then and you're likely to catch a Cantonese opera performance on a temporary stage over the road.

Heading back to town, you could always pick up the train at the next KCR station to the north instead, which you reach from the end of Ting Kok Road. Rather than cross the river again, follow the signs through the new housing estate to your right – **TAI WO**, a brand new "town" due to hold 40,000 people, was built in just four years, with its own train station, shops and arcades, and is still being finished – giving an idea of the almost indecent haste with which the New Territories are being developed.

Tai Po and Plover Cove

Plover Cove

The best thing about Tai Po is its proximity to the nearby country-side, notably **Plover Cove Country Park**, a few kilometres north-east. Bus #75K (roughly every 15min) from outside Tai Po Market KCR Station runs there in around thirty minutes, up Ting Kok Road and around the northern shore of Tolo Harbour.

The bus terminates at the few houses of **TAI MEI TUK** at the edge of the Plover Cove Reservoir. The bay here was once part of the harbour and has since been dammed to provide a huge fresh water supply for Hong Kong. Close to the terminus there's a line of bicycle rental places and a clutch of *dai pai dongs* and drinks stalls: it'll cost around $30–40 a day to rent a bike – not a bad idea if your intention is to head straight for Bride's Pool (see below), but cumbersome if you want to tackle some of the excellent walks in the neighbourhood. Over the road, the little peninsula by the main dam shelters a barbecue site, and there's a water sports centre where you can rent rowing boats. If you're going no further into Plover Cove Country Park, you could always try the circular nature trail here, which is signposted and takes approximately an hour to complete.

Bradbury Lodge youth hostel is at Tai Mei Tuk. You"ll need to book ahead as it's very popular; see p.194 for details.

The only road, Bride's Pool Road, heads north, alongside the reservoir past endless barbecue sites, to **Bride's Pool** – around an hour's stroll along a new road that gets a fair bit of traffic at the weekend. A series of waterfalls, it's home to more barbecue sites and lots of picnickers, though you can escape the worst of the crowds by taking the trail thirty minutes back downriver to Chung Mei – an abandoned old village of scallop gatherers and vegetable farmers who moved to Tai Po when the reservoir construction destroyed their livelihood.

There are plenty of other local **walks**, if you've got the energy, and none of them are particularly exacting as long as you carry water. Marked paths lead off the Bride's Pool nature trail to Wu Kau Tang, from where there's a trail to Miu Tin, which leads past some elderly, depopulated villages. Just beyond, there's a very small and basic campsite at Sam A Chung, and a circular route back to Wu Kau Tang. Better, if you're just around for the day, to follow the **Pat Sin Leng Trail**, which runs for around 5km between Bride's Pool and Tai Mei Tuk, scrambling above the road for good views of the reservoir. At the Tai Mei Tuk end of the trail, just back from the main road, there's a **Visitor's Centre** (daily except Tues 9.30–11.30am & 1.30–4.30pm) with useful information boards on local flora, fauna and geology, as well as hiking advice and other details.

You can also walk on past Bride's Pool **to Starling Inlet and Luk Keng** (see "Fanling" below). Keep on Bride's Pool Road, past the waterfall, and it's around another 3km to Luk Keng – two hours all told from Tai Mei Tuk – from where you can take the minibus on to Fanling. If you want to cut out the first part of the walk from Tai Mei

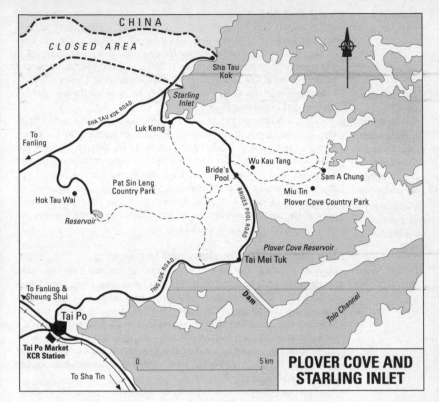

PLOVER COVE AND
STARLING INLET

Tuk, there's a **bus to Bride's Pool** (the #75R from Tai Po Market
KCR), though it only runs on Sundays and public holidays between
October and April; at other times, you'll have to walk, as described
above.

Fanling

By the time you reach **FANLING**, more than 20km from Tsim Sha
Tsui, you're deep in the New Territories and – despite the inevitable
new building – it becomes easier to appreciate the essentially rural
aspect of the countryside. The people, too, begin to look different.
Around Fanling, and especially in Sheung Shui to the north, many
families are of **Hakka** descent – traditionally farmers and much in
evidence around the area's vibrant markets. It's the women you'll
notice most, dressed in simple, baggy black suits and large fringed
hats. Besides selling their produce in the markets, they take an active
role in what would usually be seen as "male" jobs in the West – haul-
ing barrows on building sites and doing the heavy work in local
gardens and fields.

Fanling

You can reach Luen Wo market direct from Kowloon on the #70 bus from Jordan Rd Bus Terminal, an hour's ride.

Fanling itself is eminently missable, much of it in the process of being rebuilt and merged with neighbouring Sheung Shui to form another massive new housing development. Expats come out here to play golf at the swanky *Royal Hong Kong Golf Club*, founded in 1889 (and open to visitors: see p.269), but the tourist attraction touted by the HKTA is the nearby **Luen Wo market** (*Luen Wo Hui*) – certainly worth a visit, but not nearly as good as the one further up the road in Sheung Shui.

To reach the market, take bus #78K from outside Fanling KCR; they're very frequent and it takes around ten minutes to get there. There's only been a market here since 1948, though Fanling has been a market centre for the local Hakka people for much longer than that. You should get there by 10am to see it at its best; if you do, you'll be able to get **breakfast** very cheaply. The Chinese eat *congee* and a doughnut stick from one of the little noodle stalls around the covered market; for a few dollars more, other places will sell you a plate of duck or pork and rice.

Sha Tau Kok, Starling Inlet and Luk Keng

East of Fanling, the new development peters out into the rural, border area with China. Bus #78K continues past Luen Wo Market to **SHA TAU KOK**, a twenty-minute ride past quiet farming and fishing villages dotted along the valley. It's not an area you can feasibly explore, since Sha Tau Kok itself lies in a restricted area, but it's a pleasant ride. At Starling Inlet, there's a checkpoint on the road, where you'll be politely turfed off the bus: you'll have to wait for the return bus, though the Sha Tau Kok locals have passes which enable them to cross in and out freely.

You can see more of this pretty area by taking a regular maxicab instead from Fanling KCR station – the #56K – which turns off the Sha Tau Kok road at **Starling Inlet** and runs around the cove to **LUK KENG**. This is a very peaceful village, with a couple of noodle stalls on the road by the bus stop and two more old Hakka villages in the valley plain behind. If you walk down the main Luk Keng Road, it soon becomes Bride's Pool Road (see "Plover Cove" above); about five minutes from Luk Keng bus stop there's a noticeboard showing the route to Bride's Pool. It also indicates a circular half-hour "Family Walk" which takes you out along the inlet and then cuts back high above the villages and water to regain the main road. There are magnificent views as you go, across to the border village of Sha Tau Kok and China beyond, and down onto the fish farms and junks of Starling Inlet itself.

A much longer hike, though again finishing up at Plover Cove, is accessible by taking the #52K maxicab from Fanling KCR. This drops you at **HOK TAU WAI** (where there's a campsite), around 4km from Fanling, from where a trail runs past a small reservoir over the top of the Pat Sin Leng Country Park and down to Tai Mei Tuk – a lengthy walk but easily done in a day.

Sheung Shui

A few minutes beyond Fanling, **SHEUNG SHUI** is as far as you can go on the KCR without going on into China. It's only 3km from the border and is well worth coming out to visit, one of the most enjoyable of the New Territories' towns, with a centre that's small enough to appreciate and a character not yet swamped by new development – though this will surely come and great apartment blocks are already being erected on the fringes of town. For the moment, though, Sheung Shui retains something of its traditional Hakka life.

The town divides into two areas. The main part, just five minutes on foot from the KCR station, is known as **SHEK WU HUI**, an interconnected block of streets that can't be bettered as an example of a down-to-earth New Territories' market town, with its cheap clothes stalls, *dai pai dongs*, herbalists' shops and hardware stores. Hakka women on their way to the market are laden down with goods and bags, and it's one of the few places left in Hong Kong where you still see letter-writers at the roadside at small tables: for a fee, they'll write a dictated letter for those who can't manage it themselves. The food **market**, in the alleys behind San Hong Street (off the main San Fung Avenue), is one of the best in the territory, certainly the one which comes closest in appearance to those over the border. The covered stalls are stuffed with fruit and veg, preserved eggs and beancurd, while in a separate section live fish are picked from the slabs and clubbed on demand. It's no place for the squeamish, particularly when you notice the more peripheral trades going on in between the stalls: vendors selling from buckets of tied crabs and jumping prawns; the frog-seller who dispatches the beasts with a hatchet across the back, keeping the legs and throwing the twitching bodies away; the woman who spends all day wringing the necks of

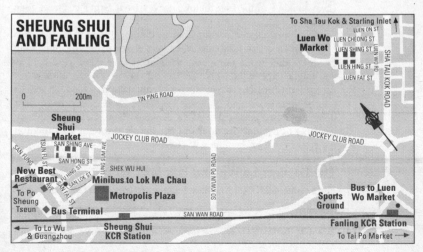

tiny birds, taken from a squeaking cage, and placing the pathetic plucked carcasses on a slab.

The other part of Sheung Shui is **PO SHEUNG TSUEN**, the original village over to the west of the town. Down the main San Fung Avenue from the KCR station, take the first left (at the traffic lights) and walk past the *Jockey Club* playground up to the main road, where you'll see the *China Light and Power* building over the way. Cross at the lights and go down the steps straight ahead of you, just to your right. Walk along the small creek, and through the car park, and behind the new apartment blocks is the old village. It's an almost medieval rag-taggle of buildings with dank alleys between the houses, just wide enough for one person to walk down and with open gutters alive with rustling rats. The houses are a strange mixture, some brand new with bright tiling, others just corrugated iron and cheap plaster. It's actually much less alarming than it appears and, though you might be stared at, there's not much to fear. Every house pays protection money to the local "security" group, so opportunistic crime is rare. Foreigners are not entirely unknown here either, since there's a military base nearby. The only thing to see is the large local **ancestral hall**, built in the eighteenth century. Giving directions to this is pointless, since the name and numbering system for the alleys is hopelessly confusing, but you'll stumble across it sooner or later and be glad that you did: unlike many such places in more touristed parts of Hong Kong, this one is firmly in use by the locals and still stands in its original crumbly surroundings, carved and decorated in traditional fashion.

Practicalities

You'll pass Sheung Shui's **bus terminal** on your way from the KCR station to the main San Fung Avenue; the #17 **minibus** to the Lok Ma Chau lookout point (see below) leaves from San Fat Street (see map).

There are lots of **restaurants** in the small centre of Shek Wu Hui, including the rambling *New Best Restaurant*, on San Fung Avenue. Other restaurants near the market have good fresh fish, as you might expect, and on San Fat Street, there's the *Malaysian Restaurant* (no. 26), which serves cheap Malaysian food, as well as European lunches and dinners. The *Thai Food Restaurant*, next door, has more good-value Asian cooking. Even cheaper meals are available at the **dai pai dongs** in the town's market – they're all at the eastern end of San Shing Avenue.

There's a review of the New Best Restaurant *on p.217.*

CHINA

THE NEW TERRITORIES

The Border: Lo Wu and Lok Ma Chau

The **border with China**, which follows the course of the Sham Chun river across the narrow neck of the New Territories' peninsula, has lost much of its erstwhile attraction for tourists since the People's Republic became more receptive to individual travel. There aren't really any compelling reasons to go and look – it is only a fence and a river when all's said and done – but if you're in the area anyway, at Sheung Shui particularly, you may want to make the trip just to say you've been.

The crossing into China used by foreign travellers is the train link through the station of LO WU, one stop after Sheung Shui and the last stop on the Hong Kong side of the border. You're only allowed here if you're equipped with valid travel documents to go on into China; otherwise it's a closed area to visitors.

Local people make the crossing at a couple of other points – Sha Tau Kok and Man Kam To, just northeast of Sheung Shui – and with the right documentation, you could cross here as well. But there's no real point without your own transport since onward connections are non-existent.

Lok Ma Chau

For years, LOK MA CHAU, four kilometres west of Sheung Shui, was the place to come and peer over the border at Red China, from a special viewing platform built above the river. It's a bit anachronistic these days, but still makes for a pleasant hour or two's diversion as Lok Ma Chau lies in some isolated, green surroundings. Even here, though, the jackhammers are falling, as the fields are dug up to accommodate the new Hong Kong–Guangzhou motorway that's under construction.

The best way here is by **bus**: either the #76K from Sheung Shui's bus terminal or minibus #17 from San Fat Street (see above). Both take about fifteen minutes to reach the general area: ask the bus driver – you need to get off at the junction of Lok Ma Chau Road and Castle Peak Road, and follow the signposts up the main road to the look-out point, which will take around another 15–20 minutes. A steep path leads up between souvenir stalls to a terrace overlooking Shenzhen, the Chinese border town; the river marks the boundary and the wire fence delineates a sort of no-man's land. There's a map to tell you what you're looking at (not much), a restaurant back down the road and frequent minibuses heading back to the main road if you can't be bothered to walk.

From the main road, you don't need to head back to Sheung Shui for the return trip. If you set out early enough to get up to this part of the New Territories, flagging down the next #76K bus that runs past takes you into Yuen Long, a New Town around twenty minutes south. From here, you can easily circle right around the western New Territories before returning to Kowloon or Central, a couple of hours' travelling all told if you don't linger.

San Tin

If the rural peace and quiet appeals, you could stick around long enough to see the traditional Chinese dwellings at the nearby village of SAN TIN, either a thirty-minute walk from Lok Ma Chau or

The Border: Lo Wu and Lok Ma Chau

reached on the same buses from Sheung Shui. On foot, return to the main Castle Peak Road (20min) and turn right, heading along the busy main road towards Yuen Long; it's another ten minutes to San Tin. By bus, take the #76K or #17 minibus from Sheung Shui and get off in San Tin by the *Esso* service station. Walk up the street beside the post office, just off the main road, and within five minutes you'll be at **Tai Fu Tai**, a fine example of a nineteenth-century home built for a wealthy Chinese family. From here, continue through the maze of quiet streets and eventually you'll stumble on the **Man Lun Fung Ancestral Hall**, built at the end of the seventeenth century, and still in use as a worship- and meeting place for local people.

The West: Tsuen Wan, Tuen Mun and Yuen Long

Access to the **western New Territories** is a simple matter, and connecting transport means you can construct a day-trip which runs through all the major towns and villages. There are basically two routes, both of which start at **Tsuen Wan**, a New Town at the end of the MTR line, or reached by hoverferry from Central. You'll want to stop here long enough to see the excellent **Sam Tung Uk Museum**, a restored Hakka village, and there are a couple of other rural diversions, including some good walks in the neighbouring **country parks**. From Tsuen Wan, the quickest and most popular route is the bus run up Route Twisk to **Yuen Long** town, which passes the famous walled villages of the **Kam Tin** area; Yuen Long is also close to the oyster beds at **Lau Fau Shan**, which is one place you might want to break for lunch. Other buses run along the southern shore to **Tuen Mun**, a route which allows you to get off at several excellent **beaches** along the way. Yuen Long and Tuen Mun are connected by bus and train (the LRT), so completing the circle is easy. Alternatively, buses run east from Yuen Long to connect up with stations on the KCR rail line, from where it's an easy trip back to Kowloon.

Tsuen Wan

Approached by bus from the north or west TSUEN WAN ("shallow bay") appears as a stack of white high-rises nestling between the hills, overlooking Tsing Yi Island and the greater harbour beyond. Arriving by hoverferry from Central is similarly exhilarating, a short skim across the water providing a rare view of the western side of Kowloon and passing tiny **Stonecutter's Island**, acquired in 1860 (at the same time as Kowloon) to provide a military base for the defence of the harbour and new colony.

The only approach that doesn't merit attention is the one that most people are likely to make: taking the tunnel-bound Tsuen Wan

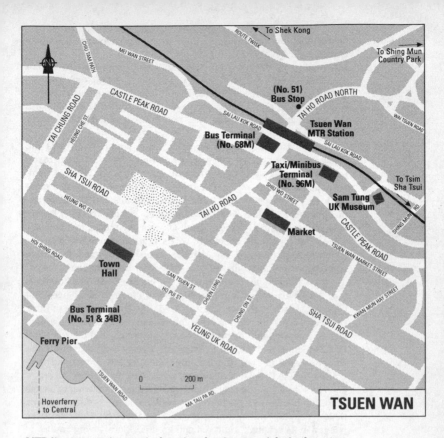

MTR line west to its terminal station, leaving you right in the centre of town, and in the midst of some major development. In 1898, there were only 3000 inhabitants, mostly farmers. Now, around a million people live and work in the area, and the town has the futuristic look favoured by planners all over Hong Kong: flyovers and walkways spin off in all directions, and signposts point into interlinking malls and gardens. There's the usual complement of shops and stores, and if it's your first New Town it merits a brief look around. Apart from the **market**, three blocks south of the MTR, the only thing worth seeing in the centre is the first-rate Sam Tung Uk Museum, though there are several attractive **walks** on the outskirts if you've got more time to spare.

The Sam Tung Uk Museum

The Tsuen Wan area was completely depopulated following the orders of the seventeenth-century Manchu government to abandon the coastal villages in response to constant pirate attacks. It wasn't populated again until the end of the century and permanent settlements only developed later, typified by the eighteenth-century Hakka walled village that survives today as the **Sam Tung Uk Museum** (daily except Tues 9am–4pm; free). Founded by a clan originally from China's Fujian province, who moved into Guangdong, the name of what was a farming village means "three-beamed dwelling" – a reference to the three roofed halls that form the central axis of the village, with new housing added on both sides as the village grew.

At the entrance there's an **orientation room** which tells the fascinating story of the village's restoration. There's a particularly revealing photograph that shows Sam Tung Uk surrounded by similar adjacent villages when Tsuen Wan was just a gleam in a planner's eye, as recently as 1977, which indicates the speed of the building here. As the New Town went up around it, the villagers moved out, and in 1980 Sam Tung Uk was declared a monument – cleaned, stripped and renovated to its original condition, with the furniture and most of the exhibits actually collected from two contemporary Hakka villages over the border in Guangdong.

It's a remarkable achievement. The enclosed pristine **buildings** may not be an authentic representation of life in these villages, but certainly show clearly how life was lived. The basic layout is of three connected halls: a common room for villagers, with carts and sedan-chairs; a central hall for banquets and gatherings; and the Ancestral Hall, which faced the main entrance. Everywhere, the walls are whitewashed and cool, the buildings sporting low lintels and well-crafted beamed roofs. The rooms, connected by narrow streets – corridors really – display traditional farming implements, some beautiful blackwood furniture, as well as more ordinary chairs, tables, cooking and cleaning tools. The Ancestral Hall has been painted in its original bright red and green colours, giving an idea of what you're missing in other parts of Hong Kong, where the halls are often engrained with decades' worth of dust and dirt. Outside, the **gardens** have been landscaped to show how there would have been a threshing ground and a fish pond, and there's a gate house beyond which would have guarded the entrance to the village.

Shing Mun and Kam Shan Country Parks

Fifteen minutes east of Tsuen Wan by bus, **Shing Mun Country Park** is a fine target if you've got a couple of spare hours and want to get out into more rural surroundings. Minibus #82 from Shiu Wo Street, two blocks south of the MTR, runs straight to the **Country Park Visitor's Centre** (daily except Tues 9.30am–4.30pm), whose exhibition hall highlights the local history – particularly the World War II defensive system (see below) – and the flora and fauna. From the centre, a signposted walk runs around the Shing Mun (Jubilee) Reservoir, a relatively easy two-hour hike with great views of the surrounding hills, much of the route shaded by trees. Back at the visitor's centre there's a summertime refreshment kiosk and toilets.

A minor detour from the round-reservoir hike takes you to the **Shing Mun Redoubt**, an undergound hilltop fortification built by the British in 1939 as part of the New Territories' defence (known as the "Gin Drinker's Line") against the subsequent Japanese invasion. Based on a series of tuunels – each named after a London street or area – the system was taken by the Japanese after a short and bloody battle in 1941. Large parts of the system still remain intact, covered by undergrowth: if you're intent upon exploring, you'll need a torch and you must be careful since the tunnels aren't maintained. To get there from the visitor's centre, walk around the reservoir in an anti-clockwise direction and when you see a big overhead sign marked "MacLehose Trail (Stage Six)", leave the road and join the trail; the tunnels start about ten minutes after the sign.

This section of the **MacLehose Trail** itself heads south towards Smuggler's Ridge, a ninety-minute climb that takes you into the neighbouring **Kam Shan Country Park**, known for its wild monkeys. The trail section ends at the Kowloon Reservoirs and the park entrance, from where you can pick up buses back to Kowloon: either the #81 to Jordan MTR station or #72 to Sham Shui Po MTR station.

Yuen Yuen Institute

To complete the tour of Tsuen Wan's outskirts, take maxicab #81 from Shiu Wo Street (two blocks south of the MTR) to the **Yuen Yuen Institute**, a ten-minute ride into the green hills overlooking the city; the bus may be marked Lo Wai Village. It's a working temple dedicated to Taoism, Buddhism and Confucianism – which makes for an interesting mix of styles – and there's a dining room where very good vegetarian food can be bought. Lunch should cost around $60.

Practicalities

The **hoverferry** from Central docks down at Tsuen Wan Ferry Pier; see p.45 for details. From the bus terminal at the pier, you can catch **bus #51 to Kam Tin**, via Route Twisk (see below), though it also makes a stop on the flyover above the MTR station. Also from the Ferry Pier, bus #34B runs along the coastal Castle Peak Road, passing the **beaches** covered in the section below.

The main **bus terminal** in Tsuen Wan is just opposite the MTR station, underneath the shopping centre. From here, you can catch **bus #68M to Tuen Mun**, which follows the new highway and not the parallel coastal road; this is the bus to take if you're heading for either the Ching Chung Koon Temple or the Mui Fat Monastery. The **taxi/minibus terminal** back along the main road (underneath the *Wilson* car park) is where you catch the #96M minibus, which skirts the coast for the beaches and the goose restaurants at Sham Tseng. **Shiu Wo Street**, a couple of blocks south of the MTR, near the market, has the minibus and maxicab stops for the country parks and the Yuen Yuen Institute.

THE NEW TERRITORIES

The coastal route: Castle Peak Road

Two parallel roads run along the coast of the western New
Territories: the new, fast highway, Tuen Mun Road, and the quieter
and original **Castle Peak Road**. Finished in 1919, this road is the
one to follow if you want to see any of the shoreline, as it winds
around the **beaches** and small headlands between Tsuen Wan and
Tuen Mun, before cutting up through the inland region to Yuen
Long, continuing all the way to Lok Ma Chau. The coastal part of
the route is best done on minibus #96M or bus #34B from Tsuen
Wan: see above for details.

Tsing Yi Island

Dominating the entire first half of the coastline is the industrial
wedge of **Tsing Yi Island**, across Rambler Channel from Tsuen Wan.
Oil depots and other filthy industrial concerns have been relegated
here over the last couple of decades, reducing the quality of life for
the 90,000 unfortunate residents of the island's housing estates.
Occasional safety scares have done nothing for its reputation either,
and in the local press Tsing Yi is luridly referred to as the "Island of
Fear", giving it an H.G. Wells-style curiosity it doesn't otherwise
warrant. For the visitor, the major concern is that the various
noxious emissions haven't helped the water quality around here,
which is already hit by the junk flowing out of developing Tsuen
Wan's harbour. This means that some of the otherwise fine beaches
along the coast here are off-limits for swimming: you'll need to check
the latest press reports or watch out for noticeboards at the beaches.

The beaches and Sham Tseng

The **beaches** nearest to Tsuen Wan are all pretty much affected by
the polluted water, but the sands are generally fine. You'll pass
Approach beach and **Ting Kau**, while further on are **Ho Mei Wan**
and **Gemini** beaches.

Otherwise the first place to stop is at **SHAM TSENG**, a little
roadside village about fifteen minutes out of Tseun Wan, from
where regular *kaidos* run across to Ma Wan Island (see p.188). For
the pier at Sham Tseng, you need to get off at the stop after the
massive *San Miguel* brewery, directly opposite which there's a line
of nine or ten **restaurants**, all specialising in roast goose and duck.
The *Chan Kee*, right opposite the factory, has an English menu and
tables under a marquee where you can spend a very pleasant lunchtime eating goose, swigging the cold, local (*San Miguel*) beer, and
avoiding the heavier Chui Chow influenced items on the menu –
"pig's ding", intestines and goose blood.

Beyond Sham Tseng, there are only a couple more **beaches** to
tempt you – **Angler's** and **Dragon**. Neighbouring Tsing Lung Tau has
a *kaido* service across to the isolated northern coast of Lantau Island
(see p.181).

Tuen Mun and around

For the rest of the ride to Tuen Mun you can sit back and appreciate the views over the water and the increasingly built-up coast. There are a few beaches on the eastern side of town, but again the water quality is dodgy. TUEN MUN itself, a large and straggling town, doesn't do much to attract you to get off and look around, with only a couple of nearby Chinese temples offering a spark of interest. The name of the town means "Channel Gate", a reminder that this was once an important defensive post, guarding the eastern approaches to the Pearl River Estuary. These days, it's a standard New Town sporting the obligatory shopping and commercial development – **Tuen Mun Town Plaza** – which at least makes an attempt at variation: there's a fake Georgian square around a fountain, planted inside the plaza.

THE NEW TERRITORIES

If you came from Tsuen Wan on the #68M bus, stick with it as it runs right through the town, passing both temples. Otherwise, get off in the centre and make your way to one of the stations of the **Light Rail Transit** system (LRT), which links Tuen Mun with Yuen Long to the north; there are terminals right in the centre, or down at the **Ferry Pier**, where the **hoverferries** from Central arrive and depart. To head back to Kowloon, bus #68X runs to Jordan Road Ferry Pier.

For more on the LRT system and a route map, see "Getting Around", p.42.

Ching Chung Koon Temple

There's a large Taoist temple complex, the **Ching Chung Koon Temple** (daily 7am–7pm), just out of Tuen Mun. It's a little complicated to find, but worth the effort: the #68M bus stop is on Castle Peak Road, just a few minutes out of the centre (ask the driver), and if you walk to the left over the small hill and cross the river you'll come to Affluence LRT station (line #507 from Tuen Mun Ferry Pier or #612 from the town centre); bear left through the housing estate to the main road, and the temple is visible to your right.

At the entrance, there's a plan which makes sense of the complex of temples, gardens and shrines, built in 1949 and dedicated to Lu Sun Young, an eighth-century "Immortal" blessed with magical and curative powers. The main temple is flanked by separate bell and drum towers, which signal the prayer times. The room to the left of here is where you book your **vegetarian lunch** (a set meal served for a minimum of two people), while next down is the **Ancestral Hall**, unusually large and crammed full of photos and records of the dead. People pray here for their ancestors' souls, and occasionally you might catch a commemoration service, when monks chant – accompanied by drums, cymbals and flutes. The best time to see this is at either of the annual festivals which commemorate the dead: Ching Ming or Yue Lan (see "Festivals", p.256–257). At the end of the buildings, there's an ornamental **garden**, carefully built in traditional style, with imported Chinese rocks, a rock pool and pagodas, setting off perfectly the air of formal prayer and devotion in the complex.

Mui Fat Monastery

The other local temple, this time strictly Buddhist in character, is the **Mui Fat Monastery**, about 4km north of Tuen Mun on Castle Peak Road, halfway to Yuen Long. You can get there on the #68M bus, which stops virtually outside, or on the #68X direct from Jordan Road Ferry Terminal; or ride the LRT from either Tuen Mun or Yuen Long – get off at Lam Tei station, and the temple is just back up the road.

The only part of the monastery you can get into is the tall, square temple set back from the main road, a garish building whose entrance is guarded by two golden dragons, their bodies writhing the whole way up the building. Also outside, on either side of the entrance, sit a toothy lion and an elephant, with pigeons perched everywhere. There are three floors inside, the top one overwhelming in its opulence, with three large golden Buddhas, massive crystal chandeliers, marble tablets and little Buddha images lining the walls, and a bell and a skin drum hanging at either side.

On the middle floor is a decorated dining room which, like Ching Chung Koon, serves tasty **vegetarian lunches** (noon–3.30pm): buy a ticket at the desk on the way in and you'll be brought platefuls of food from the kitchens.

THE NEW TERRITORIES

Route Twisk: Tai Mo Shan and Shek Kong

The other bus route through the western New Territories runs anti-clockwise, inland north of Tsuen Wan and around to Yuen Long, on the so-called **Route Twisk**, a high road pass which is sometimes blocked in part by landslides during the typhoon season. Route Twisk, incidentally, stands for "Tsuen Wan Into Shek Kong". Take the #51 bus, which you can pick up at Tsuen Wan Ferry Pier or above Tsuen Wan MTR station.

Tai Mo Shan and the MacLehose Trail

It's a splendid climb in the bus up the hillside above Tsuen Wan, with great views back to the sea. After 4–5km, just above the village of Chuen Lung, there's an entrance into the **Tai Mo Shan Country Park**, which contains Hong Kong's highest peak, **Tai Mo Shan**, 958m above sea level. The climb is straightforward enough if you're keen, and it's a nice idea to combine it with a night in the nearby **Sze Lok Yuen youth hostel**, which you reach by getting off the #51 at the junction with the smaller Tai Mo Shan Peak Road – the hostel is signposted, around an hour's walk up the road. There's a Visitor's Centre near the bus stop, too, with details of all the other local trails, including the walk to the magnificent series of waterfalls at **Ng Tung Chai**, in the north of the park.

At the hostel or the peak, you're actually on the **MacLehose Trail** (Stage 8), 22km from its western end at Tuen Mun; there's also a **campsite** here in the Tai Mo Shan Country Park, by the Management Centre, over on the western side of Route Twisk. If you just fancied a short day's hike, join the Trail here and walk west to Tin Fu Tsai (6km), from where you can drop down the 3–4km to the coast at Tsing Lung Tau for buses east or west along the coast.

Route Twisk:
Tai Mo Shan
and Shek
Kong

See p.127 for more details on the MacLehose Trail and p.159 for a sketch map.

Shek Kong

The #51 bus climbs up over the pass and rattles down the winding road into the **SHEK KONG** (pronounced "Sek" Kong) area, through rich forested slopes, offering sweeping views of the plain below. Carved into the plain, and visible from way off, is the runway belonging to Shek Kong's military garrison; as you reach ground level the road passes through neat barracks buildings. Many of the Vietnamese boat people were placed in closed camps at Shek Kong in 1989, creating an impossible situation. Security was limited since the Vietnamese were kept in tents behind wire fences in the military grounds; escapes and mass break-outs into the local area were common and, given the conditions, trouble flared both in the camp and outside in the hard-pressed neighbouring villages.

Kam Tin

The #51 bus ends its ride in **KAM TIN**, an area famous for its surviving **walled villages**. One of them at least is firmly on the tourist map, but there are a couple of others in the area, all displaying the same characteristic buildings and solid defensive walls.

KAT HING WAI is the most obvious walled village, just off the main road where the bus stops, opposite a *Park 'N' Shop* supermarket. The square walls enclose a self-contained village, encircled by a moat, which has been inhabited for nearly four hundred years by members of the Tang clan, who once farmed the surrounding area. Their ancestors moved here from central and southern China almost a thousand years ago, fortifying villages like these against pirate attacks and organising their lives with little recourse to the measures and edicts of far-off Imperial China. As late as 1898, this village was one of the ones prepared to see action against the new British landlords, when local militias were raised to resist the handing over of the New Territories to Britain.

Today, the buildings are as defensively impressive as ever, with guardhouses on each corner and a great entrance gate, but otherwise Kat Hing Wai is a rather sad sight, most of it entirely on show for tourists. Down the main street are tacky souvenir stalls and Hakka women posing for photos in their "costume" (normal wear in many parts of the New Territories). They'll want money if you try and take a photo, and it'll cost you a dollar or so to set foot through the gate in the first place.

You'd do better to make your way to **SHUI TAU TSUEN**, a few hundred metres back down the main road (towards Tsuen Wan) on the right: at the Mung Yeung Public School, follow the lane down and over the bridge. The village is much bigger, though not as immediately promising: there's new building on the outskirts and many of the old buildings are locked or falling down. But the elegant carved roofs are still apparent, and a walk around the tight alleys reveals the local temple and an ancestral hall, and gives at least some impression of normal village life. The other village in the area is **WING LUNG WAI**, up the main road in the opposite direction, beyond Kat Hing Wai, though this is mostly fenced off and inaccessible to visitors. You can get into the market here, though, for the usual mix of noise and activity.

Practicalities

The main road at Kam Tin is lined with restaurants, bars and even discos – slightly surprising in the middle of nowhere until you pass the local military HQ on the way into Yuen Long. The *Naafi* (Navy, Army, Air Force Institute) has a Friday **market** (9am–1pm) at Shek Kong Camp, selling arts and crafts; the #51 bus drops you close by.

There are a few **onward routes** to consider. As well as bus #51, which runs back to Tsuen Wan, #77K runs down the main road on its way from Yuen Long to Sheung Shui; minibus #18 runs along the same route. You can also catch bus #54 to Yuen Long, while the #64K passes the walled villages on its run between Tai Po and Yuen Long.

THE NEW TERRITORIES

Yuen Long

Since it's a major transport hub, you're more than likely to end up in the town of **YUEN LONG** if you've followed any of the routes through the western New Territories. That's about all you'll do there, though; like Tuen Mun, it's not a place to hang around. These days, Yuen Long is unrecognisable as the coastal fishing village it once was – now a built-up New Town of 250,000, it's much like the others, with the LRT train line running right through the middle of the main street. But out in the surroundings there are still-visible relics of an older life – small temples and ancestral homes scattered across the fragmented coastline. Unfortunately, without exception, they're all difficult to reach and mostly rundown. The closest you get to tradition in Yuen Long itself are the big annual celebrations of the **Tin Hau Festival**, a throwback to the town's fishing days. If you're around at the time of the Mid-Autumn Festival, it's worth knowing that Yuen Long is also renowned for the quality of its **moon cakes**, the small lotus-seed cakes with a preserved egg yolk that are eaten at this time: some of the best in the territory are the *Wing Wah* moon cakes, made by the *Tai Wing Wah Restaurant*, 11 Tai Lee Street.

On buses to the town, the destination indicator often reads "Un Long" and not "Yuen Long"; it's the same place.

The **bus terminal** is in On Tat Square, just off the main Castle Peak Road down Kik Yeung Road, from where you can catch buses #76K and #77K to Sheung Shui; #68M to Tuen Mun (for Mui Fat Monastery and Ching Chung Koon Temple); #68X to Jordan Road Ferry Pier; or the #64K to Tai Po Market KCR station. Down Castle Peak Road itself, minibus #18 runs into Sheung Shui, and there's a separate **minibus terminal** nearby on Tai Fung Street: to get to it, turn into Kuk Ting Street at 77 Castle Peak Road (*Bank of East Asia*), follow Sai Tai Street, and Tai Fung Street is over on the right. This is where to come to catch the direct #34 minibus to Lau Fau Shan.

Lau Fau Shan

The main reason to be in Yuen Long is to take the bus out to nearby LAU FAU SHAN, an oyster-gathering and fishing village a few kilometres northwest. It's the most unusual of the places in Hong Kong to come and eat seafood, a ramshackle place literally built on old oyster shells. Even better is the fact that it's the least-visited of the seafood villages, which means realistic prices and a meal in basic surroundings without the fear of being ripped off. To **get there**, you need to take minibus #34 or bus #655 from Yuen Long; the minibus leaves from the terminal on Tai Fung Street (see above), the #655 from the main Castle Peak Road

The ride takes around twenty minutes, through some fairly drastic constructions necessary to protect the local villages from floodwater. The bus stop in Lau Fau Shan is right by the only street, Ching Tai Street, which leads right down to the water past a succession of small restaurants, fishmongers' stalls and dried seafood provisions stores. The oysters are turned into excellent oyster sauce, which is on sale everywhere, while the fish market is at the very end of the street. The dried foods are interesting – oysters, scallops, mussels and fish used to make soups – but they're something of a delicacy; if you want a packet of dried scallops to take home, you can expect to pay up to $500. Walk through the fish market and you're on the main jetty, on either side of which – stretching a hundred metres to the water and away as far as you can see – are piled millions of old, opened oyster shells, enormous dunes of them hiding fishing pots and wooden skiffs. The village here looks out over Deep Bay and across to the Chinese mainland – a fine aspect.

There are plenty of **restaurants** in the village, all pretty reliable. The *Bond Kee* (9 Ching Tai St; opposite no. 19 and with a Kent cigarette sign to distinguish it) is always good: choose fish and they'll bring it wriggling to your table for inspection before whisking it away to be cooked; the deep-fried oysters are also thoroughly recommended, a massive crispy plateful, easily enough for three.

THE NEW TERRITORIES

The East: Clearwater Bay and the Sai Kung Peninsula

To visit the eastern limb of the New Territories you'll need to set aside another couple of days: one to take in the popular beaches and magnificent Tin Hau Temple at **Clearwater Bay**; the other to visit the beautiful **Sai Kung peninsula**, with its fishing town, sands and nearby islands. The whole Sai Kung area is about the closest you get in Hong Kong to real isolation, though on weekends and holidays even the large country parks here aren't big enough to absorb all the visitors. Happily, most people stick to two or three spots, and if you're prepared to do some walking, you'll be able to find a bit of space.

Access to both areas is by bus from **Choi Hung** MTR station, on the Kwun Tong line (take the Clearwater Bay North exit). All the buses leave from the bus ranks just outside the station.

THE NEW TERRITORIES

To Clearwater Bay

Bus #91 (as well as #91R on Sunday) or regular minibuses from outside Choi Hung MTR station run east and then south along **Clearwater Bay Road**, a pleasant half-hour's ride through striking countryside, much of which forms the backdrop to a succession of posh villas and houses with precarious views over the bays below. About halfway, you'll pass the **Shaw Brothers' Film Studio**, where countless Cantonese movies are churned out every year, before dropping down to **TAI AU MUN**, which overlooks **Clearwater Bay** itself.

There's a bus stop here, where you can get off for the first, smaller **beach** (known as #1 beach), though the bus does continue down the hill to stop at the terminus next to the much bigger #2 beach. You can count on this being packed at the weekend, despite its size, and you should take your own food if you've come for the day as there's only a snack kiosk here. It's no roomier in the adjacent "water world" slide area either. There is a path between the two beaches if you want to check on space at either one.

A Walk: to Joss House Bay and Back

Beyond the beaches the road climbs up and across the peninsula giving marvellous views over the sea, passing the tiny village of **PO TOI O** over the other side of a small bay, which is guarded by two temples, one on either side of the bay's headlands. At the end of the road, half an hour away, is the **Clearwater Bay Country Club**, to which the HKTA sells day-passes if you're after a bit more civilised swimming and lounging about (see p.268 for more information).

A marked path to the side leads down to **Joss House Bay**, or Tai Mui Wan, where one of Hong Kong's finest temples is situated. The short path runs past an inscribed rock, the 108-character inscription dating from 1274 (Southern Sung Dynasty) and recording a visit to the area made by an officer in charge of salt administration. Further on is the **Tin Hau Temple** itself – elaborately carved and beautifully sited, with a large terrace overlooking the bay. Built originally in 1266 (though reworked several times since, particularly in 1962 after Typhoon Wanda almost destroyed it), this is *the* major site of the annual Tin Hau celebrations in Hong Kong, and there's a long quay below the terrace where thousands of passengers disgorge from the special chartered junks and ferries to come and pay homage to the Goddess of the Sea. The temple entrance is guarded by two small stone lions with round stones in their mouths: turn the stones three times for luck.

Back at the Country Club, a second path leads, circuitously, back to Clearwater Bay beach, via the village of **SHEUNG LAU WAN**, from where there's a *kaido* service to Sai Wan Ho on Hong Kong Island. You'll see the small village down to your left as you circle the headland back towards Clearwater Bay – it has two piers at either side of its bay and fish farms. Bypassing the village, the path heads over the ridge, where you can detour to climb to the nearby summit of **Tin Ha Shan**; or simply drop straight down to the main road, just five minutes from the bus terminal. The whole walk – past Po Toi O, Joss House Bay, the temple and then around the headland – should take three to four hours depending on the heat; take water with you, and be warned that the path is sketchily marked at times. You may spend periods scampering up and down the hill looking for the route.

Tung Lung Chau

Lying just to the south of the peninsula, the small island of **Tung Lung Chau** maintains a restored eighteenth-century Chinese fort on its northern shore. Overlooking the Fat Tong Mun passage, the **Tung Lung Fort** kept a strategic eye on ships sailing from Guangzhou to Hong Kong, but it was finally abandoned to the elements at the beginning of the nineteenth century. It remained overgrown until 1979, when its rectangular walls and interior were restored and opened to the public. There's an **information centre** at the site (daily except Tues 9am–4pm), good for filling in the background to the excavations, and after poking around the fort you can walk on to Tung Lung's other historic attraction, Hong Kong's largest **rock carving**. With dimensions of roughly two by two-and-a-half metres, it represents a dragon: you reach it by taking the path from the fort, back past the ferry pier, around 1500 metres in all.

Despite the island's proximity to the Clearwater Bay peninsula, you can only reach it by **ferry from Sai Wan Ho** on Hong Kong Island, which operates on Saturday, Sunday and public holidays, and docks roughly halfway between the fort and the rock carving. Call ☎560 9929 for timetable information, or check with the HKTA.

Sai Kung Town and its beaches

North of Clearwater Bay, beaches and coves spread over a much bigger area, incorporating a series of island retreats, good walking trails, even a folk museum. The whole area is known as **Sai Kung**, and is divided into two main **country parks**, with several approaches and little centres. The main centre (and the destination of all the buses from Choi Hung) is **SAI KUNG TOWN**, a rapidly developing resort that is fast outgrowing its former fishing-village borders. Bus #92 from Choi Hung MTR, or maxicab #1, gets you there in around half an hour, following Clearwater Bay Road before heading north along Hiram's Highway, passing Hebe Haven on the way.

The Town

New building all around is rather dwarfing the little fishing village that Sai Kung once was, but for the moment it remains a pleasant enough seaside port. The bus terminal is just back from the sea, with the whole seafront promenade devoted to fish and seafood **restaurants**, most of which have outside seating overlooking the bay. A walk down the seafront takes you to the **fish market** in the older part of town, overlooking the junks tied up in the harbour. Stroll back, and you can pick up a fishing net, line and bait at one of the stalls, or choose your lunch from one of the slabs and buckets laid out along the quayside. The *Seaside Seafood Restaurant* is a good place to take your fish to be cooked, on the quay towards the fish market; or for a real treat, head for the *San Shui*, at the end of the quayside closest to the bus terminal, where the speciality is "bamboo fish".

For a review of the San Shui, *see p.222.*

There's a fairly strong expat presence in town these days, so if you wander through the few streets back from the quay you'll also come across a pub and a pizza place.

Nearby Islands and Beaches

Along the Sai Kung quayside, you'll be accosted by people selling tickets for *kaidos*, which run across to **islands and beaches** in the vicinity. It's a bit tricky to work out exactly where the boats are going sometimes, as there are no signs and few people speak English, but if you don't really mind and just want to hit a beach, take yourself off with the first that offers itself. They go and return at regular intervals all day, so you won't get stuck anywhere if you don't like it.

The most popular trip is the short run across to **Kiu Tsui Chau** (or Sharp Island), whose main beach at Hap Mun Bay, where the *kaidos* dock, is fine, though it's small and can get mobbed at the weekends. There are barbecue pits, and a snack-bar, and a rough trail leads up through thick vegetation to the island's highest point. Most of the rest of the rocky coast is inaccessible, though *kaidos* also run from Sai Kung to Kiu Tsui, a small bay to the north of the island. Be warned that getting back to Sai Kung from Hap Mun Bay

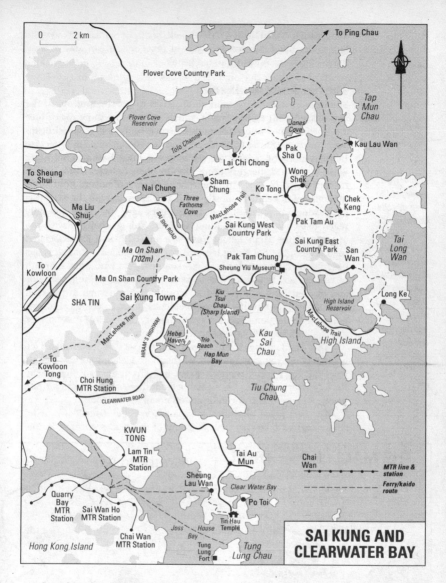

SAI KUNG AND CLEARWATER BAY

can be a bit of a scrum: you have to leave on a boat with the same coloured flag as the one that you came on, and as there's no such thing as a queue in Hong Kong it can be a fight to get on the boat.

Other *kaidos* and ferries run from Sai Kung on the longer route to **High Island**, now actually part of the mainland peninsula since dams linked it to form the High Island Reservoir. *Kaidos* also run from the yachting centre of **HEBE HAVEN** (Pak Sha Wan) across to

Sai Kung Town and its beaches

a peninsular beach, called **Trio Beach**, south of Sai Kung Town: the bus to Sai Kung passes Hebe Haven first, or you can always walk the 2–3km from Sai Kung to the beach.

The Sai Kung peninsula

You need to make a bit more of an effort to get the best out of the rest of the **Sai Kung peninsula**, which stretches all the way north to the Tolo Channel and encompasses some supremely isolated headlands and coves. The whole region is one giant, 7500-hectare **Country Park**, split into two sections, Sai Kung East and Sai Kung West, along with neighbouring **Ma On Shan Country Park**, which reaches down to Sha Tin. There have been settlements here since the fourteenth century, mostly fishing villages, though the area was never widely populated: even thirty years ago, you could still only reach most places in Sai Kung on foot. Things changed with the opening of the High Island Reservoir in 1979, and its associated road access, but Sai Kung has still not been spoiled – though it has become mightily popular with weekend-trippers who want a breath of country air. Following the marked paths through the grasslands and planted forests is indeed invigorating after a spell in the city: there's plenty of birdlife, some spectacular coastal geological formations due to the peninsula's volcanic history, and lots of quiet places just to plonk yourself down and tear into your picnic.

The **MacLehose Trail** runs right across the peninsula (see below), while you can see most of the more isolated northern coast from the **ferry** which departs twice daily from Ma Liu Shui in the New Territories to Tap Mun Chau island: there's more on this route below, and see p.135 for information about Ma Liu Shui.

The best place to start any exploration is Sai Kung Town, from where regular buses run out to many of the places covered in this

Two useful maps for the area are the Countryside Series Sheet 4 (Sai Kung and Clearwater Bay) and the Pak Tam Chung Nature Trail map; both available from the Govt. Publications Centre; see p.36.

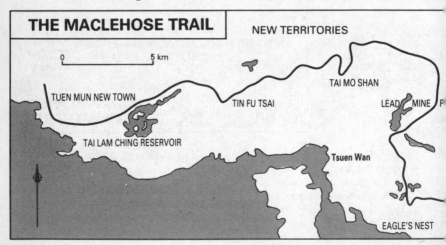

THE MACLEHOSE TRAIL

NEW TERRITORIES

0   5 km

TUEN MUN NEW TOWN

TIN FU TSAI

TAI MO SHAN

LEAD MINE P

TAI LAM CHING RESERVOIR

Tsuen Wan

EAGLE'S NEST

section; though note the alternative approach from Sha Tin on bus #89R, which circles the Ma On Shan Country Park.

Pak Tam Chung

From Sai Kung Town, bus #94 (hourly) and #96R (Sun only; starts in Choi Hung; every 20min) make the fifteen-minute run around the coast to **PAK TAM CHUNG**, which isn't anything more than a bus terminal and **Visitor's Centre** (daily except Tues 9.30am–4.30pm), where you can pick up local hiking and transport information. However, Pak Tam Chung is the effective start of the MacLehose Trail, and it also attracts visitors to the nearby **Sheung Yiu Folk Museum** (daily except Tues 9am–4pm; free), a twenty-minute walk away from the bus terminal along a nice, shady (signposted) route. The museum is based around an abandoned village, Sheung Yiu, founded 150 years ago by a Hakka family who made their living from the produce of a local lime kiln. The kiln itself is on the outskirts of the village, on the path as you approach, the lime from it used for local agriculture and building purposes. Further on, there's a line of whitewashed houses constituting the village, built on a high terrace overlooking the water and defended by a thick wall and gate tower, which kept off the pirates who roamed the area in the nineteenth century. The tile-roofed houses, including an equipped kitchen-house, have been restored and filled with farming implements, typical Hakka clothes and diagrams of how the kiln operation worked.

The MacLehose Trailhead: High Island and Tai Long Wan

Keep on down the Pak Tam Road from Pak Tam Chung, past the turn-off for the museum, and the **trailhead** for the western end of the cross-New Territories **MacLehose Trail** is just a few minutes' walk ahead of you. The first two stages of the 100-kilometre route

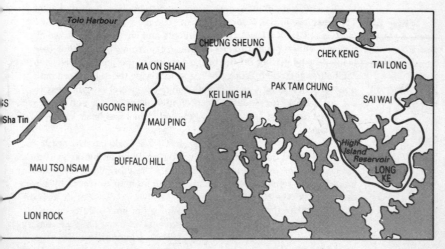

run off to the south from here, through the Sai Kung East Country Park, a twenty-kilometre hike around **High Island Reservoir** and then north to Pak Tam Road, from where you can continue the trail or cut back to Pak Tam Chung. This part of the trail would take the best part of a day to complete. There are no less than seven **campsites** along the way, one, at Long Ke Wan, on the southeastern edge of the reservoir, with a fine beach. Less committed hikers could shorten the route by just walking around the reservoir and back to the trailhead, as Sai Wan Road branches off the trail about three-quarters of the way round (at Sai Wan), heading directly back to Pak Tam Chung.

If you're looking for a beach at the end of a walk, then a path just beyond Sai Wan leads north to the bay of **Tai Long Wan** – a much better target from Pak Tam Chung if you're not interested in completing any part of the MacLehose Trail for its own sake. It'll still take three to four hours for the round trip (around 12km by concrete path), but the beach is very definitely worth it: unspoiled white sand, among the finest in the territory. The small village of Ham Tin, beside the beach, has a couple of outdoor restaurants serving basic food and drinks, though they're usually only open at the weekend. Note that the last bus back from Pak Tam Road (see above) to Sai Kung is at around 7.30pm; don't get stuck.

Wong Shek, Chek Keng and Jones' Cove

Bus #94 (also #95R on Sun from Pak Tam Chung) continues on across the neck of Sai Kung East Country Park to **WONG SHEK** – little more than a pier and a few barbecue pits really, and only worth coming out to if you're going to be staying at one of the nearby youth hostels or catching the *kaido* **to the island of Tap Mun Chau** to the north (see below).

For booking details for both hostels, see "Accommodation", p.194–195.

Two of Hong Kong's more remote **youth hostels**, both with over 100 beds, are in the Wong Shek area. The most popular, *Bradbury Hall*, is at **CHEK KENG**, the next village and bay to the west, which you can either reach directly on the ferry from Ma Liu Shui (see below); or by getting off the bus at the top of the pass, at Pak Tam Au, before you reach Wong Shek, and following the signposted path down to Chek Keng – a 45-minute walk. The hostel is right next to the sea (which, for once, is clean enough to swim in), and there's space for **camping**, too; you can get cold drinks and basic **meals** in the village.

The other hostel, *Pak Sha O*, is at **JONES' COVE**, to the north – Hoi Ha Wan on some maps. Again, you could come by ferry from Ma Liu Shui, getting off at either Lai Chi Chong or Wong Shek and following the signs, which will take around an hour to walk. But it's easier to take the #94 bus, getting off just before Wong Shek at Ko Tong. Take Hoi Ha Road, on the left, and it's around a thirty-minute walk to the hostel – though taxis are available if you hang around, and on Sundays and public holidays there's a maxicab service. Hoi

Ha beach is around another fifteen minutes' walk from the hostel, and again, you can get simple food and cold drinks in the village.

The Northern Coast and the Tolo Channel

The most remote section of the Sai Kung peninsula is its **northern coast**, though you can easily see it by taking the **ferry from Ma Liu Shui** to Tap Mun Chau island (see below). The pier is a signposted fifteen-minute walk from the University KCR station; see p.135.

The HKTA has details about the current timetable for the Ma Liu Shui–Tap Mun Chau ferry. For the addresses of their offices, see p.36.

Ma Liu Shui lies at one end of the **Tolo Channel**, which basically splits the New Territories' two most rural areas, Plover Cove and Sai Kung. The ferry ride makes for a fine half-day trip if all you're going to do is stay on board and soak up the views: the early morning departure runs up the channel for Tap Mun Chau calling on the way at isolated bays along Sai Kung's northern coast. In the order reached from Ma Liu Shui, these are: Shap Sze Heung, Sham Chung, Lai Chi Chong (for *Pak Sha O* hostel), Tai Tan (for Wong Shek), Chek Keng (for *Bradbury Hall* hostel) and Kau Lau Wan. All of these places, which are in **Sai Kung West Country Park**, are connected by paths and rougher trails, and there are campsites along the way, but you'll need to be well-equipped with a tent, food and water if you're to explore the area properly.

One place on the northern coast you can visit without too much difficulty is **NAI CHUNG**, only a ten-minute bus ride from Sai Kung Town (#99; hourly). It's one of a dozen similar places in the area, where you'll find barbecue sites, picnic areas, drinks stalls and rowing boats for rent. The others can be seen (or stopped off at) if you take the opportunity to return using **bus #89R** instead from Nai Chung. It only runs on Saturday and Sunday (every 20–30min), but connects Sai Kung Town with Sha Tin on the KCR line, following the coast north around the neighbouring **Ma On Shan Country Park**.

Incidentally, if you fancy the climb to the top of **Ma On Shan** itself – Hong Kong's second highest mountain at 702 metres – access is by the #99 bus from Sai Kung Town. About five minutes out of Sai Kung, get off at the top of the ridge by the picnic area and follow the signposts for the MacLehose Trail – most of the steep, five-kilometre route, apart from the final peak, is part of Stage 4 of the trail. A great deal of the climb can be very tough, though the extraordinary views make the effort more than worthwhile. A few words of warning, though: you'll need decent footwear, plenty of water, and don't even think of attempting the walk in bad weather.

Tap Mun Chau

Right up in the northeast of the territory, at the mouth of the Tolo Channel, **Tap Mun Chau** is an awkward island to reach, but it is becoming an increasingly popular alternative with Hong Kong's inhabitants. Chartered boats make stops here and though there's not a great deal to see, it's the relative isolation that's the main draw.

The Sai Kung Peninsula

The quickest way to **get there** is by *kaido* from Wong Shek (see above), a twenty-minute crossing: currently, departures are Monday to Saturday at 8.30am and then every two hours until 6.30pm; hourly on Sunday from 8.30am to 5.30pm. The **return** *kaidos* from Tap Mun Chau to Wong Shek leave every two hours Monday to Saturday from 7.45am to 3.45pm (with the last one at 6pm); hourly on Sunday from 8am to 5pm..

Otherwise, you'll have to take the ferry from Ma Liu Shui ferry pier (details above under "The Northern Coast and Tolo Channel"), though the timings on this route make a day-trip difficult. Perhaps the best option for both seeing the island and enjoying a long ferry trip is to cross from the Sai Kung peninsula by *kaido* and pick up the return ferry to Ma Liu Shui.

Both ferry and *kaido* dock in a sheltered inlet on the island's west side which contains the only **village** – a single line of crumbling houses and small shops overlooking the fish farms that constitute the only industry. It's a rundown, ramshackle kind of place, nice and quiet, with the houses on the only street open to the pavement. There's a Tin Hau temple along here, too (to the left of the pier), the venue for a large annual festival, while to the right of the pier, a fishermen's quarter straddles the low hill – nets and tackle stacked and stored in the huts and houses, many built on stilts over the water.

A couple of paths spread across the island, which is surprisingly green, leading to its English name of "Grass Island". After you've ambled around, the only thing to do is to head back to the main street and its one good **restaurant**, the *New Hon Kee*; left from the ferry pier and it's on the first corner. There's no English sign, but there is an English menu which offers reasonable seafood, fried rice and beer in a room overlooking the water.

Don't miss the last ferry whatever you do. There's no accommodation on Tap Mun Chau, and even the restaurant owners don't live on the island but back in the New Territories.

Chapter 5

The Outlying Islands

Hong Kong island is only one of 230-odd other islands scattered in the South China Sea that, together with the Kowloon peninsula and New Territories, make up the territory of Hong Kong proper. The vast majority of these **outlying islands** are tiny, barren and uninhabited; one, Chek Lap Kok, is currently being completely transformed by the reclamation work neccessary for it to house Hong Kong's new airport. Others are restricted areas, used as detention centres or for rehabilitating drug addicts, but the few you can visit form some of the territory's less cluttered reaches. The main destinations – the southwestern trio of **Lamma, Cheung Chau** and **Lantau** – are very popular with locals and tourists alike: Lantau is

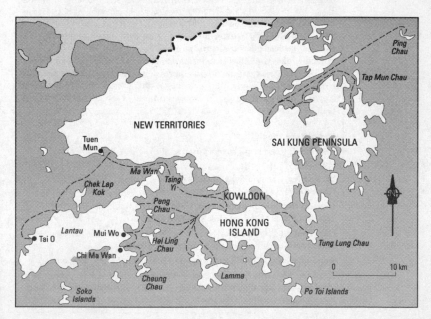

actually much bigger than Hong Kong Island, and staying overnight here is a distinct and attractive possibility. Several other islands are less accessible, though if you're determined, places like **Peng Chau** and **Ma Wan** can also be rewarding places to visit.

None of the islands are exactly uncharted territory. The easily accessible ones have suffered from the attentions of the developers over the years, and an increasing number of Hong Kongers – *gweilos* especially – choose to live on islands like Lantau and Cheung Chau.

ISLAND PRACTICALITIES

Getting There

Regular ferries run from Hong Kong Island to Lamma, Cheung Chau and Lantau. Faster (and more expensive) **hoverferries** also serve a few main destinations – like Peng Chau, or Silvermine Bay and Discovery Bay on Lantau. A couple of the more remote islands are also served by ferry, but these are much less frequent and depart from piers in the New Territories. Departure points for all these routes are given below, and check the "Travel Details" at the end of each island account for more specific information. Access to a couple of places is by **kaido**, a licensed, motorised sampan or converted fishing boat; some **inter-island connections** are also made by *kaido*. These are less frequent than the ferries and though there are timetables on some of the routes, they are often impossible to track down: you'll just have to ask around.

There are also weekend **excursion ferries** to some of the most popular destinations from the Star Ferry Pier in Tsim Sha Tsui: you have to reserve ahead for these, with the *HYFCO Travel Agency*, Shop 3, Star House, Salisbury Road, Tsim Sha Tsui (☎730 8608). Or, if you don't mind splashing out, arranging a **charter boat** is easy enough: either enquire at ferry piers on the islands, or in Central on Hong Kong Island; or contact a rental company, like *New Moonraker Motorboat Co. Ltd* at Blake Pier (☎522 1455), which rents out motorboats, junks and other boats. There are more rental companies along the quayside at the Central Government Pier (beyond the Western Arm). For organised **tours** of the islands by boat, see p.49.

Departure Piers

Aberdeen, Hong Kong Island: *kaido* to Mo Tat Wan/Sok Kwu Wan (Lamma).

Blake Pier, Central, Hong Kong Island: hoverferry to Discovery Bay (Lantau).

Central Harbour Services Pier, Central, Hong Kong Island: ferries to Yung Shue Wan (Lamma), Sok Kwu Wan (Lamma).

Government Pier, Central, Hong Kong Island: hoverferries to Cheung Chau, Mui Wo (Silvermine Bay; Lantau), Peng Chau.

Kennedy Town, Hong Kong Island: *kaido* to Yung Shue Wan (Lamma).

Outlying Districts Services Pier, Central, Hong Kong Island: ferries to Cheung Chau, Mui Wo (Silvermine Bay; Lantau); excursion ferry to Sha Lo Wan (Lantau) and Tai O (Lantau).

Some of the other islands were inhabited way before Hong Kong Island itself, but their fishing communities have been abandoned and the buildings left to rot after the people moved to new cities and jobs on the mainland. Since then things have become much more developed, but some stretches of the islands can still feel relatively deserted – especially if you're lucky enough to be invited onto a private (or chartered) boat, when you can reach some supremely isolated spots.

The islands covered here are the main ones in the southwest of the territory, to which there are regular ferries from Central and Kowloon. However, other (minor) islands are accessible from various points on Hong Kong Island and in the New Territories and are covered elsewhere in the text:

Sham Tseng, New Territories: *kaido* to Ma Wan.
Star Ferry Pier, Tsim Sha Tsui, Kowloon: weekend ferries to Cheung Chau, Mui Wo (Silvermine Bay, Lantau).

Using the Ferries

You can't reserve seats on the ferries: it's first come, first served, so get there early at busy times. **Tickets** to all main destinations cost around $7 one-way for "ordinary class" and around $12 for "de luxe class" (upstairs, on the air-conditioned top deck). These fares virtually double after noon on Saturday for the weekend; children under twelve pay half-price at all times. All return tickets are double the price of a single. **Hoverferry** tickets cost around $20 one-way: adults and children pay the same price.On some ferries you buy your ticket from a booth at the pier: the destinations are clearly marked on boards above your head. At other piers you need a supply of **small change** which you feed into a turnstile, so always make sure you've got a few loose dollars with you. If you can, especially at the weekend, buy a return ticket so you won't have to queue on the way back.

None of the journeys are very long – around an hour maximum on all the main routes – and if you can't get a seat, you can always lounge on deck; coming back into Hong Kong, especially, the views are fabulous. Each ferry also has a small **bar** selling coffee, sandwiches, hot noodles, cold drinks and beer.

On a *kaido*, you usually pay the fare to the person operating the boat. It will usually only be around $5–10, though tourists can expect to pay more than the locals on some routes. Sometimes, when there's no regular service, you'll need to charter the whole boat – the text tells you when it's neccessary and roughly how much it will cost.

When to go

Services to all the main islands are more frequent on **Sunday** for a good reason: the entire territory swaps its packed vertical apartment blocks for packed horizontal beaches. There are enormous queues at the piers, and, after noon on Saturday and all day Sunday, the fares shoot up, too. If you are planning to stay **overnight** on any of the islands, be prepared to pay vastly inflated prices at the weekend, and think about booking well in advance.

Midweek is much better for a quieter visit anywhere, when some places can seem positively secluded. Note that a major annual disruption to the timetables occurs during the **typhoon season** (May–Oct), when ferry services can be abandoned at very short notice. Listen to the bulletins and check with the harbour office if you want to avoid being stranded.

The main reason that most people head out to any of the islands is for their **beaches**, not a bad idea given the crowded state of the sands on Hong Kong Island. However, even the fine beaches on Lantau are packed if you go at the weekend or on a public holiday, and pollution often puts many other island beaches out of bounds – at least as far as swimming goes. Luckily, there are other reasons why you might want to come. Lantau is a popular target for **hiking**, and its cross-island trail, old villages and scores of monasteries make it easily the most interesting place for which to head. Lamma and, to a lesser degree, Cheung Chau are noted for their **seafood restaurants** and food stalls; while the quieter and less visited islands – including Peng Chau and Ma Wan – still offer a slice of the traditional Chinese life that was once lived all over the territory. You may want to stay over at one or two of the places: there are **hotels** on Cheung Chau and Lantau, and a couple of **hostels** on Lantau, all picked out in the text – you'll need to turn to the "Accommodation" chapter (p.193) for reviews and booking details.

There's a good **map** of the southwestern islands – Lantau, Cheung Chau, Peng Chau and Lamma – which is part of the *Countryside Series* (No.3 "Lantau and Islands"); available from the Government Publications Centre, Connaught Place, Central (next to the GPO building). The HKTA dishes out a free leaflet on all the outlying islands, as well as printed **ferry and hoverferry timetables** for all the major routes, which are well worth picking up, particularly since the prices and times given below are all subject to change.

Lamma

THE OUTLYING ISLANDS

The closest island to Hong Kong – Aberdeen is only around 3km from its northern point – **Lamma** is perhaps the best to visit if your time is limited. Its elongated fourteen square kilometres are still largely unspoiled and you can round off a trip with a meal in one of the fine seafood restaurants there. There's no motorised traffic on the island, something which attracts many expats to live on Lamma, in search of a rural existence within commuting distance of Hong Kong. By and large they've found it: what development there is is fairly low-key, and some of the more outrageous recent planning proposals have been defeated by conservationists. Much of Lamma's northern region was designated to be the site of an oil refinery in the early 1970s. Opposition, and the recession of 1974, put paid to that, though nothing could prevent the later building of the power station at Po Lo Tsui, on the northwestern coast. This is the island's major eyesore, though it's gradually being rivalled by the quarrying operations on the other side of the island, overlooking Sok Kwu Wan. Still, once you're on the hilltops following the well-marked paths and trails, Lamma regains its peace and quiet.

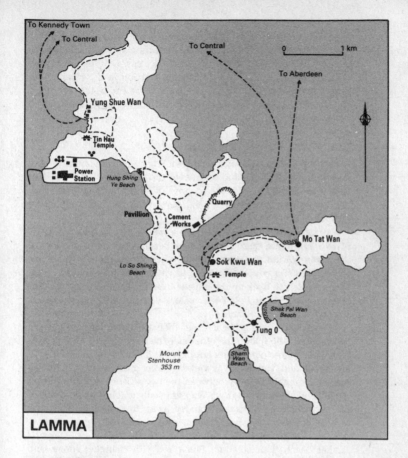

LAMMA

Yung Shue Wan

Ferries run to the two villages on the island, Yung Shue Wan in the northwest and Sok Kwu Wan at the island's squeezed middle. As it's an easy walk between the two, and the best seafood is at Sok Kwu Wan, you're best off aiming first for **YUNG SHUE WAN**, which is also connected to Hong Kong Island by regular *kaido* service from Kennedy Town. The ferry trip takes forty minutes to the little village, huddled around its harbour, and with just one street, **Yung Shue Wan Main Street**, at the end of which is a typically gloomy **Tin Hau temple** overlooking the water. The expat presence in the village is manifest in a couple of new bars and the apartment buildings spreading up behind the village, but it remains small-scale enough to be pleasant. Really, the only things that spoil the village atmosphere are the two huge chimney stacks of the power station that glare down from behind the hill.

For reviews of Yung Shue Wan's best restaurants, see p.222; accommodation is detailed on p.206.

If you've come intending to walk across the island, there's nothing much to stop you heading straight off, though the narrow seafront street has a scattering of **restaurants**, a couple with terrace tables outside. If you made the trip the other way, or if you just fancied the island air, there is **accommodation** in the village, too, including the *Man Lai Wah Hotel*, right at the end of the ferry pier, and the simpler *Lamma Vacation House*, down Main Street on the left-hand side.

The walk to Sok Kwu Wan

It's around 3–4km on foot to Sok Kwu Wan, across the hill from the northern half of the island and down through the narrow waist of land at Lo So Shing. It'll take an hour or so: from Yung Shue Wan, take the left turn off Main Street, before the Tin Hau temple; the signs say "Hung Shing Ye".

Along a good concrete path, it's a twenty-minute walk to HUNG SHING YE, where there's a tiny sand beach with first-hand views of the power station. It's nice enough when it's empty and there are barbecue pits, a couple of places to get a drink and holiday apartments stretching back up the hillside from the sand. There's another hotel, too, the *Han Lok Yuen*, where you can also eat pigeon or seafood at the terrace tables.

From Hung Shing Ye a clear footpath continues around the beach and up the hill on the other side, now signposted to "Sok Kwu Wan". It's quite a climb on a hot day, but it's not long until the path levels out and you reach a viewing point marked by a **Chinese pavilion**, roughly halfway between the two villages. Carry on down the hill and views of Sok Kwu Wan gradually unfold – as do those of the vast cement works and quarry away to your left. The path reaches down to the island's waist, and, at the small village school, there's a diversion to LO SO SHING, to the right, a bigger and sandier beach than at Hung Shing Ye, with changing rooms and showers, a snack kiosk and more barbecue pits. It's usually all right for swimming, too, though check the information board first for the current condition of the water. Back onto the main path, it's only another twenty minutes to the other village on the island, Sok Kwu Wan.

Sok Kwu Wan

The bay at SOK KWU WAN is entirely devoted to fish farming. Floating wooden frames cover the water, interspersed with rowing boats, junks and the floating canvas shelters of the fishermen and women. A concrete path runs the length of the village, from the obligatory Tin Hau temple to the main pier, along which Sok Kwu Wan's **seafood restaurants** form a line. They're the only real reason to come, though what was once a low-key array of simple eating houses has turned into a range of polished restaurants, with outdoor tables overlooking the bay and large fish tanks set back on the street. Some restaurants have special set menus in English posted on the walls, and these are worth investigating. Otherwise, just pick a likely-looking place and order what you want – though *always* ask the price first, certainly if you're choosing your fish straight from the tank. The most popular restaurants tend to get booked up in advance in the evening by groups coming over from Hong Kong: they'll have arranged a set-price meal with the particular restaurant, and, if there's a group of you and you can get someone to ring for you, that's not a bad idea at all. At lunchtime, you'll have no trouble finding a space.

The only drawback to eating on the terraces is the view over the bay: the whole hillside opposite has been quarried, scarred and despoiled by storage containers, corrugated-iron huts and a large conveyor belt; and the bay itself – sometimes known by its alternative name, Picnic Bay – is rapidly becoming soiled by the refuse generated by the intensive fish farming in the area. It's illegal for the fishermen to live on the floating rafts, but many do: they use the polystyrene floats at the pier to row themselves across to the fish frames, where they erect canvas shelters, from which they dump sewage and rubbish.

Mo Tat Wan and Mount Stenhouse

If you arrive early enough in the day, there are a couple of other targets around Sok Kwu Wan that can fill in the time before dinner. It's a 25-minute walk (left as you step off the ferry pier) to **MO TAT WAN**, another small beach village and usually quieter than the others on the island. It's one of the oldest villages in Hong Kong, here in some shape or form for over three hundred years, though there's not much to show for it. Although it's hardly worth waiting around for, the **kaido** service to Aberdeen from Sok Kwu Wan calls in regularly every day; there's a timetable posted at Sok Kwu Wan pier.

A path from Mo Tat Wan leads the kilometre or so to the bigger beach of **Shek Pai Wan** on the southeastern coast, from where you can continue on – past Tung O – to the smaller **Sham Wan** beach. This is perhaps the remotest beach on the island, and is worth heading to if only for that reason.

Cast around a bit, either in Sok Kwu Wan or at Shek Pai Wan and Sham Wan, and it's not difficult to find one of the paths that lead eventually up to the summit of **Mount Stenhouse**, 353m up in the middle of the island's southwestern bulge. Also known as Shan Tei Tong, it's quite a climb, particularly since the paths aren't wonderful, but you'll be rewarded with some fine views. It should take just under two hours from Sok Kwu Wan to climb up and down again; make sure you take plenty of water along if you're going to tackle it.

LAMMA TRAVEL DETAILS

Central
to Yung Shue Wan (10–12 daily; first at 6.50am, Sun at 8.15am, last at 11.20pm, Sat at 12.30am);
Sok Kwu Wan (7–9 daily; first at 8am, last at 11pm).

Kennedy Town
to Yung Shue Wan (regular *kaido* service).

Aberdeen
to Mo Tat Wan/Sok Kwu Wan (Mon–Sat 6–8 daily, Sun every 45min; first at 6.50am, Sun at 8am, last at 7.15pm).

Yung Shue Wan
to Central (10–12 daily; first at 6.25am, Sun at 6.50am, last at 10.35pm);
to Kennedy Town (regular *kaido* service).

Sok Kwu Wan
to Central (7–8 daily; first at 6.50am, Sun at 8.20am, last at 10pm); to Mo Tat Wan/Aberdeen (6–8 daily).

For ticket prices and other ferry details, see p.164–165. For up-to-date ferry information, call the Hong Kong Ferry Co. ☎ *542 3081.*

Cheung Chau

THE OUTLYING ISLANDS

Cheung Chau

An hour southwest of the city, **Cheung Chau** is the most congested of the outlying islands, the central waist of its dumb-bell shape crammed with buildings, its harbour and typhoon shelter busy day and night. However, unlike some of the other islands, it's not an artificial development caused by invading outsiders seeking peace and quiet – though certainly these exist on Cheung Chau. Rather, the island is one of the oldest settled parts of Hong Kong, with a prosperity based on fishing, supplemented in the past, with smuggling and piracy. There's a life here that's independent of the fortunes of Hong Kong, manifest in a surviving junk shipyard, several working temples and one of Hong Kong's best annual festivals.

Concrete **paths** cover the entire island, and, despite the name, which means "long island" in Cantonese, you can whip around the place fairly quickly. Like Lamma, no cars are allowed here, though you'll have to listen out for the buzz of the motorised scooter-like work vehicles as you walk along – the paths aren't really wide enough for you both. Much of the relatively undeveloped parts of the island are taken up by youth camps, and the two or three fine beaches are regularly crowded. But for all that, the paths repay a dawdle: traditional life thrives in the main village, with its shops and fishing boats and stalls; there are some excellent views as you go; and – as ever – sampling Cheung Chau's seafood is a major reason to visit.

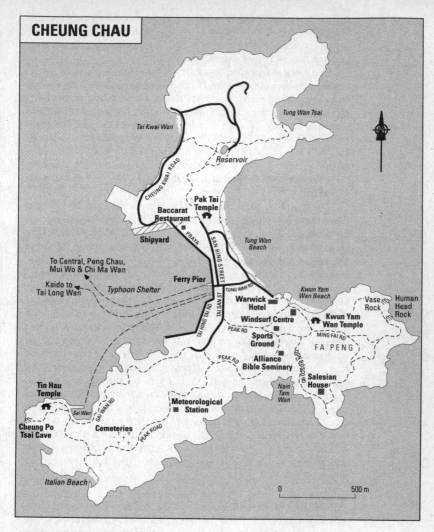

CHEUNG CHAU

Tung Wan Tsai

Tai Kwai Wan

Reservoir

CHEUNG KWAI ROAD

Pak Tai
Temple

Baccarat
Restaurant

Shipyard

PRAYA

SAN HING STREET

Tung Wan
Beach

To Central, Peng Chau,
Mui Wo & Chi Ma Wan

Ferry Pier

Kaido to
Tai Long Wan

Typhoon Shelter

TUNG WAN RD

Kwun Yam
Wan Beach

Vase
Rock

Human
Head
Rock

TAI HING TAI RD

TAI SAN ST

Warwick
Hotel

Windsurf Centre

PEAK RD

Kwun Yam
Wan Temple

MING FAI RD

FA PENG

Sports
Ground

DON BOSO RD

PEAK RD

Alliance
Bible Seminary

Tin Hau
Temple

Sai Wan

SAI WAN RD

Cheung Po
Tsai Cave

Cemeteries

PEAK ROAD

Meteorological
Station

Nam
Tam
Wan

Salesian
House

Italian Beach

0   500 m

Cheung Chau Village

The ferry from Central picks its way through the breakwaters and
junks to dock at **CHEUNG CHAU VILLAGE**, where all the population and activity is concentrated. The waterfront road, or **Praya**, is
where the fishermen still lay out their catch in water-filled trays and
buckets, and early morning and mid-afternoon this develops into a
small market, with the fishermen joined by fruit and veg and clothes
sellers. There's not much to the crowded few streets that make up
the centre of the village but it invites a leisurely stroll. From oppo-

site the ferry pier, Tung Wan Road leads across the island's waist to Tung Wan Beach (see below), a short walk through a couple of twists and turns lined with stalls and shops, the place to snap up bamboo hats and other essential beach gear.

One block in from the water, **San Hing Street** is the main street, leading up about 500m to the **Pak Tai Temple**, built in 1788 and set in its own little square. Not surprisingly, on an island once totally dependent on fishing, the inhabitants deemed it prudent to dedicate a temple to Pak Tai, the protector of fishermen and "supreme emperor of the dark heaven". Inside, there are relics appropriate to Pak Tai's status: an 800-year-old iron sword, fished out of the sea; a golden crown; a gilded nineteenth-century sedan-chair, made to carry the god's image during festivals – and a plaque recording the 1966 visit of Princess Margaret.

The temple is also the venue for the annual four-day **Cheung Chau Bun Festival**, or "Ta Chiu", in late April/early May, held since the ravages of a series of eighteenth- and nineteenth-century plagues that supposedly appeased the vengeful spirits of those wrongly killed by Cheung Chau's pirates. Outside the temple, several sets of bamboo scaffolding are erected, each around twenty metres high and topped with pink and white buns. Up until 1978, at midnight on a designated day, people were encouraged to clamber up the frames to grab the buns, which would bring good luck – the higher the bun, the better the luck. This particular activity was stopped after what the tourist authorities refer to darkly as "an unfortunate accident"*, and these days the buns are just handed out from the bottom of the frames. The festival's other great draw is the teams of costumed children riding on floats through the streets, some of their peers strapped onto stilts on which they glide over the crowds. The village is packed for the four days of the festival – extra ferries are laid on from Hong Kong – and it's a fascinating time to come: as well as the high-profile displays, there are a whole host of religious services, Chinese opera performances, unicorn and lion dances, and all the bluster and bustle that the Cantonese bring to any celebration.

North of the village

Just down from the temple, at the water, are the **boatyards**, where junk-builders still work entirely by hand, using no plans and skills that haven't changed much in 500 years – though electric drills and saws have been introduced. Even more unusually, you may also catch sight of blocks of ice being shipped out of the adjacent ice-making factory, and loaded onto boats for removal to Hong Kong.

Beyond here, the **northern** stretch of the island only has views to offer but they're worth the effort. On the seafront, just after the

---

*In fact, a couple of the towers collapsed and 24 people were injured.

fire station, some steep steps on the right lead up to a new housing estate, from where you can look down over the village and harbour. Or continue around the headland, following the waterfront Cheung Kwai Road: there's a path off to the left after a few hundred metres (marked "Family Trail") which leads up to a hilltop reservoir, from where there are splendid views right over the whole island. From the reservoir, you can descend straight back down into the village, past a small cemetery – you'll come out close to the Pak Tai Temple.

The East Coast: Tung Wan and Kwun Yam Wan

Across the waist of land from the ferry pier, a few minutes' walk up Tung Wan Road, is the island's main beach, **Tung Wan Beach**, 700–800m of fine sand and as popular as anywhere in the territory at the weekend. There are a couple of restaurants by the beach, as well as Cheung Chau's bid for the weekend set, the *Warwick* hotel, at the southern end. Just past here, around the little headland, there's another sweep of sand, **Kwun Yam Wan Beach** (or Afternoon Beach), probably the best on the island. The **Windsurf Centre** here hires out all the relevant bits and pieces: windsurfers from around $75 an hour ($250 a day), canoes $40–60 an hour. The bar/café at the centre is also a good place for a beer.

A walk around the island

If you've got a couple of hours and fancy something more strenuous than loafing on a beach, the **southern** part of the island lends itself to a good, circular walk along tree-shaded paths. From the waterfront in the village, close to the ferry pier, jump on a *kaido* to SAI WAN, across the harbour at the southwestern tip of the island: you'll hear the name of the village being called by the *kaido* operators or just ask someone on the quayside. It's a five-minute crossing and on the way the *kaido* sometimes calls at one or two of the junks in the harbour, depositing people laden with shopping at their floating homes.

From Sai Wan's pier, a path leads up to one of the island's several **Tin Hau** temples, where there's a pavilion overlooking the harbour. A path runs over the brow of the hill to a rocky bluff, part of which has been landscaped with barbecue pits. Follow everyone else scrambling over the rocks and you'll come to the so-called **Cheung Po Tsai Cave**, touted as the HQ of a notorious Cheung Chau pirate. Whether it was or wasn't, the adventurous and agile can climb through the underground passage here: unless you follow someone else, you'll need a flashlight, which you can buy from a woman sitting at the entrance: it'll cost around $30, though make it clear that you're only renting it and you'll get $20 or so back when you return it. The climb is fairly hard going, though faint hearts will be shamed by the queue of elderly women risking the drop into the abyss with their grandchildren.

Back at Sai Wan pier, follow the only road (Peak Rd) for several hundred metres and detour right down to Pak Tso Wan, known as **Italian Beach** – small and sandy, though a little grubby. The road climbs up through a series of **cemeteries**, with occasional pavilions providing views over the sea, into Lung Tsai Tseun, once a separate village but now a southern outpost of the main village. Just after the Alliance Bible Seminary building, take Fa Peng Road to the right and then follow Don Bosco Road, which leads down to Salesian House, a religious retreat, before doubling back to **Fa Peng Knoll**, the island's eastern bulge. Turn left here and the path runs down past the **Kwun Yam Temple**, at which point you're back at Kwun Yam Wan beach and only a short walk from the centre. Alternatively, you can follow a path from Fa Peng that will take you around the eastern headland, climbing down the cliffside to view a series of weirdly shaped **rocks** that have supposedly self-explanatory names – Vase Rock, Human Head Rock and Loaf Rock; in fact, they could equally be called Big Splodge Rock, Amorphus Rock and Vague Shape Rock.

Practicalities

There are **bike rental** shops on the road between the Pak Tai Temple and the Praya, as well as at the northern end of the Praya itself. There's no shortage of **holiday apartments** to let, either. During midweek, they're reasonably cheap, even more so if you can get three or four people together. The only time to avoid, or book months in advance, is the period of the Bun Festival, though staying at weekends is relatively pricey, too. Try one of the agencies opposite the ferry pier: you'll see the photo-boards, with details, as you disembark. Or there's an agency next door but one to *Dreyers' Ice Cream Store* on Tung Wan Road, which has places overlooking the beach with bathroom and kitchen for around $300 a night (for two people); more like $500 at the weekend. Of the **hotels**, the obvious – if most expensive – place to stay is the *Warwick*, overlooking Tung Wan Beach.

For hotels on Cheung Chau, see p.206; the restaurants are reviewed on p.222.

For **eating**, most of the village's waterfront Praya is lined with small restaurants, both north and south of the ferry pier. At night, the whole street is decked out with tables and chairs as the *dai pai dongs* arrive to dish out cheap and excellent seafood; take your pick of places and point to what you want. If you need a place with an English menu, try the *East Lake Restaurant*, up Tung Wan Road, on the way to the main beach; or check out those at the northern end of the Praya, nearest the Pak Tai Temple, especially the *Baccarat*. For **bottled water** and cold **beer**, there's a *Wellcome* supermarket opposite the ferry pier.

Note that if you're on Cheung Chau during the Bun Festival, the island goes **vegetarian** for a few days – no great hardship since the food on offer remains excellent.

CHEUNG CHAU TRAVEL DETAILS

Ferries: daily
Central to Cheung Chau (hourly; first at 6.25am, last at 11.30pm, Sat at 12.30am).
Tsim Sha Tsui to Cheung Chau (Sat at 4pm; Sun at 8am &10am).
Cheung Chau to Central (hourly; first at 5.35am, last at 10.30pm, Sat at 11.30pm); Tsim Sha Tsui (Sun at 12.45pm).

Hoverferries: Mon–Fri only
Central to Cheung Chau (at 9am, 10.15am, 12.15pm, 2.15pm & 4.05pm).
Cheung Chau to Central (at 9.40am, 10.50am, 12.50pm, 2.50pm & 4.50pm).

Inter-Island Ferry Service: daily
Cheung Chau to Chi Ma Wan and Mui Wo (both on Lantau) and on to Peng Chau (roughly every two hours, first at 7am, last at 10.10pm; not every departure calls at every stop, so check the timetable at the pier).

For ticket prices and other ferry details, see p.164–165. For up-to-date ferry information, call the Hong Kong Ferry Co. ☎542 3081.

Peng Chau

THE OUTLYING ISLANDS

Hoverferries on their way to Lantau (see below) call first at **Peng Chau**, a tiny horseshoe-shaped blob of land fifty minutes from Hong Kong and just twenty minutes from its larger neighbour. It's firmly part of the little southwestern archipelago of islands and is relatively densely populated, but few tourists bother to get off the hoverferry. In truth, there's no real reason why they should, though the quiet streets are a pleasant alternative to the busy antics of Mui Wo. You could see the whole of Peng Chau in the hour or so that you'll have to wait for the next connection; there are inter-island ferries to Peng Chau from Mui Wo throughout the day.

Wing On Street, just back from the pier, is a typical island street, part market, part residential, with its Tin Hau temple, noodle shops, Chinese herbalists and no traffic. Signs point you in the direction of **Tung Wan**, the island's only real beach. It's five minutes' walk away and the bay is pretty enough, with a barbecue site at one end and a few fishing boats. Really, though, you won't want to hang around, unless you've been tempted into one of the **seafood restaurants**, where the food is as good and as cheap as on any of the islands.

Hei Ling Chau

A fairly frequent service runs from the quayside to **Hei Ling Chau**, an island south of Peng Chau and around twice its size, though don't get on the ferry by mistake, since part of the island is used as a drug rehabilitation centre – the chattering trippers are actually visiting relatives.

THE OUTLYING ISLANDS

*See map
overleaf*

Lantau

Since it's by far the biggest island in the territory, you could spend
three or four days exploring **Lantau**'s fairly obvious charms. The
name means "broken head" in Cantonese, though it looks more like
the shape of a dog when viewed on a map. Twice the size of Hong
Kong Island, Lantau is wild and rugged enough in parts to make real
hiking an attractive option; some of the beaches are among the best
in Hong Kong, and for once there's a full set of cultural diversions,
including two different monasteries, both of which you can sleep at.

Much of the island is preserved as a country park. The circular
seventy-kilometre-long **Lantau Trail** loops around the southern half
of the island, passing campsites and the island's two youth hostels
along the way. We've marked the trail on our map, but if you want
more detailed information, pick up the free leaflet *Lantau Trail*,
published by the Country Parks Authority (CPA), which lists the
route stages and picks out the relevant camping and local transport
details; there's a staffed CPA booth at the ferry pier in Mui Wo, and
for anything more than an afternoon's stroll you'll need camping
equipment and all the related gear. You don't have to tackle the
whole thing at once: there are a couple of easy stages and other half-
day walks accessible from Mui Wo, the village where the ferries dock.

If you're not going to take in any of the Lantau Trail, you're
going to have to rely on some form of **transport** on the island.
Lantau has a small **bus** network, which will get you to nearly all of
the places covered below, and there are **taxis**, too. Hitching,
though, like everywhere else in the territory, is a virtual non-starter.

Mui Wo (Silvermine Bay)

The large ferries from Hong Kong all dock at **MUI WO** ("five petal
flower"), generally known by its English name "Silvermine Bay", after
the silver mine which once brought prosperity to the village but has

long since been boarded up. The walk to the site of the mine is pleasant enough, about a kilometre inland from the village and close to a waterfall. The village itself is actually about the least interesting place on the island and most people head from the ferry straight to the **bus terminal** outside, where queues build up quickly for buses to the most popular destinations on the island; even if the bus is full you shouldn't have to wait long for the next one (see the "Travel Details" box at the end of the section for routes and timetables). Taxis leave from the same square and travel information (on ferries back to Central, etc) is posted on boards at the pier building.

To the right of the bus terminal is the **Cooked Food Market** (6am–midnight) – a dozen or so covered stalls with outside tables that overlook the bay itself. They're all fairly cheap, serving bowls of noodles, seafood and the like. Other options are nearby: a *Wellcome* **supermarket** and a *Park 'N' Shop* around the main square, and the *Rome* cake shop, across the square from the ferry pier.

For details about all Lantau's hotels, turn to p.207.

Beyond the Cooked Food Market, a path leads around to the long, curving **beach**, backed by restaurants, barbecue pits, showers and toilets. Unfortunately, the water here has been considered too polluted for safe swimming for the last few years, though that doesn't seem to stop the locals fishing in it, or dredging the sands for shellfish. Still, it looks an attractive stretch of sand from a distance, and there are two **hotels** which capitalise on the nice views across the bay: the large *Silvermine Beach Hotel* (which has a reservations booth at the ferry pier) and the smaller, nicer *Mui Wo Inn*, further along.

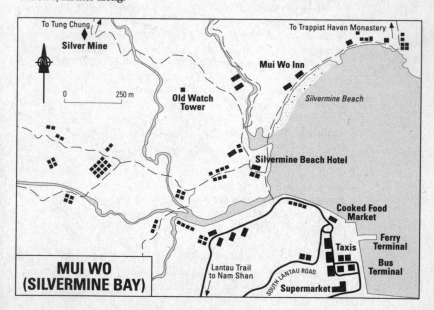

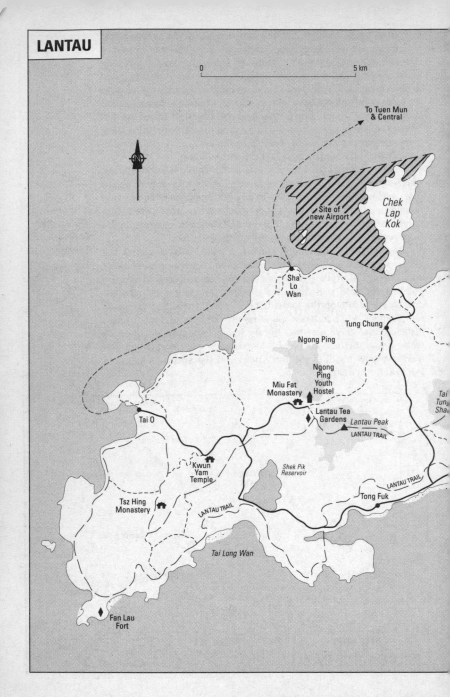

LANTAU

0   5 km

To Tuen Mun
& Central

Chek
Lap
Kok

Site of
new Airport

Sha
Lo
Wan

Tung Chung

Ngong Ping

Ngong
Ping
Youth
Hostel

Miu Fat
Monastery

Lantau Tea
Gardens   *Lantau Peak*

LANTAU TRAIL

Tai O

Tai
Tun
Sha

Kwun
Yam
Temple

*Shek Pik
Reservoir*

LANTAU TRAIL

Tong Fuk

Tsz Hing
Monastery

LANTAU TRAIL

Tai Long Wan

Fan Lau
Fort

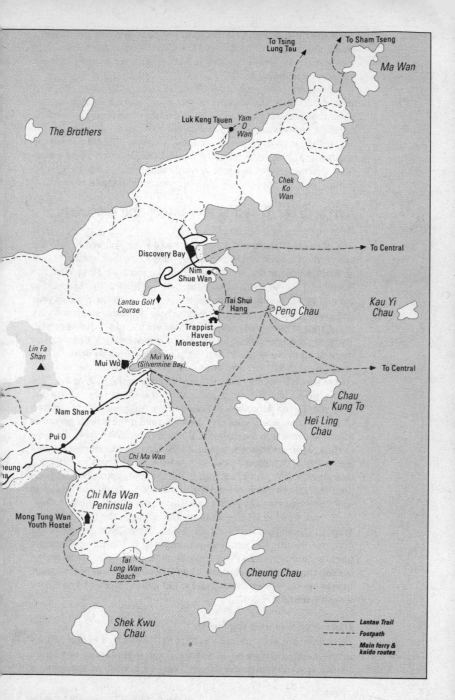

To Tsing Lung Tau

To Sham Tseng

Ma Wan

The Brothers

Luk Keng Tsuen

Yam O Wan

Chek Ko Wan

Discovery Bay

Nim Shue Wan

To Central

Lantau Golf Course

Tai Shui Hang

Peng Chau

Kau Yi Chau

Lin Fa Shan

Mui Wo

Mui Wo (Silvermine Bay)

Trappist Haven Monestery

To Central

Nam Shan

Chau Kung To

Hei Ling Chau

Pui O

Chi Ma Wan

Cheung Sha

Chi Ma Wan Peninsula

Mong Tung Wan Youth Hostel

Tai Long Wan Beach

Cheung Chau

Shek Kwu Chau

————— Lantau Trail
– – – – – Footpath
— — — Main ferry & kaido routes

If the Cooked Food Market didn't appeal, you can get Western meals and snacks at the *Silvermine Beach Hotel*; the terrace café out front has bay views, making it a good place for a beer (there's a $20 minimum charge).

Also along the beach at Mui Wo you can **rent bicycles**. It'll cost around $25 an hour, cheaper if you want one for longer, though given the steep hills between Mui Wo and everywhere else and the excellent bus service, it's difficult to see why you would want one for longer than it takes to potter around the village. Mui Wo is also the starting and finishing point of the **Lantau Trail**: section 1 (outwards) runs southwest down the road towards Nam Shan, while section 12 (return) cuts up from the Chi Ma Wan peninsula to the ferry pier.

North: to the Trappist Monastery and Discovery Bay

One of the best short hikes you can make from Mui Wo is over the hills to the Trappist Haven Monastery in the next bay north. It takes around an hour and a half: head along the seafront Tung Wan Tau Road (past the hotels) and take the path on the left by the river, at the end of the beach; keep going straight up, with the river to your left, and the path loops round eventually to the right, steep and very overgrown in parts and signposted only once, right at the very end. There are some excellent views as you go, over Peng Chau and to Hong Kong in the distance, and – if you wish – you can detour to the peak on your left, from where you'll get a view over the new golf course above Discovery Bay. Otherwise, stick to the path to the right of the peak, which brings you out at the dairy farm above the **Trappist Haven Monastery**. Founded by refugees from mainland China, the monastery supports itself by selling the milk it produces to various outlets in Hong Kong; if you wander down from the farm to the chapel, an adjacent building sells little bottles of creamy milk and boxes of "Trappist Cookies" – just the thing if you've struggled over from Mui Wo on a hot day. If the tranquil atmosphere appeals (and the monks have cornered a particularly shady and beautiful spot) you can **stay overnight** in visitors' dormitories here, though you'll have to have arranged things first: write to the Grand Master, Trappist Haven, Lantau Island, PO Box 5, Peng Chau, or ring ☎987 6292 for details; simple meals are included in the price. There's a **kaido** service across to Peng Chau from the small pier at the end of the road beyond the monastery. There are only a few daily crossings, the last one at 4.30pm, so try and avoid getting stuck or you'll have to walk back to Mui Wo.

Discovery Bay and the North

The alternative is to press on to **NIM SHUE WAN**, a couple of kilometres away; there's a path from the Trappist Monastery or a *kaido* service from the monastery's pier. There's a small beach here, at which you should be able to swim, and a road which leads down into **DISCOVERY BAY** ("Disco Bay" to the *gweilo* locals), a residential New Town with its own beach, water sports facilities, shops, markets and banks. The main attraction for visitors is the route back to Central that Disco Bay offers: a hoverferry service runs every twenty to thirty minutes throughout the day, a half-hour ride which docks in Central at Blake Pier.

Any **further north** from Discovery Bay and you'll have to rely on walking to get around. There's a fairly good network of hiking trails, though nowhere particularly exciting to hike to and nowhere – other than camping in the rough countryside – to stay. The only sights, such as they are, are at **Chek Ko Wan** (Penny's Bay), a shipyard building luxury yachts, and just to the west, at **Yam O Wan**, an inlet used as a containment centre for floating timber. If you make it this far, you can return to civilisation by catching the *kaido* from Yam O Wan (at Luk Keng Tseun) over to the New Territories: it'll drop you at Tsing Lung Tau, a jetty on the main road between Tsuen Wan and Tuen Mun. Following the sparse trails beyond Chek Ko Wan, *kaido* services also link Lantau's far northeastern coast with Ma Wan Island, only a couple of minutes across the water.

Chi Ma Wan peninsula

The other short walk from Mui Wo is to the **Chi Ma Wan peninsula**, a foot of land around 4km south of the ferry pier. The most direct route there is to follow the first section of the Lantau Trail as far as Nam Shan (where there's a **campsite**) and then switch to the last section of the trail, following it south to the peninsula: you'll come out on Chi Ma Wan Road, which runs east–west across the neck of the peninsula.

East along the road it's only a short walk to **Chi Ma Wan** itself, the bay giving its name to the detention centre there for Vietnamese awaiting resettlement. From the pier, there's a handy ferry service, either back to Mui Wo or on to Cheung Chau to the south. With a good map you could make your way around the peninsula clockwise from Chi Ma Wan (there's another campsite right at the peninsula's easternmost point), but it's easier and more rewarding to take in the **western side**. There's a youth hostel there to aim for, and you can cut out the walk from Mui Wo by taking the bus (#1 or #7) from the Mui Wo ferry pier to **PUI O**, where there's an excellent beach. It's one of the most popular on the island, and there are barbecue pits here, a campsite at its eastern end and, back on the main road, a few simple restaurants. You might find a flat for rent if you ask around, or try the reasonable *Sea Breeze Hotel* on the main road.

From the bus stop on the main road at Pui O, follow the signpost (on the left) to **HAM TIN**. A concrete footpath leads you across the fields and alongside the river to a small temple, from where another

For reservation details for Mong Tung Wan hostel, see p.195. You can reach the hostel by kaido from the waterfront at Cheung Chau. Ask for Mong Tung Wan; it should cost around $100 for the boat.

signpost points up towards **Mong Tung Wan** – just under an hour's walk, with lovely views over Pui O beach. The quiet bay has a **youth hostel**, made up of white bungalows set back from the harbour – a nice, clean place, though packed to the gills on Saturday nights from June to August.

Camping is allowed here, too, but you'll have to bring your own food as the shop only sells beer and soft drinks; there are barbecue pits. The path from the hostel leads down to a tiny harbour, where there are a couple of crumbling, empty apartment blocks and the remains of the mysteriously abandoned Mong Tung Wan Country Club – wreckage and old furniture lying on the small beach and up the hillside. You could swim here, though it's rocky and a little murky. The hostel warden can arrange for a **kaido** to pick you up from the harbour and take you over to Cheung Chau: it'll cost around $100 for the boat and you'll have to order it the night before.

Yi Long and Tai Long Wan

A footpath runs on from Mong Tung Wan around the peninsula, climbing steeply above the coast, and you can clamber down to good beaches at a couple of places. At **YI LONG**, there's a swanky new private development, *Sea Ranch*, and if you don't fancy the beach there, the next bay along, **Tai Long Wan**, has some long and usually empty sands. It's hard going, though, especially to reach Tai Long Wan, and an easier way of getting there is by *kaido* from Cheung Chau's waterfront (around $80–100, depending on numbers).

The real attraction at Tai Long Wan is the **Frog & Toad** (☎989 2300), a splendid bar/restaurant at the back of the tiny village behind the beach. A three-storey village-house with a roof terrace, at the weekend it's crowded with expats drinking enormous amounts of beer and tucking in to the great pub food – ribs, sausages, salads and the Frog & Toad burger, even set Thai meals if you book them in advance. The downstairs bar turns into a sweaty disco after about the fifteenth tequila slammer and the whole thing shuts when the last person leaves. As the only realistic way out is by *kaido*, either arrange for the one that brought you from Cheung Chau to return at a certain time, or get someone at the bar to ring for one when you're ready to go. Incidentally, it's worth a phone call to check if the place is open before you leave, certainly during the week.

The south coast: Pui O to Fan Lau

Lantau's best beaches are all on the **south coast** and most are easily accessible by **bus** from Mui Wo; bus #4 (to Tong Fuk), #5 (to Shek Pik) and #2 (to Po Lin Monastery) run along the coast, so you can get off wherever you like.

Pui O beach (see above) is the closest to Mui Wo, around a fifteen-minute bus ride away. The next one along, at **CHEUNG SHA**, is considered by many to be the best in the territory. There are a couple of cafés here, serving simple Chinese food and cold drinks; a campsite, and the possibility of renting a **room** at the *Cheung Sha Resort House*.

Cheung Sha beach stretches all the way down to **TONG FUK** (more cheap Chinese cafés), where the road strikes inland to reach the **Shek Pik Reservoir**, an impressive construction whose surroundings have been planted and landscaped to provide picnic areas and walking trails. The reservoir, with a capacity of 5500 million gallons, provides much of Hong Kong with drinking water. Collected here by tunnels and gullies, it swooshes through another tunnel to Mui Wo, where a treatment centre close to the ferry pier cleans the water and pipes it to Hong Kong Island. There's a beach below the reservoir at Tai Long Wan, a short walk away.

A longer walk from Shek Pik, following a section of the Lantau Trail, leads past a couple of fairly isolated campsites to **FAN LAU**, 5km away on the southwestern tip of the island. It takes around two hours to walk from Shek Pik, via Kau Ling Chung. There are two excellent beaches here, a large east-facing one and a smaller west-facing one a few minutes' walk away, as well as the remains of a 1300-year-old rectangular **fort**, from which there are fine views across the water. Built to garrison troops, the fort overlooked a strategic sea route into the Pearl River Estuary, but was abandoned at the turn of this century. The Lantau Trail swings north from Fan Lau, with Tai O village around two to three hours' walk further on.

Tai O and around

The largest village on Lantau, **TAI O**, on the northwestern coast, was once the centre of a thriving salt export trade to China. The salt pans are still visible, though the local fishermen have converted them into fish ponds – an enterprise which hasn't stopped the village population from falling rapidly as people move to the city to look for jobs. There are still around 3000 people left in Tai O, though, and it's a favourite tourist destination, with plenty of interest in the village's old streets, shrines and temples.

The village splits into two halves: a mainland section, where the bus stops (#1 from Mui Wo; a 45-min ride), and an island settlement, across a narrow creek. There's a **rope-ferry** between the two, a twenty-second crossing on a wooden, flat-bottomed boat pulled by two villagers, a means of transport that's existed here for nearly fifty years and will continue until at least 1995, when a pedestrian bridge is planned. It costs fifty cents to make the crossing and the ferry operates continuously from 6am to midnight. From the bus stop, walk down to the main street and turn right for the small pier. Women in *sampans* will also try and inveigle you into making a slightly longer crossing, for a much higher fee – good for photo-opportunities at any rate.

Across the other side, fishermen's houses are built on stilts at the creek, and after you've looked around the small village shops and the market you can visit the local temples, sited on the island. One – built originally in the eighteenth century – is dedicated to Kwan Tai, the God of War and Righteousness, to whom people pray for protection; the other, the Hau Wong temple, facing the sea, contains the local dragon racing boat, some sharks' bones and a whale's head, found by Tai O's fishermen. This is a five-minute walk along the main street through town – the shacks either side alive with the clack of *mahjong* tiles. At the end of the village, on a small headland, there's a barbecue area and the temple, with a lovely carved roof frieze displaying two roaring dragons.

The number of tourists that descend upon Tai O also means that you'll have no trouble getting something to eat. Cross over by the rope-ferry, and at the end of the street you'll see the *Fook Moon Lam* (open 11am–9.30pm), next to the market, whose short English-language menu includes good fresh scallops and prawns.

Kwun Yam, Ng Yuen and Tsz Hing Monastery

On the way to or from Tai O, not far from the village, the #1 bus makes a stop at the **Kwun Yam temple**, where you can get a simple vegetarian meal. If you fancy a walk, there's a half-hour route from here up to **Ng Yuen**, an ornamental garden around a kilometre away, at its best in February and March. Another kilometre beyond is **Tsz Hing Monastery** – situated in one of the most islolated spots on the island and guarded by a six-metre-long stone dragon. The monks and nuns here aren't really geared up to receiving visitors, though no one will actually object if you do turn up and have a vague interest in Buddhism: Sunday is the recommended visiting day. There is accommodation available, too, but only for those seriously interested in a meditational retreat. If you're just looking, you can descend from the monastery back through Ng Yuen and then straight down to Tai O on a direct path – about an hour's walk all told.

The Po Lin Monastery and Lantau Peak

Apart from a trip to the beach, the one place that everyone makes for in Lantau is the Po Lin Monastery in the central **Ngong Ping** region, north of the Shek Pik Reservoir. There's always a massive queue for the #2 bus from Mui Wo at the weekend, but it's worth the wait, partly for the ride – past the reservoir and slowly up the valley, with swirling views below to the coast.

Around fifty minutes later the bus pulls up in front of the gates of the **Po Lin Monastery**, founded by three monks in 1905 on a plateau surrounded by mountains, including Lantau Peak itself. The temple complex is on a much grander scale than is usual in Hong Kong, more reminiscent of a Thai temple; just to reinforce the fact, on the hill behind the compound is the tallest **statue of the Buddha** in southeast Asia, a bronze seated figure 34m high, and built at a reputed cost of $68 million. The hundred monks and nuns at the monastery led a relatively peaceful existence until the 1970s, when the main temple and its pavilions were opened, since when they've been regularly besieged by swarms of people posing for photos on the temple steps and in the gardens. The main hall houses a noted group of three statues of the Buddha – fairly restrained under the circumstances, at only around three metres high each. There's nothing at all restrained about the main temple itself, which is painted and sculpted in an almost gaudy fashion. Everything else in the grounds is firmly aimed at the weekly tourist invasion. There's a huge and chattering **dining hall**, where you can get a filling meal of inventive vegetarian food (you need a coupon from the ticket office inside the temple complex): help yourself to soup and rice, sit at the table numbered on your ticket and they'll bring the rest to you. A traditional pagoda outside the dining hall shelters a pay phone and a drinks vending machine. Fans of the bizarre might wish to spend a night in this religious circus: you can book a **dormitory bed** at the meal ticket office, three meals included in the price.

Out through the main gates, a path leads up the few hundred metres to the **Lantau Tea Gardens**, Hong Kong's only tea-producing estate. Not surprisingly, this hasn't escaped the holiday camp treatment either, and there's roller skating and horse riding available here. More importantly, there's also a café where you can get a cup of Lantau's own tea. There's more accommodation available at the Tea Gardens, either in rooms or at the adjacent **youth hostel**. If you can, it's best to book both in advance.

For booking details, see p.207 (Tea Gardens) and p.195 (youth hostel).

Lantau Peak

The only real reason to stay close to the monastery – apart from the faint hope of seeing a monk on roller skates using the pay phone – is to make the early-morning hike up Fung Wong Shan, as **Lantau Peak** is properly known. A very steep path leads up from the Tea Gardens to the 934m-high peak, the second highest in Hong Kong, and renowned as an excellent venue for sunrise watching. This will mean a crack-of-dawn start, but the views are justly famous – over as far as Macau on a clear day.

The peak is on the Lantau Trail and, depending on how energetic you feel, the path then heads east, reaching the slightly lower **Tai Tung Shan**, or "Sunset Peak", after about 5km. A fairly sharpish two-hour descent from there puts you on the road at Nam Shan and within shouting distance of Mui Wo.

Tung Chung

The other main village on the island, **TUNG CHUNG**, on the northern shore below Chek Lap Kok island, was once a trading and fishing port with close links with Tai O. These days it's a quiet,

LANTAU TRAVEL DETAILS

For up-to-date ferry information, call the Hong Kong Ferry Co. ☎542 3082.

Ferries: daily

Central to Mui Wo (hourly, first at 7am, last at 11.15pm, Sat & Sun at 12.20am); Tuen Mun/Sha Lo Wan/Tai O (Sat at 2.15pm, Sun at 8.15am).

Tsim Sha Tsui to Mui Wo (Sat at 1pm, 2pm, 3pm, 5pm & 7pm; Sun hourly 9am–6pm).

Mui Wo to Central (hourly, first at 6.10am, last at 10pm); Tsim Sha Tsui (Sat at 2pm, 3pm, 4pm & 6pm; Sun hourly noon–7pm).

Tai O to Tuen Mun/Central (Sat at 5pm, this service terminating at Tuen Mun; Sun at 5.30pm, terminating at Central).

Tai Shui Hang (Trappist Haven Monastery) to Peng Chau (Mon–Sat at 8.10am, 9.30am, 11.30am, 12.30pm, 2.45pm & 4.30pm; Sun at 8.10am, 10.15am, 12.15pm, 3pm & 4.45pm).

Tung Chung to Castle Peak Bay (3 daily).

Inter-Island Ferry: daily

Mui Wo to Peng Chau (5–7 daily; first at 6.05am, last at 10.50pm); Chi Ma Wan/Cheung Chau (8 daily; first at 6.05am, last at 9.40pm).

Hoverferries: Mon–Fri only

Central to Mui Wo (at 9.40am, 11.20am, 2.25pm & 4.25pm); Discovery Bay (every 20–30min).

Mui Wo to Peng Chau/Central (at 10.20am, 12.10pm, 3.10pm & 5.10pm).

Discovery Bay to Central (every 20–30min).

Kaidos

Kaido services operate on the following routes with varying degrees of regularity; specific details are given in the text where appropriate.

Tai Shui Hang–Nim Shue Wan.

Luk Keng Tseun (Yam O Wan)–Tsing Lung Tau.

Tai Long Wan–Cheung Chau.

Mong Tung Wan–Cheung Chau.

Buses

Fares are roughly between $3 and $8 one-way, paid on board; they're a few dollars more on Sunday. Routes from Mui Wo include:

#1 to Tai O (via Pui O and Kwun Yam Temple); half-hourly until12.30am.

#2 to Ngong Ping (Po Lin Monastery); Mon–Sat hourly, Sun every 30min.

#3 to Tung Chung; hourly, first at 7.50am, last at 6.35pm.

#4 to Tong Fuk (via Nam Shan and Cheung Sha beach); Mon–Sat hourly until 10.15pm, Sun half-hourly until 10pm.

#5 to Shek Pik; Mon–Sat hourly until 6.30pm, Sun half-hourly until 7.30pm, with an extra bus at 9pm.

#7 to Pui O (via Nam Shan); Mon–Sat hourly until 11.15pm, Sun half-hourly until 7.30pm.

crumbling place, with a bit of fish farming going on by the ferry pier and some local shallot growing but little else. The one road out of the village leads past the nineteenth-century **Battery**, which once guarded the waters here, but locked gates sadly prevent you from getting a closer look at its overgrown walls and embankments. A kilometre or so further on, the road winds inland to **Tung Chung Fort**, six cannons lining its northern wall, though these days the fortifications protect a school. There was a fortress here as long ago as the seventeenth century, though this building dates back only to 1817, built on the orders of the Viceroy of Guangdong (Canton province) to defend Lantau's northern coast. Over the road from the fort are two paths, the unmarked one on the right leading back over the fields to Ma Wan Chung, the part of the village with the ferry pier and where the bus drops you. There are several **noodle shops** here if you're hungry, and a deathly quiet atmosphere – a pleasant change after the tourist antics of Ngong Ping and Tai O.

A series of good **walks** can be made in the vicinity. The obvious one is down from the Po Lin Monastery, a pleasant two- or three-hour hike which takes you past several smaller temples scattered along the Tung Chung valley. Much longer affairs are the journey from Mui Wo and the coastal walk from Tai O, both of which will take you around five hours; don't forget to take water along with you.

The bus ride (#3 from Mui Wo) is as good a reason as any to head for Tung Chung. Like the route to Ngong Ping, it's a slow climb up over the hills, before rattling down the valley to the village. You could just return to Mui Wo by bus, too, though Tung Chung has the added attraction of a **ferry** link with Castle Peak Bay in the New Territories, an hour's ride; departures are at 8am, 1pm and 4.30pm.

Near Lantau: the Soko Islands, Chek Lap Kok and Ma Wan

Several of the much **smaller islands around Lantau** provide ample evidence of the rapid depopulation of the outlying islands, as people move to Hong Kong Island and the New Territories in search of work.

The Soko Islands

The most extreme example of depopulation is the little archipelago of the **Soko Islands**, south of Lantau, which once supported viable communities, linked to Hong Kong by ferry. As the inhabitants moved out, the islands became the target of weekenders on private yachts seeking an isolated anchorage. In 1989, the last two inhabitants, an elderly couple living on Tai A Chau, the largest island, moved out, renting their home to the government who turned the Sokos into a Vietnamese "reception" centre – a desperate move to alleviate the chronic accommodation shortage for that summer's

Near Lantau:
the Soko
Islands,
Chek Lap
Kok and Ma
Wan

newly arrived Vietnamese. There was no shelter or fresh water on the Sokos at the time, and four thousand people were crammed onto an overgrown, rubbish-laden Tai A Chau – a sad way of repopulating the islands.

Chek Lap Kok

Just north of Tung Chung (on Lantau), **Chek Lap Kok** is the site of Hong Kong's controversial new international **airport**, not due to be operational until at least 1997. Given the disaster waiting to happen at overcrowded Kai Tak airport in Kowloon (which officially reached saturation point in 1993), it was only a matter of time before a new airport was proposed, but progress has not been straightforward. The environmental consequences of using Chek Lap Kok provided the initial stumbling block: mountains and peaks in the vicinity have had to be shorn, and land reclamation undertaken on a massive scale, while road and rail links will have to be engineered to connect the new airport with the mainland. A six-lane expressway, 32-kilometre high-speed rail link, double-decker suspension bridge and tunnel link to Hong Kong Island are all planned – something that's going to cost around HK$100 billion.

Local objections were over-ridden and the project is now well under way – in order to prepare the site, some 40,000 tonnes of explosive is being used to blast out 75 million cubic metres of rock. Fishermen on nearby Cheung Chau claim that the dumping of mud from the project has killed the fish, while more vociferous objections have come from the Chinese government, worried – perhaps with some justification – that the airport is a last, grand gesture from a departing British government, which won't have to foot the bill after 1997 if things go wrong. However, a financing package has now been agreed between Britain and China, and the work continues at a merry pace.

Ma Wan

There's more interest on **Ma Wan**, off Lantau's northeastern point, a strategically placed island which was once a customs control point operated by the Ching Dynasty for foreign ships approaching Kowloon. It's a fertile island, with 900 inhabitants and a main village that's still an active fishing port. However, **getting there** is a rather long-winded process. There is an hourly **kaido** service, but it departs from Sham Tseng in the New Territories: you need to take the MTR to Tsuen Wan, then the #96M minibus from the taxi/minibus terminal there.

Tsuen Wan is covered on p.144; Sham Tseng on p.148.

The *kaido* takes about ten minutes to cross to Ma Wan, passing the fish farms that line the island's northern coast. You're dropped at the main pier in **MA WAN VILLAGE**, pervaded by the odour of the local shrimp paste industry, the ingredients for which you'll see drying everywhere in the sun, laid out on round trays. There's a Tin

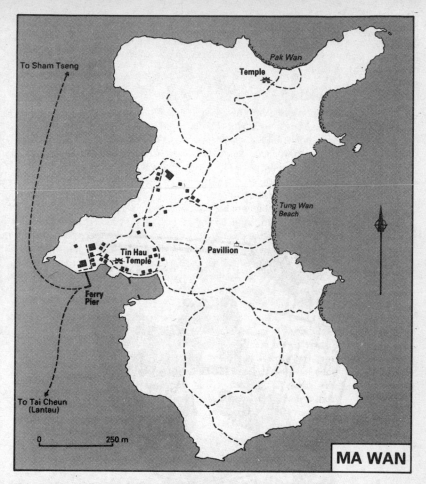

To Sham Tseng

Pak Wan

Temple

Tung Wan
Beach

Tin Hau
Temple

Pavillion

Ferry
Pier

To Tai Cheun
(Lantau)

0   250 m

MA WAN

Hau temple to the right of the pier, and one path leads off through the village to the main **Tung Wan** beach on the eastern side of the island – a 250m stretch with lifeguards and water that's all right to swim in, though you might be persuaded otherwise by the proximity of the industrial Tsing Yi Island just over the way. The rest of the island is ripe for a walk. Rather like someone's overgrown garden – lush vegetation, giant palm fronds and little ponds – it'll take around an hour to tramp the paths. Incidentally, don't think about swimming anywhere other than the east coast. The northern coast is fairly polluted, while the western shore – facing Lantau – fronts a channel known as Kap Shui Mun ("rapid water gate"). The currents here are strong, which means some entertaining manoeuvring by local boats at times. The Cheung Chau pirate Cheung Po Tsai is supposed to have lost a treasure-laden junk to the rapids here.

Hong Kong Listings

Accommodation

Accommodation in Hong Kong doesn't have to be a major expense. There are plenty of rock-bottom choices, starting at around $50 a night for a bed in a dormitory room (even cheaper if you stay in an *IYHF* hostel), which are bearable if all you're doing is passing through. However, for extended stays – even just three or four nights – they cease to be an attractive proposition: they're often crowded, dirty and hot. If you can afford a little more, then a room in a guest house with fan or air-conditioning starts at around $200–250 double, slightly more with an attached bathroom; while if money is no object, the territory has some of the world's finest hotels, offering an unparalleled degree of comfort and service.

Hong Kong has the world's highest hotel occupancy rate, and there isn't really a high or a low season as far as hotel bookings are concerned. Nevertheless, given the sheer number of options, **booking in advance** isn't strictly necessary – especially at the cheaper end of the market – if you don't mind a bit of legwork. The only time you will be chasing too few hotel beds is in the middle of Chinese New Year and at the end of March, during the Rugby Sevens weekend, but even then you should find something. Still, for peace of mind (and certainly if you want to guarantee space in one of the plusher hotels) it's as well to have your first night's accommodation sorted out before you arrive. If you want to be in Hong Kong on the last day of British rule in June 1997, note that the big

hotels are taking bookings now – and some are already full.

Airport arrivals can reserve rooms through the office of the **Hong Kong Hotel Association** in the Buffer Hall of Kai Tak airport (daily 7am–midnight; ☎383 8380). There's no booking fee, but they'll only contact hotels which are members of their association, which rules out the bulk of the budget hostels and hotels; the cheapest room you'll get through them is from around $350 double. The HKTA also issues a *Hotel Guide*, which includes maps, contact numbers and prices.

Beware of the **touts** at the airport and elsewhere, who will accost you and offer you a cheap room. The place you're taken to might, in fact, be all right, but if you decide you don't want to take the room having seen it they'll probably try and pin a charge on you for taking you there in the first place. If this happens to you, don't pay, but don't expect them to be happy about it. On the other hand, don't be too paranoid: the people handing out guest house business cards are harmless enough; you can always take the card and go and look on your own later.

The bulk of the very cheapest places – dormitories and guest houses – are Kowloon-side, in and around Tsim Sha Tsui, but with money to burn you can take your pick of the posh hotels on Hong Kong Island or in the new strip of Tsim Sha Tsui East. There is also a string of YMCAs and equivalent places, on the island and in Kowloon, offering more downmarket (but thoroughly decent)

Accommodation

hotel-style accommodation; and there's a small network of youth hostels (and a few cheap hotels) in the New Territories and on the outlying islands – both under-used options for the most part.

Dormitory Accommodation

The cheapest beds in Hong Kong are those found in **dormitory-style accommodation**, mostly located in Tsim Sha Tsui. Typically, you'll pay around $50 for a space in a multi-bedded dorm, sharing with other backpackers. There will normally be separate shower and laundry facilities, and sometimes a TV room and cooking facilities. The dorms are friendly places, good for meeting people, but can be cramped and some are less than secure. Most of the dorms are located in guest houses, which otherwise have regular rooms for rent, too. Below is a list of places with dorm space, but check the listings for more specific information.

City Guest House: p.200.

Garden Hostel: p.200.

Golden Crown Guest House: p.200.

Ocean View Guest House: p.204.

Sky Guest House: p.202.

STB Hostel: p.206.

Travellers' Hostel: p.203.

Victoria Hostel: p.204.

Youth Hostels

There are seven official *International Youth Hostel Federation* (*IYHF*) **youth hostels** in Hong Kong though only one, Ma Wui Hall on Hong Kong Island, is readily used by foreign travellers. The others are in fairly remote parts of the New Territories and on Lantau Island, but if you want to escape the cloying atmosphere of central Hong Kong, it's worth making an effort to stay at them. They are all very cheap – $25–40 per person – and have cooking and washing facilities. You'll need an *IYHF* membership card to use them, available from the national organisations in your home country: or you can buy a "Welcome Stamp" at your first Hong Kong hostel – buying six is the equivalent of having international

membership. The **head office** of the Hong Kong Youth Hostels Association is Room 225, Block 19, Shek Kip Mei Estate, Sham Shui Po, Kowloon (☎788 1638).

You must book beds at the hostels **in advance**, either by writing to or telephoning head office, or by telephoning the hostels themselves. The HKTA office in the Buffer Hall at the airport has a leaflet on how to reach the Ma Wui Hall hostel; use the free phones to check on space with the warden or the head office. The hostels are **closed** between 10am and 4pm (some are also closed one day midweek), and there are separate dormitories for men and women – although couples can sometimes get a dorm together if the hostel's empty. On Friday and Saturday nights throughout the year the New Territories hostels are nearly always packed with groups of young Chinese: go in midweek and you'll often be on your own. Also, you'll need a sheet sleeping bag, which you can hire at the hostel for a few dollars.

Mount Davis

Ma Wui Hall, Mount Davis, Hong Kong Island ☎817 5717. The most popular – and central – hostel in Hong Kong, above Kennedy Town on top of Mount Davis, with superb views. There are cooking facilities, lockers and 112 beds, but it fills quickly. Take bus #5B (destination "Felix Villas") from Des Voeux Road Central, or bus #47 from Central Bus Terminal, to beyond Kennedy Town; get off on Victoria Road at the junction with Mount Davis Road, walk back to Mount Davis Path and follow the signs up the very steep access road to the hostel – a tough, two-kilometre, half-hour climb with luggage. Or take a taxi from the Macau Ferry Terminal (around $50) or Kennedy Town (around $30).

New Territories

Bradbury Hall, Chek Keng, Sai Kung Peninsula, New Territories ☎328 2458. 100 beds; see p.160.

Bradbury Lodge, Tai Mei Tuk, Tai Po (call head office for information). 100 beds; see p.138.

Pak Sha O, Hoi Ha (Jones' Cove), Sai Kung Peninsula ☎ 328 2327. 112 beds; see p.160.

Sze Lok Yuen, Tai Mo Shan, Tsuen Wan ☎ 488 8188. 92 beds; see p.150.

Lantau

Mong Tung Wan, Chi Ma Wan peninsula ☎ 984 1389. 88 beds; see p.182.

Ngong Ping ☎ 985 5610. 48 beds; see p.185.

Guest Houses, YMCAs and Hotels

Most budget travellers end up in one of Tsim Sha Tsui's **guest houses**. Given the high rents in Hong Kong, most of them are shoe-box sized, with paper-thin walls and a turnover that's fast and furious (qualities shared by many of the owners). Often the decor looks as if someone has tried to swing a cat in the room – and failed. However, if you're prepared to spend a little more than you'd perhaps planned, you should be able to find somewhere reasonable.

Most guest houses are contained inside large mansion blocks on and **around Nathan Road** in Tsim Sha Tsui, most notoriously **Chungking Mansions** (36-44 Nathan Rd), where there are dozens of very cheap places – although many are not that inviting. Instead, you might want to try one of the other slightly more appealing, less intense blocks, like the nearby **Mirador Mansion** (56-58 Nathan Rd) or the **Lyton Building** (42-48 Mody Rd). There are periodic rumours that Chungking Mansions is to be redeveloped. It is undoubtedly a massive fire risk: fire doors (if they have them) jammed open, dangling electrical cables and few sprinkler systems. It's up to you whether you stay here or not: certainly there are other alternatives. On the other hand, Chungking Mansions has developed a reputation among travellers as a place to meet people and swap information.

When **renting your room**, *always* ask to see it first, and don't be afraid to try and bargain the price down. If you're

staying a few days, you'll often be able to get a reduction, but be wary about paying out the whole lot at once: if the guest house turns out to be roach-infested or noisy, or both, you'll have a hard job getting your money back if you want to leave early. Best advice is to take the room for a night and see what it's like before parting with your cash.

Check that the **air-conditioning** unit works – some places will make an extra charge ($20–30 per night) for air-conditioning; other rooms simply come equipped with a ceiling fan. **Bathrooms** are rarely that: rather, a tiny additional room with toilet and hand-held shower. But this is usually better than sharing what can be fairly grim communal bathrooms. Guest rooms also come with TV, though the reception in places like Chungking Mansions can leave a lot to be desired. Guest houses nearly all charge for the room, which usually sleeps two (sometimes three) people, so **single travellers** will find themselves paying over the odds – the best you can do is ask for the smallest available room, but it will often be terribly claustrophobic.

There are several **YMCAs** and **religious organisations** offering accommodation somewhere in between the most expensive of the guest houses and the cheapest of the regular hotels. The rooms are all well-appointed (with air-conditioning and TV) and comparatively spacious; most places add a ten percent service charge. Most importantly, at these prices, you can start to pick and choose the area that you want to stay in; some of the places below are in excellent locations. Rooms at all of them can be booked at the airport's accommodation office.

Hong Kong has some of the world's finest and most expensive **hotels**, competing for the massive business custom that passes through the colony. The *Peninsula* is the most famous and longest-established, an elegant colonial hotel on the Tsim Sha Tsui waterfront; of the others, the *Mandarin Oriental* is considered to be in the running for the title of the world's best hotel. There are

Accommodation

STOP PRESS: Fire regulations have recently closed down several of Chungking Mansions' guest houses. Some of those listed in this book (see p.201–203) may no longer exist; others may have re-opened under a new name or management.

Accommodation

Accommodation in this guide is classified into eight price categories. **Dormitory beds (①)** are classified according to the cost **per person per night**; the **guest house and hotel** categories refer to the amount you can expect to pay for a **double room**. Guest houses tend to have a range of rooms on offer – singles, doubles, with and without air-conditioning or bathroom – and some reviews have multiple price categories to reflect this. In hotels (roughly speaking category ④ and upwards), you can count on rooms coming with a bath-room, air-conditioning and TV. Again, most have a range of available rooms and the price categories sometimes reflect this (eg, ⑤–⑦).

① Under $60 per person
② Under $200 per room
③ $200–300 per room
④ $300–500 per room
⑤ $500–800 per room
⑥ $800–1200 per room
⑦ $1200–2000 per room
⑧ Over $2000 per room

some cheaper, mid-range hotels around if you want to avoid guest houses, though often in these you're just paying for the official designation, "hotel" – the YMCAs might prove better value. With most hotels, the only choice to be made is location since most are fitted with everything that you could possibly want – business centres, gyms and restaurants, hair stylists and gift shops.

Lots of hotels don't distinguish between singles and doubles; you're just charged for the room; breakfast is not usually included. It pays to shop around, since most places offer discounts and deals at odd times of the year. You won't find any real bargains, but you might save a couple of hundred dollars here and there. Count on adding a ten percent **service charge** and a five percent

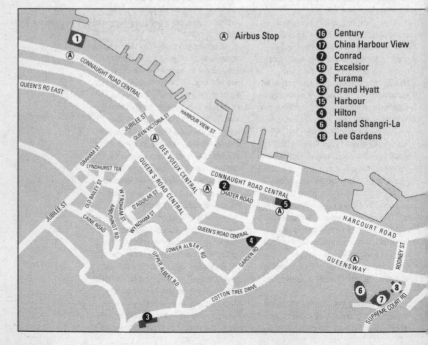

Ⓐ Airbus Stop

⑯ Century
⑰ China Harbour View
⑦ Conrad
⑲ Excelsior
⑤ Furama
⑬ Grand Hyatt
⑮ Harbour
④ Hilton
⑥ Island Shangri-La
⑱ Lee Gardens

government **tax** to the quoted room price. It's worth remembering, too, that many hotels work out better value if booked as part of an **inclusive tour**. And if you want a **harbour view**, you'll always pay much more than the standard room rate.

Central and Western

On the whole, these are the most expensive areas in Hong Kong to look for a room. There are no guest houses and the few hotels are of international quality and price – the locations, though are superb. The Airbus from the airport passes most of the hotels; otherwise, take the MTR to either Central or Sheung Wan.

Garden View International House, 1 Macdonnell Rd ☎877 3737, fax 845 6263. The only vaguely budget option in Central, this YWCA-run hotel has an excellent location, and some rooms are reserved for women only. Book well in advance. Bus #12A from Central Bus Terminal runs nearby. ⑤.

Furama Kempinski, 1 Connaught Rd ☎525 5111, fax 845 9339. Harbour or Peak views, revolving restaurant, and a faithful business clientele. ⑦

Hongkong Hilton, 2 Queen's Rd ☎523 3111, fax 845 2590. One of the island's luxury hotels, now in its fourth decade, the *Hilton* has been superseded by some of the posher, new places, but it's still supremely comfortable – with harbour views, heated pool, tennis courts and private junk for the use of guests. ⑧.

Marriott, Pacific Place, 88 Queensway ☎810 8366, fax 845 0737. Part of the flash Pacific Place complex (the first to open here) and exuding Hong Kong hi-tech. Harbour views are more expensive than the standard rooms. ⑧.

Mandarin Oriental, 5 Connaught Rd ☎522 0111, fax 810 6190. Built around the same time as the *Hilton*, the *Mandarin* is considered by many to be the best in the world: there's no faulting the service (the staff run into hundreds), facilities (the rooms have balconies) or location (close

Accommodation

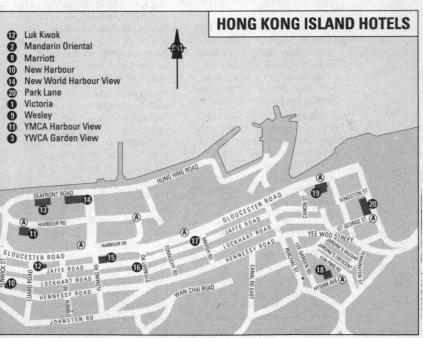

HONG KONG ISLAND HOTELS

⑫ Luk Kwok
② Mandarin Oriental
⑧ Marriott
⑩ New Harbour
⑭ New World Harbour View
⑳ Park Lane
① Victoria
⑨ Wesley
⑪ YMCA Harbour View
③ YWCA Garden View

Accommodation

① *Under $60*
per person
② *Under $200*
per room
③ *$200–300*
per room
④ *$300–500*
per room
⑤ *$500–800*
per room
⑥ *$800–1200*
per room
⑦ *$1200–2000*
per room
⑧ *Over $2000*
per room

to the Star Ferry). You don't need to stay here to appreciate its marvels – pop into the coffee shop, eat in the *Man Wah* restaurant (see p.219) or have a drink in the maritime *Clipper Lounge*. ⑧.

Hotel Victoria, Shun Tak Centre, 200 Connaught Rd ☎540 7228, fax 858 3398. Sharing the enormous Shun Tak Centre with the Macau Ferry Terminal, the *Victoria*'s large, comfortable rooms have great harbour views, and there's a pool and tennis courts – excellent value for money if you're looking for upmarket lodgings. Sheung Wan MTR, or walk along the overhead pedestrian walkway from Central. ⑦.

Wan Chai

Again, no real bargains, except for the *Wesley* and *International House*, which are popular enough to warrant booking well in advance. Mostly, the hotels here are patronised by business people: you certainly don't need to stay in Wan Chai to get the best out of its nightlife and the Arts Centre. Access is by Wan Chai MTR or from Wan Chai Ferry Pier.

Grand Hyatt, 1 Harbour Rd ☎588 1234, fax 802 0677. Part of the Convention and Exhibition Centre (along with the neighbouring *New World*), and bulging with fine harbour views, this is a prime example of the territory's bid for the business trade – massively expensive, hugely luxurious. ⑧.

 Harbour Hotel, 116–122 Gloucester Rd ☎574 8211, fax 572 2185. Mid-range hotel close to the Exhibition Centre and all the Wan Chai nightlife. There are plenty of single rooms, making this a good target for lone travellers with a budget that stretches beyond Chungking Mansions, while others have the elusive harbour view. ⑤.

 Harbour View International House, 4 Harbour Rd ☎802 0111, fax 802 9063. One of the best-value Hong Kong Island locations, and good views to boot, right next door to the Arts Centre and handy for Wan Chai ferry pier. It's operated by the YMCA, and the doubles, complete with all facilities, come at the bottom of this category. ⑥.

Luk Kwok Hotel, 72 Gloucester Rd ☎866 2166, fax 866 2622. Recently refurbished, this is one of the city's landmark mid-range hotels – famous as the hotel location used in the film *The World of Suzie Wong* (see p.83). Not that you'd recognise it anymore, with its designer treatment. Comfortable and decent value. ⑥.

New World Harbour View, 1 Harbour Rd ☎802 8888, fax 802 8833. More splendid views, as the name suggests, and the same expense-account business clientele as the *Grand Hyatt*, though the rooms are a shade cheaper. ⑧.

The Wesley, 22 Hennessy Rd ☎866, 6688, fax 866 6633. Knock-down room rates in a hotel close to the Arts Centre. ⑤–⑥.

Causeway Bay

Hong Kong's premier shopping district isn't well-endowed with decent hotels. The two listed below often feature as part of package tours, and are worth asking about if that's how you're travelling to the territory, since room rates will then be eminently affordable. Causeway Bay does have several cheap guest houses in its back streets, though most are the sort of places you rent by the hour – worth avoiding for the most part. Access is by Airbus, tram or Causeway Bay MTR.

The Excelsior, 281 Gloucester Rd ☎895 8888, fax 895 6459. Best-sited of Causeway Bay's major hotels – overlooking the water – though it's getting on in years and doesn't feature the same up-to-the-minute facilities of other similar places. Rooms are better value than at most large hotels though. ⑦.

The Park Lane, 310 Gloucester Rd ☎890 3355, fax 576 7853. With views over Victoria Park, this is the most convenient hotel for the department stores. There's a wide variety of rooms on offer. ⑦.

Tsim Sha Tsui

Most visitors – and nearly all those travelling on a budget – stay in Tsim Sha Tsui, which breaks down into several specific areas, though wherever you end up, you're supremely well sited for all the

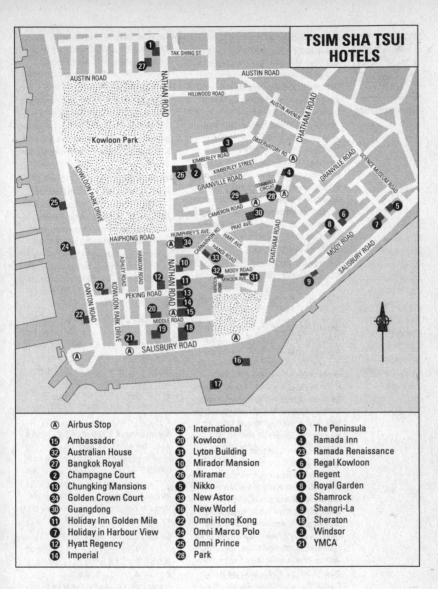

AUSTIN ROAD

TAK SHING ST

AUSTIN ROAD

HILLWOOD ROAD

AUSTIN AVENUE

CHATHAM ROAD

Kowloon Park

KIMBERLEY ROAD

OBSERVATORY RD

KIMBERLEY STREET

GRANVILLE ROAD

GRANVILLE ROAD

SCIENCE MUSEUM ROAD

KOWLOON PARK DRIVE

GRANVILLE CIRCUIT

CAMERON ROAD

MODY ROAD

HAIPHONG ROAD

PRAT AVE

HUMPHREY'S AVE

HART AVE

CARNARVON RD

HANKOW ROAD

ASHLEY ROAD

HANOI ROAD

SALISBURY ROAD

NATHAN ROAD

MODY ROAD

MINDEN AVE.

CHATHAM ROAD

CANTON ROAD

KOWLOON PARK DRIVE

PEKING ROAD

MINDEN ROW

MIDDLE ROAD

SALISBURY ROAD

N

Ⓐ Airbus Stop	㉙ International	⑲ The Peninsula
⑮ Ambassador	⑳ Kowloon	④ Ramada Inn
㉜ Australian House	㉛ Lyton Building	㉓ Ramada Renaissance
㉗ Bangkok Royal	⑩ Mirador Mansion	⑥ Regal Kowloon
② Champagne Court	㉖ Miramar	⑰ Regent
⑬ Chungking Mansions	⑤ Nikko	⑧ Royal Garden
㉞ Golden Crown Court	㉝ New Astor	① Shamrock
㉚ Guangdong	⑯ New World	⑨ Shangri-La
⑪ Holiday Inn Golden Mile	㉒ Omni Hong Kong	⑱ Sheraton
⑦ Holiday in Harbour View	㉔ Omni Marco Polo	③ Windsor
⑫ Hyatt Regency	㉕ Omni Prince	㉑ YMCA
⑭ Imperial	㉘ Park	

shops, bars, restaurants and nightlife. The main road, Nathan Road, runs the gamut from high-class hotels like the *Sheraton* and *Miramar* to the myriad cheap guest houses in Chungking Mansions and other blocks. In the streets east and west of Nathan Road, there's a similar mix: it's just to the west of the road that you'll find possibly the two best-sited hotels in the territory, the colonial *Peninsula* and the affordable *Salisbury YMCA*. The Airbus runs through the area; or Tsim Sha Tsui MTR puts you within walking distance of all the places listed below.

Accommodation

ALONG NATHAN ROAD

Ambassador Hotel, 26 Nathan Rd ☎366 6321, fax 369 0663. Right at the foot of Nathan Rd, the smart *Ambassador* is perfectly poised for jaunts over the road to the Cultural Centre. Rooms can be very good value; ones on the upper floors have views down Nathan Road (and sound-proofing keeps the traffic noise away). There's also a good restaurant here. ⑦.

City Guest House, 9th Floor, F2, Mirador Mansion, 56–58 Nathan Rd ☎724 2612. In an alternative – and slightly more appealing – mansion block to Chungking, the *City* has dorm beds as well as regular air-con rooms with TV. Discounts offered for longer stays; laundry service available. Dorms ①, rooms ③.

First Class Guest House, 16th Floor, D16, Mirador Mansion, 56–58 Nathan Rd ☎722 4935. A popular place in the Mansion, with basic singles and doubles. ②.

Garden Hostel, 3rd Floor, F4, Mirador Mansion, 56–58 Nathan Rd; entrance on Mody Road; ☎721 8567. The dorms in this well-run travellers' hostel attract small discounts if you stay more than one night; the doubles are as cheap as you'll find, with shared bathroom. Also cooking facilities, lockers, TV and noticeboard. Try and book a few days ahead since it's very popular. Dorms ①, rooms ②.

Golden Crown Guest House, 5th Floor, Golden Crown Court, 66–70 Nathan Rd ☎369 1782. Golden Crown Court is about the least awful of the blocks along Nathan Road, and this is a very friendly place, though there's not much space in the dorms and the other rooms smell musty; a couple have showers, otherwise communal bathroom. Clean, though, and with laundry facilities, China visas available and soft drinks for sale. Dorms ①, rooms ③.

Holiday Inn Golden Mile, 46–52 Nathan Rd ☎369 3111, fax 369 8016. Right next door to Chungking Mansions, which must annoy the owners, the rooms here are typically good value from the *Holiday Inn* chain, with plenty of single rooms too. There's also a pool. ⑦.

Imperial Hotel, 30–34 Nathan Rd ☎366 2201, fax 311 2360. A surprising bargain if you're looking for a real hotel on Nathan Road itself, though you'll need to book ahead. ⑤–⑥.

Kowloon Hotel, 19–21 Nathan Rd ☎369 8698, fax 739 9811. Not to be confused with the guest house in Mirador Mansion, this offers standard hotel comfort (mostly to business travellers) at reasonable rates. ⑥.

Kowloon Hotel, 13th Floor, F1 and 10th Floor, E10; reception at 13th Floor, F4, Mirador Mansion, 56–58 Nathan Rd ☎311 2523. A guest house, despite the name, the smart, well-kept rooms are looked after by a friendly set. The F1 rooms all have shower, TV and air-con – and there are fridges and an iced-water dispenser, too. The 10th floor rooms are slightly cheaper, but not as nice. Recommended. ③.

Man Hing Lung Guest House, 14th Floor, F2, Mirador Mansion, 56–58 Nathan Rd ☎722 0678 or ☎311 8807. The rooms here are very small and clean (there's barely room to dirty anything), but all come with shower, TV and air-con – the very cheapest don't have a window. The best room is no. 4, though it can be noisy. ③.

Miramar Hotel, 130 Nathan Rd ☎368 1111, fax 369 1788. Right opposite Kowloon Park, this is a fairly garish hotel, dating from the 1950s and bursting with shops. It's enormous, and pricey, but for all that is often full. If you want a view over the park, you'll need to be in a more expensive room at the top. ⑦.

Sheraton, 20 Nathan Rd ☎369 1111, fax 739 8707. Lording it over the bottom of Nathan Road, the *Sheraton* is swanky and expensive, though for the price of a cocktail you can ride the exterior elevator to the *Sky Lounge* for superb harbour views; yuppies congregate in the basement *Someplace Else* bar – both places covered in Chapter 8. The lobby, incidentally, is one of the easiest places in Tsim Sha Tsui from which to make a phonecall. ⑦–⑧.

Chungking Mansions, 36–44 Nathan Rd

Capital Guest House, Block A, 13th Floor, A6 ☎366 3455. Air-con rooms with private bathroom; fills quickly. ③.

Carlton Guest House, Block C, 15th Floor, C1 ☎721 0720. Recently refurbished, all the rooms here have private bathroom. It's friendly and good value. ③.

Centre Point Inn, Block C, 3rd Floor, C2 ☎368 5974 or ☎368 7641. Rather dated travellers' institution whose cluttered and dark interior hides no-frills singles and doubles. ④.

Chungking House, Block A, reception 5th Floor ☎366 5362. The only real hotel in the Mansions, its "de luxe" single and double rooms come with air-con, bath and TV. It's fairly large and is the only place here that the accommodation office at the airport will book for you – though, frankly, with this much money to spend, you can do better than Chungking Mansions. ④.

Dragon Garden, Block D, 5th Floor, D1 ☎311 6641. Good-value, spacious rooms with TV and air-con. ②.

Four Seas Guest House, Block D, 15th Floor, D7 ☎368 7469. Very cheap doubles. ②.

Garden Guest House, Block C, 16th Floor, C5 ☎368 0981. Clean, tidy and competitively priced doubles with shower, TV and air-con. ③.

Guangzhou Guest House, Block D, 13th Floor, D1 ☎908 38247. One small bargain bunk-bed double, and a few more expensive rooms too. Not the most welcoming management, though ②

Happy Guest House, Block B, 10th Floor, B3 ☎368 0318. Popular and friendly, you'll have to go to "reception" on the 9th floor (B3) first. Singles available, as well as doubles with fan and TV, some with bath. ②–③.

London Guest House, Block A, 6th Floor, A1 ☎366 5975. Slightly shabby, but friendly and likely to have room; the staff are very conscientious. Basic doubles, some with shower and TV, and one room with a bathtub, all at the bottom of this category. Recommended. ③

New Asia Guest House, Block A, 8th Floor, A7 ☎724 0426. There's usually room here: basic singles and doubles (some without windows), as well as bigger doubles with air-conditioning and TV; laundry service available. ②–③.

New Home Town, Block D, 10th Floor, D8 ☎723 8229. A plush place for Chungking Mansions: a carpeted hallway and comfortable twin rooms with bath and TV ("Come as a customer, go as a friend" reads the business card). ③.

New International, Block A, 11th Floor, A7 ☎369 2613. Fairly standard doubles, though each room has a fridge and TV. The staff are very helpful and speak good English; laundry service available. ③.

New Mandarin Guest House, Block E, 13th Floor, E5 ☎366 0073. Rooms with and without bath, plus air-con and TV; also singles and doubles in Block A (8th floor, A9). ②.

New Shanghai Guest House, Block D, 8th Floor, D3 ☎723 0965. Recommended place with singles, doubles and triples with shared bathroom. Rooms have fan or air-con and TV. ②

New Shangri-La, Block D, 8th Floor, D3. Favoured by long-stayers, the rooms come with air-con and TV, but the bathrooms are shared. It's popular, so getting a room might be tricky. ②.

Park Guest House, Block A, 15th Floor, A1 ☎368 1689. A guest house you can rely on, this has been renting out rooms for years. Clean, very tidy box-like singles and doubles, some with fridges and shower; rooms on the 14th floor too. ③.

Peking Guest House, Block A, 12th Floor, A2 ☎723 8320. Bargain-priced but small, doubles with air-con and TV, some with shower. The best rooms face Nathan Road, which can be a bit noisy for some; and a welcoming manager to boot. ③.

Ranjeet Guest House, Block C, 4th Floor, C1. Cramped rooms done out in lurid pink, though undeniably cheap. ②.

Rhine Guest House, Block A, 11th Floor, A8 ☎367 1991. Very friendly, family-run place with basic doubles with and without bath. ②–③.

Accommodation

① *Under $60 per person*
② *Under $200 per room*
③ *$200–300 per room*
④ *$300–500 per room*
⑤ *$500–800 per room*
⑥ *$800–1200 per room*
⑦ *$1200–2000 per room*
⑧ *Over $2000 per room*

Accommodation

*STOP PRESS:
Fire
regulations
have recently
closed down
several of
Chungking
Mansions' guest
houses. Some of
those listed in
this book may
no longer exist;
others may
have re-opened
under a new
name or
management.*

A Chungking Checklist

If you're going to stay in **Chungking Mansions** (36–44 Nathan Rd), it's as well to know what you're letting yourself in for. It's the most extreme of the mansion blocks in Tsim Sha Tsui: 17 storeys high, a festering collection of grimy, rubbish-strewn corridors, dimly lit accommodation, gift shops, basic restaurants and loitering locals.

It's next to the *Holiday Inn*. The ground and first floors are shopping arcades; the guest houses are on the floors above. Wander around and you'll find five sets of **lifts**, labelled A to E, two lifts for each block – one for the even floors, one for the odd floors. Noticeboards tell you which guest houses are on each floor: the numbers, A3, B4, etc, are the address on that floor for each guest house. Confusingly, once you're up in the Mansions, some of the **blocks** connect with each other by corridors: one wrong turn through a swing door and you could be coming down Block C having gone up Block B.

Searching for a room, it's best to leave one person downstairs with the luggage as the lifts are very small. When they get overloaded, an alarm sounds and the last one in has to get out. If you're really going to shop around, go straight to the top floor of a block and work your way down: the lists below have been drawn up on that principle.

The **drawbacks** to a stay here are immediately obvious. Big queues form for the lifts (especially Blocks A and B), and if you're staying on the 16th floor, walking up the stairs instead isn't always an option. Claustrophobics will hate the small, stainless steel lifts anyway, while some of the staircases are straight out of a Hammer horror movie. If you're lucky, the rustling noises in the large piles of abandoned rubbish are cats; and if they are cats, don't even think about stroking one.

Sheraton Guest House, Block E, 14th Floor, E5 ☎368 7981. Full marks for the optimistic name – singles and doubles with bath. A friendly enough place, you'll probably find the owner on the 3rd floor (E3). ②.

Sher-I-Punjabi, Block D, 8th Floor, D7 ☎368 0859. The extremely cheap rooms are all right, but the communal areas are less than clean and wildlife has been spotted. ②.

Sky Guest House, Block A, 3rd Floor ☎368 3960. Bargain dorm beds, kitchen and shared bathroom. Not the most salubrious place in the Mansions, but you aren't reliant on the lifts if you stay here. ①.

Sun Ying Guest House, Block A, 8th Floor, A1 ☎368 8094. There's a cheap room with bunk-beds, doubles with a shower, and scope for bargaining if you're staying more than one night – though the Saturday night prayer meetings might put off wilder types. ②–③.

Super Guest House, Block A, 17th Floor, A1; reception 12th Floor, A5 ☎368 3767. Clean singles and doubles which are larger, and – given the floor-number – quieter, than usual, away from the traffic noise. ③.

Tokyo Guest House, Block A, 13th Floor, A1 ☎367 5407. Nice big doubles and a welcoming owner. Recommended. ②.

Tom's Guest House, Block C, 16th Floor, C1 ☎367 9258. Pleasant place with a friendly owner, though the clean and cool doubles with air-con and TV (separate bathrooms) fill quickly. He has more expensive rooms with shower in Block A (8th Floor, A5), but it's worth trying here first. ②

Most of the **guest houses** themselves are all right and some are really good. A few owners run more than one place, so don't worry if you're packed off to another block or another floor when you try to check in: just make sure to see the room first and establish the price. The **lists** below let you check out the possibilities block by block, and floor by floor; cross-check with the reviews for more detailed information.

Block A

17th Floor: *Super Guest House.*
16th Floor: *Traveller's Hostel.*
15th Floor: *Park Guest House.*
13th Floor: *Capital Guest House;*
Tokyo Guest House.
12th Floor: *Peking Guest House.*
11th Floor: *New International;*
Rhine Guest House.
8th Floor: *Sun Ying Guest House;*
New Asia Guest House.
7th Floor: *Welcome Guest House.*
6th Floor: *London Guest House.*
5th Floor: *Chungking House.*
3rd Floor: *Sky Guest House.*

Block B

10th Floor: *Happy Guest House.*
9th Floor: *Wing Wah.*

Block C

16th Floor: *Tom's Guest House;*
Garden Guest House.
15th Floor: *Carlton Guest House.*
4th Floor: *Ranjeet Guest House.*
3rd Floor: *Centre Point Inn.*

Block D

15th Floor: *Four Seas Guest House.*
13th Floor: *Guangzhou Guest House.*
10th Floor: *New Home Town.*
8th Floor: *New Shanghai Guest House; New Shangri-La;*
Sher-I-Punjabi.
5th Floor: *Dragon Garden.*

Block E

14th Floor: *Sheraton Guest House.*
13th Floor: *New Mandarin Guest House.*

Accommodation

Travellers' Hostel, Block A, 16th Floor ☎368 7710. Best-known of the backpackers' hostels, with mixed dorm beds, a few singles, as well as regular doubles. Also with kitchen, TV, lockers, showers and good noticeboard. However, the wierdos the hostel sometimes attracts make it one to avoid for a long-term stay. China visas sorted out at the travel agency next door. Dorms ①, rooms ②–③.

Welcome Guest House, Block A, 7th Floor, A5 ☎721 7793. A recommended first choice; air-con doubles with and without shower. Nice clean rooms, luggage storage, laundry service and China visas available. ②.

Wing Wah, Block B, 9th Floor, B4 ☎721 9475. Good-value, clean rooms with air-conditioning and TV; communal bathrooms. ②.

EAST OF NATHAN ROAD

Australian House, 2nd Floor, 1 Minden Ave ☎368 4235. A popular place and often full. Doubles with and without bath; discounts for longer stays – worth considering for an extended stop, though it can be difficult to get in in the first place. ④.

Hotel Flora, 2nd Floor, Champagne Court, 16 Kimberley Rd ☎723 7382. Round the back of the *Miramar*, Champagne Court is not as upmarket as its name suggests, but it's a mite posher than the other mansion blocks in the area. The hotel is secure, the good rooms have attached bathrooms, and the people are friendly. ④.

Guangdong Hotel, 18 Prat Ave ☎739 3311, fax 721 1137. No real bargain, but within staggering distance of some of the better bars and restaurants. Rooms are pricier the higher up the building you go. ⑥.

① *Under $60 per person*
② *Under $200 per room*
③ *$200–300 per room*
④ *$300–500 per room*
⑤ *$500–800 per room*
⑥ *$800–1200 per room*
⑦ *$1200–2000 per room*
⑧ *Over $2000 per room*

Accommodation

International Hotel, 33 Cameron Rd ☎366 3381, fax 369 5381. One of the better of Tsim Sha Tsui's mid-range hotels. Hardly overladen with facilities, but good value if you're looking for hotel comfort. ⑤–⑥.

Lee Garden Guest House, 8th Floor, 34–36 Cameron Rd ☎367 2284. Decent singles, doubles and triples with bath, air-con and TV; at the bottom of this category. ④

Lyton House Inn, Lyton Building, 42–48 Mody Rd, rear Ground Floor; through the arcade and right; ☎367 3791. The Lyton Building (on the south side of Mody Road, beyond Blenheim Ave) has a few guest house options. This is one of the longest-standing, whose big doubles with shower are modern and clean – not a bad choice for women travellers. ④.

On Sun Tat, 7th Floor, Flat F, Champagne Court, 16 Kimberley Rd ☎723 9143. The pleasant people here have well-kept rooms with shower, air-conditioning and TV (ask in the travel agency). A good first call, since the rooms are cool and quiet, if not enormous; most of them have a window. If they don't have room, you could try the *Flora* in the same block (see above). ③.

Princess Guest House, 29 Chatham Rd South ☎366 8216. Away from the Chungking crowd, and probably worth trying for that reason alone. Reasonable rooms at the lower end of this category. ⑤.

Tourist House, Lyton Building, 42–48 Mody Rd, 6th Floor; use lift 3; ☎721 8309. Doubles with shower and TV, though the small rooms are nothing special. It might also be "full" to Westerners. ③.

Travellers' Home, 1 Minden Ave ☎723 3579. Pricier than usual doubles; and a strict 2am curfew, which may curtail your evening explorations. ④.

Victoria Guest House, 2nd Floor, 4 Minden Ave ☎366 8508. Owned by the same people who operate the hostel on Hankow Rd, the air-con rooms here aren't bad value. ③.

WEST OF NATHAN ROAD

Ramada Renaissance, 8 Peking Rd ☎375 1133, fax 375 1066. Serious prices for rooms for jaded business travellers – there are even fax machines provided, as well as TVs and all the usual comforts, including a pool. It's at the Canton Road end of the street. ⑦.

Ocean View Guest House, 5th Floor, 15 Ashley Rd. A bold name for this unmarked hostel with a green door, next to a beauty parlour. Basic dorm rooms. ①.

Omni, Harbour City, Canton Rd; *The Hongkong* ☎736 0088, fax 736 0011; *Marco Polo* ☎736 0888, fax 736 0022; *Prince* ☎736 1888, fax 736 0066. The massive Harbour City development houses three different hotels under the same *Omni* umbrella. They're all fairly fancy, and you can use each hotel's facilities at will; the rest of the time, you'll spend lost in the endless shopping mall corridors. Only the *Hongkong* (the largest) has harbour views. ⑦.

The Peninsula, Salisbury Rd ☎366 6251, fax 722 4170. Far and away the grandest hotel in Hong Kong, the *Pen*, as it's known, has been putting visitors up in unrivalled style since the late 1920s. Its elegant colonial wings have been overshadowed by the new central extension which is set to dominate the Tsim Sha Tsui skyline. Service is impeccable, as you might expect; its restaurants among the best places in the territory to eat. At least drop in for afternoon tea, which lets you gawp at the splendid lobby; and see p.112 for more on its history. ⑧.

Victoria Hostel, 33 Hankow Rd ☎376 1696. Small, mixed dorms – cheaper without air-con – cooking facilities and a little sitting-out area. ①

YMCA: The Salisbury, 41 Salisbury Rd ☎369 2211, fax 739 9315. Spruced up and expanded, this is the best semi-cheap hotel location in this part of town, next to the *Peninsula* and in the middle of Tsim Sha Tsui. It may be a Y, but the facilities are excellent, including a good café. The air-con doubles with TV and shower are booked up weeks in advance – try making a reservation *two months* ahead. ⑤.

LANTAU

Cheung Sha Resort House, Cheung Sha. Self-contained apartments big enough to sleep six (the price doubles at the weekend). ⑤–⑥.

Lantau Tea Gardens, Ngong Ping ☎985 5161. Cheap rooms available close to the monastery; very busy at the weekend, with discounts from Monday to Thursday. ③.

Mui Wo Inn, Mui Wo ☎984 8597. Further along from the *Silvermine Beach*, this small hotel has attractive rooms with a balcony and cheaper rooms at the back. ④.

Sea Breeze Hotel, Pui O ☎984 7977. On the main road and popular with weekenders who pack out the nearby beach. ④.

Silvermine Beach Hotel, Mui Wo ☎984 8295. Overlooking the beach at Silvermine Bay, this is comfortable, almost luxurious, and great value for money compared to the hotels back in the centre. Rooms are discounted from Sunday to Thursday. ⑤–⑥.

Camping

There are around forty official **campsites** throughout the territory, most in the various Country Parks. There are large concentrations on Lantau Island and on the Sai Kung Peninsula in the New Territories; several of the most usefully sited are detailed in the text. All of them cost just a few dollars and you can't reserve a space, making getting there early at the weekend or on a public holiday a good idea. All the sites have basic facilities: toilets, barbecue pits and a water supply. But generally you'll need to take your own food and equipment, and be prepared to walk to most of them as they're often well away from shops and villages. There's a free combined information sheet/map of the sites called *Campsites of Hong Kong Country Parks*, available from the HKTA.

You can sometimes camp at the youth hostels on Lantau and out in the New Territories; see the list at the beginning of this chapter and call first to check before setting out. Camping this way, you'll be able to use the hostel facilities, too.

Accommodation

Chapter 7

Eating

Don't underestimate the importance of **food** in Chinese culture. Meals are a shared, family affair, full of opportunity to show respect for others – by the way the food and drink is served, accepted and eaten. Although they're generally informal in tone, there's a structured form to each meal which reflects the importance of the food being eaten. As a visitor, especially as a foreigner, the nuances might pass you by, but it will soon become apparent that the Hong Kong Chinese live to eat – every café and restaurant is noisy and packed, the shrill interiors more reminiscent of school cafeterias than fancy eateries. On the street, too, stalls and stands do a constant, brisk trade in snacks and cheap meals.

Almost everyone eats out regularly and the vast Chinese restaurants organise their opening hours around the long working days of most of the population. You can also pick and choose from one of the world's widest selections of cuisines. Quite apart from the **regional Chinese** variations on offer – of which the local **Cantonese** cooking is the most familiar to foreigners – there isn't any kind of **Asian** food you can't sample, from Burmese to Vietnamese. Probably the biggest surprise is the number of excellent **Indian** and **Pakistani** restaurants in the territory. **American** and **European** food is well-represented, too, though it's cooked with varying degrees of skill: generally speaking, the high-class hotel, French and Italian restaurants are good, but other food can often leave a lot to be

desired. There's also a catch-all category of **international** restaurants and bars, where you can eat anything from burgers and steaks to nouvelle cuisine. At the other end of the scale, most bars and pubs put on **British**-style food of the pie-and-chips variety,

Food needn't be expensive, certainly if you stick to Chinese and Asian restaurants. The important thing is to retain your spirit of adventure at all times: some of the best dining experiences in Hong Kong are in the most unlikely-looking places, and some of the best food is eaten almost in passing, on the street or taken quickly in a *dim sum* restaurant or café.

The **listings and reviews** below should help you decide where and what to eat in Hong Kong. We've started with breakfast, street food, and snacks, cafés and delis, followed by *dim sum* restaurants and Chinese food in its various guises, succeeded by all the other cuisines available in the territory, listed in alphabetical order. At the end of the chapter are details for buying your own food in **markets and supermarkets**.

You'll find **descriptions** of Cantonese food, including *dim sum*, as well as other regional Chinese food and Asian cuisines in the introductions to the various sections. **Vegetarian** restaurants, and those that serve vegetarian meals, are included throughout, though bear in mind that the only solely vegetarian places are either Cantonese or Indian/Pakistani – there's a round-up on p.236. To go straight to the listings for the kind of food

Eating

you want to eat, check the **food index** above.

The **opening hours** given throughout are daily, unless otherwise stated. Don't count on being able to use **credit cards** everywhere. Many restaurants – especially the smaller ones – will only take cash, so always check first if you're unsure.

Breakfast

The traditional Chinese breakfast is **congee**, a gruel made from rice boiled for a long time in lots of water, served with chopped spring onions or morsels of meat or fish. It's available from some early opening restaurants or street stalls (*dai pai dongs*), and often comes with long sticks of fried dough – a bit like doughnuts. Congee is an acquired taste, but it's something that Chinese kids get used to from a very early age, since it's virtually force-fed to babies and sick children. It's more appealing to breakfast on **dim sum** (see below), served from selected restaurants, many of which erect stalls outside to sell takeaway *dim sum* to passers-by – though the stalls have usually disappeared by 9am or so. **Western breakfasts** – cooked and Continental – are available in most of the bigger hotels, and in cafés and pubs,

especially in Tsim Sha Tsui – some of the best are picked out below.

Central

Dan Ryan's Chicago Bar and Grill, 114 The Mall, Pacific Place, 88 Queensway. American restaurant (see p.226) serving classic breakfasts – eggs, pancakes and all the fixings. Served 7.30–11am.

Delifrance, 1st Floor, 16–18 Queen's Rd. Breakfast combos from $12–20, and usually a quiet place for a coffee.

Hilton Hotel Coffee Shop, 2 Queen's Road. Superb American buffet breakfast served from 7–11am for $120.

Joyce Café, The Galleria, 9 Queen's Rd. Set breakfast menus in Central's smartest café. Served 8am–noon.

Mad Dogs, 8 Wyndham St. A pub with great all-day British breakfasts, as well as a lighter continental breakfast and fresh fruit plates. There's a second branch at 32 Nathan Rd, Tsim Sha Tsui.

Mandarin Oriental Hotel, 5 Connaught Rd. ☎ 522 0111. *The* serious hotel breakfast, served in *The Grill Room*; around $220 gets you unlimited stabs at an enormous buffet, from fresh fruit juice and cereals, eggs and all the works, through to strudels and cheese. A supreme feast, served from 7–11am.

Eating

Wan Chai and Causeway Bay

Old China Hand, 104 Lockhart Rd, Wan Chai. All day fry-ups, just the thing after a night on Wan Chai's tiles.

Panash, *Daimaru*, Household Square, Kingston St/Cleveland St, Causeway Bay. Superb bakery with adjacent café for speciality breads, cakes, sandwiches, fresh fruit juices and good coffee. Open 10.30am–9.30pm; closed Wed.

Phoenix Congee and Noodle, 13–15 Cleveland St, Causeway Bay. Congee and all the trimmings for a real Cantonese breakfast; noodles too. Open 7.30am–11.30pm.

Happy Valley

Superbowl, 21 King Kwong St. Congee as an art form and as tasty as it comes, but relatively pricey. Open 11am–11pm.

Tsim Sha Tsui

An American Place, Carnarvon Plaza, 20 Carnarvon Rd. Coffee, bagels and muffins for homesick Americans.

Cherikoff, 184 Nathan Rd. Good, budget Western breakfasts, and coffee and cakes served all day.

Chungking Mansions, 36–44 Nathan Rd. Cheap curried breakfast, for those with cast-iron constitutions, at *Kashmir Fast Food* (Ground Floor, no. 17) and *Lahore Fast Food Centre* (Ground Floor, no. 19); served from around 8am.

Kowloon Shangri-La Hotel, 64 Mody Rd ☎721 2111. Enormous buffet breakfast in the *Lobby Lounge* for around $140 a head. Served Mon–Sat 7–10am.

Mall Café, Ground Floor, *YMCA*, 41 Salisbury Rd. Favourite Tsim Sha Tsui spot for a leisurely breakfast; Continental, English or Chinese for $30–40. The Hong Kong daily papers are available and there are free coffee refills from the roving staff. Served from 7–11am

South China Restaurant, 104 Austin Rd. Cut-priced Western breakfast available. Open from 8am.

Starlight Express, Cultural Centre Restaurant Block, Salisbury Rd. Standard sit-down Cantonese caff (one of a chain) with budget breakfasts for those hanging out for ham and eggs; rotten coffee, though. Open Mon–Sat 8am–10pm, Sun 9am–10pm.

YMCA International House, 23 Waterloo Road, Yau Ma Tei. Continental or American breakfast in the restaurant for around $45–55. Served 7.30–10.30am.

Street Food: Dai Pai Dongs

You'll find it hard to resist the **street food** in Hong Kong: a short walk through some of the most densely populated parts of the territory gives you the choice of dozens of different snacks, all sold at incredibly cheap prices. If you're worried about **hygiene**, most of the snacks are fairly innocuous anyway, made out of fresh or preserved ingredients, while more elaborate food – noodles and the like – is freshly cooked in front of you.

The street stalls you'll see all over the territory are called **dai pai dongs**. Most are mobile mini-kitchens and you just point to what you want and pay, usually just a few dollars for most things. Common snacks are fish, beef and pork balls (threaded onto bamboo sticks and dipped in chilli sauce), fresh and dried squid, spring rolls, steamed buns, won ton (stuffed dumplings), simple noodle soups, pancakes, congee (rice gruel served with a greasy, doughnut-type stick), cooked intestines, tofu pudding and various sweets. In some places – open-air and indoor markets and on a couple of the outlying islands – dai pai dongs are more formal affairs, grouped together with simple tables and chairs, and with more elaborate food: seafood, mixed rice and noodle dishes, stews and soups, and bottled beer. There'll rarely be a menu, but everything will still be dirt cheap, and you should be able to put together a decent meal for around $30–40.

The following central Hong Kong and Kowloon locations are the most accessible places to sample *dai pai dong* food. Every New Territories town has its own particular area for *dai pai dongs*, as do various of the outlying islands; see the text for more details.

Graham St market, at the bottom of Stanley St, Central.

Haiphong Rd, bottom of Kowloon Park, Tsim Sha Tsui.

Hau Fook St, Tsim Sha Tsui. Off Carnarvon Road, between Cameron Road and Granville Street, the street tables here serve basic Cantonese and Shanghai food, especially seafood.

Luard Rd, opposite Southorn Playground, Wan Chai.

Sheung Wan Market, Urban Council Complex, 345 Queen's Rd Central. The Cooked Food Market on the second floor is one of the more exhilarating culinary experiences in town: no frills, no foreigners, open 6am–2am.

Sutherland St and Hing Lung St, off Des Voeux Rd, Sheung Wan.

Temple St, Yau Ma Tei. Reliable seafood-based street food at the Temple Street Night Market, from 7pm; see p.119.

Fast food, Cafés and Delis

Chinese and European/American **fast-food shops** exist everywhere. All the familiar Western burger and pizza joints are represented in Hong Kong, though *McDonald's* seems to have a stranglehold on the market. Burgers here are the same as anywhere else in the world, though prices are around half (or less) of what you'd pay at home – kept low in order to establish American fast-food in a culture that has been producing its own more appetising version for thousands of years. Burger bars are now sadly popular with Chinese kids; they are also, incidentally, the cheapest places to get a cup of coffee and a welcome blast of air-conditioning. A couple of Chinese chains sell Asian-influenced snacks (radish cake, chicken wings and the like) and there are some excellent Chinese **cake shops**, too.

Cafés, often just hole-in-the-wall jobs, dish out polystyrene and foil boxes of more substantial food – rice and meat, noodles, etc – which you can generally eat perching on a stool or take away, for around $15–30 a go.

Other Western delights include a growing number of **sandwich bars** and **delis**, a few good **ice cream shops**, and some fine department store and shopping-mall **coffee shops**.

You can sometimes get non-Chinese **tea** in cafés and snack bars (but not in restaurants): it's generally *Liptons* and comes hot or cold on request. It's common to drink it with lemon; tea with milk is much more rare – if you want milk, it will normally be the condensed variety. For real milk and tea, venture into one of the big hotels for **afternoon tea**, something which is well worth doing at least once for the atmosphere. **Coffee** is the more usual hot drink, but it's invariably weak and instant and again served with condensed milk, and sugar unless you specify otherwise – for the real stuff, you'll need to visit either the hotels, a European restaurant or coffee shop. Coke and all the usual international fizzy **soft drinks** are available from stalls and shops everywhere, as are a variety of **fruit juices** – though the small boxed ones are packed with sugar and additives. Fresh fruit juice is always expensive. Try the **local soft drinks**: *Vitamilk* is a plain or flavoured soya milk drink – a few dollars a carton – while lemon tea, chocolate milk and lots of other infusions all come cold and in cartons. Regular **milk** isn't drunk very much by the Cantonese (who have a lactose intolerance), but you can buy it in supermarkets.

Territory-wide café and fast food chains

Burger King. Outlets at 59 Des Voeux Rd, Central, and 26 Granville Rd, Tsim Sha Tsui.

Café de Coral. Chinese takeaway snacks from a bright, plastic interior. Chicken wings, radish cakes, salads and sandwiches at low prices.

Ka Ka Lok. Chinese takeaway snacks and meals; cheap and plastic.

Kentucky Fried Chicken. Branches at 6 D'Aguilar St, Central; 40 Yee Woo St, Causeway Bay; 2 Cameron Rd, Tsim Sha Tsui; 241 Nathan Rd, Yau Ma Tei.

Eating

Eating

Food Courts

Hong Kong has several Food Courts – areas in shopping malls devoted to inexpensive takeaway shops serving different types of food. Pick and mix your cuisine and sit at one of the central tables. The best food courts are:

The Majestic Centre, 348 Nathan Rd, Tsim Sha Tsui.

Shop 029, Marine Deck, Ocean Terminal, Basement, Harbour City, Canton Rd, Tsim Sha Tsui.

Seibu, The Mall, Pacific Place, 88 Queensway, Central.

Maxim's. BBQ chicken legs, hamburgers, salads, roast meat dishes, drinks and sandwiches. Good cake shops, too, at MTR and KCR stations, and at the Star Ferry terminals.

McDonald's. Two 24-hour restaurants at 21 Granville Rd and 12 Peking Rd (both in Tsim Sha Tsui), plus many other branches.

Pizza Hut. The many branches, include B1, Edinburgh Tower, The Landmark, 11–19 Queen's Rd Central; 1 Kowloon Park Drive, Tsim Sha Tsui; Shop 008, Ocean Terminal, Harbour City, Canton Rd, Tsim Sha Tsui.

Starlight Express. Cantonese café chain with Western and Chinese meals and snacks.

Delis and sandwich shops

Beverly Hills Deli, Level 2, New World Centre, 18 Salisbury Rd, Tsim Sha Tsui. American-style deli; see "American" for details. Open 10.30am–10pm.

Delicatessen Corner, Shop 103, Mezzanine Floor, Hutchison House, Central; 1st Basement, *Holiday Inn Golden Mile*, Tsim Sha Tsui. Lunch boxes, soups, salads and sandwiches; Central branch is counter service only 9am–5pm; *Holiday Inn* branch open 7.30am–10.30pm

Delifrance, A1–A3 Queensway Plaza (at the entrance to the Lippo Centre), Admiralty. A pseudo-French deli selling croissants, French paté sandwiches and decent cakes – a few tables inside, too, if you want to sit down. Open 9am–6pm.

Giants Sandwiches, 53 Wellington St, Central. Recommended sandwiches; there's a small seating area. Open 7.30am–7.30pm.

Oliver's Super Sandwiches. Reliable deli and sandwich shop chain with nearly 20 branches, including Shop 104, Exchange Square II, 8 Connaught Place, Central; Shop 201–205, Prince's Building, 10 Chater Rd, Central; Shop A, Fleet House, 38 Gloucester Rd, Wan Chai; Shop G, Windsor House, 311 Gloucester Rd, Causeway Bay. All open Mon–Sat 8am–6pm.

Tiffany Delicatessen, 13–14 Connaught Rd, Central (Ground Floor of Euro Trade Centre). Takeaway sandwiches; freshly baked European-style bread, cooked meats, smoked fish, cakes and wines. Open 8am–5pm.

Victoria Deli, Shop 233a, Shun Tak Centre, 200 Connaught Rd, Central, Sheung Wan. Salads, sandwiches, cakes and freshly baked European bread to take away. Open 9am–8pm.

Cafés and coffee shops

Dragon Restaurant, 508 Lockhart Rd, Causeway Bay. Cantonese café meals, as well as cheap set European lunches. Open 7am–midnight.

Joyce Café, The Galleria, 9 Queen's Rd, Central. In a league of its own for stylish café surroundings, this is an expensive place to eat, though there are set breakfast menus and afternoon tea is served. Otherwise it's soups, sandwiches, pastas and salads for Central's smart set. Open Mon–Sat 8am–7.30pm.

Martino, 68 Paterson St, Causeway Bay. Japanese-style coffee shop serving a variety of good, freshly ground coffee and snacks. Open noon–midnight.

Pacific Coffee Company, Ground Floor, Bank of America Tower, Shop 1C, Central. Real filter coffee, good fruit juices and cakes.

Point Chaud, 15 Chiu Lung St (off Queen's Rd), Central. Stand-up café and French bakery with set lunches, sandwiches, salads, crepes/waffles and coffee and (Western) tea.

Afternoon Tea

If you're gasping for a real cup of tea, British-style with proper milk and all the trimmings, then some of Hong Kong's most splendid hotels do the honours. The lobby lounges are generally the places to head for, among which the **Peninsula** (Salisbury Rd, Tsim Sha Tsui) is the most magnificent – all gilt and soaring pillars and a string quartet playing as you munch at the tea and scones. Other marvellous venues for afternoon tea are at the **Regent** (Salisbury Rd, Tsim Sha Tsui); the **Omni Hongkong Hotel** (3 Canton Rd, Tsim Sha Tsui), the Grand Hyatt (1 Harbour Rd, Wan Chai) and the **Mandarin Oriental** (5 Connaught Rd, Central). At all these places, expect to pay around $120 per person for a set tea.

Sweet Things

Ice cream: best either from *Haagen Dazs Ice Cream Shop* (World Wide Plaza, Pedder St, Central; 132 Nathan Rd, Tsim Sha Tsui); branches of *Dairy Farm Ice Cream Express* (central ones at Hong Kong-side and Kowloon-side Star Ferry terminals, and at 74 Nathan Rd, Tsim Sha Tsui); and *Movenpick* (44 Hankow Rd, Tsim Sha Tsui).

Pancakes: from the vendor at the bottom of Blake Pier, Central; freshly cooked pancakes smeared with margarine, peanut butter and condensed milk; always a queue.

Pokka, *Daimaru*, Household Square, Kingston St, Causeway Bay. Coffee by the cup in the department store coffee shop, or buy the beans from a fine variety on offer.

Queen's Café, 39–41 Lee Garden Rd, Causeway Bay. Three-course Western meals for under $75, plus affordable curries, spaghetti, hamburgers, sandwiches and drinks. An attached bakery, too, for cakes and pastries. Open 11am–11.30pm.

South China Restaurant, 104 Austin Rd, Tsim Sha Tsui. A cheap café with reasonably priced European set meals. Open 8am–11pm.

Uncle Russ, Lippo San Plaza, Ground Floor, 406 Canton Rd, Tsim Sha Tsui. Excellent filter coffee and cookies too. Open 9am–6pm.

Wing Lok Yuen, 19 Chiu Lung St (off Queen's Rd), Central. Set lunches (Chinese and European) – soup, main dish and coffee/tea for around $40. Open 8am–9pm.

Dim Sum

Some of the most exciting of all Cantonese food is **dim sum**, which, literally translated, means "to touch the heart". Basically, it's steamed or braised stuffed dumplings, small cakes and other appetisers served in little bamboo baskets. This might not sound like much, but there are scores of different varieties. There's a list of the most common dishes given below, but everyday items include pork, prawn, crab, beef or shark's fin dumplings, as well as spring rolls, prawn toast, rice and cooked meats in lotus leaves, curried squid, chicken feet, turnip cake, stuffed peppers, pork and chicken buns, custard tarts and steamed sweet buns.

Restaurants that specialise in *dim sum* **open early** in the morning, from around 7am, and serve right through lunch up until around 5pm; nearly all regular Cantonese restaurants also serve *dim sum*, usually from 10–11am until 3pm. If you can't make breakfast, the best time is before the lunch rush – say around noon; after lunch there won't be much left. The opening hours given in the reviews below (daily, unless otherwise stated) are the *dim sum* hours for that particular restaurant: most of the places convert into regular restaurants for the evening session.

Getting in and finding a table

Most *dim sum* restaurants are enormous, often with tables on several floors; in the smarter places, staff with two-way radios check on space before letting you through. Also, many are decorated in a completely

DIM SUM TERMS

If you can't find what you want, try approximating the following sounds to order *dim sum*.

Savouries

Steamed prawn dumplings	*har gau*	虾餃
Steamed beef ball	*au yuk*	牛肉丸
Steamed spare ribs in spicy sauce	*pai gwat*	排骨
Steamed pork and prawn dumpling	*siu mai*	烧卖
Steamed bun stuffed with barbecued pork	*cha siu bau*	叉烧包
Gelatinous rice-flour roll stuffed with shrimp/meat	*cheung fun*	長粉
Steamed glutinous rice filled with assorted meat, wrapped in a lotus leaf	*nor mai gai*	糯米鸡
Deep-fried stuffed dumpling served with sweet and sour sauce	*won ton*	云吞
Half-moon shaped steamed dumpling with meat/shrimp	*fun gwor*	粉角
Congee (thick rice gruel, flavoured with shredded meat and spring onion)	*djuk*	粥
Spring roll	*chun kuen*	春卷
Turnip cake	*law bak go*	蘿蔔糕
Chicken feet	*fung jao*	鳳爪
Stuffed beancurd	*yeung do fu*	釀豆腐
Taro/yam croquette	*woo kok*	蕃薯糊角
Crabmeat dumplings	*hie yuk gau*	蟹肉餃
Shark's fin dumplings	*yu chi gau*	魚翅餃
Curried squid	*gar li yau yu*	咖喱丝魷魚卷
Steamed, sliced chicken wrapped in beancurd	*gai see fun kuen*	雞丝粉卷
Fried, stuffed green pepper	*yeung chen jiu*	釀青椒
Deep-fried beancurd roll with pork/shrimp	*seen chuk guen*	鮮春卷
Steamed dumpling with pork and chicken	*guon tong gau*	猪肉雞水餃
Steamed chicken bun	*gai bau tsei*	雞仔包
Barbecued pork puff	*cha siu so*	叉烧酥
Mixed meat croquette	*ham shui kok*	咸水角

Sweets

Water chestnut cake	*ma tai go*	馬蹄糕
Sweet beancurd with almond soup	*do fu fa*	豆腐花
Sweet coconut balls	*nor mai chi*	糯米池糕
Steamed sponge cake	*ma lai go*	馬孔果布丁
Mango pudding	*mango bo din*	芒蓉飽
Sweet lotus seed paste bun	*lin yung bau*	蓮蓉飽
Egg-custard tart	*daan tat*	蛋撻

over-the-top fashion: they're used for wedding receptions and parties, and so are covered in dragons, swirls and painted screens, ornate backgrounds that can easily cost millions of Hong Kong dollars.

Going in, you'll either be confronted by a *maitre'd*, who'll put your name on a list and tell you when there's space, or you can just walk through and fight for a table yourself. It's busiest at lunchtime and on Sunday when families come out to eat, when you'll have to queue. This is not an orderly concept: just attach yourself to a likely looking table where people appear to be finishing up, and hover over the seats until they leave. Any hesitation and you'll lose your table, so keep an eye out.

It's best to **go in a group** if you can, in order to share dishes. As all the tables seat about ten or more, you'll be surrounded by others anyway, which is fun if the experience is new to you.

How to order, how to pay

Sit down and you'll be brought **tea** – apt since if you're Chinese you don't go just to eat *dim sum*, but to *yam cha* ("drink tea"). You don't pay for this, though in some places there'll be a small cover charge. Foreigners will generally be given jasmine tea (*heung ping*), which is light and fragrant, but the Chinese mostly drink *bo lay*, a strong black or fermented tea which is good at cutting through the oil and stodge. If you want this (and hot water too, to dilute it), ask for *bo lay gwan soy*. When you want a refill, just leave the top off the teapot and it'll be replaced for free.

At this stage, if you're Chinese you'll have already started to wash your chopsticks and rinse your bowls in the hot tea or water: everything's clean anyway, but it's almost an obsession with some people.

In most places you'll see **trolleys** being wheeled through the restaurant. They contain the bamboo baskets which, typically, contain three or four little dumplings or similar-sized bites to eat. Somewhere, too, there'll be people frying stuffed vegetables at mobile stands, others with trays of spring rolls and cakes,

and different trolleys dispensing noodle soups, congee and other food. Just flag down the trolleys as they pass and see what you fancy by lifting the lids. Each time you pick something, the basket or plate will be dumped on the table, and a mark made on a card left at your table when the tea was brought. In some of the more upmarket *dim sum* restaurants, you'll have to order your dishes from the kitchen, in which case there'll invariably be a short menu in English on the table.

When you've finished, cross your chopsticks over the pile of rubble left on your table and flag down a waiter, who will take your card. He or she counts the number of empty baskets/plates on the table, checks it off against the ticks on your card and goes away to prepare the bill. Most things **cost** the same, just twenty to thirty dollars a basket. Even if you absolutely stuffed yourself on *dim sum*, you'd find it hard to spend more than $70–80 a head, perhaps as much as $120 if you ate in one of the fancier, famous *dim sum* places. On top of this, you'll nearly always pay a ten percent service charge.

Central

Blue Heaven, Manning Building, 2nd & 3rd floor, 48 Queen's Rd ☎ 524 3001. Rowdy and spacious, and though the food is only average it's a pretty fair first stop for the *dim sum* novice. Open 7am–5pm.

City Hall Chinese Restaurant, 2nd Floor, City Hall Low Block ☎ 521 1303. Harbour views and a good range of *dim sum* served by friendly types throughout the day. You'll have to wait for a lunchtime table; take a ticket at the door. Open Mon–Sat 10am–3pm, Sun 8am–3pm.

Diamond Restaurant, 267–275 Des Voeux Rd ☎ 544 4708. A swarming Cantonese diner on several floors, you may have to wait (or share a table), but it's loud, authentic and cheap. Trolley women shout out their wares and you'll have to speak up if you want to eat anything – learn the names of a few dishes before you go. It's in Sheung Wan, near Western Market. Open 6.30am–5pm.

Eating

For more details about restaurants – etiquette, the bill, service charges, etc – see "Restaurants", p.218.

Eating

Luk Yu Teahouse, 24–26 Stanley Street ☎523 5464. Excellent, if rather pricey, *dim sum* from this traditional wood-panelled and screened Chinese tea-house, with service by white-coated waiters. You order from a Chinese order-paper, but a waiter will choose a selection for you if you ask – though don't expect the service to be particularly welcoming. You really need to book, or be prepared to wait if you're not a regular, but it's worth persevering for the experience. Open 7am–6pm.

Tai Woo, 15–19 Wellington St ☎524 5618. All-day *dim sum* ordered from a short English menu – a lunchtime favourite with local office workers and shoppers, and good value. Open 10am–5pm.

Tsui Hang Village Restaurant, 2nd Floor, New World Tower, 16–18 Queen's Rd ☎524 2012. Get there early for the good *dim sum* in splendid, traditional surroundings. Open Mon–Sat 2.30–6pm, Sun 10am–6pm.

Yung Kee Restaurant, 32–40 Wellington St ☎522 1624. Classic Cantonese restaurant which gets mobbed for its fine *dim sum*.. Open 2–5.30pm.

Zen, LG1, The Mall, Pacific Place, 88 Queensway ☎845 4555. Sharp designer-style and expertly cooked *dim sum*, which means slightly higher prices than usual. Open Mon–Fri 11.30am–3pm, Sat 11.30am–4.30pm, Sun 10.30am–4.30pm.

Wan Chai

Dynasty Restaurant, 3rd Floor, *New World Harbour View*, 1 Harbour Rd ☎584 6971. Harbour views from one of Hong Kong's best hotels and excellent, if pricey, *dim sum*. Open Mon–Sat noon–3pm, Sun 11.30am–3pm.

East Ocean Seafood Restaurant, 3rd Floor, Harbour Centre, 25 Harbour Rd ☎827 8887. Just across from Wan Chai ferry pier (opposite China Resources Building), the smart interior resembles a ship's dining room with its wood paneling and port-hole motifs. Not much English spoken, and few tourists, but if you perservere you should end up with decent *dim sum* from roving trolleys. Open 11am–6pm.

Round Dragon Chinese Restaurant, 60th Floor, Hopewell Centre, 183 Queen's Rd East ☎861 1668. *Dim sum* sixty floors up, with views to match, which on the whole is what you're paying for, since the food is unremarkable. There's an English menu to help you out. Open 11.30am–3pm.

Causeway Bay

Jade Garden, branches at 1 Hysan Ave ☎577 9332; and 1st Floor, Hennessy Centre, 500 Hennessy Rd ☎895 2200. Part of the *Maxim's* chain, these mainstream Cantonese restaurants serve reliable *dim sum*. Hysan Ave. branch open 7.45am–midnight, Hennessy Rd, 8am–midnight.

Kwan Tong Restaurant, 380–394 Hennessy Rd ☎803 4388. Large resturant with lots of *dim sum* variety. Open 7am–3pm.

Maxim's Palace, 1st Floor, World Trade Centre, 280 Gloucester Rd ☎576 0288. Swanky surroundings for your *dim sum*. Open 7.45am–3pm.

Rainbow Room, 22nd Floor, *Lee Garden Hotel*, 33 Hysan Ave ☎895 3311. A short *dim sum* menu, impeccably served by a phalanx of elegantly turned out waiters in high-class surroundings. The restaurant has a decent reputation, and is very popular with the lunchtime business crowd, so it's best to get there by 12.30pm (there's no advance booking). It's pricey as *dim sum* goes, but is one of Hong Kong's finer experiences. Open noon–3pm.

Aberdeen

Blue Ocean, 9th Floor, Aberdeen Marina Tower, 8 Shum Wan Rd ☎555 9415. Aberdeen harbour views and reliable *dim sum*. Open noon–5.30pm.

Jumbo Floating Restaurant, Shum Wan, Wong Chuk Hang ☎553 9111. The famous floating restaurant (see "Cantonese" below) serves *dim sum* from breakfast onwards, as does its neighbouring sister ship, the *Jumbo Palace*. It's the cheapest way to have a meal aboard, so worth considering. Open 7.30am–5pm.

Tsim Sha Tsui

Beijing Restaurant, 34–36 Granville Rd ☎366 9968. A Beijing restaurant that trots out northern-style *dim sum* at lunchtime – stodgy dumplings a speciality. There's not a huge choice and it's very meat-orientated: the noodle soups and mixed cold cuts of meat are popular. Open 11am–5pm.

Fontana Restaurant, 6–8a Prat Ave ☎369 9898. *Dim sum* palace, where *maitre d's* with two-way radios find you a table in the bowels of the restaurant. There's a wider range of dishes than usual, served from trolleys, but get there early as it attracts a bustling local clientele. Open 11am–3pm.

Harbour View Seafood Restaurant, 3rd Floor, Tsim Sha Tsui Centre, West Wing, 66 Mody Rd ☎722 5888. Harbour views from Tsim Sha Tsui East and particularly good seafood *dim sum*; the staff should help you out. Open 11am–5pm.

Jade Garden, 4th Floor, Star House, 3 Salisbury Rd, by the Star Ferry terminal ☎730 6888. Part of the *Maxim* chain, serving *dim sum* with harbour views. There's another branch, also with reasonable *dim sum*, at 25–31 Carnarvon Rd ☎369 8311. Open 10am–3pm.

New Territories

House of Canton, Shop 701, Riviera Plaza, Riviera Garden, Tsuen Wan ☎406 0868. One of a small chain; a good place if hunger strikes out in the New Territories. Open 11am–5pm.

New Best Restaurant, San Fung Ave, Sheung Shui. *Dim sum* restaurant on two floors: head up the escalators and try and attract the attention of the *maitre'd*. The food is great, and very cheap – and you'll be the only tourist in the place. Open 8am–5pm.

Sha Tin Treasure Restaurant, New Town Plaza, 6th Floor, 602–637, Sha Tin. Enormous New Territories' *dim sum* palace, where it's worth the wait for a table. Sunday is usually the best day to come, but it will be very busy. Open 10am–3pm.

Yuet Loy Heen, 2nd Floor, *Kowloon Panda Hotel*, 3 Tsuen Wah St, Tsuen Wan ☎409 1111. Highly rated *dim sum*; the seafood choices are especially good. Open 8am–4.30pm.

Vegetarian dim sum

Bodhi Vegetarian Restaurant. A reliable vegetarian restaurant chain that usually has a takeaway/stand-up *dim sum* section as well as waiter service. Worth trying at least once even for committed carnivores. Branches include: 56 Cameron Rd, Tsim Sha Tsui ☎739 2222; 384–388 Lockhart Rd, Wan Chai ☎573 2155; 36 Jordan Road, Yau Ma Tei ☎735 4686; 32–34 Lock Rd/81 Nathan Rd, Tsim Sha Tsui ☎366 8283; 60 Leighton Rd, Causeway Bay ☎890 5565. All branches open for *dim sum* 11am–5pm.

Lotus Garden, 60 Yee Wo St, Causeway Bay ☎895 4333. Small vegetarian restaurant, with *dim sum* to eat in or take away. Open 8.30am–11.30pm.

Natural Vegetarian Food, Ground Floor, 36 Lyndhurst Terrace, Central ☎851 6811. Convenient stop for veggie *dim sum* and other snacks and meals. Open 8am–noon.

Pak Bo Vegetarian Kitchen, Ground Floor, 106 Austin Rd, Tsim Sha Tsui ☎380 2681. Point to what you want from the window and eat inside; it's cheap and very good.

Vegi-Food Kitchen, 8 Cleveland St, Causeway Bay ☎890 6660. One of Hong Kong's best-known vegetarian restaurants (p.221) serves *dim sum*, too. Open 11am–5pm.

Wishful Cottage, 336 Lockhart Rd, Wan Chai ☎573 5603 and 573 5645. Truly marvellous vegetarian restaurant (see p.220), which serves *dim sum* throughout the day. Open 10.30am–5pm.

Restaurants

If you've mastered the *dim sum* palaces, no Chinese or Asian **restaurant** in Hong Kong need hold any fears. Almost everywhere will have a **menu** in English and the only real problem is that often the translations leave a lot to be desired. Also,

Eating

These restaurants serve solely vegetarian food: you can be sure there's no minced pork or prawn lurking in the dumplings, even if they look exactly like their meaty counterpart.

Eating

Restaurant Price Categories

The restaurants reviewed in this book have been given price categories as follows:

Inexpensive under $120

Moderate $120–250

Expensive $250–400

Very Expensive $400–750

The prices are for a **three-course meal**, or Asian equivalent, **per person exclud-**ing drinks and service. Alcohol in Hong is expensive: count on an extra $25–40 for each beer, and from $180 for a bottle of house wine. It's also worth noting that anything sold at the market rate – shark's fin and abalone dishes, and fresh fish and lobster plucked from restaurant fish tanks – can be wildly expensive. If you make them part of your Chinese meal, expect to nudge into the Expensive or Very Expensive category nearly every time.

the English-language menu is generally much less extensive and exciting than the Chinese one: you may have to point at what other Chinese diners are eating if you want good, seasonal, traditional food rather than the more bland tourist menu.

Most Cantonese restaurants are **open all day**, from early in the morning until midnight or beyond – until 3–4am in certain parts of the city, like Tsim Sha Tsui and Wan Chai. The ones that serve *dim sum* start serving their regular menu from mid- to late afternoon onwards. Other regional Chinese and Asian restaurants keep pretty much the same long hours, though perhaps not opening up until around 11am or so. Western restaurants generally have shorter hours, but you'll never have a problem finding somewhere to eat up until around midnight.

For the intricacies of **eating and ordering** in a Chinese restaurant, see the box below. To ask for **the bill** you say *mai dan*, which – with the wrong intonation – can also mean to "buy eggs". Sign language works just as well. Nearly all restaurants will add a ten percent **service charge** to your bill; if there are nuts and pickles or other nibbles on your table, you'll often pay a small cover charge, too. In places where there is no charge leaving ten percent is fine, though you can just leave the few dollars or coins from your change. Even if you've paid service, the waiter may wave your change airily above your head in the leather wallet that the bill came in; if you want the change, make a move for it or that will be deemed a tip too.

Chinese

Cantonese cuisine is the most common cooking style in Hong Kong, but most types of Chinese food can be eaten here, if not in specialist **regional restaurants**, then as individual dishes in places that are otherwise firmly Cantonese – the waiter should always be able to point you towards the house speciality. One thing common to most of the regional cuisines is the inclusion of things that Westerners often baulk at eating at all. Chinese food over the centuries has been essentially a starvation food: nothing can ever afford to be wasted, and intestines, bone marrow, fish heads, chicken feet and blood are all recycled as food in various forms. Some are not as disgusting as they sound; others – like braised chicken blood – can challenge even the most robust palates.

Lots of restaurants (Cantonese especially) will offer a standard **tourist menu** – set meals which are often good value. The drawback is that they won't be very adventurous, and may well stray into the sweet-and-sour-pork-ball area of "Chinese" food. It's worth shopping around, as there are some very good deals to be had. Also, it's worth noting that if you're going on **into China**, you'd do best to sample all the foods first in Hong Kong: the quality and choice here is infinitely better than on the mainland.

CANTONESE

Cantonese cuisine, from China's southeastern Guangdong (or Canton) province, is that which has been exported in bastardised forms to virtually every country in the world by Cantonese immigrants, and it is at its supreme best in Hong Kong. Throw away all your ideas of "Chinese" food when you sit down at a good Cantonese restaurant: apart from the cooking methods – mainly stir-frying and steaming – there's little similarity, and no self-respecting Chinese person would eat what they dismiss as the "foreign food" they serve up in takeaway shops at home.

Ingredients are based around fish and seafood, pork, beef and vegetables, either lightly fried with a little oil, or steamed, or braised, and flavoured with fresh ginger, spring onion, soy and oyster sauce. Everything is bitingly fresh and full of natural flavour, as a walk around any market proves – too fresh for some sensibilities, who can't bring themselves to choose their dinner from a restaurant fish tank. The **fish and seafood** is excellent: apart from the various types of fish (garoupa, mullet and bream especially), which are often steamed whole, prawns are the most common item, but you'll also find scallops, crayfish, mussels, clams, crabs, oysters, abalone, squid, octopus and lobster. Prawns and crabs, served in spicy black bean sauce, are classic dishes.

Chicken is the most widely eaten meat, and duck is popular too: commonly, it'll either come sliced and stir-fried with vegetables, or marinaded and braised with things like lemon and soy or black bean sauce. Other **specialities** are *dim sum* (for which, see above), and roast and barbecued meats, especially pork and duck, as well as pigeon, all of which you'll see hanging up in restaurant windows, served with plain rice. Frog's legs are eaten, too; snake (see p.70) is one of the territory's more notorious delicacies, along with various intestinal dishes, and (more appealing) preserved eggs (p.68).

For some Cantonese recipes, turn to p.361. And as well as the restaurants listed below, look at the "Dim Sum" listings above for the details of other Cantonese restaurants.

Central

Fat Heung Lam, 94 Wellington St ☎593 0404. It's hard to fault this small, cheap and cheerful vegetarian restaurant. Inexpensive.

House of Canton, Century Square, 1 D'Aguilar St ☎868 2988. Showpiece branch of the small *House of Canton* chain – traditional dishes with a nouveau twist, upmarket surroundings but reasonable prices. Open 11am–midnight. Moderate.

Jade Garden, 1st Floor, Swire House, 11 Chater Rd ☎5226 3031. Reliable member of the *Maxim* restaurant chain with a decent – if unsurprising – menu. There'll be plenty that's recognisable, all well-cooked, and served by English-speaking staff. Mon–Sat 11.30am–11pm, Sun 10am–midnight. Moderate.

Man Wah, 25th Floor, *Mandarin Oriental Hotel*, 5 Connaught Rd ☎522 0111. If you've got the cash for one extravagantly priced Cantonese meal, blow it here on some beautiful food (which follows a seasonal menu) and spectacular views. If they don't take your breath away, the bill will. Reservations are essential. Open noon–3pm & 6.30–11pm. Very Expensive.

Tsui Hang Village Restaurant, 2nd Floor, New World Tower, 16–18 Queen's Rd ☎524 2012. Named after the home town of Sun Yat-sen, the restaurant is well thought of – the food and decor traditional and prices reasonable. Open Mon–Sat 11.30am–midnight, Sun 10am–midnight. Moderate.

Yung Kee Restaurant, 32–40 Wellington St ☎522 1624. Impressive eating-house on several floors with immaculately laid tables and excellent food. Diners are presented with "hundred-year-old eggs" and preserved ginger as they sit down – traditional Cantonese appetisers – and the house speciality is roast goose (there's a roaring trade in takeaway roast goose lunch boxes during the week). You can also try frog served in several forms and some interesting hot pot dishes. Open 11am–11.30pm. Moderate.

Eating

Eating

EATING CHINESE FOOD

Don't be unnecessarily intimidated by the prospect of eating in a Chinese restaurant in Hong Kong. The following tips will help smooth the way – and they apply to all Chinese and many other Southeast Asian restaurants.

Chopsticks and other Utensils

You eat, naturally enough, with **chopsticks**, which – with a bit of practice and patience – are easy enough to master.

The basic idea is to use them as pincers, between thumb and forefinger, moving the bottom one to get a grip on the food; but really, any method that gets the food into your mouth is acceptable. If you can't manage, use the china spoon provided, or shrink with shame and ask for a fork and spoon – many restaurants will have them. You eat out of the little bowl in front of you (the smaller cup is for your tea), putting your rice in and plonking bits of food on top. Then, raise the bowl to your lips and shovel it in with the chopsticks (much easier than eating with chopsticks from a plate), chucking bones and other grungy bits onto the tablecloth as you go. They'll change the cloth when you leave, so it's no problem if your table looks like culinary Armageddon.

Etiquette demands that you don't stick your chopsticks upright into your bowl when you're not eating (it's a Taoist death sign); place them across the top of the bowl, or flat on the table, or on the chopstick rests.

There may well be one or two tiny **dishes** laid at your place too: at some stage someone will come round and fill one of them with soy sauce, the other with chilli sauce, and you dip your food into either.

Zen, LG1, The Mall, Pacific Place, 88 Queensway ☎845 4555. Unique, in that the *Zen* operation first opened in London, the restaurant is at the forefront of the designer-led, new Cantonese cuisine – which means hi-tech surroundings, imaginative Cantonese food which borrows influences extensively from the rest of Asia and competent, English-speaking staff. Open Mon–Fri 11.30am–3pm & 6–11pm, Sat 11.30am–4.30pm & 6–11pm, Sun 10.30am–4.30pm & 6–11pm. Expensive.

Wan Chai

Bodhi Vegetarian Restaurant, 384–388 Lockhart Rd ☎573 2155. A territory-wide chain serving uniformly good vegetarian food. There are appealing set menus, too, if you're not sure what to order. Open 11am–11pm. Inexpensive.

> ### Street Food
>
> For the very cheapest Cantonese food, you'll need to head for the nearest *dai pai dong* (street stall); see p.211 for locations.

Fook Lam Moon, 35–45 Johnston Rd ☎866 0663. Among Hong Kong's finest – and most famous – Cantonese restaurants, this is no place to come if you're skimping on costs. Classic cooking, pricey ingredients (shark's fin, bird's nest) and consistently reliable quality. Open 11.30am–11.30pm. Expensive–Very Expensive.

Healthy Mess, Ground Floor, 51–53 Hennessy Rd ☎527 3918. Bright and busy Cantonese vegetarian restaurant that specialises in *tofu* (beancurd) dishes. Open 10.30am–11.30pm. Inexpensive.

Man Yu, 159 Johnston Rd ☎572 0337. An unusually quiet Cantonese restaurant that comes recommended. Open 7.30am–11pm. Inexpensive–Moderate.

Steam & Stew Inn, Hing Wong Court, 21–23 Tai Wong St East ☎529 3913. Typical Cantonese family cooking: soups, stews and braised dishes, guaranteed MSG-free. Open 11.30am–11.30pm. Inexpensive.

Wishful Cottage, 336 Lockhart Rd ☎573 5603 and 573 5645. Small vegetarian restaurant with an extensive Cantonese menu. Large portions mean that the

Eating

Ordering Food and Drink

For **ordering Chinese food**, you're best off in a group; as a rough guide, order one more dish than there are people. The idea is that you put together a balanced meal, including the "five tastes" – acid, hot, bitter, sweet and salty – best achieved by balancing separate servings of meat, fish and vegetable, plus rice and soup. **Soup**, incidentally, is drunk throughout the meal rather than as a starter – normally meat, fish or vegetable stock that will come in a tureen – though if you want your individual bowl of chicken and sweetcorn soup you'll usually be able to get that too. **Rice** with food is white and steamed; fried rice comes as a fancier dish as part of a large meal. It's bad manners to leave rice, so don't order too much. The food will either come with various **sauces** (like plum sauce or chilli sauce), which are poured into the little dishes provided, or you can use the soy sauce and sesame oil on the table to flavour your food. Bear in mind that you use the sauces as dips: sloshing soy sauce over your rice and food will pick you out as an uncouth foreigner straight away. They'll rarely serve **dessert** in Cantonese restaurants (maybe ice cream in some places), though you'll often get a sliced orange with which to cleanse the palate.

The classic **drink** with your meal is tea (for which see *"Dim Sum"*, above), and you'll always be brought this as a matter of course. If you want alcohol, beer is good with most Chinese food. Wine is generally prohibitively expensive in Hong Kong's restaurants, and in any case isn't as suitable an accompaniment; if you must drink wine, go for a dry white so as not to kill the taste of the food. Other than beer, Chinese people drink very little alcohol with their food: if it's a party or a celebration, they're most likely to drink neat brandy or whisky.

---

excellent noodle soup and one main dish will fill you up; try the unusual deep-fried walnuts in sweet and sour sauce. Open 10.30am–10.30pm. Moderate.

Causeway Bay

Ah Yee Leng Tong, Basement, Hang Lung Centre, 2–20 Paterson St ☎576 8385; 503–505 Lockhart Rd ☎834 3480; and Lai Chi Building, 42 Leighton Rd ☎895 0192. Old-style Cantonese cafés serving warming soups and casseroles. Open 11.30am–11.30pm. Inexpensive.

Bodhi Vegetarian Restaurant, 60 Leighton Rd ☎890 5565. A territory-wide chain serving uniformly good vegetarian food. There are appealing set menus, too, if you're not sure what to order. Open 11am–11pm. Inexpensive.

Lotus Garden, 60 Yee Wo St ☎895 4333. Small vegetarian restaurant, with a takeaway counter too. Open 8.30am–11.30pm. Inexpensive.

Vegi-Food Kitchen, 8 Cleveland St ☎890 6660. A sign at the entrance warns "Please do not bring meat of any kind into this restaurant", which gives you an inkling of what to expect – decent Cantonese vegetarian food at very fair prices. Open 11am–11.30pm. Moderate.

Happy Valley

Pigeon Club Seafood Restaurant, 5a Sing Woo Rd ☎591 0298. An unassuming location, but the food is wonderful and very good value. Open 11.30am–11.30pm. Moderate.

Aberdeen

Floating restaurants, Shum Wan, Wong Chuk Hang. Docked in Aberdeen harbour, Hong Kong's famous floating restaurants are, in truth, a bit of a disappointment. You can eat better, cheaper seafood at various other venues around the territory. But you can't eat it floating aboard something that looks like it fell off the set from Bertolucci's *The Last Emperor* anywhere else. There are three: the *Jumbo* ☎553 9111; the *Jumbo Palace* ☎554 0513; and the *Tai Pak* ☎552 5953. Each has its own private boat that will run you there across the harbour. The two *Jumbos* are open 7.30am–11.30pm, the *Tai Pak* 11.30am–11.30pm. Moderate–Expensive.

The restaurants reviewed in this book have been given price categories as follows:

Inexpensive under $120

Moderate $120–250

Expensive $250–400

Very Expensive $400–750

These are per person prices; see box on p.218 for more details.

Eating

The restaurants reviewed in this book have been given price categories as follows:

Inexpensive under $120

Moderate $120–250

Expensive $250–400

Very Expensive $400–750

These are per person prices; see box on p.218 for more details.

Tsim Sha Tsui

Bodhi Vegetarian Restaurant, 32–34 Lock Rd/81 Nathan Rd, ☎366 8283. Possibly the best branch of this territory-wide chain, serving good vegetarian food. There are appealing set menus, too, if you're not sure what to order. Open 11am–11pm. Inexpensive.

East Ocean Seafood Restaurant, B1, East Ocean Centre, 98 Granville Rd ☎723 8128. Noisy basement dining with excellent seasonal cooking and approachable waiters. Open 11am–midnight. Moderate-Expensive.

New Year Seafood Restaurant, 8 Ashley Rd ☎376 0926. One of Tsim Sha Tsui's better Cantonese choices – it may have only a basic menu with few surprises, but the restaurant is always busy. Open 11am–11.30pm. Inexpensive.

Orchard Court, 37 Hankow Rd ☎317 5111. Good-value seasonal Cantonese cuisine, dishes cooked with fruit in the summer, casseroled in winter. Open 11am–midnight. Moderate.

Shang Palace, Basement 1, *Kowloon Shangri-La Hotel*, 64 Mody Road, Tsim Sha Tsui East ☎721 2111. Marvellous restaurant with over-the-top Imperial decor, which seems to cook everything well, including pigeon. It's busy at lunchtime – go early. Open Mon–Sat noon–3pm & 6.30–10pm, Sun 11am–3pm & 6.30–11pm. Expensive-Very Expensive.

Sun Tung Lok, Shop 63–64, Ocean Galleries, Harbour City, 17–19 Canton Rd ☎730 0288. Famous shark's fin restaurant, serving the (wildly expensive) delicacy in several different ways, alongside other excellent food. For a cheaper meal try the eel in black bean sauce and one of the chicken or pigeon dishes – all authentically Cantonese. (There's a second branch at 125 Sunning Rd, Causeway Bay ☎852 2899). Open 11am–midnight. Expensive.

The Sweet Dynasty, 88 Canton Rd ☎375 9119. Decorative Chinese tea house which specialises in Cantonese desserts – there's inventive use of *tofu*, exotic fruits and nuts, and the red bean soup is a house speciality. Savoury dishes are available, too. Open 11.30am–midnight. Inexpensive.

New Territories

Lung Wah Hotel and Restaurant, 22 Ha Wo Che, Sha Tin ☎691 1594. The best place in Hong Kong to eat hot, greasy pigeon – a Cantonese speciality. It's tricky to find, but the effort is worth it for this traditional New Territories' restaurant, with a garden full of *mahjong* players and outdoor tables, which gets packed at the weekend. Get there by taxi or minibus #60X from Sha Tin KCR, or bus #48 – from Tsuen Wan ferry to Wo Che – to Sha Tin Police Quarters; then take the footbridge at the end of Wo Che Street. Open 11am–11pm. Inexpensive.

San Shui, Ground Floor, Siu Yat Building, Lot 941, Sai Kung Town ☎792 1828. The speciality is "bamboo fish": carp, stuffed with preserved turnip and grilled over charcoal outside on a hand-rotated bamboo pole – pricey but delicious. This is just one of a line of harbourside restaurants here serving excellent fresh fish and seafood. Open noon–midnight. Moderate.

Yucca de Lac, Ma La Shui ☎692 1835. Long-established open-air restaurant in the hills overlooking the Chinese University and Tolo Harbour. There's an extensive menu – the pigeon is recommended, as are the beancurd dishes. It's on the old Tai Po Road, above Tolo Highway – take a taxi from Sha Tin and walk back down on foot to University KCR; or take bus #70, from Jordan Rd Ferry Terminal to Sheung Shui, which passes the restaurant. Open 11am–11pm. Moderate.

Outlying Islands

Baccarat, 9 Pak She Praya St, Cheung Chau ☎981 0606. Good choice for garlic fried prawns or scallops, served with fried rice; the beer is cold here, too. Inexpensive-Moderate.

East Lake Restaurant, Tung Wan Rd, Cheung Chau. On the way to the main beach from the ferry pier, this is a reliable spot for a decent fish meal. Inexpensive-Moderate.

Lancombe, 47 Main St, Yung Shue Wan, Lamma ☎982 0881. No-nonsense food and prices: fish, as usual, a speciality. Open 11am–10pm. Moderate.

Man Fung Seafood Restaurant, 5 Main St, Yung Shue Wan, Lamma ☎982 1112. One of the better of Yung Shue Wan's terrace restaurants, with *dim sum* in the morning, fresh fish and a long list of budget rice or noodle combination dishes, which will set you up for an afternoon's walk. Open 6am–9pm. Inexpensive–Moderate.

HAKKA

The **Hakka** people originated in northern China, but migrated south over the years and have been farming in what are now the New Territories for centuries. Their food is often taken to be Cantonese, and although there are few Hakka restaurants in Hong Kong, most Cantonese restaurants serve some Hakka dishes. These use beancurd a lot, and salted and preserved food, deriving from the days when the Hakka carried their food with them as they moved: salted, baked chicken, pork and preserved cabbage, intestines and innards cooked in various ways are staple dishes. One real speciality is boned duck, stuffed with rice, meat and lotus seeds.

Chuen Cheung Kui, 108 Percival St, Causeway Bay ☎577 3833. Large portions of family style cooking make this a popular place with locals – weekends are always packed. Not much English spoken; you may have to point. Open 11am–11pm. Moderate.

New Home Hakka & Seafood Restaurant, 19–20 Hanoi Rd, Tsim Sha Tsui ☎366 5876. Fairly austere tile and mirror decor, but reasonably attentive service and authentic Hakka food. The tangy salt-baked chicken is excellent (and half a bird is big enough for two), as are the beancurd dishes and soups. Open 7am–midnight. Moderate.

BEIJING (PEKING)

Beijing food is a northern style of cooking which relies more on meat, and supplements rice with bread and dumplings.

Meals are heavier, one of the specialities a Mongolian-influenced **hot pot** of sliced meat, vegetables and dumplings cooked and mixed together in a stock that's boiled at your table in a special stove; you eat the food as it's cooked and then drink the soup at the end of the meal. The most famous Beijing food of all is **Peking duck**, a recipe that's existed in China for centuries – slices of skin and meat from a barbecued duck, wrapped in a pancake with spring onion and radish and smeared with plum sauce. If you order this, be sure to ask for the duck carcass to be taken away after carving and turned into soup with vegetables and mushrooms, which is then served later.

American Restaurant, 20 Lockhart Rd, Wan Chai ☎527 7277. Misleadingly named, averagely priced Beijing restaurant with a large menu that's a favourite with tourists. Open 11.30am–11.30pm. Inexpensive–Moderate.

Beijing Restaurant, 1st–3rd Floor, 34–36 Granville Rd, Tsim Sha Tsui ☎366 9968. Peking duck buffet dinners served from 7–9pm for around $120 a head, plus a full menu too. Reservations advised for the buffet. Open 11am–11.30pm. Moderate.

Cheung Kee, 1st Floor, 75–79 Lockhart Rd, Wan Chai ☎529 0707. Despite the unprepossessing entrance, and the lack of an English menu, this place is highly recommended for delicious Beijing-style food – try the smoked fish. Open noon–11pm. Inexpensive.

New American Restaurant, 177–179 Wan Chai Rd, Wan Chai ☎575 0458 or 575 0851. Great noodles plus all the usual dishes. Open 11am–10.30pm. Moderate.

Peking Garden, branches at Basement, Alexandra House, 6 Ice House St, Central ☎526 6456; Shop 003, The Mall, Pacific Place, 88 Queensway, Central ☎845 8452; and 1st Floor, *Excelsior Hotel* Shopping Arcade, 281 Gloucester Rd, Causeway Bay ☎577 7231. Reliable food in all three restaurants, with good Peking duck and interesting desserts. Open 11.30am–3pm & 5pm–midnight. Moderate–Expensive.

Eating

Eating

Spring Deer, 1st Floor, 42 Mody Road, Tsim Sha Tsui ☎723 3673. Long-established place noted for its Peking duck (which is carved at the table), among a barrage of authentic dishes. The duck starts at $200 a portion, so single diners are in trouble, but the rest of the food is magnificent and filling – and served in three dish sizes. Try the smoked chicken, and the beancurd with minced pork. Open noon–11pm. Moderate.

SHANGHAINESE

Shanghainese is also a heavier cuisine than Cantonese, using more oil and spices, as well as preserved vegetables, pickles and steamed dumplings. It's warming, starchy food, popular in the winter. Meals often start with cold, smoked fish, and include "drunken chicken", cooked in rice wine. Seafood is widely used, particularly fried or braised eels, while the great speciality is the expensive hairy crab – sent from Shanghai in the autumn, it is steamed, and accompanied by ginger tea; the roe is considered a delicacy.

Andy's Kitchen, 25 Tung Lo Wan Rd, Causeway Bay ☎577 1819. Despite the name, this small, local restaurant serves terrific and affordable Shanghai cooking. The smoked fish is worth trying – dry pieces of aromatic fish – and you'll get a plate of nuts and pickled cabbage to nibble on while you make up your mind about the rest. Open 11am–10pm. Moderate.

Dim Sum Burger, 13–15 Cleveland St, Causeway Bay ☎577 7199. The *dim sum* is Shanghainese, as are the "burgers", which are in fact steamed or fried dumplings. Pleasant Shanghai food in busy café surroundings. Open 7.30am–midnight. Inexpensive.

Great Shanghai, 26 Prat Ave, Tsim Sha Tsui ☎366 8158. One of the most reliable of Hong Kong's Shanghai restaurants, with well-presented food (fine fish and seafood) served in small or large portions. A good choice for a first Shanghai meal and extremely good value. Open 11am–11pm. Moderate.

Kung Tak Lam, 15 Hanoi Rd, Tsim Sha Tsui ☎367 7881; 55 Tung Lo Wan Rd, Causeway Bay ☎890 3127. Shanghai vegetarian resturant, owned by Lau-Wo Ching, whose wife was a 1960s' Cantonese movie star and whose Causeway Bay branch catered for John Major's 1992 visit to the territory. Very reasonably priced food – beancurd, thick soups and dishes that mock their meat and fish counterparts. Open 11am–11pm. Inexpensive.

Shanghai Garden, Hutchison House, 10 Harcourt Rd, Central ☎524 8181. More upmarket than the Tsim Sha Tsui Shanghai eating places, the *Shanghai Garden* also mixes in dishes from other regions. But the food is authentic and tasty and prices aren't too extreme for Central (though they are higher than all the other places listed in this section). Open 11.30am–3pm & 5.30pm–midnight. Moderate.

Shanghai Tai Woo, 10 Ashley Rd, Tsim Sha Tsui ☎376 0225. Poor service and little character, but the portions are ample. It's a good place to experiment safely if you're unsure about the cuisine. Open 11am–11pm. Inexpensive.

Shanghai Village, 9 Lan Fong Rd, Causeway Bay ☎849 9705. No frills, but authentic Shanghainese cooking. Open noon–11pm. Moderate.

Wu Kong Shanghai Restaurant, Basement, Alpha House, 27 Nathan Rd, Tsim Sha Tsui ☎366 7244. Crowded, popular restaurant with a wide menu, and – given its handy position – reasonably priced to boot. Go early for dinner or expect to wait in line. Open 11.30am–11pm. Moderate.

SZECHUAN (SICHUAN)

Szechuan food is spicy and hot, using garlic, fennel, coriander, chillis and pepper to flavour the dishes, which are served with hot dips and bread and noodles. Salted bean paste is a common cooking agent. Marinades are widely used and specialities include smoked duck (marinaded in wine, highly seasoned and cooked over camphor wood and tea leaves to provide the characteristic taste). Other dishes you'll see are braised aubergine, which is always good, beancurd with chilli sauce, prawns with garlic, chilli and ginger, and braised beans. As you might expect, you'll get through a lot of beer with a Szechuan meal.

Fung Lum, 1st Floor, 23 Prat Ave, Tsim Sha Tsui ☎367 8686. Popular with tourists and with English-speaking staff, but don't let that put you off – there's plenty of good things on the menu, with dishes split into "small" and "medium" sizes; stick with the small dishes (which feed two in any case) and increase your choices. Try the chicken in garlic and chilli oil; and drink *Tsing-tao* or *Kirin* beer. Open 11am–11pm. Inexpensive–Moderate.

Kam Kong Restaurant, 60 Granville Rd, Tsim Sha Tsui ☎367 3434. Good, no-nonsense food, highly spiced and coming with lashings of hot green and red chillis. Try the "green fish", the dumplings (*won ton*) and the smoked fish; the reasonably priced dishes come in three sizes so you don't need to over-order. Open noon–11pm. Inexpensive–Moderate.

Pep 'n' Chili, Shop F, 12–22 Blue Pool Rd, Happy Valley ☎573 8251. Good, well-cooked food (fine smoked duck and special noodles) in modern surroundings, though a bit on the expensive side. The more alarmingly hot dishes are picked out on the menu to avoid patrons suffering unlooked-for death by chilli. Open noon–3pm & 6–11pm. Expensive.

The Red Pepper, 7 Lan Fong Rd, Causeway Bay ☎577 3811. The name says it all – a good choice for devilishly hot food and a favourite with expats. The smoked duck and beancurd are standard favourites here. You might want to book in advance, since it can get very busy. Open noon–midnight. Moderate.

Szechuan Lau, 466 Lockhart Rd, Causeway Bay ☎891 9027. Classic Szechuan food, with all the best-known dishes served in relaxed surroundings. The chilli prawns are great, and there are more interesting seafood dishes, too. Open noon–midnight. Moderate.

CHIU CHOW

Another southeastern cuisine (from the Swatow district of Guangdong), **Chiu Chow** food is strong on seafood, including thick shark's fin soup and eel, and also encompasses the famous (and very expensive) bird's nest soup – made from the dried saliva which binds the nests of the sea-swallow. The food uses much the same ingredients but is oilier than Cantonese (roast goose is another favourite), and you assist the digestion with a drink of bitter tea, known as "Iron Maiden" or "Iron Buddha".

Carrianna Chiu Chow Restaurant, 151 Gloucester Rd, Wan Chai ☎574 1282. Large servings and good value for money make this a popular spot – it's always noisy and busy. Open 11am–11.30pm. Moderate.

Chiu Chow Garden, Basement, Jardine House, 1 Connaught Place, Central ☎525 8246; 3rd Floor Vicwood Plaza, 199 Des Voeux Rd, Central ☎545 7778; 2nd & 3rd Floor, Hennessy Centre, 500 Hennessy Rd, Causeway Bay ☎577 3391; 2nd Floor, Tsim Sha Tsui Centre, 66 Mody Rd, Tsim Sha Tsui East ☎368 7266. Chiu Chow food from the *Maxim* people. Always reliable and not expensive; goose is a speciality. All open 11am–3pm & 5.30pm–midnight. Moderate.

City Chiu Chow Restaurant, 1st Floor, East Ocean Centre, 98 Granville Rd, Tsim Sha Tsui East ☎724 5383. One of a chain (look for the words "City Chiu Chow" in the name) selling reasonably priced food, even if the cooking doesn't always inspire. Open 11am–midnight. Moderate.

Kai Kung Chiu Chow Restaurant, 8 Minden Row, Tsim Sha Tsui. Basic café with Chiu Chow specialities. Open 10am–9pm. Inexpensive.

Kornhill Chiu Chow Restaurant, Kornhill Plaza, 1 Kornhill Rd, Quarry Bay ☎885 4461. The roast goose on display is the best thing to have here, but other dishes are equally authentic and the prices are very fair. Open 11am–3pm & 5.30pm–midnight. Inexpensive–Moderate.

Eating

The restaurants reviewed in this book have been given price categories as follows:

Inexpensive under $120

Moderate $120–250

Expensive $250–400

Very Expensive $400–750

These are per person prices; see box on p.218 for more details.

Eating

The restaurants reviewed in this book have been given price categories as follows:

Inexpensive under $120

Moderate $120–250

Expensive $250–400

Very Expensive $400–750

These are per person prices; see box on p.218 for more details.

Pak Lok, 25 Hysan Ave, Causeway Bay ☎576 8886. An enormous Chiu Chow menu, with good shark's fin soup. Avoid this (it's always very expensive) and the rest of the food is reasonably priced, given the restaurant's good reputation. Open noon–1am. Moderate–Expensive.

HANGZHOU, HOT-POT AND HUNAN

City Restaurant, 659–668, 6th Floor, New Town Plaza, Sha Tin, New Territories ☎606 4141. A seafood hot-pot restaurant (called *for wok*); order fish, seafood, veg and noodles and cook them over a boiling stock pot on your table, finishing off with the soup. The deluxe hot pot will feed two or three. Open 11am–11.30pm. Moderate.

Hunan Garden, 3rd Floor, The Forum, Exchange Square, 8 Connaught Place, Central. ☎868 2880. Hunan province features spicy dishes akin to those from Szechuan; the menu points out what's hot and what isn't. An attractive place with harbour views. Open 11.30am–3pm & 5.30pm–midnight. Expensive.

Tien Hung Lau, 18c Austin Ave, Tsim Sha Tsui. ☎368 9660. Food from the south-western city of Hangzhou, including the famous "Beggar's Chicken", a whole chicken baked and covered in mud and lotus leaves (which you must order in advance), and West Lake fish with vinegar sauce. You'll need to book. Open noon–2pm & 6–10pm. Moderate–Expensive.

African

Cafe Afrikan, 7 Glenealy St, Central ☎868 9299. One of Hong Kong's latest culinary experiments, the *Afrikan* dishes up a mean *couscous*, as well as more exotic creations – including soup served in a bread shell and some highly rated desserts. No alcohol is served, but there's terrific coffee and other drinks available; good music too. Open Mon–Sat noon–midnight. Inexpensive–Moderate.

American

Apart from the burger bars that are swamping Hong Kong, there are some more upmarket **American** restaurants and steak houses that may take your fancy. A couple are excellent, if very pricey. There's been an explosion in the number of designer diners, too, especially around Central – all very stylish but not places for a budget meal.

Al's Diner, 39 D'Aguilar St, Lan Kwai Fong, Central ☎869 1869. Straightforward diner food – burgers, dogs, chilli and sand-wiches – and late opening at weekends for ravenous clubbers. Open Mon–Thurs 11am–1am, Fri & Sat 11am–3am. Inexpensive–Moderate.

American Pie, 4th Floor, California Entertainment Building, 34–36 D'Aguilar St, Lan Kwai Fong, Central ☎877 9779. Forget the overpriced meals, with the exception of brunch, and hog out instead on the superb desserts and cakes. A terrace gives the place added attraction. Open Mon–Thurs 11am–2.30pm & 6.30pm–midnight, Fri–Sun noon–midnight. Moderate–Expensive.

Beverly Hills Deli, Level 2, 55 New World Centre, 18 Salisbury Rd, Tsim Sha Tsui ☎369 8695. Despite the name, New York-style deli and kosher food – bagels, pastrami, lox, the works – at inflated prices. Mouthwatering stuff though and takeaway food available. Open 10.30am–10.30pm. Moderate.

Bostonian, *Ramada Renaissance Hotel*, 8 Peking Rd, Tsim Sha Tsui ☎375 1133. American-style hotel restaurant which excels in meat dishes. If you can eat the 46oz rib of beef, they'll tear up your bill (and if you were wondering, the record is *seven minutes . . .*). Good salads, too, and desserts to die for. Open noon–3pm & 6–11pm. Expensive–Very Expensive.

California, 30–32 D'Aguilar St, Lan Kwai Fong, Central ☎521 1345. Restaurant/café/bar that oozes Americana and serves a classic menu – burgers, potato skins, salads and barbecues. Pricey and flash. Mon–Sat noon–1am, Sun 5pm–1am. Expensive.

Dan Ryan's Chicago Bar and Grill, 114 The Mall, Pacific Place, 88 Queensway, Central ☎845 4600. Bumper American-size portions of ribs, steaks, salads and homemade desserts. You'll get enough food to sink a battleship, but it doesn't come cheap. Open Mon–Sat 8.30am–midnight, Sun 9.30am–midnight. Expensive–Very Expensive.

Graffiti, 17 Lan Kwai Fong, Central ☎521 2202. Typical of Lan Kwai Fong's recent arrivals, this is a favourite with Central's suits – American-style pizzas, burgers, pasta and a good salad bar. The gimmick here is the crayons provided for you to decorate your tablecloth. The best efforts go on the wall. Drinks are pricey, but eat before 8pm and you can take advantage of Happy Hour. Open Mon–Wed noon–midnight, Thurs–Sat noon–2am. Moderate.

LA Café, Ground Floor, Lippo Centre, Admiralty ☎526 6863. The *LA Café* sports a *Harley Davidson* above the bar, Californian cuisine and international beer served by staff with attitude. Open noon–midnight, later at the weekend. Moderate–Expensive.

Prince's Tavern, Mezzanine Floor, Prince's Building, 10 Chater Rd, Central ☎523 9352. Good Cajun and Creole cooking as well as American standards and appetising set lunches. Open Mon–Fri 11am–8.30pm, Sat 11am–7pm. Moderate.

Top Dog, 1 Lan Kwai Fong, Central ☎868 9196. Chic, retro café serving good hot dogs and other snacks. Open 11am–late. Inexpensive.

British

Restaurants serving solely British food are remarkably thin on the ground, though there are dozens which incorporate classic British dishes as part of a wider international menu (for which, see "International", below). However, if you want no-nonsense portions of fish and chips, steak and kidney pie or an all-day English breakfast, most **pubs** can do the honours; in fact, if you're looking for a filling, low-priced, one-plate meal, pub food is your best bet outside a *dai pai dong*.

Bentley's Seafood Restaurant & Oyster Bar, B4 Basement, Prince's Building, 3 Des Voeux Rd, Central ☎868 0881.

British fish and seafood/oyster restaurant serving classic grills alongside a smattering of Southeast Asian-inspired dishes. Open Mon–Sat 11am–3pm & 6.30pm–midnight. Expensive.

Harry Ramsden's, Wu Chung House, 213 Queen's Rd East, Wan Chai ☎832 9626. The famous British fish-and-chip shop moves out East – and remains remarkably true to its origins. The best fish and chips for thousands of miles, served under imported Yorkshire chandeliers. Full takeaway service too. Open 11.30am–11.30pm. Moderate.

PUB FOOD

The following is a selection of the pubs and bars in Hong Kong that serve mostly British food, usually at lunchtime but often right through the day, from breakfast onwards. For opening times and more details see "Bars and Pubs" in the next chapter. They're all Inexpensive.

The Blacksmith's Arms, 16 Minden Ave, Tsim Sha Tsui. Regular pub food and set lunches.

Hardy's, 35 D'Aguilar St, Central. German specials, pie and chips.

Horse and Carriage, 117 Lockhart Rd, Wan Chai. Very cheap set lunches.

Horse and Groom, 161 Lockhart Rd, Wan Chai. Cheap set lunches.

Joe Bananas, 23 Luard Rd, Wan Chai. Same owners as *Mad Dogs*, same good pub food.

Kangaroo Pub, 35 Haiphong Rd, Tsim Sha Tsui. Aussie pub with good-value breakfast, steaks and snacks.

Mad Dogs, 8 Wyndham St, Central; 32 Nathan Rd, Tsim Sha Tsui. All-day breakfasts, burgers, salads, pies, peas, and fish and chips. Strong on vegetarian options too.

Ned Kelly's Last Stand, 11a Ashley Rd, Tsim Sha Tsui. Aussie pub with lashings of burgers, pies, beans and salad.

Old China Hand, 104 Lockhart Rd, Wan Chai. Good all-day breakfasts.

Schnurrbart, 29 D'Aguilar St, Central. German specials, herring and sausage.

Eating

Eating

The restaurants reviewed in this book have been given price categories as follows:

Inexpensive under $120

Moderate $120–250

Expensive $250–400

Very Expensive $400–750

These are per person prices; see box on p.218 for more details.

Buffets and set meals

Most of the larger hotels in Hong Kong (and some restaurants) put on an excellent self-service **buffet** lunch and dinner. It's generally European-style food, though there are some good Asian exceptions. Often, there will be a **set meal**, too, a three-course lunch and dinner, which is the most inexpensive way to eat in the grander hotel restaurants. Check the "Hotel Fare" section on the *What's On* page of the daily *South China Morning Post* for details of special deals; the places listed below are all reliably good. Lunch is usually noon–2.30pm, dinner 6.30–10pm, but ring for exact times – set and buffet dinners, particularly, have a habit of being over by around 9.30pm. For a buffet lunch, expect to pay around $100, buffet dinner and set meals $160–250; ten percent service will be added in all cases and drinks are extra.

Excelsior Hotel, 281 Gloucester Rd, Causeway Bay ☎894 8888. Daily buffet lunch and dinner in the *Coffee Shop*; set lunch in *The Grill*.

Furama, 1 Connaught Rd, Central ☎526 7662. Expensive lunch and dinner buffets in the revolving, top-floor *La Ronda*; superb views while you eat.

Island Shangri-La, Pacific Place, 88 Queensway, Central ☎877 3838. High-class breakfast, lunch and dinner buffets in the *Island Café*.

Marriott, Pacific Place, 88 Queensway, Central ☎810 8366. International buffet lunch and dinner in the *Marriott Café*; Sunday brunch too.

New World Harbour View, 1 Harbour Rd, Wan Chai ☎802 8888. Health-conscious buffet lunch in the 8th floor *Oasis*.

Omni Prince, Harbour City, Canton Rd, Tsim Sha Tsui ☎736 1888. Southeast Asian lunch and dinner buffet in the *Spice Market*, set lunch and pasta dinner buffet in the *Coffee Shop*. The other *Omni* hotels also have a good choice of well-priced buffets and set meals.

Regal Riverside, Tai Chung Kiu Rd, Sha Tin, New Territories ☎649 7878. Excellent daily Southeast Asian buffet served in the *Asian Delights* restaurant.

Sheraton, 20 Nathan Rd, Tsim Sha Tsui ☎369 1111. Buffet lunch at the *Sidewalk Café*, dinner buffet in the *Coffee Shop* and set Indian lunch at *Bukhara*.

Windsor Hotel, 39–43 Kimberley Rd, Tsim Sha Tsui ☎739 5665. A good-value daily dinner buffet with Japanese delicacies.

Filipino

Filipinos are the territory's largest immigrant group, so it's surprising that there are only a few restaurants where you can try out the food, which consists of good mixed stews, casseroles, soups, seafood and rice-based dishes – some of which show a decided Spanish influence.

Chungking Café, Ground Floor, no. 24, Chungking Mansions, 36–44 Nathan Rd, Tsim Sha Tsui. Cheap, filling food at a café at the back of the Mansions' ground floor. Open 10.30am–10.30pm. Inexpensive.

Cinta Restaurant, Basement, *Hotel New Harbour*, 6 Fenwick St, Wan Chai ☎527 1199. Extensive Filipino menu (as well as Malaysian standbys and an Indonesian *rijstafel*). As the lounge bar features Filipino singers after 9pm, it's good for a drink, too. Open 11am–2am. Moderate.

Cinta-J, Malaysia Building, 50 Gloucester Rd, Wan Chai ☎529 6622. Just around the corner from the associated *Cinta*, this has good value Filipino set lunches served from noon–3pm (and a long Happy Hour that starts shortly afterwards). Inexpensive.

Mabuhay, 11 Minden Ave, Tsim Sha Tsui ☎367 3762. Crispy fried pig's intestines is fairly typical of the authentic dishes offered here, but there are plenty of other choices – hearty soups, garlicky baked clams (actually green mussels) and grilled fish. Basic, bustling canteen dining accompanied by Western pop and cheap schooners of beer. Thoroughly recommended. Open 8.30am–11pm. Inexpensive.

French

Au Trou Normand, 6 Carnarvon Rd, Tsim Sha Tsui ☎366 8754. This long-standing restaurant dishes up fine provincial French food in rustic surroundings, with Calvados to wash it all down. It's even more affordable at the buffet lunch – around $120 for salad, pâté, grills, dessert and coffee, served between 11.45am and 3pm. Open noon–3pm & 7–11pm. Moderate.

Gaddi's, 1st Floor, *Peninsula Hotel*, Salisbury Rd, Tsim Sha Tsui ☎366 6251. The most famous Western restaurant in Hong Kong. Extraordinary food, extraordinary prices (at least $800 per person for a full meal); advance booking and smart dress essential. Open noon–3pm & 6.30–11pm. Very Expensive.

Stanley's French Restaurant, 86 Stanley Main St, Stanley ☎813 8873. Chic French restaurant in Stanley village which is winning a lot of friends with its imaginative, regularly changing menu and bay views. You'll need to book in advance at weekends. Open noon–3pm & 7pm–midnight. Expensive.

German, Austrian and Swiss

Baron's Table, 1st Floor, *Holiday Inn Golden Mile*, 46–52 Nathan Rd, Tsim Sha Tsui ☎369 3111. Grand and expensive German meals, including smoked specialities. Servings are enormous, while the Teutonic surroundings are absurdly out of place in Hong Kong. Open noon–2.30pm & 7pm–11.30. Very Expensive.

Chesa, 1st Floor, *Peninsula Hotel*, Salisbury Road, Tsim Sha Tsui ☎366 6251.The *Pen's* top-price Swiss restaurant with great fondue and superb meat and fish dishes. Not too outrageously pricey either (the set lunches are especially good value), given the hotel's pedigree. Reservations essential. Open noon–3pm & 6.30–11pm. Expensive.

Mozart Stub'n, 8 Glenealy St, Central ☎522 1763. Meat dishes predominate in this small Austrian restaurant. If you're looking for filling central European food, this is about the best value on offer in the territory – book ahead for dinner. Open Mon–Sat noon–3pm & 6.30pm–midnight. Moderate–Expensive.

Greek, Turkish and Lebanese

Bacchus, Basement, Hop Hing Centre, 8–12 Hennessy Rd, Wan Chai ☎529 9032. Disappointing food, though the virtually compulsory plate-smashing and contorted dancing makes for a fun evening out. Open noon–2.30pm & 6–10.30pm.. Moderate–Expensive.

Beirut, Shop A, Winner Building, 26–39 D'Aguilar St, Central ☎804 6611. A chic setting for Lebanese food, kebabs and mixed grills. Open noon–3pm & 6–11pm. Moderate.

Midnight Express, 3 Lan Kwai Fong, Central ☎525 5010. Pitta bread stuffed with all kinds of fillings at bargain prices. Just the place after a drinking bout in Lan Kwai Fong. Open Mon–Sat 11.30am–3am, Sun 6pm–12.30am. Inexpensive.

Zorbas, 6–7 Ichang St, Tsim Sha Tsui ☎375 1567. Cosy Greek restaurant charging fair prices for some of the best food of its kind in the territory. Open noon–2.30pm & 6.30–10.30pm. Moderate.

Indian, Pakistani, Sri Lankan, Burmese and Nepalese

After Chinese food, one of Hong Kong's biggest culinary concentrations is that of the innumerable **Indian** and **Pakistani** restaurants and cafés – with one each of **Sri Lankan** (*Club Sri Lanka*), **Nepalese** (*Hong Kong Nepalese Association*) and **Burmese** (*Rangoon*), whose cuisines are closely related. Most are found either in or around Chungking Mansions in Tsim Sha Tsui, where they're nearly all very basic, unlicensed places, very cheap and some of them very good. There's a slightly more expensive cluster over on Hong Kong Island, on and around Wyndham Street, as well as a few in Wan Chai and Causeway Bay. Some are established as "private clubs" or "Mess Clubs", ostensibly for members only, but don't let this put you off. You'll generally only need to sign a register, if that, though a few places might hand over a membership card in return for a few dollars.

CENTRAL

The Ashoka, 57–59 Wyndham St ☎524 9623. A comfortable restaurant serving highly recommended Northern Indian food. There are very good-value set lunches and dinners, and several vegetarian choices. Open noon–2.30pm & 6–10.30pm. Moderate.

Eating

Eating

Club Sri Lanka, Basement, 17 Hollywood Rd ☎ 526 6559. Very good Sri Lankan restaurant (at the Wyndham St end) with some fine vegetarian dishes and a different bread baked every day; the food is similar to southern Indian, although it can be highly spiced. There's a help-yourself buffet meal as well as a limited menu. Extra friendly staff and nice surroundings make this one of Central's better choices. Open 12.30–2.30pm & 7–10.30pm. Inexpensive.

Gunga Din's Club, Lower Ground Floor, 59 Wyndham St ☎ 523 1276. What used to be among the very best of Hong Kong's Indian restaurants has lost its edge under new management, but meals – served in pastel surroundings – can still be memorable and the prices are good; booking recommended. Open 11.30am–2.30pm & 6–10.30pm. Moderate.

India Curry Club, 3rd Floor, 10 Wing Wah Lane, Winner Building (off D'Aguilar Street) ☎ 523 2203. A very limited menu, but fine food (always some vegetarian) and friendly service in basic, cramped surroundings. Open 11.30am–2.30pm & 6.30–10.30pm. Inexpensive.

The Mughal Room, 1st Floor, Carfield Commercial Building, 75–77 Wyndham St ☎ 524 0107. Upmarket Northern Indian restaurant, with costumed staff, historical notes on a decent-looking menu that's strong on tandoori dishes. The food can be a bit hit-and-miss though, but the surroundings are worth paying for. Open noon–3pm & 6–11pm (evening only on Sun). Moderate.

Shalimar Club, 2nd Floor, 28a Stanley St ☎ 522 8489. A wider menu than usual, including kebabs and tandoori food. A small place with friendly service. Open 11.30am–2.30pm & 6–10.30pm. Inexpensive.

WAN CHAI AND CAUSEWAY BAY

Club Aparmar, 1st Floor, 16 Lee Tung St, Wan Chai ☎ 574 2643. Cheap and extremely good food in a small, badly lit restaurant. Open 11.30am–3pm & 6–11pm. Inexpensive.

Jo Jo Mess Club, 1st Floor, 86–90 Johnston Rd, Wan Chai (entrance on Lee Tung St) ☎ 527 3776. Good tandoori restaurant. Open 11am–3pm & 6–11pm. Inexpensive.

Maharaji, 222 Wan Chai Rd, Wan Chai ☎ 574 9838. Fine food (including halal options) and even better prices; a good first choice. Open noon–2.30pm & 6–10.30pm (Sun, evening only). Inexpensive.

Rangoon, Ground Floor, 265 Gloucester Rd, Hoi Kung Mansion, Causeway Bay ☎ 892 1182 or ☎ 893 0778. This quiet Burmese restaurant is a real treat, with a high-quality menu (with vegetarian dishes) that's not particularly expensive – beautifully presented and hefty portions. Open 11.30am–11.30pm. Moderate.

Shahanshah, 16 Leighton Rd, Causeway Bay ☎ 895 1533. Halal Indian food that comes with a very good reputation. A bit pricey, though. Open 11am–3pm & 6–11pm. Moderate.

Viceroy of India, 2nd Floor, Sun Hung Kai Centre, 30 Harbour Rd, Wan Chai ☎ 827 7777. Food from all parts of India and terrace dining, too, with harbour views, make this a popular spot. The lunch buffet is particularly well regarded. Open noon–3pm & 6–11pm. Moderate.

TSIM SHA TSUI

Delhi Club Mess, Block C, 3rd Floor, C3, Chungking Mansions, 36–44 Nathan Rd. A curry house par excellence, once you ignore the spartan surroundings and slap-down service. The ludicrously cheap set meal would feed an army. Open noon–2.30pm & 6–11.30pm. Inexpensive.

Hong Kong Nepalese Association, Block D, 15th Floor, D3, Chungking Mansions, 36–44 Nathan Rd ☎ 367 0487. Spartan but clean café with an outstanding (and very cheap) buffet lunch. Open 11.30am–3pm & 6–11.30pm. Inexpensive.

Kashmir Club, Block A, 3rd Floor, A3, Chungking Mansions, 36–44 Nathan Rd. Almost comfortable by Chungking standards – tablecloths and air-conditioning – and serving good Indian and Pakistani food. The staff are friendly too. Open noon–2.30pm & 6–10pm. Inexpensive.

Khyber, 2nd Floor, Wing Lok Building, 16b Peking Rd (entrance on Lock Road) ☎368 9014. Despite an unprepossessing entrance, this is one of the best Indian restaurants in town, with an unusually good selection of vegetable dishes, served in brasserie-style surroundings. Open 12.30–2.30pm & 6–11.30pm. Moderate..

Koh-i-Noor, 1st Floor, 16c Mody Rd, 3–4 Peninsula Apartments (on corner with Minden Row) ☎368 3065. The garish, upmarket decor hides fairly average food, though it does have a tandoori menu and all the usual snacks, breads and accompaniments. There's a second branch in Central. Open 11.30am–3.30pm & 6–11.30pm. Moderate.

Mumtaj Mahal Club, Block C, 12th Floor, C6, Chungking Mansions, 36–44 Nathan Rd ☎721 5591. Halal Indian cuisine in a restaurant with a decent view over Tsim Sha Tsui East – the food's better than in most around here. Open 12.30–3pm & 7–10.30pm. Inexpensive.

Nanak Mess, Block A, 11th Floor, A4, Chungking Mansions, 36–44 Nathan Rd ☎368 8063. Punjabi-style food served in a spacious (for Chungking Mansions) dining room. Open noon–3pm & 7–11pm. Inexpensive.

Woodlands, 8 Minden Ave ☎369 3718. Part of an international chain, this is a terrific, mainly southern Indian restaurant serving strict vegetarian food, with a menu that describes each dish in detail. Snacks as well as full meals, including biryani and excellent thalis, the portions large enough to share. Always popular, with friendly service. Open noon–3.30pm & 6.30–11pm. Inexpensive.

Indonesian

Spicy **Indonesian** food is easy to come by in Hong Kong, and on the whole it's very good. *Satay* is the most famous dish, but look out for good deals on the *rijstafel* ("rice table") – a buffet of ten or more little dishes which give you a taste of everything. Sweets and desserts are always tempting as well, often displayed in the windows of the restaurants, and available to take away.

Bali Restaurant, 10 Nanking St, Yau Ma Tei ☎330 2902. Affordable, but fairly unimaginative, Indonesian food, (though the fish in chilli sauce is very tasty) served in extremely kitschy surroundings – lanterns, bamboo and drapes as far as the eye can see. Open noon–11pm. Inexpensive–Moderate.

Cinta Restaurant, Basement, *Hotel New Harbour*, 6 Fenwick St, Wan Chai ☎527 1199. Good and filling *rijstafel* among other authentic meals. Open 11am–2am. Moderate.

Java Rijstafel, 38 Hankow Rd, Tsim Sha Tsui ☎367 1230. Bang in the middle of Tsim Sha Tsui, the *rijstafel* is worth considering here, though it's only served for a minimum of two people. The satay is good too. Open noon–10.30pm. Moderate.

Restaurant Indonesia, 514 Lockhart Rd, Causeway Bay ☎575 7827. Restaurant with a good reputation and a takeaway counter. Open 11.30am–midnight. Inexpensive–Moderate.

International

Hong Kong is infested with **international** restaurants with an identity crisis. The old, established places tend to serve classic European bistro/brasserie meals; new arrivals follow their counterparts in the West with menus strong on Mediterranean and Californian flavours. And others draw from East and West, serving up steaks or fried noodles to a mixed clientele.

Finealley's, 2 Glenealy St, Central ☎523 3595. Generous European meals in a quiet, central location. Dishes come from the Med, as well as Germany and France; there are always some vegetarian choices, too. Open Mon–Fri noon–2.30pm & 6.30–10.30pm, Sat & Sun 6–10.30pm. Moderate.

IFJ Food Plaza, 2nd Floor, Chungking Mansions, 36–44 Nathan Rd, Tsim Sha Tsui ☎724 4933. Twenty-four hour servings of assorted European and Asian meals – *IFJ* stands for "Italy, France, Japan", though the foods of Vietnam, Thailand and Cambodia also get a look in. Open 24 hours. Inexpensive.

Eating

The restaurants reviewed in this book have been given price categories as follows:

Inexpensive under $120

Moderate $120–250

Expensive $250–400

Very Expensive $400–750

These are per person prices; see box on p.218 for more details.

Eating

The restaurants reviewed in this book have been given price categories as follows:

Inexpensive under $120

Moderate $120–250

Expensive $250–400

Very Expensive $400–750

These are per person prices; see box on p.218 for more details.

Jim's Euro Diner, Ground Floor, Tak House, 5–11 Stanley St, Central ☎868 6886. Spotless, modern diner serving three-course set meals comprising Italian, French, German and British dishes. Open noon–3pm & 6–10pm. Inexpensive–Moderate.

Jimmy's Kitchen, Basement, South China Building, 1–3 Wyndham St, Central ☎526 5293; 1st Floor, Kowloon Centre, 29 Ashley Rd, Tsim Sha Tsui ☎376 0327. Old, reliable European restaurant, popular with expats and serving a menu of standards from French onion soup to steak pie. It's relatively cheap given its decent-sized portions. Open noon–midnight. Moderate–Expensive.

Peak Café, 121 Peak Rd, The Peak ☎849 7868. Refurbished in Californian designer-style, the East-West food at the Peak is spot on, as are the views out to sea from Hong Kong's finest vantage point. Set meals are good value and there are weekend barbecues and good vegetarian choices, too. Open 10.30am–11.30pm. Expensive.

Parc 27, 27th Floor, *Park Lane Hotel*, 310 Gloucester Rd, Causeway Bay ☎890 3355 x3344. Come for the views and the food – both are worth the admittedly high tab. Open noon–3pm & 6–11pm. Expensive.

Post 97, 1st Floor, 8–11 Lan Kwai Fong, Central ☎810 9333. Mediterranean café food in the *Nineteen 97* complex (for details of which see the next chapter), with a daily vegetarian choice. Mon–Thurs 9am–2am, Fri–Sun 24hrs. Moderate–Expensive.

Stanley's Oriental Restaurant, 90b Stanley Main St, Stanley ☎813 9988. Excellent location, with a terrace overlooking Stanley's bay, and featuring an enterprising mix of Indian, Thai, Cajun and Chinese cooking. Daily specials are always worth trying. Open 9am–11pm. Moderate–Expensive.

Italian

La Boheme, 2nd Floor, 151 Lockhart Rd, Wan Chai ☎511 7717. Value-for-money restaurant with classic, northern Italian dishes; the *risotto* is particularly well-regarded. It also hosts rave dance parties on occasional Saturdays. Open noon–2.30pm & 7–10.30pm. Moderate–Expensive.

Jaffe's, 1st Floor, *Century Hong Kong Hotel*, 238 Jaffe Rd, Wan Chai ☎598 8888. An excellent bet for lunch; there's a fine salad bar as well as pasta and pizza. Open 11.30am–3pm & 6–11.30pm. Moderate.

Marco Polo Pizza, 23 Lan Kwai Fong, Central ☎868 1013. Great takeaway pizzas and free deliveries in Central, Western, Stanley and south side Hong Kong. Open Mon 11am–9pm, Tues–Thurs 11am–midnight, Fri & Sat 11am–2am, Sun 5–9pm. Inexpensive.

Il Mercato, Basement, 34–36 D'Aguilar St, Central ☎868 3068; 126 Stanley Main St, Stanley ☎813 9090. Fine pizzas, or spend a little more and dine out on fresh, superior Italian food. Set lunches are always good value. *Marco Polo* (see above) will deliver their food too. Open noon–3pm & 6.30pm–midnight (Central branch closed Sun lunch). Moderate.

Numero Uno, 1 Village Rd, Happy Valley ☎838 8118; 66b Bonham Rd, Mid-Levels ☎559 0225. Award-winning pizza and a respectable salad bar, though neither branch is particularly central. Open 11am–11pm. Inexpensive–Moderate.

The Pizzeria, 2nd Floor, *Kowloon Hotel*, 19–21 Nathan Rd, Tsim Sha Tsui ☎369 8698. Smart and highly rated pizzeria, with pricier pasta dishes and main courses too. Open noon–3pm & 6–11pm. Moderate.

Rigoletto's, 14–16 Fenwick St, Wan Chai ☎527 7144. Established Italian restaurant whose decent food draws lots of visitors. Open Mon–Sat noon–3pm & 6pm–midnight, Sun 6pm–midnight. Moderate.

Spaghetti Factory, 8 Granville Rd, Tsim Sha Tsui ☎311 3657. Mostly pasta, but some pizzas as well, all at very reasonable prices – the drawback being that it's not the most authentic Italian food you'll ever eat. Open 11.30am–11.30pm. Inexpensive.

Eating

Tivoli, 130 Austin Rd, Tsim Sha Tsui ☎366 6424. A popular, candlelit, checked-tablecloth joint, serving good pasta and authentic thin-crust pizzas. Very good value. Open noon–midnight. Moderate.

Va Bene, 58–62 D'Aguilar St, Lan Kwai Fong, Central ☎845 5577. Stylish new Venetian restaurant that requires a full wallet (and a reservation) – authentic Italian cuisine like this (including great fresh pasta) doesn't come cheap in Hong Kong. Open noon–3pm & 7pm–midnight. Expensive.

Japanese

Eating **Japanese** food is not a budget choice in Hong Kong, but it's still good value compared to what you'd pay at home – especially if you're eating fish, which, in Hong Kong, is as fresh as it ever comes. Good lunch deals abound if you're looking for quantity rather than quality. If you're unfamiliar with the food, try *sushi*, raw fish wrapped in rice or seaweed; *sashimi* is sliced raw fish served with spicy horseradish sauce (*wasabi*). More mainstream dishes include *tempura*, deep-fried seafood or vegetables in batter, and *teppanyaki*, which is grilled, sliced meat/seafood. Drink *sake* (hot rice wine), or good *Sapporo* or *Kirin* beer, with your meal.

Department stores. For informal, cheap Japanese food, try the supermarkets in the *Sogo* (555 Hennessy Rd) and *Daimaru* (Household Square, Kingston St) department stores, which feature takeaway *sushi* and Japanese snack bars. Inexpensive.

Ganruku, 27a Chatham Rd, Tsim Sha Tsui ☎369 9728. The S-shaped conveyor belt delivers your food – about the cheapest way to eat Japanese in Hong Kong. There are half a dozen other branches too. Open 11am–11pm. Inexpensive.

Kiku Express, Lower Ground Floor, Jardine House, Connaught Rd, Central ☎845 9541. Popular Japanese café serving *sushi*, noodles and other dishes, as well as takeaway lunch boxes. Open Mon–Sat 7.30am–7pm. Inexpensive.

Momoyama, Shop 15, Lower Ground Floor, Jardine House, Connaught Rd, Central ☎845 8773. Jardine House's other Japanese option, this time for the flash and speedy business lunch brigade. Medium to pricey set meals. Open Mon–Sat 11am–3pm & 5.30–10.30pm. Moderate–Expensive.

Orba, Ground Floor, 107 Hennessy Rd, Wan Chai ☎528 3853. Japanese counter lunches providing excellent value for money, particularly the *sashimi*. Open noon–11pm. Moderate.

Unkai, 3rd Floor, *Sheraton Hotel*, 20 Nathan Rd, Tsim Sha Tsui ☎369 1111 x2. If you're going to blow your money on one ridiculously expensive meal, it may as well be somewhere reasonably true to its Japanese origins. In this case, the chefs are from Osaka and the food is beautifully presented. Open noon–2.30pm & 6.30–10.30pm. Very Expensive.

Yorohachi, 5–6 Lan Kwai Fong, Central ☎524 1251. A small restaurant in the trendy heart of Central serving good *sushi* and decent food at reasonable prices. It's popular, so book in advance. Open 11am–3pm & 6–11pm. Moderate.

Korean

Korean food is one of Hong Kong's treats. Nearly all of the restaurants feature a "barbecue" (*bulgogi*) as part of the menu – the table contains a grill, over which you cook marinaded slices of meat, fish or seafood; assorted pickles (including *kimchi*, spicy, pickled cabbage), rice and soup come with the meal. For this kind of food, the more of you there are, the better – order one barbecue dish each, and even with a beer and some noodles you'll not spend more than $120 or so a head. Korean beer is good if they have it, or go for the Japanese alternatives which most places carry. One odd feature of many restaurants is the ginseng-flavoured chewing gum handed out when you leave.

Busan Korea Restaurant, 21a Ashley Rd, Tsim Sha Tsui ☎366 2543. Cheap and cheerful place, usually with room to spare. Open noon–10pm. Inexpensive.

Eating

Joongo, 1st Floor, Great Eagle Centre, 23 Harbour Rd, Wan Chai ☎827 9287; Kimchi House, 195–197 Johnston Rd, Wan Chai ☎838 0121. Serving both Korean and Japanese food, the cooking here can be a bit hit-and-miss, but worth it for the spectacle of stereo TVs – Chinese- and English-language – blasting away. Open 11am–10.30pm. Moderate.

Korea House, 101–106 Blissful Building, 247 Des Voeux Rd, Sheung Wan ☎541 6930. Recommended by those in the know, and with excellent *kimchi*. Open 11.30am–11pm. Moderate.

Koreana, 55 Paterson St, Causeway Bay ☎577 5145. Decently priced barbecue restaurant with all the standard dishes as well as some interesting vegetable choices. Open noon–11.30pm. Moderate.

Laisan Korean BBQ, New Town Plaza, 6th Floor, 657–658, Sha Tin. Decent New Territories' restaurant that's popular with Sha Tin youth. The combination barbecue meals for two are excellent value. Open noon–11pm. Inexpensive.

Manna Korean Restaurant, Basement, 83b Nathan Rd, Tsim Sha Tsui ☎721 2159; 6–6a Humphrey's Ave, Tsim Sha Tsui ☎368 2485; 32b Mody Rd, Tsim Sha Tsui ☎367 4278. Crowded barbecue restaurants where you can fill up cheaply. The Mody Rd branch is the best, but you'll probably have to queue; the Nathan Rd one is a cavernous place, whose smoke funnels over the tables make it look like a ship's engine room. No frills, plenty of clatter and great food; get a plate of Korean noodles to soak up the barbecue sauce. Open 11am–11pm. Inexpensive.

Malaysian and Singaporean

For cheap, filling food, the territory's **Malaysian** restaurants are a good first stop: there are lots in Tsim Sha Tsui and they all serve mountainous noodle and rice dishes, along with more elaborate food that echoes the local Cantonese style. Many restaurants, Malaysian and Cantonese, also serve dishes that are strictly **Singaporean** in character, mixing spicy, traditional food with Malay dishes and ingredients.

Banana Leaf Restaurant, Ground Floor, Lockhart House, 440 Jaffe Rd, Wan Chai ☎382 8189; 3rd Floor, 440 Prince Edward Rd (at Lung Kok St), Kowloon City. Malaysian and Singaporean standards, served on banana leaves, as is traditional. Curries are notable, too, particularly fish-head curry; pad out your meal with satay, samosas and breads. Open 11am–3pm & 6pm–midnight. Inexpensive.

Eastern Hot Pot Restaurant, 41 Ashley Rd, Tsim Sha Tsui ☎376 0323. Nothing of the kind, but a bright, basic restaurant with a fairly cheap Malaysian menu and daily lunch specials. Open 11.30am–11pm. Inexpensive.

Nam Ah, 27 Ashley Rd, Tsim Sha Tsui ☎376 0707. Plonk yourself down in the diner-style booth seating and dig in – mostly Malaysian, but with Chinese and European food, too; noodle and rice plates and a few bargain set meals. Open 11am–11pm. Inexpensive.

Satay Hut, Houston Centre, Mody Rd, Tsim Sha Tsui East ☎723 3628. Authentic satay dishes and other Singaporean staples in a friendly restaurant. Open noon–3pm & 6–11pm. Moderate.

Seefah Restaurant, 1–3a Hart Ave, Tsim Sha Tsui ☎721 3270. A large restaurant with some good-value Malaysian dinners, and other Asian dishes, too. Open 11am–11pm. Inexpensive.

Singapore Mandarin, 93–99 Hennessy Rd, Wan Chai ☎866 3098. Meals of quality, although the staff can be a little overbearing. Open 11.30am–10pm. Moderate.

SMI Curry Centre, 1st Floor, 81 Lockhart Rd (junction with Luard Rd), Wan Chai ☎527 3107. Reliable Malaysian dishes, along with Singaporean meat and fish *sambal* and other curries (SMI stands for "Singapore, Malaysian, Indian"). Budget prices and pleasant surroundings. Open noon–11.30pm. Inexpensive.

Mexican

Casa Mexicana, Ground Floor, Victoria Centre, 15 Watson Rd, North Point ☎566 5560. Ropey Mexican food but everyone comes to get blind on the *margheritas* and beer. Not a particularly cheap evening, but there's a $150 Sunday buffet after 6pm. Open 11.30am–midnight. Moderate.

Mexican Association, 11th Floor, Hankow Centre, 1c Middle Rd, Tsim Sha Tsui ☎367 4535. The food's OK here, though most concentrate their attention on the frozen pitchers of *margheritas*, the best in town. The building is behind the YMCA. Open noon–midnight. Moderate.

Mongolian

Kublai's, 1st Floor, 151 Lockhart Rd, Wan Chai ☎511 2287; and 55 Kimberley Rd, Tsim Sha Tsui. Mongolian "barbecue" restaurant: pick your own ingredients – noodles, spices, vegetables, sliced meat and fish, and sauces – and then take it to be cooked. Highly entertaining if there's a crowd, and you can keep going back for more – though the whole affair can be a little rushed at busy times. Open noon–3pm & 6.30–11pm. Inexpensive.

Thai

It's only recently caught on in the West, but **Thai** food has been well-established in Hong Kong for years. There are some classy places about, especially in Central, but almost without exception the best places are the cheaper restaurants in Kowloon City, near the airport, where the food is a dream. To reach them, take buses #11 (from Jordan Rd Ferry), #5, #5C and #9 (Star Ferry), or #5K and #5C (Kowloon Station) and get off at Carpenter Road, opposite the airport. The fiery cuisine includes *tom yam*, a classic soup with prawns, lemon grass, chillis and straw mushrooms; spicy fish or prawn cakes, served with cucumber and chilli sauce; meat or fish served in violently hot red or green-paste curry sauces; and flat noodles, garnished with nuts and vegetables (*pad thai*). Wash it all down with a Thai beer, like *Singha*.

Baan Thai, 4th Floor, Causeway Bay Plaza 1, 489 Hennessy Rd, Causeway Bay ☎831 955. Lots of Thai style and spice make this one of the most authentic of Hong Kong's Thai restaurants – a good

place to splash out on the more expensive fish dishes. Steer clear of those and a meal can be a bargain, given the slick service and quality food. Open noon–3pm & 6–11.30pm. Moderate.

The Chili Club, 88 Lockhart Rd, Wan Chai ☎527 2872. A recommended Thai restaurant, which is more expensive than those at the airport but excellent. It's a small place, so booking – especially at night – is a good idea. Open noon–3pm & 6–10.30pm. Moderate.

Golden Harvest, 21 Kai Tak Rd, Kowloon City ☎383 6131. Serving some of the best Thai food in Hong Kong – a select menu which features excellent *tom yam* and fishcakes, and good beer. Couldn't be better value. Open 11.30am–11.30pm. Inexpensive.

Her Thai, Shop 1, Promenade Level, Tower 1, China Hong Kong City, Canton Rd, Tsim Sha Tsui ☎735 8898. New, high-class Thai restaurant with harbour views and a nice line in interior decor. The food's extremely good – especially the seafood – but expect to pay more than usual. Open noon–3pm & 6–11pm. Moderate–Expensive.

Shek O Chinese Thai Seafood Restaurant, near the bus stop, main corner, Shek O ☎809 4426. On Hong Kong Island's east coast (see p.102 for transport details), this open-air café gets crowded quickly, and deservedly so. Excellent food from an extensive menu, and a fine atmosphere. Open noon–10pm. Inexpensive.

Silk's, 4–6 On Lan St, Central ☎524 2567. Just off Wyndham Street (opposite *Mad Dogs*), this is surprisingly reasonably priced for Central, serving good food in an elegant, smart interior – the *pad thai* is good and the baked chicken with coconut a revelation. Open noon–3pm & 6–11pm. Expensive.

Supatra's, 50 D'Aguilar St, Lan Kwai Fong, Central ☎522 5073. Chic setting and decor, as befits the trendy end of town (which you can view from the window-side tables), though the food doesn't always live up to its promise. Open noon–11.30pm. Moderate.

Eating

The restaurants reviewed in this book have been given price categories as follows:

Inexpensive under $120

Moderate $120–250

Expensive $250–400

Very Expensive $400–750

These are per person prices; see box on p.218 for more details.

Eating

The restaurants reviewed in this book have been given price categories as follows:

Inexpensive under $120

Moderate $120–250

Expensive $250–400

Very Expensive $400–750

These are per person prices; see box on p.218 for more details.

Thai Delicacy, 44 Hennessy Rd, Wan Chai ☎527 2598. Recommended low-budget, high-quality Thai restaurant. Open 11.30am–11.30pm. Inexpensive.

Thai Food Restaurant, 1st Floor, *King's Hotel*, 473 Nathan Rd, Yau Ma Tei ☎780 1281. The large pictorial menu makes this plain-looking restaurant a good choice if you're unsure what to order. The spicy, tasty dishes are keenly priced; you won't spend a fortune whatever you order. Open noon–9pm. Inexpensive.

Thai Wah, 24 Kai Tak Rd, Kowloon City ☎716 7432. A small restaurant serving all the classic dishes, including a fiery *tom yam* in three sizes (the middle-sized bowl is enough for two or three people). Check out the daily specials – and be sure to have the prawn cakes. Open 11am–midnight. Inexpensive–Moderate.

Vegetarian food

The main problem with being **vegetarian** in Hong Kong is the language barrier in restaurants; often, even when the waiters do speak English, they will insist that things like chicken or pork aren't really meat. In Chinese restaurants, it's better to say "I eat vegetarian food" (*ngor sik tzai*), or Buddhist monk's food as it's thought of, which is an accepted concept. Even committed Chinese meat-eaters eat strictly vegetarian meals fairly regularly in order to clean out the system and balance their diet, while a fair number of the population are vegetarian for religious reasons, either permanently or on certain religious holidays.

It's fairly easy to stick to vegetarian Chinese food, either eating the mainstream vegetable, mushroom and beancurd (*tofu*) dishes on the menu or ordering a regular noodle dish without the meat. Bear in mind, though, if you're a purist, that many Chinese dishes start off life with a meat stock. Some good, strictly vegetarian **dishes** to order are *lo hon tzai* ("monk's vegetables"; a mixture of mushrooms, vegetables and beancurd) and *bak choy* (Chinese cabbage), usually stir-fried and served with oyster sauce.

To avoid any problems, it's easiest to eat in one of the excellent **Cantonese**

vegetarian restaurants, where the food is based on *tofu*, which can be shaped into – and made to taste of – almost anything. Several places also specialise in **vegetarian dim sum**, where all the food looks exactly like its meaty counterpart (you even call it by the same names), but is all strictly vegetarian. In regular *dim sum* restaurants, you'll have a much harder time eating widely and well unless you eat prawns, though the various cakes and puddings are usually harmless enough.

Other than these places, you're best off in the territory's **Indian and Pakistani restaurants** (p.229), which have lots of non-meat choices, at a **pizza** (p.232) place, or a hotel buffet (p.228), which will always have a good salad bar and other vegetarian options. A meal at one of the **Buddhist monasteries** in Hong Kong will also consist of good, solid – and cheap – vegetarian food; see especially Lantau (Chapter 5) and the various temples in the New Territories (Chapter 4).

VEGETARIAN RESTAURANTS

The places listed below are completely vegetarian, and are reviewed elsewhere in this chapter.

Dim Sum: for vegetarian *dim sum*, see p.217.

Everywhere: *Bodhi Vegetarian Restaurant*; several locations in Hong Kong and Kowloon; see "Chinese: Cantonese", above

Fat Heung Lam, 94 Wellington St, Central; p.219.

Kung Tak Lam, 15 Hanoi Rd, Tsim Sha Tsui; p.224.

Healthy Mess, Ground Floor, 51–53 Hennessy Rd, Wan Chai; p.220.

Vegi-Food Kitchen, 8 Cleveland St, Causeway Bay; p.221.

Wishful Cottage, 336 Lockhart Rd, Wan Chai; p.220.

Woodlands, 8 Minden Ave, Tsim Sha Tsui; p.231.

Vietnamese

The growing band of **Vietnamese** restaurants in Hong Kong reflects the growing number of immigrants. It can be snacky food – barbecued chicken pieces, spring rolls (which you wrap in lettuce leaves and dip in sauce) and noodle soups – though the availability of traditional ingredients means that more complicated dishes are common, too. The most elaborate meal is the traditional seven-course set meal where all the dishes are various treatments of beef. Flavour things with the fermented fish sauce and chilli on the table. The best beer to drink is "33", a French brew popular in Vietnam.

Golden Bull Restaurant, Level 1, 17, New World Centre, 18 Salisbury Rd, Tsim Sha Tsui ☎369 4617. Impressive, top-of-the-range Vietnamese restaurant with a long menu – the barbecued prawns are always good. Ring first to book a table as it's generally busy. Open noon–11.30pm. Moderate–Expensive.

Lisa (Fat Dat) 41 Morrison Hill Rd, Causeway Bay ☎573 7806. Recommended, even if some of the spark has gone lately. Try the French beef and broccoli. Open noon–10pm. Moderate.

Loy Loy, 9 Ashley Rd, Tsim Sha Tsui ☎376 0778. Cheerful canteen-style restaurant with a largely Cantonese clientele; you may have to share a table. The bumper-sized set menus are particularly good value, but the staff will talk you through the rest of the dishes, too. Open noon–11pm. Moderate.

Mekong, Arcade 2, *Hotel Miramar*, 130 Nathan Rd, Tsim Sha Tsui ☎311 3303. A rated restaurant, with a strong menu, including the seven-types-of-beef set dinner. Open 11.30am–11.30pm. Moderate.

Myer, 10 Cheung Lok St, Jordan ☎771 2401. North of Jordan MTR, down the second street on the right, this cheap café has excellent spring rolls and other snacks. Open 11.30am–10.30pm. Inexpensive.

Paterson, Shop A, Marco Polo Mansion, 10 Cleveland St, Causeway Bay ☎890 6146. One of the best Vietnamese restaurants in Hong Kong, with a large menu, good soups and seafood; try one of the clay-pot dishes. Open 11.30am–11.30pm. Moderate.

Special Diets

Some of the Pakistani restaurants in Chungking Mansions advertise themselves as serving **halal** food (see p.229), as does the occasional Chinese Muslim restaurant. For **kosher** food, there's no specific restaurant, but try the *Beverly Hills Deli* (see "American", p.226); or enquire about the kosher kitchen and restaurant at the Ohel Leah synagogue, 76 Robinson Road, Mid-Levels ☎559 4820. Any other dietary requirements can probably be catered for by the biggest hotel restaurants; it's always worth a phone call. Or check the list of **supermarkets** given under "Buying your own food" (p.238), if you want to play safe and buy your own provisions.

Saigon Beach Restaurant, 66 Lockhart Rd, Wan Chai ☎529 7823. Good little restaurant that's popular with young travellers and locals because it sticks to the basics and cooks them well. Open noon–3pm & 6–10pm. Inexpensive.

Vietnam City, Lower Ground Floor, Energy Plaza, 92 Granville Rd, Tsim Sha Tsui ☎366 7880. More upmarket Vietnamese, with French and Chinese influences apparent in the menu. Open noon–11.30pm. Moderate.

Buying Your Own Food: markets, supermarkets, bakeries and barbecues

With hot food and snacks so cheap in Hong Kong, there isn't much incentive to buy **picnic food**. However, you'll probably want to buy bread, cakes and fruit from the **markets**, and more elaborate food if you're going to use any of the hundreds of **barbecue sites** throughout the territory. If you're on any kind of special diet – or simply want to know exactly what you're eating – there are **supermarkets** right across Hong Kong. Be warned, though, that for anything recognisably Western, you'll pay a lot more than you would at home.

Eating

Eating

Markets

A walk around a Cantonese **market** is a sight in itself, and several are detailed in the text, including Hong Kong Island's Central Market (p.63), Sheung Wan market (p.69) and Luen Wo (p.140) and Sheung Shui markets (p.141) in the New Territories. A market is where the bulk of the population buys its fresh food, shopping at least once a day for meat, fish, fruit and vegetables. All the towns and residential blocks, especially in the developments in the New Territories, have a market hall.

They can look a bit intimidating at first, but no one minds you wandering around and checking out the produce. Most food is sold by the **catty**, which equals 1.3lb or 600g. Prodding and handling **fruit and veg** is almost expected: just pick out the items you want and hand them over. They'll invariably be weighed on an ingenious set of hand-held scales, and, although the metric system is in official use, will almost certainly be priced according to traditional Chinese weights and measures. No one's out to cheat you, but it can help to know some Cantonese numbers and prices. Some stallholders will let you sample some of the more obscure fruit: one to watch for is the durian, a yellow, spikey fruit shaped like a rugby ball, that is fairly pricey and decidedly smelly – very much an acquired taste.

Buying **meat and fish** is also straightforward, though if you're going by sight alone make sure that the pretty fish you're pointing at isn't extremely rare and very expensive. It's perfectly all right to have several things weighed until you find the piece you want. For the best fish, either get to the market early in the morning, or come back in the mid-afternoon when the second catch is delivered. Every market will also have a **cooked meat** stall, selling roast pork, duck and chicken, which can perk up a picnic lunch no end.

Supermarkets

There are plenty of **supermarkets** around, but apart from a couple of notable exceptions they're pricey and concentrate on tinned and packet foods. Territory-wide **supermarket chains** include *Wellcome*

and *Park 'N' Shop* . For addresses of these, and other specialist supermarkets, see below; they're generally open daily from around 8am to 8pm, though stores throughout the territory vary their hours.

TERRITORY-WIDE SUPERMARKETS

Park 'N' Shop: branches at Pedder St, Central; Admiralty Centre, Central; and the Peak Tower.

Wellcome: branches at The Forum, Exchange Square, Central; 78 Nathan Rd, Tsim Sha Tsui.

SPECIALIST STORES

Asia Provisions Co. Ltd, 14 Pottinger St, Central; 31 Granville Rd, Tsim Sha Tsui. Despite the name, this is full of British and European brand names – the place to get jams, baked beans and cornflakes.

Daimaru, Household Square, Kingston St, Causeway Bay. Excellent Japanese supermarket inside the department store; takeaway food, too.

Indian Provision Store, Ground Floor, nos. 65–68, Chungking Mansions, 36–44 Nathan Rd, Tsim Sha Tsui. Indian spices, sweets and pickles as well as tins and dairy products.

Mok Po Food Co., 16th Floor, Korean Centre, no. 7, Sheung Wan. Korean supermarket.

Sogo, East Point Centre, 555 Hennessy Rd, Causeway Bay MTR. There's a Japanese supermarket inside the department store – takeaway Japanese snacks and food as well.

Thai Corner, 1A, Level 3, Sha Tin Plaza, Sha Tin, New Territories. Thai spices and sauces, noodles and pickles.

Yaohan, New Town Plaza, 18 Sha Tin Centre Rd, Sha Tin, New Territories. The ground floor of this department store has a huge Japanese supermarket, fresh meat and fish, alcoholic drinks, takeaway *sushi* and a Japanese snack bar.

Bakeries

The bread sold in supermarkets tends to be white and horrible, and you're better off buying it from the **bakeries** you'll find in every market and on most street corners. It'll be substantially the same – brown and wholemeal are virtually unknown – but will at least be fresher, and costs only a couple of dollars for a small sliced loaf. **Cakes** from bakeries are cheap, too, only a dollar or two for very sweet and very addictive creations. More elaborate cream cakes and buns are sold from the *Maxim's* chain of shops, which you'll find in most MTR and KCR stations, as well as at the Star Ferry terminals.

Barbecues

Almost everywhere of scenic interest you go in Hong Kong (and at some youth hostels and campsites) there are special **barbecue pits** provided in picnic areas. They're inordinately popular and getting the ingredients together for a barbecue isn't difficult. Supermarkets sell fuel, barbecue forks and all the food, as do kiosks at some of the more enterprising sites; either buy ready-made satay sticks or pick up cuts of meat and fish from the market.

Eating

Chapter 8

Nightlife: Bars, Pubs and Clubs

If you're not making eating your sole evening's entertainment, then Hong Kong has plenty to occupy you, lots of it carrying on until the small hours. There's no shortage of **bars, pubs, discos and clubs** in which you can while away the night, and because Hong Kong doesn't have that desperately trendy edge that bedevils London and New York, most of them are good, down-to-earth fun. That doesn't mean they're scruffy. Some are, but plenty are expensively decorated and dripping with sophistication, so if you're planning some extensive investigation, bring (or buy) clothes that won't wilt under a supercilious Hong Kong glare. Also,

pubbing and clubbing are comparatively **expensive** and you'll need a fairly substantial amount of money to party every night. The Chinese don't drink much, so most bars and pubs are the province of the territory's expats and tourists. You will, however, catch lots of the local youth in the brash, glittery discos, where the emphasis is more on dancing than posing.

Bars and Pubs

There's a wide range of **places to drink** in Hong Kong, most of them in Tsim Sha Tsui, Central and Wan Chai, and varying

---

Alcoholic drinks

The most readily available alcoholic beverage is **beer**, lager-style and served ice-cold. The main brews are *San Miguel* and (better) *Tsingtao*, the latter a sharp Chinese beer made originally from a German recipe. If you can't get either of these, there's locally brewed *Carlsberg*, though some bars and restaurants (and lots of supermarkets) sell good foreign beer, like the Japanese *Kirin* or *Sapporo*, *Guinness* and even cider. Beer costs from around $6–7 a small can, $10–12 a litre in the supermarket; in a restaurant, it's around $17–25 a large bottle; while in bars and pubs, this rises dramatically – anything from $25–35 for a draught half-litre.

Drinking **wine** is very expensive, starting at around $180 a bottle for even the most average of wines – considerably more for anything halfway decent. Buy your own in a supermarket, and you'll pay at least $70–80 for basic French plonk – the alternatives are often South African, though Australasian wine is fairly well-represented. You can get wine from the Chinese mainland but it's not common, and is unspectacular. Most internationally known **spirits** are available in bars and restaurants, again at a price. Cheaper, though much nastier and guaranteeing a miserable morning-after, are the various brands of Chinese **rice wine**, some of the cheaper examples of which are best left for cooking.

from chic, international cocktail bars to rowdy pubs. Although many of the pubs are, as you might expect, British in style – complete with horse brasses and dart boards – lots of others are either Australian or American, with food and drink to match.

Most bars and pubs are **open** from around lunchtime until well after midnight; some, especially in Wan Chai, stay open until breakfast time, and a couple keep serving drinks right around the clock. Lockhart Road (particularly between Luard Rd and Fleming Rd) is lined with late-opening, hard-drinking dens. You can get **food** in many places, especially at lunchtime – the Australian and British ones are good for pies and peas, and fish and chips – and it's usually good value; see p.227 for more details. Some places also put on **live music**, mostly folk (ie, singer-guitarists mangling "Yesterday") and jazz: these are picked out in the lists below, but for fuller details of live music, turn to the following chapter.

The other thing to watch out for is the prevalence of **Happy Hours**, where you'll get two-for-one drinks, or at least substantial discounts. They generally lasts a lot more than an hour: some time between 5pm and 8pm is usual (though some places sell cheap drinks all afternoon). Blackboards and notices in pubs and bars have details, and check the reviews below.

Central

Blake Pier. Outdoor bar/café on the upper level of the pier. Cheap draught beer and food (including breakfast), and good harbour views. Open 8am–9pm.

Cactus Club, 13 Lan Kwai Fong ☎525 6732. Fashionable bar which mixes a mean *margherita* for a young crowd; good beer selection too. Open Sun–Thurs noon–2am, Fri & Sat noon–4am.

Café Flipp, Ground Floor, California Building, 34–36 D'Aguilar St ☎801 4946. Stylish open-fronted bar; cool but not pretentious. Open Mon–Sat noon–midnight.

California, 24–26 Lan Kwai Fong ☎521 1345. Expensive American bar and restaurant, though open late and with a tiny dance floor. Open Mon–Sat noon–1am, Fri & Sat until 4am.

The Gallery & Pier One, Shop 12, Basement, Jardine House, 1 Connaught Rd ☎526 3061. Dark, nautical surroundings – oak barrels, ropes and maritime bric-a-brac – for this basement British pub with a city clientele and Filipino musicians struggling with "Smoke on the Water". Open Mon–Sat 8am–midnight.

Godown, Ground Floor, Tower II, Admiralty Centre, 18 Harcourt Rd ☎866 1166. Traditional expat haunt with regular live jazz sessions – which is the only time it's worth going. Open 10am–2am.

Hardy's, 35 D'Aguilar St ☎526 7184. Popular pub with folk singers and a decent, party atmosphere, particularly on Fridays – make sure you know the words to "American Pie". Happy Hour 5.30–8.30pm. Open Sun–Thurs 5.30pm–midnight, Fri & Sat 5.30pm–2am.

The Jazz Club, 2nd Floor, 34–36 D'Aguilar St ☎845 8477. The narrow bar is open to non-members, who can drink to the jazz sounds coming from the video CD provided for customers' use. Happy Hour 5–8pm. Opening hours vary according to who's playing; see "Live Music", p.248.

The Jockey, 1st Floor, Swire House, 11 Chater Rd ☎526 1478. Expensive British-style pub which attracts the suits and portable phones; food, too. Open Mon–Sat 11am–11pm.

LA Café, Ground Floor, Lippo Centre, Queensway ☎526 6863. American designer bar: *Harley Davidson* in the bar, TVs in the toilets, trendies lurking in the corners. There's live music and stand-up comedy at times, too. Open noon–midnight.

Mad Dogs, 8 Wyndham St ☎810 1000. Unashamedly British pub, with pictures of Queen Victoria, British beer on draught and comfy seating. It mostly attracts a business district clientele, all of whom pack in for the 4–8pm Happy Hour. Open Mon–Thurs 7am–2am, Fri & Sat 7am–3am, Sun 10am–2am.

Nightlife:
Bars, Pubs
and Clubs

Nightlife: Bars, Pubs and Clubs

Post 97, Upper Ground Floor, 9 Lan Kwai Fong ☎810 9333. A trendy café-bar in the *Nineteen 97* complex which doubles as an art gallery; Happy Hour is 5–7pm. Open Mon–Thurs 9am–2am, Fri–Sun 9am–5am.

Schnurrbart, Ground Floor, Winner Building, 29 D'Aguilar St ☎523 4700. Good German bar with bar stools, herring and sausage snacks, and some of the best beer around. Serious headaches are available courtesy of the 25 different kinds of *schnapps*. Open noon–2am.

The Time Is Always Now, 19–27 Wyndham St ☎877 1100. Another café-bar with pretensions as an art gallery. This at least has big, comfortable chairs and magazines available to read. Open noon–midnight.

The Vintage, 19 On Lan St ☎586 1421. Dripping with Hong Kong style, this place opens for breakfast and stays open, catering to the young and determinedly cool. Open 7am to whenever the manager decides to close.

Wan Chai

Horse and Groom, 161 Lockhart Rd. Drinks any time of the day or night; and worth visiting for the cheap food. Open 24hr.

Horse and Carriage, 117 Lockhart Rd. Basic drinking, very cheap food and budget drinks during the 11am–8pm Happy Hour. Open 11am–6am.

Hunter's Castle, 114 Lockhart Road. Serious pub drinking, especially during the long, long Happy Hour (noon–9pm). Open 24hr.

Joe Bananas, 23 Luard Road ☎529 1811. Lively American bar with a late disco, occasional live music and marathon weekend opening hours; Happy Hour 11am–9pm. There's a strict door policy – men need a shirt with a collar – which makes a mockery of the non-PC wet T-shirt contests on offer at times. Open Mon–Thurs 11.30am–4am, Fri & Sat 11.30am–6am, Sun 6pm–4am.

Old China Hand, 104 Lockhart Rd ☎527 9174. For hard-core drinkers, hung-over clubbers (who come for breakfast), and

those with a taste for formica surfaces. Open 24hr.

The Wanch, 54 Jaffe Rd ☎861 1621. Another venue for all those party animals who know the words to various 1960s' song classics – and want to sing along, loudly. Open 11am–1am.

Causeway Bay

The China Jump, 7th Level, Causeway Bay Plaza 2, 463 Lockhart Rd ☎832 9007. Popular expat haunt with a small dance-floor (see "Discos and Clubs", below) and loud pop and rock. Open Mon–Wed noon–2am, Thurs–Sat noon–5am.

Dickens Bar, Lower Ground Floor, *Excelsior Hotel*, 281 Gloucester Rd ☎894 8888. One of the few decent hotel bars, this also features regular jazz sessions. Sun–Thurs 11am–2am, Fri & Sat 11am–3am.

Tsim Sha Tsui

Amoeba, 22 Ashley Rd ☎376 0389. Tsim Sha Tsui's trendiest venue and refreshingly different – a New York-style café-bar with minimalist surroundings, attracting a youthful crowd for the good food and nightly live music sessions. Open noon–2.30am.

The Blacksmith's Arms, 16 Minden Ave ☎369 6696. An enjoyable and fairly authentic British pub with a solid pub food menu, a dartboard and a 3–8pm Happy Hour. Open noon–1am.

Jousters II, 19–23 Hart Ave ☎723 0022. Ludicrous drining venue – mock medieval interior, suits of armour, coats-of-arms and other baronial trappings, washed down with loud rock music and very cheap drinks right up until 9pm. Open Mon–Thurs noon–2am, Fri & Sat noon–3am, Sun 6pm–2am.

Kangaroo Pub, 1st Floor, 35 Haiphong Rd ☎312 0083. New location for an old favourite, popular with travellers – split-level Australian pub, with windows overlooking the bottom of Kowloon Park. Australian beer, sports on the video, a fine juke box and snacks or a full menu in the restaurant. Happy Hour 4–7pm. Open 11am–3am.

Bars With Views

The places below all offer views while you drink – mostly of the harbour, though the *Flying Machine* gives you a great vantage point over the airport runway. Some have already been covered in the listings, but where they haven't (especially if they're hotel bars), you can expect to pay more than usual for your drink.

Blake Pier, upper level, Central.

Harbour View Lounge, 1st Floor, *Holiday Inn Harbour View*, 70 Mody Rd, Tsim Sha Tsui East ☎ 721 5161.

Harlequin, 25th Floor, *Mandarin Oriental*, 5 Connaught Rd, Central ☎ 522 0111.

Flying Machine, 14th Floor, *Regal Airport Hotel*, 38 Sa Po Rd, Kowloon City ☎ 718 0333.

Peak Café, 121 Peak Rd, Victoria Peak ☎ 899 7868.

La Ronda, 30th Floor, *Hotel Furama*, 1 Connaught Rd, Central ☎ 525 5111.

Sky Lounge, 18th Floor, *Sheraton*, 20 Nathan Rd, Tsim Sha Tsui ☎ 369 1111 x3342.

Tiffin Bar, *Grand Hyatt*, 1 Harbour Rd, Wan Chai ☎ 588 1234.

Nightlife: Bars, Pubs and Clubs

Mad Dogs Kowloon, 32 Nathan Rd ☎ 301 2222. More entertaining than the Central branch, this basement pub elevates serious drinking to an art form. Live musicians kick off the evening proceedings, which degenerate later on as guest DJs whip up the beer monsters. Great fun. Happy Hour 4–7pm, plus two-for-one deals most nights on selected drinks. Mon–Thurs 8am–2am, Fri–Sun 8am–4am.

Ned Kelly's Last Stand, 11a Ashley Rd ☎ 376 0562. Dark Australian bar with great live trad jazz after 9pm; good beer and meaty Aussie food served at the tables. It's a real favourite with travellers and good fun – after 9pm you'll be lucky to get a seat. Open 11am–2am.

Sky Lounge, 18th Floor, *Sheraton Hotel*, 20 Nathan Rd ☎ 369 1111 x3342. Marvellous city and harbour views in stylish surroundings; dress up for the impeccable service, and free nibbles, accompanied by nightly crooners and instrumentalists. It's cheaper before 8pm, after which there's a steep minimum charge per person. Open Sun–Thurs 11am–1am, Fri & Sat 11am–2am. Open 3pm–1am.

Someplace Else, Basement, *Sheraton Hotel*, Nathan Rd ☎ 369 1111 x5. The Sheraton's other bar (entered at the junction with Middle Rd) is much more accessible – an upmarket meeting place, whose large, rowdy two-floor bar-

restaurant has live music, free popcorn nibbles, Tex-Mex and Asian snacks and a good cocktail list. Happy Hour 4–7pm. Open Sun–Thurs 11am–1am, Fri & Sat 11am–2am.

Waltzing Matilda Arms, 12–14 Hart Ave ☎ 368 8046. Popular bar, frequented by Hong Kong's gay community. Open 10am–4am.

Discos and clubs

Hong Kong has some excellent **discos and clubs** if you're simply looking for a fun night out. There's a selection given below, but bear in mind that favourites change and others close down: check local listings magazines for an accurate rundown of what's happening where. Also note that some of the discos are, at least nominally, private clubs; you may have to join before you're allowed in.

Prices are fairly reasonable, though, and on the whole you shouldn't have to pay more than $150 total for entry to most places. Some include a drink or two in the entry price, and lots only charge an entrance fee at the weekend, on the busy Friday and Saturday nights. Most places stay **open** until around 3–4am; some don't stop until 6am.

The **music** is generally mainstream European and American pop and dance music, although plenty of places also play Canto-pop (see "Live Music", p.247), and others have recently introduced Japanese-

Nightlife: Bars, Pubs and Clubs

style karaoke lounges. The **rave scene** has made a belated appearance in Hong Kong, but it's all fairly low-key and likely to stay that way: venues hosting occasional raves include *DD II* (see below) and *Amoeba* (see "Bars and Pubs") and, bizarrely, the *Viceroy of India* restaurant in Wan Chai (see p.230 for address and phone number).

Central

California, 24–26 Lan Kwai Fong ☎521 1345. Smart American restaurant-bar with a tiny dance floor on which the local yuppies strut their stuff three times a week. Open Wed, Fri & Sat night only until 1am or so.

Club 97, 9 Lan Kwai Fong ☎810 9333. A popular ground-floor disco, with a small dance floor and good Western rock and pop. Mobbed at the weekend, when there's a cover charge, but free and emptier during the week. Open until around 5am.

DD II, 38 D'Aguilar St ☎524 8809. Swish disco that attracts a gay clientele, as well as dance fiends. Some of the territory's earliest raves were held here and it still hosts sporadic dance parties. Open Sun–Thurs 9.30pm–3.30pm, Fri & Sat 9.30pm–4.30am.

Wan Chai and Causeway Bay

The China Jump, 7th Floor, Plaza Two, 463 Lockhart Rd, Causeway Bay ☎532 9007. If you make it past the self-opinionated fashion police masquerading as bouncers, then entertainment is split between the small dance floor and the performance art of the bar tenders. Escapes being a cattle market by the skin of its teeth. Open Mon–Wed until 2am, Thurs–Sat until 5/6am.

JJ's, *Grand Hyatt*, 1 Harbour Rd, Wan Chai ☎588 1234. Classy mainstream disco with a smart dress code, two bars, snooker and darts. Open Sun–Thurs 5.30pm–2am, Fri & Sat 5.30pm–3am.

Joe Bananas, 23 Luard Rd, Wan Chai ☎529 1811. American disco nights in a lively bar/restaurant. Men will need a shirt with a collar; non-drinkers will require tolerance and understanding. Open Mon–Thurs until 5am, Fri & Sat until 6am, Sun until 4am.

Neptunes, Basement, 62 Lockhart Rd, Wan Chai. Typical of Wan Chai's traditional hangouts, the dingy but good-natured environment is the backdrop for mostly Western pop, interspersed with bouts of the Filipino house band playing cover versions. The clientele is mainly Filipino, too – which means significant numbers of sad Western men on the prowl. Open 10pm–4am.

Westworld, 4th Floor, *New World Harbour View*, 1 Harbour Rd, Wan Chai ☎836 3690. Hip new dance club that's visually and financially extravagant – a decidedly non-Canto-pop experience. Open until 4am.

Stanley

Beaches, Stanley Main St, Stanley Village ☎813 7313. Expat haunt which pounds out 60s' and 70s' sounds nightly. Open until 2am.

Tsim Sha Tsui

Bar City, Basement 2, New World Centre, 18 Salisbury Rd ☎369 8751. Curious just about covers it: three different bars promising Canto disco, cabaret entertainment and "live bands in a Las Vegas-style pub setting". Open 9pm–2.30am.

The Catwalk, *New World Hotel*, 22 Salisbury Rd ☎369 4111. Mirrors and chrome and bland Western pop – which doesn't seem to have prevented it from acquiring a reputation as a Triad hangout. Open 9pm–3am.

Falcon, Basement, *Royal Garden Hotel*, 69 Mody Rd ☎721 5215. Posh surroundings and mainstream Canto-pop for the well-heeled. Open 9pm–3am.

Hostess Clubs

Hong Kong is notorious for its plethora of **hostess clubs**, or "girlie bars", which the HKTA tries hard to push as a tourist experience. Frankly, they're pathetic places for pathetic patrons, exploitative in every way, whose sleazy offers of "one drink $30" are distinctly worth resisting Still, whatever your feelings about them, some have almost entered into Hong Kong legend. *Bottoms Up* (14 Hankow Rd, Tsim Sha Tsui) is a case in point, famous simply because parts of the James Bond film *The Man With the Golden Gun* were shot there. *Red Lips* (1a Lock Rd, Tsim Sha Tsui) is notori-ous for the advanced age of its host-esses, most of whom are over sixty. And *Club BBoss* (New Mandarin Plaza, 14 Science Museum Rd, Tsim Sha Tsui East) is reputedly the largest hostess club in the world, an enormous, super-plush haunt, where a full-sized Rolls Royce-shaped model car drives you to your table. It was forced to change its name – from *Club Volvo* – after losing a court action brought by *Volvo* cars about the use of the name. The club argued, unsuccessfully, that the name was merely a transliteration of its Chinese name, *Dai Fu Ho*, or "big wealthy tycoon".

Chapter 9

Live Music: Rock, Pop, Folk and Jazz

Hong Kong is never the first place that touring Western bands think of, but even so the **live music** scene has picked up considerably over the last couple of years. Venues, however, remain few: apart from the *Hong Kong Coliseum* and the *Queen Elizabeth Stadium*, where the mega-stars play, there's no real middle-ranking concert hall for rock and pop music. If you're in Hong Kong during a quiet period for Western bands, check to see if any of the big names in the homegrown pop music scene are playing: **Canto-pop**, a Chinese-language variety of ballads and disco music, is easily the most popular music in Hong Kong – there are more details in the feature below.

There's a thriving local **jazz** scene, based around regular gigs in pubs and clubs, while many bars offer evening punters what is euphemistically referred to as **folk music**. You'll never see anyone very exciting, but if all you want to do is drink to the strains of Eagles' cover versions, there's plenty of opportunity. Finally, most of the large **hotels** feature resident bands and visiting "international artists" in their bars – invariably mood music and crooning as an accompaniment to expensive cocktail-sipping.

To find out **what's on**, look in the free listings magazine *HK Magazine*, available at many of the venues listed below and at bars and restaurants, particularly in and around Lan Kwai Fong. The *South China Morning Post* also has a daily "What's On" page (which lists the hotel-bar music in detail) and a weekly "Gig Guide".

Rock and pop

Outside the big venues, less well-known bands tend to appear in bars and pubs, or are served up as PAs ("personal appearances" singing or miming to backing tapes) in one or two of the discos. You'll find details of forthcoming events in the local press, or contact the places listed below direct. **Ticket prices** vary, but you'll usually pay from $50–100 for local bands and visiting second-rank groups and artists, more like $200–400 for someone famous.

Academic Community Hall, Baptist College, 228 Waterloo Rd, Kowloon Tong ☎ 338 6121. Major pop concerts by Chinese and international stars.

Amoeba, 22 Ashley Rd, Tsim Sha Tsui ☎ 376 0389. Live local bands most nights, including Thursday night's *Radio Free Hong Kong*, showcasing the best (and worst) of the territory's alternative and Indie bands.

Fringe Club, 2 Lower Albert Rd, Central ☎ 521 7251. Occasional rock and pop gigs by local bands.

Hong Kong Coliseum, 8 Cheong Wan Rd, Hung Hom, Kowloon ☎ 765 9234. Fairly regular performances by major inter-

For details of where to hear classical music in Hong Kong, see the following chapter.

Canto-pop

The origins of **Canto-pop** lie in the Cantonese movie musicals of the 1950s and 1960s, whose soundtracks became enormously popular in post-war Hong Kong. But until the 1970s, most true pop music in Hong Kong was either imported from the West or from Taiwan, whose Mandarin pop singers were among the first to receive star treatment. **Sam Hui**, in the mid-1970s, was the first Hong Kong-based artist to mix Cantonese lyrics with Western pop music – a style that quickly became known as Canto-pop. To Western ears, it's often fairly bland stuff – ballads are easily the most popular song form – but to the practitioners it's anything but straightforward. The nine tones in the Cantonese language cause major problems, since they limit the expressiveness that singers can put into the songs; singing in Mandarin is actually much easier.

Hui – the "Elvis Presley of the Orient" – retired in 1992, but by then he had been superseded by a phalanx of young (and not so young) hopefuls, including **Alan Tam, Jacky Cheung** and **Andy Lau**. It's largely a male dominated scene, though there are notable women singers, too. For years, undisputed Canto-pop Queen was **Anita Mui**, unearthed in a *TVB* talent contest in 1982. Mui, too, has recently announced her "retirement", but there are several others hoping to follow her – **Sally Yeh, Sandy Lam, Sammy Cheung, Vivian Chow** and **Shirley Kwan** are among the best known..

And let there be no doubt how popular these singers are. Michael Jackson or Madonna would be able to fill the 12,000-seater *Coliseum*, but Sam Hui's retirement concerts saw 41 sold-out nights there; Paula Tsui performed 43 sell-outs in 1992, while Alan Tam has played at the *Coliseum* 121 times in his career. If you get the chance to see one of the big names live in Hong Kong, it's an experience worth catching – more cabaret than pop concert.

Live Music: Rock, Pop, Folk and Jazz

---

national rock and pop bands, and lengthy concert series by Canto-pop superstars.

Joe Bananas, 23 Luard Rd, Wan Chai ☎529 1811. Disco-bar with very occasional rock and blues gigs.

LA Café, Ground Floor, East Tower, Lippo Centre, Queensway, Admiralty ☎526 6863. Fairly regular rock and pop performances by local bands and artists.

Queen Elizabeth Stadium, 18 Oi Kwan Road, Wan Chai ☎575 6793. Major rock and pop bands.

Folk

Entrance to all these bars and pubs is free, but you must expect to buy a drink or two.

Cinta Restaurant and Lounge, Basement, *Hotel New Harbour*, 6 Fenwick St, Wan Chai ☎527 1199. Filipino singers after 9pm.

Hardy's, 35 D'Aguilar St, Central ☎526 7184. Inoffensive folk singers most nights doing cover versions.

Mad Dogs, 8 Wyndham St, Central ☎810 1000; 32 Nathan Rd, Tsim Sha Tsui ☎301 2222. Early evening singer-guitarists most nights at both pubs.

Someplace Else, Basement, *Sheraton Hotel*, 20 Nathan Rd, Tsim Sha Tsui ☎369 1111 x 5. Regular live singers doing all the regular cover versions.

The Wanch, 54 Jaffe Rd, Wan Chai ☎861 1621. Solid folk and pub rock venue, with live music five nights a week from 9pm to 2am.

Jazz

Mostly, entrance to pub jazz gigs is free (except where stated below), and the standard of playing is very high. Visiting name acts play at the *Jazz Club*, while August sees the annual two-day *Select Live Under the Sky* **jazz festival**, which attracts some top people, though it's become less jazz-orientated and more middle-of-the-road of late; details from the HKTA.

Live Music: Rock, Pop, Folk and Jazz

Dickens Bar, Lower Ground Floor, *Excelsior Hotel*, 281 Gloucester Rd, Causeway Bay ☎894 8888. Jazz sessions every Sunday.

The Godown, Ground Floor, Tower II, Admiralty Centre, 18 Harcourt Rd, Admiralty ☎866 1166. Jazz night with the resident band on Wednesday, after 8pm.

Fringe Club, 2 Lower Albert Rd, Central ☎521 7251. Occasional jazz gigs; cover charge for non-members.

The Jazz Club, 2nd Floor, 34–36 D'Aguilar St, Central ☎845 8477. A unique venue in Hong Kong. Live jazz nightly: Sun–Thurs after 9.30pm, Fri & Sat after 10.30pm. Admission to non-members $200–250; more expensive tickets for big name bands and soloists throughout the year.

Ned Kelly's Last Stand, 11a Ashley Road, Tsim Sha Tsui ☎376 0562. Trad and Dixieland jazz every night after 9pm from the stomping resident band, the "Kowloon Honkers". Recommended.

Chapter 10

The Arts and Media

For years Hong Kong has had a poor cultural reputation, something that's only partially been put to rights by a series of good, annual **festivals** and the opening of the **Cultural Centre** in Tsim Sha Tsui, a conglomeration of theatre, studios and concert hall. Before this, artistic and cultural life depended on the not inconsiderable efforts of the **Hong Kong Arts Centre** and the adjacent **Academy for Performing Arts**, in Wan Chai, both of which continue to put on high-quality work. However, the formal, mostly Western arts, remain limited in scope in Hong Kong. The only art form that commands a mass audience is **film**, with the cinemas packed for every new Hollywood release, and – more pertinently – for every new Chinese film that comes out. Local **Chinese culture** is less formally presented in the territory, though, as you might expect, there's much more of it around. The main venues host traditional dance, opera and music performances, but you're just as likely to see something exciting in the night markets, or during religious holidays at temples and on the street.

Cantonese might be the language of the overwhelming majority in Hong Kong, but for tourists it's the preponderance of the English-language **media** that makes the territory such an easy place to come to terms with. Television, radio and newspapers are immediately accessible to English-speaking visitors – something that you may, or may not, be grateful for, depending on how keen you are to get away from things.

Information, Listings and Tickets

Information about cultural events and performances can be picked up at any of the venues listed below. For detailed **listings** of forthcoming events, there are three free magazines: the Urban Council's dual-language monthly *City News* (available in City Hall and other government buildings); the Hong Kong Arts Centre's monthly *Artslink* magazine; and *HK Magazine* (available at bookshops, bars, clubs and restaurants throughout the centre). Take a look, too, at the weekly *TV & Entertainment Times*, as well as in the two main English-language daily newspapers, the *Hong Kong Standard* and the *South China Morning Post*, whose weekend editions have good reviews and listings.

Tickets for most events can be bought at any of the main venues, and from offices called **URBTIX** outlets; there's a list below of venues and outlets.

Cultural events are very good value in Hong Kong. Many are subsidised by the government and accordingly, you won't pay anything like the prices you would at home. Generally, expect to pay $50–100 for seats for most local productions, rising to $200–400 for anything international.

Main Venues

Academy for Performing Arts, 1 Gloucester Rd, Wan Chai ☎584 1500. Six separate stages for local and international drama, modern and classical dance. Box office 10am–8pm.

The Arts and Media

Arts Festivals

There are several main **arts festivals** in Hong Kong each year. More information about all of them can be obtained from the HKTA, but it's worth knowing that tickets for the best performances can be hard to come by; book well in advance, or be prepared to settle for what performances you can get into.

Hong Kong Arts Festival (Jan/Feb). Wide-ranging international arts festival, mixing traditional Chinese and western cultural influences in a variety of song, dance and drama.

Hong Kong International Film Festival (April). A month's worth of international films shown at various venues – very popular and very imaginative. The City Hall has specific information if you want to try booking in advance.

Festival of Asian Arts (Oct/Nov). An event which gathers together artists from all over Asia for singing, dancing and acting.

Fringe Festival (Jan/Feb). Runs in conjunction with the official HK Arts Festival, supplementing (and clashing with) its offerings. Information from the *Fringe Club*.

Lan Kwai Fong Street Festival (Aug). Around a week's worth of street entertainment, food promotions and special events based around the trendy Central street.

Alliance Française, 123 Hennessy Rd, Wan Chai ☎ 527 7825. Films and culture at the French Cultural Institute. Box office 8.30am–9.30pm.

City Hall, 7 Edinburgh Place, Central ☎ 522 9928. Two blocks which put on drama, concerts, recitals, exhibitions and lectures. Box office 10am–10pm.

Cultural Centre, 10 Salisbury Rd, Tsim Sha Tsui ☎ 734 2009. Dance, drama and concerts in Hong Kong's newest and most controversial building, drawing on local and international performers. See p.108 for more details about the building. Box office 10am–9pm.

Fringe Club, 2 Lower Albert Rd, Central ☎ 521 7251. Offbeat venue for local performance art, jazz, concerts, poetry and drama, as well as classes and workshops. Pick up the schedule from the venue; temporary membership available. Box office 5–11pm.

Goethe Institute, 14th Floor, Hong Kong Arts Centre, 2 Harbour Rd, Wan Chai ☎ 802 0088. Films and events at the German Cultural Institute.

Hong Kong Arts Centre, 2 Harbour Rd, Wan Chai ☎ 582 0200. Local art, drama, concerts and film screenings, galleries and exhibitions. Box office 10am–8pm.

Hong Kong Coliseum, 9 Cheong Wan Rd, Hung Hom ☎ 765 9234. Hong Kong's largest venue (12,000 seats) for concerts, dance and sports events. Box office 10am–6.30pm.

Hong Kong Convention and Exhibition Centre, 1 Harbour Rd, Wan Chai ☎ 582 8888. Major concerts and performances. Box office varies according to the promoter; check press for details.

Ko Shan Theatre, Ko Shan Rd (off Chatham Rd North), Hung Hom ☎ 334 2331. Hong Kong's first open-air theatre, located in a disused quarry. Film, theatre, Chinese opera and concerts.

Ngau Chi Wan Civic Centre, 11 Clearwater Bay Rd, New Territories ☎ 726 0854. Drama, dance and film. Box office 10am–6.30pm.

Queen Elizabeth Stadium, 18 Oi Kwan Rd, Wan Chai ☎ 575 6793. 3500-seat stadium for large concerts and sports events. Box office 10am–6.30pm.

Sha Tin Town Hall, 1 Yuen Wo Rd, New Town Plaza, Sha Tin, New Territories ☎ 694 2536. Drama, dance and concerts. Box office 10am–9.30pm.

Sheung Wan Civic Centre, 345 Queen's Rd, Sheung Wan ☎ 853 2689. Drama, concerts, lectures and exhibitions. Box office 10am–6.30pm.

Tsuen Wan Town Hall, Yuen Tun Circuit, Tsuen Wan, New Territories ☎414 1355. Large venue for concerts, dance and drama. Box office 10am–9.30pm.

URBTIX Outlets
Telephone bookings can be made on ☎734 9009 (10am–8pm). Otherwise, central URBTIX outlets include: City Hall, the Cultural Centre and the Hong Kong Arts Centre.

Chinese Cultural Performances

Chinese cultural performances are widespread in Hong Kong, every town and village having its hall, theatre or outdoor space where traditional opera and dance can take place. All performances are highly theatrical; coming across one by accident can be a real highlight of your stay.

The best known is the Chinese opera, which you'll see performed locally at festivals, on religious holidays, and in some of the larger venues by visiting and local troupes. In Hong Kong, the style is mostly Cantonese (though visiting mainland Chinese groups perform Peking Opera on occasion, too) – a highly stylised affair, a musical drama with mime, set songs and responses based on well-known legends and stories. The costumes and garish make-up are magnificent, and while the strident operatic singing and percussion is decidedly awkward to untuned Western ears, it becomes compelling after a while – particularly as the story is interspersed with bouts of elaborate, skilful swordfighting and acrobatics. Performances often go on for three hours or more, but the ones held in or near temples at festivals are usually informal, people walking about, chatting and eating right the way through.

Other cultural shows you might catch include traditional Chinese music, puppet theatre, folk dancing, acrobatics and tumbling, magic and martial arts – all things that are soon evident if you're in Hong Kong for any length of time. Street markets and festivals are good places to look; or check in the local press for specific performances at some of the main venues listed above.

Obviously, it's most rewarding to stumble on performances as you travel around the territory: religious festival events (see p.255–258) and cultural shows out in the New Territories (often listed in the press) are put on for the locals and have few pretensions. But if you want to ensure you see at least something of the traditional culture during your stay, the HKTA organises free hour-long shows every week at various places in the territory. Main venues are in the New World Centre (Tsim Sha Tsui) and Cityplaza (Taikoo Shing), where there'll usually be a bit of everything on display from opera extracts to glove puppetry. For more information, contact any of the HKTA offices (see p.36).

There are also daily Chinese craft and culture displays at the Sung Dynasty Village in Lai Chi Kok (p.124) and events and performances in Middle Kingdom, Ocean Park (p.97). And make an effort to visit the Temple Street Night Market (p.119), where you can see enthusiastic amateurs performing Cantonese opera – pay a few dollars, and you'll be allowed into a seated enclosure and served tea while you watch.

Film

There are at least thirty cinemas in Hong Kong, with the current trend firmly towards multi-screen complexes, which show a mixture of new Hollywood and Cantonese releases. Going to the cinema is cheap and it's worth taking in one of the Chinese-language films if you can: most are lightweight pot-boiler films, slapstick comedies, gangster movies and martial arts thrillers, though increasingly some very interesting films from the mainland are on view, too. There are English sub-titles, and reviews of current films in both English-language daily newspapers to help you choose which to see. All the major English-language films make it to Hong Kong soon after release, and are shown in their original language, with Chinese sub-titles.

You'll often have to queue to get into cinemas, and all the major venues are computer-controlled: you pick your seat

The Arts and Media

The Arts and Media

from the available ones left, shown on the video monitor by the box office, and pay the cashier. Entrance is around $40 a ticket (the *loge*, incidentally, is equivalent to the dress circle).

Films are participatory experiences in Hong Kong. There's plenty of clapping and booing, and as the Hollywood films are sub-titled, the Chinese audience talks right through them. It can be hard to concentrate as the couple in front of you argue heatedly and the chicken feet snacks fly overhead, but it's undeniably fun.

The **major cinemas**, and a few interesting minor ones, are listed below, but for a full rundown of what's on where, consult the local press. If you're just wandering and fancy a movie, the biggest concentration of cinemas is in Causeway Bay. There are also some small **private cinemas** in Hong Kong, normally showing re-runs and foreign films, and there are regular film shows (often free) at the *Alliance Française* and *Goethe Institute*; see "Main Venues" above for addresses.

Real film buffs will want to try and coincide with the annual **film festival**, which always has an excellent and entertaining international programme, though it can be hard to get seats (see "Arts Festivals" feature, above, for more details).

Astor Classics, 380 Nathan Rd, Jordan ☎781 1833. Sister cinema of *Columbia Classics*, below, with a similar programme of new releases.

Cine Art House, Sun Hung Kei Centre, Harbour Rd, Wan Chai ☎827 4778. Arty foreign films in two mini-cinemas.

Columbia Classics, Great Eagle Centre, 23 Harbour Rd, Wan Chai ☎827 8291. Usually an interesting programme of non-blockbuster films as well as new releases.

Hong Kong Arts Centre, 2 Harbour Rd, Wan Chai ☎582 0200. Seasons of alternative film and Chinese cinema.

Majestic Cinema, 348 Nathan Rd, Jordan ☎782 0272. Long runs for new releases – it's at Saigon St.

New York Cinema, 463–483 Lockhart Rd, Plaza II, Causeway Bay ☎838 7380. Plush cinema for new Western and Chinese releases.

Ocean Theatre, 3 Canton Rd, Tsim Sha Tsui ☎730 5444. Kowloon-side screen for all the latest releases.

Palace Theatre, 1st Floor, 280 Gloucester Rd, Causeway Bay ☎895 1679. In the World Trade Centre (behind the *Excelsior*), this is one of the most comfortable places to watch new releases and old favourites.

United Artists, One Pacific Place, 88 Queensway, Central ☎869 0322; level 2, Whampoa Plaza, Hung Hom ☎303 1040; New Town Plaza, Sha Tin, New Territories ☎698 0651. Modern multi-screen venues for all new releases.

Zuni Icosahedron, 12th Floor, Rhenish Centre, 248–250 Hennessy Road, Wan Chai ☎893 8704. Avant-garde video and animation features. Ring for membership details.

Music: Classical and Chinese

The main exponent of **Western classical music** is the *Hong Kong Philharmonic Orchestra*, formed in 1975, whose season runs from September through to June, and which employs guest conductors and soloists from time to time. Performances are at a variety of venues, including the Cultural Centre; information on ☎832 7121. Less formally, there are **free lunchtime concerts** every Wednesday in St John's Cathedral, Garden Rd, Central, from around 1.15pm to 2pm; details on ☎526 5539.

For **Chinese orchestral music**, look for performances by the *Hong Kong Chinese Orchestra*, founded in 1977, the territory's only professional Chinese music group. The orchestra plays at City Hall and the Cultural Centre. Its repertoire takes in traditional Chinese instruments and reworkings of western classical music, a combination which is not to everyone's taste but is certainly worth hearing. For other types of Chinese music, see "Chinese Cultural Performances", above.

Televison and Radio

You may end up watching more **television** than you'd bargained for. Every hotel and most guest houses lay them on for their guests, and you're hard pushed to escape them in bars and restaurants.

There are four main domestic channels, two English-language and two Chinese, operated by two companies. *Television Broadcasts (TVB)* run Jade (Chinese) and **TVB Pearl** (English); *Asia Television (ATV)* run Home (Chinese) and **ATV World** (English). In addition, hotel TVs often receive satellite channels, including *Star TV*, which incorporates regular *BBC* news and current affairs programmes, as well as *MTV* and a sports channel.

Much of the domestic **English-language programming** is imported – documentaries, soaps and sitcoms – while on the whole, the homegrown product is unbelievably bad, barely literate link-people and presenters holding together programmes that look like they were conceived by five-year-olds. Things won't get any better. In the run-up to 1997 and the handover to the Chinese, English-language broadcasting (in both TV and radio) is becoming ever more marginalised. It's of distinct minority appeal in a territory where almost six million of the inhabitants speak Chinese as a first language – the way forward has already been signalled by *TVB*, which now carries Mandarin news and financial reports on its English-language Pearl channel.

In the meantime, however, the saving grace of both English-language channels is that each features at least one **film** every night, some made for TV but plenty of recent Hollywood productions too. Also, they're fairly good on **sporting events** and you can count on getting live coverage of important soccer matches, as well as tennis, rugby and other sports – though often shown here in the early hours because of the time difference. Be warned, though, that the constant commercials are no respecter of film plot or goalmouth action.

If you speak Cantonese, then the **Chinese channels** put on a lot more locally produced stuff – including some good Cantonese and mainland Chinese feature films – but on the whole it's a diet of soaps and variety shows.

The Arts and Media

Radio Stations

RTHK Radio 3 (567 kHz, 1584 kHz). News, finance and current affairs.

RTHK Radio 4 (97.6 to 98.9 mHz). Western and Chinese classical music.

RTHK Radio 6 (675 kHz). The BBC World Service relay station.

Quote AM (864 kHz). Commercial radio; pop and easy listening.

BFBS (96.6, 102, 104.8, 107.4 mHz FM). The British Forces Broadcasting Service – classic British radio.

Metro News (1044 kHz AM). Local and Asian news and finance.

Pearl starts up in the early afternoon and runs through to late at night, World doesn't close down (though the late night/early morning programming relies on America's *CNN Live*). **Programme details** are contained in the *South China Morning Post* and the *Hong Kong Standard* and in the week's *TV & Entertainment Times*.

If you've got a **radio** there's plenty in English to tune in to. Stations include those operated by the main broadcasting outfit, *Radio Television Hong Kong (RTHK)*; there's a commercial station too, as well as British Forces radio and the BBC World Service. Again, radio listings are in the daily papers and *TV & Entertainment Times.*

For details of Hong Kong's daily newspapers, see p.283.

Theatre and the Performing Arts

Hong Kong has recently become the home of excellent local **drama and performance art**, alongside the usual international touring companies and artists who enliven the cultural year. There's a wealth of **venues** to check for forthcoming performances (details above), most dominant of which is the Cultural Centre. Most of the other main venues host drama and performance art throughout the year, too: the only thing to check is whether the **productions** are in English or Cantonese.

Other than straight drama, some of the most exciting local performances are **dance**-orientated, which don't have the

The Arts and Media

disadvantage of a language barrier and often mix Western and Chinese forms very successfully. **Fringe events** are common, too: the *Fringe Club*, especially, hosts its fair share of mime, magic, cabaret and tumbling.

Some interesting local **companies** to watch out for, who play at venues all over the territory, include:

Actor's Rep. A professional group covering English-language drama.

American Community Theatre. Performances of American classics.

Chung Ying Theatre Company. English and Cantonese performances, including Chinese opera .

City Contemporary Dance Company. Full-time professionals who usually perform at the Arts Centre.

Hilton Hotel Dinner Theatre. Light comedy from visiting British West End stars in the *Hilton* hotel; expensive and infrequent.

Hong Kong Ballet Company. Classical and contemporary ballet performances at various venues.

Hong Kong Dance Company. Modern and classical Chinese dance.

Hong Kong Singers. Musical comedy of the Gilbert and Sullivan variety.

Stage Renegades. Trendy PC productions which merit a look.

Zuni Icosahedron. Avant-garde theatre in Cantonese and English.

Visual Arts: galleries and exhibition space

Some of the main venues listed above have **gallery and exhibition space** that's worth checking for current displays. Otherwise, keep an eye on all the territory's **museums**, which host occasional lectures and exhibitions based around their subject. Also, the Urban Council's **district libraries** put on year-round lectures, displays and exhibitions that might be of interest; full details in each month's *City News* magazine (available from City Hall).

There are many **private galleries** in Hong Kong which display art and fine art. The *South China Morning Post* always highlights a good selection of current exhibitions in its daily *What's On* section. The places listed below are always worth dropping in on.

Alisan Fine Arts, 315 Prince's Building, 10 Chater Rd, Central ☎526 1091.

Asia Horizons Gallery, 20th Floor, Kailey Tower, 16 Stanley St, Central ☎868 0077.

JR Guettinger Gallery, 2 Lower Albert Rd, Central ☎537 1482.

Pottery Workshop, 2 Lower Albert Rd, Central ☎525 7634.

Wattis Fine Art, 2nd Floor, 20 Hollywood Rd, Central ☎524 5302.

Zee Stone Gallery, 11 The Forum, Exchange Square Three, Central ☎845 4476.

Chapter 11

Festivals

Timimg your trip to coincide with one of Hong Kong's traditional **Chinese festivals** can greatly add to its interest. Below is a round-up of the year's events, with details of what to expect and where to see the associated celebrations. We've given the likely months and dates for the festivals (as well as the lunar dates), but for the exact dates look in one of the HKTA's free publications, which should summarise them. Also, the *South China Morning Post* records each lunar day on its daily listings page. The festivals below are dealt with **chronologically**, starting with the Chinese New Year.

Chinese New Year

Most famous and most important of the Chinese festivals, **Chinese New Year** falls some time between the end of January and the end of February. Decorations go up everywhere, there's a huge **flower market** in Victoria Park on Hong Kong Island (and in Fa Hui Park and Cheung Sha Wan playground in Kowloon), where locals buy lucky flowers – peach and plum blossom – fruit, lanterns and sweets. You might also catch an impromptu **lion dance**. These are mostly held in residential areas, but ask the tourist office which large hotels are likely to put on a dance display. The most obvious manifestation of New Year is the red scrolls and posters that are pasted to walls and houses all over the territory: the Chinese characters wish long life, prosperity and happiness.

This aside, though, there's not actually a great deal to see at Chinese New Year.

It's a family festival, when people will settle debts, visit friends and relations, buy new clothes and generally ensure a fresh start for the year. Married couples hand out lucky money in red envelopes (*lai see*) to their families and tip dustmen and cleaners in the same way; people on salaries get a bonus; and shop assistants and waiters are feasted by their employers. Traditionally, services like hairdressing cost double in the run-up to the festival. Lots of shops, businesses and restaurants close down for three days or even longer (traditional New Year celebrations last fifteen days), but plenty stay open since families also eat out to celebrate. To wish someone a "Happy New Year", you say **kung hay fat choi**.

Arriving in Hong Kong and trying to find a room during Chinese New Year is something you should avoid. And don't even think about travelling to China during the festival: everything is jam-packed solid as the Hong Kong Chinese stream across the border to visit relatives.

Yuen Siu (Lantern) Festival

The **Yuen Siu Festival** marks the last official day of the Chinese New Year celebrations (the fifteenth day of the first moon), when traditionally designed and brightly coloured lanterns are hung in restaurants, shops, temples and houses. It falls a couple of weeks after the start of the New Year – and is also known as a kind of Chinese Valentine's Day. There's a second lantern festival in September; see "Mid-Autumn Festival" below.

Not all the Chinese festivals are also public holidays. For a full rundown of public holidays in Hong Kong, see p.20.

Festivals

Ching Ming Festival

Generally held in April, **Ching Ming** is when families visit their ancestral graves to perform traditional rites. The day – the beginning of the third moon, a public holiday – signals the beginning of spring and a new farming year, but it's more noted for the sweeping of graves at the territory's cemeteries. Whole families take along joss sticks, incense and food offerings (roast pork and fruit), which are left for the dead at the graves while prayers are said for the departed souls and blessings sought for the latest generations of the family. Extra public transport is laid on to the cemeteries, on Hong Kong Island and out in the New Territories, as well as extra ferries to carry people to the outlying islands: it's one enormous scrum.

Tin Hau Festival

A traditional fishing festival, this is one of the most spectacular of the year's events. Falling in late April or May (on the 23rd day of the third lunar month), it is in honour of **Tin Hau**, a legendary fisherman's daughter of a thousand years ago, who could forecast the weather, calm the waves and generally assist the fishermen to a decent catch; not surprisingly, she is regarded as the Goddess of Fishermen and protector of those at sea. Fishing boats are colourfully decorated with flags, streamers and pennants as fishermen and others who follow the goddess gather at the various Tin Hau temples throughout the territory to ask for luck in the coming year and to offer food, fruit and pink dumplings as a mark of respect. The main temple is the one at **Joss House Bay** in Sai Kung (p.155), where massive crowds congregate every year, and there is always a good celebration in **Yuen Long** in the New Territories, another large centre of Tin Hau worship. Special ferry services run out to some of the temples; the temples themselves are brightly decorated and there are usually Chinese opera displays, dances and parades at most of them.

Tam Kung Festival

The second patron saint of the fishing people is **Tam Kung**, whose festival is celebrated in May (eighth day of the fourth lunar month) at the temple in Shau Kei Wan on Hong Kong Island (p.102).

Birthday of the Lord Buddha

A low-key celebration in May when the Buddha's statue is taken out of the various Buddhist monasteries in the territory and "bathed" in scented water. The monasteries on Lantau are an obvious place to head for to see the rites being performed, but there are important monasteries in the New Territories, too, at Sha Tin and Lam Tei (see Chapter 4).

Tai Chui (Cheung Chau Bun) Festival

A week-long extravaganza in May (starting on the eighth day of the fourth moon) on Cheung Chau Island, the **Tai Chiu Festival** is one of the highlights of the festival year. The buns that give the festival its English name are distributed for luck at the end of the celebrations, which consist of dances, operas, parades – and the famous "floating children" and bun towers. See "Cheung Chau" (p.172) for more details; and expect the island and all the transport there and back to be in a state of siege during this time.

Tuen Ng (Dragon Boat) Festival

The **Tuen Ng Festival** is one of the oldest of Cantonese festivals, held to commemorate the Chinese hero Ch'u Yuen, an advisor to the king who committed suicide by jumping in a river in Hunan Province and drowning, in protest against a corrupt third-century-BC government. The local people tried to save him in their boats, while others threw rice dumplings into the water to feed the fish that would otherwise have eaten his body.

Today, the festival is celebrated in early June (fifth day of the fifth moon) with noisy **dragon boat races** – narrow rowing boats with a dragon's head and tail – throughout the territory, while rice dumplings are eaten, too. The boats are crewed by anything up to eighty people (though most are smaller), the oar-strokes set by a drummer, and the races are accompanied by cymbals and watched from scores of junks and launches. You can see races in many places (try Tai Po, Stanley and Yau Ma Tei, and watch the local press for details or ask the tourist office), and since 1976 there's been an annual International Dragon Boat Race, with teams from all over the world competing.

Birthday of Lu Pan

Held in July, this is a holiday for anyone connected with the building trades. **Lu Pan** was a Master Builder in around 600 BC, a skilled carpenter and possessor of miracle powers. Banquets are held in his honour on his festival day (the thirteenth day of the sixth moon) and there are ceremonies at the Lu Pan Temple in Kennedy Town (p.75).

Maiden's Festival

Also known as the Seven Sister's Festival, the **Maiden's Festival** is held in mid-August, on the seventh day of the seventh moon. It is observed mostly by young girls and lovers, and prayers and offerings are made to the six sisters of Chih Nu, separated from her lover by the Queen of Heaven – a celebration that dates back more than 1500 years. One place you can see the devotions and offerings is at the Bowen Road Lover's Stone Garden at Wan Chai Gap (p.81).

Yue Lan Festival

The **Yue Lan Festival** is held in late August (the fifteenth day of the seventh moon). It's known as the "Festival of the Hungry Ghosts", commemorating the lunar month when ghosts are released from the underworld to roam the earth. It's generally seen as an unlucky day, when accidents or sinister events can happen. To forestall that, people give offerings to the ghosts in the form of paper models of food, cars, houses, money, furniture, etc – which are then ceremoniously burnt so that the ghosts can take them back to the underworld with them. It's not a public holiday, but you may see fires on the pavements and at the roadside during this time where the elaborate models are burnt. See the account of the Pak Tai Temple in Wan Chai (p.85) for more details about the dying craft of making the paper models.

Festivals

Mid-Autumn Festival

Another major festival, the **Mid-Autumn Festival** is also called the **Moon Cake Festival** after the sweet cakes eaten at this time – mostly made from sesame and lotus seeds and stuffed with a duck egg. The festival takes place in September (on the fifteenth day of the eighth moon), is roughly similar to the western Harvest Festival, and purportedly commemorates a fourteenth-century revolt against the Mongols, when the call to arms was written on pieces of paper, stuffed inside the cakes and distributed to the population. Today, there are various kinds of moon cake (*yuek beng*) on sale around this time, all wonderfully sickly: you will see them stacked up in bakeries, costing from around $100 for a box of four, though the better, more elaborate double-yolk cakes are pricier. The festival also combines with lantern displays, which take place on hillsides throughout the territory. The Peak and various spots in the New Territories are favourite places to go and light your lantern while watching the moon rise – at which point you scoff the cakes. There's a lantern display, too, in Victoria Park on Hong Kong Island. The day after the festival is a public holiday, and expect transport to anywhere near a hill (like the Peak Tram) to be packed the night before.

Birthday of Confucious

The **birthday of Confucius**, in September, is marked by low-key religious ceremonies at the Confucius Temple in Causeway Bay.

Festivals

Cheung Yeung Festival

A public holiday in October (on the ninth day of the ninth month), the **Cheung Yeung Festival** relates to a tale from Han Dynasty times, when a soothsayer advised an old man to take his family to the mountains for 24 hours to avoid disaster. On his return, everything else in the village had died. The same trip to high places is made today in remembrance, with the result again that all transport to hilly areas is packed. Lots of people also take the opportunity to visit family graves.

Chapter 12

Shopping

The stories you've heard about bargain-basement prices for electrical goods, clothes and other items are broadly accurate – the only imported goods to attract duty in Hong Kong are alcohol, tobacco, perfumes, cosmetics and cars. However, don't be misled into thinking that you're going to pick up goods for next to nothing. The picture has changed over recent years as other Southeast Asian countries have begun to rival the territory: clothes from Bangkok are probably better value these days, while prices for hi-fi and photographic equipment are not the steal they once were. Approach your shopping as you would at home: buy something because you like it, shop around, and always check the small print on the never-to-be-repeated special offers.

Shopping: A Survival Guide

Although it may sometimes seem like it, not everyone's out to rip you off, but there are some rules to follow and dodges to be aware of before you part with any cash. The most important ground rule is to **shop around** to get an idea of what things cost: pirate goods are common, so if you see something that's spectacularly cheap, always check it out elsewhere. Obviously, buying a calculator or cheap digital watch on the street, you're not going to expect it to work for ever. But with expensive hi-fi gear you need to be more circumspect; take your

time, ask for demonstrations, and don't buy the first one you see.

Choosing a Shop

For expensive items, it's often recommended that you use shops that are **members of the Hong Kong Tourist Association (HKTA)**; they pay an annual membership fee and identify themselves by a sign in the window of a red junk within a red circle. Obviously, only a fraction of the territory's shops and stores are in the HKTA and the ones that aren't aren't necessarily all villains – far from it. But it's a starting point if you're worried.

All the registered shops are listed in the HKTA's *Shopping* guide (available free from HKTA offices), which has plenty of information on shopping for various items and goods. Look, too, at the newspaper *Hongkong* and the monthly *Hong Kong Guide*, both available from HKTA offices, for their articles on shopping and factory outlets.

For questions about shopping in Hong Kong, or **complaints against HKTA members**, ring ☎ 801 7278 (Mon–Fri 9am–5pm, Sat 9am–1pm).

Agents and Importers

Many of the products sold in Hong Kong are handled by a sole **agent or importer**, who can give you reliable information about the particular model you're interested in if the shop is vague or unhelpful. The agents' and importers' names and telephone numbers are given in the HKTA *Shopping* guide.

Shopping

Guarantees

Always check the **guarantee** you're given for photographic, electronic or electrical goods. Some are international guarantees, in which case they should carry the name of the sole agent in Hong Kong for that product; others are purely local guarantees, which are *only valid in Hong Kong*, usually for a period of twelve months. All guarantees should carry a description of the product, including a model number and serial number, as well as the date of purchase, the name and address of the shop you bought it from and the shop's official stamp.

Deposits and Refunds

You don't need to put down a **deposit** on anything unless it's being made for you. For tailored clothes for example, expect to put down up to fifty percent of the price. On other items, if the shop insists (to secure the item, or to order a new one because they're "out of stock"), go somewhere else – there are always plenty of alternatives. Generally, goods are not returnable or **refundable**, though if something is faulty or missing, the better stores will replace your goods. To make sure, always have your receipt itemised and go straight back to the shop if there's something wrong.

Compatibility

It's important to check that electrical goods are compatible with your domestic mains voltage, and that television sets and VCRs are compatible with each other, and with your domestic broadcasting system.

Customs, Shipping and Insurance

Before making large puchases, check with the relevant consulate (there's a list on p.280) or the HKTA about **customs** regulations for the country you want to import the goods to. Most shops can arrange to have your purchase packed and sent overseas, but make sure you have it **insured** to cover damage in transit as well as loss. To send items home yourself, you need to go to a main post office (see p.283), where you can also arrange insurance. Parcels usually take at least six weeks by surface mail and one week by airmail to reach Europe or North America.

Avoiding rip-offs

Having checked all the main points, you still need to be armed against the out-and-out bad guys – or simply against the shopkeepers who see their chance to make a little extra cash from a tourist.

•**Always ask the price**.

•**Bargaining**: for most large items in the bigger shops and department stores, the price will be fixed and you won't be able to bargain, though you might be able to wangle extra accessories and the like before completing the sale. However, you can bargain in markets and smaller shops, though bear in mind that the seller always wins.

• **Switching goods**: if you've paid for goods, don't let them out of your sight as it's not unknown for bits and pieces to have mysteriously vanished by the time you get home, or for cheaper gear to have been substituted. Either pack your purchases yourself, or check everything before you leave the shop. If things like camera cases or electrical leads are part of the package, make sure they're there and itemised on the receipt: otherwise, return later to complain and you may be told that they're "extras" which you now have to pay for.

•**Fake and pirate gear**: sometimes you know that goods are fakes and it doesn't matter. Hong Kong's ubiquitous fake Rolex watches, for instance, are definitely worth the money, and fake designer-label gear from markets has a certain cachet. But if you want the real McCoy, don't buy anything from anyone on the street; also, don't be tempted by stupid bargains – pay the going rate and get receipts and guarantees. Lots of the traffic in pirated things like watches and cameras has been stamped upon recently by the customs authorities in any case, although pirate computer gear is something of a growth industry right now.

Boycotting Products

There's nothing you can't buy in Hong Kong, which means that there are markets in several products you may not feel entirely happy about – **furs, leather and skin** goods made from rare and exotic or endangered species and, most importantly, **ivory**. There are huge stocks of ivory in Hong Kong, one of the world's largest markets in the product and, while lots of countries have recently placed import bans on the stuff, the British government initially refused to ban sales in Hong Kong because stocks were so great and the ivory lobby so powerful – Hong Kong is home to the biggest ivory processing centre in the world and employs about 3000 people in the business. However, the government is a party to CITES (the Convention on International Trade in Endangered Species) and since 1990, the Hong Kong authorities have abided more stringently by the rules of the worldwide ban. But, without compensation paid to the merchants here, it seems likely that illegal trading will continue, further undermining the efforts to save the elephant from exploitation.

The trade in endangered species also rears its head in **traditional Chinese medicine**, much of which utilises the body parts of animals like tigers and rhinos. A lot of the medicines (surprisingly) carry bilingual ingredient lists – if you're going to buy anything, check first.

Shops

You don't need our help to find designer gear or hi-fi electrical equipment in Hong Kong: all the big names are sold absolutely everywhere and specific addresses, if you need them, are given in the HKTA's *Shopping* guide and a dozen other publications and leaflets. We've listed more mainstream places – markets, bookshops and department stores – that should be useful for anyone stopping in Hong Kong, as well as a selection of miscellaneous shops, any of which can occupy a spare half-hour or so, or provide an offbeat souvenir.

Shop opening hours vary according to what part of Hong Kong you shop in.

> ### Shopping Hours
>
> Central and Western: daily 10am–6pm.
>
> Wan Chai and Causeway Bay: daily 10am–10pm.
>
> Tsim Sha Tsui, Yau Ma Tei and Mongkok: daily 10am–10pm.
>
> Tsim Sha Tsui East: daily 10am–7.30pm.

Shopping

Mostly, shops are open seven days a week; some department stores close on Sunday, while Japanese department stores open on Sunday but close for one day mid-week instead. Otherwise, the only time that shops close is for two to three days around Chinese New Year, and even then by no means all do so. Shops mostly stay open during Western holidays like Christmas and Easter. Opening hours for street **markets** are even longer – open daily and until late at night, though with a couple of exceptions which are dealt with in the text.

Antiques, Arts and Crafts

There are great opportunities to buy Chinese antiques, arts and crafts in Hong Kong, in hundreds of specialist stores and markets, but you'll rarely come across bargains. If you're looking for something specific, be prepared to pay for it. Art and antiques more than 100 years old should come with a certificate of authenticity; such items are also allowed into most countries duty-free, though check first with your consulate if unsure (there's a list on p.280).

A FEW IDEAS

Art Galleries. There's a list of art galleries with regular exhibitions and sales on p.254.

Chinese Products Stores. See "Department Stores" below for a list of stores specialising in arts, crafts and goods from the Chinese mainland.

Hollywood Road, Central. The main venue for antique, art and craft shops, with scores of shops open Mon–Sat 10am–6pm.

Shopping

Markets. Check the list on p.266 for the addresses of markets specialising in arts and crafts.

SPECIFIC STORES

The Asian Collector, 19–27 Wyndham St, Central. Constantly changing exhibitions in this small gallery – old Hong Kong photos, Asian maps, etc – and always worth a look.

Chinese Arts and Crafts Bazaar, Level II, New World Shopping Centre Mall, 18–24 Salisbury Rd, Tsim Sha Tsui East. Displays of traditional arts and crafts – painting, seal carving, calligraphy, doll-making and tea-making; closed Mon.

Creative Hands, Shop 34, Western Market, 323 Des Voeux Rd, Sheung Wan. Original paintings, prints, watercolour materials.

Mountain Folkcraft, 12 Wo On Lane (off D'Aguilar St), Central. Beautiful handmade folk art and crafts from Southeast Asia and elsewhere.

Museum Shop, Hong Kong Arts Centre, Cultural Centre, Salisbury Rd, Tsim Sha Tsui. Art books and supplies, calligraphy materials, prints, postcards, gifts and stationery.

The Pottery Workshop, 2 Lower Albert Rd (entrance on Wyndham St), Central. Small gallery for locally produced pottery and ceramic art. Affordable and interesting.

Welfare Handicrafts, Shop 7, Jardine House, 1 Connaught Place, Central; Salisbury Rd, Tsim Sha Tsui. Store selling arts and crafts on behalf of charities.

Bookshops

All the **bookshops** below sell English-language books, and in some you can buy foreign-language newspapers and magazines, too. There are, of course, hundreds of other bookshops that only sell Chinese-language books.

Bookazine, 102–103, Alexandra House, Chater Rd, Central; Basement, Jardine House, 1 Connaught Rd, Central; Shop UG34, Tsim Sha Tsui Centre, Tsim Sha Tsui East. Excellent selection of foreign magazines and books, especially good for cookery books and novels.

Cosmos Books, 1st Floor, 30 Johnston Rd, Wan Chai. Good for travel, novels and history.

Government Publications Centre, Ground Floor, GPO Building, Connaught Place, Central. Official government publications, Hong Kong maps, exhibition catalogues, and books on local flora, fauna, politics, environment, industry and anything else you can think of.

Hong Kong Book Centre, Basement, On Lok Yuen Building, 25 Des Voeux Rd, Central. Cramped, library-like interior, but well-stocked with novels and travel books, and good on Chinese history and politics. Foreign newspapers, too.

Joint Publishing, 9 Queen Victoria St, Central. Sole agent/distributor for mainland Chinese publications, with a good stock of Marxist-Leninist works, foreign-language books and magazines, and books published in Hong Kong and Taiwan.

Kelly and Walsh, Shop 348, Pacific Place Shopping Mall, 88 Queensway, Central. Big, central, general bookshop, good on travel and art.

Low Price Shop, 47 Hollywood Rd, Central. Secondhand English-language books – as well as old photos, records, dubious antiques and junk.

Museum Shop, Hong Kong Museum of Art, Cultural Centre, Salisbury Rd, Tsim Sha Tsui. Books on art and artists, as well as art supplies, stationery and postcards.

South China Morning Post Family Bookshop, Star Ferry Concourse, Central; 313 Ocean Centre, Harbour City, Canton Rd, Tsim Sha Tsui; Basement One, New World Centre, 18–24 Salisbury Rd, Tsim Sha Tsui East. Fine selection of English-language novels, travel guides, dictionaries, maps and books on Hong Kong and China, and foreign newspapers.

Swindon Book Co. Ltd, Star Ferry Concourse, Tsim Sha Tsui; 13–15 Lock Rd, Tsim Sha Tsui; 249 Ocean Terminal, Harbour City, 3 Canton Rd, Tsim Sha Tsui; 310 Ocean Centre, Harbour City, 5 Canton Rd, Tsim Sha Tsui. A general bookshop with a fairly large travel section; the Star Ferry branch is particularly good for books on Hong Kong.

Wanderlust Books, 30 Hollywood Road, Central. Hong Kong's best selection of guides, walking tours, travel writing, maps and related topics.

Yaohan, New Town Plaza, 18 Sha Tin Centre Road, Sha Tin, New Territories. The bookshop in the massive Japanese department store has a good selection of English-language novels, as well as Chinese and Japanese magazines.

Clothes

For the addresses of the big-name **designers** – from Armani to Valentino, as well as local Hong Kong whizz-kids – look no further than the HKTA *Shopping* guide, which lists them all in exhaustive detail. Otherwise, it's best simply to check out all the options as you wend your way around the city. Typically, you'll save up to 25 percent by buying designer gear here rather than in its country of origin, but as it all starts highly priced in the first place you're still going to need substantial amounts of money. For cheaper clothes shopping, track down the factory outlets

(see below), where shirts and jackets with snipped-out labels really start to save you money. For other ideas, visit the various **markets** (p.266) that specialise in clothes – Stanley Market is famous for its **silk** – and don't neglect the department stores (see below), either. The Japanese department stores are particularly good on designer labels; the Chinese products stores are excellent for fabrics.

Shopping

FACTORY OUTLETS

One unusual aspect of shopping in Hong Kong is the chance to buy something from a wide variety of **factory outlets** – in commercial buildings selling clothes, fabrics and jewellery direct to the public. Prices here are very competitive, either because there's no retail mark-up, or because you're buying seconds whose imperfections are minimal. The HKTA puts out a brochure, *Factory Outlets*, which details all the main clothing and jewellery businesses that deal in this way, as well as opening times and the average prices of the goods on offer. Some of the shops

Clothing and shoe sizes

Dresses

USA	8	10	12	14	16	18	20
UK	10	12	14	16	18	20	22
Continental	40	42	44	46	48	50	52

Women's shoes

USA	4.5	5.5	6.5	7.5	8.5	9.5
UK	3	4	5	6	7	8
Continental	35.5	36.5	37.5	38.5	39.5	40.5

Men's suits/coats

USA	36	38	40	42	44	46
UK	36	38	40	42	44	46
Continental	46	48	50	52	54	56

Men's shirts

USA	14	15	16	17
UK	14	15	16	17
Continental	36	38	41	43

Men's shoes

USA	6	7	8	9	10	11
UK	6	7	8	9	10	11
Continental	39	41	42	43	44	46

Shopping

provide free transport, so if you know what you want, ring first and see if it's worth the trip.

Two areas to browse in are along **Granville Road** in Tsim Sha Tsui (off Nathan Rd), which has a long run of cheap, discount clothing shops; and around **Man Yue Street/Man Lok Street** in Hung Hom, where there're lots of jewellery and clothing businesses. Also try Johnston Road in Wan Chai; and the shops near the Caroline Centre in Causeway Bay.

TAILORS

Hong Kong has always been famous for the speed and good value of its **tailors**, but whatever you've heard, if you're foolish enough to buy a suit made in 24 hours, it either won't fit, will fall apart, or both. You'll need at least two or three fittings for a decent tailor to make you a decent suit, spread over several days, and though it won't be spectacularly cheap it will be considerably better value than the same suit made at home. Personal recommendation is the best way to find a tailor in Hong Kong, but if you are willing to spend the money, it's safe to go to one of the long-established tailors in the arcades of the main hotels. Or visit *Sam's Tailors*, 94 Nathan Road, Tsim Sha Tsui; almost a Hong Kong institution.

Computers

Hong Kong is an excellent place to stock up on hardware and software, but be warned that there's a huge piracy problem. Always check that what you're buying is compatible with your country's electrical system and, if it's a game, with your television system. You'll need to check customs' requirements for some purchases, too. Two main places for which to head are:

Asia Computer Plaza, Lower Ground Floor, Silvercord, 30 Canton Rd, Tsim Sha Tsui. Reliable computer mall on two floors, specialist computer bookshop, too.

Golden Shopping Arcade, 156 Fuk Wah St, Sham Shui Po, Kowloon. Famous for its supply of cheap computer goods, but notorious as a centre for pirate gear.

Department stores

One of Hong Kong's great joys is the diverse selection of mammoth, air-conditioned **department stores**, owned by parent companies from different countries; pick your culture and dive in. Most have cafés and coffee shops inside, too.

CHINESE PRODUCTS STORES

All the following department stores specialise in products made in mainland China – clothes, furniture, antiques, herbal medicines, fine art, porcelain, electrical goods, jewellery, etc. There are some occasional bargains to be had, and if you treat the furniture and art departments as museums, you'll be able to spend whole afternoons inside.

China Products, 19–31 Yee Wo St, Causeway Bay; 488–500 Hennessy Rd, Causeway Bay.

China Resources Artland Centre Department Store, China Resources Building, Low Block, 26 Harbour Rd, Wan Chai.

Chinese Arts and Crafts, Shell House, 24 Queen's Rd, Central; 230 The Mall, Pacific Place, 88 Queensway, Central; Ground Floor, Prince's Building, 3 Des Voeux Rd, Central; Star House, 3 Salisbury Rd, Tsim Sha Tsui; Silvercord, 30 Canton Rd, Tsim Sha Tsui; 233–239 Nathan Rd, Yau Ma Tei.

Chinese Merchandise Emporium, Chiao Shang Building, 92–104 Queen's Rd, Central.

Chung Kiu Chinese Products Emporium, 17 Hankow Rd, Tsim Sha Tsui; 528–532 Nathan Rd, Yau Ma Tei; 47–51 Shan Tung St, Mongkok.

Yue Hwa Chinese Products Emporium, Mirador Mansion, 54–64 Nathan Rd, Tsim Sha Tsui; Park Lane Shoppers' Boulevard, 143–161 Nathan Rd, Tsim Sha Tsui; 301–9 Nathan Rd, Yau Ma Tei.

HONG KONG STORES

Lane Crawford, 70 Queen's Rd, Central; Levels 1–3, The Mall, One Pacific Place, 88 Queensway, Admiralty; Ground Floor, Windsor House, 311 Gloucester Rd,

Causeway Bay; Ground Floor, 74 Nathan Rd, Tsim Sha Tsui; Shop 100, Ocean Terminal, Harbour City, 3 Canton Rd, Tsim Sha Tsui. Hong Kong's oldest Western-style department store – the first branch listed is the main one.

Sincere, 173 Des Voeux Rd, Central; 83 Argyle St, Mongkok. A more downmarket store, though with the same range of products; the Argyle St branch is good for shoes.

Wing On, 26 Des Voeux Rd, Central; 211 Des Voeux Rd, Central; 183 Queen's Rd East, Wan Chai; Cityplaza I, 1111 King's Rd, Taikoo Shing; 361 Nathan Rd, Yau Ma Tei; Wing On Plaza, 62 Mody Rd, Tsim Sha Tsui East; Site 11, Whampoa Garden, 6 Tak Hong St, Hung Hom. Standard department store with branches all over the territory.

JAPANESE STORES

Daimaru, Household Square, Kingston St, Causeway Bay; Fashion Square, Paterson St/Great George St, Causeway Bay. The first branch has a Japanese supermarket and snack bar and specialises in household goods, the second is mainly fashion and sportswear. Closed Wed.

Isetan, Shopping Mall, *Sheraton Hotel*, 20 Nathan Rd, Tsim Sha Tsui. Central Japanese shopping.

Matsuzakaya, Hang Lung Centre, 2–20 Paterson St, Causeway Bay; Queensway Plaza, 93 Queensway, Admiralty. Good for clothes; closed Thursday.

Mitsukoshi, Hennessy Centre, 500 Hennessy Rd, Causeway Bay; Sun Plaza, 28 Canton Rd, Tsim Sha Tsui.

Seibu, Pacific Place, 88 Queensway, Admiralty. Upscale Japanese store.

Sogo, East Point Centre, 555 Hennessy Rd, Causeway Bay. Ten floors' worth of consumerism, including a good Japanese supermarket.

Yaohan, Ground Floor, Whampoa Garden, Hung Hom; New Town Plaza, 18 Sha Tin Centre Rd, Sha Tin, New Territories; Tuen Mun Town Plaza, Tuen Mun, New Territories. The Sha Tin branch is Hong Kong's biggest department store – a place to spend days rather than hours.

OTHER STORES

Marks & Spencer, Shop 120 & 229, The Mall, Two Pacific Place, 88 Queensway, Admiralty; Ground–2nd Floor, Excelsior Plaza, East Point Rd, Causeway Bay; Shop 102 & 254, Ocean Centre, Harbour City, 5 Canton Rd, Tsim Sha Tsui. Classic British department store selling sensible underwear, even in the Far East.

Food and drink

For a list of **bakeries, delicatessens, take-aways** and **supermarkets**, consult the relevant sections of Chapter 7. You'll find accounts of **markets** where you can buy food throughout the book. The main ones are Central and Sheung Wan markets (Chapter 2); Temple Street Night Market (Chapter 3); and Luen Wo Market and Sheung Shui Market (both Chapter 4).

For **wines and spirits** and other drinks, most of the supermarkets have decent selections: *Yaohan* in Sha Tin and *Wellcome* in The Forum, Exchange Square, Central, are particularly well-stocked. A good specialist shop is *Remy Fine Wines* (117 Swire Arcade, Swire House, Central; and elsewhere), worth checking for bin end sales and other offers.

If you're buying food in markets (or fish in restaurants), you need to know that **Chinese weights and measures** are different from western ones. Most things are sold by the **catty**, which is the equivalent of 1.3 lb or 600g; the smaller unit is the **tael**, equivalent to 1.3 oz or 38g. That said, unless you can speak and read Chinese, you'll probably find that simply picking up the amount you want and handing it to the stallholder is the best way to go about things.

Jewellery

Jewellery prices are relatively low in Hong Kong (since precious stones can be imported without paying duty) and there are probably more jewellers' shops in the territory than any other kind. If you're going to buy, first get hold of the HKTA's free *Shopping Guide to Jewellery*, which explains about the different quality and grade of various precious stones sold in Hong Kong. This is particularly important if

Shopping

Shopping

you're buying **jade**, which is very popular here: there's a special Jade Market in Kansu Street, Yau Ma Tei (see p.117).

If you need help or information on buying **diamonds**, you can contact the *Diamond Importers' Association Ltd*, Room 1707, Parker House, 70 Queen's Road, Central ☎ 523 5497.

For **opals**, a fun place to visit – without any pressure to buy at all – is *The Opal Mine* (Burlington House, Ground Floor, 92 Nathan Rd, Tsim Sha Tsui), an informative exhibition on the mining of opal in Australia, where ninety percent of the world's opal comes from. It also describes its manufacture as jewellery, and details how to distinguish between the various types.

Markets: clothes, fabrics and bric-a-brac

You'll get the cheapest clothes and fabrics in markets, but shop around and haggle. You'll not be able to try anything on and you'll never be able to take anything back, but be sensible and you shouldn't go too far wrong. The list below is just a round-up; full details appear in the text at the given page number.

Jade Market, Yau Ma Tei. Jade jewellery and artefacts; p.117.

Jardine's Bazaar, Causeway Bay. Clothes and household goods; p.91.

Li Yuen Street East and West, Central. Women's and children's clothes; p.63.

Man Wa Lane, Sheung Wan. Traditional Chinese seals; p.69.

Marble Street, North Point. Shirts and shorts; p.101.

Stanley Market, Stanley Village. Clothes, fake designer labels a speciality; p.99.

Temple Street, Yau Ma Tei. The best night market: clothes, tapes, watches, jewellery, digital bits and pieces, everything; p.119.

Tung Choi Street, Mongkok. Women's and children's clothes and accessories; p.120.

Upper Lascar Row, Central. Flea market; p.72.

Western Market, Sheung Wan. Fabrics, arts and crafts; p.69.

Music: CDs and tapes

You'll be able to buy most mainstream CDs and tapes in Hong Kong: prices are generally around 20–30 percent lower than in the UK (and slightly higher than in the US), though there are even greater bargains to be had if you shop around. Records are pretty much considered a novelty item these days; the ones you see stacked in shops are in fact laser discs. Check out the locally produced Canto-pop releases, as well as recordings of mainland Chinese artists.

Chungking Mansions, 36–44 Nathan Rd, Tsim Sha Tsui. Cheap tapes and CDs at various stalls inside Nathan Road's most labyrinthine shopping centre.

DoReMi Records, D16, Queensway Plaza, 93 Queensway, Admiralty. A bit limited in range, but with the odd bargain.

Good Times Music Store, Shop 109, Ocean Centre, Harbour City, 5 Canton Rd, Tsim Sha Tsui. You can listen to your selection before buying here.

Hong Kong Records, Shop G31, Hutchinson House, 10 Harcourt Rd, Central; Shop 252, The Mall, Pacific Place, 88 Queensway, Admiralty. Good mixture of styles and prices; no vinyl in sight, despite the name.

Radio City, 500 Hennessy Rd, Causeway Bay. Next to the MTR, this is the closest Hong Kong gets to a megastore – several floors of CDs, classical to Canto-pop. It has its own café; look out for bargain compilations.

Satellite Record Co, B9–10, United Centre, Queensway Plaza, 93 Queensway, Admiralty. Good for classical music.

Strange Time Records, 1 Lan Kwai Fong, Central. New and rare CDs, laser discs and vinyl in trendy Lan Kwai Fong.

Works Record Company, 38 Hankow Rd, Tsim Sha Tsui. Mainly Canto-pop and classical.

Shopping Malls

Even if you hate shopping, it's impossible to avoid walking through a **shopping mall** on any visit to Hong Kong, since half the pedestrian overpasses and walkways in

Central and Tsim Sha Tsui East pass straight through one or more of them. You're not even immune in hotels – most of the larger ones have ground-floor arcades so that you run the gauntlet on every trip in and out. You may as well accept that you're going to see the inside of more shopping malls than you thought existed; you may even enjoy them, since they are at least air-conditioned.

The main concentrations are in Central, Tsim Sha Tsui and Tsim Sha Tsui East, with a few in Causeway Bay and a couple of other major malls in the New Territories. They are almost sights in themselves, gleaming, climate-controlled consumer paradises, filled with slick, chic shops, serviced by state-of-the-art elevators and computer directories, enlivened by galleries, lights and fountains, and sustained by bars, cafés and restaurants. All the important ones are covered in the text, but a quick checklist of the best includes:

Cityplaza, 111 King's Road, Taikoo Shing, Hong Kong Island.

The Landmark, Des Voeux Rd, Central.

Shun Tak Centre, 200 Connaught Rd, Sheung Wan.

Swire House, Connaught Rd, Central.

New Town Plaza, Sha Tin, New Territories.

New World Centre, 20 Salisbury Rd, Tsim Sha Tsui.

Ocean Terminal, Canton Rd, Tsim Sha Tsui. Incorporating Harbour City and Ocean Centre.

Pacific Place Mall, 88 Queensway, Admiralty.

Times Square, Causeway Bay.

Tea shops

Buying **Chinese tea** in little tins and boxes is a nice idea for a souvenir, and Hong Kong has lots of specialist tea shops, some of which are listed below. Buy in small amounts, from any of a hundred different types, since tea loses its flavour over long periods of time, and don't be afraid to ask if you can taste various varieties. Not all shops will oblige, but some are quite prepared to let you taste before you make your choice.

Chan Chuan Lan Tea Co., 26 Cochrane St, Central.

Chinese Merchandise Emporium, 92–104 Queen's Rd, Central.

Fook Ming Tong Tea Shop, Ground Floor, Pedder Building, 8 Theatre Lane, Central; Western Market, 323 Des Voeux Rd, Sheung Wan; LG3, Mitsukoshi, Hennessey Centre 500 Hennessy Rd, Causeway Bay; Shop 200A, Ocean Terminal, Harbour City, Canton Rd, Tsim Sha Tsui

Kee Heung Chun Tea Co., 67 Wellington St, Central.

Ten Zen, 290 Queen's Rd, 18 Sha Tin Centre Rd, Central, Sheung Wan.

Ying Kee, 151 Queen's Rd, Central; 170 Johnston Rd, Wan Chai; LG1, Two Pacific Place, 88 Queensway, Admiralty; 139 Shanghai St, Yau Ma Tei; 446A Nathan Rd, Yau Ma Tei.

Shopping

Chapter 13

Sport

The only drawback to Hong Kong's varied range of **sporting opportunities** is the inevitable lack of space for such things. **To play** some sports – particularly racquet sports – you'll have to book well in advance, or just be lucky with vacancies, which is why so many residential blocks have private sports facilities. Still, as a tourist, you will be able to find something energetic to do, and all the possibilities are detailed below in alphabetical order, with advice on how to participate. **Spectator sports** are more limited, primarily because the territory's available space restricts the number of stadiums and sports grounds, not to mention teams. That said, there are events throughout the year – some of them of international standard – and again, you'll find details below.

The major municipal stadiums and sports grounds are run by the Urban Council, whose free monthly magazine *City News* (from City Hall) carries a "Sports Diary" listing current events and competitions. For more information, contact the **Sports Promotion Office** at the territory's main sporting venue, the **Queen Elizabeth Stadium**, 18 Oi Kwan Road, Wan Chai ☎591 1346.

One privately run sports centre is the **Hong Kong Sports Institute** in Sha Tin (☎605 1212), which has excellent facilities and is open to non-members during off-peak hours (ie Mon–Fri 8am–6pm). Ring for information if you're interested, and see the various sports listings below; a free shuttle bus runs from Sha Tin KCR station every half an hour from 9.15am–

9.45pm. A second centre offering visitor's passes for $10 is the **South China Athletic Association** (Caroline Hill, Causeway Bay; ☎577 6932), founded in 1904 and with facilities for all kinds of sports and keep-fit activities; again, ring first for details.

Finally, you can let someone else do the organising by signing on for the HKTA's **sports and recreation tour** (information from any HKTA office). Around $320 gets you a day-return trip to the Clearwater Bay Golf and Country Club, in the Sai Kung peninsula, which includes admission, lunch and transport. Table tennis, swimming and the sauna and jacuzzi are free; there's a small charge for squash, badminton and tennis; and a heftier charge if you want to play golf. You have to book a day in advance (departures are at around 8am). There's a bar and restaurants there, too.

Badminton

You can hire **badminton** courts for around $45 an hour at the two places listed below. More general information is available from the **Hong Kong Badminton Association** ☎838 4066.

Hong Kong Sports Institute, Sha Tin ☎605 1212. Off-peak hours only for visitors; Mon–Fri 9.30am–5.45pm.

Queen Elizabeth Stadium, 18 Oi Kwan Road, Wan Chai ☎591 1346.

Bowling

For **ten-pin bowling**, try one of the bowling alleys below. At each, a game costs around $10, usually slightly more after 5pm. Avoiding weekends is a good idea, as alleys are extremely popular. For **lawn bowls**, which costs from around $30 an hour, try the green at Victoria Park, Causeway Bay (☎570 6186).

Fourseas Bowling Centre, Cityplaza, Taikoo Shing ☎567 0703. Open 9.30am–1am.

South China Bowling Centre, 88 Caroline Hill Rd, Causeway Bay ☎890 8528. Open 10am–midnight.

Top Bowl Ltd, Whampoa Garden, Hung Hom ☎764 0811. Open 9am–3am.

Fishing

The **fishing** season in Hong Kong's reservoirs lasts from September to March; if you're over thirteen, you can get a licence from the Water Supplies Department, 7 Gloucester Rd, Wan Chai (☎824 5000). They'll also give you information about what you can and can't catch.

Golf

Golf is a pricey sport in Hong Kong, as elsewhere, and you'll have to be keen to make the arrangements to play at the various clubs in the territory. The Hong Kong Open Golf Championship is held every February. Less serious golf is catered for by the **minigolf** course at Shek O, right by the beach, and a similar set-up, with a driving range, at Sha Tin's New Town Plaza.

Clearwater Bay Golf and Country Club ☎719 1595. The HKTA runs an inclusive day-trip to this club. Green fees here are around $450, caddies and clubs extra.

Discovery Bay, Lantau ☎987 7273. Among the newest of Hong Kong's golf clubs, with a course spectacularly laid out on top of the island's hills. Fees here are around $700 from Monday to Friday, weekends around $1500, plus extras.

Royal Hong Kong Golf Club (*RHKGC*), Fanling, New Territories ☎670 1211. The territory's major club, and site of the HK Open, there are three 18-hole courses at which visitors can play on weekdays for

around $1100 per person, plus caddies ($200) and clubs ($350). The *RHKGC* also operates an 18-hole course at Deep Water Bay on Hong Kong Island (☎812 7070), which costs visitors around $400 plus extras, again on weekdays only. You should book well in advance for all these courses.

Shek O. The swishest golf course, on the south side of Hong Kong Island, open to members only – with membership restricted to only 300 people.

Horses: racing and riding

The only sport in Hong Kong to command true mass appeal, **horse racing** is a spectating must if you're here during the season, which runs from September to May. There are two courses, both run by the **Royal Hong Kong Jockey Club** (*RHKJC*): the original one at Happy Valley (☎833 1333) and a much newer, state-of-the-art affair at Sha Tin in the New Territories (☎697 3261), to which the HKTA can organise tours and tickets for the enclosures. If you want to go on your own, and not as part of a package, then take your passport to the racecourse a couple of days before the races (over 18s only) and the RHKJC will sell you a guest badge for $50; or you can just turn up and pay $10 to get into the public stands. See p.92 and p.133 for full details of each course.

If you want to get on the back of one of the beasts, then there are a couple of places where you can go **horse riding**, though it's necessarily a limited option given the terrain. One venue is the Lantau Tea Gardens (☎985 5718; 9–11.30am & 1–5pm) on Lantau, by the Po Lin Monastery, where half an hour on a trotting track costs around $130, more serious stuff outside from $300. Otherwise, there's the **Pokfulam Public Riding School**, at 75 Reservoir Road, Pokfulam, Hong Kong Island (☎551 0030; Sept–June only, closed Mon), which costs around $250 an hour for lessons – book well in advance. This last, incidentally, has riding facilities especially designed for disabled people.

Sport

Indoor sports: snooker, billiards, pool and darts

There are dozens of private clubs at which you can play table games like **billiards**, **snooker** and **pool**. You usually have to join, though sometimes you only need pay a nominal fee, and then pay for your games. Look in the Yellow Pages (under "Billiards") for a club near you and ring for opening hours and membership details before setting out.

Less formal is a game of **darts** in one of the pubs. Several have boards (including the *Kangaroo Pub* and *The Blacksmith's Arms*, both in Tsim Sha Tsui); check the pub listings in Chapter 8 for more possibilities.

Martial Arts

As in China, **martial arts** are phenomenally popular in Hong Kong, where every second film released features combat of some sort or other. Though born in the United States, **Bruce Lee** (1940–73) spent the later part of his childhood in Hong Kong, and every kid still wants to be him, or one of the dozens of other movie practitioners who have emerged since. Bruce's actor son, Brandon Lee, died tragically young like his father, of an accident on a film set in 1993; meanwhile Jackie Chan remains one of the most prolific of the current stars – you'll see his name everywhere in magazines and on film posters.

The martial art you see most of in Hong Kong outside the cinema, however, is **tai chi**, also known as shadow boxing – a series of slow, balletic exercises designed to stimulate both the mind and the body. Early morning in most of the parks and gardens is the best time to watch or participate in this extraordinarily uplifting exercise. Popular venues include Kowloon Park, Victoria Park, Chater Gardens and the Botanical and Zoological Gardens.

Hong Kong Chinese Martial Arts Association, 687 Nathan Rd ☎ 394 4803.

Hong Kong Tai Chi Association, 60 Argyle St, Mongkok ☎ 395 4884.

Rugby

Rugby is generally of a good standard (Union, not League) and each Easter a couple of days are devoted to a series of Rugby Sevens matches, with international teams competing for the prize – though this is largely an excuse for the expats to get drunk. The event is organised by the **Hong Kong Rugby Football Union** (Block A, Room 1401, Watson's Estate, North Point; ☎ 566 0719), which can provide more information and tell you how to go about joining a team in Hong Kong.

Running: jogs, runs and marathons

You'll see people **jogging** at dozens of places throughout the territory, some of which have marked routes and exercise stops along the way. A few of the most popular spots are along Bowen Road in Mid-Levels; around the roads at the top of Victoria Peak; along the Tsim Sha Tsui East waterfront; around Victoria Park, Causeway Bay; and in Kowloon Park, off Nathan Road. If you do run or jog, remember that the summer heat and humidity are crippling; run in the early morning or evening and take some water along.

Two annual **races** to watch out for are the **Hong Kong Marathon**, held in January, and the **Coast of China Marathon**, which takes place in March. You can get information, and entry forms, for the HK Marathon from the *Hong Kong Amateur Athletic Association* (☎ 574 6845); for the Coast of China from *Athletic Promotions Ltd* (☎ 573 5292). Both events start early, and in the past the Hong Kong Marathon has attracted a large contingent of disabled athletes in wheelchairs.

More offbeat running is provided by the **Orienteering Association of Hong Kong** (c/o Queen Elizabeth Stadium, 18 Oi Kwan Rd, Wan Chai ☎ 891 2691), which runs an orienteering course in Pokfulam Country Park on Hong Kong Island. The Association issues a map showing the course, which you can get by writing to them.

Skating

There are two **ice-skating** rinks in Hong Kong and a couple of fairly central **roller-skating** rinks, too. And although it's hardly a spectator sport in Hong Kong yet, you can get into the mood of things by cuffing the ears of the little blighters who **skateboard** over your toes on all the pedestrian walkways in Central; Blake Pier and the bottom of Jardine House are favourite venues, so watch your step.

Ice-skating

Cityplaza Ice Palace, Cityplaza, Taikoo Shing ☎885 4697; Taikoo Shing MTR. Open 7am–10pm; around $30, including the skates.

Whampoa Super Ice, Whampoa Garden, Hung Hom ☎774 4899. Open 10am–11pm; $35 including skates.

Roller-skating

Lantau Tea Gardens, Lantau. Rink open 8.30am–dusk; around $15 an hour.

Rollerworld, Cityplaza, Taikoo Shing ☎567 0391. Open 9am–9pm; $35–40 a session.

Sportsworld Association, Telford Gardens, Kowloon Bay ☎757 2211. Open 9am–11.15pm; $35 a session.

Soccer

Soccer is widely played throughout the territory, Hong Kong's First Division littered with has-been or never-were players from other countries (mostly Britain) – teams are allowed five overseas players. Good local talent is fairly thin on the ground, but games can be entertaining, not least because the foreign players tend to be bought as strikers – and consequently face local defences comprised of people much shorter than themselves.

If you're sufficiently interested, teams to watch are Happy Valley, South China and recent champions, Eastern. The "national team", such as it is, usually has a torrid time in the World Cup qualifying matches, making heavy weather against such footballing giants as Bahrain, Lebanon and China. The best advice for soccer fans is to find a TV on Sunday evenings during the English soccer season, when you get an hour's worth of the previous week's top English matches; most major cup and international matches are televised, too.

Squash

Squash is about the most popular indoor racquet sport. You'll need to book well in advance, and you'll pay around $45–50 an hour at the public courts listed below. For beginners, the Urban Council (☎529 7960) organises courses, and the Hong Kong Squash Association (☎529 7611) has private lessons for intermediate players.

Hong Kong Sports Institute, Sha Tin ☎605 1212; off-peak hours only Mon–Fri 9.30am–6.45pm.

Hong Kong Squash Centre, Cotton Tree Drive, Central ☎869 0960; book seven days in advance.

Lai Chi Kok Sports Hall, Lai Chi Kok, Kowloon ☎745 2796.

Queen Elizabeth Stadium, 18 Oi Kwan Rd, Wan Chai ☎591 1346.

Victoria Park, Causeway Bay ☎570 6186.

Swimming

If you don't want to risk the water at any of the territory's **beaches** – the best of which are covered in the text – then you'll have to take your dip in one of the few, and crowded, **swimming pools** operated by the Urban Council: call the Urban Services Department for information (Hong Kong ☎832 2616; Kowloon East ☎320 6542; Kowloon West ☎309 1058). Some of the bigger hotels have pools, though these are usually open to residents only.

Aberdeen, 2 Shum Wah Rd, Aberdeen ☎553 3617. Daily 7am–9pm; adults $15, children $7. Good facilities for the disabled.

Hong Kong Sports Institute, Sha Tin ☎605 1212. You can use the pool in the off-peak hours – daily 7–9am, Mon–Fri noon–2pm. Call first; $30 per person.

Sport

Sport

Kowloon Park, Nathan Rd, Tsim Sha Tsui ☎724 3577. July and August only. Open 6.30–11.30am & 1–10pm; adults $15, children $7.

Kowloon Tsai, Inverness Rd, Hung Hom ☎336 5817. Daily 7am–9pm; adults $15, children $7.

Morrison Hill, Oi Kwan Rd, Wan Chai ☎575 3028. Daily 6.30–11.30am, 1–6pm & 8–10pm; adults $15, children $7.

Victoria Park, Hing Fat St, Causeway Bay ☎570 4682. Daily 7–11.15am & 1–9.45pm; adults $15, children $7.

Tennis

Public **tennis** courts are often solidly booked, but if you can get a court you'll pay around $35–50 an hour. Try at one of the following places. The Queen Elizabeth Stadium also has the facilities for **table tennis**, which costs about half as much per hour.

Hong Kong Sports Institute, Sha Tin ☎605 1212. Off-peak hours only for visitors; Mon–Fri 9.30am–5.45pm.

Tennis Centre, Wong Nai Chung Gap Rd, Happy Valley ☎574 9122.

Victoria Park, Causeway Bay ☎570 6186.

Watersports

As you might expect, there's plenty of choice for watersports in a territory of 230 islands. **Sailing** enthusiasts, who are members of an overseas club, can contact the prestigious *Royal Hong Kong Yacht Club* on Kellet Island, Causeway Bay (☎832 2817), which has reciprocal arrangements with many foreign clubs. For plain **boating and pleasure cruising**, contact any of the tour companies listed under "Organised Tours", p.49, or ask the HKTA for recommendations.

You can rent **windsurfing** equipment at quite a few of the territory's beaches: try the *Windsurf Centre* (☎981 8316) on Kwun Yam Wan Beach on Cheung Chau (p.173) , or the *Tai Po Sail Board Centre* (☎661 1818), 77 Chau Uk Chuen, Shun Wan, Ting Kok Rd, Tai Po, both of which offer courses and rental. The **Hong Kong Windsurfing Association** (PO Box 1083, Central) can help with other enquiries. Some of these beachside operations also offer **water-skiing** and **canoeing** (particularly at the Cheung Chau *Windsurf*

Chapter 14

Children's Hong Kong

It's some kind of achievement in itself to have got the children unscathed through a long-haul flight, so once here it's nice to know that in many ways Hong Kong is made for them. Not that there's an enormous amount in the way of specialised activities and events, but the territory itself can be a playground. Most of the things that you'll want to do anyway – from visiting island beaches to trawling through space-age shopping malls – are of sufficient general interest to keep everyone amused. The transport, particularly the trams and ferries, is exciting, most of the views and walks more so; and there is a hard core of venues with a real family slant – Ocean Park is only the best-known. It's good to know, too, that restaurants in Hong Kong (certainly Chinese restaurants) mostly welcome kids with open arms. Eating is a family affair,

as a trip to any *dim sum* restaurant shows, and you don't need to worry about children running up and down the aisles and shrieking: they'll be considered abnormal if they don't.

The sections below should give you some ideas for day-to-day **activities**. You'll need to follow the page references for the full accounts of each sight, activity or sport. There's also a round-up of **dangers** to be aware of if you're travelling with small children.

Outings

Base a day-trip around the places and activities below, all of which can occupy several hours with kids in tow.

Hong Kong Park, Central (p.66). Enormous aviary, greenhouses, gardens, picnic areas, restaurant and excellent play areas.

Babysitting

Most large hotels can organise **babysitting** for you if you contact reception; the HKTA has a full list of ones that will oblige, if you want to check before you leave.

Playgroups and Information

Playgroups and parent-toddler groups are run by a variety of organisations. Information from – among others – the *Pre-School Playgroups Association* (Mon, Wed & Fri only; ☎523 1611); St Andrew's Church, 138 Nathan Rd, Tsim Sha Tsui (☎367 1478); St John's

Cathedral, Central (☎523 4157). There's also a bi-monthly *Mother and Baby* magazine published in Hong Kong, available in many kids' clothes stores and toddler shops.

Clothes and Supplies

Hong Kong has branches of specialist store *Mothercare* (Shop 338–340, Prince's Building, Chater Rd, Central; Shop 137, Ocean Terminal, Harbour City, Canton Rd, Tsim Sha Tsui); for details of kids' clothes shops, check the listings in HKTA's *Shopping* guide (available free at HKTA offices).

Children's Hong Kong

Also close to the pedestrian walkways that snake off into the hi-tech buildings of Central.

KCR train to Sheung Shui and back, New Territories (Chapter 4). A train ride, with stops at traditional markets, brand new towns and shopping centres, and a railway museum.

Ocean Park and Water World, Deep Water Bay, Hong Kong Island (p.96). Multi-ride amusement and theme park, with marine animals, shows, gardens, and an adjacent slide-and-splash park.

Outlying islands (Chapter 5). Ferry rides to all the main islands, where there are beaches, walks, temples and watersports.

Sea cruises (see "Organised Tours", p.49). Cruises lasting anything from an hour to a whole day through the harbour and around the outlying islands; many include a picnic lunch.

Stanley Village, Hong Kong Island (p.99). Beaches, watersports, a market, restaurants, and a good bus ride there and back.

Sung Dynasty Village and Lai Chi Kok amusement park, Lai Chi Kok, Kowloon (p.124). Historical Chinese theme park, waxworks museum, a small-scale amusement park and zoo.

Victoria Peak (p.76). A trip up on the Peak Tram; walks around the Peak, panoramic views and picnic areas.

Whampoa Gardens, Hung Hom (p.116). Huge concrete ship-shaped shopping mall, with musical fountain, coffee shop, ice-skating rink, cinema and children's play area.

Museums and Temples

The following places will interest an inquisitive child. The museums are ones where participation is encouraged – operating robots, clambering on old train carriages, walking through a renovated village – and while nearly all the temples in Hong Kong are unusual enough for most visitors, the ones listed below are particularly large and colourful.

Ching Chung Koon Temple, Tuen Mun, New Territories (p.149).

Po Lin Monastery, Lantau (p.184).

Railway Museum, Tai Po Market, New Territories (p.136).

Sam Tung Uk Folk Museum, Tsuen Wan, New Territories (p.145).

Science Museum, Science Museum Rd, Tsim Sha Tsui East (p.116).

Space Museum, Salisbury Rd, Tsim Sha Tsui (p.112).

Wong Tai Sin Temple, Kowloon (p.122).

Sport

Consult Chapter 13, "Sport", for details of all **sporting activites** in Hong Kong. You should be able to persuade even the most slothful child that there's something there that they'd enjoy, whether it's bowling, skating or swimming. If you want your sport self-contained, think about the HKTA trips to the Clearwater Bay Golf and Country Club, where there's a variety of activities on offer in one well-equipped complex.

Entertainment

Obvious ideas include **cinemas**, which show the latest films in English; the HKTA-organised **cultural shows**, with song, dance and mime in various venues; and a visit to a **Chinese opera** for the singing and costumes. Some places, like the Arts Centre and local libraries, organise **special events** for children throughout the school summer holiday: the HKTA will have current information, or call into City Hall and look at the noticeboards, and pick up the *City News* magazine. There's more information on all these activities and events in Chapter 10.

Coinciding with one of Hong Kong's **festivals** (see p.255 for details) is another way to expose kids to a bit of cultural entertainment. They'll particularly enjoy the Cheung Chau Bun Festival, the dragon boat racing, and any of the colourful Tin Hau celebrations.

Shopping

Shopping can keep children amused, too, especially when it's raining, since if you pick one of the huge shopping malls you don't have to set foot outside for hours on end, even to eat.

There's a list of the main malls on p.267; while specific **shops** that you might want to take in include the enormous *Toys R Us* (Shop 003, Basement, Ocean Terminal, Harbour City, Canton Rd, Tsim Sha Tsui; Shop A197–199, Level I, New Town Plaza, Sha Tin, New Territories), and the Japanese department stores in Causeway Bay (see p.265), which feature games, toys, comics and cafés.

Eating

Chapter 7 details all the eating possibilities. You can get fish and chips in Hong Kong (Yorkshire's famous *Harry Ramsden's* has a branch here), as well as pizzas, hamburgers and all manner of calorific junk, so no one needs to starve. For more of an occasion, visit one of the specialist **fish restaurants** in Lau Fau Shan (Chapter 4) or Lei Yue Mun (Chapter

Children's Hong Kong

Dangers

• Hong Kong can be extremely hot and **humid**: small children should wear a hat; and make sure they're drinking enough liquids.

• Keep a close eye on children when riding **public transport**. Tram rides on Hong Kong Island, the Peak Tram, and the MTR are all exciting, but they're nearly always packed. Keep kids away from tram windows, and from the edges of the cross-harbour ferries.

• Don't encourage or allow children to play with **animals** found on the street. Rabies is still a problem here, and if your child gets bitten or scratched by a stray kitten, you're in for lengthy hospital visits.

3) or on one of the outlying islands (Chapter 5), where youngsters can pick dinner out of the fish tanks.

Chapter 15

Staying On: Working and Living in Hong Kong

Hong Kong is – and always has been – full of foreigners working and living in the territory. As ties with the UK weaken, fewer of them are British and these days the biggest immigrant group in Hong Kong is from the Philippines, mostly women who come here to work as servants and house maids (*amahs*). What European expatriate workers (expats) there are tend more and more to have been posted to the territory by their company, or have applied for jobs with Hong Kong firms from abroad. That said, the dream still persists with many travellers that they can turn up, find work and make their fortune; and you *can* find work and accommodation in Hong Kong. However, mostly you'll need to lower your sights and be aware that you're in competition with five million other people.

Hong Kong isn't an easy place to live, job or no job. It's crowded, hot and humid, with few prospects of getting away from it all and all the frustrations of living in a country where you don't speak the native language. You'll find the basic rules below, together with ideas about how to get a job and somewhere to live. However, there are no short-cuts to making the kind of money Hong Kong is famous for – though you can be happy with the thought that it's several times easier to become a Hong Kong dollar millionaire than a sterling or US dollar millionaire.

Finding Work

If you're a British citizen you get an automatic year-long stamp in your passport and don't require an **employment visa**. Everyone else needs a visa, which you have to apply for at any British Embassy or Consulate, before you arrive. Any general enquiries should be addressed to the Immigration Department, Wan Chai Tower, Gloucester Road, Wan Chai ☎829 3000. Staying and working longer than six months, you'll also need an ID card (see below).

The kind of work where vacancies are currently on offer is **skilled, professional work**: there's a brain drain occurring right now from the territory, due to uncertainty about Hong Kong's future, and there's never been a better time to look to plug the gaps, provided you aren't worried about what Chinese rule will bring. Flick through the *South China Morning Post* and its jobs pages – it's on sale in foreign Chinatowns – and you might be able to apply before you leave. Note, though, that if you need an employment visa and find a job while you're a visitor in Hong Kong, you'll have to leave the territory and apply for a visa before being allowed to take up the position.

If you don't want to apply for anything specific, you can always try **writing and ringing around** once you're in Hong Kong. Ideally, you'll need a base (ie your own or someone else's flat and phone), plenty of experience in the field you're trying to bust into, and lots of time. Bring copies of all relevant qualifications. You can get a free list of many different Hong Kong companies from the **Employment Services Division**, Labour Department, 17th Floor, Harbour Building, 38 Pier Road, Central.

Failing that, the other option is to look for **semi- and unskilled work**, which is more widely available, but has the disadvantage of being fairly badly paid. Some ideas are listed below and though you'll make enough to live on with most of the jobs, you're in competition with young Chinese people, who are mostly well-educated, bilingual and prepared to accept lower wages than you'd expect for the same job.

Employment Agencies

Employment agencies are listed in the Yellow Pages. Most will ask to see your CV/résumé before registering you. And the longer you plan to work, the more chance you have of getting a job – you might need to be economical with the truth about the length of time you intend to spend in Hong Kong. The following agencies will register people looking for as little as six weeks' clerical work:

Adia Personnel Services Ltd, Room 1113, Swire House, 11 Chater Rd ☎ 525 1257.

Drake International, 18th Floor, Peregrine Tower, Lippo Centre, Drake St, Central ☎ 848 9288.

Swift Recruitment Ltd, Room 504, Luk Yu Building, 24–26 Stanley St, Central ☎ 845 3280.

Career Opportunities?

• **Bar and restaurant work**. Poorly paid – around $35 an hour plus tips – but there are always vacancies in English and Australian pubs and often in non-Chinese restaurants. Ask around the bars, look in windows for notices of "help wanted", check the noticeboard in the *Travellers' Hostel*, Chungking Mansions.

• **Film extras**. Hong Kong is a huge filmmaking centre and there are reputed to be jobs going as extras for films and commercials, paying around $250 a day.

Nice work if you can get it; again, watch noticeboards and newspapers.

• **Hostess/modelling/escort work**. You might see adverts seeking any of these three categories of people, though in general they're worth avoiding. At best, hostessing/escort work consists of drinking lots of champagne with fat old businessmen; at worst it consists of sleeping with them as well.

• **Hotel work**. Fairly hard to come by for foreigners, but watch out for advertising by the big hotels for cleaning, kitchen and desk staff. Some of the hostels in Chungking Mansions also occasionally take on helpers; ask at the ones used to western travellers, like the *Travellers' Hostel*.

• **Office work**. The Hong Kong papers are full of office jobs – clerking, dogsbodies, gofers and sales people – but you'll often need to speak Cantonese. Law companies are among the few businesses which employ only English-speaking people; phoning them direct can be very effective. Reckon on earning from $5000 a month and upwards, not a fortune by any means, though many jobs also offer commission.

• **Smuggling**. The noticeboards at the *Travellers' Hostel* and elsewhere sometimes advertise for people to take items – electronic gear and the like – to other countries, where it can be sold at a premium. You'll get the air ticket for your trouble, and maybe paid too, but if customs stamp the gear in your passport you'll be expected to have it when you leave the country you've brought it into – and if you don't know exactly what it is you're taking, or haven't checked the goods, it could well be drugs. Not at all recommended.

• **Teaching**. Eminently possible, though again not brilliantly paid (around $70–100 an hour). However, you don't always need experience or a TEFL qualification. Look in the *South China Morning Post* for jobs in private and government schools, or for people wanting private tuition; or advertise yourself. The language schools listed in the Yellow Pages are worth checking.

Staying On: Working and Living in Hong Kong

Staying On: Working and Living in Hong Kong

Finding an Apartment

If you're staying in Hong Kong for any length of time, you'll need to get out of your hostel or hotel and into an apartment. Space is at a premium in the territory and rents aren't cheap, nor will you get the same space for your money as at home. But as long as you don't want to live on Hong Kong Island itself, you should be able to find somewhere that's reasonably priced, especially if you can share accommodation with someone else.

If you've been sent to Hong Kong by your company, or have come for a job that's been offered to you by a large company, then you won't pay most or all of your rent: your initial hotel bills should be paid, too, while you look for apartments on **Hong Kong Island** – perhaps in the nice areas on the south side by the beaches, or in Mid-Levels above Central. If you *are* paying your own rent, however, these places are likely to be way out of your price range. A flick through the papers at the property pages will show you that you're talking telephone numbers, and living on The Peak itself has always been reserved for the phenomenally wealthy. Mere mortals will have to look elsewhere for accommodation; generally, the further out of Kowloon you get, the cheaper it becomes. The **New Territories** towns are good places to look: Sha Tin is probably the closest place you'll be able to afford, only a quick train ride from Kowloon Tong; Tsuen Wan and Tuen Mun are further out and plagued by rush-hour congestion, but connected with Central by hoverferry. If you don't mind the travelling time, and being fairly isolated as one of the few foreigners around, towns further up the KCR railway line are substantially cheaper: like Tai Po and developments in and around Fanling and Sheung Shui. Living on one of the **outlying islands** (Lamma, Cheung Chau or Lantau particularly) is popular with many foreigners and certainly it's quieter and often cheaper. But commuting in every day can be a real pain, and in typhoon season the ferry services are often suspended altogether.

You can start **to look** for apartments in the classified sections of the *South China Morning Post* and the *Hong Kong Standard*. Places are mostly rented unfurnished and are advertised by the square footage of the apartment; you'll soon work out what's big and what isn't. The price in dollars will be the monthly **rent** – around $10,000 and upwards for anything halfway decent – and you might well have to pay two months' rent as a deposit as well. If nothing comes up, or at the same time, look for lettings agencies in the Yellow Pages and have them put you on their lists. Or wander around the shopping centres in the New Territories towns, like Sha Tin, and go into the agents you see to ask about apartments: they're the shops with coloured cards in the windows, generally in Chinese, but with explicable square footage and price signs.

Once you're in your apartment, you'll be responsible for furnishing it and all the bills. Lots of the new blocks have security guards and video-protection services, but otherwise give some thought to **securing your apartment**: change the locks or get a steel door like everyone else.

ID Cards

Every resident of Hong Kong has to have and carry an **identity card**, which you should get hold of as soon as possible; you use it often in everyday life. Technically, you're supposed to apply for one within thirty days of arrival if you're going to stay in Hong Kong.

ID cards are **issued** free of charge at the territory's Immigration Department at Wan Chai Tower, Gloucester Road, Wan Chai ☎ 829 3000. Take your passport, and a few dollars in change which you'll need for making photocopies and having a couple of photos taken. They'll take your name and address and you'll have to return about a month later to pick the card up. Lose it and a replacement costs $170.

> There are several **organisations** you might find useful as you settle in to Hong Kong – from the Community Advice Bureau to the Samaritans; they're all listed in the next chapter, "Directory".

Chapter 16

Directory

AIDS *AIDS Concern* counselling service ☎522 5665; Thurs & Sat 7–10pm.

AIRLINES All the airlines in Hong Kong are listed in the Yellow Pages under "Air Line Companies". The main ones include:

Air India, 10th Floor, Gloucester Tower, The Landmark, 11 Pedder St, Central ☎521 4321.

Air New Zealand, Suite 902, Three Exchange Square, Connaught Place, Central ☎845 8063.

British Airways, 30th Floor, Alexandra House, 7 Des Voeux Rd, Central ☎868 0303; and c/o *Royal Garden Hotel*, 69 Mody Rd, Tsim Sha Tsui East ☎368 9255.

Cathay Pacific, Ground Floor, Swire House, Chater Rd, Central ☎884 1488; and c/o *Royal Garden Hotel*, Room 109, 1st Floor, 69 Mody Rd, Tsim Sha Tsui East ☎767 3888.

China Airlines, Ground Floor, St George's Building, 2 Ice House St, Central ☎868 2299.

Gulf Air, 18th Floor, Euro Trade Centre, 13–14 Connaught Rd, Central ☎868 0832.

Japan Air Lines, Gloucester Tower, The Landmark, 11 Pedder St, Central ☎523 0081; and c/o *Harbour View Holiday Inn*, Mody Rd, Tsim Sha Tsui East ☎311 3355.

KLM, Ground Floor, Fu House, 7 Ice House St, Central ☎525 1255.

Korean Air, Ground Floor, St George's Building, 2 Ice House St, Central ☎523 5177.

Lufthansa, 6th Floor, Landmark East, 12 Ice House St, Central ☎868 2313.

Philippine Airlines, Room 1801, Swire House, Chater Rd, Central ☎522 7018.

Qantas, Room 1422, Swire House, Chater Rd, Central ☎842 1430.

Royal Nepal Airlines, Room 1114–1116, Star House, Salisbury Rd, Tsim Sha Tsui ☎730 9151.

SAS, Room 2407, Edinburgh Tower, The Landmark, 11 Pedder St, Central ☎526 5978.

Singapore Airlines, Ground Floor, Alexandra House, 7 Des Voeux Rd, Central ☎520 2233.

Swissair, 8th Floor, Tower II, Admiralty Centre, 18 Harcourt Rd, Admiralty ☎529 3670.

Thai International, Shop 122, 1st Floor, World Wide Plaza, Pedder St, Central ☎529 5601.

United Airlines, 29th Floor, Gloucester Tower, The Landmark, 11 Pedder St, Central ☎810 4888.

AIRPORT ENQUIRIES Hong Kong International (Kai Tak) Airport ☎769 7531.

AMBULANCE Call ☎999, or the St John's Ambulance Brigade, which runs a free ambulance service – on ☎576 6555 (Hong Kong Island), ☎713 5555 (Kowloon), or ☎4639 2555 (New Territories).

AMERICAN EXPRESS Ground Floor, New World Tower, 16–18 Queen's Rd, Central

Directory

(Mon–Fri 9am–5.30pm, Sat 9am–noon; ☎844 8668); report stolen cheques on ☎811 6122.

AMNESTY INTERNATIONAL The local branch of the campaigning organisation is at 3rd Floor, Besto Best Building, Unit C, 32–36 Ferry St, Kowloon ☎300 1251.

BANKS AND EXCHANGE There are banks of every nationality and description throughout Hong Kong, seemingly on every street corner. Opening hours are Mon–Fri 9am–4.30pm, Sat 9am–12.30pm, with small fluctuations – half an hour each side – from branch to branch. Most charge commission for exchanging travellers' cheques, though generally, the *Hang Seng Bank, Wing On Bank* and the *Union Bank of Hong Kong* don't. There's no commission either if you change *American Express* or *Thomas Cook* cheques at their respective offices (see above and below). You can also change money and cheques at a licensed money changer – there are several in Tsim Sha Tsui which are open late (and on Sun). They won't rip you off, but they do charge a big commission (around 9 percent of the sum changed). The signs on the windows of the money changers which say "No Commission" only apply if you're *selling* Hong Kong dollars. Otherwise, you can change travellers' cheques and cash at the big hotels and in some stores, but the rates will be lower than at the bank.

BIKE RENTAL Not an option in central Hong Kong, though possible on the islands and in the New Territories. Check with the HKTA; or contact the *Hong Kong Cycling Association*, at the Queen Elizabeth Stadium, 18 Oi Kwan Rd, Wan Chai ☎573 3861.

BRITISH COUNCIL At 255 Hennessy Rd, Wan Chai ☎879 5145; bus #11 stops outside. There's a lending library on the first floor (Mon, Tues, Thurs & Fri 9.30am–8.30pm, Wed noon–8.30pm, Sat 9.30am–6.30pm) which costs $120 a year to join, a reference library with the same opening times, British newspapers available and free films (watch the local press). For

French and German equivalents, see "Cultural Groups" below.

CAR PARKS The biggest garaging firm is *Wilson*, which, among other places, has car parks at Kowloon (Hung Hom) Station, City Hall (Central), 310 Gloucester Rd and 475 Lockhart Rd; other central car parks are at Exchange Square and Prince's Building.

CAR RENTAL You'll pay from around $300 a day, $2000 a week, for the smallest available car. You need to be over eighteen and have a valid overseas driving licence (with which you can drive in Hong Kong for a year) or an international driving licence. Remember that you drive on the left. Agencies include: *Avis*, Ground Floor, Bonaventure House, 85 Leighton Rd, Causeway Bay ☎890 6988 and Zung Fu Car Park Building, 50 Po Loi St, Hung Hom ☎3346007; *Holiday Rental*, Ground Floor, 237A Prince Edward Rd, Mongkok ☎713 0113; *Intercontinental Hire Cars Ltd*, 21st Floor, Lane Crawford House, 70 Queen's Rd, Central ☎532 1388.

COMMUNITY ADVICE BUREAU St John's Cathedral New Hall, 8 Garden Rd, Central ☎524 5444 (Mon–Fri 9.30am–4pm). Deals with day-to-day problems and advice for newcomers and tourists.

CONSULATES AND EMBASSIES British citizens who need consular assistance, particularly with regard to passport issues, should contact the *Hong Kong Immigration Department*, 7 Gloucester Rd, Wan Chai ☎829 3000. The other main consulates and embassies are:

Australia, Harbour Centre, 23rd Floor, 25 Harbour Rd, Wan Chai ☎522 8086.

Canada, 12th Floor, One Exchange Square, Central ☎810 4321.

China, 5th Floor, China Resources Building, Lower Block, 26 Harbour Rd, Wan Chai ☎835 3657.

Denmark, 2402b Great Eagle Centre, 23 Harbour Rd, Wan Chai ☎827 8101.

France, Admiralty Centre, 26th Floor, 18 Harcourt Rd, Admiralty ☎529 4351.

Germany, 21st Floor, United Centre, 95 Queensway, Admiralty ☎ 527 1334.

India, 16th Floor, 16D, United Centre, 95 Queensway, Central ☎ 528 4028.

Indonesia, 127 Leighton Rd, Causeway Bay ☎ 890 4421.

Ireland: no permanent diplomatic mission; for consular assistance, contact the Immigration Dept (see above).

Japan, 24th Floor, Bank of America Tower, 12 Harcourt Rd, Admiralty ☎ 522 1184.

Korea, 5th Floor, Far East Financial Centre, 16 Harcourt Rd, Central ☎ 527 2724.

Malaysia, 50 Gloucester Rd, Malaysia Building, 23rd Floor, Wan Chai ☎ 527 0921.

Netherlands, China Building, Room 301, 29 Queen's Rd, Central ☎ 522 5127.

New Zealand, Room 3414, Jardine House, Connaught Rd, Central ☎ 525 5044.

Norway, Room 1401, AIA Building, 1 Stubbs Rd, Wan Chai (☎ 574 9253).

Pakistan, China Resources Building, 26 Harbour Rd, Wan Chai ☎ 827 0681.

Philippines, 22nd Floor, Wah Kwong Regent Centre, 88 Queen's Rd, Central ☎ 810 0183.

Portugal, 10th Floor, Two Exchange Square, Connaught Place, Central ☎ 522 5789.

Singapore, Admiralty Centre Tower, Unit 901, 19th Floor, 18 Harcourt Rd, Admiralty ☎ 527 2212.

South Africa, 27th Floor, Sunning Plaza, 10 Hysan Ave, Causeway Bay ☎ 577 3279.

Sweden, Hong Kong Club Building, 8th Floor, 3a Chater Rd, Central ☎ 521 1212.

Switzerland, Room 3703, 11 Pedder St, Gloucester Tower, Central ☎ 522 7147.

Thailand, 8th Floor, Fairmont House, 8 Cotton Tree Drive, Central ☎ 521 6481.

Taiwan, 4th Floor, East Tower, Lippo Centre, 89 Queensway, Admiralty ☎ 525 8315.

USA, 26 Garden Rd, Central ☎ 523 9011.

Vietnam, 20th Floor, Kam Chung Building, 19–21 Hennessy Rd, Wan Chai ☎ 527 0221.

CONTRACEPTION Condoms are available in supermarkets, the Pill on prescription from pharmacists. For anything else, contact a Family Planning Clinic: the HQ is at Ground Floor, 8b, Wing Lot House, Fu Loi Estate, Cheung Wan ☎ 493 3318. There's a more central clinic at 130 Hennessy Rd, Wan Chai.

COURIER FIRMS For international courier flights, contact *Cathay Pacific* ☎ 735 2163; *Polo Express* ☎ 303 1286; *International Courier Co.* ☎ 761 1516; or *Globenet* ☎ 736 1577.

CULTURAL GROUPS *Alliance Française*, 123 Hennessy Rd, 2nd Floor, Wan Chai (Mon–Fri 10am–1pm & 2–6pm; bus #11 passes by) has a French-language library and films; *Goethe Institute*, 14th Floor, Hong Kong Arts Centre, 2 Harbour Rd, Wan Chai (Mon–Fri 9.30am–7.45pm; ☎ 527 0088) has a general purpose German-language library (as well as some English-language books), and also newspapers and a video library.

DENTISTS Dentists are listed in the Yellow Pages (under "Dental Practitioners"); or you can ring the *Hong Kong Dental Association* (☎ 528 5327) for a list of qualified dentists. Treatment is expensive.

DEPARTURE TAX Don't forget to hang on to enough Hong Kong dollars for your airport departure tax: $150 for anyone over 12.

DISABLED TRAVELLERS A special twelve-seater bus service, *Rehabus*, operates on a dial-a-ride system during off-peak hours and at the weekend; phone ☎ 817 8154 in advance to make a reservation. Other useful numbers include: *Joint Council for the Physically and Mentally Disabled* ☎ 549 7700 (general information centre for all voluntary agencies); *Hong Kong Red Cross* ☎ 802 2021 (wheelchair loans and other services); *Hong Kong Society for the Blind* ☎ 778 8332; *Hong Kong Society for the Deaf* ☎ 527 8969.

DRESS As you would in any city where it's hot and humid, though bear in mind that a lot of the posher hotels and restaurants insist on some kind of dress code: no

Directory

Directory

shorts, sandals or flip-flops if you're going for tea at the *Peninsula* and a jacket and tie if you're eating in an expense-account restaurant. For dinner with the Governor, you'll need the penguin suit and tie hire services of *Tuxe Top Co. Ltd*, 1st Floor, 18 Hennessy Rd, Wan Chai & 3rd Floor, 16 Peking Rd, Tsim Sha Tsui (both branches open daily 10am–7pm).

DOCTORS Look in the Yellow Pages (under "Physicians and Surgeons"), or contact the reception desk in the larger hotels. Most doctors speak English. You'll have to pay for a consultation and any medicines they prescribe, but it'll be no more than $150 for anything fairly basic; pick up the medicine at the doctor's surgery and ask for a receipt for your insurance. It's cheaper to visit the nearest local government clinic (often with the words "Jockey Club" in the title, since that's who partly funds them): they stay open late, and you'll only pay a few dollars if you need a basic prescription or treatment at the casualty desk – though you may have to queue. All the clinics are listed in the Hong Kong phone book (at the beginning, in the Government directory).

DRY CLEANING There are shops inside the MTR stations at Jordan, Admiralty, Causeway Bay, Central and Tsim Sha Tsui.

ELECTRICITY Current is 200 volts AC. Plugs are either square three-pin or two round pins, so a travel plug is useful.

EMERGENCIES Call ☎999 for Fire, Police or Ambulance; also see "Ambulance" and "Doctors" above, and "Hospitals" and "Samaritans" below.

ENVIRONMENTAL MATTERS Contact *Friends of the Earth* (2nd Floor, 53–55 Lockhart Rd, Wan Chai ☎528 5588) for details of local issues and campaigns.

GAY LIFE Until very recently, in law homosexuality was completely illegal – the statutes carried a maximum penalty of life imprisonment for committing a homosexual act. The law was brought into line with Britain's in 1990, but there is still no gay scene to speak of in the

territory. Few people are prepared to speak about their homosexuality, and there's no open, obvious place for gay men and women to meet people. There's an advisory service, *Horizons* (☎893 0208) for gays and lesbians; other than that, you'll have to rely on one of a very few places where you might meet other gay people, listed in the box on p.244.

HOSPITALS Government hospitals are the cheapest; they're listed in the Hong Kong phone book. You'll pay around $2000 a day if you're admitted, though casualty visits are free – the government hospitals below have 24-hour casualty departments. Private hospitals are more expensive, but the standard of care much higher.

Government Hospitals *Princess Margaret Hospital*, Lai King Hill Rd, Lai Chi Kok, Kowloon ☎310 3111; *Queen Elizabeth Hospital*, Wylie Rd, Kowloon ☎710 2111; *Queen Mary Hospital*, Pokfulam Rd, Hong Kong Island ☎819 2111; *Tang Shiu Kin Hospital*, Queen's Rd East, Hong Kong Island ☎831 6800.

Private Hospitals *Baptist Hospital*, 222 Waterloo Rd, Kowloon ☎337 4141; *Canossa Hospital*, 1 Old Peak Rd, Hong Kong Island ☎522 2181; *Hong Kong Adventist Hospital*, 40 Stubbs Rd, Hong Kong Island ☎574 6211; *St Teresa's Hospital*, 327 Prince Edward Rd, Kowloon ☎711 9111.

LAUNDRY There's a same-day service in most hotels, and lots of the guest houses in Chungking Mansions (see "Accommodation", p.193) will do your laundry fairly cheaply. Otherwise, try *Fabric Care*, 87 Kimberley Rd, Tsim Sha Tsui; or *Singclean*, 1st Floor, Room 114, Worldwide Plaza, Pedder St, Central. Places charge by the weight of your washing.

LEFT LUGGAGE There's an office in the departure lounge at the airport (daily 6.30am–1am); or leave luggage at various guest houses in Chungking Mansions – though you'll have to be happy with the owners/general security to leave anything valuable here.

LIBRARIES The main English-language library is in the City Hall High Block in Edinburgh Place, Central, open Mon–Thurs 10am–7pm, Fri 10am–9pm, Sat 10am–5pm, Sun 10am–1pm: Junior Library (2nd Floor), Lending Library (3rd Floor), Reference Library (4th Floor), Newspaper Reading Room and Record Library (5th Floor); to join, you need a passport and $100 deposit (ID card holders free). There's also the British Council library (see above) and the *American Library*, 1st Floor, United Centre, 95 Queensway, Admiralty (Mon–Fri 10am–6pm), which is free to join; apply in person with your passport/ID card.

LOST PROPERTY Police ☎860 2000; MTR, Admiralty station (daily 11am–6pm); KCR, 8th Floor, KCR House, Sha Tin, NT ☎606 9392 (Mon–Sat 9am–noon).

NEWSPAPERS There are four English-language newspapers published in Hong Kong. The *South China Morning Post* is the most reliable, a firmly centrist publication that's the best thing to read on the various problems that face Hong Kong. It carries a good, daily "what's on" listings section. The *Hong Kong Standard* is the Post's main rival, duller and notable only for its reasonable daily listings section. The other two papers are the *Asian Wall Street Journal* and the *International Herald Tribune* – the first business-led, the second culled mostly from American newspapers. Published in China, but widely available in Hong Kong, the *China Daily* makes interesting reading in an Alice-in-Wonderland kind of way – straight-down-the-line government propaganda. There are also over forty Chinese newspapers published daily in Hong Kong of various political hues. Beijing objects to the hard reporting of several of them, though there are a few pro-China papers as balance.

British, European and American newspapers are widely available too, normally a couple of days late. They're on sale at both Star Ferry concourses; or try inside the *South China Morning Post Family Bookshop* in Central's Star Ferry concourse. For magazines, check the newsstand in Theatre Lane, just off Queen's Rd Central, or – again – either of the Star Ferry concourses. For local listings magazines and freesheets, see p.249.

PHARMACIES The largest Western-style pharmacist is *Watson's*, which has branches all over Hong Kong (open daily 9am–6pm) and stocks toiletries, contact lens fluid and first aid items. For the nearest branch to you, phone ☎606 8833. Central branches are at Hutchison House (☎526 1736) and the Admiralty Centre (529 6603); in Tsim Sha Tsui there are branches at 132 Nathan Rd (☎368 2396) and in China Hong Kong City (☎736 7362).

PHOTOCOPYING There's a cheap photocopy service in the City Hall library (see "Libraries" above for address).

POLICE Main police stations are as follows: *Hong Kong Island HQ*, Arsenal St, Wan Chai ☎860 2000 and *Kowloon Regional HQ*, 190 Argyle St ☎761 2200. General Enquiries ☎866 6166. For lost property, call ☎860 2000 and you'll be given the address and telephone number of the local police station that will deal with your loss. For Crime Hotline and Taxi Complaints, call ☎527 7177; and for Complaints Against the Police, call ☎527 7226 x200.

POST OFFICES The main General Post Office (GPO) building is at 2 Connaught Place, Central (Mon–Fri 8am–6pm, Sat 8am–2pm ☎922 2222), just behind the Star Ferry on Hong Kong Island, to the right as you get off: the ground floor is for collecting registered letters and parcels, and there are public pay phones there as well; the first floor is for stamps, sending registered letters and other counter services. Kowloon-side, the Kowloon Central Post Office is at 405 Nathan Rd (Yau Ma Tei MTR; same hours as above). Letters sent poste restante will go to the Central GPO building; there's a separate office to collect them from, at the end of Connaught Place, next to the Government Publications Centre, open Mon–Sat 8am–6pm: take your passport.

Directory

Directory

PUBLIC TOILETS You'll find them at all major beaches, sights and country parks – there's usually no paper, though there might be an attendant on hand to sell you a couple of sheets. Public toilets are more scarce in the centre, but that's no problem given the number of restaurants and hotels in Tsim Sha Tsui and Central. The swankier the place, the less likely you'll be challenged; indeed some of the very top hotels have "rest rooms" incorporated into their high-class ground-floor shopping arcades. The finest (and most intimidating) toilet experience is in the arcade of the *Peninsula* hotel: attendants turn on the taps, hand over the soap and retrieve the towels amid brass and marble elegance; you're expected to tip.

RAPE HOTLINE Call ☎572 2733.

SAMARITANS Call ☎896 0000. There's an English-speaking 24-hr service.

TELEPHONES For local calls, you'll find phones at public transport terminals, in shops, hotels, restaurants and bars – local calls are free, except for a $1 charge in coin-operated phones. For long-distance calls, either use an IDD pay phone – many accept phone cards or credit cards – or go to a *Hong Kong Telecom Service Centre*: 102A, One Exchange Square, Central (open 24hr); 3 Gloucester Rd, Wan Chai (Mon–Fri 8am–9pm, Sat 8am–3pm); 3 Hennessy Rd, Wan Chai (Mon–Fri 9am–6pm, Sat 9am–4pm); Hermes House, 10 Middle Rd, Tsim Sha Tsui (open 24hr); Unit D37, Kai Tak Airport, Kowloon (daily 8am–11pm). See p.21 for more information.

Useful telephone numbers include:

Calls to China ☎012

Collect calls ☎010

Directory Enquiries (English) ☎1081

Emergencies (ambulance, police or fire) ☎999

IDD and Cardphone enquiries ☎013

International Operator ☎013

Telefax operator ☎014

Telephone problems/repair ☎109

Time and temperature ☎18501

Tourist information (multi-lingual) ☎801 7177

THOMAS COOK Change travellers' cheques at 18th Floor, Vicwood Plaza, 199 Des Voeux Rd, Central (Mon–Fri 9am–5.30pm, Sat 9am–1pm; ☎545 4399); Ground Floor, Mirador Mansion, 58a Nathan Rd, Tsim Sha Tsui (daily 8am–10pm; ☎366 9687). —

TIME Eight hours ahead of the UK (seven in summer); 16 hours ahead of Los Angeles, 13 hours ahead of New York.

TIPPING Large hotels and most restaurants will add a 10 percent service charge to your bill. In restaurants where there's no service charge, they'll expect to pick up the dollar coins change. In taxis, make the fare up to the nearest dollar. Porters at posh hotels and at the airport aren't carrying your bags for the love of the job – tip at your discretion.

TRANSPORT ENQUIRIES See "Getting Around", p.37, for public transport information.

TRAVEL AGENCIES As well as flights to the rest of Southeast Asia and beyond, most of the places below can help with travel to China, including organising visas.

China Travel Service (CTS), 4th Floor, CTS House, 78–83 Connaught Rd, Central ☎853 3533; 2nd Floor, China Travel Building, 77 Queen's Rd, Central ☎525 2284; 1st Floor, Alpha House, 27–33 Nathan Rd, Tsim Sha Tsui ☎721 1331; 10–12, 1st Floor, China Hong Kong City, 33 Canton Rd, Tsim Sha Tsui ☎736 1863. China visas, tours and tickets.

Global Union Express Ltd, Room 96A, New Henry House, Ice House St, Central ☎845 4232. Trans-Siberian train specialists.

HKFS-STB, Room 501–9, Trade Square 681, Cheung Sha Wan Rd, Kowloon ☎725 3983. Agent in Hong Kong for the well-respected STA Travel.

Hong Kong Student Travel Ltd, 10th Floor, Room 1021, Star House, Salisbury Rd, Tsim Sha Tsui ☎730 3269; right by the Kowloon-side Star Ferry. Very popular place for flights, package tours, boats and trains to China, visas, ISIC and YIEE cards. Open Mon–Fri 9.30am–7pm, Sat 9.30am–6pm, Sun noon–5pm. Branches at 1812 Argyle Centre, 688 Nathan Rd, Mongkok; 11th Floor, Circle Plaza, 499 Hennessy Rd, Causeway Bay; 305 Entertainment Building, 30 Queen's Rd, Central.

Honour Tourist Company, Room 807, Universal Commercial Building, 69 Peking Rd, Tsim Sha Tsui ☎311 4211. Worth trying for flights.

Phoenix Services, Milton Mansions, 6th Floor, Room B, 96 Nathan Rd, Tsim Sha Tsui ☎722 7378. Chinese visas, train tickets, and flight and hotel booking services.

Shoestring Travel, 4th Floor, Alpha House, 27–33 Nathan Rd, Tsim Sha Tsui ☎723 2306 (entrance on Peking Rd). Flights, visas and bus tickets to Guangzhou.

Time Travel, Block A, 16th Floor, Chungking Mansions, 36–44 Nathan Rd, Tsim Sha Tsui ☎366 6222. Helpful place with visas, tickets, passport photos and telex/fax service.

Traveller Services, Room 704, Metropole Building, 57 Peking Rd, Tsim Sha Tsui ☎367 4127. Friendly and helpful with tickets and visas.

Wah Nam Travel, Room 602, Sino Centre, 582–592 Nathan Rd, Kowloon ☎332 0367. Visas, boat and train tickets.

Wallem Travel Ltd, 46th Floor, Hopewell Centre, 183 Queen's Rd East, Wan Chai ☎865 1618. Trans-Siberian train specialists.

VACCINATION CENTRES At Room 903–905, Kowloon Government Office, 393 Canton Rd, Tsim Sha Tsui ☎368 3361 (Mon–Fri 9am–1pm & 2–4.30pm, Sat

Building, 181 Gloucester Rd, Wan Chai ☎572 2056 (Mon–Fri 9am–1pm & 2–4.30pm, Sat 9am–12.30pm).

WOMEN'S HONG KONG Historically, Chinese women have shouldered the domestic work burden, while fulfilling their social relationships through the framework of the extended family. In effect, seeking education and independence as a woman is seen as a Western idea, foreign to a society which still places enormous emphasis on marriage and the family. The possibility of independence is further eroded by the general lack of welfare facilities and the cost of health care and education – a situation worsened by the way in which middle-class women in Hong Kong exploit other, poorer women, by employing them as maids on low wages. There isn't a well-developed women's movement, although the *Association for the Advancement of Feminism in Hong Kong*, Room 1202, Yam Tze Commercial Building, 17–23 Thomson Rd, Wan Chai (☎528 2510), run by local Chinese women, collects information on social and political measures affecting women in Hong Kong. The main women's organisation is the *Hong Kong Council of Women* (PO Box 819, Hong Kong, or 4 Jordan Rd, Yau Ma Tei, Kowloon), dominated by expats and not overtly radical. It does, however, maintain a library, support groups and a refuge – *Harmony House* (☎522 0434) –for battered women and their children; the telephone number is a 24-hr hotline. It's also worth knowing that there's a long-term residential hotel/club for women in Hong Kong, the *Helena May*, but you'll have to book well in advance: more information from the *Helena May*, 35 Garden Road, Mid-Levels ☎522 6766.

Directory

Macau

Chapter 17

Introducing Macau

The territory (or enclave, as it's often called) of **Macau** is 60km west of Hong Kong and 145km south of Guangzhou. It's split into three small, distinct parts – a peninsula and two islands – and the whole enclave covers less than 18 square kilometres (making it the fourth smallest country in the world), in which lives a population of roughly half a million.

The **city** of Macau itself is built on a peninsula of the Chinese mainland, about 4km by 2km at its widest points and easy to negotiate on foot. It's here that you'll find most of the real sights, colonial buildings and historical interest, lots of restaurants and the bulk of the casinos, for which Macau is famous. A three-kilometre-long bridge links the peninsula with **Taipa** island, from where a slightly shorter causeway runs across to the southernmost **Coloane** island. Both islands are small, easily reached by bus, and feature some fine beaches, more good restaurants and the odd church and temple.

Although the bulk of the population is Chinese, at times it's easy to imagine yourself in the Mediterranean. The pace of life is slower than in Hong Kong: there's time to have a drink at an outdoor café overlooking the harbour and walk along the waterfront. As you climb up to old fortresses through hilly, cobbled streets, you pass small squares lined with pastel-coloured mansions and cracked, whitewashed Catholic churches. But Macau is gradually losing its sleepy colonial image by embarking on a series of **construction projects** that will allow it to compete with the other burgeoning Southeast Asian economies. An airport is being built, off Taipa, which should be in operation well before Chek Lap Kok in Hong Kong is up and running: this, and a new container port, are designed to attract new trade and investment, challenging Hong Kong's current dominance. A highway from Macau and the neighbouring Chinese Special Economic Zone of Zhuhai will run up to Guangzhou, linking with the new Hong Kong–Guangzhou highway – firmly linking the enclave with the rapidly expanding southeastern Chinese economy.

For Macau's visa regulations, customs and currency matters, turn to the relevant sections of Basics.

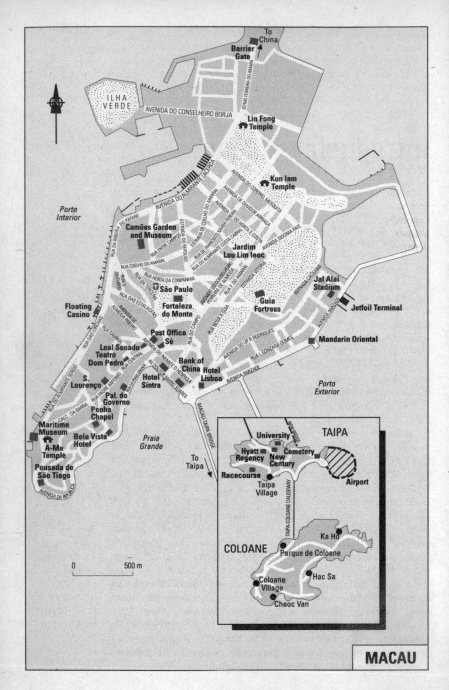

If you're really pushed for time, a day-trip from Hong Kong can take in most of the interesting things in the whole of Macau, but it really warrants a longer visit. Three or four days is enough time to get around everything comfortably and gives you the chance to sample a few of the excellent restaurants. It's also worth considering leaving **for China** from Macau – you don't need to return to Hong Kong to move on, since there are regular bus and ferry connections.

Getting to Macau

Until Macau's airport is operational (see below), the only current air link to the enclave is the helicopter service from Hong Kong. Otherwise, most people will arrive **by sea from Hong Kong**, the journey taking one to two hours, depending on the vessel. Most departures are from the Macau Ferry Terminal in Central, on Hong Kong Island, though there are links with Kowloon too. **From China**, you can approach by ferry; while there's also a straight land route from Guangzhou, which allows you to take the bus or walk across the border into Macau.

By Air

Macau's **airport** is currently being built off the islands of Taipa and Coloane, supervised by the Civil Aviation Authority of Macau (*Autoridade de Aviação Civil de Macau*; see "Directory" for address). It's due to become operational by 1995 (though delays have already held the project up) for direct flights from Asia, Europe and North America; the passenger terminal will be located at the eastern end of Taipa.

In the meantime, the gap is plugged by a **helicopter service** between Hong Kong and Macau. There are nine departures a day, operated by *East Asia Airlines* (☎859 3359), which cost around $1000 one-way ($1100 at the weekend) for the twenty-minute flight. Departures are from the helipad at Hong Kong's Macau Ferry Terminal (see below), where you can buy tickets (counter 8, 3rd Floor); see "Directory", p.333, for telephone number of *East Asia Airlines* in Macau.

By Sea

Most departures by sea **from Hong Kong** – by Jetfoil (the quickest service), High-speed Ferry and Jumbocat – are from the **Macau Ferry Terminal** (☎859 3359), in the Shun Tak Centre, 200 Connaught Road, Central, Hong Kong Island (Sheung Wan MTR). Other, less frequent departures – by Jetcat and Hoverferry – are from the **China Ferry Terminal** at 33 Canton Road, Tsim Sha Tsui. All the ticket details are covered in the boxed feature below.

Hong Kong–Macau By Sea

The Hong Kong government charges a **departure tax** of $26 per person on sea journeys to Macau, which is generally included in the price of your ticket; if you buy a return ticket, you'll also be charged a Macau departure tax of 20ptcs. At the Macau Ferry Terminal, you can book same-day and advance tickets for all services, as well as tickets for the Jetfoils up to 28 days in advance. Advance Jetfoil tickets are also available from any *Ticketmate* office, which you'll find in Hong Kong at the MTR station concourses of Tsim Sha Tsui, Jordan, Mongkok, Tsuen Wan, Kwun Tong, Causeway Bay and Wan Chai.

Try and **book in advance** for all crossings, especially at the weekend and on public holidays, when all the transport is packed; getting a return ticket saves you time anyway at the other end. Standby tickets are available, but you'll have to join the queue – though as departures from the Macau Ferry Terminal are so frequent, you shouldn't have too long a wait. All **prices** given below are for one-way fares; returns are exactly double. All tickets are for a specific **departure time**; aim to be at the ferry terminal thirty minutes before departure as you'll have to fill in immigration forms before boarding. Luggage on the jetfoils is limited to hand luggage. You'll be allowed on with a suitcase or rucksack, but anything more and you should think about taking the High-speed Ferry.

Jetfoils

Run by the *Far East Jetfoil Company* (☎859 3333), **Jetfoils** provide the quickest ride to Macau, getting there in 55 minutes. There's a daily 24-hour service from the Macau Ferry Terminal, with **departures** every 15–30 minutes during the day, less frequently (though still regularly) at night. **Tickets** are priced according to class and departure time, but broadly day services from 7am–6pm cost around $90 for economy class (lower deck) and $100 first class (upper deck); weekend prices are around $100 and

Coming **from China**, many people choose to bypass Hong Kong and make their way first to Macau, using the once-daily (overnight) **ferry from Guangzhou** (from Zhoutouzui Wharf). Tickets for this – available from the wharf, or from the *CITS* office in Guangzhou next to the main train station (see "Onwards Travel", p.365) – are comparable in price to those for the equivalent trip from Guangzhou to Hong Kong by ferry (HK$150–200 one-way). There's also a longer, twice-weekly, ferry service – the *Macmosa* – from **Taiwan**, though this has been under threat for some time due to falling passenger numbers.

By Land

Buses operate from Guangzhou direct to Macau, a six-hour trip. They cross the border at Gongbei, the town immediately over the border from Macau, in the Zhuhai Special Economic Zone; if you've got off in Gongbei for a look around, the Barrier Gate border into Macau is open daily 7am–9pm.

$110 respectively. Night services, from 6pm–7am, cost around $115 (economy) and $140 (first class).

Telephone credit card bookings in Hong Kong for Jetfoil services can be made on ☎859 6596; *Visa, Mastercard, American Express* and *Diners Club* are all accepted.

Catamarans

Two types of **catamaran** make the crossing from Hong Kong to Macau, both operated by *Hong Kong and Macau Hydrofoil Company* (☎523 2136). The **Super-Shuttle Jumbocat** takes 65 minutes, with half-hourly departures between 7.30am and 6pm from the Macau Ferry Terminal; tickets cost around $95 Monday to Friday, $105 at weekends. *American Express* and *Visa* card holders can book by telephone on ☎559 9255. The **Jetcat** – a smaller version of the Jumbocat – takes around ten minutes longer and makes ten trips daily, with departures from Kowloon's China Ferry Terminal; around $70 Monday to Friday and $80 at weekends.

High-speed Ferries and Hoverferries

Hong Kong Ferries' (☎542 3038) **Hoverferries** run twelve times daily from the China Ferry Terminal between 8.30am and 6pm (two night services, too). They take around 70 minutes, for a fare of around $70 Monday to Friday, $85 at weekends and $100 at night. You can book at the terminal or at Jordan Road Ferry Pier in Kowloon and the Central Harbour Services Ferry Pier in Central.

Despite the name, **High-speed Ferries** (*Hong Kong Hi-Speed Ferries Ltd*; ☎815 3043) take longer – around 90–100 minutes. There's more room for luggage, though, and there are five daily departures (six at weekends) between 8am and 8pm from the Macau Ferry Terminal. Tickets cost around $35 economy ($55 weekend), $52 tourist class ($75 weekend) and around $70 first class ($90 weekend).

Arriving in Macau

All Jetfoils, Jet cats, Jumbocats, Hoverferries and High-speed Ferries dock at the several piers on Avenida da Amizada in the Outer Harbour (Porto Exterior), on the eastern side of the Macau peninsula. The terminal has several names, but it's most commonly known as the **Jetfoil Terminal**, which is what it says on the buses that run past there. The **helicopter** service from Hong Kong lands on a pad above the terminal; and the ferry service from Taiwan also docks here. If you're only staying for the day, there's a **left luggage office** (daily 8am–3am), the *Bagageiro*, in the terminal's ground-floor ticket office.

Pick up a map at the Visitor Information Centre inside the terminal (see below) and you could **walk into central Macau**: it takes around twenty minutes to reach the *Hotel Lisboa*. Otherwise, **buses** from the stops right outside the terminal run into the centre and out to the two outlying islands: #3, #3A, #10, #12, #13, #28A and

For all
departure
details from
Macau, see
"Directory",
p.333 and 334.

#28C all go past the *Lisboa*; #28A goes on to Taipa island; and #13 continues to Coloane island. Other transport options from the terminal are taxis and pedicabs, for details see "Getting Around" below.

The **ferry from Guangzhou** docks at the pier next to the Floating Casino, from where it's a short walk to the main avenue, Avenida de Almeida Ribeiro. If you've walked over the **border with China**, or been dropped there by bus (though it's more likely that a bus from Guangzhou would take you into the centre), jump on a #5 which will take you to Avenida de Almeida Ribeiro and to Rua da Praia Grande.

Information

It's easy to pick up information on Macau before you arrive: there's an office of the **Macau Tourist Information Bureau** (*MTIB*) in **Hong Kong** at the Shun Tak Centre, Room 3704, 200 Connaught Road (Mon–Fri 9am–1pm & 2–6pm, Sat 9am–1pm; ☎540 8180), which has lots of useful leaflets and maps. Otherwise, **in Macau**, you can pick up the same information at various *MTIB* offices, including the Visitor Information Centre at the Jetfoil Terminal (daily 9am–6pm; ☎555424). The main office is central, at Largo do Senado 9 (Mon–Fri 9am–1pm & 3–6pm, Sat 9am–12.30pm; ☎397 1115), and there are smaller information counters at a few of the fortresses in Macau.

Free **literature** to look out for includes separate leaflets on Macau's churches, temples, outlying islands and walks; a bus timetable; hotel brochures; and the free monthly newspaper, *Macau Travel Talk*, which lists forthcoming cultural events and entertainment, and carries useful reviews of hotels and restaurants.

Getting Around

You'll be able to **walk** almost everywhere in Macau, though to reach the outlying islands and a couple of the more far-flung sights, you'll have to take a bus. To get the most out of Macau's bus system, pick up a map and a bus route timetable from one of the tourist offices in the city. **Buses and minibuses** are run by two companies, *Transportes Colectivos de Macau* (*TCM*) and *TRANSMAC*, and operate on circular routes from 7am daily until around 11pm–midnight; a few stop running after 6–8pm, though the short distances mean you shouldn't get stuck. **Fares** are low: 1.80ptcs for any single trip on the city routes, 2.30ptcs to Taipa, 3.30ptcs to Coloane Village and 3.50ptcs to Hac Sa – pay the driver as you get on with the exact fare.

Main **terminals** and stops for the buses are outside the Jetfoil Terminal; close to the *Hotel Lisboa;* at Barra (around from the A-Ma temple); along Avenida de Almeida Ribeiro; and at Praça Ponte e Horta (for the Floating Casino). The main routes from these places are listed in the box above, while the text gives details of buses for particular destinations where appropriate.

Taxis, Pedicabs, Car and Bike Rental

It's cheap enough to get around Macau by **taxi**, and you'll find ranks outside all the main hotels and at various points throughout the enclave. All rides are metered: minimum charge is 6.50ptcs (for the first 1500m), after which it's 80 *avos* for every 250m, plus 1ptca for each piece of luggage. Going by taxi to the islands of Taipa and Coloane, there's a 5ptcs and 10ptcs surcharge respectively, though there's no surcharge if you're coming back the other way.

Outside the Jetfoil Terminal and the *Hotel Lisboa* you'll be accosted by the drivers of **pedicabs** – three-wheeled bicycle rickshaws. They're more for short tourist rides – say along the harbour – than for serious getting around, since Macau's hills prevent any lengthy pedalling. You're supposed to bargain for the ride, which will will cost around 25ptcs for a short turn along the harbour, 60–70ptcs for an hour's sightseeing.

Renting a car doesn't make an awful lot of sense in Macau, simply because it's so easy to get around cheaply by public transport and on foot. But you might want to pay for the novelty of driving a **moke** – effectively a low-slung jeep – particularly if you intend to see a bit of the two outlying islands where transport is less common. There are two agencies, *Avis* and *Macau Mokes*; see "Directory" for prices, addresses and driving details.

For organised tours of Macau, see "Directory", p.335.

Renting a **bicycle** is the best bet if you want a little more mobility, though be warned that the traffic in the centre is as manic as in Hong Kong, and that you're not allowed to ride over the Macau–Taipa bridge. Bike-riding is most enjoyable on the islands: in Taipa village, you can rent bikes either from the shop in the main square where the buses stop, or from Largo do Camões, next to the Pak Tai temple; in Coloane, the bike rental shop is at the bottom of Coloane village's main square, towards the water. They cost around 10ptcs an hour, depending on the bike, or 40ptcs a day. Note that if you want a bike for Coloane it's better to rent one there than ride over the causeway from Taipa.

Language and Addresses

Roughly 95 percent of the population of Macau is Chinese, three percent Portuguese and two percent of other origins. Nevertheless, as in Hong Kong, the colonial power has retained the primacy of its language and Macau's two official languages are Portuguese and Cantonese. In practice, for visitors, this means becoming familar with Portuguese street and office signs, which are explained throughout the text if there's any confusion; a few useful Portuguese words are given below to help decipher signs and some of the *MTIB* maps. Otherwise, you won't need Portuguese to get around, though you may find the menu reader on p.324–325 useful. Although taught in schools, English is patchily spoken and understood – and a few words of Cantonese will always help smooth the way (for which see "Language", p.369).

Addresses are written in the Portuguese style: ie, street name followed by number. Abbreviations to be aware of are Av. (Avenida), Est. (Estrada), Calç. (Calçada) and Pr. (Praça).

Some Useful Portuguese Words		*Jardim*	Garden
		Largo	Square
Alfandega	Customs	*Lavabos*	Toilets
Avenida	Avenue	*Mercado*	Market
Baia	Bay	*Museu*	Museum
Beco	Alley	*Pensão*	Guest house
Bilheteira	Ticket office	*Ponte*	Bridge
Correios	Post office	*Pousada*	Inn/Hotel
Edifício	Building	*Sé*	Cathedral
Estrada	Road	*Praça*	Square
Farmácia	Chemist	*Praia*	Beach
Farol	Lighthouse	*Rua*	Street
Fortaleza	Fortress	*Travessa*	Lane
Hospedaria	Guest house	*Vila*	Guest house

Chapter 18

Macau, Taipa and Coloane

O ver four hundred years of foreign trade and colonial rule has shaped **MACAU** into arguably the most intriguing of the southern Chinese settlements ceded to European powers over the centuries. When the **Portuguese** arrived off the southern Chinese coast at the turn of the sixteenth century, they were looking for trading opportunities to add to their string of successes in India and the Malay peninsula. In particular, they were hoping to break the Venetian monopoly of the Far Eastern spice trade, something that had seemed possible since the seizure of the Malay port of Malacca in 1510. Three years later, the first European to set foot in southern China, Portuguese explorer Jorges Álvares, opened up trade with the Chinese Empire. Later, with the Portuguese "discovery" of Japan in 1542 – accidentally, as it happens, by a ship blown off course – it became vital for the Portuguese to find a base from where they could direct trading operations between China and Japan, as well as between both countries and Europe. This base was Macau, first settled in 1557, and by the end of the sixteenth century 900 Portuguese settlers were living here. The area was already well-known to the local Chinese, who knew it as **A-Ma-Gao** ("Bay of A-Ma"), after the goddess of the sea A-Ma, who was reputed to have saved a ship from a storm off the Macau coast. From A-Ma-Gao is derived the modern name, Macau, linking it firmly with the territory's seafaring and trading history.

Most of the interest is contained on the fist-shaped **peninsula** of land that reaches south from the Barrier Gate and the border with China. You can easily walk around the central streets, making separate visits to various points of interest further north and south – all of which can also be reached by bus or taxi if you run out of puff. It's harder going than you might at first think: Macau's hills make for tiring climbing in the heat of the day, though you're always rewarded by excellent views from the churches and fortresses that crown the summits, most notably the ruined church of **São Paulo** and the adjacent **Fortaleza do Monte**. Other attractions include a couple of **temples** that are the equal of any of the better known ones in Hong Kong, an excellent **Maritime Museum** – which illumi-nates the enclave's long associations with fishing and trade – and a series of quiet **gardens** and squares that reflect the enclave's more laid-back approach to life. Spare time, too, for trips out to the two islands: **Taipa**, best known for the fine restaurants in its one village, and Coloane, which sports a couple of good **beaches**, including the black sands at Hac Sa.

A little history

Following the intitial Portuguese settlement, a city soon grew up on the peninsula, becoming influential as a centre for sending Christian **missionaries** to China and Japan. The Jesuit Francis Xavier had visited Japan from 1549–51 and he was followed by a series of missionaries, who travelled through Macau and left an indelible mark on the settlement. The **Jesuits** were pioneers, using the vast trading funds to build great churches in a European Baroque style, the most notable of which was the church of São Paulo. Given city status in 1586, Macau's civil and religious importance to the Portuguese was confirmed in a decree which named it as *Cidade do Nome de Deus de Macau*: "City of the Name of God, Macau".

Throughout the sixteenth and early seventeenth century Macau prospered, but from 1612 onwards the authorities were forced to build **fortifications** on the city's hills to ward off attacks from the **Dutch**, who had their eyes on the valuable trade which emanated from the city. The Dutch came close to taking Macau in 1622, but were beaten off, only to move in elsewhere in the Far East, encour-aged by the failing Spanish Empire, which since 1580 had incorpo-rated Portugal. Before long, the Dutch had gained a foothold in Japan, turning the Japanese against the Jesuit missions there, and by 1639 Japan was closed to the Portuguese for trade, removing one of Macau's vital links. Another disappeared in 1641 with the Dutch capture of Malacca, and although Portugal regained its inde-pendence from Spain at around the same time, it was too late to restore the country's – and Macau's – trade with the Far East. From the end of the seventeenth century onwards Macau became impov-erished, adversely affected by the loss of trade and its proximity to a meddling Imperial Chinese authority. At its lowest political point, in the mid-eighteenth century, it was known rather contemptuously as the "City of Women", a reference to the number of child slaves and prostitutes abandoned in what was rapidly becoming a miserable backwater.

Ironically, it was the growing importance of other foreign trad-ers in the South China Sea during the eighteenth century that saved Macau. Forced to spend the summers away from the trading "factories" in Guangzhou by the Chinese, who wouldn't allow perma-nent foreign settlement on their soil, the British, Americans, Dutch, French and others moved to Macau instead. The city became a sort of halfway house for foreign companies, whose merchants built fine mansions to live in. However, even this position was undermined after 1841, with the **founding of Hong Kong** as a British colony and free port, and the opening up of the other Chinese Treaty Ports in 1842 for direct trade.

The **nineteenth century** saw modern Macau begin to take shape. A new Governor, João Ferreira do Amaral, arrived in 1846 to stake a claim for Portuguese sovereignty over the peninsula; he annexed the neighbouring island of Taipa, expelled the Chinese customs officials from Macau, and built new roads – although sovereignty wasn't ceded by China until 1887. Macau prospered again in a minor way, yet it was always clear that it was second-best to Hong Kong, whose rapidly expanding infrastructure now attracted all the direct trade with China that Macau once monopolised. The enclave became renowned for less salubrious methods of money-making, notably with the advent of **gambling** and prostitution rackets, which existed alongside the well-established opium trade that had been run through Macau since the very earliest days.

Lurching on in its down-at-heel way, Macau's last great upheavals came with the great **population movements** in Southeast Asia earlier this century. The population increased rapidly after the Sino-Japanese War in the 1930s; many Europeans moved in during World War II as the Japanese respected Portuguese neutrality; and it was the turn of Chinese refugees, after 1949 and the Communist victory in the civil war, to migrate to Macau in massive numbers. The fairly cordial relations between Portugal and China were strained in 1966 when the Chinese **Cultural Revolution** led to a series of riots in Macau, during which demonstrators were shot dead. Yet even this failed to provide the impetus for China to take back the land it had claimed for so long. In fact, since the late 1960s China has had complete political control over Macau, finding a benefit in Portugal's sovereignty not frightening away western business and investment. This position became clear in 1974, after the **revolution in Portugal**. The new left-wing government there began to disentangle itself from its remaining colonial ties in Mozambique, Angola and elsewhere, yet was told firmly by the Chinese that they'd prefer things to remain as they were, with the Portuguese holding nominal sovereignty while it continued to make money for China. By now, a tourist-industry infrastructure in Macau was well in place, with new hotels and sports facilities going hand-in-hand with the vast amounts of money generated by the gambling industry.

With Britain and China reaching agreement in 1984 over the future of Hong Kong, it was only a matter of time before Macau would also be **returned to China** – something that, following agreement in 1987, is now due to happen on 20 December 1999, when the last chapter in the long history of colonialism in the South China Sea will be closed. Officially Macau – like Hong kong – will get to keep its capitalist structure intact for at least fifty years. In practice, though, Macau has always been far more under China's influence than Hong Kong: the enclave's Basic Law – agreed with China – retains the indirect elections and appointed legislature seats that the Hong Kong Governor is currently trying to remove. Local liberals and pro-democracy activists are in the minority and on the defensive, concerned that the enclave will rapidly lose its Portuguese heritage once it returns to China. They point – with some justification – to the way the conservatives in government accede to China's every wish; most recently to the removal of a long-standing statue of a former Macau governor, which Beijing regarded as too "colonial". The conservatives, for their part, talk of the need for "convergence" with China if Macau is to continue to be economically viable after 1999. Quite how Macau will develop as a "Special Administrative Region" (SAR) of China is literally anyone's guess.

Around the peninsula

In the early days of the Portuguese settlement at Macau, a thriving town emerged at the bottom half of the **peninsula**. Grand buildings were erected around a network of streets which still exists, including a fine central avenue which ran across the peninsula. The central focus of the town was the Praia Grande, a large, handsome bay from which all the streets radiated, and around which the locals worked and rested, promenading in the evenings along the waterfront much as they would have done back home in Portugal.

Along the Praia Grande

MACAU

The **Praia Grande** is still the most colonial part of Macau, a fine banyan-planted sweep with benches at strategic intervals and views across to Taipa and down to the southernmost tip of the peninsula. An evening walk or pedicab ride along the bay is one of the rightly touted attractions of Macau, though enjoy it while you can, since redevelopment is currently underway designed to enclose the bay, forming two artificial lakes and reclaiming land for residential and commercial building – losing its classic simplicity for ever.

The northern edge of the bay has two prominent landmarks, both at odds with much of colonial Macau. The modern snub-nosed **Bank of China** building is the latest addition to an increasingly built-up waterfront, while just to the east sits the orange polka-dot bulk of the **Hotel Lisboa**, whose low flanks are fronted by a multi-storey circular drum done up like a wedding cake and lit to extravagant effect at night. No one should miss a venture into the hotel's 24-hour casinos, or a wander through the hotel's gilt and marble surroundings, past the gift shops, and the ten restaurants and bars inside. Outside the hotel is a good place to pick up a pedicab around the bay.

The Lisboa's casinos are covered on p.330.

Along Avenida de Almeida Ribeiro

Macau's central avenue stretches from the *Hotel Lisboa* right across to the Inner Harbour on the west side of the peninsula. The first section is known as Avenida do Infante d'Henrique, changing its name as it crosses Rua da Praia Grande to **Avenida de Almeida Ribeiro**. Dead central, it's a fine thoroughfare, shops and banks tucked into shady arcades on either side of the road, and there's plenty to stop off for as you make your way up it.

On the right, the steps of Rua da Sé climb past some graceful balconied houses before dipping down into a large square which holds the squat **Sé** itself – Macau's Cathedral, hidden from the rest of town in a natural hollow. It's not a particularly distinguished church, rebuilt in stone in the mid-nineteenth century on top of its original sixteenth-century foundations, and completely restored again in 1937, though it's spacious enough inside and flanked by some rather pretty colonial buildings. What must once have been a handsome cathedral square now serves as a car park.

To the local Chinese, the avenue is known as San Ma Lo ("new road").

From the Sé, a side road drops down into the rather grander **Largo do Senado** or Senate Square, though it's better approached from the main avenue. Like the avenue, the square is arcaded, its elegant buildings painted pale pink, yellow or white and set off by a small fountained park with benches and flowers. In the arcade on one side sit fortune tellers and newspaper vendors, while off to one side, down Rua Sul do Mercado de São Domingos and adjacent streets, is a **market**: a quadrangle of clothes stalls and *dai pai dongs* around a covered building which deals mostly in fish and meat.

At the bottom of Largo do Senado, the arcaded buildings peter out in the adjacent Largo São Domingos, which holds the fine seventeenth-century Baroque church of **São Domingos** (usually open afternoons; ring the bell at the side gate). Built for Macau's Dominicans, its restrained cream and stucco facade is echoed inside by the pastel colours on display, on the pillars and walls and on the statue of the Virgin and Child which sits on top of the altar. There's a small museum of sculpture and church art at the back of the building, and on May 13 every year the church is the starting point of the major procession in honour of Our Lady of Fatima.

The Senate House itself, the **Leal Senado** ("Loyal Senate"), faces the main square on Avenida de Almeida Ribeiro, earning its name from a grateful Portuguese monarchy in recognition of the loyalty Macau had shown to the crown during the Spanish occupation of Portugal in the seventeenth century. Founded as early as the 1580s, it's one of the truly great buildings in Macau, of traditional Portuguese design and with interior courtyard walls decorated with *azulejo* tiling. These days it's used by the municipal government of Macau, whose powers are a shadow of those of the democratic forum that once met here. But as a public building it's open to visi-

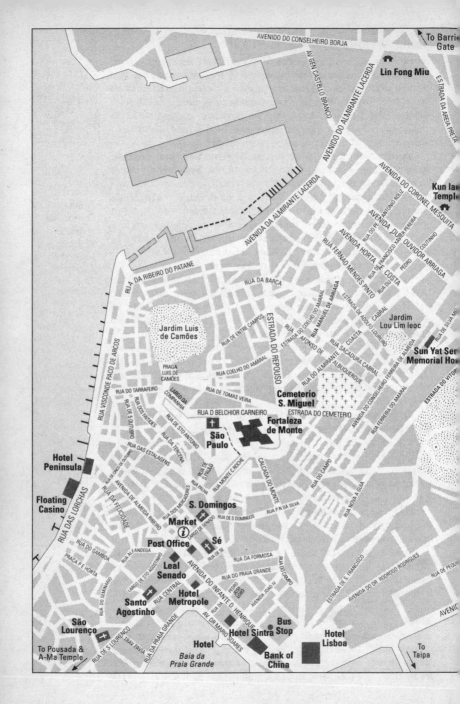

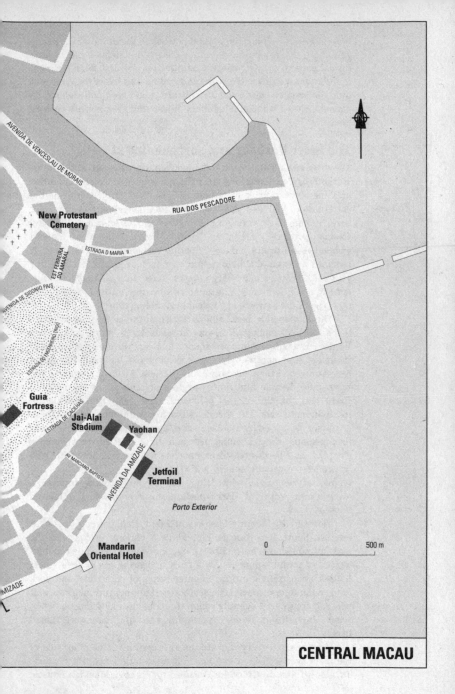

AVENIDA DE VENCESLAU DE MORAIS

RUA DOS PESCADORE

New Protestant Cemetery

ESTRADA D MARIA II

EST FERREIRA DO AMARAL

AVENIDA DE SIDONIO PAIS

ESTRADA AV ENGENHEIRO TRIGO

Guia Fortress

ESTRADA DE CACILHAS

Jai-Alai Stadium

Yaohan

AV MARÇIANO BAPTISTA

AVENIDA DA AMIZADE

Jetfoil Terminal

Porto Exterior

MIZADE

Mandarin Oriental Hotel

0   500 m

CENTRAL MACAU

tors (Mon–Sat 1–7pm; free), and if you ask in the office on the left as you enter, you're allowed to climb the main staircase, past a little formal garden, to the **Senate Chamber** on the first floor – a rich, grand room with panelled walls and ceiling and excellent views out over the square. Adjacent is the **library**, two-tiered and elaborately carved, whose wooden chambers house musty sixteenth-century books.

The Inner Harbour and surrounding streets

The main avenue ends on the peninsula's western side, at the **Inner Harbour** or Porto Interior – the main harbour of Macau for centuries until the new terminals were built over on the Porto Exterior on the eastern side. You still take the ferry to Guangzhou from the pier here, though the overriding attraction is the so-called **Floating Casino** (properly called the *Casino Macau Palace*), a moored wooden vessel that was once a floating restaurant in Hong Kong. It replaced an even shabbier casino that had been moored here for years, and remains incredibly popular, filled with all kinds of different ways to lose money, and punters who stay in the nearby cheap hotels so as not to waste any valuable gambling time.

The harbourside here retains a turn-of-the-century atmosphere that's worth sampling. Rua das Lorchas leads down past **Praça Ponte e Horta**, an elongated square that was obviously once grand though it now sports only one surviving old building, the green four-storeyed, balconied house on the left. From the square, the harbourside **Rua do Almirante Sergio** is arcaded all the way down to Barra and the tip of the peninsula (see below), a fascinating twenty-minute walk. The arcade pillars are painted red with Chinese characters which advertise each shop, and you'll pass chandlers and fishing-supply shops (selling nets and great steel hawsers), greasy electrical and hardware stores, incense sellers, peddlers with jade ornaments, vegetable sellers and *dai pai dongs*. There's a small temple at no. 131, while the side streets around conceal a tumbledown world of dark, peeling, tatty shops and mildewed houses.

Closer to the Floating Casino you'll find similar streets of similar interest. Some, like **Rua da Felicidade** – almost parallel with the main avenue – have been spruced up, and what was once a red-light district of sordid repute is now a fairly endearing run of small guest houses, shops selling luridly coloured strips of cured beef and pork (a local Cantonese speciality), seafood restaurants and cake shops. It was still considered suitably rough to double as old Shanghai, when scenes in *Indiana Jones and the Temple of Doom* were filmed here.

More basic in every way are the streets over on the other side of the main avenue, which can have changed little since last century. Turn down **Rua de Cinco de Outubro** for its traditional tea houses, one at no. 126–130, another at no. 159, and the splendid *Farmacia Tai Neng Tong* on the left at no. 146, which has a remarkable decorated facade and sculpted interior. Beyond, the street opens out into **Largo do Pagode do Bazar**, a small square with market stalls and a temple, past which things become more intense as the very old surrounding streets degenerate into a noisome wholesale market: wicker baskets full of vegetables and roots, chickens in coops waiting to be killed and plucked, and whole side alleys turned over to different trades – one full of ironmongers, another of street-barbers.

São Paulo and the Fortaleza do Monte

Macau's most enduring monument – and its most famous image – is the imposing facade of the church of São Paulo, which stands high above the nest of streets to the north of the main avenue. Building began in 1602 on a Jesuit church here, known as Madre de Deus ("Mother of God"), and its rich design reflected the precocious, cosmopolitan nature of early Macau. Designed by an Italian, it was built largely by Japanese craftsmen who produced a stunning Spanish-style retable-facade that took twenty-five years to complete. The church and adjacent Jesuit college became a noted centre of learning, while the building evoked rapture in those who saw it: "I have not seen anything that can equal it, even in all the beautiful churches of Italy, except St Peter's" wrote one visitor in the 1630s. However, following the expulsion of the Jesuits from Macau, the college did duty as an army barracks and on a fateful day in 1835 a fire, which had started in the kitchens, swept through the entire complex leaving just the carved stone facade.

Approaching from the little square on Rua de São Paulo, up the impressive wide swathe of steps (floodlit at night), you can just about convince yourself that the church still stands, but on reaching the terrace the **facade** is revealed, like a misplaced theatre backdrop, rising in four tiers and chipped and cracked with age and fire damage. The statues and reliefs carved on the facade over 350 years ago have lost none of their power and are worth a cricked neck to study more closely: a dove at the top (the Holy Spirit) is flanked by the sun and moon; below is Jesus, around whom reliefs show the implements of the crucifixion – a ladder, manacles, a thorn crown, a flail. Below are the Virgin Mary and Angels, flowers representing China (a peony) and Japan (chrysanthemum), a griffin and a rigged galleon, while the bottom tier holds four Jesuit saints, and the crowning words "Mater Dei" above the central door.

Fortaleza do Monte

To the right of the church, a path and steps lead up the few hundred metres to the solid **Fortaleza do Monte** (daily 9am–5.30pm; free), a fortress that was part of the Jesuit complex of São Paulo and dates from the same period. It saw action only once, when its cannon helped drive back the Dutch in 1622, and like São Paulo fell into misuse after the Jesuits had gone. From the ramparts you can appreciate its fine defensive position, cannon still pointing out to the Macau–Taipa bridge and giving fine views around almost the whole peninsula – only the Guia fort and lighthouse to the east is higher. The well-kept grounds contain a meteorological station (in the pale yellow colonial building), and, most welcome after the climb, a small bar at the entrance; there's a tourist information counter here, too.

The Camões Garden and Museum; the Old Protestant Cemetery

Just to the north of São Paulo is a square, **Praça Luís de Camões** (buses #17, #18 & #19 all run past), at the head of which the **Jardim Luís de Camões** is a garden of banyans, ferns and flowers commemorating the sixteenth-century Portuguese poet who is supposed to have visited Macau and written part of his epic *Os Lusías* (about Vasco de Gama's voyages) in the vicinity. There's a bust of Camões, encircled by rocks, and although there's no real evidence that he ever did come to Macau, the Macanese have awarded themselves an annual holiday in his name, just in case. The garden was once part of the grounds of the adjacent building, a stylish late eighteenth-century country villa, originally called the Casa Garden, and later the headquarters of the British East India Company in Macau. Now known as the **Museu de Luís de Camões** (daily 11am–5pm; 1ptca), its historical and art collection pertaining to Macau is wide-ranging, and includes some attractive old prints of the enclave.

For the full rundown of grave inscriptions, the MTIB sells a fascinating book called The Protestant Cemeteries of Macau, *by Manuel Teixera, which covers both this cemetery and the New Protestant Cemetery – over by the Kun Iam temple, off Avenida do Coronel Mesquita.*

To the side of the museum, you might need to knock in order to gain entrance to the **Old Protestant Cemetery**, established in 1814 as a plaque above the door records. In here lie many of the non-Portuguese traders and visitors who passed through Macau, some of them shifted to this cemetery in later years as the pre-1814 gravestones show. This was because for decades Protestants who died in Macau had no set burial place: the Catholic Portuguese didn't want them cluttering up the city and the Chinese objected if they were interred on ancestral lands. The older graves were moved here from various resting places outside the city walls after the East India Company bought the land to set up their own cemetery. The most famous resident is the artist **George Chinnery** (on the cemetery's upper tier), who spent his life painting much of the local Chinese coast, though the real interest in roaming around is to seek out the various poignant graves, many belonging to ordinary seamen who died in the seas nearby. There's also the grave of the missionary Robert Morrison, who translated the Bible into Chinese, and his wife who died in childbirth.

East: Across to the Outer Harbour

The largest cemetery on the peninsula is over to the east from here, the otherwise undistinguished **Cemeterio São Miguel**, from where Avenida do Conselheiro Ferreira de Almeida – with its fine colonial mansions set back from the road – takes you to the quiet **Jardim Lou Lim Ieoc** (daily 6am–10pm; 1ptca, free on Fri). A formal Chinese garden with the usual grottoes, pavilions, carp ponds, shrubs and trees, it was built in the nineteenth century and modelled on the classical gardens of Suzhou, in China. It's enclosed by a high wall that hides completely its serene charms from the road outside.

Around the corner, on Avenida de Sidonia Pais (at the junction with Rua de Silva Mendes), the **Sun Yat-sen Memorial Home** (Mon & Wed–Fri 10am–1pm, Sat & Sun 3–5pm), a Moorish-style building, was built by the republican leader's family to house relics and photos. Sun Yat-sen lived in Macau for a few years, practising as a doctor, before developing his revolutionary beliefs, and while there's no massive interest here, if you can coincide with the brief opening hours there's half an hour to be spent quite happily in the odd building.

Above here, the severe hill leads up to the nearby **Guia Fortress**, built in 1637–8 on the highest point in the territory. It was originally designed to defend the border with China, though it's seen most service as an observation post given its extraordinary perch above the whole peninsula. It's a long, hot walk up the quiet lane to the fort, but you'll be rewarded by the pick of the views in Macau and a small seventeenth-century chapel within the walls dedicated to Our Lady of Guia, which contains an image of the Virgin that local legend says left the chapel and deflected Dutch bullets with her robe during the Dutch attack of 1622. You can only get into the chapel once a year, on August 5 (6–9am), the saint's day. The chapel's other function was to ring its bell to warn of storms, something now taken care of by the fortress's lighthouse, built in 1865 and crowning the hill. From the fortress walls, among other sweeping views are those over the **Outer Harbour**, the Porto Exterior, where you probably arrived.

Within the ramparts (daily 9am–5.30pm), there's a small tourist information office whose most useful function is to provide much-needed drinks in an adjacent bar.

North to the Barrier Gate

There are a couple of stops worth making on the way north to the Barrier Gate, though you're going to have to be very energetic to want to do it all on foot. By public transport, the best way is to use bus #5, which you can catch on the main Avenida de Almeida Ribeiro, getting off about halfway down Avenida Horta e Costa.

From here, it's only a couple of blocks north to the parallel Avenida do Coronel Mesquita and the splendid **Kun Iam Temple** (daily 7am–6pm), entered through a banyan-planted courtyard. Dedicated to the Buddhist Goddess of Mercy (Kwun Yum or Kuan Yin in Hong Kong), and venue of the signing of the first ever Sino-

American treaty in 1844, the temple complex is around 400 years old and one of the most interesting in both Hong Kong and Macau. There's an overpowering smell of incense inside, and from the formal gardens outside you can look up to the porcelain tableaux that decorate the eaves and roofs of the main buildings. A flight of stone steps approaches the three altars of the main temple, one behind the other, the third one dedicated to Kun Iam herself, dressed in a Chinese bridal suit. She is surrounded by other statues of the eighteen wise men of China; the figure on the left, nearest the fortune teller's desk, with the moustache, round eyes and pointy beard, is Marco Polo, said to have become a Buddhist during his time in China. If you want your fortune told, shake one of the cylinders on the fortune teller's desk in the main temple until a bamboo sliver falls out, when it's matched with the "correct" fortune hanging behind the desk – the Chinese characters are explained to you and you hand over a few *patacas* in return. Elsewhere in the complex, there are plenty of other opportunities to bring yourself good luck, though you'll probably have to join a queue each time. You can touch the miniature tree shaped like the Chinese character for "long life", and turn the stone balls in the mouths of the lions on the main steps three times to the left for luck.

Pick up the #5 bus again and it runs on, up Avenida do Almirante Lacerda, past a second temple, the **Lin Fong Miu**, or Lotus Temple – smaller than the Kun Iam and Taoist rather than Buddhist. Built in 1592 in order to provide overnight accommodation for mandarins travelling between Macau and Guangzhou, it has a fine nineteenth-century facade, and altars dedicated to a variety of Chinese deities.

By bus, take the #10 or #11 from the Hotel Lisboa (or direct from the Barrier Gate), or the #21 from the main avenue, each of which drops you at Barra bus terminal, just around the corner from the A-Ma temple.

The Barrier Gate

The #5 bus from Lin Fong Miu runs through the less edifying parts of the Macau peninsula, primarily apartments and roadworks, before stopping right outside the imposing stucco **Barrier Gate**, built in the late nineteenth century and marking the border with China. Called the *Portas do Cerco* in Portuguese (or "Siege Gate"), a gate here has always marked the entrance to Portuguese territory, even when the old city walls were much further south. Once upon a time, all you could do was peer through the gate at the other side, but these days it's possible to walk or bus across if you've got the right documents – though you'll join the queue of bulging goods trucks that line up all day in both directions.

South to Barra: the A-Ma Temple and the Maritime Museum

Having exhausted the central streets, and made the northern jaunt to the Barrier Gate, the other move is south down the finger of the peninsula to the area known as Barra.

Walking, following Rua Central, the whole route shouldn't take more than half an hour. Up a small side street, on the right, you pass

SOUTHERN MACAU
PRAIA GRANDE
TO BARRA

the peppermint-coloured **Teatro Dom Pedro V**, built in 1873, across
from which is the early nineteenth-century church of **Santo
Agostinho**, whose pastel walls are decorated with delicate piped
icing – the monthly accounts are pinned to the inside of the door,
showing expenditure on flowers and "Liturgical Comestibles".
Further down Rua Central, the square-towered **São Lourenço** on Rua
de São Lourenço also dates from the early nineteenth century,
though like Santo Agostinho it's built on much older foundations,
both parishes having existed since the very early Portuguese days.
Both churches are in need of a lick of paint, and will probably be
locked, but the faded grandeur is impressive, only adding to Macau's
lazy-day atmosphere. Beyond the churches lies the **Barra district** of
Macau, the road lined with cheap Chinese cafés, clothes-making
workshops, car repairers and the workspaces of various craftsmen.

By the water, turn left for the **A-Ma Temple** (*A-Ma Miu* in
Cantonese), built underneath Barra Hill and probably the oldest

temple in Macau, parts of it dating back 600 years. A-Ma, the Goddess of the Sea and Queen of Heaven (known in Hong Kong as Tin Hau), is supposed to have saved a ship from a storm; where the ship landed, the goddess ascended to heaven and a temple was built on the spot. She subsequently gave her name to the whole territory and is honoured here in a convoluted complex of temples and altars dotted among the rocks. Red is the predominant colour, in the buildings and in the characters painted on the grey and green rocks. Paths lead you above the carved roof joints, curved like prows and topped by dragons; inside the cluttered pavilions are fortune tellers and incense burners. The busiest time to come is during A-Ma's festival (late April/May; the 23rd day of the third moon), when alongside the devotions there's Cantonese opera in a temporary theatre erected at the site.

The Maritime Museum

Over the road from the temple, in new purpose-built premises designed to look like wharf buildings, is Macau's superb **Maritime Museum** (*Museu Marítimo de Macau*: daily except Tues 10am–5.30pm; 5ptcs, children 2ptcs), a place where you could easily spend an hour or so. Ranged across three storeys is an engaging and well-presented collection relating to local fishing techniques and festivals, Chinese and Portuguese maritime prowess and boat building. Poke around and you'll find navigational equipment, a scale model of seventeenth-century Macau, traditional local clothing used by the fishermen, even a small collection of boats moored at the pier, including a naval tug and a dragon racing boat. The whole collection is made eminently accessible with the help of explanatory English-language notes, video displays and boat models. There's an outdoor café where you can get a beer, and it's possible to take a half-hour **junk ride** from the museum around the Inner Harbour, which is very definitely worth doing – giving you a different perspective of the enclave's comings and goings by water as you chug past warehouses, floating homes, dredgers and tug boats. Daily departures are at 10.30am, 11.30am, 3.30pm and 4.30pm (15ptcs); buy tickets in the museum (which then allows you free entry into the museum).

From the Fortaleza da Barra to the Palácio do Governo

Keep on past the museum and the road swings around the tip of the peninsula past the swanky **Pousada de São Tiago**, built over the ruins of arguably the most important of Macau's fortresses, the **Fortaleza da Barra**. The fortress was finished in 1629, designed to protect the entrance to the Inner Harbour, a function it achieved by hiding two dozen cannon within its ten-metre-high walls. Over the centuries, it fell into disrepair along with all Macau's other forts, and was rescued in 1976 when it was converted into a *pousada* or inn. Don't worry if you can't afford the outlandish prices to stay here, since if you've a genuine interest in seeing the foundations and eight-

For full details of the pousada, see "Accommodation", p.322.

eenth-century chapel inside, no one will mind if you have a look. The *pousada*'s terrace-bar is reasonably priced too, and makes a good venue for a pot of tea overlooking the water.

Continue around the Praia Grande and the energetic can detour up to the left via **Penha Hill**, another steep climb, this time rewarded by the nineteenth-century Bishop's Palace and **Penha chapel** (daily 9am–4pm) – with more grand views over the city. The restored, colonial **Bela Vista** hotel (see p.322) is close by and has an excellent restaurant, with bay views – you'll need to reserve in advance if you want to stop here for lunch. Dropping down again to the harbourside road, Rua da Praia Grande, and heading back to the centre, you'll pass the pink **Palácio do Governo** (Government House), built in the mid-nineteenth century and as graceful as any of the colonial buildings already seen.

Taipa

In the eighteenth century the island of **Taipa** – just to the south of the peninsula – was actually two adjacent islands, whose sheltered harbour was an important anchorage for trading ships unloading their China-bound cargo at the mouth of the Pearl River. Silting of the channel between the two islands eventually caused them to merge, providing valuable farming land. With the emergence of Hong Kong and the development of the Macau peninsula, Taipa was left to get on as best it could, and nowadays it's a quiet, laid-back sort of place – though that will undoubtedly change once the new airport (under construction on the island's east coast) is up and running. Airport construction apart, there's little industry here – just a couple of fireworks factories – and the island's three square kilometres provide a pleasant and easily manageable hour or two's worth if you rent a bike on arrival. Give yourself time for lunch or dinner, too, to make the most of Taipa – the village contains some fine places to eat.

Take the #11, #22 or #28A if you're heading directly for Taipa village. The #13, #21, #21A and #28A stop outside the Hyatt Regency *and at a stop close to the* Taipa House Museum, *before running on to* Coloane.

Buses from the avenue close to the *Hotel Lisboa* cross the 2.5km **Macau–Taipa bridge**, and going either way there are terrific views from its highest section about halfway across. A new bridge, further to the east, should also be in operation, too, once the airport starts to generate extra traffic.

The first bus stop on the island is outside the **Hyatt Regency** hotel, just up from the end of the bridge, from where buses continue to Taipa village, about another five minutes away. Up from the hotel on the left, on the hill overlooking the water, is the **University of East Asia**, just down from which – on a ledge east of the bridge – is a small **Kun Iam Temple**. Further back towards the bridge, on the other (western) side of the hotel, is the more interesting **Pou Tai Un Temple** (daily 9am–6pm). Brightly painted, it's the largest temple on the island and is still being added to, with gardens and pavilions, and a large dining room which serves up vegetarian Chinese meals.

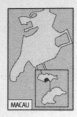

MACAU

Taipa village

Buses pull up in **TAIPA VILLAGE**'s main square, the **Largo Governador Tamagnini Barbosa**, just back from the sea – a big name for such a half-pint place. There are a couple of cafés here, a bike rental shop and – around the corner, to the side of the garage – the local **Tin Hau Temple**, a small greybrick building whose doorway is lined with painted red paper.

There are only a few streets to the village and a wander through them takes in a couple of faded squares and some pastel-painted houses in narrow, traffic-free alleys. Largo do Camões, a more spacious square just behind the main one (off Rua Regedor) could be straight out of rural Portugal, with its peeling, balconied houses and shady trees, if it wasn't for the large **Pak Tai Temple** here. Inside, there's a carved altar whose figures are echoed in the impressive carved frieze above the entrance.

The half an hour it'll take to stroll around all this can be finished off by walking to the older waterfront area of the village, where the

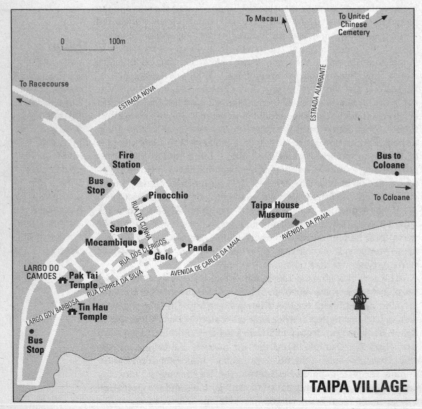

TAIPA VILLAGE

Portuguese gentry of Taipa used to live. Head down Rua Correia da Silva from the main square and look for a flight of steps on the right, called Cascada do Coxo, from where a cobbled road leads up to Taipa's hundred-year-old church (usually locked). Below here, on the tree-planted waterfront Avenida da Praia, are several late nineteenth- and early twentieth-century **mansions**, built with shutters and verandahs and commanding fine views over the sound to Coloane. One of the houses has been opened to the public as the **Taipa House Museum** (*Casa Museu*: daily except Mon 9.30am–1pm & 3–5.30pm; free), which shows off the house as it appeared a century ago. Its airy, wooden interior is filled with period blackwood and rosewood furniture, an equipped kitchen, and assorted chinoiserie and Portuguese-influenced bits and bobs. This is only the first house to be restored along the Praia; the others, once spruced up and open, are intended to form a complete cultural and historical exhibition for Taipa.

For reviews of Taipa Village's best eating places, see p.326–327; check their locations on the map opposite.

Back in the centre of the village, narrow Rua do Cunha has evolved into a sort of "Food Street" over the years, and it now incorporates an impressive array of **restaurants** – indeed this is one of the main reasons to come. Lunchtime is especially good, when you'll be sharing the restaurants with the expat Portuguese businessmen who come here for authentic Portuguese food.

The rest of the island

Rent a bike (see p.296 for locations and prices) and you can cycle around the **eastern half** of Taipa in under an hour. Retrace your route back to the main junction outside Taipa village and head straight over, following Estrada Coronel Nicolau de Mesquita, which leads uphill, past the university and above the island's north coast. At the top of the rise is the **United Chinese Cemetery**, with stepped rows of graves leading down to the water. The whole coast below is in the process of being reclaimed and as you move on, what would once have been fairly nice beaches are now disfigured by water drainage pipes, dumper trucks and foundation works. Still, it's an exhilarating ride as the road swoops down the other side of the island, passing the causeway to Coloane and the Avenida da Praia before reaching the main road junction again.

To the **west** of Taipa village, the only draw is the **racecourse**, operated by the Macau Jockey Club. It used to host horse-trotting races, no serious rival to the money-making horse racing in Hong Kong, until a new grass track was laid here at the end of 1989 and regular horse racing started up; the season runs from September to June. A satellite dish beams out the racing to other Asian countries, giving Hong Kong a run for its money at last. The **Four-Faced Buddha Shrine** outside the stadium brings much-needed luck to the punters. Incidentally, most of the buses come this way on their way back to Macau from Taipa village.

Coloane

Coloane island is around twice the size of Taipa, a base for pirates as late as the turn of this century who hid out in the cliffs and caves, seizing the cargoes of trading ships passing between Macau and Guangzhou. Like Taipa, there's little specifically to attract you, other than some eminently peaceful surroundings and a village with the same mix of temples and colonial leftovers. This doesn't make it any less enticing, though, especially as the island has a couple of good sand **beaches** and – with bike rental possible – the means to waste time gently in some fairly isolated bays and hills.

On the way around the west coast of the island, the buses from the peninsula and Taipa pass the **Parque de Coloane** (Tues–Sun summer 8am–9pm, winter 9am–5pm; free), a twenty-hectare site with gardens, ponds, pavilions and views out over the water. There's an aviary (5ptcs) here, too, and a display of the local flora and fauna, as well as picnic and barbecue areas.

Coloane village

Direct from the Macau peninsula, take buses #13, #21 or #21A, which run through Taipa and over the causeway to Coloane village. Moving on from Taipa, either take the same buses from the stop near Taipa House Museum, or the #14, which leaves every 20min from Taipa village's main square.

Most of the buses end their run in COLOANE VILLAGE, in a dusty central square surrounded by cafés, whose focal point is the village TV set up in the middle. Signs point off to the few local attractions, down roads that are all cobbles and cart-tracks. There's little traffic, chickens scratching around the pot-holes, and a ramshackle air about the low, crumbling Chinese houses, mouldering shrines and temples.

Stroll down to the peaceful waterfront and turn left for the tiny, pale yellow chapel of **St Francis Xavier**, set back from the sea. Built in the same style as others in Macau, the chapel dates from 1928 and honours the eponymous sixteenth-century missionary who passed through Macau on his way to China and Japan. If the friendly priest is around, you'll be let into the sacristy to see St Francis's elbow and a fine selection of other bones of the "Martyrs of Japan" – seventeenth-century Christians killed in Japan after the missionaries were expelled. The bones were rescued from the fire at São Paulo in Macau, kept in the Sé and then transferred here in 1976, since when an increasing number of Japanese visitors have come to pay their respects. The priest was born in Italy, but speaks excellent English and Cantonese. In front of the chapel, the **monument** with the embedded cannonballs commemorates the repelling of the last pirate attack in Coloane, which took place on 12 and 13 July 1910. The latter date is now an annual celebration on the island.

Further along the waterfront, past the library, the even tattier and smaller **Kun Iam Temple** is set back among the houses, though the **Tam Kong Temple** at the end of the road is more interesting, facing China across the narrow channel. The prize piece here is a whalebone shaped into a dragon boat with oarsmen – though the locally caught shark's snout runs it a close second. Like St Francis's chapel, if there's someone around to point out all the exciting religious exhibits you'll probably get stung for 10ptcs or so. Dig deep, as there's not much else to spend your money on in Coloane.

The other way along the harbour, past the junks moored offshore and people loafing around the rocks, it's not far to the village's last temple, the small **Sam Seng Temple**. Beyond here, shops are built out over the water, selling dried fish and seafood, while the road leads on to a tiny pier and police station. On the other side of the hill is Coloane's working **shipyard** – a fascinating place where junk building still takes place. Wooden planks fashioned from tree trunks lie around waiting to be seasoned, while work goes on on the two or three half-finished boat hulls, pervaded by the intoxicating smell of sawdust and grease.

Coloane's beaches

Coloane's good **beaches** are all easily reached by bike from the village, or by bus.

The closest sandy beach to the village is at **CHEOC VAN**, just a couple of kilometres east. It's fairly well-developed, featuring cafés, the *Pousada de Coloane* (see "Accommodation", p.322) and generally murky seawater – though it's mud from the Pearl River rather than anything unsavoury. There's a swimming pool here, too (daily 9am–1pm), which you'll have to pay a few *patacas* to use.

A few kilometres further east, **HAC SA** is much the better choice, since the grey-black sand beach (*hac sa* means "black sand") is very long and backed by a pine grove, with plenty of picnic places amid the trees. You can rent windsurfers here, and even go horse-riding, while if you don't fancy the sea or sands, there's a swimming pool and sports complex behind the beach (daily 9am–10pm). On the sands there's a beach-bar, as well as a couple of **restaurants** near the bus stop, (including the excellent *Fernando's*; see p.327), while at the northeastern end of the beach the new, upmarket *Westin Resort* complex sprawls across the headland.

KÁ HO, at the far eastern end of the island, is really only for the curious, since the beach has disappeared under the local cement works. It's a nice ride there and back though.

Bus #14 or #21A, from Taipa every 20–40min, stop in Coloane village before moving on to Cheoc Van beach and Hac Sa. Bus #15 also runs every two hours from Coloane to Ká Ho.

Macau Listings

Chapter 19

Accommodation

There is a huge number of places to stay in Macau, but weekends and public holidays are always busy with gamblers coming over from Hong Kong, so think about **booking in advance** if you're travelling to Macau at these times. You can do this through the MTIB office in Hong Kong in the Shun Tak Centre (though not for the cheapest hotels), through the Hong Kong reservations offices of the larger hotels (see the reviews below), or directly with the hotels and guest houses themselves in Macau. Other busy times are at Chinese New Year, Easter and during the Macau Grand Prix in late-November. If you've arrived without a booking, there's a **courtesy phone** at a desk in the Jetfoil Terminal, by the Visitor Information Centre, from where you can make reservations at one of the larger hotels.

It's worth noting that there are no youth hostels or campsites in Macau. However, the guest houses and hotels are, for the most part, much better value than in Hong Kong – at the bottom end of the market you'll often be able to find a self-contained room for around the same price as a sweatbox Kowloon dormitory.

Guest Houses and Hotels

The scores of **cheap hotels** – called either a *vila*, *hospedaria* or *pensão* – are located in two main areas: around the *Hotel Lisboa* and *Hotel Sintra* (the area bounded by Rua da Praia Grande, Av. do Infante d'Henrique, Rua Dr. P. J. Lobo and Av. de Dom João IV) and around the Floating Casino (bus #3A from the Jetfoil Terminal).

There's no shortage of choice, though many of the available rooms are small, dark and grubby. They're mostly used by weekend gamblers from Hong Kong who aren't too bothered about where they get their two hours' sleep a night before heading off to lose yet more money. Few of the owners speak English, so telephoning in advance isn't always an option. The other problem is that many places are highly prejudiced against taking Westerners, particularly young ones with backpacks. Often, a place is "full", even when it patently isn't; sometimes you won't even get your foot in the door. You'll increase your chances by leaving your bags with someone while you look around, and by looking presentable, but basically you'll have to accept that there's no consistency – a hotel that we've said is all right, or you've found OK before, might just change its mind the next time you turn up.

The places around the *Hotel Lisboa* are generally a better bet than the ones in the more traditional Chinese streets around the Floating Casino, though there are notable exceptions in both areas. Bear in mind that you may have to grab the first available place you see at busy times, looking around later for something better.

You'll have no such problems with the **mid-range** and **top-of-the-range** places, some of which offer very good value for money. Even if you're not particularly wealthy, it's worth the extra cash to stay somewhere decent for a night or so (especially after a few days in crowded Hong Kong), and midweek **discounts** some-

**Macau:
Accommmodation**

Hotels and guest houses in this section are classified into seven **price categories**, which refer to the minimum you can expect to pay for a double room. In the cheaper places (categories ①, ② and ③) you will often have to share a bathroom, and there might only be a fan to keep you cool. In all mid-range and top-of-the-range hotels – ④ and ⑤ and above – bathrooms are usually attached, and your room should have air-conditioning and a TV; most smarter hotels also have a range of available rooms (standard and deluxe doubles, suites, etc), so sometimes the price categories reflect that (eg ⑥–⑦). In all hotels, you'll also pay ten percent **service charge** and five percent **government tax** on top of your bill; the price categories don't reflect these extra charges.

You'll find prices drop during midweek in many places, and you may sometimes be able to negotiate a room rate lower than those suggested.

① Under 90ptcs
② 90–150ptcs
③ 150–300ptcs
④ 300–500ptcs
⑤ 500–800ptcs
⑥ 800–1200ptcs
⑦ Over 1200ptcs

times make it possible to undercut the official prices. The swankiest hotels are the three in the south of the peninsula – the *Bela Vista* and the two *pousadas*. Mere mortals will choke at the prices being asked, but you can't beat the location or the facilities: at least think about stumping up for a drink in one of the terrace café-bars to see what all the fuss is about.

There are only a few choices out on the **islands** of Taipa and Coloane, and they're all fairly expensive too. Still, it's an attractive idea to stay out of the centre, particularly at one of those hotels right on the beach on Coloane, but bear in mind the extra bus trips to and from the centre.

Around the Floating Casino

Hotel Cantao, Rua do Guimarães ☎922416. Off Av. de Almeida Ribeiro, this rickety old hotel has an endearingly antiquated feel. The basic, airy rooms come with shutters, fan and balcony (shared shower) – not a bad first call, though with only forty or so rooms it fills quickly. ①.

East Asia Hotel, Rua da Madeira 1 ☎922433. In the heart of old Macau, the *East Asia* is a long-standing gamblers' haunt, recently renovated so that many of the rooms now have attached bath. ④.

Hotel Grande, Av. de Almeida Ribeiro 146 ☎921111. Another 1930s hotel catering for serious gamblers. Rooms are reasonably good value (at the bottom of this category), and there are lots of them. ⑤.

Hoi Keng Hotel, Rua do Guimarães 153 ☎572033. Just up from the Floating Casino, and facing the *Peninsula*, this very small hotel is worth trying if you want your own bathroom; cheaper rooms available, too. The entrance is on Rua Caldeira. ③.

Hou Kong Hotel, Travessa das Virtudes 1 ☎937555. On an alley down Ruada Felicidade and off Travessa do Auto Novo, More welcoming than most along here, a real hotel with clean, balconied rooms. ④.

Hotel Ko Wah, 3rd Floor, Rua da Felicidade 71 ☎375599. A pleasant hotel on one of Macau's most interesting streets. Most of the refurbished rooms have bath and TV, making this one of the most attractive budget choices. ③.

Vila Kuan Heng, Praça Ponte e Horta 6 ☎573629. The best of the budget options on this square, which is just off Rua das Lorchas. The spick and span rooms have attached bathroom; prices are at the bottom of this category. ③.

Hotel London, Praça Ponte e Horta 4 ☎937761. Well-equipped rooms (singles, doubles and triples) in a decent location, featuring a thirty percent discount every day except Saturday. ③.

Hospedaria Nam Kio, Rua das Lorchas 13. Fronted by a *mahjong* school and a bit dingy, but the owner speaks English and you won't find better prices. ①

Hotel Peninsula, Rua das Lorchas, Ponte Cais 14 ☎318899. Almost next to the

Floating Casino, your money buys a modern, clean room in a block overlooking the water. Air-conditioning too. ④.

Hotel Ung Ieong, Rua das Lorchas 15; ☎573857 or ☎573814. Basic but large rooms with fan; shared bathrooms. You won't always be welcomed with open arms. Entrance is around the corner on Rua do Bocage. ①

Hospedaria Vong Kong, Rua das Lorchas 45 ☎574016. Opposite the *Gulf* service station, this has singles and larger doubles; fairly spartan facilities, though. ①.

Around the Hotel Lisboa and Hotel Sintra

Hotel Fortuna, Rua de Cantão ☎786333, fax 786363; Hong Kong reservations on ☎559 2010. New 350-room hotel, behind the *Lisboa*, typical of the latest wave of building to hit Macau; steel and glass outside, Chinese decor inside. ⑥.

Vila Kimbo, 1st Floor, Av. do Infante d'Henrique 59 ☎710010. Clean rooms with TV, toilet and shower – worth a try even if they might not take you. ③.

Hotel Lisboa, Av. da Amizade ☎377666, fax 567193; Hong Kong reservations on ☎559 1028. A monstrous orange circular drum on the waterfront (with new adjacent annexe) that has roughly 1100 rooms and a bundle of 24-hour casinos, shops, bars and restaurants – some people never set foot outside the door. A splendid if hectic experience. Rooms in the rear block don't have the same atmosphere, but are cheaper than those at the front; you can also pay considerably more than the price category shown for a superior double or suite. ⑤–⑥.

Vila Loc Tin, Rua Dr P. J. Lobo ☎710018. Use the entrance at no. 27; up to the 1st floor, follow corridor around, cross the central stairwell and it's on the 2nd floor. Reasonable double rooms with a shower. ③.

Hotel Metropole, Rua da Praia Grande 63–63A ☎388166, fax 330890; Hong Kong reservations on ☎833 9300. Well-placed, central hotel, just back from the Praia Grande, and good value if you're looking for rooms with all the fixings. ⑤.

Vila Nam Kok, Rua da Praia Grande 95 ☎555523. Fairly large, bright rooms with bath – and more chance you'll be allowed in than at the *Va Lai* over the road. ③.

Vila Nam Tin, Travessa da Praia Grande 4; ☎81513. A friendly place whose largish, bright rooms come with attached bathroom – a good first choice. The street is off Av. de Dom João IV. ③.

Hotel Sintra, Av. de Dom João IV ☎710111, fax 510527; Hong Kong reservations on ☎540 8028. Close to the *Lisboa* and all the action, this is a good budget choice for some hotel-standard comfort; it's at the bottom of this category. The smart rooms with bath and TV have been recently renovated and many have views across the bay to Taipa. ⑤.

Va Lai Vila, Rua da Praia Grande 42. A modern, clean hotel, whose rooms have bath and TV, though you might find they won't take you. ③.

Wai Lee Guest House, Avenida de Dom João IV 38 ☎710199. The sign outside says *Vila Vai Lei* – nice, quiet and friendly and although the rooms are gloomy, they do have TV and shower. One of the better-value options. ②.

From Av. Almeida de Ribeiro to São Paulo

Hotel Central, Av. de Almeida Ribeiro 26–28 ☎372404 or ☎373309, fax 3322275. One of Macau's oldest hotels, open since 1928. It's a good location, right on the central avenue, and many of the rooms have a bathroom. But ask to see the room first, since others don't even have windows. ③.

Holiday, Estada do Repouso 36 ☎361696. Close to the Fortaleza and São Paulo. The compact rooms are just about worth the money. ③.

Pensão Ka Va, Calçada de São João 5 ☎574022. Just below the Sé, this smart, central *pensão* has affordable rooms with bath. ③.

Vila Long Va, 8th floor, Av. de Almeida Ribeiro 21 ☎76541. Above *Wing Heng* bank, there are lovely large rooms with bath, though you might well be told it's "full". ③.

Macau: Accommmodation

Macau: Accommmodation

Southern Macau

Bela Vista, Rua Comendador Kou Ho Neng 8 ☎965333, fax 965588; Hong Kong reservations on ☎881 1688. The finest colonial hotel in Macau, the *Bela Vista* is a grand block with balconied suites and a high-ceilinged dining room where splendid meals are served on the terrace (see p.326). Recently renovated using imported Portuguese materials and specialist craftsmen, there are just eight sumptuous suites: book well in advance if you want to stay at the weekend (or you want an unencumbered bay view), at least a few days ahead at other times. ⑦.

Pousada Ritz, Rua da Boa Vista ☎339955, ax 317826; Hong Kong reservations on ☎739 6993. Above the *Bela Vista*, and accordingly graced with superb views from its terrace and best rooms. There's an indoor pool and billiards room, among other amenities. ⑦

Pousada de São Tiago, Av. da República ☎378111, fax 552170; Hong Kong reservations on ☎739 1216. A gloriously preserved seventeenth-century fortress now turned into an upmarket hotel with all the creature comforts and an unbeatable location at the foot of the peninsula. Rooms with views at remarkable prices; swimming pool and terrace bar. Again, book well in advance for one of the 23 rooms. ⑦.

Between the Jetfoil Terminal and Guia Fortress

Hotel Guia Macau, Estrada do Eng. Trigo 1–5 ☎513888, fax 559822; Hong Kong reservations on ☎770 9303. Closer to the fort than the *Matsuya* (below) and altogether posher, with an atrium and swish elevators. Decently priced, though, for this sort of style, and with a shuttle bus to the *Lisboa* to save you the walk. ⑤.

Mandarin Oriental, Av. da Amizade ☎567888, fax 594589; Hong Kong reservations on ☎881 1688. Swanky comforts, including a pool and a casino, at prices considerably less than the sister hotel in Hong Kong. It's the white block close to the Jetfoil Terminal, which makes it a little far from the centre for an evening stroll. ⑥–⑦.

Hotel Matsuya, Calçada de São Francisco 5 ☎577000 or ☎575466, fax 568080. Good hillside location, on the way up to the Guia fortress. Pleasant rooms, fine views, and a terrace café. Book in advance, since there are only 41 rooms. ⑤.

Hotel Royal, Estrada da Vitoria 2 ☎552222, fax 563008; Hong Kong reservations on ☎540 6333. A modern highrise, close to the Guia fortress and well-equipped, with standard and deluxe doubles, suites and a pool. ⑥.

Taipa

Hyatt Regency, Estrada Almirante Marques Esparteiro 2 ☎831234, fax 830195; Hong Kong reservations on ☎559 0168. Just over the bridge from Macau (all the Taipa buses run past it), it's what you'd expect from the *Hyatt* chain: smart rooms, casino, swimming pool and attentive staff. Rooms overlooking the water cost most; specify when booking if that's what you want. ⑥–⑦.

New Century, Estrada Almirante Marques Esparteiro ☎831111, fax 832222; Hong Kong reservations on ☎548 2213. This new, five-star hotel is enormous – and is also a good bit cheaper than the *Hyatt*, just over the way. Views are good, and the *Silver Court* restaurant here is also highly recommended. ⑤–⑥.

Coloane

Pousada de Coloane, Praia de Cheoc Van ☎328143, fax 328251; Hong Kong reservations on ☎540 8180. For years the only choice on Coloane, the *pousada* is surprisingly inexpensive given its location and facilities. It's a small place, whose 22 rooms have balconies overlooking the beach: book in advance. ⑤.

Westin Resort, Estrada de Hac Sa ☎871111, fax 871122; Hong Kong reservations on ☎803 2015. Coloane's newest hotel, the *Westin* lies at the far end of Hac Sa's fine beach. Ideal for a quiet day or two, and offering excellent private sports facilities, including an 18-hole golf course. You're a little stranded once the sun goes down, though *Fernando's* restaurant (see p.327) is within walking distance. ⑥–⑦.

Chapter 20

Eating and Drinking

As in Hong Kong, most of the **food** eaten in Macau is Cantonese. If this is all you eat, however, you would be missing out on a lot, since Macau's unique combination of Portuguese and Asian cuisine – called **Macanese** – is well worth trying. A variety of cafés and restaurants serve straightforward and excellent **Portuguese** food – from *caldo verde* (a cabbage and potato soup), through different varieties of *bacalhau* (dried salted cod, Portugal's national dish), to milk puddings. Staples like steak, rabbit and sausages, grilled chicken, fried fish, sardines and other seafood dishes are also available, all served in huge quantities. From **Africa** and **India** (Goa particularly) the Portuguese took spices and chillis, and Macanese restaurants nearly always serve enormous spicy prawns and "African Chicken" – Macau's most famous dish, chicken grilled with peppers and chillis. Food from Angola, including fine spicy meat and vegetable stews, is served in at least one of Macau's restaurants. From **Brazil**, there is *feijoda*, an elaborate meal traditionally made from meat, beans, sausage and vegetables.

Most restaurants mix and match all these influences, also using local **Cantonese** ingredients and dishes, so that pigeon, quail and duck, as well as seafood (like crab and sole), are all available alongside the Macanese standbys. One result of this cross-fertilisation of culinary ideas is that the Cantonese influence in some supposedly Macanese restaurants is very heavy-handed. Thus steaks

are sometimes small, thick and grilled, rather than flat and fried with garlic; Portuguese staples can be inexpertly cooked; and everything comes at once, like in a Cantonese meal. None of this matters very much, but it's annoying if you've taken the trouble to search out a "Portuguese" restaurant.

Eating in a **Portuguese/Macanese restaurant** in Macau is, however, a revelation if you've already spent time in Hong Kong's Cantonese diners. For a start, freshly baked **bread** is common; all meals are washed down with cheap imported **Portuguese wine** – fine, heavy reds, chilled whites and slightly sparkling *vinho verde*, as well as any number of **ports** and brandies; and you can get decent **coffee** too. In most places, the **menu** is in Portuguese and English as well as Chinese; check the lists below for descriptions of the food you don't recognise.

Vegetarians should do well for themselves. Every Portuguese restaurant serves excellent mixed salads; and most places will fry eggs and serve them up with some of the best french fries around. *Caldo verde* is always good (though you might have to fish out the piece of Portuguese sausage); *sopa álentejana* (garlic and bread soup) is harder to come by, but much tastier than it sounds.

People eat out earlier in Macau than in Hong Kong – you should aim to be at the restaurant by 8pm – and they rarely stay open later than 11–11.30pm. As for the **price of a meal**, it's uniformly good

Macau: Eating and Drinking

value, certainly compared to similar meals in Hong Kong: soup or salad, a main course, half a bottle of wine and coffee comes to around 150–170ptcs almost everywhere; dessert and a glass of port adds another 40–50ptcs – though two courses in most restaurants will fill you to the brim since servings are so large. Eating Macanese specialities – curried crab, grilled prawns, etc – pushes the price up a little, since these are charged at the daily market rate. To all restaurant bills, add 15 percent service charge and tax; it'll usually be included in the total.

There isn't the **bar scene** that there is in Hong Kong, and most of your drinking will be done with your meal – much the most civilised way to while away an evening. If you really just want a beer or a glass of wine, several of the Portuguese restaurants can accommodate you; *Jimmy's Kitchen Garden Esplanade* (see

"Cafés") is nice for an early evening drink, while all the posher hotels have bars too.

Cafés

You'll find small **cafés** all over Macau, many serving a mixture of local Cantonese food and Portuguese-style snacks. Some are known as a *Casa de Pasto*, a traditional Portuguese workers' dining room, though in Macau, as often as not, they're thoroughly Chinese in cuisine and atmosphere.

Café Safari, Patio do Coto Velo 14 ☎574313. Close to the Leal Senado, off the main avenue, this has good-value European breakfasts, plus other snacks, tea and coffee, and regular meals. Open 9am–1am.

Casa de Pasto San Pou, Rua de Camilo Pessanha 10 ☎594292. Very cheap snacks and meals in a cake shop-cum-

---

A Portuguese/Macanese Menu Reader

Basics and Snacks

Arroz	Rice
Batatas fritas	French fries
Legumes	Vegetables
Manteiga	Butter
Omeleta	Omelette
Ovos	Eggs
Pimenta	Pepper
Prego	Steak roll
Sal	Salt
Salada mista	Mixed salad
Sandes	Sandwiches

Meat

Almondegas	Meatballs
Bife	Steak
Chouriço	Spicy sausage
Coelho	Rabbit
Cordoniz	Quail
Costeleta	Chop, cutlet
Dobrada	Tripe
Figado	Liver
Galinha	Chicken
Pombo	Pigeon
Porco	Pork
Salsicha	Sausage

Fish and Seafood

Ameijoas	Clams
Bacalhau	Dried, salted cod
Camarões	Shrimp
Carangueijo	Crab
Gambas	Prawns
Linguado	Sole
Lulas	Squid
Meixilhões	Mussels
Pescada	Hake
Sardinhas	Sardines

Soups

Caldo verde	Green cabbage and potato soup, often served with spicy sausage
Sopa álentejana	Garlic and bread soup with a poached egg
Sopa de mariscos	Shellfish soup
Sopa de peixe	Fish soup

Cooking Terms

Assado	Roasted
Cozido	Boiled, stewed
Frito	Fried
Grelhado	Grilled
No forno	Baked

---

café. Large portions of Portuguese and Chinese food.

Garden Terrace, Pousada de São Tiago, Av. da República ☎ 378111. Excellent breakfasts served on the *pousada* terrace: fresh fruit juices, eggs, home baked pastries and bread and good coffee – a thoroughly civilised way to start the day. Open 7–11am.

Jimmy's Kitchen Garden Esplanade, Av. Dr. Mário Soares. Opposite the *Sintra*, in the esplanade between road and bay, you can sit outside here and sink a cheap *San Miguel* and eat plates of inexpensive Chinese food.

Leitaria I Son, Largo do Leal Senado 7. A dairy-products café, with an endless variety of inexpensive milk puddings, ice cream and milkshakes, as well as fried-egg breakfasts and tea with real milk. Recommended.

McDonald's, Rua do Campo 17–19. Burgers, fries, etc, all at the usual low, Southeast Asian prices. Open 7am–10pm.

Sopa de Fitas Boa Fortuna, Av. do Infante d'Henrique 41. Late-opening noodle soup specialist. A bowlful for around 15ptcs. Open 11am–4.30am.

Sopa de Fitas Infante, Av. do Infante d'Henrique 65 ☎ 593392. No English menu in this cheap noodle shop, so you'll have to point. Bowls of noodles for around 15ptcs.

Tomas, Av. Ouvidor Arriaga 12. Set breakfasts and run-of-the-mill two-course European and Chinese meals at bargain-basement prices. Open 10am–midnight.

Restaurants

The reviews below concentrate on the excellent Portuguese and Macanese restaurants in Macau, but there are other

Macau: Eating and Drinking

Specialities	
African Chicken (Galinha á Africana)	Chicken baked or grilled with peppers and chillis; either "dry", with spices baked in, or with a thick, spicy sauce
Camarões	Huge grilled prawns with chillis and peppers
Cataplana	Pressure-cooked seafood with bacon, sausage and peppers (named after the dish in which it's cooked)
Cozido á Portuguesa	Boiled casserole of mixed meats (including things like pig's trotters), rice and vegetables
Galinha á Portuguesa	Chicken baked with eggs, potatoes, onion and saffron in a mild, creamy curry sauce
Feijoda	Rich Brazilian stew of beans, pork, sausage and vegetables
Pasteis de bacalhau	Cod fishcakes, deep-fried
Porco á álentejana	Pork and clams in a stew

Pudim flá	Creme caramel
Arroz doce	Portuguese rice pudding

Drinks	
Água mineral	Mineral water
Café	Coffee
Chá	Tea
Cerveja	Beer
Sumo de laranja	Orange juice
Vinho	Wine (*tinto*, red; *branco*, white; *rosé*, rosé)
Vinho do Porto	Port (both red and white)
Vinho verde	Green wine – ie a young wine, slightly sparkling and very refreshing. It can be white, red or rosé in Portugal but in Macau is usually white

Meals	
Almoço	Lunch
Comidas	Meals
Jantar	Dinner
Prato dia/ Menu do dia	Dish/menu of the day

Macau: Eating and Drinking

options in the unlikely instance that you tire of this kind of food. You can buy wine at the same inexpensive prices in all Macau's restaurants, Portuguese or not.

Macanese and Portuguese

Afonso III, Rua Central 11 ☎586272. Two-storey café-restaurant presided over by Afonso – former chef at the *Hyatt* – who will decipher the Portuguese menu for you. Provincial dishes feature, like a mammoth, oily serving of Álentejo pork with clams, drenched in fresh coriander. Other seafood dishes are pricier. Check the daily list of specials to see what the mainly Portuguese clientele is eating. Open noon–11pm.

Bela Vista, Rua Comendador Kou Ho Neng 8 ☎965333. Macau's most exclusive hotel has a fine restaurant open to all – make a reservation and ask for a terrace seat, so that you can drink in the views as you tuck into the decent Portuguese and Continental food. There's a good *cataplana* (pressure-cooked fish and seafood in spicy sauce) and a separate port list that runs from around 30ptcs a glass to 7500ptcs a bottle. It's more expensive than all the other restaurants in this section, though if careful you could still get away for 200ptcs for two courses and wine; more like 300ptcs once coffee, dessert and service have been added.

Estrela do Mar, Travessa do Pavia 11 ☎322074. A small and friendly restaurant, with Portuguese and Macanese specialities, including a selection of *bacalhau* dishes. Not the best food in town, but cheaper than most and fine as an introduction to the local cuisine – and you can just pop in for a coffee and a brandy if you want. It's off Rua da Praia Grande, close to the Palácio do Governo. Open 11am–1am.

Fat Siu Lau, Rua da Felicidade 64 ☎573585. The oldest and most famous of Macau's restaurants, with pigeon the speciality, best eaten with the excellent French fries. Nice, relaxed atmosphere, but – pigeon apart – not the best food in Macau by any means, whatever the adverts say. Open 11am–1.30am.

Henri's Galley, Av. da República 4 ☎556251. The spicy prawns are renowned as the best in Macau, though try the *caldo verde* and any of the immense chicken dishes – the *Galinha á Portuguesa* is brilliant. The tables outside overlooking the bay get the traffic noise; go for a window seat instead and soak up some of the best food and wine in Macau. The restaurant is at the southern end of the peninsula, below the *Bela Vista*. Open noon–11pm.

A Lorcha, Rua do Almirante Sergio 289 ☎313193. Just around the corner from the Maritime Museum, this attractive wood-beamed restaurant is always busy – it's best to reserve in advance for lunch when the Portuguese business community are out in force. There's a large menu of Portuguese staples, superbly cooked, which the Governor of Macau is reputed to enjoy on regular visits. Open 1–3pm & 7pm–midnight. Closed Tues.

Pele, Rua de São Tiago da Barra 25 ☎965624. The African Chicken comes swimming in sauce and there are great spicy prawns to start. But there's a funereal café atmosphere and no great surprises on the menu. The restaurant is close to the *pousada*. Open noon–11.30pm.

Restaurante Portugues, Rua do Campo 16 ☎551386. Reasonably priced and popular, though it's best to avoid the African Chicken here and go instead for one of the fish dishes. Most main courses come with vegetables. Decent wine, too, and friendly service. Open 11am–1am.

Solmar Restaurante, 11 Rua da Praia Grande ☎574391. Old, averagely priced Macanese restaurant with reliable if unadventurous food, including sardines and all the other classics. Open 11am–11pm.

TAIPA

Galo, Rua do Cunha 47 ☎327318. Decorated in Portuguese country style with the cock (*galo*) – the national emblem of Portugal – much in evidence. The photographic menu is very Portuguese – plenty of boiled meats and pig's trotters – but mainstream dishes include steaks, great grilled squid and large mixed salads. You can eat very well, very cheaply, though the staff are a bit grumpy. Open 11.30am–10pm.

Mocambique, Rua dos Clerigos 28a ☎321475. Small restaurant serving tasty Portuguese colonial food, with various dishes from Goa and Africa – from *samosas* to African Chicken. Standard prices and a popular place, so book ahead. Open 12.45–3pm & 7.30–10pm.

Panda, Rua Carlos Eugénio 4–8 ☎327338. Reasonably priced and with good sardines but betrays its Chinese influence in the kitchen – unless you order your courses separately, everything comes at once. Open 11am–10.30pm

Pinocchio's, Rua do Sol 4 ☎327128. Good Macanese food served at tables in an outdoor garden – fish cakes and prawns are well regarded. Open noon–11.30pm.

O Santos, Rua do Cunha 20 ☎327508. The best place on Taipa for authentic, traditional café food – *bacalhau*, rabbit, sardines, Portuguese sausage, steak and fries, fried fish and rice. It's great value, and serves huge portions washed down with decent Portuguese wine, port and strong espresso coffee. Open noon–3pm & 6–10pm.

COLOANE

Fernando's, Hac Sa Beach ☎328264. The sign is hidden, but this is very close to the bus stop, at the end of the car park, under the *Coca Cola* sign – the nearest to the sea in a small line of cafés. Walk through to the back and there's a huge barn-like dining room, where Fernando explains the menu to novices – clams and crab are house specials, the grilled chicken is enormous and succulent. Slightly pricier than usual, but then better than usual, and backing on to the beach. Open noon–10pm.

Pousada de Coloane, Praia de Cheoc Van ☎321844. Reserve a table if you want to eat here – deservedly popular for the *cataplana* dishes and other seafood specialities. Often, tables are set on the terrace. Open noon–10.30pm.

Chinese

Dai pai dongs. Along Rua Escola Comercial, off Av. do Infante d'Henrique (to the side of the sports ground between the hotels *Sintra* and *Lisboa*). Cheap and cheerful noodle and seafood dishes, eaten outdoors.

Long Kei, Largo de Senado 7b; ☎573970. A huge menu takes in good *dim sum* and Cantonese food. Open 11am–11pm.

Shanghai 456, New Wing, Mezzanine Floor, *Hotel Lisboa*, Av. da Amizade ☎388474. Long-established Shanghai restaurant which does the rounds of other regional cuisines, too, including Szechuan and Beijing dishes. Open 11am–11pm.

Silver Court, *New Century Hotel*, Estrada Almirante Marques Esparteiro, Taipa ☎831111. Wonderful Cantonese seafood restaurant that's pricier than most by virtue of its position in a fairly new hotel, but is fine value compared to equivalents in Hong Kong. Specialities are from the Shun-de region, south of Guangzhou, like carp mousse dumplings and pigeon. Open 9am–3pm & 6–11pm.

Other Asian Restaurants

Ali's Curry House, Av. da República 4 ☎555856. Strange restaurant which curries virtually everything on the menu, not always to tasty effect. Still, if you've had too much Portuguese food, it makes a change and it's inexpensive. Open noon–1am.

Baan Thai, Rua de Henrique de Macedo ☎344663. Authentic Thai food, which might be too hot for some. It's close to the *Hotel Royal*, one of several Thai places in this district. Open 6.30pm–6am.

Delhi Restaurant, Av. Sidonio Pais 43 ☎571330. Southern Indian cuisine, which means plenty of vegetarian dishes; fish and squid also gets curried. One of Macau's better deals and very friendly. Open noon–11pm.

Ko Ka, Rua Ferreira do Amaral 21. Across the gardens from the *Hotel Royal*, this late-opening Thai restaurant is one of the most reasonably priced in town. Open 5.30pm–6am.

Macau:
Eating and
Drinking

Macau: Eating and Drinking

Tee Jei, Estrada Nova, Edificio Va Fai Un, Loja C, Taipa ☎320203. Tandoori Indian cooking; try the mixed grill for a taste of everything. Open noon–3pm & 6.30–11pm.

Italian

Café Luso, Rua Central 33b ☎570142. A good Italian/Mediterranean restaurant with some interesting daily specials (squid is always excellent, as is the stuffed tiger prawn), and very reasonably priced pasta and pizzas. Friendly staff. Open 11am–11pm.

Pizzeria Toscana, Rua Formosa 28b ☎592267.Genuine Italian food and not just pizzas, though these are superb. Open 11am–11.30pm.

Buying your own food and wine

Apart from the market on Rua Sul do Mercado de São Domingos, where you can buy fruit and veg, there are branches of the **supermarket** *Park "N" Shop* at Av. Sidonio Pais 69 and Praça Ponte e Horta 11. *Days and Days*, at Rua da Praia Grande 57b, also sells cheap wine and spirits, while for chocolates and alcoholic **drinks** of all kinds, try *Tong San*, Largo do Senado 33.

Chapter 21

Gambling, Entertainment, Sports and Festivals

Eating out is one of the two main entertainments in Macau. The other is **gambling** in various shapes and forms, and most people spend their evenings lurching from restaurant to casino. This is no bad thing in moderation – a couple of nights in Macau is all you need to get around the more interesting venues for losing your money. In lots of cases, too, just being a spectator is entertainment enough, particularly at the "sporting" venues – horse- and dog-racing stadiums – which encourage betting.

There are various other **sports** on offer too, from squash to horse-riding, though most people will probably be content with a swim at one of the good beaches on Coloane. **Cultural** activities of any kind are thin on the ground, though a couple of annual music and arts festivals do their best to bridge the gap. However, because of Macau's Portuguese Catholic past, the enclave celebrates several other religious and national **festivals and holidays** that you don't find in Hong Kong. Some are very definitely worth coinciding with if you want to catch the fairly rare sight of Christian processions and celebrations in a Far Eastern country.

Gambling

The main thing about gambling in Macau is that – with the exception of the casinos in the *Mandarin Oriental* and *Hyatt Regency* hotels – it's a downmarket, no-

frills occupation, designed to rake in the largest amount of money in the shortest possible time. If you're expecting the gilt and glitter of Las Vegas (as well as the free drinks and cheap buffet dinners), you're in the wrong town.

The vast majority of the **punters** in Macau's casinos are Hong Kong Chinese, deprived of the legal right to pursue games of chance in their own territory – some deprivation bearing in mind that gambling is second only in importance to breathing in China. It's not a subdued, high-class operation, and the casinos are noisy, frenetic places – nearly always packed, especially at the weekend, with a constant stream of people who leg it off the jetfoil and into the games.

Given that the sole object of the casinos is to take money off ordinary people, there aren't the **dress restrictions** that you might expect, and in most places you'll be fine as you are. However, **cameras** aren't allowed in any of the casinos and if you've got a bag you'll have to check it in, noting down the serial number of any valuable items in there on a pad provided.

How to win

Basically, you won't win unless you're very lucky, so don't look upon Macau as the way out of your money troubles. You can bet on a series of casino games, some of which are outlined below, or on one of

Macau: Gambling, Entertainment, Sports & Festivals

several sporting events which take place regularly throughout the year. Wherever you go, and whatever you do, the same **warnings** apply. Gamble for fun only; *never bet more than you can afford to lose*. It's notoriously easy to get carried away, particularly if you're trying to make up for money that you've already lost. The best advice is to decide beforehand how much you're prepared to lose and then walk away when it's all gone. The same applies if you actually win, since the speed with which you can pour it all back is phenomenal. Remember, too, that the only system that works is the casino's. Recent figures show Macau's casinos pulling in around US$450 million a year.

The Casino Games

There's an astounding number of games on offer in any of Macau's six casinos. Lots are familiar: you'll need no coaching to work the **one-armed bandits** or slot-machines (called "hungry tigers" locally), which either take Hong Kong dollars or *patacas* and pay out accordingly. The same goes for **roulette** (only available in the *Hotel Lisboa*), and many of the card games are the ones you would expect, like **baccarat** and **blackjack**.

However, local variations and peculiarly **Chinese games** can make a casino trip more interesting. To sort them all out, ask at the tourist information centres where you can buy the *A-O-A Macau Gambling Guide*, which details all the games, rules and odds (a simplified version appears in *Macau Focus*, which the MTIB gives away). The easiest to follow is **boule**, like roulette but with a larger ball and fewer numbers (25) to bet on. **Pai kao** is Chinese dominoes and is utterly confusing for novices. **Fan tan** is easier to grasp, involving a cup being scooped through a pile of buttons which are then counted out in groups of four, bets being laid on how many are left at the end of the count – about as exciting as it sounds. In **dai-siu** ("big-small" in Cantonese) you bet on the value of three dice, either having a small (3–9) or big (10–18) value. In all the games, the **minimum bet** is usually $20.

The casinos

The gambling franchise in Macau is held by the *Sociedade de Turismo e Diversoes de Macau* (*STDM*), which operates eight **casinos**. Each has its own character and variation of games. To get in them, visitors officially need to be (or look) 18; there's no entry fee. Except for the *Victoria*, all the casinos are open 24 hours a day.

Casino Jai-Alai, Outer Harbour, by the Jetfoil Terminal. All-night table action in a stadium that used to host *Jai-Alai* (Basque pelota) games. Also has an off-course betting centre for the dogs.

Casino Kam Pek, Av. de Almeida Ribeiro. Known also as the Chinese Casino on account of the mainly Chinese card and dice games played here. Very popular and very intense. Also has an off-course betting centre for the dogs.

Casino Macau Palace, Inner Harbour, Av. de Almeida Ribeiro. Otherwise known as the Floating Casino, recently replaced by a new two-decked vessel, though still delightfully downmarket.

Hyatt Regency, Taipa. Among the newest and smallest of the casinos. Very select and for high-rollers only.

Hotel Kingsway, Rua de Luis Gonzaga Gomes. Most recent casino to open, fairly flash and not terribly interesting unless you've come to risk your all.

Hotel Lisboa, Av. da Amizade. The biggest casino in Macau, a four-level extravaganza covering all the possible games; it's the only casino in Macau with roulette tables. There are enough comings-and-goings here to entertain you without losing a cent. Bars, restaurants and shops are all within chip-flicking distance and there's also an off-course betting centre for the dog track.

Mandarin Oriental Macau, Av. da Amizade. Upmarket hotel casino, worth popping into for the contrast. Still no Las Vegas, but you'll need decent clothes to play the small range of games.

Victoria, Macau Jockey Club. Over on Taipa, this is only in operation in the evening and on race days.

Racing

You can vary your casino visits with a trip to one of the racing stadiums in Macau, either to watch or for a flutter. **Horse racing** is as popular as it is in Hong Kong, races held on the enlarged and converted race track on Taipa. There's also **dog racing** at the Macau Canidrome, though spotting form is notoriously tricky.

HORSE RACING

The Macau Jockey Club hosts regular weekend **horse racing** from September to June; more information on ☎321888, and consult the MTIB. The minimum bet on a race is $10. The buses to Taipa (#11, #28A or #33) from close to the *Hotel Lisboa* all return via the racecourse.

GREYHOUND RACING

There's **greyhound racing** at the Canidrome (*Canidromo*; ☎574413) in Av. General Castelo Branco, very close to the Lin Fong Temple; buses #1, #2 and #5 from the Floating Casino go right past it. There are races on Tuesday, Thursday, Saturday and Sunday starting at 8pm, and on Sunday afternoons; entrance is 2ptcs to the public stand, 5ptcs for the members' stand. Again, the minimum bet is $10. You'll find a bar and a restaurant there, alongside the betting facilities. If you need any further incentive, the stadium is owned by one Donny Osmund – though, disappointingly for pop fans, he's actually a Chinese banker.

Cultural Events

The free newspaper, *Macau Travel Talk*, lists the month's **concerts and exhibitions**, the usual **venues** for which are the gallery in the Leal Senado, which puts on temporary art displays; the University of East Asia on Taipa, whose auditorium is used for concerts; and – more rarely – the Jardim Lou Lim Ieoc which also hosts recitals and concerts. Other occasional concert venues are a couple of the central churches (like São Lourenço) and the **Macau Forum** (Av. da Amizade), which puts on rock gigs now and then.

Annual events worth catching include the **International Music Festival**, held in October, when Chinese and Western orchestras and performers stage concerts at all the above venues over a seven-day period. Tickets go for 100–300ptcs; check with the MTIB for details. There's also the **Macau Arts Festival**, usually held in February/March, which features a month's worth of events and performances by local cultural and artistic groups.

For the last few years, Macau has also held an international **fireworks festival**, when teams compete with each other to produce the biggest and brightest bangs over the Praia Grande. There's no fixed date, so check with the MTIB.

Sports and Recreation

Apart from horse and dog racing, Macau's biggest sporting draw is the annual **Macau Grand Prix**, held on the third weekend in November, a Formula 3 event (plus a motorbike race, too) which takes place on the enclave's streets, part of the circuit following the enlarged shoreline Avenida da Amizade. Accommodation and transport is mobbed over this weekend, and you'll need to book well in advance if you want to see it.

Walking and Running

Walking/jogging trails criss-cross the land around the Guia Fortress, the most popular a 1700-metre trail reached from the lower car park, just up the hill from the *Guia Hotel*. There are also signposted walking trails on Coloane: the *Trilho de Coloane* and *Trilho Nordeste de Coloane*. The latter is the more accessible, a six-kilometre walk that begins/ends near Ká Ho beach.

If you're feeling especially energetic, in the first week of December the **Macau Marathon** clogs up the enclave's streets, the course running across the peninsula and both islands.

Participatory Sports

Participatory sports available include **squash**, which you can play at the *Hyatt Regency* (☎831234) or the *Mandarin Oriental* (☎567888). Otherwise, head for the *Hotel Lisboa* (☎377666), whose labyrinthine twists and turns conceal a **swim-**

Macau:
Gambling,
Entertainment, Sports
& Festivals

ming pool open to the public and a snooker and billiards room.

Hac Sa beach (p.315) on Coloane has a recreation centre (Mon–Fri 9am–9pm, Sat & Sun 9am–10pm; 5ptcs) with swimming pool (another 15ptcs), roller-skating, mini-golf, children's playground and tennis courts. You can rent windsurfing equipment on the beach here, too.

Finally, the Macau Horse Riding Centre (Tues–Sun; ☎328303), also at Hac Sa beach, rents out the beasts and arranges instruction.

Festivals and Holidays

Macau's mostly Cantonese population celebrates the same Chinese religious and civil holidays and festivals as in Hong Kong: there's a round-up of the events and celebrations associated with the festivals on p.255–258. But the enclave also celebrates several holidays and festivals lent to Macau by Portugal, often marked by parades, special exhibitions and concerts. The major ones are:

February: procession of Our Lord of Passos. An image of Christ is carried in procession from Santo Agostinho to the Sé for an overnight vigil and then returned via the stations of the cross.

Lent (first Sunday): procession of Our Lord of Passion. The statue of Christ is carried in procession from Santo Agostinho church to the Sé, with stations of the cross set up as it goes.

April 25: anniversary of the 1974 Portuguese revolution. A public holiday.

May 13: procession of Our Lady of Fatima, from São Domingos church to the Penha chapel to commemorate a miracle in Fatima, Portugal, in 1913. The biggest annual Portuguese religious celebration, though not a public holiday in Macau.

June 10: Camões Day (Portuguese Communities Day). A public holiday to commemorate Portugal's national poet.

June 24: procession in honour of St John the Baptist (the patron saint of Macau), with a special Mass in the cathedral. Also in June is a procession in honour of St Anthony of Lisbon.

July 13: holiday on Taipa and Coloane celebrating the defeat of pirates in 1910.

October 5: Portuguese Republic Day; a public holiday to mark the establishment of the Portuguese Republic in 1910.

December 1: Portuguese Independence Day; a public holiday.

Chapter 22

Directory

AIRLINES *East Asia Airlines* (Hong Kong helicopter service; ☎550777); *Air France* (c/o *Agencia de Viagens Turisticas Luis Chou*, Av. do Dr. Mário Soares ☎575438); *Air India* (c/o STDM Air Travel Dept, *Hotel Lisboa*, new wing, ground floor ☎375068); *British Airways* (c/o *Agencia de Viagens Turisticas F. Rodrigues*, Rua da Praia Grande 71 ☎581777); *Swissair* (*Agencia de Viagens Turisticas C&O*, Rua Dr. Pedro José Lobo 15, Room 1501 ☎311313).

AIRPORT Information about the new airport from *Autoridade de Aviação Civil de Macau*, Rua Dr. Pedro José Lobo 1-3, Edifício Luso Internácional, 26th Floor ☎511213.

BANKS AND EXCHANGE Banks are generally open Monday–Friday 9am–4pm, Saturday 9am–noon, though a bank in the arcade of the *Hotel Lisboa* keeps much longer hours than this. Most of the main banks will exchange travellers' cheques. These include *Banco Nacional Ultramarino (BNU)*, Av. de Almeida Ribeiro 2; *Standard Chartered Bank*, Av. Infante d'Henrique; and *Hongkong and Shanghai Bank*, Rua Praia Grande 75, which gives cash advances with a *Visa* card. The large hotels will also change money, though obviously at a price; and there are licensed money changers, too (*casa de cambio*), including one at the Jetfoil Terminal. There's also a bank on both Taipa and Coloane.

BOOKSHOPS It's hard to find bookshops in Macau that carry English-language books; do your book shopping in Hong Kong. However, books about Portugal and Macau are available from the *Portuguese Bookshop and Cultural Centre*, Rua de Pedro Nolasco da Silva (near the Sé).

CAR RENTAL Contact *Avis* (at the shopping arcade/car park, *Mandarin Oriental Macau*, Av. da Amizade ☎567888; 2nd Floor, Burfield Building, 143 Connaught Rd, Central, Hong Kong ☎541 2011) or *Macau Mokes* (Jetfoil Terminal ☎378851; 806 Kai Tak Commercial Building, 317–321 Des Voeux Rd, Central, Hong Kong ☎543 4190). For moke rentals, expect to pay 300–330ptcs for 24 hours, with slightly cheaper midweek rates available; there's also a charge of 50ptcs for insurance and a 300ptcs deposit. You need to be at least 21, to have held a driving licence for two years and have your own, or an international, driving licence with you. Remember to drive on the left.

CHINA AND TAIWAN DEPARTURES Ferry tickets to Guangzhou can be bought from *Yuet Tung Shipping Co.*, next to the Floating Casino on the quayside (daily 8am–noon & 2–5.30pm). The ferry departs daily at 8pm and arrives the next morning at 7.15am; fares range from around 100ptcs (2nd-class dorm) to 180ptcs (2-bed cabin) one-way. Departures, too, to Kongman (daily at 1.40pm, arrive 3.40pm, around 80ptcs, reserve 3 days in advance); and Shekou (daily at 2.30pm, arrive 4pm, around 100ptcs). Tickets to Taiwan on the *Macmosa* ferry (1–2 weekly; 24hr) are

Macau: Directory

available from the office at the Jetfoil Terminal; tickets cost from around 1000ptcs one-way.

DEPARTURE TAX 20ptcs per person, usually included in the price of your jetfoil/ferry ticket.

DOCTORS Go to the hospital casualty departments (see below) or look in the telephone directory Yellow Pages under "Médicos".

DRINKING WATER It comes straight from China and is perfectly all right to drink. It doesn't always taste wonderful, though, and you might be happier with bottled water, sold in shops everywhere.

ELECTRICITY Most of Macau's electricity is supplied at 220v, although some buildings in the older parts of the city still use power at 110v. Plugs use three round pins.

EMERGENCIES Call ☎999 for police, ambulance or fire brigade services. Other numbers include Fire Brigade ☎572222; Ambulance ☎577199 or ☎378311; Public Security Force ☎573333.

HONG KONG DEPARTURES Ferry and jetfoil tickets to Hong Kong can be bought at the Jetfoil Terminal ticket office on the ground floor. The various companies' windows sell tickets for all immediate sailings; for advance tickets, use the ticket office at the *Hotel Lisboa* (Mon–Sat 9.30am–11.30pm, Sun 9.30am–7.30pm) or the *STDM* office, opposite the *Peninsula* hotel at Rua das Lorchas 161. The *Hongkong and Macau Hydrofoil Co.* also has an advance booking office for the Super-Shuttle Jumbocat services at Av. de Almeida Ribeiro 34 (daily 8.30am–8pm), or call ☎711166 for credit card bookings. For high-speed ferry enquiries, call ☎57068. Departure frequencies are the same as from Hong Kong (see "Getting to Macau", p.291), as are the prices – though they're expressed in *patacas*.

HOSPITALS There are 24-hour casualty departments at *Centro Hospitalar Conde São Januário*, Calç. Visconde São Januário

☎577199 (English-speaking); and *Hospital Kiang Wu*, Est. Coelho do Amaral ☎378311 (mostly Chinese-speaking).

LAUNDRY There are laundries (*lavanderia*) opposite the *Fat Siu Lau* restaurant on Rua da Felicidade, and on Rua Sul do Mercado, close to the market.

NEWSPAPERS You can buy Hong Kong's English-language daily newspapers in Macau, as well as imported copies of foreign newspapers, from the newspaper stands along the central avenida. Macau's local newspapers are, of course, in Cantonese and Portuguese.

PHARMACIES *Farmácia Popular*, Largo do Leal Senado 16 ☎355085; *Farmácia União*, Rua Ferreira do Amaral 17 ☎370198; *Farmácia Tsan Heng*, Av. de Almeida Ribeiro 7 ☎572888; *Farmácia Lap Kei*, Calç. do Gaio 3D ☎343054; *Farmácia Chun Cheong*, Rua de S. Domingos 8 ☎371264. Each takes it in turn to open for 24hr; details posted on the door.

POLICE The main police station is at Av. Dr. Rodrigo Rodrigues ☎573333.

POST OFFICES The main post office is the large granite building on the central Largo do Leal Senado, just off Avenida de Almeida Ribeiro (Mon–Fri 9am–1pm & 3-5.30pm, Sat 9am–12.30pm); this is where poste restante mail is sent. Otherwise, little booths all over Macau sell stamps, as do the larger hotels, and there's a post office on each of the two outlying islands, Taipa and Coloane. If you're looking for signs, *Correios* is Portuguese for "post office"; *selos* is "stamps".

TELEPHONES Local phone calls from pay phones cost 1ptca though like Hong Kong, local calls are free from courtesy phones in hotels and restaurants. There are groups of pay phones around the Largo do Leal Senado and at the Jetfoil Terminal. Some take telephone cards, available from the telephone office at the back of the main post office (open 24hr), from where you can make international calls. See p.22 for details of dialling abroad.

Useful telephone numbers include:

Directory Enquiries ☎185 (Portuguese);
☎181 (Chinese and English)

Emergencies ☎999

Home Direct Information ☎101

Time ☎140 (English)

Weather Information ☎911 (Portuguese)

TELEVISION You can pick up Hong Kong's television stations in Macau, as well as some from mainland China; there's also a local station, *Teledifusao de Macau* (*TdM*), whose programmes are mostly in Cantonese and Portuguese, though a few are in English. *TdM*'s programme listings are carried in Hong Kong's daily newspapers.

TIME Macau is eight hours ahead of GMT; 13 hours ahead of New York, 16 hours ahead of Los Angeles.

TOUR OPERATORS There's no shortage of companies which will show you the sights by bus. There are endless tour combinations available – half-day whisks around the peninsula and islands, from around 100ptcs a head, to pricey three- or four-day trips that take in Zhuhai and parts of Guangdong province. Most can be booked in Hong Kong as well, though it's generally cheaper to book in Macau.

For details, ask at any of the *MTIB* offices in Hong Kong or Macau or contact one of the tour operators, some of which are listed below (there's a full list in *Macau Travel Talk*) and all of which offer the same tours at broadly similar prices.

China Travel Service, Rua da Praia Grande 63 ☎782331.

International Tourism, Trav. do Padre Narciso 9, Ground Floor ☎975183.

Macau Star, Room 511, Tai Fung Bank Building, Av. de Almeida Ribeiro 34 ☎558855.

Macau Tours, Av. Dr. Mário Soares 35 ☎385555.

Sintra Tours, Hotel Sintra, Room 207–8, Av. Dom João IV ☎710111.

VACCINATION CENTRE At *Direcção dos Serviços de Saúde* (Health Dept), Av. Conselheiro Ferreira de Almeida ☎562235.

VISAS For China visas, visit the *China Travel Service*, Rua da Praia Grande 63 (Mon–Sat 8.30am–1pm & 2.30–5.30pm), which issues visas and tickets (including tickets for the bus to Guangzhou), and organises tours. Most other tour agencies can sort out a visa for you, too; see "Tour Operators", above, for addresses.

Macau: Directory

The Contexts

Hong Kong: a History

To Western eyes, the history of Hong Kong starts with the colonial adventurers and merchants who began settling on the fringes of southeast China in the mid-sixteenth century. The Portuguese arrived in Macau in 1557; almost 300 years later, the British seized Hong Kong Island. However, the whole region has a long, if not greatly distinguished, history of its own that is thoroughly Chinese – a tradition that can only intensify with the handing back of both Hong Kong and Macau to China at the end of this century.

Early Times

Archeological finds point to settlements around Hong Kong dating back 6000 years, and while there's little hard evidence, it's accepted that the archipelago off the southeastern coast of China was inhabited in these very early times by fishermen and farmers. There was no great living to be made: then, as now, it was a largely mountainous region, difficult to cultivate and with trying, tropical weather. Disease was common, and though the sea was rich in fish, the islands formed a base for bands of marauding pirates. Later, though far from the Imperial throne in Peking, the land became a firm part of the great Chinese Empire, which was unified in 221 BC. Throughout the series of ruling dynasties that dominated the next 1500 years, the area around Hong Kong was governed – after a fashion – by a magistrate who reported to a provincial Viceroy in Guangdong (Canton province).

The local population was made up of several **races**, including the Cantonese – who were the most powerful and divided into clans – the Hakka people, a peripatetic grouping who had come down from the north, and the Tankas, who mostly lived on the water in boats. Villages were clan-based, self-contained and fortified with thick walls, and the inhabitants owned and worked their nearby ancestral lands. The elders maintained temples and ancestral halls within the villages, and daily life followed something of an ordained pattern, activities and ceremonies mapped out by a geomancer, who interpreted social and religious ideas through a series of laws known as **fung shui** or "wind and water".

Examples of these **walled villages** still survive in the New Territories, most notably at Kam Tin and Tsang Tai Uk (near Sha Tin), while geomancy is a flourishing art in modern Hong Kong, where the design of all new buildings takes into account the ancient principles of favourable location.

This village-based life continued uneventfully for centuries, the small population of the peninsula and islands mostly untroubled by events elsewhere in the empire. Recorded history made its mark only in the thirteenth century AD, when one of the rulers of the **Song Dynasty**, a boy-emperor, was forced to flee to the peninsula of Kowloon in order to escape the Mongols who were driving south. They cornered him in 1279 and he was killed, the last of his dynasty. The Mongol victory caused a great movement of local tribes in southern China, and a general lawlessness and unrest followed, characterised by continuing pirate activity based on Lantau Island.

Trade and the Chinese

The wider Chinese Empire, however, had begun to engineer links with the Western world that were to bring Hong Kong into the historical mainstream. Although the empire considered itself superior to other lands, supreme and self-sufficient, there had been **trade** between China and the rest of the known world for hundreds of years, often conducted under the guise of "tribute" from other countries and leaders, so as to the idea of Chinese pre-eminence. Out China went silk, tea and fine art; in came horses, cloth and other luxuries.

The concept of superiority was a resilient one, with foreigners seen as "barbarians" by the Chinese and kept at arm's length. Foreign merchants had to petition the authorities to be allowed to trade; they were not allowed to live within the borders of the empire; they were forbidden to learn the Chinese language, and were generally treated with disdain by Chinese officials.

The relationship changed slightly in the sixteenth century, when some of the first of the Western traders, the **Portuguese**, were given a toehold in the Chinese Empire by being granted permission to establish a trading colony at **Macau**, 60km west of Hong Kong. To the Chinese, it was a concession of limited importance: the Portuguese were confined to the very edge of the empire, far from any real power or influence, and when the same concessions were given to other Western nations in the eighteenth century, the Chinese saw things in the same light. As long as the barbarians kept to the fringes of the Celestial Empire, their presence was accepted – and mostly ignored.

For the West, and especially Britain, such trading territories were viewed altogether differently. Allowed to establish trading operations in **Canton** (Guangzhou) from 1714 onwards, many Western countries saw it as a first step to opening up China itself, and by the turn of the nineteenth century, the Dutch, American and French had joined the British in Canton hoping to profit from the undoubtedly massive resources at hand.

For the time being, however, foreign traders in Canton had to restrict themselves to the peculiar dictates of the Chinese rulers. Their **warehouses** (called "factories") were limited to space outside the city walls on the waterfront, and there they also had to live. All their operations were supervised, their trade conducted through a selected group of Chinese merchants, who formed a guild known as a **Cohong** (from which is derived the Hong Kong word *hong*, or company). In the summer, foreigners had to leave for Portuguese Macau, where most of them kept houses (and often, their families). Under these circumstances foreign merchants somehow prospered and trade thrived. The British East India Company was only one of the firms involved, seeing their Chinese enterprises as simply an extension of the world-wide trade network they'd built up on the back of the British victory over Napoleon and mastery of the seas.

The Opium Trade

The problem that soon became apparent was that trade took place on eminently favourable terms for the Chinese. Foreigners had to pay for Chinese tea and silk in silver, while the Chinese wanted little that the Westerners had. The breakthrough was the emergence of the trade in **opium**, in demand in China but illegal and consequently little-grown. The Portuguese had been smuggling it into Macau from their Indian territories for years, and as it became clear that this was the one product that could reverse the trade imbalance, others followed suit. Most energetic were the British, who began to channel opium – "foreign mud" as the Chinese came to call it – from Bengal to Canton, selling it illegally to corrupt Chinese merchants and officials in return for various goods. Illegal or not, the trade mushroomed and opium became the linchpin of the relationship between the Chinese and the ever-richer foreign merchants.

Familiar Hong Kong names began to appear in Canton, most of whom were connected with the opium trade. **William Jardine** and **James Matheson** were two of the most successful and unscrupulous traders, both Scottish Calvinists who had no qualms about making fortunes from an increasing Chinese reliance on drugs. The trade was also encouraged by the British government, and by corruptible Chinese government officials who ignored what had become an overt smuggling operation. By 1837, around 40,000 chests of the drug were landed annually in China, unloaded at Lin Tin Island in the Pearl River estuary, transferred onto Chinese barges and floated upriver to Canton.

As silver began to flow out of China to pay for the increasing amounts of the drug being imported, the trade imbalance came to the attention of the Chinese Emperor in Peking (Beijing), who also began to show concern for the adverse effect that the opium was having on the health of his population. In 1839, the Emperor appointed an opponent of the trade, the Governor of Hunan province, **Lin Tse-Hsu**, to go to Canton to end the import of opium – something he'd achieved fairly spectacularly in his own province by brute force. Once in Canton, Lin Tse-Hsu ordered the surrender and destruction of all the foreigners' opium chests, 20,000 in all, and much to the disgust of the enraged merchants, the British Chief Superintendent of Trade, **Captain Charles Elliot**, did just that. His was a difficult position, since he represented the traders, yet personally stood against the opium trade, and his actions did nothing to diffuse the affair. Governor Lin ordered a blockade against the merchants' factories and demanded they each sign a bond, promising not to import opium into China in future. Under Elliot's direction, the traders left Canton and retreated to Macau and their boats, anchored in Hong Kong harbour, fearing further trouble. The situation deteriorated when Lin reminded the Portuguese of their official neutrality, which they upheld by refusing Elliot a secure base on Macau and by forbidding the selling of supplies to the British merchant fleet, which still waited nervously off Hong Kong.

The First Opium War

If it was Governor Lin's intention to force the British back to Canton to trade on his terms, then he miscalculated disastrously. The mood in Britain, where Lord Palmerston was Foreign Secretary in the Whig government of Lord Melbourne, was one of aggressive expansionism. Merchants like Jardine and Matheson had long been urging the government to promote British free trade in China, demanding gunboats if necessary to open up the Chinese Empire. The first Superintendent of Trade in China, Lord Napier, had been given precisely those instructions, but had been humiliated by the Chinese when he had tried to press British claims in the region. Canton had been closed to him and his frigates forced to retreat, a disgrace in British eyes that Palmerston had not forgotten.

Captain Elliot had already begun the skirmishes that would degenerate into the so-called **First Opium War**, having replied to Lin's threats by firing on a Chinese fleet in September 1839 and sinking a number of ships. It was these threats, rather than the protection of the opium trade, that gave Britain the excuse it sought to expand its influence in China. There was opposition to the trade in Britain, particularly among the ranks of the Whigs, who had already made their mark with the abolition of the slave trade. But potential attacks on British personnel and overseas livelihoods couldn't be ignored.

Palmerston ordered an **expeditionary fleet** from India, comprising 4000 men, which arrived

off Hong Kong in June 1840 with the express purpose of demanding compensation for the lost opium chests and an apology from the Chinese, and – most importantly – acquiring a base on the Chinese coast, which could be used like Portuguese Macau to open up the country for free trade. Several ports up and down the Chinese coast had been suggested by traders over the years, including Canton itself, and the expedition (led by Admiral George Elliot, a cousin of Charles) was authorised to grab what it could. The British fleet soon achieved its military objectives: it attacked the forts guarding Canton, while other ships sailed north, blockading and firing on ports and cities right the way up the Chinese coast. When part of the fleet reached the Yangtze river, approaching Beijing itself, the Chinese were forced to negotiate.

Governor Lin was dispensed with by the Emperor, who appointed a new official, Kishen, to deal with the British fleet, by now again under the command of Charles Elliot. The fighting stopped and the British withdrew to the Pearl River to negotiate, but after six weeks of stalling by the Chinese, the fleet once again sailed on Canton and knocked out its forts. Kishen capitulated and Elliot **seized Hong Kong Island**; the British flag was planted there on January 26, 1841.

Fighting began again soon after, when in August 1841 Elliot was replaced by Sir Henry Pottinger, who was determined to gain more than just Hong Kong Island. The fleet sailed northwards, taking ports as they went, which were later recognised as free trade "Treaty Ports" by the 1842 **Treaty of Nanking**, which halted the fighting. In this way, Shanghai, Amoy (Xiamen), Fuzhou, Canton and others were opened up for trade, the Chinese were forced to pay an indemnity to the British; but most important of all, the treaty ceded Hong Kong Island to Britain in perpetuity.

The New Colony

Not everyone was thrilled with Britain's new imperial acquisition. The small island was called Hong Kong by the British, after the Cantonese name (*Heung Gong*), most commonly translated as meaning "Fragrant Harbour". But aside from the excellent anchorage it afforded to the British fleet, Palmerston for one saw Elliot's action as a lost opportunity to gain further parts of China for Britain. It was a move which cost Elliot his job, while at home Queen Victoria was amused by the apparent uselessness of her new out-of-the-way colony.

Nevertheless, the ownership of Hong Kong – which formally became a British Crown Colony in 1843 – gave a proper base for the opium trade, which became ever more profitable. By 1850 Britain was exporting 52,000 chests of opium a year to China through the colony.

Sir Henry Pottinger, who replaced Elliot, became the colony's first **Governor**, a constitution was drawn up, and from 1844 onwards, a Legislative Council and a separate Executive Council were convened – though the governor retained a veto in all matters. In colonial fashion, pioneered elsewhere in the world by the British, government departments were created, the law administered and public works commissioned. At first, though, the colony remained something of a backwater, since the British were still ensconced at Canton and most of the China trade went through the other Treaty Ports. The population of around 15,000 was mostly made up of local Chinese, lots of whom were attracted by the commercial opportunities they thought would follow; many of them sold land rights (that often they didn't own in the first place) to the newly arrived British, who began to build permanent houses and trading depots.

The first buildings to go up were around Possession Point, in today's Western district – offices, warehouses (called "godowns") and eventually European-style housing. This area was abandoned to the Chinese when the first colonists discovered it to be malarial and mistakenly moved to Happy Valley – which turned out to be even more badly affected. Gradually, though, sanitation was improved. Happy Valley was drained and turned into a racecourse; summer houses were built on The Peak; and a small, but thriving town began to emerge – called **Victoria**, on the site of today's Central. The number of Europeans living there was still comparatively small – just a few hundred in the mid-1840s – but they at least now existed within a rigid colonial framework, segregated from the Chinese by early governors and buoyed by new colonial style and comforts. Streets and settlements were named after Queen Victoria and her ministers; Government House was finished in 1855; the Zoological and Botanical Gardens laid out in 1864; St John's Cathedral opened in 1849; and the first path up The Peak cut in 1859. As Hong Kong began to come into its own as a

trading port, the British merchants who lived there started to have more say in how the colony was run: in 1850, two merchants were appointed to the Legislative Council.

The Second Opium War and Colonial Growth

Relations between Britain and China remained strained throughout the early life of the colony, flaring up again in 1856 when the Chinese authorities, ostensibly looking for pirates, boarded and arrested a Hong Kong registered schooner, the *Arrow*. With London always looking for an excuse for further intervention in China, this incident gave Britain the chance to despatch another fleet up the Pearl River to besiege Canton – instigating a series of events sometimes known as the **Second Opium War**. Joined by the French, the British continued the fighting for two years and in 1858 an Anglo-French fleet captured more northern possessions. The **Treaty of Tientsin** (Tianjin) gave foreigners the right to diplomatic representation in Peking, something Palmerston and the traders saw as crucial to the future success of their enterprise. But with the Chinese refusing to ratify the treaty, the Anglo-French forces moved on Peking, occupying the capital in order to force Chinese concessions.

This second, more protracted series of military engagements finally ended in 1860 with the signing of the so-called **Convention of Peking**, which ceded more important territory to the British. The southern part of Kowloon peninsula – as far north as Boundary Street – and the small Stonecutter's Island (which is still restricted to the military) were handed over in perpetuity, increasing the British territory to around 36 square miles. This enabled the British to establish control over the fairly lawless village that had grown up on the peninsula at Tsim Sha Tsui, while the fine Victoria Harbour could now be more easily protected from both sides. Almost as a by-product of the agreement, the opium trade was legalised, too.

The period immediately after was one of **rapid growth**. With a more secure base, the colony's commercial trade increased and Hong Kong became a stop for ships en route to other Far Eastern ports. They could easily be repaired and refitted in the colony, which began to sustain an important shipping industry of its own. As a result of the increased business, the **Hongkong and Shanghai Bank** was set up in 1864 and allowed to issue banknotes, later building the first of its famous office buildings. The large foreign trading companies, the **hongs**, established themselves in the colony: Jardine, Matheson was already there, but it was followed in the 1860s by Swire, which had started life as a shipping firm in Shanghai. The town of Victoria spread east and west along the harbour, around its new City Hall, taking on all the trappings of a flourishing colonial town, a world away from the rather down-at-heel settlement of twenty years earlier. One of the major changes was in the size of the **population**: the Taiping rebellions in China greatly increased the number of refugees crossing the border, and by 1865 there were something like 150,000 people in the colony. With Hong Kong soon handling roughly a third of China's foreign trade, the colony began to adopt the role it assumes today – as a broker in people and goods.

By **the 1880s**, Hong Kong's transformation was complete. Although the vast majority of the Chinese population were poor workers, the beginnings of today's meritocracy was apparent as small numbers of Chinese businessmen and traders flourished. One enlightened governor, **Sir John Pope Hennessy**, advocated a change in attitude towards the Chinese that didn't go down at all well: he appointed Chinese people to government jobs, there were Chinese lawyers, and even a Chinese member of the Legislative Council. It was an inevitable move, but one that was resisted by the bigoted colonialists, who banned the Chinese from living in the plusher areas of Victoria and on The Peak.

1898: The Leasing of the New Territories

Following Japan's victory in the **Sino-Japanese War** (1894–95), China became subject to some final land concessions. Russia, France and Germany had all pressed claims on Chinese territory in return for limiting Japanese demands after the war, and Britain followed suit in an attempt to defend Hong Kong against possible future attack from any foreign source in China. One British gain was the lease of Weihaiwei in Shandong, in the north, to be held as long as the Russians kept Port Arthur (Lushun), on which they'd secured a 25-year lease in 1897.

More significant, though, was the British government's demand for a substantial lease on the land on the Kowloon peninsula, north of Boundary Street. Agreement was reached on an area stretching across from Mirs Bay in the east to Deep Bay in the west, including the water and islands in between, and this territory was **leased from China for 99 years**, from July 1, 1898. It came to be known as the **New Territories**, and provides the legal focus for the return of the whole colony to China in 1997. Although the British undoubtedly thought they'd got a good deal in 1898 – a 99-year lease must have seemed as good as an outright concession – it was to become clear over the years that Hong Kong would never survive as a viable entity once the greater resources of the New Territories were handed back. Thus had the British authorities effectively provided a date for abolition of one of their most dynamic colonies.

The colony of Hong Kong was now made up of just under 1100 square kilometres of islands, peninsula and water, but there was an indigenous Chinese population of around 100,000 in the newly acquired territory which resisted the change. Many villagers feared that their ancestral grounds would be disturbed and their traditional life interfered with, and local meetings were called in order to form militias to resist the British. There were clashes at **Tai Po** in April 1899, though British troops soon took control of the main roads and strategic points. Resistance in the New Territories fizzled out and civil administration was established, but the villagers retained their distrust of the authorities. One further problem caused by the leasing agreement was the anomalous position of **Kowloon Walled City**, beyond the original Boundary Street – a mainly Chinese garrison that had evolved into a fairly unpleasant slum by 1898. For some reason, the leasing agreement didn't include the Walled City, and China continued to claim jurisdiction over it, hastening its degeneration over the years into an anarchic settlement and a flashpoint between the two sets of authorities.

The Years to World War II

By the turn of the **twentieth century**, the population of Hong Kong had increased to around a quarter of a million (and more came after the fall of the Manchu Dynasty in China in 1911), and the colony's trade showed an equally impressive performance, finally moving away from opium – which had still accounted for nearly half of the Hong Kong government's finances in 1890. In 1907, an agreement was reached between Britain and China to end the opium trade, and imports were cut over a ten-year period – though all that happened was that the cultivation of poppies shifted from India to China, carried on under the protection of local Chinese warlords. Opium smoking wasn't made illegal in Hong Kong until 1946 (three years later in China).

Alongside the trade and manufacturing increase came other improvements and developments. The **Kowloon Railway**, through the New Territories to the border, was opened in 1910 (and completed, on to Canton, by the Chinese, in 1912); the **University of Hong Kong** was founded in 1911; **land reclamation** in Victoria had begun; and the **Supreme Court** building was erected in the first decade of the new century (and still stands today, in Central, as the Legislative Council building).

Despite this activity, movements outside the colony's control were soon to have their effect, and the years following World War I saw a distinct economic shift away from Hong Kong. Shanghai overtook it in the 1920s as *the* Chinese trading city, and Hong Kong lost its pre-eminence for the next thirty years or so. The polarisation in Chinese politics began to have an effect, too. Sun Yat-sen was elected President of the Republic in Canton, and a militant movement on capitalistic Hong Kong's doorstep was bound to cause trouble. Most of Hong Kong's Chinese were desperately poor and there had been the occasional riot over the years, which erupted in 1926 (following Sun Yat-sen's death) into a total **economic boycott** of the colony, organised and led by the Chinese Nationalists (the Kuomintang), based in Canton. There was no trade, few services and – more importantly – no food imports from China, a state of affairs which lasted for several months and did untold damage to manufacturing and commercial activity. Expat volunteers had to keep things going as best they could, while the strike leaders in Hong Kong encouraged many Chinese people to leave the colony so as to press home their demands – a shorter working day, less discrimination against the local Chinese population and a reduction in rent.

The strike didn't last, but the colony's confidence had been badly dented. And although business picked up again, new worries emerged in the 1930s as the **Japanese occupied southern China**. Hundreds of thousands of people fled into the colony, almost doubling the population, and many saw the eventual occupation of Hong Kong itself as inevitable.

Japanese Occupation 1941–45

The Japanese had been advancing across China from the north since 1933, seizing Manchuria and Beijing before establishing troops in Canton in 1939 – an advance which had temporarily halted the civil war then raging in China. What was clear was that any further move to take Hong Kong was bound to succeed: the colony had only a small defensive force of a few battalions and a couple of ships, and couldn't hope to resist the Japanese army.

Some thought that the Japanese wouldn't attack, and certainly, although Hong Kong had been prepared for war since 1939, there was a feeling that old, commercial links with the Japanese would save the colony. However, when the Japanese occupied Indo-China, the colony's defences were immediately strengthened. A line of pillboxes and guns was established across the New Territories, the so-called Shing-mun redoubt, which was hoped would delay any advancing army long enough for Kowloon to be evacuated and Hong Kong Island to be turned into a fortress from which the resistance could be directed.

On December 8, 1941 the **Japanese army invaded**, overran the border from Canton, bombed the planes at Kai Tak airport and swept through the New Territories' defences. They took Kowloon within four days, the British forces retreating to Hong Kong Island where they were shelled and bombed from the other side of the harbour. The Japanese then moved across to the island, split the defence forces in hard fighting and finished them off. The **British surrender** came on Christmas Day, after around 6000 military and civilian deaths, with 9000 more men captured. The soldiers were held in a prisoner-of-war camp at Sham Shui Po, in Kowloon, while those British civilians who had not previously been evacuated to Australia were interned in Stanley Prison on the island.

It was a dark time for the people of Hong Kong, who faced a Japanese army out of control. Although some Chinese civilians collaborated, many others helped the European and Allied prisoners by smuggling in food and medicines, and helping to organise escapes. It wasn't necessarily a show of support for the British, but an indication of the loyalty most Hong Kong Chinese felt towards China, which had suffered even worse under the Japanese. Atrocities faced the Allied prisoners, too: during the short campaign, the Japanese had murdered hospital staff and prisoners, and in prison, beatings, executions for escape attempts, and torture were commonplace. Life in Stanley meant disease and malnutrition, and being a civilian was no guarantee of safety: in 1943, seven people were beheaded on the beach for possessing a radio.

The Japanese meanwhile sent a military governor to Hong Kong to supervise the **occupation**, but found the colony to be much less use to them than they had imagined. It wasn't incorporated into the Japanese-run parts of China, and apart from changing the names of buildings and organisations – and adding a few Japanese touches to Government House – nothing fruitful came of their time there. The New Territories became a battleground for bandits, various factions of the Chinese defenders and the Japanese invaders; towns and villages emptied as many of the local Chinese were forcibly repatriated to the mainland; food and supplies were run down; the cities on either side of the harbour were bombed out. As the Japanese gradually lost the battle elsewhere, Hong Kong became more and more of an irrelevance to them, and when the **Japanese surrendered to the Allies** in August 1945, colonial government picked itself up surprisingly quickly.

Post-War Reconstruction: the 1950s and 1960s

The immediate task in Hong Kong was to rebuild both buildings and commerce, something the colony undertook with remarkable energy. By the end of 1945 the population was again at the level it stood at before occupation, and the colonial administration was firmly in place. Within a couple of years the harbour had been cleared and the trading companies were back in business. This was, however, achieved at a price, and Hong Kong lost out on the democratic reforms that were sweeping the rest of the world. There had been suggestions that the colony become a free-trading "international" state after the war, or that it be handed back to China, but quick thinking by the imprisoned British leaders on Japan's surrender – who declared themselves the acting government – ensured that Hong Kong remained a British colony. Liberal measures designed to introduce at least some democratic reforms into the running of the colony were treated with virtual disdain by the population, which was interested only in getting its business back on its feet.

The boost the economy needed came in 1949–50, when the **Communists came to power in China**, unleashing a wave of new immigration across the border. The civil war in China had been fought in earnest since the end of World War II, and with the fall of Nationalist China, traders and businessmen were desperate to escape. Thousands arrived, many from Shanghai, to set up new businesses and provide the manufacturing base from which the colony could expand. By 1951, the population had grown to around two-and-a-half million, and Hong Kong had moved from being a mere entrepôt to become an industrial centre. New, lucrative industries – directly attributable to the recent refugees – included textiles and construction. A further incentive for a change in emphasis in the colony came with the American embargo on Chinese goods sold through Hong Kong during the **Korean War**, so that the territory was forced into manufacturing goods as a means of economic survival.

The new immigrants unleashed new problems for the colony. Virtually all of them were ardently anti-Communist, many supporting the Kuomintang, and they took every opportunity during the 1950s to unsettle the relationship between Hong Kong and China. This resulted in **riots** in the colony between Communists and Nationalists, pointing the way towards future conflict. In an attempt to solve the problem thousands of ex-Kuomintang soldiers and their families – who had been unable to join the bulk of their colleagues in Taiwan – were forcibly moved to the village of Rennies Mill, on Hong Kong Island, which remains today a bastion of Nationalist support.

This uneasy link with China was exploited by both sides throughout the 1960s, each action emphasising Hong Kong's odd position as both a British colony and a part of China, prey to the whims and fortunes of the Chinese leadership. In 1962, the point was made by the Chinese government in the so-called **trial run**, which allowed (and encouraged) upwards of 60,000 people to leave China for Hong Kong. The border was flooded, and though the British authorities were determined to keep such an influx out, there was little they could do in the face of blatant provocation from the Chinese army, which was directing the flow of people.

Things finally got out of hand in 1966–67, as the worst excesses of the Chinese **Cultural Revolution** began to spill over into the colony.

There had already been serious rioting in Hong Kong in April 1966, ostensibly against a price rise in the first-class Star Ferry fare. Against the background of increasing political turmoil in mainland China (where the Red Guards emerged in Beijing in August 1966), local strikes and unrest began to dominate the colony in spring of the following year. After deaths and rioting in neighbouring Macau, where the Portuguese authorities were overrun by Red Guard agitators, the situation in Hong Kong deteriorated, and May and June 1967 saw the worst violence yet: Government House was besieged by pro-China activists, there were cases of Europeans being attacked in the streets, and some policemen were killed on the Hong Kong–Chinese border. There were also riots and strikes, and a curfew was imposed; and in July a bomb exploded on Hong Kong Island, injuring nine people. However, apart from supportive and vociferous press reports in the pro-China newspapers, and a virulent anti-Imperialist/British poster campaign taken directly from the mainland, the organisers of the riots and unrest took little comfort from the attitude of Beijing. Chairman Mao was intent upon pursuing the Cultural Revolution to its fullest extent in China and had little time for what was happening in Hong Kong. Mao was also keen to avoid destabilising the colony, as it was an important source of revenue – a pragmatic attitude that determined the Chinese approach towards Hong Kong throughout this period. Although there were more disturbances throughout the rest of 1967, the protests fizzled out as tourism and confidence in the local economy gradually picked up again.

The 1970s: Social Problems

The economic gains of the postwar period were accompanied by the growth of a number of social problems that still trouble the colony today. The **population** continued to grow, bolstered by the ever-increasing number of immigrants, legal and (mostly) illegal, from China. There had been a housing shortage since the end of World War II, which this growth exacerbated, and **squatter huts** evolved throughout Hong Kong. Despite an emergency housing programme, these habitations still exist in places, prey to storms and fires which over the years have wrought havoc on various settlements. The first **New Town**, Tuen Mun, opened in 1973, was a prototype of the gleaming cities that now spread across the New Territories, housing

hundreds of thousands. It's hoped that these will eventually take the rest of Hong Kong's dispossessed, though in the meantime many thousands of people wait in grim resettlement camps, barrack-like tin huts with few facilities.

The rise in population caused concern in Hong Kong for other reasons. Although there was no unemployment, there were water and power shortages over the years, limited welfare facilities and poor public services, all of which had to be shared by more and more people. Resentment against the new arrivals was nothing new but was to have an importance after 1975, when the first of the **Vietnamese boat people** – fleeing their country after the North Vietnamese victory – fetched up in the colony. Although no one was turned away (a credit to the Hong Kong authorities even now), the numbers involved soon soared to frightening proportions – 65,000 refugees in 1979, many of whom had no chance of subsequent resettlement in other parts of the world.

The other major problem during this period was that of **crime and corruption**, endemic in Hong Kong since the founding of the colony. In modern times, crime was fuelled in particular by the number of Chinese illegal immigrants, who had little else to turn to once the Hong Kong authorities began to make it harder for them to secure official papers and earn a living. This was mirrored by the emerging scale of **official and police corruption** throughout the 1960s, which touched most aspects of life, from accepting bribes from street traders through to police cover-ups of serious illegal activity – a state of affairs only partly redeemed by the setting up in 1974 of the **Independent Commission Against Corruption**.

The Triads

Behind much of the major crime and corruption in Hong Kong were the various secretive **Triad** organisations, akin to the Sicilian Mafia in scale and wealth, though probably unrivalled in terms of sheer viciousness. Triads (so-called because their emblem was a triangle denoting harmony between Heaven, Earth and Man) were first established in the seventeenth century in China, in an attempt to restore the Ming Dynasty after its overthrow by the Manchus. They moved into Hong Kong early in the colony's history, where they were able to organise among the new immigrants, splitting up into separate societies with their own elaborate initiation rites and ceremonies. The Triad organisations relied on a hierarchical structure, with ranks denoted by numbers which begin with 4 – representing the four elements, compass points and seas.

After World War II, with the colony in tatters, refugees and immigrants from newly Communist China moved into Hong Kong, many to the Walled City in Kowloon, which became a notorious criminal haven, protected by the Chinese assertions of legal rule over this small enclave on Hong Kong territory. The Walled City became a no-go area for the Hong Kong police, while the number of groups operating throughout the colony rose to around fifty – with possibly 100,000 members in all, operating everything from street gangs upwards to organised crime.

Towards 1997: The Political Moves

As China began to open up to the wider world in the early 1970s, Hong Kong's relationship with its neighbour improved dramatically. Trade between the two increased, as did Hong Kong's role as economic mediator between China and the West. Chinese investment in Hong Kong became substantial – in Chinese-owned banks, hotels, businesses, shops – and Hong Kong was a ready market for Chinese food products, even water. This shift in relationship was recognised in the mid-1970s, when the word "colony" was expunged from all official British titles in Hong Kong: in came the concept of Hong Kong as a "territory", which sounded much better to sensitive Chinese ears.

Against this background came the realisation that 1997 – and the handing back of the New Territories – was fast approaching. There was a general belief that it would be absurd to pretend that Hong Kong could survive without the New Territories, and that it was unlikely that China would want them without the money-making parts of Kowloon and Hong Kong Island.

The first tentative moves towards finding a solution occurred in **1982**, when British Prime Minister Margaret Thatcher visited China and Hong Kong. Certain injudicious remarks by her on that tour, concerning British responsibility to Hong Kong's citizens and the validity of the original treaties ceding the territory to Britain, caused the Chinese to make an issue of the sovereignty question. As far as they were concerned, Hong Kong and its people were Chinese, so any

responsibility was that of Beijing. To the Chinese government, historically the treaties had been "unequal" (that is, forced by a strong nineteenth-century Britain on a weak China) and therefore illegal. After Thatcher had gone home, and the dust had settled, talks continued, with both sides agreeing that their aim was the "prosperity and stability" of a future Hong Kong, while arguing about the question of sovereignty. It became clear during 1983 that Britain would eventually concede sovereignty to China, and that Britain would abandon all claims to Hong Kong, not just the New Territories.

After two years of debate and uncertainty, which had a negative influence on business and confidence in the colony, the **Sino-British Joint Declaration** was signed in September 1984, with Britain agreeing to hand back sovereignty of the entire territory to China in 1997. In return, Hong Kong would continue with the same legal and capitalistic system for at least the next fifty years, becoming a "Special Administrative Region" (SAR) of China, in which it would have virtual autonomy – a concept the Chinese labelled as "one country, two systems". Almost immediately, the declaration haunted the British government: no changes to the document were allowed after it was signed and, as people began to point out in the colony, with virtually no democratic institutions in place in Hong Kong, the Chinese would effectively be able to do what they liked after 1997. Only the economic necessity to retain Hong Kong's wealth-producing status would limit their actions, and even that wouldn't be enough in the face of any radical change in leadership in Beijing.

The declaration was followed by the publication in Beijing in 1988 of the **Basic Law**, a sort of constitutional framework for explaining how the SAR of Hong Kong would work in practice. Again, in theory, the Basic Law guaranteed the preservation of the existing capitalist system in Hong Kong, along with various freedoms – of travel, speech, of the right to strike, etc – that were deemed necessary to sustain confidence. But, in spite of this, concern grew steadily in Hong Kong. Only a third of the Legislative Council seats were to be directly elected by 1997 (with half elected by 2003); vague references to the outlawing of "subversion" were disturbing to anyone who was even remotely critical of Beijing's actions; and China refused a referendum in Hong Kong on the provisions of the Basic Law. Despite a consultation exercise in Hong Kong, where the Hong

Kong government invited direct comment from the public on the Basic Law, confidence wasn't restored. Liberals in Hong Kong, in the Legislative Council and elsewhere, accused the British government of a sell-out, and of failing to implement democratic reforms that would at least provide some guarantee of stability after 1997. The **brain drain** of educated, professional people leaving Hong Kong for new countries, which had been picking up ever since 1984, began to increase more rapidly.

1989: Shattered Confidence

1989 was a grim year for Hong Kong. On June 4, following student-dominated pro-democracy demonstrations in China, Deng Xiaoping sent in the tanks to **Tiananmen Square** in Beijing to crush the protest – an act which killed hundreds, possibly thousands, of people, with many more arrested, jailed and executed in the following weeks. This put China on show as never before, and confirmed the worst fears of almost the entire Hong Kong population that the British government had indeed sold them out to a dangerous and murderous regime. No one now doubted that with the People's Liberation Army due to be stationed on Hong Kong territory after 1997, any future dissent in the colony against Chinese authoritarian rule could be stamped upon as easily as in Beijing, whatever the Basic Law said. And to indicate the seriousness of this view, the Hang Seng Index, the performance indicator of the Hong Kong Stock Exchange, dropped 22 percent on the Monday following the massacre.

Tiananmen Square was a particularly galling experience for Hong Kong's own **pro-democracy movement**, which had staged extraordinary rallies in support of the Beijing students – and which spirited several dissident Chinese students out of China to safety in the following months. Successive protest rallies in Hong Kong had brought out up to a million people on to the streets – almost twenty percent of the population – to demand democracy in China, and more significantly, more democracy in Hong Kong itself. A copy of Beijing's Goddess of Liberty was erected in Hong Kong after the massacre; Cantonese pop stars recorded a song, For Freedom, in support of the Chinese students; while in typical Hong Kong fashion, manufacturers cashed in on the protests with stores selling democracy armbands, headbands and T-shirts. Everywhere, the point was being made loudly

and angrily that without democratic institutions in place well before 1997, the territory and its people would be entirely at the mercy of the whims of the leaders in Beijing.

If there had been a brain drain from Hong Kong before June 4, it was now a flood. Embassies and consulates were swamped by people desperate for an escape route should things go wrong in the future. Singapore's announcement that it would be taking up to 25,000 Hong Kong Chinese over the next five to eight years led to fighting for application forms. Surveys and opinion polls showed that sixty percent of the population wished (and expected) to qualify for a foreign passport, and that one in six people would leave anyway before 1997.

On top of all this, the territory was enduring the worst problems yet caused by the continuing influx of the **Vietnamese boat people**. The summer sailing season saw the numbers top 50,000, the highest for a decade – and with fewer countries prepared to accept new immigrants, most Vietnamese arrivals were doomed to a protracted and unpleasant stay in Hong Kong's closed camps. As the camps filled and then burst, isolated and uninhabited outlying islands were used to hold the boat people. Shelter was in makeshift tents, conditions were unsanitary, food was poor, and, not surprisingly, trouble followed. There were disturbances in some of the camps – fighting between rival groups of Vietnamese, break-outs into the local villages, a few attempted suicides and the occasional murder – all of which the Hong Kong authorities could see no end to, given the numbers still arriving daily from across the South China Sea.

Into the 1990s

The turn of the decade brought no respite for Hong Kong. The two main problems were still the question of what would happen in 1997 and what to do with the Vietnamese. They were complicated and, in many ways, related questions, attracting emotional debate both in the territory and in Britain. Both matters affected the quality of life in Hong Kong, with many feeling that there was no assured future. Yet certain features of life in Hong Kong, like the **economy**, were still to be envied. The territory ranks eleventh in the world league of trading nations; it's the biggest container port in the world, the largest exporter of watches and radios (second largest of clothes and toys), and the fourth most important financial centre. Its economic growth has averaged eight percent a year for a decade; there's full employment; and it has a per capita income of around US $10,000 (second only to Japan in Asia). In addition, 60 percent of all China's exports pass through Hong Kong, while the territory accounts for 70 percent of foreign investment in China. It's a formidable record for a place that was devastated only forty years ago, and founded just a century before that.

Domestic Troubles

However, to pretend that everything else was rosy in this capitalistic garden would be naive in the extreme. **Crime** was on the increase throughout the period – although the Triads seemed intent upon moving out of Hong Kong before 1997, setting up shop in places like London and Amsterdam, Australia and Canada – while **drug addiction** was a major worry, with estimates of around 40,000 active drug users, 96 percent of them heroin addicts. And though the Far Eastern **sex trade** had shifted substantially to Thailand during the 1980s, the combination of prostitution and needle-sharing contributed to marked increases in the AIDS figures.

Most disturbing of all, however, was that despite Hong Kong's long association with Britain, and British protestations that she had a duty to the territory's citizens, Hong Kong had few of the **rights and privileges** that people in Britain enjoyed and expected. There was no democracy worth the name (see below); citizens could be stopped and searched by the police at any time, and forced to carry an ID card; public welfare provision was limited; while over the years, the citizens of Hong Kong had been stripped of the right of abode in Britain by successive racist Immigration Acts. Told to consider themselves British for a century and a half for the purposes of government and administration, the vast majority of the Hong Kong Chinese – having given up Chinese nationality in order to become subjects of the British Crown – were effectively stateless.

The Passport Question

The problem of the duty of the British government to the territory's population was crystallised into the **passport question**. Since the events in Tiananmen Square, increasing numbers in Hong Kong had sought a second passport so that if China went back on the promises enshrined in the Joint Declaration they would have an "insurance policy" – the right to leave the territory and live elsewhere.

The issue was not strictly whether or not people were able to get hold of such passports. Many countries, from Paraguay to The Gambia were willing virtually to sell passports (and thus citizenship) to the large numbers of Hong Kong Chinese wishing to leave. All it took was the money. However, this was obviously an option open only to the wealthy and the well-connected. The moral question faced by the British government was whether or not to grant the **right of abode** to all the citizens of Hong Kong, so that people would have a choice of where to live after 1997.

After 1997, anyone without a passport automatically becomes a citizen of the PRC. The view **in Hong Kong** was that Britain had a duty to the territory's people, which involved overturning the various Immigration Acts passed in Britain and restoring their right of abode in Britain by giving them full British passports. It was argued that most people wanted to stay in Hong Kong anyway, and that, given the choice, most certainly wouldn't want to come to Britain – by far the most popular destinations for Hong Kong Chinese leaving the territory are Canada and Australia, where there are large Chinese populations. But the right to a passport would give the residents of Hong Kong more security, and thus lend the territory more stability.

The view of the **British government** was confused from the start. Having effectively made many Hong Kong people stateless through the provisions of the 1981 British Nationality Act (Hong Kong people hold a British "dependent territories" or "overseas national" passport), the government argued that insurance policies exist to be used. It claimed all those with passports would in fact come to Britain, which would be disastrous for housing and social security measures, and for race relations in the UK. The figures were uncertain (it depends whether you count the whole Hong Kong population or just those with dependent territory passports), but the spectre of between three and a half million and five million people flooding into Britain was raised. Instead, the government – by way of the British Nationality (Hong Kong) Act – offered full passports and space in Britain for 50,000 "key personnel", in effect, high-ranking civil servants and police officers, technical and professional people, businesspeople and the wealthy, plus their families – a figure of around 225,000 in all. This was designed to ensure that these people stayed in Hong Kong, unless things became intolerable; placements were determined by a points system and the governor had the final judgement on the matter.

This was clearly a tokenistic offer, and although it's arguable whether anything like three and a half million people would have come in any case, there was fierce opposition in the UK to the plan. In fact, with 1992 and the single European market looming, those who did come would have had the right to settle anywhere in the European Community, not just Britain (which most Hong Kong Chinese people find cold and economically backward).

The situation was further confused by the **attitude of the British people**, who in opinion polls said that they opposed letting any substantial number of Hong Kong Chinese settle in Britain. The opposition Labour Party particularly was torn between its moral heart and its political head: it knew that to call for a large influx of non-white immigrants into Britain would cost it dear in terms of support from the very people it needed to put it back into power.

The Chinese government, too, started to criticise Britain for supposedly reneging on the terms of the Joint Declaration, saying that whatever happened, it wouldn't honour the full British passports issued, as the people in Hong Kong would be Chinese citizens after 1997 – and thus not entitled to leave or enter the territory on so-called "foreign" passports.

The Vietnamese

There was an ironic twist to the nationality debate for the people of Hong Kong regarding the fate of the **Vietnamese boat people**, who had been landing in the territory since 1975. While seeking overseas passports themselves, the people of Hong Kong were increasingly adamant that the unfortunate refugees from Vietnam should not be allowed to stay in the territory. From having initially offered sanctuary to the boat people – the only Southeast Asian state to do so – Hong Kong now felt inclined to tow the Vietnamese back out to sea.. Partly it was frustration with the lack of any progress in finding an international solution to the problem – successive Geneva conferences failed to come up with sufficient quotas from countries prepared to take the boat people. But it was a little rich

from a people which one day hoped to seek sanctuary itself.

The situation became even more ironic once the British government decided upon its course of action towards the boat people in Hong Kong. Those deemed "economic migrants" were to be repatriated to Vietnam – forcibly if necessary – while long screening procedures would sort out the genuine refugees, thought to be ten percent of the total, who would be guaranteed resettlement in a third country. The first **forced repatriation** took place in December 1989, and a pathetic sight it was, as 51 men, women and children were herded into trucks by armed police and forced on to an aeroplane back to Vietnam. It drew worldwide condemnation, but was supported in Hong Kong at most levels – though quite what the distinction was between Vietnamese economic migrants and those Chinese who fled China in the 1950s to set up in Hong Kong, or those who now seek to flee Hong Kong for whichever third country will have them, was never satisfactorily explained.

Britain's tougher stance led to a marked decrease in the numbers sailing to Hong Kong, though there is considerable evidence that the Vietnamese simply headed to other nearby countries instead – shifting rather than alleviating the problem. There was also an upturn in the Vietnamese economy at the turn of the decade, which perhaps persuaded many would-be migrants to stay. Whatever the truth, the last boat recorded as entering Hong Kong was in late 1991 (with only the odd refugee adding to the total since).

Meanwhile, in Hong Kong, conditions deteriorated in the nine **camps** in which the Vietnamese were held. At its peak, the camps' population was just over 64,000 people – conditions were basic and exacerbated by violent clashes between the different Vietnamese factions contained within. In the worst incident, 21 people died at Shek Kong camp in a fire set during a fight between north and south Vietnamese groups.

By mid-1993, the camps' population had diminished to around 42,000 as the number of **voluntary returnees** steadily increased. Of these, only 2400 were considered to be genuine refugees (and will be resettled elsewhere), though 9000 are still to be screened. The other 30,000 will return to Vietnam either voluntarily or compulsorily. There has been an average return rate of 1000 a month since Britain and Vietnam finally reached agreement in October 1991 on the method of return. Overseen by the United Nations High Commission for Refugees (UNHCR), those who volunteer to return to Vietnam receive a US$50 bonus and US$30 a month during their first year back; forced returnees are supervised by the Orderly Return Programme and get the $30 a month but not the bonus. The Hong Kong government hopes to have the screening process for refugee status finished by 1994 and the camps closed down, with their entire populations returned to Vietnam by the end of 1995.

The New Politics

The **Basic Law** - the projected "constitution" for Hong Kong as a Special Administrative Region of China after 1997 - was finally approved by China's National People's Congress in April 1990, and immediately provided a focus around which people in Hong Kong began to question the lack of democratic progress in the territory.

Leaders in Hong Kong were particularly outraged by the attitude of the British government, which - in their eyes - during the consultations on the Basic Law had capitulated every step of the way to the Chinese. China, for obvious reasons, is keen to have as little democracy as possible in place in Hong Kong by 1997, and the final draft of the Basic Law as passed had worrying implications for the future - a promise of eventual universal suffrage was deleted, Beijing will have the power to declare martial law in Hong Kong, and an anti-subversion clause was added.

Out of the protests against the Basic Law grew a new **political awareness**, which expressed itself in a number of emerging pressure groups and fledgling political parties. The **Hong Kong Alliance in Support of the Patriotic and Democratic Movement** organised a 10,000-strong rally in April 1990, defying warnings from China to stop this kind of "provocation". One of the leading liberal activists in Hong Kong, Martin Lee, a barrister, became head of a new pro-democracy party **United Democrats of Hong Kong** (UDHK); the other main grouping is the conservative, business-led (and confusingly named) **Liberal Democratic Federation**.

In **elections** in September 1991 - the territory's first direct elections - United Democrat candidates swept the board, winning 16 of the 18 seats on the 60-seat Legislative Council (Legco) that were up for grabs. It was a limited exercise in democracy - 21 other candidates were selected by so-called "functional constituencies," consisting of trade and professional groups, while the rest were appointed by the Governor - but it sent a powerful message to Beijing that Hong Kong people were dissatisfied with the provisions of the Basic Law. Even more alarming for Beijing was the fact that pro-China candidates failed to win a single seat.

Despite the advance of the United Democrats, the Governor, David (later Sir David) Wilson refused to appoint liberals to his Executive Council (Exco) - a move welcomed in Beijing, though denigrated in Hong Kong. Indeed, Wilson's role in Hong Kong's government became increasingly suspect in the eyes of many, who accused him of giving in too readily to the Chinese. His fate was sealed when new British Prime Minister John Major was forced to travel to Beijing to sign the agreement for Hong Kong's new airport. Major's presence at the signing ceremony was virtually a condition of the agreement, and it was seen very much as an embarrassment for the British that Wilson, with his diplomatic skills, should have avoided.

Fortuitously, as it turned out for the Prime Minister, his close ally **Chris Patten** - Conservative Party chairman - lost his parliamentary seat in Britain's April 1992 elections, even as his party was returned to power. Major offered him the governorship, which he eventually accepted, ushering in a new political era in Hong Kong.

The Last Governor - and the Future

Chris Patten was the 28th - and almost certainly last - **Governor** to be appointed, but uniquely he was the first career politician to take the post. His arrival caused consternation all round: among the local population, who complained about having Britain's cast-off politicians imposed upon them; and among the Chinese leadership who - rightly as it turned out - feared Patten's motives for taking the job.

Any thoughts that Chris Patten was there to make up the numbers until 1997 soon disappeared. He quickly jettisoned much of the colonial paraphernalia associated with his position, while in talks with Beijing it became clear that he - and Britain - sought an extension in the **franchise** for Hong Kong before the handover to China, that went beyond the provisions made in the Basic Law. Under the Basic Law, in elections scheduled for 1995, Legco will still have 60 members, but the number of elected members will rise from 18 to 20 (to 30 by 2003). This had already been dismissed by Hong Kong liberals as too slow a move towards democracy: United Democrats want 50 percent of Legco directly elected in 1995, rising to 100 percent by 2003. Patten's proposal was to stick to the number of directly elected members agreed with China, but to widen the franchise, by lowering the voting age from 21 to 18; by increasing the number of indirectly elected council members; and by creating extra "functional constituencies", which would effectively enfranchise 2.7 million Hong Kong people – as opposed to the roughly 200,000 voters that the present system allows, which is vociferously supported by China.

The Chinese government began a loud campaign against the new Governor and his proposals, and **relations between Britain and China** worsened considerably. The Chinese were adamant that the franchise should not be extended in this way, seeing the move – correctly – as a Western attempt to import democracy into China by the back door. As talks dragged on, and relations soured, new threats were made to Hong Kong's stability. China vowed to renege on all contracts and commercial agreements signed by the Hong Kong government without its consent as soon as the colony was returned to its control in 1997 – something that threatened the future of several major projects, including the new Chek Lap Kok airport. The Hang Seng Index reflected a general lack of confidence in the territory's future by recording massive falls; and rumours of destabilisation by the Chinese government caused huge runs on two of Hong Kong's largest banks, Citibank and the Standard Chartered. China also reiterated its non-recognition of the UK passports offered to the 50,000 key Hong Kong personnel. In the meantime, Britain had announced a new British National Overseas (BNO) passport to replace the British Dependent Territories passport after 1997 – the BNO passport would grant British consular protection outside China, but not the right of abode in the UK.

The situation has reached something of a **stalemate**, with both sides playing a nerve-wracking poker game with the territory's future.

Meetings throughout 1993 consistently failed to provide any breakthrough with China hostile to Governor Patten's very presence in any negotiations and Britain adamant that its limited democratic proposals should prevail.

In the end, though, it's China that holds all the aces: in simple terms, the Chinese government can afford to wait until 1997, when – once back in control of Hong Kong – they can do what they please. China has already vowed to overturn any change in the election laws and hold elections on its own terms in 1997. It is also insisting on the right to veto any "subversive" legislators appointed before 1997, a move which hits at the heart of the Patten proposals since the victors in the 1995 elections are almost certain to be those liberals associated with United Democrats leader, Martin Lee, and his close ally, Szeto Wah. Britain and Hong Kong, for their part, insist on a "through train", whereby legislators in place by 1997 should be allowed to remain.

The National People's Congress (NPC) in China has also approved the establishment of a "working body" on Hong Kong – in effect, a parallel administration that could replace the existing one on the day after the handover. Advisers appointed by China include an erstwhile acting governor, Sir David Akers Jones and Allen Lee, a former senior Legco member and one-time supporter of the colonial government – both expected to become leading players when China takes over in 1997.

Governor Patten's firm line commands respectable support in Hong Kong, but all sides sport weaknesses in their negotiating positions. China itself needs the Western investment that Hong Kong provides and is desperate to retain Most Favoured Nation (MFN) status with the USA; above all, it's keen to re-establish itself in the eyes of the world following the break in relations that occurred after the events in Tiananmen Square in 1989. In Hong Kong, conservative business groups press for an accommodation with China, arguing that the territory's future prosperity rests on co-operation and not confrontation, but the various conservative and pro-Beijing factions have commanded little popular support so far. Conversely, United Democrats and other liberals see full democracy by 1997 as the only safeguard against future Chinese clampdowns – but privately concede that there is little hope of this happening, given the constraints of the Basic Law within which they have to operate.

However, in many ways the most indefensible position is that adopted by the British government and its representative in Hong Kong, the Governor. Adopting the high moral ground and arguing forcefully for democracy now, Britain conveniently forgets the past. For 150 years, there has been no real democracy in Hong Kong. Successive governments have shown no interest in establishing a democratic forum, and liberal reforms – like the abolition of the death penalty and the legalisaion of homosexuality – have only occurred in the past few years, decades after similar reforms were enacted in Britain itself. In April 1992 the International Commission of Jurists (ICJ) claimed that Britain had broken the law when deciding to give only 50,000 key citizens the right to settle in Britain. The ICJ maintained that the people of Hong Kong had a right to self-determination which should have been tested in a referendum before the Joint Declaration was signed in 1984. It concluded that all three million British Dependent Territory citizens should be given the right of abode in the UK – something that the British government has never had any intention of doing. Moreover, Governor Patten's movements are circumscribed by Britain's long-term wish to maintain cordial relations with China because of the trading opportunities that are involved.

Time is rapidly running out for the people of Hong Kong, whose only real hope is that the aged leadership in Beijing is defunct by 1997. As they were for centuries, the stability and prosperity of Hong Kong are once again dependent on China.

Books

There's no shortage of books written about Hong Kong and Macau, especially as the time approaches when they'll both be handed back to the Chinese. You'll find that you can get most of them in Hong Kong, too; for a list of main bookshop addresses in Hong Kong, see p.262. What there is a lack of – certainly in translation – is books about both territories written by Chinese authors; only Timothy Mo redresses the balance. In the reviews below, the UK publisher is listed first, followed by the publisher in the US – unless the title is available in one country only, in which case we've specified the country; o/p signifies out of print.

Hong Kong

History and Politics

Nigel Cameron *Power* (OUP East Asia in UK). Immensely detailed history of the *China Light & Power Co*, one of Hong Kong's biggest economic successes. More interesting, though, for the insight it offers into one of the territory's main power-broking families, the Kadoories.

Austin Coates *Myself a Mandarin* (OUP East Asia in UK). Light-hearted account of the author's time as a magistrate in the colonial administration during the 1950s. For more from the prolific Coates, see "Macau" below.

Maurice Collis *Foreign Mud* (Gordon Brash Singapore, Norton in US – o/p). Useful coverage of the opening up of China to trade and of the opium wars.

Robert Cottrell *The End of Hong Kong: The Secret Diplomacy of Imperial Retreat* (John Murray in UK). One of the most recent perusals of the manoeuv-

rings between Britain and China, this is a lucid enough account for anyone interested in how Hong Kong will be handed over to the Chinese. Well written and perceptive.

E. J. Eitel *Europe in China* (OUP East Asia in UK). First published in 1895, this is an out-and-out colonial history of early Hong Kong – lively, biased and interesting.

G. B. Endacott *A History of Hong Kong* (OUP in UK and US – o/p), *Hong Kong Eclipse* (OUP East Asia in UK). Hong Kong's most important postwar historian, Endacott's is still the standard history and usually available in public libraries. *Hong Kong Eclipse* deals with the fraught period 1941–45, the Japanese occupation, and is a comprehensive, general account relying on first-hand accounts and official records.

Jean Gittins *Stanley: Behind Barbed Wire* (HK Univ. Press – o/p). Well-written and moving eyewitness account of time spent behind bars at Stanley Prison during the internment of civilians by the Japanese in World War II.

Kevin Rafferty *City on the Rocks: Hong Kong's Uncertain Future* (Penguin in UK and US). One of the latest surveys of Hong Kong's history, people and institutions. Wide-ranging and knowledgable, this big book marshals all the usual views and looks to the future, putting Hong Kong firmly on the world's economic and political stage.

Gerald Segal *The Fate of Hong Kong* (Simon & Schuster in UK). Excellent current round-up of the various interests at work in deciding Hong Kong's future, and incorporating informed accounts of what the effects of 1997 are likely to have on the rest of the region.

Peter Wesley-Smith *Unequal Treaty 1898–1997* (OUP in UK and US). Sound and detailed review of the leasing of the New Territories to Britain in 1898, recording the reaction of both the British and Chinese authorities along the way. Written before the Joint Declaration, but full of pertinent comment about the future difficulties concerning the expiry of the lease.

Gavin Young *Beyond Lion Rock* (Penguin in UK). Dismal account of the history of *Cathay Pacific*

Airways, which although started in Shanghai after World War II, came to international prominence from its later base in Hong Kong under the wing of the Swire company. On the whole a full-blown apology for some fairly unappealing characters.

Travel, Reference and Contemporary Life

Emily Hahn *China to Me* (Virago/Da Capo). A breathless account of pre- and postwar jinks in (mainly) Shanghai and Hong Kong, including time when the American author and her child lived under Japanese rule in the territory as her friends were interned. In print for the first time in over forty years, it's a good read.

Susanna Hoe *The Private Life of Old Hong Kong* (OUP in UK and US). A history of the lives of Western women in Hong Kong from 1841–1941, recreated from contemporary letters and diaries. A fine book, and telling of the hitherto neglected contribution of a whole range of people who had a hand in shaping modern Hong Kong.

Hong Kong (Hong Kong Government Press). The HK government's official yearbook, published annually, and a detailed – if uncritical – mass of photos, statistics, essays and information. Available in most HK bookshops, or from the Hong Kong Government Office, 6 Grafton St, London W1 (☎071/499 9821).

Jan Morris *Hong Kong: Epilogue to an Empire* (Penguin/Vintage). Hong Kong – historical, contemporary and future – dealt with in typical Morris fashion: which means an engaging mix of anecdote, solid research, acute observation and lively opinion. One of the best introductions there is to the territory.

Eric Pang (ed.) *The Guide Maps of Hong Kong Streets* (Art's Publishing Co). Massively detailed book of maps and indexes that's a must if you're spending more than a few days in Hong Kong. Updated fairly regularly and available in Hong Kong bookshops, if not in Britain before you come.

Jackie Pullinger *Chasing the Dragon* (Hodder & Stoughton/Servant Publications). The missionary author spent the best part of two decades – the 1970s and 1980s – grubbing around in the Walled City and saving souls. Fine on Hong Kong low-life, but you soon get tired of the proselytising and doubt her success rate with hardened heroin addicts and Triad members. Her *Crack in the Wall* (Hodder & Stoughton in UK)

details Triad life in the Walled City and makes more interesting reading.

Madelaine H. Tang (and others) *Historical Walks: Hong Kong Island* (The Guidebook Company). An invaluable little book detailing five walks through parts of Hong Kong Island, with clear maps and directions. Available in most Hong Kong bookshops.

Fiction

James Adams *Taking the Tunnel* (Michael Joseph in UK). Ruthless Hong Kong-based Triad members hold a trainload of passengers hostage on the Channel Tunnel – a pacy thriller that ticks along nicely, incorporating authentic background touches throughout.

James Clavell *Tai-Pan* (Coronet/Dell), *Noble House* (Coronet/Dell). Big, thick bodice-rippers set respectively at the founding of the territory and in the 1960s, and dealing with the same one-dimensional pirates and businessmen. There's no real Hong Kong atmosphere in either. A much better read, incidentally, is his *King Rat*, set in Changi prisoner-of-war camp in Singapore where Clavell was a POW.

John Le Carré *The Honourable Schoolboy* (Coronet/Bantam). Taut George Smiley novel, with spooks and moles chasing each other across Hong Kong and the Far East. Accurate and enthusiastic reflections on the territory and the usual sharp eye trained on the intelligence world.

Elizabeth Darrell *Concerto* (Michael Joseph in UK). Blockbuster novel set against the background of the Japanese invasion of Hong Kong in 1941.

Somerset Maugham *The Painted Veil* (Mandarin/Viking Penguin). Colonial story of love, betrayal and revenge which unfolds in Hong Kong and moves on to cholera-ravaged mainland China. First published in 1925.

Timothy Mo *An Insular Possession* (Pan/Random House). A splendid novel, recreating the nineteenth-century foundation of Hong Kong, taking in the trading ports of Macau and Canton along the way. Mo's ear and eye for detail can also be glimpsed in *The Monkey King* (Vintage/Faber), his entertaining first novel about the conflicts and manoeuvrings of family life in postwar Hong Kong, and his filmed novel *Sour Sweet* (Vintage in UK and US) – an endearing tale of an immigrant Hong Kong family setting up business in 1960s London.

Macau

C. R. Boxer *Seventeenth Century Macau* (Heinemann in UK). Interesting survey of documents, engravings, inscriptions and maps of Macau culled from the years either side of the restoration of the Portuguese monarchy in 1640. An academic study, but accessible enough for some informative titbits about the enclave.

Daniel Carney *Macau* (Corgi/Zebra). Improbable characterisation in a Clavell-like thriller set in the enclave.

Austin Coates *Macao and the British* (OUP East Asia in UK), *A Macao Narrative* (OUP East Asia in UK), *City of Broken Promises* (OUP East Asia in UK). Coates has written widely about the Far East, where he was Assistant Colonial Secretary in Hong Kong in the 1950s. *Macao and the British* follows the early years of Anglo-Chinese relations and underlines the importance of the Portuguese enclave as a staging-post for other traders. *A Macao Narrative* is a short but more specific account of Macau's history up to the mid-1970s; *City of Broken Promises* is an entertaining historical novel set in Macau in the late eighteenth century.

Cesar Guillen-Nunez *Macau* (OUP in UK and US). Decent, slim hardback history of Macau, worth packing for the insights it offers into the churches, buildings and gardens of the city.

Books About China

David Bonavia *The Chinese* (Penguin/Viking Penguin). Excellent introduction to the Chinese – their lives, aspirations, politics and problems. Intended as a discussion of the Chinese of the People's Republic, it remains useful and instructive for all travellers to Asia.

John King Fairbank *The Great Chinese Revolution 1800–1985* (Pan/Harper & Row). Readable and enjoyable account of the opening up of China since the turn of the nineteenth century. Good for straightforward explanation of the tricky manoeuvring before and after the Revolution in 1949.

Michael Fathers and Andrew Higgins *Tiananmen: the Rape of Peking* (Doubleday in UK and US). Eyewitness account of the events leading up to the massacre in and around Tiananmen Square in 1989. A studied report of horror which leaves you feeling numb.

Christopher Hibbert *China and the West 1793–1911* (Penguin/Viking Penguin). Superbly entertaining account of the opening up of China to Western trade and influence. Hibbert leaves you in no doubt about the cultural misunderstandings that bedevilled early missions to China – or about the morally dubious acquisition of Hong Kong and the other Treaty Ports by Western powers.

Astrology: the Chinese Calendar and Horoscopes

Most people are interested to find out what sign they are in the Chinese zodiac system, particularly since – like the Western system – each person is supposed to have characteristics similar to those of the sign which relates to their birthdate. There are twelve signs of the Chinese zodiac, corresponding with one of twelve animals, whose characteristics you'll find listed below. These animal signs have existed in Chinese folk tradition since the sixth century BC, though it wasn't until the third century BC that they were incorporated into a formal study of astrology and astronomy, based around the device of the lunar calendar. Quite why animals emerged as the vehicle for Chinese horoscopy is unclear: one story has it that the animals used are the twelve which appeared before the command of Buddha, who named the years in the order in which the animals arrived.

Each **lunar year** (which starts in late January/early February) is represented by one of the twelve animal symbols. Your sign depends on the year you were born – check the **calendar chart** below – rather than the month as in the western system, but beyond that the idea is the same: born under the sign of a particular animal, you will have certain characteristics, ideal partners, lucky and unlucky days. The details below will tell you the basic facts about your character and personality, though it's only a rough guide: to go into your real Chinese astrological self, you

need to be equipped with your precise date and time of birth and one of the books listed below, which can explain all the horoscopical bits and pieces. The **animals** always appear in the same order so that if you know the current year you can always work out which one is to influence the following Chinese New Year. 1993 was the Year of the Rooster.

The Rat

Characteristics: usually generous, intelligent and hard-working, but can be petty and idle; has lots of friends, but few close ones; may be successful, likes challenges and is good at business, but is insecure; generally diplomatic; tends to get into emotional entanglements.

Partners: best-suited to Dragon, Monkey and Ox; doesn't get on with Horse and Goat.

Famous Rats: Wolfgang Amadeus Mozart, William Shakespeare, Marlon Brando, Doris Day, Yves St Laurent, Leo Tolstoy, Jimmy Carter and Prince Charles.

The Ox

Characteristics: healthy; obstinate; independent; usually calm and cool, but can get stroppy at times; shy and conservative; likes the outdoors and old-fashioned things; always finishes a task.

Partners: best-suited to Snake, Rat or Rooster; doesn't get on with Tiger, Goat or Monkey.

Famous Oxen: Walt Disney, Adolf Hitler, Napoleon Bonaparte, Richard Nixon, Vincent Van Gogh, Peter Sellers, Dustin Hoffman, Robert Redford, Margaret Thatcher, Shirley Bassey, Jane Fonda, Pieter Paul Rubens.

The Tiger

Characteristics: adventurous; creative and idealistic; confident and enthusiastic; can be diplomatic and practical; fearless and forward, aiming at impossible goals, though a realist with a forceful personality.

Calendar Chart

Date Of Birth	Animal	Date Of Birth	Animal
1.2.1900–18.2.1901	Rat	10.2.1948–28.1.1949	Rat
19.2.1901–7.2.1902	Ox	29.1.1949–16.2.1950	Ox
8.2.1902–28.1.1903	Tiger	17.2.1950–5.2.1951	Tiger
29.1.1903–15.2.1904	Rabbit	6.2.1951–26.1.1952	Rabbit
16.2.1904–3.2.1905	Dragon	27.1.1952–13.2.1953	Dragon
4.2.1905–24.1.1906	Snake	14.2.1953–2.2.1954	Snake
25.1.1906–12.2.1907	Horse	3.2.1954–23.1.1955	Horse
13.2.1907–1.2.1908	Goat	26.1.1955–11.2.1956	Goat
2.2.1908–21.1.1909	Monkey	12.2.1956–30.1.1957	Monkey
22.1.1909–9.2.1910	Rooster	31.1.1957–17.2.1958	Rooster
10.2.1910–29.1.1911	Dog	18.2.1958–7.2.1959	Dog
30.1.1911–17.2.1912	Pig	8.2.1959–27.1.1960	Pig
18.2.1912–5.2.1913	Rat	28.1.1960–14.2.1961	Rat
6.2.1913–25.1.1914	Ox	15.2.1961–4.2.1962	Ox
26.1.1914–13.2.1915	Tiger	5.2.1962–24.1.1963	Tiger
14.2.1915–3.2.1916	Rabbit	25.1.1963–12.2.1964	Rabbit
4.2.1916–22.1.1917	Dragon	13.2.1964–1.2.1965	Dragon
23.1.1917–10.2.1918	Snake	2.2.1965–20.1.1966	Snake
11.2.1918–31.1.1919	Horse	21.1.1966–8.2.1967	Horse
1.2.1919–19.2.1920	Goat	9.2.1967–29.1.1968	Goat
20.2.1920–7.2.1921	Monkey	30.1.1968–16.2.1969	Monkey
8.2.1921–27.1.1922	Rooster	17.2.1969–5.2.1970	Rooster
28.1.1922–15.2.1923	Dog	6.2.1970–26.1.1971	Dog
16.2.1923–4.2.1924	Pig	27.1.1971–14.2.1972	Pig
5.2.1924–23.1.1925	Rat	15.2.1972–2.2.1973	Rat
24.1.1925–12.2.1926	Ox	3.2.1973–22.1.1974	Ox
13.2.1926–1.2.1927	Tiger	23.1.1974–10.2.1975	Tiger
2.2.1927–22.1.1928	Rabbit	11.2.1975–30.1.1976	Rabbit
23.1.1928–9.2.1929	Dragon	31.1.1976–17.2.1977	Dragon
10.2.1929–29.1.1930	Snake	18.2.1977–6.2.1978	Snake
30.1.1930–16.2.1931	Horse	7.2.1978–27.1.1979	Horse
17.2.1931–5.2.1932	Goat	28.1.1979–15.2.1980	Goat
6.2.1932–25.1.1933	Monkey	16.2.1980–4.2.1981	Monkey
26.1.1933–13.2.1934	Rooster	5.2.1981–24.1.1982	Rooster
14.2.1934–3.2.1935	Dog	25.1.1982–12.2.1983	Dog
4.2.1935–23.1.1936	Pig	13.2.1983–1.2.1984	Pig
24.1.1936–10.2.1937	Rat	2.2.1984–19.2.1985	Rat
11.2.1937–30.1.1938	Ox	20.2.1985–8.2.1986	Ox
31.1.1938–18.2.1939	Tiger	9.2.1986–28.1.1987	Tiger
19.2.1939–7.2.1940	Rabbit	29.1.1987–16.2.1988	Rabbit
8.2.1940–26.1.1941	Dragon	17.2.1988–5.2.1989	Dragon
27.1.1941–14.2.1942	Snake	6.2.1989–26.1.1990	Snake
15.2.1942–4.2.1943	Horse	27.1.1990–14.2.1991	Horse
5.2.1943–24.1.1944	Goat	15.2.1991–3.2.1992	Goat
25.1.1944–12.2.1945	Monkey	4.2.1992–22.1.1993	Monkey
13.2.1945–1.2.1946	Rooster	23.1.1993–9.2.1994	Rooster
2.2.1946–21.1.1947	Dog	10.2.1994–30.1.1995	Dog
22.1.1947–9.2.1948	Pig	31.1.1995–18.2.1996	Pig

Partners: best-suited to Horse for marriage; gets on with Dragon, Pig and Dog; avoid Snake, Monkey and Ox.

Famous Tigers: Karl Marx, Queen Elizabeth II, Alec Guinness, Stevie Wonder, Ludwig van Beethoven, Marilyn Monroe, Princess Anne, Diana Rigg, Charles de Gaulle, Rudolf Nureyev.

The Rabbit

Characteristics: peace-loving; sociable but quiet; devoted to family and friends; timid but can be good at business; needs reassurance and affection to avoid being upset; can be vain; long-lived.

Partners: best-suited to Pig, Dog and Goat; not friendly with Tiger and Rooster.

Famous Rabbits: Fidel Castro, Bob Hope, Harry Belafonte, David Frost, Martin Luther King, Josef Stalin, Queen Victoria, Ali McGraw and Albert Einstein.

The Dragon

Characteristics: strong, commanding, a leader; popular, athletic; bright, chivalrous and idealistic, though not always consistent; likely to be a believer in equality.

Partners: best-suited to Snake, Rat, Monkey, Tiger and Rooster; avoid Dog.

Famous Dragons: Joan of Arc, Ringo Starr, Mae West, John Lennon, Frank Sinatra, Salvador Dali, Jimmy Connors, Kirk Douglas, Che Guevara, Shirley Temple Black and Yehudi Menuhin.

The Snake

Characteristics: charming, but possessive and selfish; private and secretive; strange sense of humour; mysterious and inquisitive; ruthless; likes the nice things in life; a thoughtful person, but superstitious.

Partners: best-suited for marriage to Dragon, Rooster and Ox; avoid Snake, Pig and Tiger.

Famous Snakes: J. F. Kennedy, Abraham Lincoln, Edgar Allen Poe, Mao Zedong, Pablo Picasso, Brahms, Franz Schubert and Ferdinand Marcos.

The Horse

Characteristics: nice appearance and deft; ambitious and quick-witted; favours bold colours; popular, with a sense of humour, gracious and gentle; can be good at business; fickle and emotional.

Partners: best-suited to Tiger, Dog and Goat; doesn't get on with Rabbit and Rat.

Famous Horses: Neil Armstrong, Barbara Streisand, Paul McCartney, Chris Evert, Theodore Roosevelt, Rembrandt, Raquel Welch, Leonid Brezhnev and Igor Stravinsky.

The Goat

Characteristics: a charmer and a lucky person who likes money; unpunctual and hesitant; too fond of complaining; interested in the supernatural.

Partners: best-suited to Horse, Pig and Rabbit; avoid Ox and Dog.

Famous Goats: Andy Warhol, Billie Jean King, Liberace, Mohammed Ali, Michelangelo, Laurence Olivier, James Michener and Diana Dors.

The Monkey

Characteristics: very intelligent and sharp, an opportunist; daring and confident, but unstable and egoistic; entertaining and very attractive to others; inventive; a sense of humour but with little respect for reputations.

Partners: best-suited to Dragon and Rat; doesn't get on with Tiger and Ox.

Famous Monkeys: Leonardo da Vinci, Mick Jagger, Bette Davis, Charles Dickens, Julius Caesar, Paul Gauguin, Joan Crawford and Rene Descartes.

The Rooster

Characteristics: frank and reckless, and can be tactless; free with advice; punctual and a hard worker; imaginative to the point of dreaming; likes to be noticed; emotional.

Partners: best-suited to Snake, Dragon and Ox; doesn't get on with Pig, Rabbit and Rooster.

Famous Roosters: Michael Caine, Prince Philip, Charles Darwin, Peter Ustinov, Elton John, Katharine Hepburn, Peter O'Toole and Yves Montand.

The Dog

Characteristics: alert, watchful and defensive; can be generous and is patient; very responsible and has good organisational skills; spiritual, home-loving and non-materialistic.

Partners: best-suited to Rabbit, Pig, Tiger and Horse; avoid Dragon and Goat.

Famous Dogs: David Niven, Henry Moore, Brigitte Bardot, Liza Minnelli, Zsa Zsa Gabor, Winston Churchill, Elvis Presley, Golda Meir, Sophia Loren and Voltaire.

The Pig

Characteristics: honest; vulnerable and not good at business, but still materialistic and ambitious; outgoing and outspoken, but naive; kind and helpful to the point of being taken advantage of; calm and genial.

Partners: best-suited to Dog, Goat, Tiger and Rabbit; avoid Snake and Rooster.

Famous Pigs: Alfred Hitchcock, Ronald Reagan, Maria Callas, Henry Kissinger, Woody Allen, Julie Andrews, Humphrey Bogart, Al Capone, Ernest Hemingway and Johnny Mathis.

Cantonese Recipes

Cantonese cooking is generally quick and simple, and with a few basic utensils and ingredients you can create a tasty, nutritious Cantonese meal in your own home. The recipes given below can either be attempted individually and eaten as snacks, or as part of a wider meal, making changes and additions as suggested. There's nothing particularly complicated about the recipes; they're examples of good, basic home cooking, the sort of things you'd eat every day in a Chinese home in Hong Kong – though not necessarily in a restaurant, where people take the opportunity to eat more elaborate, expensive food.

Utensils

The main utensil you need is a **wok**, a thin metal frying pan with deep sides and a curved bottom, designed to spread the heat evenly around the whole surface. A normal frying pan is not really a substitute. Woks generally come with either one long handle or two wooden side-handles, the first type for stir-frying, the second for steaming or deep-frying. Bought in Chinatown supermarkets, they're fairly inexpensive – the long-handled sort is best for general use. Fancy ones with plastic fittings, or "non-stick" ones, sold in department stores as "wok sets" are inferior in every way. Once you have your wok, you need to season it before use: rinse it in water, dry it, then heat it slowly for ten minutes or so wiped with a little oil; let it cool, and wipe the wok, repeating the whole process until the paper wipes clean. When in use, never clean a wok with detergent; always use plain water and dry thoroughly before storing it. If it rusts, scrub it off and season the wok again before use.

Really, the only other equipment you need for basic Cantonese cooking is a large **lid** for the wok, for use when steaming, and a **wok stand**, which makes a base for the wok over the gas flame or electric ring (gas is best for Cantonese cooking, since you can turn the heat off immediately; with electricity you have to take a little more care). You can use the **spatulas** and other ordinary kitchen utensils you already have, though if you're going to cook lots of Chinese

food, a long-handled metal spatula, a sieve and wooden chopsticks are all useful things to have. You can also buy **bamboo steamers**, which you place on a little metal stand inside your water-filled wok. They come in various sizes, but again, unless you're mad keen, you can make do with steaming fish and the like on a heat-resistant plate, which you place on top of the stand.

Ingredients

If you live near a Chinatown you'll be able to get all the ingredients you need for even the most elaborate of Cantonese meals. But most supermarkets and grocers carry the basics, certainly all the things you'll need to make all the recipes below. The main things to have in large supply are **garlic**, fresh **ginger** root (powdered is no good), **spring onions** and **peppers**, both capsicums and chilli peppers. Other flavourings are **soy sauce**, **oyster sauce** and **sesame oil**, and **vegetable oil** (or any mild-flavoured oil) to fry in.

Common **vegetables** are Chinese cabbage, baby corn, mushrooms and beansprouts. If you're lucky enough to have a specialist shop near you, stock up whenever you can on tinned (unless you can get fresh) **bamboo shoots**, **straw mushrooms** and **water chestnuts**; fresh **beancurd**; preserved **black beans**; and dried **Chinese mushrooms** – which you need to soak in hot water, preferably overnight, before use. With all these, a bottle of **rice wine**, some small, **dried shrimps**, and a selection of **nuts**, **noodles** and **rice**, there's barely a recipe you're not prepared for.

If you can't get all the right ingredients, don't worry. Chinese cooking is nothing if not adaptable. Remember, though, that the ingredients must complement the food being cooked, so don't substitute strong flavours for delicate ones; it's better to leave an ingredient out, than put in one that's overpowering. The most important rule of all is wherever possible to use **fresh food**.

The Recipes

All the recipes below will feed four people, unless otherwise stated. The beauty of Chinese food, though, is that since it's eaten communally, you can easily spin out meals to accommodate more, by cooking more of the basic things, like rice and soup. The other rule to follow is that you should aim to cook one more dish than the number of people present, and maintain the general balance between meat, fish and vegetable dishes.

Soup

Soup is an indispensable part of a Cantonese meal, drunk throughout the meal and not just at the beginning as in the west. Mostly the soups are clear, and their basis is a good stock, which you should prepare in advance, keeping it in the fridge or freezing it for future use.

Chicken carcass or bones/spare ribs/root vegetable chunks
4 slices fresh ginger
2 cloves garlic, sliced
Pinch of salt

Put the ingredients in large saucepan of water (using meat or vegetable, as you like) and boil on a low heat for 2 to 2½ hr, adding more water if necessary. Skim the pan as it boils and strain at the end, reserving the liquid as the basis for any soup. Heat with diced vegetables, seafood chunks, dried shrimp, slices of meat or beaten egg (or any combination of these) for a clear, hot soup.

Plain rice

The other indispensable part of any meal, rice accompanies the other dishes and is generally eaten just plain boiled. Use only long grain white rice; any other variety is just not the same. Unless you've got an expensive rice cooker, follow these steps for perfect rice. Using one cup of rice per person, place rice in a saucepan and wash and rinse well under a running tap, draining the water off each time until it stops appearing cloudy (about six or seven rinses). To the drained rice, then add just under twice the amount of cups of water to rice. Cover with tight-fitting lid and bring to boil; then turn heat down to minimum and simmer for 10min. Then turn off heat and keep covered for another 10–15min. Only now should you take the lid off, when it's ready to eat.

Basic fried rice

In a more elaborate meal, fried rice can become one of the main dishes. In Hong Kong and China, it's always prepared with leftover cooked rice from the day before – if you're starting from scratch, cook the rice well in advance and only use it when cold.

3 tablespoons vegetable oil
1 large onion, thinly sliced
2–3 eggs, beaten
4 bowls cooked rice
2 spring onions, chopped
Soy sauce

Heat oil in wok and stir-fry onions for a minute or so. Add cooked rice and toss well, heating through, adding a little more oil if necessary to prevent sticking. Make a well in the rice and pour in beaten eggs. Let them set on the bottom, then worry eggs into the rice, adding splashes of soy sauce as they cook. The rice is ready when the egg is set; garnish with chopped spring onion. For more elaborate fried rice, add shrimp, peas, bacon, strips of meat or mushrooms (or any combination) when you add the onion, making sure they're cooked before you add the rice.

Simple steamed fish

This is the most common way to eat fish, which is cleaned and served whole, with head and tail intact; cut them off if you prefer. Or simply use fillets; chunky haddock is good (and can be used frozen for this recipe).

1–1½ lb white fish
4 slices fresh ginger, cut into strips
2 cloves garlic, sliced
Vegetable oil
Salt
Soy sauce
2 spring onions, chopped
3 Chinese mushrooms, thinly sliced
1 tablespoon Chinese preserved vegetables

Prepare fish and place on steaming plate or shallow dish. Sprinkle with garlic, ginger and salt, pushing some into cavities if it's a whole fish. Pour over a little vegetable oil and soy sauce and sprinkle with spring onions, Chinese mushrooms, and Chinese preserved vegetables (which you can buy in tins); the last two are not essential. Cover and steam over boiling water in wok for 15–20min.

Easier, and just as common, is to steam the fish on its own, heat oil in a wok with a dash of soy sauce and serve by pouring the hot oil over the fish – this ensures that the fish is cooked thoroughly and you use the remaining sauce as a dip.

Braised fish in sweet tomato sauce

The Cantonese generally eat their fish steamed, but this is a simple recipe for a dish with plenty of sauce.

2lb mackerel, cleaned and cut across into 2-inch chunks
2 cloves garlic, chopped
4 slices fresh ginger, chopped
3 tablespoons vegetable oil
1lb fresh tomatoes, skinned and halved
2 tablespoons soy sauce
1–2 tablespoons sugar
1 teaspoon cornflour

Heat oil in wok and fry chunks of fish for 5min, turning so that they brown on all sides. Remove and put aside, adding garlic and ginger to remaining oil and stir-fry for 30secs. Then add tomatoes and stir-fry on high heat until they break down into a thick sauce, adding water as necessary to prevent sticking. In a cup, mix soy sauce, sugar and cornflour into paste and add to tomatoes, turning down heat. Cook together until sauce is right consistency (fairly thick, not liquidy), adding water as necessary and more sugar to taste – the sweet taste should complement the tomatoes, not overpower them. Finally, add cooked fish, stir together and serve.

Lemon chicken

A dish with an unusual mix of flavours; good for a dinner party.

1 small chicken, jointed and cut into largish chunks
3 slices fresh ginger, chopped into strips
2 cloves garlic, sliced
3–4 tablespoons vegetable oil
2 large lemons, sliced
3 spring onions, chopped
2 tablespoons chicken stock
1 tablespoon rice wine (or dry sherry)
Cornflour
1 tablespoon soy sauce
Salt

Heat oil in wok, add chicken pieces and stir-fry for 5min until they start to brown. Remove chicken, add garlic, ginger and half the spring onion and stir-fry for 1min. Add stock, rice wine, soy sauce and pinch of salt and stir. Put the chicken back in, add the lemon slices and a little cornflour and cover. Cook over low heat until chicken pieces are done (20–30min), adding a little sugar if the sauce is too sharp. The secret is not to add water: the sauce should not be wet, but cooked in and clinging to the chicken.

Steamed spare ribs in black bean sauce

Spare ribs in Hong Kong are not the long Tex-Mex variety, but cut into short sections 2–3 inches long. Buy what you can and cut them to size.

1–1½ lb pork spare ribs
2 tablespoons black beans
1 onion, finely chopped
½ teaspoon salt
2 tablespoons vegetable oil
2 tablespoons stock
2 teaspoons sugar
1 tablespoon soy sauce
1 tablespoon rice wine (or dry sherry)
Cornflour
1 tablespoon red chillis, chopped
3 cloves garlic, crushed

Blanch spare ribs in boiling water for 2min, then drain and put aside. Soak black beans in hot water for 10min, drain and crush lightly with back of spoon. Heat oil in wok, stir-fry onion for less than a minute, add black beans, stock, sugar, salt, rice wine and soy sauce and continue to stir-fry for 30secs more. Mix result in bowl with spare ribs, adding cornflour to thicken. Then put ribs on dish, sprinkle with chilli and garlic and steam for 30min.

Vegetable in oyster sauce

In Hong Kong this is a standard dish, made with whatever vegetable happens to be in season. Use green vegetables and try, variously, Chinese cabbage, white cabbage, spinach, broccoli, greens and even brussel sprouts (cut them in half to get the best results).

Green vegetable
2 tablespoons vegetable oil
2 cloves garlic, chopped
2 slices fresh ginger, chopped finely
1 teaspoon sugar
1 tablespoon soy sauce
2 tablespoons oyster sauce
½ teaspoon cornflour mixed in a little water

Wash vegetable, cut into large strips or separate leaves. Heat oil in wok and stir-fry garlic and ginger for 30secs, adding vegetable. Continue to cook, stir-frying for 2min. Add sugar and soy sauce, water and cornflour and mix in. Add oyster sauce and heat through before serving. Place on dish and drip more oyster sauce over before eating.

Cook Books

Learning by trial and error is the best way to get to grips with the basic recipes; don't be afraid to experiment. However, if you want to improve your Cantonese cooking skills rapidly, get yourself a decent **cook book**. There are plenty on the market, though if you're a beginner get one with good pictures so that you can see what the end result is supposed to look like. One thing to check is that you're buying a knowledgable book. Most are classed as "Chinese" cook books, which generally means that they cull their recipes from all over China – no bad thing, but skimpy if you want to concentrate on Cantonese (ie southern Chinese) cooking. A good book should tell you where in China the recipes come from, so you can make up your own mind; one with Chinese characters next to the recipes can be handy if you're going to Hong Kong and want to test out the genuine article once there.

The longest-serving master of the Chinese cook book is **Kenneth Lo**: anything by him is straightforward, informative and inspiring. Of recent publications, **Yan-Kit So's** Classic Food of China is erudite and full of good sense (and includes all the classic Cantonese recipes); while **Ken Hom's** Fragrant Harbour Taste: The New Chinese Cooking of Hong Kong details modern Hong Kong cooking (as dished up in some of the swankier, designer restaurants), which culls its influences from all over Asia as well as the West.

On the subject of recipes and books, two Cantonese foodie **jokes** seem relevant here (both originally noted by the writer and journalist Paul Levy). First, when casting about for suitable ingredients, always bear in mind what the northern Chinese say about their southern neighbours: "The Cantonese will eat anything with four legs except a table and anything that flies except an aeroplane." Second, and hardly any less graphic, is the story of the day that an alien lands on earth and appears before an Indian and a Cantonese person – the Indian prostrates himself before the alien and prays to it, while the Cantonese person hurries off to consult a recipe book

Onwards Travel: China

Very few visitors to Hong Kong spend the whole of their time in the territory, as there are a couple of very obvious side trips to be made. The quickest, to Macau, is covered fully in the guide. The other, to China, is perhaps the more intriguing, especially if you travel independently of a tour group. A trip to the nearest Chinese city of note, Guangzhou (Canton), is easily done and the city itself is simple to negotiate. If Guangzhou is part of a longer Chinese trip, then note the other routes into China from Hong Kong that are detailed below.

If you want someone else to organise your trip for you, several tour operators can oblige, starting at around $250 for a day trip to Shenzhen – the Chinese border city – though more like $1000 for a day trip to Guangzhou itself. More details are available from some of the operators listed on p.49, or from any Hong Kong travel agent (see p.284 for list).

Into China: Red Tape and Visas

To enter China you need a valid passport and a **visa**, easily obtained in Hong Kong and generally valid for one month from the date of issue (*not* the date of entry). It's easy to extend your stay in China once there. As well as the two official visa-issuing organisations listed below, just about any travel agency in Hong Kong can arrange a visa for you, and can also sort out your transport to China and accommodation once there if you wish; for the visa only, take along two passport photographs. All the agencies are much of a muchness, the only difference being how quickly they can arrange the visa for you: it usually takes 1–3 working days, for which you'll pay around $150–200, but some places can get a same-day visa for you, for around $350–400.

> **Ministry of Foreign Affairs of the PRC**, Visa Office, 5th Floor, Lower Block, 26 Harbour Rd, China Resources Building, Wan Chai (☎827 9569; Mon–Fri 9am–12.20pm & 2–5pm, Sat 9am–12.20pm).
>
> **China Travel Service** (*CTS*), 4th Floor, CTS House, 78–83 Connaught Rd, Central (☎853 3533); 2nd Floor, China Travel Building, 77 Queen's Rd, Central (☎525 2284); 1st Floor, Alpha House, 27 Nathan Rd, Tsim Sha Tsui (☎721 1331); 10–12, 1st Floor, China Hong Kong City, 33 Canton Rd, Tsim Sha Tsui (☎736 1863); all open Mon–Fri 9am–5.30pm, Sat 9am–5pm, Sun 9am–1pm & 2–5pm.

At the border, **Chinese customs** will ask you to declare all your valuables (including things like personal stereos and cameras) and how much money and travellers' cheques you're carrying. This is entered onto a declaration form, which you keep until you leave China; don't lose it, as it's designed to prevent you selling such items in China. As always, don't carry anything through customs for anyone else, however innocent it may seem.

Getting There By Train

There are two methods of getting to China (Guangzhou) by **train**, though both use the same length of track. The cheapest method, though a little time-consuming, is to take any of the **local trains** from the Kowloon–Canton Railway Station, at Hung Hom, to the border station of **LO WU**; the one-way, fifty-minute trip costs $25. Lo Wu is on the Hong Kong side of the border but is a restricted area: you must be going on into China to come here. From here, you simply follow the signs and walk across the river bridge over the border, through passport control and customs, into **SHENZHEN**, the Chinese frontier town. It's more a city these days, a high-rise economic zone designed to attract Western and Hong Kong investment – no place to linger. Its train station is immediately across the border, and if you keep following the signs and crowds you'll wind up at the ticket office, where you can buy a ticket for the hourly trains to Guangzhou. There's a bank at the border if you want to buy local currency (see below), but you can pay for your Guangzhou ticket in Hong Kong dollars, and the journey takes around another two to three hours, depending on the train and the time of day. Note that the **last border-crossing train to Lo Wu** from Hung Hom is currently at 9.54pm; ie, the border closes at around 10.30pm. This local route to Guangzhou is to be avoided at all costs on public and religious holidays, at Easter and at Chinese New Year, when most Hong Kong families decide to visit their relations over the border.

The other method has the virtue of complete simplicity and although it costs more than twice as much, it's still not a major expense. There are currently four daily **express trains**, which travel directly from the Kowloon–Canton Railway Station to Guangzhou in three hours. These cost around $200 one-way and though the departure times occasionally change, there are usually two early morning and two early afternoon trains. You can buy tickets in advance from some of the CTS offices in Hong Kong (see above for addresses), and at the office on the first floor of the Kowloon–Canton Railway Station; at both you'll pay a small commission. It's generally not necessary to buy in advance, though, and cheaper same-day tickets can be bought from the CTS office on the ground-floor concourse of the station.

Getting There By Boat

Hong Kong is a major departure point for **boats** of all descriptions to China, and not just to Guangzhou. It's a grand way to approach China and for the most part isn't at all expensive: many people heading for Guangzhou take the train one way and the ferry the other, so as to experience both approaches.

To Guangzhou

The once-daily **ferry** to Guangzhou leaves from the China Hong Kong Ferry Terminal (Canton Rd, Tsim Sha Tsui) and costs around $170–200 one-way for a bed in a dormitory bunk or a small cabin. The journey takes eight to nine hours and you can buy tickets at CTS offices, most travel agents, or directly at the ferry terminal (where they might be a bit cheaper). There's no ferry on the last day of each month, and it's wise to book a few days in advance.

There's also a **Jetcat** service from the China Hong Kong Ferry Terminal, departing once daily and taking around three hours. Tickets cost roughly the same price as the ferry and, again, are available from CTS offices or the ferry terminal.

Other Chinese Destinations

There are several other regular services to China from Hong Kong, outlined below. For current ticket prices and departure times, contact CTS or the ferry terminals.

Shekou, the port closest to Shenzhen, is served by hoverferry three times daily from China Hong Kong Ferry Terminal (Tsim Sha Tsui) and four times daily from the Macau Ferry Terminal (Central). There's also a Jetcat service to **Zhuhai**, the Special Economic Zone across the border from Macau, west of Hong Kong; three daily from the China Hong Kong Ferry Terminal, Tsim Sha Tsui. More long-distance connections include services to **Hainan Island** (three monthly to Haikou, two monthly to Sanya); **Shantou**, in Guangdong province, east of Hong Kong (once-daily); and **Xiamen**, in Fujian province, northeast of Shantou (once-daily). Longer term China travellers might also consider the two-and-a-half-day ferry voyage to **Shanghai** (departures every five days from the China Hong Kong Ferry Terminal); or the hovercraft link between Hong Kong and **Wuzhou**, a ten-hour trip (departing even-numbered dates) which means if you're heading ultimately for the Guilin area, you can cut out the long ferry ride from Guangzhou to Wuzhou.

Getting There By Bus

There are plenty of **bus** services into China's Guangdong province (which encompasses both Shenzhen and Guangzhou), but mostly it's a more complicated business than taking the train, used by locals rather than tourists. There's a daily CTS bus to **Guangzhou**, which takes around five hours and costs a little less than the express train fare. The only problem is that the overseas department at CTS won't sell you a ticket: you'll have to try the office for the Overseas Chinese (in Alpha House, just over the corridor), though they may refuse too, on the grounds that as you don't speak Cantonese you won't be able to follow the signs and instructions. It's all a bit silly, but if you don't speak Cantonese, tell them you're travelling with a Cantonese speaker – or try buying the ticket at a Hong Kong travel agency instead.

Even more convoluted is the bus ride to **Shenzhen**. There's a service operated by Citybus (☎736 3888), which departs from the corner of

Middle Road and Kowloon Park Drive in Tsim Sha Tsui (behind the *YMCA*) four to five times daily, a one-to-two-hour drive. The service uses the Man Kam To/Sha Tau Kok bording crossing to Shenzhen, and from there – to go all the way by bus – minibuses outside Shenzhen train station (prices posted on signs at the bus stop) make the trip on to Guangzhou.

Getting There By Air

Flights from Hong Kong to China are competitively priced. To Guangzhou, it'll cost you about $400 one-way and the trip takes 35 minutes; and there are services, too, to Beijing and Shanghai. There are several daily flights to each destination with various airlines, and you can get more information at any *CTS* office, or from any of the travel agents listed on p.284.

Getting There From Macau

You can also move on into China **from Macau**, though the choices are more limited. There's a *CTS* office next to the *Metropole* hotel at 63 Rua da´ Praia Grande, which issues visas and tickets; and one at the Jetfoil Terminal.

The simplest move is just to **walk across the border** at the Barrier Gate (open 7am–9pm) into **GONGBEI**, an area of the Zhuhai Special Economic Zone, from where there are frequent minibuses to Guangzhou. The whole trip should take around five hours. There is a direct bus from Macau, though this involves stopping at the border while everyone goes through customs; it's quicker to walk across and pick up the minibus. A more popular approach is to take the **ferry to Guangzhou**, all the details are given on p.333: there's also a less useful Jetcat service from Macau to Shekou, the port for Shenzhen.

Guangzhou: some Practicalities

If you're just visiting from Hong Kong for a day or two, you'll find some details below which will help smooth your way in Guangzhou – it's a very big, sprawling city. For a longer trip, you'll need a decent guidebook and a map, both of which are available in Hong Kong bookshops. You'll also be able to get a map from any of the major hotels once you're there.

Costs and Money

Guangzhou is not typical of the rest of China, either in terms of life and conditions there or simply in how much things **cost**: for China, you'll find Guangzhou pricey, though it's still much cheaper to live here than in Hong Kong.

The **currency** is the *yuan* (¥), which is divided into ten *jiao* (which is divided into ten *fen*) and it comes in small and confusing notes. It's known as Renminbi ("People's Money") or RMB, to distinguish it from the so-called Foreign Exchange Certificates (or FECs) which you'll get as a foreigner when you exchange money or travellers' cheques at a bank. Don't panic: FECs are simply a different set of notes in various *yuan* denominations. You're supposed to use them to pay for transport, accommodation and goods while in China, and in places which only serve foreigners, like Friendship Stores. The current official exchange rate is around ¥10–11 to the pound sterling/¥6 to the US dollar. Naturally, there's a **black market** in FECs, and in Hong Kong and US dollars (which the local Chinese use to buy expensive, imported Western goods) and one of your first experiences in China will be people offering to sell you RMB in return for these currencies. This can be a dangerous business – rip-offs are common, and in any case the current black market rate makes it barely worth the risk. It's certainly not worth it if you're visiting for just a couple of days as things are cheap enough anyway. If you do change on the black market, check the going rates with other travellers and play it safe with the people who approach you: don't change money on the street; the best place is in a shop or restaurant. Always count their money first and hold onto it before counting out your own; and don't be panicked by anything – if they try the "police coming!" gambit, hand back their cash and walk away.

The train station in Guangzhou contains a *Bank of China*, opposite the Customs Hall, where you may as well change your travellers' cheques into FECs. Keep the receipt you're given because when you come to change them back into hard currency, you'll need receipts which are at least equal to the amount of Chinese currency you want to change; you can't change RMB back into dollars, only FEC.

Arriving

If you're staying at one of the big tourist hotels, there are staffed hotel reservation desks on the way out of the **train station**, which either have free shuttle buses or will give you full instructions on how to reach your hotel.

Transport leaves from outside: bus #5 (to the right of the station and over the other side of the road, going east) runs down to Shamian Island; #7 (from the terminal to the right of the station) to Dashatou Wharf, for ferries to Wuzhou; #30 runs east along the main road, Huanshi Lu, to the Friendship Store/*Holiday Inn*; #31 (from same place as #7) runs to Zhoutozui Wharf, for ferries to Hong Kong. **Taxis** are available from outside the station, and are cheap enough, though they'll expect to be paid in FEC; if you've got RMB you want to unload, be prepared for a big argument.

For other kinds of onward travel, there's a **CITS office** (the branch of the *CTS* in China for foreigners) just out the train station on the left, on Huanshi Lu (open 8.30am–12.30pm & 2–5pm), which is relatively friendly, has people who can speak English and is good for train tickets to Beijing and for general information. Train tickets to other destinations are bought inside the station itself. There's a **telephone office** right opposite the train station.

Accommodation

The cheapest **accommodation** is in the *Guangzhou Youth Hostel* (☎8884298) on Shamian Island, close to the *White Swan* hotel. If you're coming on the #5 bus, get off at the footbridge on Liuersan Lu, cross onto the island and keep going straight on for the *Guangzhou*; around ¥25–30 a night in a clean dormitory bed, more expensive doubles available, too.

A **mid-range hotel** on Shamian Island is the *Shamian Hotel* (☎8888124), opposite the *White Swan*, whose double rooms with bath go for around ¥100. Close to the river, at Haizhu Square, there's also the *Guangzhou Hotel* (☎3338168) and the *Huaqiao Hotel* (☎3336888), both with doubles from around ¥170; get there on the #29

bus from the terminal to the right of the train station. There are any number of **expensive** hotels in Guangzhou, most of which have a reservations desk at the train station and most of which you can book in advance from Hong Kong at travel agencies. They tend to be a little far out, though, and if you want to be close to the action and you've got the money, you'd do better to stay at the *White Swan* (☎8886968), on the southern shore of Shamian Island – one of the most elegant places in Guangzhou (and China). Prices are around ¥400 a night for waterfront opulence. Go in for a look anyway, even if you can't afford the room rates, as the waterfall and shops in the lobby are good for a stroll, and there's an excellent deli attached.

Eating

There are lots of good-looking eating houses along Changdi Damalu (bus #5 runs along here before reaching Shamian Island). *Datong*, at 63 Yanjiang Lu nearby, is a great Cantonese restaurant on eight floors, with *dim sum* on the sixth floor.

There are also lots of *dai pai dongs* in the streets around the noisome and fascinating Qinping Market, which starts just opposite the bridge to Shamian Island, off Liuersan Lu. Many of them sell very cheap, tasty hot pots – clay pots with rice, vegetables and meat, baked on a range. If you've not been put off by Qinping Market, whose covered streets are full of fish, turtles, dogs, racoons, owls, monkeys, kittens snakes and frogs – all on sale for eating purposes – then walk past the famous **snake restaurant** at 43 Jianglan Lu (off Renmin Lu), where you can have the creatures skinned and cooked in a variety of ways, along with other unfortunate animals, domestic and otherwise.

Language: a Cantonese Survival Guide

The language spoken by the overwhelming majority of Hong Kong and Macau's population is Cantonese, a southern Chinese dialect used in the province of Guangdong – and the one primarily spoken by the millions of Chinese emigrants throughout the world. Unfortunately, Cantonese is one of the world's most difficult languages for Westerners to learn: it's tonal, and the same word can have several different meanings depending on the pitch of the voice; there are nine different tones. To learn to speak it fluently would take years, and even mastering the basics can be fraught with misunderstanding. Things are further made difficult by the fact that written Chinese is a different matter altogether – meaningful phrases and sentences are formed by a series of characters, or pictographs, which individually represent actions and objects.

Still, most visitors get by without knowing a word of Cantonese. Hong Kong is officially **bilingual**, and all signs, public transport and utility notices and street names are written in English, as well as Chinese characters; about the only problem is making out the small English script written on the front of the buses. Also, nearly everyone you'll have dealings with in Central and Tsim Sha Tsui, as well as most of the other tourist destinations, will speak at least some English. In Macau, the dominant colonial language is Portuguese (for more on which, see p.296), but English is increasingly spoken there, too.

To help out, we've provided a small, basic guide to **everyday Cantonese** below – the sort of things you'll want to say to people on the street and in hotels and restaurants. The problem with it is that the accepted way the Cantonese words are written in English often bears little relation to

---

Cantonese Words and Phrases

Basics

Good morning	*jo san*
Hello/how are you?	*nei ho ma*
Thank you	*m goy*
Goodnight	*jo toe*
Goodbye	*joy gin*
What is your name?	*nei gwei sing ah?*
My name is...	*or sing...*
What time is it?	*cheung mun, gay dim le?*
How much is it?	*cheung mun, gay dor chin?*
Where is the train station/	*cheung mun, for che tjam hay been doe ah/*
bus stop/	*ba-si tjam hay been doe ah/*
ferry pier?	*ma-tou hay been doe ah?*
Hong Kong	*heung gong*
China	*chung kwok*
Britain	*ying kwok*

Transport and Essentials

Train	*for che*
Bus	*ba-si*
Ferry	*do shun*
Taxi	*dik-si*
Airport	*gei-cheun*
Hotel	*lui dim*
Restaurant	*fan dim*
Campsite	*yer ying way ji*
Toilets	*chi sor*
Police	*ging-tchak*

Numbers

1	*yat*
2	*yih*
3	*saam*
4	*sei*
5	*ngh (um)*
6	*luk*
7	*tchat*
8	*baat*
9	*gau*
10	*sahp*
11	*sahp yat*
12	*sahp yih*
20	*yih sahp*
30	*saam sahp*
100	*yat baak*
1000	*yat tin*

Note that the number two changes when asking for two of something – *long wei* (a table for two) – or stating something other than counting – *long mung* (two dollars).

---

how they're actually **pronounced** by a Chinese person: the romanised word is at best an approximation of the Chinese sound and, in any case, no one will understand you without the correct intonation. You'll only get it right by listening and practising. As far as the **characters** go, we've provided some examples of the most important **signs and place names**, but that's all – it's incredibly difficult for the untrained eye to read them, and anyway, they don't help with pronunciation.

SOME SIGNS

Entrance	入口	Danger	危险
Exit	出口	Customs	關稅
Toilets	厕所	Bus	公共汽車
Gentlemen	男厕	Ferry	渡船
Ladies	女厕	Train	火車
Open	营业中	Airport	飛機場
Closed	休业	Police	警察
Arrivals	到達	Restaurant	飯店
Departures	出發	Hotel	旅店
Closed for holidays	休假	Campsite	野营位置
Out of order	出故障	Beach	海灘
Drinking/mineral water	礦泉水	No swimming	禁止游泳
No smoking	請勿吸烟		

PLACE NAMES

Hong Kong	香港	Jordan	佐敦
Hong Kong Island	香港岛	Central	中建
Tsim Sha Tsui	尖沙咀	Wan Chai	灣仔
Kowloon	九龍	Causeway Bay	銅鑼灣
New Territories	新界	Aberdeen	香港仔
Happy Valley	跑馬地	Stanley	赤柱
Sha Tin	沙田	Lantau	大嶼山
Tsuen Wan	荃灣	Cheung Chau	長洲
Mongkok	旺角	Lamma	南丫島
Yau Ma Tei	油蔴地		

Glossary of Hong Kong Words and Terms

Lots of strange words have entered the vocabulary of Hong Kong people, Chinese and Westerners alike, and you'll come across most of them during your time here. Some are derivations of Cantonese words, adapted by successive generations of European settlers; others come from the different foreign and colonial languages represented in Hong Kong – from Chinese dialects to Anglo-Indian words.

Amah Female housekeeper/servant.

Ancestral Hall Main room or hall in a temple complex where the ancestral records are kept, and where devotions take place.

Cheongsam Chinese dress with a long slit up the side.

Chop A personal seal or stamp of authority.

Dai pai dong Street stall selling snacks and food.

Expat Expatriate; a foreign worker living in Hong Kong.

Godown Warehouse.

Gweilo Literally "ghost man"; used by the Cantonese for all Westerners (*gweipor*, "ghost woman"); originally derogatory, but now in accepted use.

Hong Major company.

Kaido Small boat used as a ferry, a sampan (also *kaito*).

Junk Large flat-bottomed boat with a high deck and an overhanging stern.

Mahjong A Chinese game played with tiles, like souped-up dominoes.

Miu The Cantonese word for temple.

Nullah Gully, ravine.

Praya The Portuguese word for waterfront promenade.

Sampan Small flat-bottomed boat.

Shroff Cashier.

Taipan Boss of a major company.

Acronyms

HKTA Hong Kong Tourist Association.

MTR Mass Transit Railway.

KCR Kowloon–Canton Railway.

LRT Light Rail Transit.

LEGCO Legislative Council.

EXCO Executive Council.

Index

Map Index

Help Us Update

We've gone to a lot of effort to ensure that this new edition of *The Rough Guide to Hong Kong and Macau* is up-to-date and accurate. However, information changes fast: new bars and clubs appear and disappear, museums alter their displays and opening hours, restaurants and hotels change prices and standards. If you feel there are places we've under-praised or overrated, omitted or ought to omit, please let us know. All suggestions, comments or corrections are much appreciated and we'll send a copy of the next edition (or any other Rough Guide if you prefer) for the best letters.

Please mark letters "Rough Guide to Hong Kong update" and send to:

Rough Guides, 1 Mercer Street, London WC2H 9QJ

or Rough Guides, 375 Hudson Street, 4th Floor, New York NY10014.

Many thanks to those **correspondents** who wrote in following the first edition of this book with comments and corrections: I. Esmann, J. Driver, Simon Sapper, Beverly Fitzsimmons, Andrew Dembina, Tat-Wah Liu, Anthony Lyons, R. Ramelli, Simon Smith, Ralph Lawson, Jo Goodberry, Henrik Eriksson, Kaomi Goetz, Alton Bader, Richard Trott, Wendy Hart, Robert Jones, Adrian Davenport, Peter White, Michael Sims, C.J. Morgan, Robert Wyburn and James Byrne.

DIRECT ORDERS IN THE USA

Title	ISBN	Price
Able to Travel	1858281105	$19.95
Amsterdam	1858280869	$13.95
Australia	1858280354	$18.95
Berlin	1858280338	$13.99
Brittany & Normandy	1858280192	$14.95
Bulgaria	1858280478	$14.99
Canada	185828001X	$14.95
Crete	1858280494	$14.95
Cyprus	185828032X	$13.99
Czech & Slovak Republics	185828029X	$14.95
Egypt	1858280753	$17.95
England	1858280788	$16.95
Europe	185828077X	$18.95
Florida	1858280109	$14.95
France	1858280508	$16.95
Germany	1858280257	$17.95
Greece	1858280206	$16.95
Guatemala & Belize	1858280451	$14.95
Holland, Belgium & Luxembourg	1858280877	$15.95
Hong Kong & Macau	1858280664	$13.95
Hungary	1858280214	$13.95
Italy	1858280311	$17.95
Kenya	1858280435	$15.95
Mediterranean Wildlife	1858280699	$15.95
Morocco	1858280400	$16.95
Nepal	185828046X	$13.95
New York	1858280583	$13.95
Paris	1858280389	$13.95
Poland	1858280346	$16.95
Portugal	1858280842	$15.95
Prague	185828015X	$14.95
Provence & the Côte d'Azur	1858280230	$14.95
St Petersburg	1858280303	$14.95
San Francisco	1858280826	$13.95
Scandinavia	1858280397	$16.99
Scotland	1858280834	$14.95
Sicily	1858280370	$14.99
Thailand	1858280168	$15.95
Tunisia	1858280656	$15.95
USA	185828080X	$18.95
Venice	1858280362	$13.99
Women Travel	1858280710	$12.95
Zimbabwe & Botswana	1858280419	$16.95

Rough Guides are available from all good bookstores, but can be obtained directly in the USA and Worldwide (except the UK*) from Penguin:

Charge your order by Master Card or Visa (US$15.00 minimum order): call 1-800-255-6476; or send orders, with complete name, address and zip code, and list price, plus $2.00 shipping and handling per order to: Consumer Sales, Penguin USA, PO Box 999 – Dept #17109, Bergenfield, NJ 07621. No COD. Prepay foreign orders by international money order, a cheque drawn on a US bank, or US currency. No postage stamps are accepted. All orders are subject to stock availability at the time they are processed. Refunds will be made for books not available at that time. Please allow a minimum of four weeks for delivery.

The availability and published prices quoted are correct at the time of going to press but are subject to alteration without prior notice. Titles currently not available outside the UK will be available by January 1995. Call to check.

* For UK orders, see separate price list

DIRECT ORDERS IN THE UK

Title	ISBN	Price
Amsterdam	1858280869	£7.99
Australia	1858280354	£12.99
Barcelona & Catalunya	1858280486	£7.99
Berlin	1858280338	£8.99
Brazil	0747101272	£7.95
Brittany & Normandy	1858280192	£7.99
Bulgaria	1858280478	£8.99
California	1858280575	£9.99
Canada	185828001X	£10.99
Crete	1858280494	£6.99
Cyprus	185828032X	£8.99
Czech & Slovak Republics	185828029X	£8.99
Egypt	1858280753	£10.99
England	1858280788	£9.99
Europe	185828077X	£14.99
Florida	1858280109	£8.99
France	1858280508	£9.99
Germany	1858280257	£11.99
Greece	1858280206	£9.99
Guatemala & Belize	1858280451	£9.99
Holland, Belgium & Luxembourg	1858280036	£8.99
Hong Kong & Macau	1858280664	£8.99
Hungary	1858280214	£7.99
Ireland	1858280516	£8.99
Italy	1858280311	£12.99
Kenya	1858280435	£9.99
Mediterranean Wildlife	0747100993	£7.95
Morocco	1858280400	£9.99
Nepal	185828046X	£8.99
New York	1858280583	£8.99
Nothing Ventured	0747102082	£7.99
Paris	1858280389	£7.99
Peru	0747102546	£7.95
Poland	1858280346	£9.99
Portugal	1858280842	£9.99
Prague	185828015X	£7.99
Provence & the Côte d'Azur	1858280230	£8.99
Pyrenees	1858280524	£7.99
St Petersburg	1858280303	£8.99
San Francisco	1858280826	£8.99
Scandinavia	1858280397	£10.99
Scotland	1858280834	£8.99
Sicily	1858280370	£8.99
Spain	1858280079	£8.99
Thailand	1858280168	£8.99
Tunisia	1858280656	£8.99
Turkey	1858280133	£8.99
Tuscany & Umbria	1858280559	£8.99
USA	185828080X	£12.99
Venice	1858280362	£8.99
West Africa	1858280141	£12.99
Women Travel	1858280710	£7.99
Zimbabwe & Botswana	1858280419	£10.99

Rough Guides are available from all good bookstores, but can be obtained directly in the UK* from Penguin by contacting:

Penguin Direct, Penguin Books Ltd, Bath Road, Harmondsworth, West Drayton, Middlesex UB7 0DA; or telephone our credit line on 081-899 4036 (9am–5pm) and ask for Penguin Direct. Visa, Access and Amex accepted. Delivery will normally be within 14 working days. Penguin Direct ordering facilities are only available in the UK.

The availability and published prices quoted are correct at the time of going to press but are subject to alteration without prior notice.

* For USA and international orders, see separate price list

SLEEP EASY
BOOK AHEAD

AUSTRALIA
02 261 1111

CANADA
FREEPHONE 0800 663 5777

DUBLIN
01 301766

LONDON
071 836 1036

BELFAST
0232 324733

GLASGOW
041 332 3004

WASHINGTON
0202 783 6161

NEW ZEALAND
09 379 4224

IBN INTERNATIONAL BOOKING NETWORK

Call any of these numbers and your credit card secures a good nights sleep …

in more than 26 countries

up to six months ahead

with immediate confirmation

HOSTELLING INTERNATIONAL

*Budget accommodation you can **Trust***

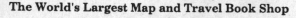

You are
A STUDENT

You travel
THE WORLD

You want
TO SAVE MONEY

Here's how

The International Student Identity Card

Available at Student Travel Offices Worldwide.

Entitles you to discounts and special services worldwide.